Pro Visual C++/CLI and the .NET 2.0 Platform

Stephen R. G. Fraser

Apress®

ISBN: 978-1-4842-2088-7

DOI 10.1007/978-1-4302-0139-7

Library of Congress Cataloging-in-Publication data is available upon request.

9 8 7 6 5 4 3 2 1

Trademarked names may appear in this book. Rather than use a trademark symbol with every occurrence of a trademarked name, we use the names only in an editorial fashion and to the benefit of the trademark owner, with no intention of infringement of the trademark.

Lead Editor: Ewan Buckingham
Technical Reviewer: Don Reamey
Editorial Board: Steve Anglin, Dan Appleman, Ewan Buckingham, Gary Cornell, Tony Davis, Jason Gilmore, Jonathan Hassell, Chris Mills, Dominic Shakeshaft, Jim Sumser
Project Managers: Laura Cheu, Richard Dal Porto
Copy Edit Manager: Nicole LeClerc
Copy Editors: Freelance Editorial Services, Ami Knox, Liz Welch
Assistant Production Director: Kari Brooks-Copony
Production Editor: Katie Stence
Compositor: Susan Gilnert
Proofreader: Elizabeth Berry
Indexer: John Collin
Artist: April Milne
Interior Designer: Van Winkle Design Group
Cover Designer: Kurt Krames
Manufacturing Director: Tom Debolski

Distributed to the book trade worldwide by Springer-Verlag New York, Inc., 233 Spring Street, 6th Floor, New York, NY 10013. Phone 1-800-SPRINGER, fax 201-348-4505, e-mail orders-ny@springer-sbm.com, or visit http://www.springeronline.com.

For information on translations, please contact Apress directly at 2560 Ninth Street, Suite 219, Berkeley, CA 94710. Phone 510-549-5930, fax 510-549-5939, e-mail info@apress.com, or visit http://www.apress.com.

The information in this book is distributed on an "as is" basis, without warranty. Although every precaution has been taken in the preparation of this work, neither the author(s) nor Apress shall have any liability to any person or entity with respect to any loss or damage caused or alleged to be caused directly or indirectly by the information contained in this work.

The source code for this book is available to readers at http://www.apress.com in the Source Code section. You will need to answer questions pertaining to this book in order to successfully download the code.

To my wife, Sarah, and my daughter, Shaina, my energy and happiness.

Contents at a Glance

PART 1 ■■■ The C++/CLI Language

PART 2 ■■■ .NET Framework Development in C++/CLI

PART 3 ■■■ Unsafe/Unmanaged C++/CLI

Contents

PART 1 ▪▪▪ The C++/CLI Language

PART 2 ■■■ .NET Framework Development in C++/CLI

PART 3 ■■■ Unsafe/Unmanaged C++/CLI

Foreword by Stanley B. Lippman

It is with great satisfaction that I introduce you to Stephen's excellent new book, *Pro Visual C++/CLI and the .NET 2.0 Platform*, the first detailed treatment of what has been standardized under ECMA as C++/CLI. Of course, any text, no matter how excellent, is itself incomplete, like a three-walled room. The fourth wall, in this case, is you, the reader. You complete the text by exercising the code samples, poking around with them, and finally writing your own code. That's really the only way to develop a deep understanding of this stuff. But having an experienced guide to step you through the hazards of any new language is priceless, and this is what Stephen's text accomplishes. I cannot recommend it too highly.

With Stephen's indulgence, I would like to give you a short overview of the ideas behind the language's original design and place it in the context of the design and evolution of C++ itself. The first question people ask is, "So what is C++/CLI?"

C++/CLI is a self-contained, component-based dynamic programming language that, like C# or Java, is derived from C++. Unlike those languages, however, we have worked hard to integrate C++/CLI into ISO-C++, using the historical model of evolving the C/C++ programming language to support modern programming paradigms. Historically, one can say that C++/CLI is to C++ as C++ is to C. More generally, one can view the evolution leading to C++/CLI in the following historical context:

- BCPL (Basic Computer Programming Language)
- B (Ken Thompson, original Unix work ...)
- C (Dennis Ritchie, adding type and control structure to B ...)
- C with Classes (~1979)
    - C84 (~1984) ...
    - Cfront, release E (~1984, to universities) ...
    - Cfront, release 1.0 (1985, to the world)—20th birthday !!!
- Multiple/Virtual Inheritance Programming (~1988) (MI)
- Generic Programming (~1991) (Templates)
    - ANSI C++/ISO-C++ (~1996)
- Dynamic Component Programming (~2005) (C++/CLI)

C++/CLI represents a tuple. The first term, *C++*, refers of course to the *C++ programming language* invented by Bjarne Stroustrup at Bell Laboratories. It supports a static object model that is optimized for the speed and size of its executables. It does not support runtime modification of the program other than, of course, heap allocation. It allows unlimited access to the underlying machine, but very little access to the types active in the running program, and no real access to the associated infrastructure of that program.

The third term, *CLI*, refers to the *Common Language Infrastructure*, a multitiered architecture supporting a *dynamic component* programming model. In many ways, this represents a complete reversal of the C++ object model. A runtime software layer, the virtual execution system, runs between the program and the underlying operating system. Access to the underlying machine is fairly constrained. Access to the types active in the executing program and the associated program infrastructure—both as discovery and construction—is supported.

The second term, slash (/), represents a *binding* between C++ and the CLI.

So, a first approximation of an answer as to "What is C++/CLI?" is to say that it is a binding of the static C++ object model with the dynamic component object model of the CLI. In short, it is how we do .NET programming using C++ rather than, say, C# or Visual Basic. Like C# and the CLI itself, C++/CLI is undergoing standardization under ECMA (and eventually under ISO).

The *common language runtime* (CLR) is the implementation of the CLI that is platform specific to the Windows operating system. Similarly, *Visual C++ 2005* is our implementation of C++/CLI.

So, as a second approximation of an answer, I would say that C++/CLI integrates the .NET programming model within C++ in the same way as, back at Bell Laboratories, we integrated generic programming using templates within the then existing C++. In both cases, both your investment in an existing C++ code base and in your existing C++ expertise are preserved. This was an essential baseline requirement of the design of C++/CLI.

What Does Learning C++/CLI Involve?

There are three aspects in the design of a CLI language that hold across all languages: (1) a mapping of language-level syntax to the underlying Common Type System (CTS); (2) the choice of a level of detail to expose the underlying CLI infrastructure to the direct manipulation of the programmer; and, (3) the choice of additional functionality to provide over that supported directly by the CLI. A fourth element of designing a CLI extension to an existing language, such as C++ or Ada, requires a fourth aspect: (4) that of integrating the managed and native type systems. We'll briefly look at an example of each in turn.

How Does C++/CLI Map to the CTS?

One aspect of programming C++/CLI is learning the underlying Common Type System, which includes three general class types:

1. A polymorphic *reference* type that is used for all class inheritance
2. A nonpolymorphic *value* type that is used for implementing concrete types requiring runtime efficiency such as the numeric types
3. An abstract *interface* type that is used for defining a set of operations common to a set of either reference or value types that implement the interface

This design aspect, the mapping of the CTS to a set of built-in language types, is common across all CLI languages, although of course the syntax varies in each CLI language. So, for example, in C#, one writes

```
abstract class Shape { ... } // C#
```

to define an abstract Shape base class from which specific geometric objects are to be derived, while in C++/CLI one writes

```
ref class Shape abstract { ... }; // C++/CLI
```

to indicate the exact same underlying CLI reference type. The two declarations are represented exactly the same in the underlying CIL. Similarly, in C#, one writes

```
struct Point2D { ... } // C#
```

to define a concrete Point2D class, while in C++/CLI one writes

```
value class Point2D { ... }; // C++/CLI
```

The family of class types supported with C++/CLI represents an integration of the CTS with the native facilities, of course, and that determined our choice of syntax. For example:

```
class native {};
value class V {};
ref class R {};
interface class I {};
```

The CTS also supports an enumeration class type that behaves somewhat differently from the native enumeration, and we provide support for both of those as well:

```
enum native { fail, pass };
enum class CLIEnum : char { fail, pass};
```

Similarly, the CTS supports its own array type that again behaves differently from the native array. And again we provide support for both:

```
int native[] = { 1,1,2,3,5,8 };
array<int>^ managed = { 1,1,2,3,5,8 };
```

It is not true to think of any one CLI language as closer to or more nearly a mapping to the underlying CTS than is another. Rather, each CLI language represents a view into the underlying CTS object model.

What Level of Detail of the CLI Does C++/CLI Expose?

The second design aspect reflects the level of detail of the underlying CLI implementation model to incorporate into the language. How does one go about determining this? Essentially, we need to ask these questions:

- What are the kinds of problems the language is likely to be tasked to solve? We must make sure the language has the tools necessary to do this.

- What are the kinds of programmers the language is likely to attract?

Let's look at an example: the issue of value types occurring on the managed heap. Value types can find themselves on the managed heap in a number of circumstances:

- Implicit boxing

  - We assign an object of a value type to an Object.

  - We invoke a virtual method through a value type that is not overridden.

- When a value type serves as a member of a reference class type

- When a value type is being stored as the element type of a CLI array

The design question a CLI language has to ask is, "Should we allow the programmer to manipulate the address of a value type of this sort?"

What are the issues?

Any object located on the managed heap is subject to relocation during the compaction phase of a sweep of the garbage collector. Any pointers to that object must be tracked and updated by the runtime; the programmer has no way to manually track it herself. Therefore, if we were to allow the programmer to take the address of a value type potentially resident on the managed heap, we would need to introduce a tracking form of pointer in addition to the existing native pointer.

What are the trade-offs to consider? On the one hand, simplicity and safety.

- Directly introducing support in the language for one or a family of tracking pointers makes it a more complicated language. By not supporting this, we expand the available pool of programmers by requiring less sophistication.

- Allowing the programmer access to these ephemeral value types increases the possibility of programmer error—she may purposely or by accident do bad things to the memory. By not supporting this, we create a potentially safer runtime environment.

On the other hand, efficiency and flexibility.

- Each time we assign the same Object with a value type, a new boxing of the value occurs. Allowing access to the boxed value type allows in-memory update, which may provide significant performance ...

- Without a form of tracking pointer, we cannot iterate over a CLI array using pointer arithmetic. This means that the CLI array cannot participate in the STL iterator pattern and work with the generic algorithms. Allowing access to the boxed value type allows significant design flexibility.

We chose in C++/CLI to provide a collection of addressing modes that handle value types on the managed heap.

```
int ival = 1024;

// int^ provides a tracking handle for
//       direct read/write access to a boxed value type ...
int^ boxedi = ival;

array<int>^ ia = gcnew array<int>{1,1,2,3,5,8};

// interior_ptr<T> supports indexing into the GC heap ...
interior_ptr<int> begin = &ia[0];

value struct smallInt { int m_ival; ... } si;
pin_ptr<int> ppi = &si.m_ival;
```

We imagine the C++/CLI programmer to be a sophisticated system programmer tasked with providing infrastructure and organizationally critical applications that serve as the foundation over which a business builds its future. She must address both scalability and performance concerns and must therefore have a system-level view into the underlying CLI. The level of detail of a CLI language reflects the face of its programmer.

Complexity is not in itself a negative quality. Human beings, for example, are more complicated than single-cell bacteria, but that is, I think we all agree, not a bad thing. When the expression of a simple concept is complicated, that is a bad thing. In C++/CLI, we have tried to provide an elegant expression to a complex subject matter.

What Does C++/CLI Add Over That of the CLI?

A third design aspect is a language-specific layer of functionality over that directly supported by the CLI. This may require a mapping between the language-level support and the underlying implementation model of the CLI. In some cases, this just isn't possible because the language cannot intercede with the behavior of the CLI. One example of this is the virtual function resolution in the constructor and destructor of a base class. To reflect ISO-C++ semantics in this case would require a resetting of the virtual table within each base class constructor and destructor. This is not possible because virtual table handling is managed by the runtime and not the individual language.

So this design aspect is a compromise between what we might wish to do, and what we find ourselves able to do. The three primary areas of additional functionality provided by C++/CLI are the following:

- A form of *Resource Acquisition is Initialization* (RAII) for reference types. In particular, to provide an automated facility for what is referred to as *deterministic finalization* of garbage collected types that hold scarce resources.

- A form of deep-copy semantics associated with the C++ copy constructor and copy assignment operator; however, this could not be extended to value types.

- Direct support of C++ templates for CTS types in addition to the CLI generic mechanism—this had been the topic of my original first column. In addition, we provide a verifiable version of the Standard Template Library for CLI types.

Let's look at a brief example: the issue of deterministic finalization.

Before the memory associated with an object is reclaimed by the garbage collector, an associated `Finalize()` method, if present, is invoked. You can think of this method as a kind of super-destructor since it is not tied to the program lifetime of the object. We refer to this as *finalization*. The timing of just when or even whether a `Finalize()` method is invoked is undefined. This is what is meant when we say that garbage collection exhibits *nondeterministic finalization*.

Nondeterministic finalization works well with dynamic memory management. When available memory gets sufficiently scarce, the garbage collector kicks in and things pretty much just work. Nondeterministic finalization does not work well, however, when an object maintains a critical resource such as a database connection, a lock of some sort, or perhaps native heap memory. In this case, we would like to release the resource as soon as it is no longer needed. The solution currently supported by the CLI is for a class to free the resources in its implementation of the `Dispose()` method of the `IDisposable` interface. The problem here is that `Dispose()` requires an explicit invocation, and therefore is liable not to be invoked.

A fundamental design pattern in C++ is spoken of as Resource Acquisition is Initialization. That is, a class acquires resources within its constructor. Conversely, a class frees its resources within its destructor. This is managed automatically within the lifetime of the class object.

This is what we would like to do with reference types in terms of the freeing of scarce resources:

- Use the destructor to encapsulate the necessary code for the freeing of any resources associated with the class.

- Have the destructor automatic invocation tied with the lifetime of the class object.

The CLI has no notion of the class destructor for a reference type. So the destructor has to be mapped into something else in the underlying implementation. Internally, then, the compiler does the following transformations:

- The class has its base class list extended to inherit from the `IDisposable` interface.

- The destructor is transformed into the `Dispose()` method of `IDisposable`.

That gets us half the way to our goal. We still need a way to automate the invocation of the destructor. A special stack-based notation for a reference type is supported; that is, one in which its lifetime is associated within the scope of its declaration. Internally, the compiler transforms the notation to allocate the reference object on the managed heap. With the termination of the scope, the compiler inserts an invocation of the Dispose() method—the user-defined destructor. Reclamation of the actual memory associated with the object remains under the control of the garbage collector.

Let's look at a code example.

```
ref class Wrapper {
    Native *pn;
public:
    // resource acquisition is initialization
    Wrapper( int val ) { pn = new Native( val ); }

    // this will do our disposition of the native memory
    ~Wrapper(){ delete pn; }

    void mfunc();
protected:

    // an explicit Finalize() method - as a failsafe ...
    ! Wrapper() { delete pn; }
};

void f1()
{
    // normal treatment of a reference type ...
    Wrapper^ w1 = gcnew Wrapper( 1024 );

    // mapping a reference type to a lifetime ...
    Wrapper w2( 2048 ); // no ^ token !

    // just illustrating a semantic difference ...
    w1->mfunc(); w2.mfunc();

    // w2 is disposed of here
}

//
// ... later, w1 is finalized at some point, maybe ...
```

C++/CLI is not just an extension of C++ into the managed world. Rather, it represents a fully integrated programming paradigm similar in extent to the earlier integration of the multiple inheritance and generic programming paradigms into the language. I think the team has done an outstanding job.

Integrating C++/CLI with ISO-C++

The type of a string literal, such as "Pooh", is treated differently within C++/CLI; it is more nearly a kind of System::String than a *C-style* character string pointer. This has a visible impact with regard to the resolution of overload functions. For example:

```
public ref class R {
public:
  void foo( System::String^ ); // (1)
  void foo( std::string );     // (2)
  void foo( const char* );     // (3)
};

void bar( R^ r )
{
  // which one?
  r->foo( "Pooh" );
}
```

In ISO-C++, this resolves to instance (3)—a string literal is more nearly a kind of constant pointer to character than it is an ISO-C++ standard library string type. Under C++/CLI, however, this call resolves to (1)—a string literal is now more nearly a kind of System::String than pointer to character. The type of a string literal is treated differently within C++/CLI. It has been designed to be more nearly a kind of System::String than a C-style character string pointer.

```
void foo( System::String^ ); // (1)
void foo( std::string );         // (2)
void foo( const char* );         // (3)

void bar( R^ r ){  r->foo( "Pooh" ); }  // which foo?

ISO-C++: // (3) is invoked ...
C++/CLI: // (1) is invoked ...
```

So, What Did You Say About C++/CLI?

C++/CLI represents an integration of native and managed programming. In this iteration, we have done that through a kind of separate but equal community of source-level and binary elements:

- Mixed mode: source-level mix of native and CTS types plus binary mix of native and CIL object files. (Compiler switch: \clr.)

- Pure mode: source-level mix of native and CTS types. All compiled to CIL object files. (Compiler switch: \clr:pure.)

- Native class can hold CTS types through a special wrapper class only.

- CTS classes can hold native types only as pointers.

Of course, the C++/CLI programmer can also choose to program with the .NET managed types only, and in this way provide verifiable code, using the \clr:safe Visual C++ compiler switch.

How Was C++/CLI Invented?

People often ask, "Who invented C++/CLI?" and, really, that's like asking, "Who invented quantum physics?" The answer to both questions is, well, it was actually a number of different folks, because the problem was too hard for any one of us to do it all, but too important to let more than one person do each part. In a sense, the way you got to do it was by wanting to do it more than anyone else. In that way, the design of C++/CLI is more like an improvisatory jazz composition than the studied design of a master, such as the original invention of C++—then called C with Classes—by Bjarne Stroustrup within Bell Laboratories. Let me see if I can explain that.

There are four people primarily responsible for C++/CLI: David Burggraaf, myself, Herb Sutter, and Brandon Bray. From a programmer's perspective, the primary creator of C++\CLI is Brandon Bray. That will probably surprise some of you because it is unlikely that all of you have (as yet) heard of Brandon, while most of you have certainly heard of both Herb Sutter and myself. The thing to remember, of course, is that at one time, no one had heard of either Herb or myself either. (In fact, the lab manager at Bell Laboratories back in 1985 when I was working on my first edition of *C++ Primer*, asked my boss, Barbara Moo, during our group's dog and pony show, "Why is he writing a book?") So, from now on, whenever you hear Brandon's name, you should think, oh, he's the one who, as we say in animation, skinned the beast and located it in world space.

Brandon won this job literally through a form of corporate natural selection. He wanted it more, and he rose to its many, many difficulties—in particular, Herb's compassionate but firm shepherding and my sheepdog's growls and yapping, always to the same point: Don't go there unless you are certain it is the correct direction and you are able and willing to defend it. That was the standard Brandon was held to, and within that boundary lies C++\CLI. It is a largely homogeneous, coherent, and thoughtful invention. It would, in my opinion, be unfair and incorrect to characterize it as complicated or ill-formed. It is complex, but only because it integrates nearly 30 years of technological change in one interoperative language: Visual C++ 2005.

From an origin's perspective, the primary visionary behind C++\CLI is David Burggraaf, the program manager of Visual C++, although he had no real idea of what C++\CLI would be, except that it would (1) reinvigorate C++ within Microsoft, (2) reengage C++ on the .NET platform, (3) reengage Microsoft within the larger C++ community, and (4) create the best and most leading-edge C++ language development group in the world.

That was David's agenda, and obviously the same person cannot be successful in leading the Visual C++ product unit of Microsoft and detailing a 300++ C++\CLI language specification for ECMA standardization! But had someone other than David been hired by Craig Symonds, general manager of all Visual Studio, Brandon would never had his opportunity—and I would not be writing this, nor would you be reading Stephen's excellent book.

When I joined Microsoft back in the winter of 2001, it was on the condition that they accept the fact that I considered their new product, *Managed Extension for C++*, an *abomination*. When I was later asked to explain what I felt was wrong with it—no one at the time accepted that evaluation— I thought it more productive to show them how I would have done it rather than simply criticize what they had done. Using the reference (&) addition to C invented by Bjarne as an analogy, I introduced the concept of the CLR reference type as a hat (^)—actually, I first proposed % as the token, since it physically mirrors the duple nature of a reference type (a named handle that we manipulate and an unnamed instance of the type allocated on the managed heap).

I also insisted we view our binding as an additional paradigm added to C++ similar to adding multiple inheritance or generic programming using templates—that is, adding keywords and tokens unique to this paradigm. To circumvent the problem of breaking existing code with new keywords, I proscribed contextual keywords. And I said our specification should be mapped as closely as possible to the existing ISO-C++ standard.

This was back in October, 2001. My manager said I had three months to develop the entire language, and another three months to deliver an implementation spec. I was a bit naïve at the time as to how

Microsoft schedules its releases, and so I took him at his word. I delivered both by March, 2002, and that pretty much ended my direct participation in the language design. Three-and-a-half years later, September, 2005, Brandon Bray delivered the specification to ECMA, and an implementation was released as part of Visual C++ 2005.

As the Grateful Dead once wrote, it's been a long, strange trip!

So, returning back to the question, *What is C++/CLI?* It is a first-class entry visa into the .NET programming model. With C++/CLI, there is a C++ migration path not just for our C++ source base, but for our C++ expertise as well. I for one find great satisfaction in that.

Stanley B. Lippman
Architect, Visual C++
Microsoft Corporation

About the Author

STEPHEN R. G. FRASER has over 15 years of IT experience working for a number of consulting companies, ranging from the large consulting firms of EDS and Andersen Consulting (Accenture) and smaller consulting firms like Allin Consulting to startup e-business and medical companies. His IT experience covers all aspects of application and Web development and management, from initial concept all the way through to deployment. He lives in Silicon Valley with his wife, Sarah, and daughter, Shaina.

About the Technical Reviewer

DON REAMEY is a software development engineer for Microsoft's Office Business Applications Group, where he works on applications that integrate with Microsoft Office. Don has 16 years of experience in the software industry, with 10 of those years building C++ and Java applications for the financial industry. Don holds a bachelors of science degree in Information Systems from Pfeiffer University.

Introduction

In the first edition of this book, I said .NET is the future. I need to correct that—C++/CLI is the future. Microsoft seems to have a set pattern when it comes to releasing their products. It takes them three versions to come out with a superior and polished product. Well, true to form, even though they call it .NET 2.0, this is version three and, to put it bluntly, Microsoft has hit the nail on the head once again.

Don't get me wrong; C# and Visual Basic .NET are still great development languages (and version three is as well), but neither have the flexibility or the pedal-to-the-metal power of C++/CLI. With .NET 2.0's version of C++/CLI, you no longer have a forced kludge of .NET concepts and C++. Instead, C++/CLI is now a true implementation of the C++ language from which you can implement .NET applications. If you're one of the legions of established C++ developers out there, this is a godsend, as you no longer have to learn a completely new language to get the benefits of .NET.

Best of all, with C++/CLI, you can practically mix and match .NET code and legacy C++ code at will. Of course, doing so comes at a cost (we'll get to that later in the book), but the benefits of this and not having to rewrite a lot of code may be worth it. As a designer, architect, or developer, it will be your task to determine whether performing this mixing and matching is worth the cost.

Unfortunately, not all is sunshine. All the code you wrote for version 1.1 of .NET can no longer be compiled with the new .NET 2.0 C++/CLI compiler option because the language syntax has changed (for the better, I think). The changes, for the most part, are fairly straightforward. There is, though, a legacy compiler option if you need it to compile your old Managed Extension for C++ v1.1 code. Also, the C++/CLI language has a few new operators, but all of them make sense and provide the language much clearer syntax to work with.

Microsoft has put a lot of effort into the new Managed C++ compiler, or more correctly, C++/CLI compiler. With this version, I feel there will be a large migration of all the old C++ developers back from C# to C++/CLI. C++/CLI will become the premier language, as it should be, to develop .NET code.

What Is This Book About?

This is a book about writing .NET 2.0 applications using C++/CLI. You'll cover a lot of ground in a short period of time. In the end, you'll be proficient at developing .NET applications, be they console applications, Windows applications, Windows services, or Web services.

While you're learning the ins and outs of .NET application development, you'll be learning the syntax of C++/CLI, both traditional to C++ and new to .NET 2.0. You will also gain a good understanding of the .NET architecture.

But, unlike the previous version, this book does not leave legacy developers out in the cold, as it also shows how to integrate your previously built C++ code and/or COM, DCOM, COM+, and ActiveX components with your new .NET 2.0 code. It should be noted that this book does not show you how to build any of this legacy code (other than some very simple example code). Instead, it shows you how to code in the world of .NET 2.0 and how to access this legacy code only when it is needed.

Changes in the Second Edition

Microsoft has made many changes to C++/CLI between versions 1.1 and 2.0; in fact, every program example in this book has been changed, though in almost all cases the output result is exactly the same as in the previous version of this book.

The first major difference is that, when appropriate, the book uses the well-established, standard two-part (declaration and implementation) approach of C++ coding. This version of the book does not advocate the use of C# inline coding style, although it's sometimes easier to code in the inline style, due to the autogenerated code by Visual Studio 2005.

The second major difference in the second edition is that it *does* cover unsafe and unmanaged C++. The book goes into how to use it, but it does not go into detail about the technologies that are developed in it, like COM+ or ATL. You will be notified that the code is unsafe when the following note first mentions it:

Unsafe Code The following is unmanaged code or unsafe code.

The third difference is that this book codes using C++ predefined data types as opposed to .NET Framework data types. Ultimately, they compile to the same thing anyway, and I thought that using .NET Framework data types everywhere in the previous book just complicated things unnecessarily.

Basically, this is a C++/CLI book, not a C# want-to-be book, where some of the readers felt my previous version of this book had strayed. With these three changes, I try to reflect this. An unfortunate side effect is that the preceding three changes forced a lot of alterations to be made throughout the book. In particular, Chapters 2 though 4 of the book have been updated considerably (although in truth, almost every chapter went through a major overhaul).

In addition to this move to make the book truly a C++/CLI book, I also added several new chapters:

- Chapter 6, "Integrated XML Documentation": C++/CLI has integrated the documentation that C# developers have been enjoying for some time.

- Chapter 14, "Windows Services": The basics of creating Windows services using C++/CLI.

- Chapter 17, "Network Programming": The basics of network programming and the Socket assembly.

- Chapter 19, "Security": The basics of .NET security and how to add it to your C++/CLI code.

- Chapter 20, "Unsafe C++ .NET Programming": A look at some of the easier unsafe C++ topics like unsafe classes, mixing managed and unsafe code and wrapping unsafe code.

- Chapter 21, "Advanced Unsafe/Unmanaged C++ .NET Programming": A look at some of the more advanced unsafe C++ topics like PInvoke, COM object integration, and data marshalling.

Who Should Read This Book?

If you're new to the Visual C++/CLI language, plain and simple, this book is for you. The software world is changing, and learning a new language is hard enough without getting unnecessarily bogged down with a complex set of old technologies before you learn about the new ones.

If you're an experienced Visual C++ or Managed Extension for C++ programmer, this book is also for you. Microsoft is changing your world. This book will show you these changes. You'll find many books on the market that try to teach you how to force your old world into this new one. This book isn't one of those. Instead, you'll learn the right way to develop .NET code, as the only focus here is the new world: .NET development.

This book is for Visual C++ programmers who don't care about COM, DCOM, COM+, or ActiveX components, either because they already know them or because they never had any reason to learn to code them. You'll use a pure .NET development environment. The only time you'll use components is when you access them—a necessary evil, as there are thousands of them out there that may never be converted to .NET.

This book is also for the (gasp!) non-Microsoft C++ developer who wants to dive into the .NET world without getting bogged down with all the things that he or she disliked about pre-.NET Windows development.

What Does This Book Cover?

This book addresses the topic of C++/CLI in three parts.

The first four chapters cover the basics and background information that make up the C++/CLI and .NET worlds. I recommend that you read these chapters first, as they provide information that you'll need to understand the remainder of the book. I also recommend that you read the chapters in sequential order because they build on one another.

The main body of the book is the next fifteen chapters of the book, which are stand-alone and cover specific topics. Here, you can pick and choose the chapters that interest you the most (hopefully every chapter) and read them in any order.

The final two chapters cover unsafe code and how to integrate it with C++/CLI. Like the first four chapters, I recommend you read them in order as they build on each other.

Chapter 1: "Overview of the .NET Framework"

In this chapter, you address the basics of the .NET architecture. You're bombarded with many new .NET terms such as "assemblies," "common language runtime (CLR)," "Common Language Specification (CLS)," "common type system (CTS)," "just-in-time (JIT) compilation," "Microsoft intermediate language (MSIL or IL)," and "manifests." This chapter tries to soften the blow of your first foray into the .NET world.

Chapter 2: "C++/CLI Basics"

This chapter should be a refresher course on the basics of C++, but be careful when you read it because there have been several changes, some of them subtle. This chapter covers the core syntax of C++/CLI. Old-time C++ programmers should pay attention to this new feature: the handle.

Chapter 3: "Object-Oriented C++/CLI"

Now, with the basics covered, you delve into object-oriented development (OOD). This chapter covers topics that old-time C++ programmers will take for granted, such as inheritance, encapsulation, polymorphism, classes, methods, and operator overloading. But be careful with this chapter, as .NET makes some significant changes—in particular in the areas of properties, constructors, and destructors.

Chapter 4: "Advanced C++/CLI"

In this chapter, I start to discuss things that should make even seasoned C++ programmers sit up and take notice, because most of the topics I cover are new to C++/CLI. This chapter's topics include multifile programming, exception handling, and delegates.

Chapter 5: "The .NET Framework Class Library"

In this chapter, you start to work with .NET as you make your first strides into the .NET Framework class library. This chapter is just an overview and takes a cursory look at many of the .NET Framework's base classes. I focus on helping you learn how to find the classes that you need. In later chapters, I go into some of these base classes in much more detail.

Chapter 6: "Integrated XML Documentation"

In this chapter, you will learn how to add, generate, and finally view XML documentation that you will embed in your C++/CLI code. This much-needed and welcome feature is a new addition to C++/CLI in version 2.0 and closely maps to the documentation that has been available to the C# developer since the release of .NET.

Chapter 7: "Collections"

Working with collections should be nearly second nature to the average software developer. Because collections are so commonplace, most programmers expect powerful and feature-rich ways of handling them, and .NET doesn't disappoint. This chapter covers the six common collections provided by .NET and then touches on a few less common ones.

Chapter 8: "Input, Output, and Serialization"

Many programs that you'll write in your career will involve moving, copying, deleting, renaming, reading, and/or writing files. More recently, with object-oriented programming, many of the file's I/O activity in a program involve serialization. With this in mind, you'll explore the System::IO and System::Runtime::Serialization namespaces.

Chapter 9: "Basic Windows Forms Applications"

Almost all Windows developers, sometime in their careers, will create a Windows application. This chapter shows you how to do it ".NET style." You'll explore how Visual Studio 2005 simplifies your development experience. You'll also explore the basic controls found in the System::Windows::Forms namespace in some detail.

Chapter 10: "Advanced Windows Forms Applications"

Having a handle on the basics is all well and good, but, as a .NET developer, I'm sure you will want to add more elaborate controls to your Windows applications. This chapter takes what you learned in Chapter 9 and expands on it by exploring some of the more advanced controls available to you in the System::Windows::Forms namespace.

Chapter 11: "Graphics Using GDI+"

If you're like me, you like a little pizzazz in the form of graphics to spice up a boring Windows appli-cation. This chapter shows you how .NET has made adding images and graphics a whole lot easier with the System::Drawing namespace.

Chapter 12: "ADO.NET and Database Development"

What is software development without databases? In most cases, the answer would be "not much." Microsoft is well aware of this and has gone to great lengths to make database programming easier. Their solution is ADO.NET. In this chapter, you'll explore the many features of ADO.NET that you can find in the System::Data namespace.

Chapter 13: "XML"

XML is the new world order when it comes to data storage. Microsoft has embraced XML in a big way. This chapter shows the many ways that you can now access XML data in the .NET environment.

Chapter 14: "Windows Services"

The C++ language has long been a stronghold for Windows services development. This will not change with C++/CLI. In fact, I predict that some of the defection to C# in this area may return because of the power of C++/CLI. In this chapter, you will see just how easy it is to create Windows services using C++/CLI.

Chapter 15: "Web Services"

The concept of Web services is not unique. In this chapter, you'll explore Web services within the .NET Framework. You'll examine how to design and create them by walking through the process yourself, creating a simple Web service and three different clients (console, Windows application, and Web application) to interact with the service.

Chapter 16: "Multithreaded Programming"

Being able to run multiple threads at the same time allows for better CPU usage and is a powerful feature. This chapter explores how the .NET Framework makes working with multiple threads concurrently a snap as you cover the .NET Framework's built-in multithreading capabilities.

Chapter 17: "Network Programming"

In this chapter, you'll examine the different methods of moving data over a network using .NET. Or, more specifically, you will examine socket coding in C++/CLI for both TCP and UDP in both synchro-nous and asynchronous approaches.

Chapter 18: "Assembly Programming"

In traditional C++, application and library developers had few choices regarding what went into .exes and .dlls. With .NET assemblies, this has changed, and you now have plenty of choices. This chapter explores those choices by looking at how you can augment your assemblies with resources, localiza-tion, attributes, and reflection.

Chapter 19: "Security"

.NET is touted as being an extremely secure software environment, and this is evident with the plethora of .NET Framework security features. In this chapter, you will see how you can access many of them using C++/CLI.

Chapter 20: "Unsafe C++ .NET Programming"

This chapter takes a look at what is involved in mixing and matching unsafe C++, also known as unmanaged C++ or traditional C++, with Safe/Managed C++/CLI. If you have some legacy C++ code that you want to migrate to .NET, this is the chapter for you.

Chapter 21: "Advanced Unsafe or Unmanaged C++ .NET Programming"

Unlike other books, which cover this topic, this book looks at advanced unsafe C++ from the eyes of someone who is coding in C++/CLI and wants to integrate some unsafe or unmanaged code into his or her existing code. (Usually the approach is the opposite, i.e., a developer is coding unsafe or unmanaged code and trying to force it into the C++/CLI environment.) It will regard the unsafe/unmanaged code as a black box that you will attach to your C++/CLI code in different fashions, depending on the type of unsafe/unmanaged code to which you are connecting.

What You Need to Use This Book

The first thing you should probably do is download the code for this book from the Downloads section of the Apress Web site (http://www.apress.com) or from http://www.ProCppCLI.net. Most of the code in the book is listed in its entirety, but some of the larger programs (in particular, the Windows Forms applications) list only relevant code.

In addition to the source code, you should have a copy of Visual Studio 2005 final beta or later. Note that most, but not all, the features mentioned in the book work with the Visual C++/CLI Express 2005 version.

As long as you have the .NET Framework version 2.0 and its associated C++/CLI compiler, however, you should be able to build nearly everything in the book (though with a lot more effort).

■**Caution** This book contains material that isn't supported in Visual Studio .NET 2003 and the .NET Framework 1.1 or earlier.

This Book Is Not the End of the Story

A book is a pretty static thing, and once you finish reading it, you have to go elsewhere for more information. Fortunately, I have built a Web site devoted entirely to Visual C++/CLI and the .NET 2.0 Platform: http://www.ProCppCLI.net.

On this site, you will find not only all the source code for this book, but also further writings on C++/CLI by me and other authors. The Web site's goal is to promote further exploration of C++/CLI and thus it will also contain news, a discussion area, an area to upload your code, and an area to download third-party code.

How to Reach Me

I would like to hear from you. Feel free to e-mail me at Stephen.Fraser@apress.com or srgfraser@ProCppCLI.net. If you have a question and you think others would benefit from the answer, ask it on the http://www.ProCppCLI.net discussion board. I will respond to every e-mail and discussion entry that I can. Questions, comments, and suggestions are all welcome.

Oh, by the way, thank you for buying my book. Now, let's get started!

PART 1

The C++/CLI Language

CHAPTER 1

■ ■ ■

Overview of the .NET Framework

First off, let's get one thing straight. This book is about developing code within the confines of the Microsoft .NET Framework 2.0. Therefore, it only makes sense that you start by getting acquainted with the underlying architecture with which you will be developing your code: the .NET Framework.

I cover a lot of material in this chapter, mostly at the 30,000-foot level. The main goal here isn't to make you a .NET Framework expert. This chapter is designed to provide you with a level playing field from which to start your C++/CLI code development while exploring this book.

I start with a brief description of what the .NET Framework is and why we programmers need it. Then, I briefly examine the assembly, which is the central building block for all .NET Framework application distribution and execution. Next, I move on to the core of .NET Framework: the common language runtime (CLR), the common type system (CTS), and the common language specification (CLS). Finally, I discuss, at a very high level, the software components available to .NET Framework developers.

What Is .NET?

To put it in the simplest of terms, .NET is Microsoft's strategy to move from a client-centric model to a network-centric model. Another way of looking at it is that the impact of .NET will be the following:

- *For programmers*: A paradigm shift in the approach to software development and deployment.
- *For architectures*: Internet processing power to be distributed more on the Web clients and less on the Web servers via Web deployment, enabling much better use of the Internet.
- *For the future of the Internet*: Ultimately, the Internet will become more an operating system and less a means of simply connecting computers together.

These things are mostly about the future. What does .NET mean to programmers here and now? The first major change that you will see with .NET is that the medium for software deployment will change from full-functionality CD-ROM installations to much smaller, as-needed-functionality Internet downloads. Microsoft calls this "Click-once" deployment or smart clients.

.NET provides the functionality to place small elements of your application programs on a Web server. These elements can then be downloaded on an as-needed basis, when that application is executing. Basically, applications run as described in these steps:

1. A user attempts to start an application using the .NET runtime.

2. The runtime checks to see if an up-to-date version of the application is in the system's global assembly cache. If it is, the runtime executes it from the cache; otherwise, the runtime downloads the updated version and then executes it.

3. While the application is running, it may require other elements. When one such element is required, the runtime checks the cache to see if it exists. Then, the runtime makes one further check to ensure the element is up to date. If there is no version in the cache, or it is not up to date, then the element is downloaded.

As you can see, this is considerably different from how it is done now, whereby everything is placed on a CD-ROM and installed at one time. I'm sure you can see that the .NET method ensures that the "latest and greatest" are always being executed.

Does this mean that the only way of distributing software is via the Internet? No, there is nothing stopping you from distributing the old way or even combining the two methods, in which you install everything up front and then use the Internet to keep everything up to date.

As you can imagine, developers now have to start designing their software in a much more modular fashion. Developers also have to be conscious of what modules will likely go together so that those modules can be downloaded concurrently to mitigate the amount of time a user has to wait between running different functionalities of the application. This will also allow for more efficient usage of the Internet.

Another major aspect of .NET that developers will become quickly aware of is that applications are no longer restricted only to the computer on which they are running. It is now possible to execute code from Web services on computers anywhere around the world. True, with some complex coding such as DCOM, COM+, and CORBA, you could, before the advent of .NET, escape the sandbox of the application host computer. But now with .NET, the code to access the resources of the Internet is nearly effortless. Equally as easy, it is possible to make your resources available to the Internet. With .NET, IIS, and a domain or IP, a computer does not have to be an island.

■ **Note** Wherever you read the word "Internet," you can assume "intranet" and "extranet" apply as well.

What Is the .NET Framework?

The .NET Framework comprises all the pieces needed to develop, deploy, and execute Web services, Web applications, Windows services, Windows applications, and console applications. (Well, almost all the pieces. IIS is needed for Web services and Web applications.) I discuss each of these in more detail later in the chapter. You can think of the .NET Framework as a three-level hierarchy consisting of the following:

- Application development technologies like Web services, Web Forms, and Windows Forms
- .NET Framework base classes
- CLR

This hierarchy is illustrated in Figure 1-1.

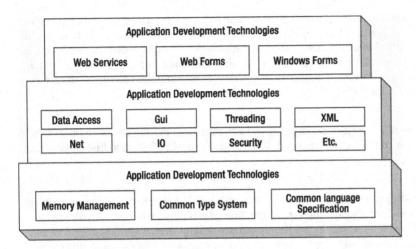

Figure 1-1. *The .NET Framework hierarchy*

Each of the layers in Figure 1-1 is dependent on the layer beneath it. The CLR lies just above the operating system and insulates the programmer from its intricacies. The CLR is what actually loads, verifies, and executes Web services, Web Form applications, Windows services, Windows applications, and console applications.

The .NET Framework base classes are a large number of classes broken up by namespaces containing all the predeveloped functionality of .NET. They contain classes to handle things such as file I/O, database access, security, threading, graphical user interfaces, and so on. As a C++/CLI developer, you will spend many hours perusing and using these classes.

The application development technologies provide a higher layer of abstraction than the base classes. C++/CLI developers will use these technologies to build their Web applications, Web services, and Windows applications. Most of the functionality a developer needs can be found at this level of abstraction, but in those cases where more control is needed, the developer can dive down into the base classes level.

.NET Programming Advantages

The .NET Framework was designed and developed from day one to be Internet aware and Internet enabled. It uses technologies such as SOAP and XML as its underlying methods of communication. As a developer, you have the option of probing as deeply as you wish into each of these technologies, but with the .NET Framework, you have the luxury, if you want, of staying completely ignorant of them.

You have probably heard that .NET is language neutral. This key feature of .NET is handled by .NET compilers. It is currently possible to develop code using the languages provided by Microsoft, (C++/CLI, C#, J#, JScript .NET, and Visual Basic .NET) or in one of the many other languages provided by third parties (such as COBOL, Delphi, and Perl). All .NET-compatible languages have full access to the .NET Framework class library. I cover .NET multilanguage support briefly in this chapter.

Another thing you have probably heard whispers about is that .NET can be platform independent. This means that it is possible to port the .NET Framework to non-Windows platforms and then run it without recompiling .NET applications and services. The reason for this is that .NET-compatible code is compiled into something called *assemblies*, which contain code, along with several other things, in an intermediate language. I cover assemblies briefly in this chapter and then delve into the art of working with them in Chapter 18.

Note It is true that the .NET Framework can be ported. Two such ports, Mono and DOTGNU, for the Linux platform are probably the best-known ports of the .NET Framework. Microsoft has also provided Rotor for multiple platforms such as MAC and BSD Unix.

If you've been coding and deploying Windows code in C++ for any length of time, I'm sure you've become painfully aware that it's anything but simple. Now, if you've gone beyond this to build distributed applications, the complexity has multiplied many times over. A key design goal of the .NET Framework is to dramatically simplify software development and deployment. Some of the most obvious ways that the .NET Framework does this are as follows:

- It usually shelters you from the complexities of the raw Windows Application Programming Interface (API). However, there are several APIs in the Win32 that don't exist in .NET and still require the use of P/Invoke to gain access. I cover P/Invoke in Chapter 21.

- It provides a consistent, well-documented object model, and with it, users can create their own consistent self-documented object models.

- Managed code is used to create objects that can be garbage collection. You no longer have to worry about memory loss because you forgot to delete allocated pointers. In fact, if you use managed code, you don't even have to deallocate pointers because the .NET Framework does not use pointers; instead it uses handles, and the .NET Framework does the deleting of allo-cated memory for you.

- The intricacies of COM and COM+ have been removed. To be more accurate, COM and COM+ are not part of the .NET Framework. You can continue to use these technologies, but .NET supports them by placing COM and COM+ components in a class-library-derived wrapper. You no longer have to worry about things such as the VARIANT, IUnknown, IDL, and so on.

- Deployment components no longer use the registry or special directories.

- Deployment is frequently as simple as an xcopy.

A Closer Look at the .NET Framework

Okay, you have looked at .NET and the .NET Framework in general terms. Now, let's break it into the elements that are relevant to a C++/CLI programmer and then look at each element in some detail. There are five major elements that a C++/CLI developer should have at least a basic knowledge of before attempting to code:

- Assemblies
- CLR
- CTS
- CLS
- .NET Framework class library

Each element impacts the C++/CLI programmer differently. Assemblies are a new form of binary distribution. The CLR is a new way of executing. The CTS is a new way of defining data-storage types. CLS is a specification of language-neutral support. The .NET Framework class library is a whole new set of development objects to learn. I discuss each of these elements in more detail in the following sections.

Assemblies

You need a basic understanding of assemblies before you can learn about any other element of the .NET Framework. I cover some basic information about assemblies in this chapter and then discuss working with them in detail in Chapter 18.

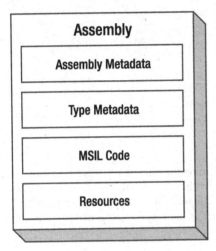

Figure 1-2. *The basic assembly structure*

Assemblies are the core building blocks for all .NET Framework application distribution and execution. They are generated after compiling C++/CLI code. Like pre-.NET application deliverables, they end with either .exe or .dll, but that is pretty well as far as the similarities go.

Basic Structure

Assemblies are a self-describing collection of functionalities stored in an intermediate language and/or resources needed to execute some portion of an application. Assemblies are made up of four sections: the assembly metadata, type metadata, Microsoft intermediate language (MSIL) code, and resources (Figure 1-2). All sections except the assembly metadata are optional, though an assembly made up of just assembly metadata sections won't do anything.

Assemblies can be either private or shared. *Private assemblies* reside in the same directory as the application itself or in one of its child directories. *Shared assemblies*, on the other hand, are stored in the global assembly cache (GAC). The GAC is really nothing more than a directory structure that stores all the assemblies that are globally available to the computer (Figure 1-3). A neat feature of the GAC is that more than one version of the same assembly can reside in it.

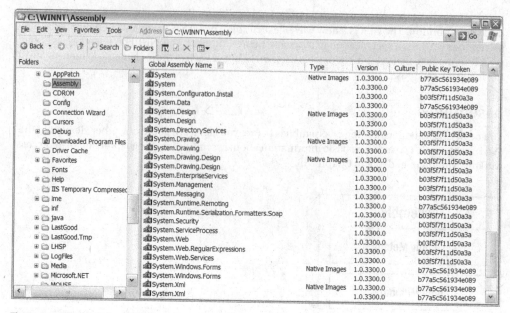

Figure 1-3. *The global assembly cache*

A key feature of all assemblies is that they are self-describing. In other words, all information needed to understand how to use the assembly can be found within the assembly itself. An assembly does this by including metadata directly within itself. There are two different metadata sections in an assembly: the assembly metadata and the type metadata. You gain access to this metadata using reflection, which I cover in Chapter 18.

Metadata

The *assembly metadata* is also known as the *assembly manifest*. As its name suggests, the assembly metadata describes the assembly. Here is a list of some of the assembly metadata's contents:

- The name of the assembly.
- The version number.
- The culture used by the assembly (i.e., language, currency, number formatting, and so on).
- Strong name information. This is a uniquely identifiable name that can be used for shared assemblies.
- A list of all files that make up the assembly.
- A list of all reference assemblies.
- Reference information for all exported classes, methods, properties, and so on, found in the assembly.

The *type metadata*, however, describes the types within the assembly. The type metadata generated depends on the type being created. On the one hand, if the type were a method, then the metadata generated would contain things such as the name, return types, number of arguments and their types, and access level. A property, on the other hand, would reference the get and set methods; these methods in turn would contain names, return types, and so on.

A nice feature of metadata is that it can be used by many of the tools available to the C++/CLI developer. For example, Visual Studio .NET's IntelliSense statement completion functionality (Figure 1-4) is actually driven using the reference assembly's metadata and not some secondary description file. Because it comes directly from an assembly, IntelliSense will also work for assemblies you have written yourself without any additional effort on your part.

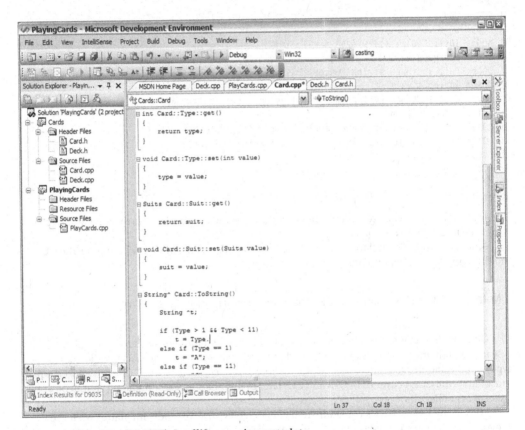

Figure 1-4. *Visual Studio .NET's IntelliSense using metadata*

Versioning

Application assemblies are very version-aware when they're referencing strong-named assemblies within the GAC. Every assembly has a version number. Also, every referencing assembly stores the version number of any assembly that it references. It's not until the referenced assembly is strong named and in the GAC that the referencing assembly automatically checks when executing, via the CLR, that the versions match before it continues to execute. I cover assembly versioning in detail in Chapter 18.

Microsoft Intermediate Language

A major change that is hidden for the most part under the covers but that you should be aware of as a C++/CLI programmer is that C++/CLI code gets compiled to MSIL and not machine code. MSIL is a CPU-independent set of instructions similar to an assembly language. For example, it contains arithmetic and logical operators and flow control. But, unlike the average assembly language, it also contains higher-level instructions to load, store, initialize, and call class objects.

Just for some grins and giggles, here is an example of some MSIL generated from a simple C++/CLI program. See if you can figure out what it does.

```
IL_0000: ldarg.0
IL_0001: ldarg.1
IL_0002: add
IL_0003: stloc.0
IL_0004: ldstr "{0} + {1} = {2}"
IL_0009: ldarga.s val1
IL_000b: call instance string [mscorlib]System.Int32::ToString()
IL_0010: ldarga.s val2
IL_0012: call instance string [mscorlib]System.Int32::ToString()
IL_0017: ldloca.s total
IL_0019: call instance string [mscorlib]System.Int32::ToString()
IL_001e: call void [mscorlib]System.Console::WriteLine(string,
object,
object,
object)
IL_0023: ret
```

For those of you who are curious, the preceding code adds two numbers together and then writes the result out to the console.

MSIL is easily converted to native code. In fact, just prior to the MSIL code running, the CLR rapidly compiled it to native code.

■ **Note** The MSIL in an assembly is compiled prior to execution. It is *not* interpreted at runtime.

One key characteristic of MSIL is that it is an object-orientation–based language with the restriction of single class inheritance, although multiple inheritance of interfaces is allowed. All types, both value and reference, used within the MSIL must conform to the CTS. Any exposed types must follow the CLS. I cover both CTS and CLS later in this chapter. Error handling should be done using exceptions.

MSIL is the key to .NET's capability to be language neutral. All code, no matter what the programming language, is compiled into the same MSIL. Because all languages ultimately compile to the same MSIL, it is now possible for encapsulation, inheritance, polymorphism, exception handling, debugging, and so on, to be language neutral.

MSIL will also be one of the keys to .NET's capability to be platform independent. With MSIL, you can have "write once, run anywhere" ability, just as you do with Java. All that is required for an assembly to run on a non-Windows platform is for the ported CLR to compile MSIL into non-Windows-specific code.

With the combination of MSIL and metadata, .NET is capable of providing a high level of security. For example, strong names found in metadata can ensure that only trusted assemblies are run. If you add code verification to this, provided when your code is compiled with the /clr:safe option, then the CLR can ensure that only managed code running with valid privileges is executed.

Resources

In .NET, resources (i.e., string tables, images, cursors, etc.) can be stored in two places: in external .resources files or directly within an assembly. Accessing the resources in either location is extremely easy, as the .NET Framework class library provides three straightforward classes for access within the System::Resources namespace. I cover these classes in detail in Chapter 18, but if you want to get a head start and look them up yourself, here they are:

- ResourceManager: Use to access resources from within an assembly

- ResourceWriter: Use to write resources to an external .resources file

- ResourceReader: Use to read resources from an external .resources file

In addition to these classes, the .NET Framework provides the utility resgen.exe, which creates a .resources file from a text file containing key/value pairs.

The resgen.exe utility is very useful if you wish to make your Windows applications support multiple (human) languages. It's easy to do this. Simply create multiple .resources files, one for each language. From these, build satellite assemblies for each language. Then the application will automatically access the correct language resource based on the current culture specified on the computer. You'll learn how to do this in Chapter 18.

Common Language Runtime

Runtimes are hardly a new concept when it comes to code execution. Visual Basic 6.0 has msvbvm60.dll, and Java, of course, has the Java Virtual Machine (JVM). The common language runtime (CLR) is .NET's runtime system.

Do we need another runtime? What makes this one that much better than all the rest? It is simply the fact that the CLR is designed to be the runtime for all languages and (possibly) all platforms. Or, in other words, you no longer need a myriad of different runtimes to handle each programming language and platform. Instead, all you need is the CLR.

It's a pretty big claim. Does it hold water?

There are two common roles for runtimes: to execute code and/or to add common functionality used by most applications. The CLR performs both of these roles for the .NET Framework. But these roles are only the tip of the iceberg. The CLR also performs several other services, such as code verification, access security, garbage collection, and exception handling, and it also handles multilanguage support and compiles MSIL into the native language of the platform (Figure 1-5).

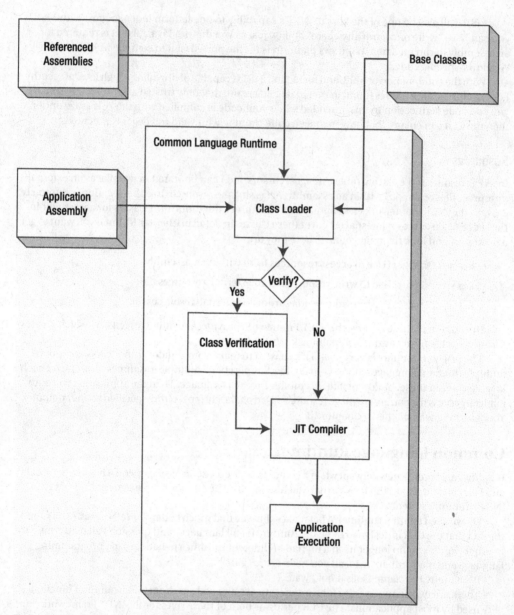

Figure 1-5. *The CLR start-up process flow*

Starting up an application in .NET is conceptually very simple. The CLR loads the application assembly, any referenced developer assemblies, and any referenced base class library assemblies. Then, the application is optionally verified for type safety and valid access security. Next, the loaded MSIL, with the help of information found in the metadata from the assemblies, is compiled into native code. Finally, the application is executed.

The CLR was designed to help provide the following:

- *Simplified programming infrastructure*: Much of the low-level plumbing (memory management, local and remote process communication, etc.) is handled automatically or hidden unless access is needed.

- *Scalability*: Areas that allow for scalability (memory management, process communication, component management, and so on) are contained, already optimized, within the framework.

- *Simple, safe deployment*: A simple xcopy is usually all that is required for deployment.

Managed Data

Managed data is data that is allocated by an application and then deallocated by the CLR's garbage collector. All .NET languages except C++/CLI default to managed data. To create managed data in C++/CLI, you must create a reference type within your source code. Chapter 3 will explore how to create managed data in C++/CLI.

Managed Code

Basically, *managed code* is code targeted for the .NET Framework's CLR, which provides things such as memory management, code access security, and multilanguage integration. Essentially, if the code is compiled into MSIL within assemblies, then usually you are creating managed code.

Conversely, *native code*, sometimes known (inaccurately) as unmanaged code, is not targeted for the CLR. Native code runs outside of the CLR sandbox, meaning that you lose things like garbage collection and code security. It is possible for the .NET Framework to access C DLLs, COM, and COM+ services, even though all of these are native. I cover native code in detail in Chapters 20 and 21.

New to .NET version 2.0 is the ability to create *safe code* or managed code that is verifiable by the CLR. *Unsafe code* as you may expect is code that can't be verified and is usually in the form of native code, but that is not a requirement, and unsafe code can also be compiled to MSIL and run in the CLR (thus, managed code by definition). I cover unsafe code in detail in Part 3. I will also be pointing it out in passing throughout the book.

All the compilers that come with the .NET Framework default to generating managed code except C++/CLI. To create managed code in C++/CLI, you need to add one of the .NET command-line switches (/clr:oldSyntax, /clr, /clr:pure and /clr:safe) when compiling.

- /clr:oldSyntax: This switch is used to compile of C++/CLI code from .NET versions 1.0 and 1.1. It will generally create a mixed image of native and managed code.

- /clr: This switch is used for the new C++/CLI code syntax of .NET 2.0. It will generally create a mixed image of native and managed code.

- /clr:pure: This switch is used to generate managed code and unmanaged data. If you use unsafe code, the compile will fail.

- /clr:safe: This switch is used to generate managed code and managed data. If you use unsafe code and/or unmanaged data, the compile will fail.

When you use Visual Studio .NET, simply select one of the C++/CLI project templates, and these will set the /clr switch for you. However, I suggest that you change the switch to /clr:safe if you plan to use only managed code, as this book does in most examples.

Common Language Runtime Services

Along with loading and executing an assembly, the CLR provides several other services. Code verification and code access verification are optional services available before the assembly is loaded. Garbage collection, on the other hand, is always active while the assembly is being executed.

Code Verification

The *code verification* service is executed prior to actually running the application. Its goal is to walk through the code, ensuring that it is safe to run. For example, it checks for things such as invalid handle references and reading past the end of arrays. The goal of code verification is to ensure that the code does not crash, and that if an error happens to occur, it is handled by the CLR by throwing an exception. This gives the application more control over how to recover or exit gracefully.

Code Access Verification

Code access verification also walks through the code and checks that all code has the permission to execute. The goal of this service is to try to stop malicious attacks on the user's computer.

A simplified way of looking at how this service works is that the CLR contains a list of actions that it can grant permission to execute, and the assembly contains a list of all the permissions it requires to run. If the CLR can grant all the permissions, then the assembly runs without problems. If, however, the CLR can't grant all the permissions, then it runs what it can but generates an exception whenever it tries to do something that it doesn't have permission to do.

Garbage Collection

Garbage collection is the mechanism that allows a runtime to detect and remove managed objects from the managed heap that are no longer being physically accessed within the application. The .NET Framework's garbage collector has the added bonus of compacting the memory after it removes the unused portion, thus keeping the fingerprints of the applications as small as possible. This bonus can complicate things sometimes, as managed objects in .NET do not have a fixed location, but you can overcome this with the pin_ptr<> keyword. I cover pin_ptr<> in Chapter 20. Also, because managed objects are referenced using handles and not pointers, pointer arithmetic is gone except in unsafe sections of the code.

Garbage collection presents a big change to average C++/CLI programmers, because it means an end to most of those annoying memory leaks that plague them while developing. It also has an added bonus: Programmers when dealing with memory management no longer have to figure out where to call the delete command to the classes that they've created using the gcnew command.

■**Caution** We will see in Chapter 3 that programmers still have to be aware of when to call the delete command if they are working with computer resources.

Garbage collection is not the default for C++/CLI. Because this is the case, there are a few things (covered in Chapter 3) that C++/CLI programmers need to learn before they can use garbage collection—in particular, the keyword ref. Fortunately, with version 2.0 of .NET, unlike in prior versions of C++/CLI, programmers have gained control of when a managed object gets deleted.

■**Note** Well, there actually isn't a prior version of C++/CLI. What came before C+/CLI was Managed Extensions for C++, or Managed C++. If you want to learn about Managed C++, you can read about it in my previous book, *Managed C++ and .NET Development*.

Attributes

Attributes are a way for developers to provide additional information about the classes, methods, or data types to the assemblies they are creating. This additional information is stored within the assembly's metadata.

There are several predefined attributes that the compiler can use to help during the compile process. For example, the `System::Obsolete` attribute causes the compiler to generate a warning when it encounters an obsolete method in a class library assembly.

You will see in Chapter 18 how to work with attributes and how it is possible to add your own custom attributes to the assembly metadata.

All attributes—developer code-created and compiler-generated—can be extracted using reflection.

Reflection

An interesting service provided by the CLR is *reflection*. This is the ability to programmatically examine the metadata within an assembly, including the one executing the reflection code. This service allows access to the metadata information, such as details about classes, methods, properties, and so on, contained within the assembly.

Most likely, you will use reflection mainly to get attribute information out of the assembly metadata. For more advanced C++/CLI developers, reflection provides the ability to extract type information within a class so that they can use it to generate types dynamically.

Reflection is accomplished using the myriad classes in the `System::Reflection` namespace. Chapter 18 covers reflection.

Multiple Language Support

.NET had the ambitious goal of creating a completely language-neutral environment for developing software. Some of the features the .NET Framework and Visual Studio .NET developers had in mind were the following:

- Common data types should be shared by all languages.
- Object handles and/or references from any language should be able to be passed as an argument to a method.
- Calling methods from classes created in other languages should be possible.
- Classes should be able to contain instances of other classes created in a different language.
- Inheriting from classes created in another language should be possible.
- The development and debugging environment for all languages should be the same.

Believe it or not, every one of those features is now supported by the CLR and MSIL.

The idea is to pick the best language for the job. Each language has its strong and weak points when it comes to software development. With language-neutral development, you can select the language that best suits the type of development needed.

Will developers accept this concept? In this age of computer-language holy wars, it seems a little doubtful. Plus, allowing the use of multiple languages during the development of a project does add complexity. Having said that, though, I've worked on a large project that used C, C++, COBOL, HTML, Macro (Assembler), and SQL, plus an assortment of batch scripting languages. To make things worse, each of these languages had different tools for development, and debugging was a nightmare. I don't even want to talk about passing data between modules created in different languages. What I would have given for .NET back then!

How does the .NET Framework create a language-neutral environment? The key is a combination of MSIL and metadata. Basically, the MSIL code tells the CLR what to do (which commands to execute), and the metadata tells it how to do it (which interfaces to use). For a language to be .NET Framework compliant, it obviously needs to be compiled into MSIL code and metadata and placed in an assembly (Figure 1-6).

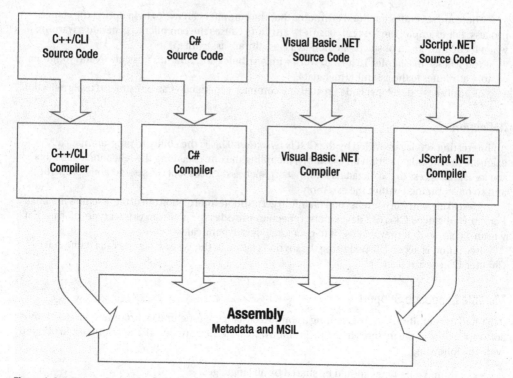

Figure 1-6. *Many compilers, one output*

Because all languages have this requirement, Microsoft was able to tweak each compiler they developed so that it created code to conform to their MSIL and metadata language-neutral requirements. Also, all languages were changed to conform to the common type system (CTS). I cover the CTS later in this chapter.

Multiple Platform Support

By its architecture, the .NET Framework is conducive to multiple platform support. The CLR enables platform independence by providing a runtime layer that sits between the operating system and the application. The just-in-time (JIT) compiler generates machine-specific native code. JIT is covered in the next section, "Just-in-Time Compilation." The MSIL and metadata allow for the "write once, run anywhere" capability that is the claim to fame of Java.

Currently, the only multiple platform support provided by the .NET Framework is for Windows-based platforms such as Windows 2000 and Windows XP. With .NET version 2.0, Microsoft has added 64-bit support to the existing 32-bit support, but the operating system is still only Windows-based.

What does platform independence mean to C++/CLI programmers? It means a new way of looking at things. C++/CLI programmers think of multiple platform support as coding generically and recompiling on each new platform. With the .NET Framework, developers only need to develop the code and compile it once. The resulting assembly could be run on any supported platform without change.

True, to develop real platform-independent code, developers must only use managed code. If a developer were to use unmanaged code, the assembly generated would become closely coupled with the architecture on which it was compiled.

Note This book focuses, for the most part, on creating code that is platform independent. Though, unlike the previous version of the book, it does delve into unsafe code, which is not platform independent.

Just-in-Time Compilation

Even though .NET applications are stored in an intermediate language, .NET applications are not interpreted. Instead, they are compiled into a native executable. It is the job of the JIT compiler, a key component of the CLR, to convert MSIL code into machine code with the help of metadata found in the executable assembly.

The JIT compiling process is, in concept, very easy. When an application is started, the JIT compiler is called to convert the MSIL code and metadata into machine code. To avoid the potentially slow start-up time caused by compiling the entire application, the JIT compiler only compiles the portions of code that it calls, when they are called (hence the name, *just-in-time compiler*). After the code is compiled, it is placed in cached memory and then run. The compiled code remains in the cached memory for as long as the application is executing. This way, the portion of code can be grabbed from cached memory, instead of having to go through the compile process each time it is called. There is a bonus in compiling this way. If the code is not called, it is not compiled.

Microsoft claims that managed code should run as fast as native code. How can Microsoft make this claim? The JIT compiler is amazingly fast, but there still is the overhead of having to compile the application each time it is run. This leads one to believe that managed code would be slower.

The key to Microsoft's claim is that JIT compilers generate code specific to the processor type of the machine they are running on. On the other hand, traditional compilers generate code targeting a general range of processor types. For example, the Visual Studio 6.0 C++ compiler generates generic Pentium machine code. A JIT compiler, knowing that it is run on, let's say, a quad processor Pentium IV, would generate code specific to that processor. The execution time between these two sets of machine code will in many cases be quite different and always in the favor of the JIT compiler-generated code. This increase in speed in the managed code should offset the JIT compiling overhead and, in many cases, make the overall execution faster than the unmanaged code.

Common Type System

The common type system (CTS) defines how all types are declared, used, and managed within the .NET Framework and, more specifically, the CLR. It is also a key component for the CLR's multiple language support. The CTS was designed to perform the following functions:

- Provide an object-oriented data model that can support the data types of all .NET Framework-compatible programming languages.

- Provide a set of constraints that the data types of a .NET-compatible language must adhere to so that it can interact with other .NET-compatible programming languages.

- Provide a framework for .NET-compatible interlanguage integration and data type safety.

There are two categories of data types defined by the CTS: the value type and the reference type. *Value types*, such as int, float, or char, are stored as the representation of the data type itself. *Reference types*, such as handles, classes, or arrays, are stored on the managed heap as references to the location of the data type.

Note Unmanaged pointer types are stored on the C Runtime (CRT) heap, which differs from the managed reference type's managed heap.

As you can see in Figure 1-7, all data types fall into one of these two categories.

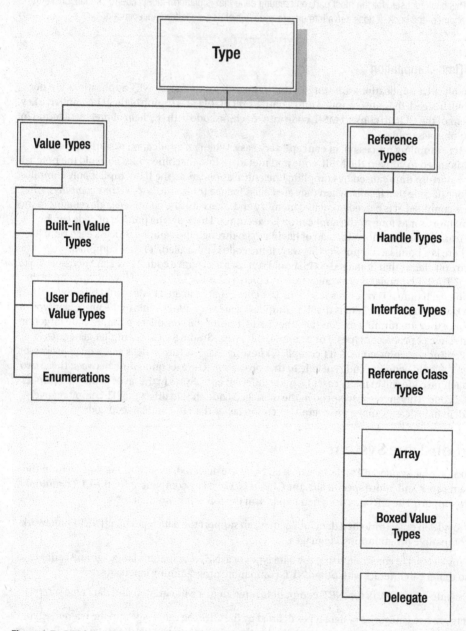

Figure 1-7. *CTS hierarchy*

Let's briefly walk through the hierarchy of all CTS types:

- *Arrays*: A single or multidimensional indexed grouping of types
- *Boxed value types*: A temporary reference to a value type so that it can be placed on the heap

- *Built-in value types*: Primitive value types that represent integers, real numbers, Booleans, and characters
- *Reference class types*: A user-defined grouping of types and methods
- *Delegates*: A type that holds a reference to a method
- *Enumerations*: A list of named integer constants
- *Interface types*: A class type where all methods are abstract
- *Handler types*: A reference to a type
- *User-defined value types*: User-defined expansion to the standard, primitive value types

A point worth mentioning is that the CLS defines all .NET-compatible language data types, but a .NET-compatible language does not need to support all CLS-defined data types. In versions prior to .NET 2.0, even Microsoft Visual Basic .NET did not support all data types. This has changed in .NET version 2.0, as you can see in the comparison of the built-in value and reference types supported by Visual Basic .NET, C#, and C++/CLI (Table 1-1).

Table 1-1. *Built-in Value and Reference Types and Their Language Keywords*

Base Class	Visual Basic .NET	C#	C++/CLI
System::Byte	Byte	byte	unsigned char
System::Sbyte	SByte	sbyte	char
System::Int16	Short	short	short or __int16
System::Int32	Integer	int	int, long or __int32
System::Int64	Long	long	long long or __int64
System::UInt16	UShort	ushort	unsigned short or unsigned __int16
System::UInt32	UInteger	uint	unsigned int, unsigned long or unsigned __int32
System::UInt64	ULong	ulong	unsigned long long or unsigned __int64
System::Single	Single	float	float
System::Double	Double	double	double
System::Object	Object	object	Object^
System::Char	Char	char	__wchar_t
System::String	String	string	String^
System::Decimal	Decimal	decimal	Decimal
System::IntPtr	IntPtr	IntPtr	IntPtr
System::UIntPtr	UIntPtr	UIntPtr	UIntPtr
System::Boolean	Boolean	bool	bool

Note The ^ character in Table 1-1 is not a typo. This is C++/CLI's new handle symbol, which I will cover in Chapter 2.

Caution You should take care when using UInt64, as unpredictable results are possible on Intel 32-bit platforms because they are not thread-safe and do not load the registers atomically.

Common Language Specification

Given that not all of the CTS data types need to be supported by every .NET-compatible language, how then does the .NET Framework maintain that these languages are, in fact, compatible? This is where the common language specification (CLS) comes in. The CLS is a minimum subset of the CTS that all languages must support to be .NET compatible (Figure 1-8).

To ensure interlanguage operability, it is only the CLS subset that can be exposed by assemblies. Because you can be assured that all languages' building assemblies are using this subset, you can thus also be assured that all languages will be able to interface with it.

Note When you develop your .NET code, it is completely acceptable to use the entire CTS. It is only exposed types that need to adhere to the CLS for interlanguage operability.

There is no imposed restriction on using the CLS. If you know that your assemblies will only be used by one language, then it is perfectly acceptable to use all the types available to that language, even those that are exposed. Just be aware that if there comes a time when you want to use your assemblies with another language, they may not work because they do not adhere to the CLS.

If you want to view the CLS, you can find it in the .NET documentation. Just search for "What is the common language specification?" The key points that you should be aware of as a C++/CLI programmer are as follows:

- Global methods and variables are not allowed.
- The CLS does not impose case sensitivity, so make sure that all exposed types differ by more than their case.
- The only primitive types allowed are Byte, Int16, Int32, Int64, Single, Double, Boolean, Char, Decimal, IntPtr, and String.
- Variable-length argument lists are not allowed. Use fixed-length arrays instead.
- Pointers are not allowed.
- Class types must inherit from a CLS-compliant class. System::Object is CLS compliant.
- Array elements must be CLS compliant.

Some other requirements might also affect you, if you get fancy with your coding. But you will most likely come across the ones in the previous list.

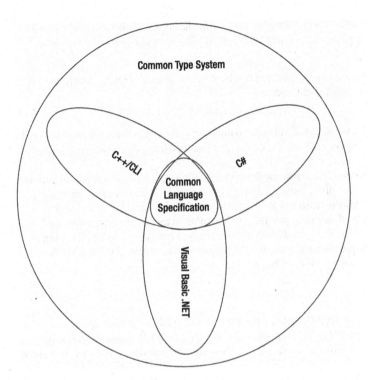

Figure 1-8. *CLS intersection diagram*

.NET Application Development Realms

.NET application development falls primarily into one of five realms: Web applications, Web services, Windows applications, Windows services, and console applications. Using languages such as C#, Visual Basic .NET, and Visual Studio .NET provides a simple, powerful, and consistent environment to develop all five. Unfortunately, for C++/CLI, only four are supported: console applications, Windows applications, Windows services, and Web services.

Prior to version 2.0 of .NET, Web applications were indirectly supported by C++/CLI, but that is no longer true as ASP.NET does not support C++/CLI even indirectly anymore.

Console Applications

Console applications are basically extinct as a final software delivery in the Windows world. Okay, developers and administrators still use them a lot, but the average nontechnical user has GUI-based applications as their final delivery. For developer tools, there is nothing like them. If you need to figure out how to do something, write out a console application. There is nothing simpler and nothing with less overhead. This book is full of console applications for just those reasons.

The key elements of all console applications are the `main()` function and the `System::Console::WriteLine()` method. In fact, that is almost all you need to write a console application.

Windows Applications

Windows applications may be the biggest change for C++/CLI programmers. C++/CLI does not support the Microsoft Foundation Class (MFC) library. Wow, don't panic—believe it or not, the .NET Framework has a better solution. It's called Windows Forms, and I'm sure you'll think, as I do, that it's a godsend. With Windows Forms, you get the ease of Visual Basic along with the power of C++/CLI when you develop Windows applications. I cover Windows applications in Chapters 9 and 10.

■**Note** With .NET version 2.0, you can now use MFC and Windows Forms somewhat interchangeably, but if you do, the generated assembly will be classified as unsafe.

When you create Windows Forms, you will use the massive System::Windows::Forms namespace. Though this namespace is large, it is consistent and well laid out. It will not take you long to get good at using it.

Just to add some variety to your Windows applications, .NET also provides a new and improved Graphical Device Interface (GDI) called, conveniently, GDI+. With GDI+, you can play with fonts, change colors and, of course, draw pictures. GDI+ is almost worth learning just for one class, System::Drawing::Image, which allows an application to load almost any commonly supported graphic file formats, including GIF, JPEG, and BMP, into memory, where they can be manipulated and drawn to the screen. To implement GDI+ in the .NET Framework, you need to explore the System::Drawing namespace. I cover GDI+ in Chapter 11.

Web Applications

ASP.NET is a large part of developing Web applications. But unlike traditional Web application development, .NET has changed things. Web applications no longer are run using interpreted scripts. Now they use full-blown compiled applications. These applications are usually written using C# and Visual Basic .NET.

Unfortunately, with .NET 2.0 and C++/CLI you can no longer write Web applications. The reason for this is primarily because Microsoft introduced a new construct in C# and Visual Basic .NET called the partial class, which has no equivalent in C++/CLI, and partial classes are heavily relied upon in ASP.NET Web applications.

■**Note** Unlike my last book, *Managed C++ and .NET Development,* this book contains no chapter on Web application development. Instead, I replaced it with Chapter 14, which concentrates more on C++/CLI and Windows Services.

Windows Services

A Windows service is a Windows application that can be started automatically when the operating system boots. However, this is not a requirement, as it is possible to start the Windows service manually.

With the Windows service there is no need for an interactive user or an interface. You will see in Chapter 14 that you do have some limited ability to interface with the service, but to do so, you need a separate control program.

Not only do Windows services not need an interactive user, but they can also continue to run after a user logs off.

Web Services

You might want to think of a Web service as programmable functionality that you execute over the Internet. Talk about remote programming! Using a simple HTTP request, you can execute some functionality on some computer on the opposite side of the world. Okay, there are still some kinks, such as the possible bandwidth problems, but they will be overcome with the current technology advancement rate—that much I am certain of. Chapter 15 covers Web services.

Web services are based on XML technology and, more specifically, the XML-derived Simple Object Access Protocol (SOAP). SOAP was designed to exchange information in a decentralized and distributed environment using HTTP. For more technical details about SOAP, peruse the World Wide Web Consortium's Web pages on SOAP (http://www.w3.org/TR/SOAP).

When you code Web services, you will be working primarily with the System::Web::Services namespace. You also get to look at attributes again.

Web services are a key part of Microsoft's plans for .NET because, as you may recall, .NET is about delivering software as a service.

.NET Framework Class Library

Everything you've learned so far is all fine and dandy, but the thing that is most important, and where C++/CLI programmers will spend many a day, is the massive .NET Framework class library. There are literally hundreds of classes and structures contained within a hierarchy of namespaces. C++/CLI programmers will use many of these classes and structures on a regular basis.

With such a large number of elements in the class library, you would think that a programmer could quickly get lost. Fortunately, this is not true. The .NET Framework class library is, in fact, well organized, easy to use, and virtually self-documenting. Namespaces, class names, properties, methods, and variable names usually make perfect sense. The only real exceptions to this that I have found are class library wrapped native classes. I am sure there are other exceptions, but by and large, most namespaces and classes are understandable just by their names. This, obviously, differs considerably from the Win32 API, where obscure names are more the norm.

With the .NET Framework class library, you can have complete control of the computer. That's because the class library functionality ranges from a very high level, such as the MonthCalendar class—which displays a single month of a calendar on a Windows Form—down to a very low level, such as the PowerModeChangedEventHandler, which notifies the application when the computer is about to be suspended, resumed, or changed from AC to battery or vice versa.

There are two hierarchies of namespaces in the .NET Framework class library: the platform-neutral System namespace and the Microsoft-specific (and aptly named) Microsoft namespace. Table 1-2 shows a brief subset of the namespaces that the average C++/CLI programmer will run into.

Table 1-2. *Common .NET Framework Class Library Namespaces*

Namespace	Description
Microsoft::win32	Contains classes to handle events raised by the operating system and to manipulate the system registry
System	Contains classes that handle primitive types, mathematics, program invocation, and supervision of applications
System::Collections	Contains classes that define collections of objects, such as lists, queues, arrays, hash tables, and dictionaries
System::Collections::Generic	Contains classes that allows classes, structures, interfaces, methods, and delegates to be declared and defined without specific types
System::Data	Contains classes that handle database access
System::Data::OleDb	Contains classes that handle access to OLE DB databases
System::Data::SqlClient	Contains classes that handle access to Microsoft SQL Server databases

Table 1-2. *Common .NET Framework Class Library Namespaces (Continued)*

Namespace	Description
System::Diagnostics	Contains classes that allow you to debug your application and trace application execution
System::DirectoryServices	Contains classes to access Active Directory
System::Drawing	Contains classes to handle the GDI+ graphics functionality
System::Drawing::Drawing2D	Contains classes that handle advanced two-dimensional and vector graphics functionality
System::Drawing:Imaging	Contains classes to handle advanced GDI+ imaging functionality
System::Drawing::Printing	Contains classes to handle custom printing
System::Globalization	Contains classes that define culture-related information, such as language, currency, and numbers
System::IO	Contains classes to handle reading and writing of data streams and files
System::Net	Contains classes to handle many of the protocols and services found on networks
System::Reflection	Contains classes that examine loaded types, methods, and fields, and also dynamically create and invoke types
System::Resources	Contains classes to create, store, and manage various culture-specific resources
System::Runtime::InteropServices	Contains classes to access COM objects and native APIs
System::Runtime::Remoting	Contains classes to create and configure distributed applications
System::Security	Contains classes to handle the CLR security system
System::Threading	Contains classes to handle multithreaded programming
System::Web	Contains classes to handle communication between browser and server
System::Web::Mail	Contains classes to create and send an e-mail using the SMTP mail service built into Microsoft Windows 2000
System::Web::Security	Contains classes to handle ASP.NET security in Web applications
System::Web::Services	Contains classes to build and use Web services
System::Web::UI	Contains classes to create controls and pages in Web applications
System::Windows::Forms	Contains classes to create Windows-based applications
System::XML	Contains classes to handle XML

Summary

This chapter created a level playing field on which to start your exploration of C++/CLI, beginning with the big picture, examining what exactly .NET is. I then explored the .NET Framework generically and finally broke it down piece-by-piece, examining such things as assemblies, the common language runtime (CLR), the common type system (CTS), and the common language specification (CLS). The chapter ended with a look at the myriad classes available to the C++/CLI developer.

The journey has begun. In the next chapter, you'll look at the basics of C++/CLI. Let's continue.

CHAPTER 2

■ ■ ■

C++/CLI Basics

You have a little work to do before you can have some fun. This chapter covers many basic but important aspects of C++/CLI programming.

This chapter starts out with variables and data types. Then you will learn about comments, literals, expressions, and operations. Next, you will explore looping and flow control. Finally, you will end with functions, focusing on C++/CLI and its infrequently used capability to be strictly a procedure language. The next chapter will look at C++/CLI as an object-oriented language, its true claim to fame.

Caution Even though you may know C++ very well, don't skip this chapter—several things vary between traditional C++ and C++/CLI. True, some of the changes may not be significant, but recognizing and understanding these changes now may make your life easier in the future.

The Obligatory "Hello World!" Program

It seems like all the programming books I read always start with a "Hello World!" program. Who am I to do things differently? Here is the "Hello World!" program, C++/CLI style:

```
using namespace System;

// The Obligatory Hello World!
void main(void)
{
    Console::WriteLine("Hello C++/CLI World");
}
```

You can create the Hello.cpp program by typing it in with any text editor. You can use Edit or Notepad, as both come with all versions of Windows. To compile it into an assembly called Hello.exe, simply execute the following line from the command prompt:

```
cl Hello.cpp /clr:safe /doc
```

Note You need the command prompt to be configured for the .NET development environment. Unless you have configured your default command prompt for this environment, I recommend that you use the command prompt provided by Visual Studio 2005.

Even though this is an assembly, you run it as you would any other executable. If you run it from the command line, you should get something like Figure 2-1.

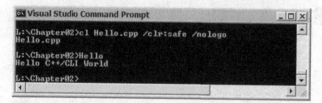

Figure 2-1. *Executing Hello.exe from the command line*

I don't cover namespaces until later in this chapter, but for now you can think of them as a way of combining a bunch of code into a uniquely named group. When you want to access this group, you use the using statement and provide its unique name. Basically, the next line

```
using namespace System;
```

says you are going to use the stuff in this System namespace.

Every C++/CLI program must start with a main() function, and every program can have only one main() function. When the main() function finishes executing, so does the program. In the case of Hello.cpp, it also happens to be the only function. The first line of the main() function is this:

```
void main(void)
```

There are other variations of main(), including the WinMain() function used to start Windows programs. I cover those other variations later in this chapter. In the preceding variation of main(), you are receiving no parameters, which is signified by the (void) placed after the main, and you are also expecting the function to return no value so void is placed before the function call, as well.

■ **Tip** The void parameter is optional when no parameters are used by the method. Instead, you can just use a pair of empty brackets. Therefore, you could also declare the above main method as void main().

A *function* is a block of code referenced by name, in this case main. It starts with an open curly bracket ({) and ends with a closed curly bracket (}). Within a function is the set of statements that it will execute. The main() function of Hello.cpp contains only one statement:

```
Console::WriteLine("Hello Managed World");
```

If more than one statement were present, the statements would be executed sequentially from beginning to end, unless a statement specifically altered the flow, either by looping back or by conditionally bypassing some of the code. You will see how this is done later in this chapter.

In C++/CLI, displaying text strings, which are enclosed in quotation marks (""), to a console window is handled using the static WriteLine() method of the class Console. Don't panic if that doesn't mean much to you—it will shortly. You will learn about classes and static methods in Chapter 3. You will also examine text strings and namespaces in Chapter 3. For now, all you need to know about displaying your own text is to replace "Hello Managed World" with whatever you want.

Statements

C++/CLI's most basic element is the statement. A *statement* is a coding construct that performs a single C++/CLI action. You will learn about different types of statements as you progress through this book, but the main thing to remember about all statements is that they end with a semicolon (;). If you forget the semicolon, your compiler will throw up all over you. Here are some statements:

```
using namespace System;
System::Console::WriteLine("Hello Managed World");
bool IsOpen;
y = GetYCoord();
```

Not much to look at, are they?

C++/CLI provides a construct for compound statements. To create a compound statement, you simply enclose several simple statements within curly brackets:

```
{
    x = x + y;
    PrintAnswer(x);
}
```

These statements execute as a group and can be placed anywhere a simple statement can be placed. You will see them in the "Flow Control Constructs" and "Looping Constructs" sections later in this chapter.

Variables and C++/CLI Data Types

One of the key differences between traditional C++ and C++/CLI, believe it or not, is found at this low level of the language. If you have worked with C++, then it may come as a little surprise that the data types int, long, float, and so on, are no more. They have been replaced with .NET fundamental types. To simplify things for traditional C++ programmers, C++/CLI allows the use of the old data types, but they are, in fact, just aliases.

Alas, I'm getting ahead of myself. I'll start at the beginning, and that is how to create or, more accurately, declare variables.

Declaring Variables

To use a variable in C++/CLI, you must first declare it. The minimum declaration of a variable consists of a data type and a variable name:

```
int counter;
double yCoord;
```

Variable declarations can go almost anywhere in the code body of a C++/CLI program. One of the few criteria for declarations is that they have to occur before the variable is used. It was once required that all declarations occur as the first statements of a function, as a result of C++'s original C background. You will still see this in practice today, because some programmers feel it makes the code cleaner to read. Personally, I prefer to place the variable closer to where it is first used—that way, I don't have to scroll to the top of every function to see how I declared something. How you code it is up to you. Following the standards of your company is always a good rule of thumb, or if you are coding on your own, stay consistent. You will find that it will save you time down the line.

There is an assortment of more complex declarations. For example, you can string together several comma-delimited variable names at the same time:

```
int x, y, z;
```

There are two special data types called a *handle* and a *pointer* (which I'll explain in more detail later). A handle requires a carat [^] in front of the variable name or after the data type, and a pointer requires an asterisk [*]:

```
String^ handlename;
String ^handlename;

String* pointername;
String *pointername;
```

Unsafe Code *Pointers* are classified as unsafe code because they cause data to be placed in the CRT heap and not the managed heap. Therefore, you need to handle all memory management yourself. The primary reason pointers are unsafe is that they allow a programmer to specify a memory location to access or reference; thus, with knowledge of the operating system, a programmer could potentially allow the executing of code unprotected by .NET.

You might think of these as saying "String handle called handlename" or "handlename handle to a String" and "String pointer called pointername" or "pointername pointer to a String." They are equivalent. There is a complication with string handles, as shown here:

```
int^ isaHandle, isNOTaHandle;
int* isaPointer, isNOTaPointer;
```

The preceding line actually declares one handle and one pointer to an int and two variables of type int. This is probably not what you are expecting. If you want two handles and two pointers to an int, you need to declare it like this:

```
int ^aHandle, ^anotherHandle;
int *aPointer, *anotherPointer;
```

You have two possible ways to initialize the variable within the declaration statement. The first is by using a standard assignment:

```
int counter = 0;
double yCoord = 300.5;
```

The second is by using what is known as *functional notation*, as it resembles the calling of a function passing the initialization value as a parameter. In C++/CLI, you should probably call this *constructor initialization*, as you are actually calling the data type's constructor to create these variables:

```
int counter(0);
double yCoord(300.5);
```

Again, use caution when initializing a variable within the declaration statement using standard assignment. This code may not do what you expect:

```
int x, y, z = 200;
```

Only z is initialized to 200; all the other variables take on the default value of the data type. Enter the following to code this so that all variables are initialized to 200:

```
int x = 200, y = 200, z = 200;
```

or

```
int x = y = z = 200;
```

It is always a good thing to initialize your variables before you use them. If you don't initialize a variable, its contents can be almost anything when it is used. To help remind you of this, the compiler displays a warning about uninitialized variables while it is compiling.

Variable Name Restrictions

For those of you with a C++ background, there are no big changes here. Variable names consist of upper- and lowercase letters, digits from 0 to 9, and the underscore character (_). The variable name must start with a letter or an underscore character. Also, variable names cannot be the same as C++/CLI reserved keywords, including all variable names starting with two underscores, which C++/CLI has also reserved. Table 2-1 contains a list of more commonly used C++/CLI reserved keywords. For a complete list of all reserved words, look in the documentation provided in Visual Studio 2005.

Table 2-1. *Common C++/CLI Reserved Keywords*

Keywords				
asm	auto	bool	break	case
catch	char	class	const	const_cast
continue	default	delete	do	double
dynamic_cast	else	enum	explicit	export
extern	false	float	for	friend
gcnew	goto	if	inline	int
long	mutable	namespace	new	nullptr
operator	pin_ptr	private	protected	public
register	reinterpret_cast	restrict	return	safe_cast
short	signed	sizeof	static	static_cast
struct	switch	template	this	throw
true	try	typedef	typeid	typename
typeid	_typeof	union	unsigned	using
virtual	void	volatile	wchar_t	while

In addition to the single-word keywords in Table 2-1, in C++/CLI double-word keywords have been added. Any white space, including comments and new lines (but excluding XML documentation comments and new lines in macros), is permitted between the double-word keywords. Table 2-2 contains a list of all C++/CLI reserved double-word keywords.

Table 2-2. *C++/CLI Reserved Double-Word Keywords*

Double-Word Keywords			
enum class	enum struct	for each	interface class
interface struct	ref class	ref struct	value class
value struct			

To add one more wrinkle to variable name mess, C++/CLI also has added some context-sensitive keywords words, or what Microsoft calls *identifiers*. These words can be used as variable names unless they are placed in a specific location in the code. I will describe each of these identifiers later in this chapter or in subsequent chapters where appropriate. Table 2-3 contains a list of all the C++/CLI identifiers.

Table 2-3. *C++/CLI Identifiers*

Identifiers			
Abstract	delegate	event	finally
Generic	in	initonly	literal
Override	property	sealed	where

Variables should probably be self-descriptive. However, there is nothing stopping you from writing a program that uses variable names starting with a0000 and continuing through z9999. If you do this, though, don't ask me to debug it for you.

There are also people who think that you should use Hungarian notation for variable names. This notation allows other programmers to read your code and know the data type by the prefix attached to its name. I find this notation cumbersome and don't use it myself unless, of course, company standards dictate its use.

■ **Note** You can find out the data type of a variable within Visual Studio 2005 by just placing your cursor over the variable name.

Predefined Data Types

All data types, even the simplest ones, are truly objects in C++/CLI. This differs from traditional C++, where primitive types such as int, float, and double were strictly stored values of data types themselves.

As a C++/CLI programmer, you have the luxury of programming simple data types just as you would in traditional C++, knowing that you can convert them to objects if needed.

Predefined data types fall into two different types: fundamental types and reference types. *Fundamental types* are the data types that default to just storing their values for efficiency on the stack but can be boxed to become full objects. *Reference types,* on the other hand, are always objects and are stored on the managed heap.

Fundamental Types

All the standard C++ data types are available to the C++/CLI programmer. Or, at least, so it appears. In reality, the standard data types are just an alias for the .NET Framework's fundamental types. With .NET 2.0, there is now no difference between using the standard C++ data types and .NET Framework's fundamental types. It's a matter of taste (or company standards) which ones you choose. My feeling, given that this is C++/CLI, is that I'm going to use C++ data types. Plus, the Visual Studio 2005 editor defaults to color-coding the data type keywords, which make things easier.

There are five distinct groups of fundamental value types:

1. Integer

2. Floating point

3. Decimal

4. Boolean

5. Character

Programmers with a C++ background should readily recognize four of these groups. Decimal, most probably, is new to all. Let's go over all of them so that there are no surprises.

Integer Types

Eight different integer types are provided to C++/CLI programmers. These can all be broken down into unsigned and signed numbers. (In other words, can negative numbers be represented or just positive numbers?) Table 2-4 shows the integer types.

Table 2-4. *Integer Fundamental Types*

C++/CLI Alias	Class Library	Description	Range
unsigned char	System::Byte	8-bit unsigned integer	0 to 255
char	System::SByte	8-bit signed integer	−128 to 127
short	System::Int16	16-bit signed integer	−32,768 to 32,767
unsigned short	System::UInt16	16-bit unsigned integer	0 to 65,535
int or long	System::Int32	32-bit signed integer	−2,147,483,648 to 2,147,483,647
unsigned int or long	System::UInt32	32-bit unsigned integer	0 to 4,294,967,295
long long or __int64	System::Int64	64-bit signed integer	−9,223,372,036,854,775,808 to 9,223,372,036,854,775,807
unsigned long long or __int64	System::UInt64	64-bit unsigned integer	0 to 18,446,744,073,709,551,615

Byte and SByte are the smallest of the integer types, at 1 byte each, hence their names. Their C++/CLI aliases are unsigned char and char, respectively. A Byte can range from 0 to 255, and an SByte can range from −128 to 127, inclusive. In traditional C++, char usually represents ASCII characters.

■**Caution** The C++/CLI alias char is not the same as the .NET Framework class library System::Char. A char is an 8-bit unsigned integer that frequently represents an ASCII character, whereas a System::Char is a 16-bit Unicode character.

The remainder of the integer types has fairly self-descriptive .NET Framework class library names, with their type and size merged into their name. Int16 are 16-bit integers, UInt16 are unsigned 16-bit integers, and so on. Personally, I think these names make more sense than short, int, and long. Plus, long and int are the same size (4 bytes), so you have to throw in __Int64 or long long.

■**Note** Given that short and int are the norm to a C++ programmer, I'll use them but, because there really isn't a 64-bit integer standard keyword, I use the .NET Framework's System::Int64 or the more convenient Int64.

There is nothing complex about declaring integer type variables. Whenever you declare an integer type variable in C++/CLI, it is immediately initialized to the value of zero. This differs from traditional C++ compilers, where the initialization is optional and up to the compiler. For traditional C++, it is possible that the value of a variable remains uninitialized and, thus, contains just about any numeric value.

To initialize integer types, you simply declare a variable and assign it a character: octal, decimal, or hexadecimal literal. I examine literals later in this chapter.

Listing 2-1 is a simple piece of code showing integer types in action.

Listing 2-1. *Integer Types in Action*

```
using namespace System;

// Integer Fundamental Types in Action
void main()
{
    char    v = 'F';                // Intialize using charater literal
    short   w(123);                 // Intializing using Functional Notation
    int     x = 456789;             // Decimal literal assigned
    long    y = 9876543211;         // long integer literal assigned
    Int64   z = 0xFEDCBA9876543210; // Hex literal assigned

    Console::WriteLine( v );              // Write out a char
    Console::WriteLine( w );              // Write out a short
    Console::WriteLine( x );              // Write out a int
    Console::WriteLine( y );              // Write out a long
    Console::WriteLine( z );              // Write out a Int64
    Console::WriteLine( z.ToString("x") ); // Write out a Int64 in Hex
}
```

Figure 2-2 shows the results of this little program.

Figure 2-2. *Results of IntegerTypes.exe*

For those of you from traditional C++ backgrounds, the ToString() appended to the integer variables in the Console::WriteLine() method might be a little confusing. Remember, in C++/CLI, integer types are objects and have several methods attached to them, and ToString() happens to be one of them.

Floating-Point Types

C++/CLI provides only two different floating-point types. Table 2-5 describes the details of each.

Table 2-5. *Floating-Point Fundamental Types*

C++/CLI Alias	Class Library	Description	Significant Digits	Range
float	System::Single	32-bit single-precision floating point	7	significant digits $\pm1.5\times10^{-45}$ to $\pm3.4\times10^{38}$
double	System::Double	64-bit double-precision floating point	15	significant digits $\pm5.0\times10^{-324}$ to $\pm1.7\times10^{308}$

Note C++/CLI also supports a long double, but on the Microsoft platform long double and double are the same.

The .NET Framework class library System::Single has the smaller range of numbers it can represent of the two floating-point types available to C++/CLI. Its alias for C++ programmers is the better-known float type. A float can represent numbers from $\pm1.5\times10^{-45}$ to $\pm3.4\times10^{38}$, but only seven of the digits are significant.

The System::Double class library has the larger range of the two. Its alias is double. A double can represent numbers from $\pm5.0\times10^{-324}$ to $\pm1.7\times10^{308}$, but only 15 of the digits are significant.

Listing 2-2 is a simple piece of code showing floating-point types in action.

Listing 2-2. *Floating-Point Types in Action*

```
using namespace System;

// Floating-point Fundamental Types in Action
void main()
{
    float w = 123.456f;    // standard decimal notation
    float x = 7890e3f;     // exponent notation
    double y = 34525425432525764765.76476476547654; // too big will truncate
    double z = 123456789012345e-300; // exponent will be reset

    Console::WriteLine( w ); // Write out Single
    Console::WriteLine( x ); // Write out Single with more zeros
    Console::WriteLine( y ); // Write out Double truncated
    Console::WriteLine( z ); // Write out Double shift back decimal
}
```

Figure 2-3 shows the results of this little program.

Figure 2-3. *Results of FloatingPoint.exe*

The .NET Framework class library double is the default value used by most functions and methods that deal with floating-point numbers.

Decimal Type

C++/CLI supports only one decimal type. This type has no traditional C++ equivalent and thus has no alias. Table 2-6 describes the decimal type.

Table 2-6. *Decimal Fundamental Type*

Class Library	Description	Significant Digits	Range
System::Decimal	128-bit high-precision decimal notation	28	$\pm 7.9 \times 10^{-28}$ to $\pm 7.9 \times 10^{28}$

This fundamental type was designed specifically for calculations requiring a lot of significant digits, as it provides 28 significant digits. Within those 28 digits, you can put a decimal. In other words, you can place a very big number in a System::Decimal that will have a small fractional area, or you can make a very small number with a very big fractional part.

System::Decimals are not a native C++ data type and, as such, they need a little magic to get them initialized if the number of significant digits you want to capture is larger than 15. The significance of 15 is that it is the number of significant digits provided by a double, the closest data type available to initialize a Decimal.

Here are three ways to load a number with more than 15 significant digits (there are other ways, I'm sure):

1. The first method is to load the digits into a String and convert the String to Decimal.

```
Decimal w = System::Convert::ToDecimal("123456789012345678901.2345678");
```

2. The second method is to use one of the Decimal constructors. Most of the constructors are pretty self explanatory. Basically convert a numeric type to a Decimal. Two constructors are more complex. The first takes an array of integers to represent the binary format of the Decimal. The second is this monstrosity:

```
public: Decimal(
    int lo,              // The low 32 bits of a 96-bit integer.
    int mid,             // The middle 32 bits of a 96-bit integer.
    int hi,              // The high 32 bits of a 96-bit integer.
    bool isNegative,     // false is positive.
    unsigned char scale  // A power of 10 ranging from 0 to 28.
);
```

3. The third method is to add two doubles together using the combined significant digits of both to make up the Decimal.

All three of these methods are shown in Listing 2-3. Also, for grins and giggles, I decided to use the Decimal method GetBits() to break the Decimal into its parts and then use the constructor to put it back together again. Don't fret if you don't understand C++/CLI arrays, as that portion of the code is not essential to the understanding of the Decimal type. I cover arrays in detail later in the chapter.

Listing 2-3. *Decimal Types in Action*

```
using namespace System;

// Decimal Fundamental Type in Action
void main()
{
    Decimal w = System::Convert::ToDecimal("123456789012345678901.2345678");
    Console::WriteLine( w );

    Decimal x = (Decimal)0.12345678901234567890123345678; // will get truncated
    Decimal y = (Decimal)0.00000000000000000789012345678; // works fine

    Console::WriteLine( x );
    Console::WriteLine( y );

    // Decimal constructor
    Decimal z(0xeb1f0ad2, 0xab54a98c, 0, false, 0); // = 12345678901234567890
    Console::WriteLine( z );

    // Create a 28 significant digit number
    Decimal a = (Decimal)123456789012345000000.00000000;
    Decimal b = (Decimal)678901.23456780;
    Decimal c = -(a + b);
```

```
Console::WriteLine( c );                        // display prebroken Decimal

// Break it up into 4 parts
array<int>^ d = Decimal::GetBits(c);

// Reassemble using Decimal constructor
Decimal e(d[0], d[1], d[2],                     // digits
        ((d[3] & 0x80000000) == 0x80000000), // sign
        ((d[3] >> 16) & 0xff) );             // decimal location

Console::WriteLine( d[0] );                   // display part 1
Console::WriteLine( d[1] );                   // display part 2
Console::WriteLine( d[2] );                   // display part 3
Console::WriteLine( d[3].ToString("X") ); // display part 4
Console::WriteLine( e );                      // display reassembled Decimal
}
```

Figure 2-4 shows the results of this program.

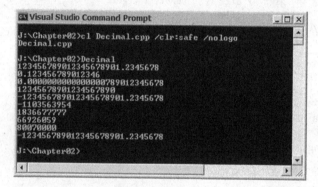

Figure 2-4. *Results of Decimal.exe*

Boolean Type

C++/CLI provides only one Boolean type. Table 2-7 describes the details of it.

Table 2-7. *Boolean Fundamental Type*

C++/CLI Alias	Class Library	Values
bool	System::Boolean	true | not 0 or false | 0

The System::Boolean fundamental type has the C++/CLI alias of bool. A bool can only have a value of true or false.

C++/CLI is a little lenient when it comes to initializing bools, as it allows them to be assigned with the value of zero for false and any number other than zero for true. The compiler does give a warning if the value assigned is not one of the following: true, false, 1, or 0.

Listing 2-4 is a simple piece of code showing the Boolean type in action.

Listing 2-4. *Boolean Type in Action*

```
using namespace System;

// Boolean Fundamental Type in Action
void main()
{
    bool a = 18757;   // will give a warning but set to true
    bool b = 0;       // false
    bool c = true;    // obviously true
    bool d = false;   // obviously false

    Console::WriteLine( a );
    Console::WriteLine( b );
    Console::WriteLine( c );
    Console::WriteLine( d );
}
```

Figure 2-5 shows the results of this little program.

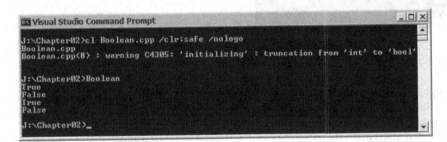

Figure 2-5. *Results of Boolean.exe*

Character Type

C++/CLI provides only one character type. Table 2-8 describes the details of this character type.

Table 2-8. *Character Fundamental Type*

C++/CLI Alias	Class Library	Value
wchar_t	System::Char	A single 16-bit Unicode character

The .NET Framework class library System::Char is a 16-bit Unicode character, which has a C++/CLI alias of __wchar_t (or wchar_t, if the Zc:wchar_t flag is set on the compiler).

Listing 2-5 is a simple piece of code showing the Char type in action.

Listing 2-5. *Char Type in Action*

```
using namespace System;

// Character Fundamental Type in Action
void main()
{
    Char  a = L'A';       // character literal 'A'
    Char  b = L'\x0041';  // hex notation for hex 41 which happens to be 'A'

    Console::WriteLine ( a );
    Console::WriteLine ( b ); //Even though I put hex 41 in b, the ASCII 'A'
                              //is printed due to b being a Char
}
```

Figure 2-6 shows the results of this little program.

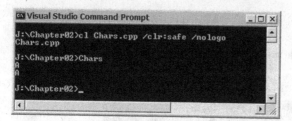

Figure 2-6. *Results of Chars.exe*

Not long ago, all Windows programs used ASCII, an 8-bit, English-only character set. Unfortunately, this was not very helpful for languages such as Chinese, which requires more than the 256-character limit imposed by ASCII. To try to solve this obvious problem, a new encoding protocol was developed called *Unicode*, within which many character sets could be defined. Unicode uses 16 bits to represent each character instead of ASCII's 8. ASCII is a subset of Unicode.

■**Caution** Traditional C++ programmers must be wary of the C++/CLI alias char, as it is not the same as the .NET Framework's class library Char. A char is an 8-bit ASCII character, whereas a Char is a 16-bit Unicode character.

Reference Types

As a C++/CLI programmer, you can think of reference types as a handle to data in the managed heap that you don't have to worry about deleting. Handles and pointers have many similarities; they both reference data in a heap (Managed and CRT). Where handles differ considerably from pointers is that a handle's address can't be manipulated, or in other words, you can't add or subtract offsets to a handle as you can with a pointer.

There are many reference types in .NET; the .NET Framework is full of them, but all C++/CLI developers almost always use only two. One is the Object type, the root of all classes in the .NET Framework class library. The other is the String type.

I deal with these two reference types now, but throughout the book I'll cover many more.

Object Type

The System::Object is the root type of the entire .NET Framework class library hierarchy. In other words, every object found in the .NET Framework ultimately has, as a parent, the Object type.

Because all objects in the .NET Framework derive from System::Object, all objects inherit several general-purpose methods, such as

- Object(): Creates a new instance of an object
- Equals(): Compares two object instances to see if they are equal
- GetHashCode(): Returns a hash code for the object
- GetType(): Returns the data type of the object
- ReferenceEquals(): Checks if two instances of an object are the same
- ToString(): Returns a string representation of the object

A developer can replace a few of these methods. For example, replacing ToString() allows an object to represent itself in a way that is readable to the user.

String Type

As a C++/CLI programmer, you will probably become very intimate with System::String. Many of your programs will involve character strings. The String type was built to handle them. Traditional C++ programmers can now forget character arrays, CString or STL's string class—you now have a powerful, predefined .NET Framework reference type to manipulate strings with. As an added bonus, it is completely garbage collected!

Being a reference type, Strings are allocated to the managed heap and referenced using a handle. String types are also immutable, meaning their value cannot be modified once they have been created. This combination allows for the optimized capability of multiple handles representing the same character string managed heap location. When a String object changes, a completely new character string is allocated in the managed heap and, if no other handle references the original String object, then the original String object is garbage collected.

Listing 2-6 is a little program showing the String type in action.

Listing 2-6. *String Type in Action*

```
using namespace System;

// String Type in Action
void main()
{
    // Create some strings
    String^ s1 = "This will ";
    String^ s2 = "be a ";
    String^ s3 = "String";
    Console::WriteLine(String::Concat(s1, s2, s3));

    // Create a copy, then concatenate new text
    String^ s4 = s2;
    s4 = String::Concat(s4, "new ");
    Console::WriteLine(String::Concat(s1, s4, s3));
```

```
// Replace stuff in a concatenated string
String^ s5 = String::Concat(s1, s2, s3)->Replace("i", "*");
Console::WriteLine(s5);

// Insert into a string
String^ s6 = s3->Insert(3, "ange Str");
Console::WriteLine(String::Concat(s1, s2, s6));

// Remove text from strings
s1 = s1->Remove(4, 5);  // remove ' will' from middle
s2 = s2->Remove(0, 3);  // remove 'be ' from start
Console::WriteLine(String::Concat(s1, "is ", s2, s3));
}
```

Figure 2-7 shows the results of this little program.

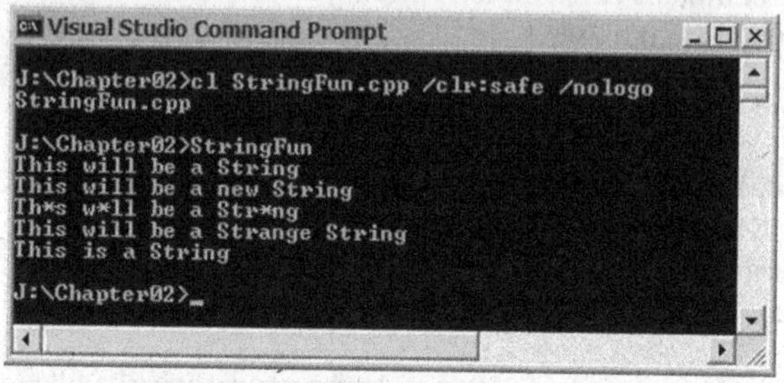

Figure 2-7. *Results of StringFun.exe*

User-Defined Data Types

With C++/CLI, you can create your own data types. User-defined data types fall into two groups: value types or reference types. As I pointed out earlier, value types are placed directly on the stack, whereas reference types are placed on the managed heap and referenced via the stack.

Value Types

Only three kinds of user-defined value types can be created using C++/CLI:

- enum class or enum struct (equivalent)
- value struct
- value class

The enum class and enum struct types are simply named constants. The value struct and value class types are identical, except that the default access value struct members are public, whereas value class members are private.

Native enums, enum classes, and enum structs

Conceptually, enums and consts share a lot of similarities. Both enable better readability of code. They also allow for the actual value being represented to be maintained at one location in your code, thus enabling the value to be changed at one location and have that change reflected throughout the code. Where enums and consts differ is that enums allow for grouping of common values within a single construct, creating a new data type. Then you can use this new data type to enforce that only specific enum values be placed in a specified variable. A const, on the other hand, is just a representation of a value and cannot be used to define a new data type.

Like the fundamental types already discussed, enums default to being placed on the stack but can beused automatically as objects when required.

There are two different syntaxes for declaring enums in C++/CLI. Ultimately, both syntax generate the same metadata and inherit from System::enums.

The first syntax is the pre-C++/CLI style, better known as a native enum. C++/CLI has augmented the native enum with the addition of an optional ability to declare the underlying data type. The data type of a native enum can be explicitly declared as one of the following data types: bool, char, unsigned char, signed char, short, unsigned short, int, unsigned int, long long, unsigned long long, float, or double. Here is an example of a native enum with and without the optional declaration of the data type:

```
enum Creature { Dog, Cat, Eagle };
enum Vehicle : char { Car, Boat, Plane };
```

The second syntax, know as CLI enums, is the preferred one for managed code (according to Microsoft) and mirrors more the syntax of the other value type declarations:

```
enum class Creature { Dog, Cat, Eagle };
enum struct Creature { Dog, Cat, Eagle };
```

CLI enums are different from native enums in that the names of the CLI enums' values, better known as enumerators, can only be found through the scope of the enums' name, and the declaring of the enums' data type has no meaning with a CLI enum. What this means to you is that to code a native enum like this:

```
Creature animal;
animal = Cat;
```

you code a CLI enum like this:

```
Creature animal;
animal = Creature::Cat;
```

The following example creates a CLI enum of all the primary colors. Then the function prints the string equivalent of the primary color enum using a switch statement. I describe the switch statement later in this chapter.

The System::Enum from which enums originate provides a simpler way of doing this exact same thing. The ToString() method for enums prints out the enum name as a character string.

Listing 2-7 is a little program showing enums in action.

Listing 2-7. *Enums in Action*

```
using namespace System;

enum class PrimeColors { Red, Blue, Yellow };

// Enum Type in Action
void main()
{
    PrimeColors color;

    color = PrimeColors::Blue;
```

```
    switch (color)
    {
        case PrimeColors::Red :
            Console::WriteLine("Red");
            break;
        case PrimeColors::Blue :
            Console::WriteLine("Blue");
            break;
        case PrimeColors::Yellow :
            Console::WriteLine("Yellow");
            break;
    }

    Console::WriteLine(color.ToString());
}
```

Figure 2-8 shows the results of this program.

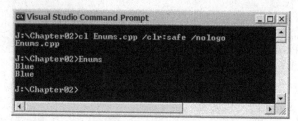

Figure 2-8. *Results of Enums.exe*

value struct and value class

The value struct and value class data types are basically C++/CLI's equivalent to traditional C++'s class and struct data types but with an added bonus. Both are unmanaged (not garbage collected) constructs used to combine multiple data types and methods (or functions) into a single data type. Then when a new instance of the data type is created, it is allocated either to the stack or CRT heap.

The added bonus is that a copy of value struct or value class can be assigned to a variable on the managed heap. Notice I said "a copy," because the original value struct and value class remains unmanaged. For those of you new to the C++ world, I cover the class and struct in detail in Chapter 21.

■**Unsafe Code** A struct and class without the prefix value or ref are unsafe code, as they are referenced using pointers and not handles. Thus, a struct and a class are placed on the CRT heap, which you have to maintain yourself.

The only difference between a value struct and a value class is the default access of their members; value struct members are public, whereas value class members are private. I cover public and private access in Chapter 3.

The value struct and value class are C++/CLI's way of providing programmers with a method of creating their own value types, thus allowing for expansion beyond the basic fundamental types.

All value structs and value classes are derived from the .NET Framework class library's System::ValueType, which allows for the value struct's and value class's ability to be placed on the stack. A value struct and value class can inherit from only interfaces. Trying to inherit from a value struct or value class results in a compile time error.

Listing 2-8 is a simple example of a value class called Coord3D. It is made up of three doubles, a constructor, and a Write() method. I cover constructors and overriding in Chapter 3. The main() function creates the two copies of Coord3D on the stack, with one using the default constructor, and the other using the one user-defined constructor. Notice that to assign a value class to another, you simply use the equal sign (=).

Listing 2-8. *A value class in Action*

```
using namespace System;

// Value class in Action
value class Coord3D
{
public:
    double x;
    double y;
    double z;

    Coord3D (double x, double y, double z)
    {
        this->x = x;
        this->y = y;
        this->z = z;
    }

    String^ Write()
    {
        return String::Format("{0},{1},{2}", x, y, z);
    }
};

void main()
{
    Coord3D coordA;
    Coord3D coordB(1,2,3);

    coordA = coordB;  // Assign is simply an =

    coordA.x += 5.5;  // Operations work just as usual
    coordA.y *= 2.7;
    coordA.z /= 1.3;

    Console::WriteLine(coordB.Write());
    Console::WriteLine(coordA.x);
    Console::WriteLine(coordA.y);
    Console::WriteLine(coordA.z);
}
```

Figure 2-9 shows the results of this program.

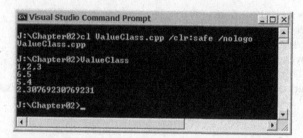

Figure 2-9. *Results of ValueClass.exe*

Reference Types

User-defined reference types are data types a programmer develops that are accessed using handles, and where the actual data object is located on the managed heap. All reference types in C++/CLI are garbage collected.

C++/CLI provides four kinds of user-defined reference types: arrays, classes, interfaces, and delegates. All four of these types share one thing: to create an instance of them required the gcnew operator.

new vs. gcnew

The gcnew operator is new to all C++/CLI developers. It appears for the first time with .NET version 2.0 and replaces the well-known new operator, which was used in all prior versions of C++/CLI (Managed Extensions for C++). Its purpose is to create an instance of a reference type object on the managed heap and return a handle to this instance. This differs from the new operator, which creates an instance of a native class on the CRT heap and returns a pointer to this instance.

Unsafe Code The new operator is used to create an instance of an object on the CRT heap and create a pointer to this object, and thus you lose the benefits of the .NET version 2.0 CLR.

Why a new operator? The gcnew and new operators do different things. When you think of it, it sort of makes sense. Why confuse things by using the same operator? Why not improve readability of the code and make it obvious which types of object you are creating? Hence, the new operator gcnew and the new handle with the caret [^] symbol were created.

Arrays

Arrays, like all other data types in C++/CLI, are objects, unlike their traditional C++ counterparts, which are simply pointers into CRT heap memory. In fact, the only resemblance between a C++/CLI and a traditional C++ array is its single-dimension syntax when being referenced.

All C++/CLI arrays are garbage collected. Also, they can be made up of any data type that derives from System::Object. If you recall, that is every data type in the .NET Framework class library.

C++/CLI arrays have specific dimensions that, when violated, generate an exception. All arrays are derived from a System::Array object, which provides them with many helpful methods and properties, in particular, the Length property for single-dimension arrays and the GetLength() method for single- or multidimensional arrays. Both of these provide the dimensions of the array.

There are no stack base declarations of C++/CLI arrays using subscripts, as in traditional C++. All C++/CLI arrays are references and created on the managed heap.

Unsafe Code For the experienced C++ programmer it is still possible to create stack-based declarations of unsafe C++ arrays, just as you would in traditional C++, because that syntax is still available to you. But arrays declared in this fashion lose the benefits of .NET's CLR given that they compile to unmanaged data.

Unlike what you have seen so far when declaring data types, arrays are declared with syntax very similar to C++/CLI templates or .NET 2.0 generic classes. Also, to declare an array requires the namespace stdcli::language:

```
using namespace stdcli::language;
```

For those coders who had to struggle with the declaration syntax of an array in the previous version of .NET (1.0 and prior), the new syntax should seem like a breath of fresh air, as I believe is a little easier to work with due to three aspects of the declaration:

- The declaration points out that it is derived from that array class.
- The declaration is more or less consistent with other reference type declarations.
- The declaration of arrays made of value types is the same as one made up reference types.

To declare an array requires a handle to the keyword array followed by the data type enclosed in angle brackets:

```
array<datatype>^ arrayname;
```

To create an instance of the array, use the constructor initialization format. Also, because you are allocating the array to the managed heap, the gcnew operator is required. Therefore, to create an array of five ints and an array of seven Strings would require the following statements:

```
using namespace stdcli::language;

array<int>^ fiveInts = gcnew array<int>(5);
array<String^>^ sevenStrings = gcnew array<String^>(7);
```

Unsafe Code It is possible to create arrays of unmanaged data types, as well, so long as the data type is of type pointer. Because the data type is a pointer and thus allocated to the CRT heap, you have to make sure that you handle the memory management yourself. In other words, you need to call delete on all allocated data.

```
class CLASS {};

array<CLASS*>^ pClass = gcnew array<CLASS*>(5);
for (int i = 0; i < pClass->Length; i++)
    pClass[i] = new CLASS();
...
for (int i = 0; i < pClass->Length; i++)
    delete pClass[i];
```

It is also possible to directly initialize an array at the time of declaration with the following syntax:

```
array<String^>^ name = gcnew array<String^> {"Stephen", "R", "G", "Fraser"};
```

Multidimensional arrays also have a template-like syntax. All you have to do is add a rank after the data type:

```
array<datatype, rank>^ arrayname;
```

The rank specifies the number of dimensions of the array and can range from 1 to 32. Any other value generates an error. The rank must also be explicit. Therefore, the rank cannot be a variable. It must be either a numeric literal or a numeric const value. When this rank is greater than 1, then the array is multidimensional. Notice, with this syntax it is possible to write single and multidimensional array declarations the same way:

```
using namespace stdcli::language;
```

```
array<int, 1>^ Ints_5     = gcnew array<int>(5);
array<int, 2>^ Ints_5x3   = gcnew array<int>(5, 3);
array<int, 3>^ Ints_5x3x2 = gcnew array<int>(5, 3, 2);
```

Multidimensional arrays declared in the preceding fashion all have dimensions of uniform size or, in the case of a two-dimensional array, are rectangular. It is also possible to have arrays that have different sizes within a dimension. This form of declaring multidimensional arrays, usually known as jagged arrays, is made up of arrays of arrays. With the new array syntax, declaring an array in this format is a breeze:

```
array< array<datatype>^ >^
```

Notice all you do is make the data type of the outer array declaration another array declaration. Initializing the array takes a little more effort, but then again it is not complicated. Here we create a two-dimensional array, in which the first dimension is 4 and the second dimension varies from 5 to 20.

```
array< array<int>^ >^ jagged = gcnew array< array<int>^ >(4);

for (int i = 0; i < jagged->Length; i++)
{
    e[i] = gcnew array<int>((i+1) * 5);  // each row 5 bigger
}
```

In the preceding example, I show how to subscript into an array, or in layman's terms, how to access an element of an array. For those of you with prior C++ experience, this should look familiar. It's the name of the array followed by the index to the element enclosed in square brackets:

```
variable_name[index];
```

Be careful though: Multidimensional arrays are accessed in a different syntax than traditional arrays. Instead of the name of the array followed by each dimension index in its own square bracket, the syntax is now the name of the array followed by a comma-delimitated list of dimension indexes enclosed in a single set of square brackets:

```
variable_name[index1,index2,index3];
```

■ **Caution**   Just to complicate things, jagged arrays use the traditional syntax to access an element of an array.

Unlike traditional C++, subscripting is not a synonym for pointer arithmetic, and it is not commutative. Thus, the only way to access data from an array is by using subscripts with all dimensions starting at a value of zero.

Two very helpful static methods of the System::Array are Sort() and Reverse(), which provide quick ways to sort and reverse the order of the elements in an array. Reverse() is shown in the following example.

Listing 2-9 is a program showing C++/CLI arrays in action.

Listing 2-9. *C++/CLI Arrays in Action*

```
using namespace System;

// Arrays in Action
void main()
{
    // Single dimension
    array<int>^ a = gcnew array<int>(4);
    array<String^>^ b = gcnew array<String^>(4);

    for (int i = 0; i < a->Length; i++)
    {
        a[i] = i;
    }

    for (int i = 0; i < b->Length; i++)
    {
        b[i] = a[i].ToString();
    }

    for (int i = 0; i < b->Length; i++)
    {
        Console::WriteLine(b[i]);
    }

    Console::WriteLine();
    Array::Reverse(b);
    for (int i = 0; i < b->Length; i++)
    {
        Console::WriteLine(b[i]);
    }

    // Multi dimension uniform
    array<int,2>^ c = gcnew array<int,2>(4,3);
    array<String^,2>^ d = gcnew array<String^,2>(4,3);

    for (int x = 0; x < c->GetLength(0); x++)
    {
        for (int y = 0; y < c->GetLength(1); y++)
        {
            c[x,y] = (x*10)+y;
        }
    }

    Console::WriteLine();
    for (int x = 0; x < d->GetLength(0); x++)
    {
        for (int y = 0; y < d->GetLength(1); y++)
        {
            Console::Write("{0,-5:00}", c[x,y]);
        }
        Console::WriteLine();
```

```
    }

    // Multidimension jagged
    array< array<int>^ >^ e = gcnew array<array<int>^>(4);

    for (int x = 0; x < e->Length; x++)
    {
        e[x] = gcnew array<int>(4+(x*2));   // each row 2 bigger
        for(int y = 0; y < e[x]->Length; y++)
        {
            e[x][y] = (x*10)+y;
        }
    }

    Console::WriteLine();

    for (int x = 0; x < e->Length; x++)
    {
        for (int y = 0; y < e[x]->Length; y++)
        {
            Console::Write("{0,-5:00}", e[x][y]);
        }
        Console::WriteLine();
    }
}
```

Figure 2-10 shows the results of this little program.

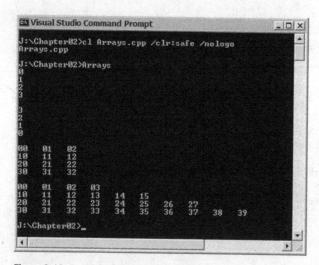

Figure 2-10. *Results of Arrays.exe*

Classes

A *class* is a fundamental building block of most C++/CLI programs. Classes are made up of data members, properties, and methods. Classes are designed to provide the object-oriented nature of the C++/CLI programming language. In other words, they provide the ability to implement encapsulation, inheritance, and polymorphism.

Chapter 3 covers classes in detail.

Interfaces

An *interface* is a collection of methods and properties, without actual definitions, placed into a single unit. In other words, an interface has no implementations for its own methods and properties. You might want to think of an interface as a binding contract of all the methods and properties that an inheriting class must provide.

Chapter 3 covers interfaces.

Delegates and Events

A *delegate* is a reference type that acts as a "function pointer" that can be bound to either an instance or a static method within a C++/CLI class. Delegates can be used whenever a method needs to be called in a dynamic nature, and they are usually used as callback functions or for handling events within .NET Framework applications. I examine delegates in Chapter 4.

An *event* is a specialized implementation of a delegate. An event allows one class to trigger the execution of methods found in other classes without knowing anything about these classes or even from which classes it is invoking the method. I examine events in Chapter 4, and they are implemented quite extensively in Chapters 9 and 10.

Boxing and Unboxing

In previous versions of C++/CLI (Managed Extensions for C++ versions 1.1 and prior) boxing was a big deal, but now with .NET version 2.0, you can almost not worry about it at all. *Boxing* is the CLR technique for converting value types into reference types. And, conversely, *unboxing* is the technique for converting reference types into value types.

The default form of storage for the .NET Framework value types is on the stack, in its machine native form. In this form, a data type cannot access its methods, such as ToString(), because the value type needs to be in an object (reference) format. To remedy this, the value type implicitly (automatically) is boxed whenever the ToString() method is called.

Note In prior versions of C++/CLI (Managed Extensions for C++), implicit boxing only occurred with fundamental value types. In .NET version 2.0, all value types are implicitly boxed.

For example, to box the following simple POINT value type:

```
value class POINT
{
public:
    int x, y;
    POINT(int x, int y) : x(x) , y(y) {}
};
```

```
POINT p1(1,2);
```

would take either of the following lines of code:

```
Object ^o = p1;
// -or-
POINT ^hp = p1;
```

Caution The created boxed object is a copy of the value type. Therefore, any modifications made to the boxed object will not be reflected in the contents of the originating value type.

Unboxing a reference type back into its value type simply requires a type cast. You will probably find that unboxing comes in handy when you have stored your boxed value types in a collection (which store reference types) and want to convert them back to their value types. I cover type casting in the "Type Conversions" section later in this chapter and collections in Chapter 7.

Here's how you would unbox the preceding two boxed value types.

```
POINT p2 = (POINT)o;
POINT p3 = (POINT)hp;
```

Type Modifiers and Qualifiers

Three modifiers and one data type qualifier are provided to C++/CLI programmers. They provide a little information to help define the variables they precede.

auto

The auto modifier tells the compiler that it should create the variable when entering a block and destroy it when exiting the block. If this sounds like most variables to you, you would be right, as it is the default modifier for all variables. Placing the auto keyword in front of variables is optional. In fact, I have never seen it used myself, but if you like typing, here is how you would use it in a program:

```
auto int normalInteger;
```

const

The const qualifier tells the compiler that the variable it is associated with cannot change during execution. It also means that objects referenced to by a const handle or pointed to by a const pointer cannot be changed. Constants are the opposite of variables. The syntax to create a const data type is simply this:

```
const Int32 integerConstant = 42;
```

Note that you need to initialize a const at the time of declaration.

Caution C++/CLI does not support const member methods on managed data types. For example, bool GetFlag() const {return true;} is not allowed within a value struct or ref class, nor is it supported by an interface.

---

extern

The extern modifier tells the compiler that the variable is defined elsewhere, usually in a different file, and will be added in when the final executable or library is linked together. It tells the compiler how to define a variable without actually allocating any storage for it. You will see this variable modifier usually when a global variable is used in more than one source file. (I discuss multifile source file assemblies in the Chapter 4.)

Note An error will occur during the linking of the application if an external variable is not defined in some other source file.

Using the `extern` modifier looks like this:

```
extern int externVariable;
```

static

The `static` modifier has four meanings based on where it is used.

When the `static` modifier is applied to a global variable, the variable's global nature is restricted to the source file in which it is declared. In other words, the variable is accessible to all functions, classes, and so on, declared within the file, but an `extern` variable or class in another source file will not have access to it.

When the `static` modifier is applied to a variable within a function (see the "Functions" section), then the variable will not go out of scope or be deleted when the function exits. This means that the next time the function is called, the `static` variable will retain the same value it had when the function was left the previous time.

When the `static` modifier is applied to a variable within a class (I discuss classes in Chapter 3), then only one copy of the variable is created, and it is shared by all instances of the class.

When the `static` modifier is applied to a method within a class, then the method is accessible without the need to instantiate the class.

Here are some basic examples of the static modifier in use:

```
static int staticVariable;
static void staticFunction ( int arg) { }
```

Type Conversions

Any time the data type on the left side of an assignment statement has a different data type than the evaluated result of the right side, a type conversion will take place. When the only data types used in the statement are fundamental types, then the conversion will happen automatically. Unfortunately, converting automatically may not always be a good thing, especially if the left side data type is smaller, because the resulting number may lose significant digits. For example, when assigning a `UInt16` to a `Byte`, the following problem may occur:

```
UInt16 a = 43690;
Byte b = a;      // b now equals 170 not 43690.
```

Here is what happened. `UInt16` is a 16-bit number, so 43690 decimal represented as a 16-bit number is 1010 1010 1010 1010 in binary. `Byte` is an 8-bit number, so only the last 8 bits of the `UInt16` can be placed into the `Byte`. Thus, the `Byte` now contains 1010 1010 in binary, which happens to equal only 170 decimal.

The C++/CLI compiler will notify you when this type of error may occur. Being warned, the compiler and, subsequently, the program it generates go merrily on their way.

If you don't want the warning, but you still want to do this type of conversion, then you can do something called an *explicit cast*. It's the programmer's way of saying, "Yes, I know, but I don't care." To code an explicit cast, you use one of the following syntaxes:

```
safe_cast<data-type-to-convert-to>(expression)
// --or--
(data-type-to-convert-to) expression
```

Here's an actual example of both syntaxes:

```
char b = safe_cast<char>(a);
// --or--
char b = (char) a;
```

Note Unlike prior versions of C++/CLI (Managed Extensions for C++) the use of the old type conversion syntax: (datatype) variable will first try to do a safe_cast, which, in most cases, will make the two syntaxes the same.

In C++/CLI, when resolving an expression, all data types that make up the expression must be the same. If the expression is made up of more than one type, then type conversion occurs to make all the data types the same. If all the data types are integer types, then the data types are converted to an int or Int64 data type. If a data type is a floating-point type, then the all data types in the expression are converted to a float or double.

All these types of conversions happen automatically. There are cases, though, where you may want all data types to be converted to a data type of your choosing. Here again, you use explicit casting, as shown here:

```
double realA = 23.67;
double realB = 877.12;
int intTotal = safe_cast<int>(realA) + safe_cast<int>(realB);
// -or-
int intTotal = (int) realA + (int) realB;
```

Variable Scope

There are two different scopes: global and local. They have subtleties that might bend these scopes a bit, but that's something most programmers don't care about.

Global scope for a variable means that it is declared outside of all functions, classes, and structures that make up a program, even the main() functions. They are created when the program is started and exist for the entire lifetime of the program. All functions, classes, and structures can access global variables. The static modifier has the capability to restrict a global variable to only the source file in which it is declared.

Local variables are local to the block of code in which they are declared. This means that local variables exist within the opening and closing curly brackets within which they were declared. Most commonly, local variables are declared within a function call, but it is perfectly acceptable to declare them within flow control and looping constructs, which you will learn about in the "Flow Control Constructs" and "Looping Constructs" sections. It is also valid to create a block of code only to reduce the scope of a variable.

The following code shows some global and local variable declarations:

```
int globalVariable;
int main()
{
    int localFunctionVariable;
    { int localToOwnBlock; }
}
```

Namespaces

Some programmers work in an isolated world where their code is the only code. Others use code from many sources. A problem with using code from many sources is that there is a very real possibility that the same names for classes, functions, and so on, can be used by more than one source.

To allow the same names to be used by multiple sources, namespaces were created. *Namespaces* create a local scope declarative region for variables, functions, classes, and structures. In other words, namespaces allow programmers to group their code under a unique name.

Creating a namespace simply requires combining all of the code within a named region, such as

```
namespace MyNamespace
{
    // classes, structs, functions, namespace-global variables
}
```

It is possible to use the same namespace across multiple source code files. The compiler will combine them into one namespace.

To reference something out of a namespace requires the use of the : : operator. For example:

```
MyNamespace::NSfunc();
```

Typing the namespace repeatedly can get tiring, so C++/CLI allows the programmer to bring a namespace into the local scope using

```
using namespace MyNamespace;
```

Now, with the namespace brought into local scope, the function NSfunc from the previous example can be accessed just like any other function of local scope:

```
NSfunc();
```

Caution Bringing multiple namespaces into the local scope could cause duplicate function, class, and struct names to occur.

Literals

Other than Decimals, each of the preceding data types has literals that can be used for things such as initializing variables or as constants. In the preceding programs, I have shown many different literals. In this section, I go over them in more detail.

Numeric Literals

Numeric literals come in five flavors:

- Octal numbers
- Integer numbers
- Hexadecimal numbers
- Decimal numbers
- Exponential numbers

Octal numbers are hardly ever used anymore. They are mainly still in use just for backward compatibility with some ancient programs. They are base-8 numbers and thus made up of the numbers 0 through 7. All octal numbers start with a 0. Some examples are as follows:

0123 (an integer value of 83)   01010 (an integer value of 520)

You need to be aware of octal numbers because if you mistakenly start an integer number with a 0, then the compiler will happily treat it as an octal number. For example, if you type in **0246**, the compiler will think its value is equivalent to the integer value 166.

Integer numbers are straightforward. They are simply whole numbers. Some examples are as follows:

1234   –1234   +1234

The symbols – and + are not actually part of the number but, in fact, are unary operators that convert the whole number into a negative or positive number. The + unary operator is assumed, so 1234 and +1234 mean the same thing.

Hexadecimal numbers are the most complex of the numeric constants. They are base-16 numbers and are made up of the numbers 0 through 9 and the letters A through F (or a through f, as case does not matter). The letters represent the numbers 10 through 15. A hexadecimal literal always starts with 0x. Some examples of hexadecimal numbers are as follows:
0x1234 (an integer value of 4660)0xabcd (an integer value of 43981)

Decimal numbers are the same as integer numbers, except they also contain a decimal and a fractional portion. They are used to represent real numbers. Some examples are as follows:

1.0   3.1415   –1.23

Just as in integer numbers, the minus symbol (–) is a unary operator and not part of the decimal number.

The last numeric literals are the *exponential numbers*. They are similar to decimal numbers except that along with the decimal—or more accurately, the mantissa—is the exponent, which tells the compiler how many times to multiply or divide the mantissa by 10. When the exponent is positive, the mantissa is multiplied by 10 exponent times. If the exponent is negative, the mantissa is divided by 10 exponent times. Some examples are as follows:

1.23e4 (a decimal value of 12300.0)   1.23e-4 (a decimal value of 0.000123)

An interesting feature that comes along with C++/CLI is that numeric literals are also objects. This means that they also have the ToString() method. Listing 2-10 shows a numeric literal object in action. Note that you need to surround the numeric literal with brackets.

Listing 2-10. *Numeric Literals in Action*

```
using namespace System;

// Integer Literals in Action
void main()
{
    Console::WriteLine (  010 );  // An Octal 10 is a base-10 8
    Console::WriteLine ( -010 ); // Negative Octal 10 is a base-10 -8

    Console::WriteLine (  0x10 ); // A Hex 10 is a base-10 16
    Console::WriteLine ( -0x10 ); // Negative Hex 10 is a base-10 -16

    // This is kind of neat. Number literals are objects, too!
    Console::WriteLine ( (1234567890).ToString() );
    Console::WriteLine ( (0xABCDEF).ToString("X") );
}
```

Figure 2-11 shows the results of this little program.

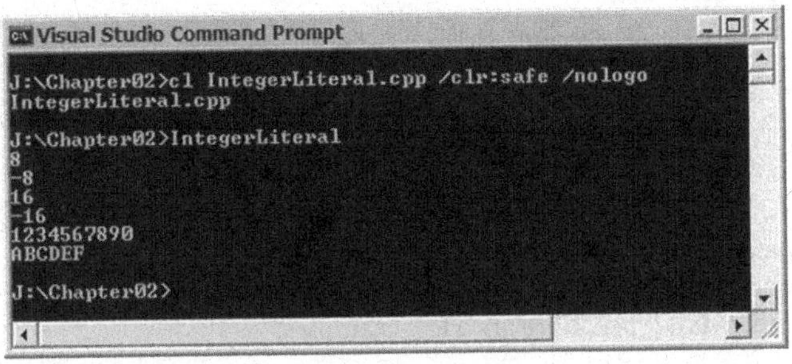

Figure 2-11. *Results of IntegerLiteral.exe*

Boolean Literals

There are only two Boolean literals: the values true and false.

Like numeric literals, *Boolean literals* are objects in C++/CLI. Thus, they too provide the ToString() method. Listing 2-11 shows a Boolean literal object in action.

Listing 2-11. *Boolean Literals in Action*

```
using namespace System;

// Boolean Literals in Action
void main()
{
    bool isTrue = true;
    bool isFalse = false;

    Console::WriteLine ( isTrue );
    Console::WriteLine ( isFalse );

    // This is kind of neat. Boolean literals are objects, too!
    Console::WriteLine ( true.ToString () );
    Console::WriteLine ( false.ToString () );
}
```

Figure 2-12 shows the results of this little program.

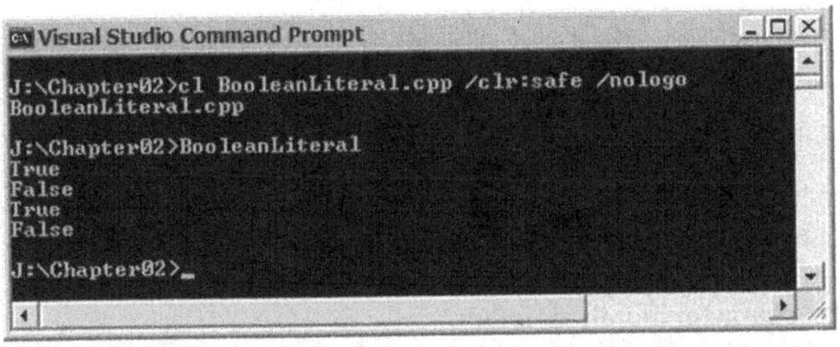

Figure 2-12. *Results of BooleanLiteral.exe*

Character Literals

C++/CLI provides two different types of character literals:

- Character
- Escape sequence

Character literals are the most basic form and are simply a printable letter, number, or symbol enclosed in single quotes. These literals can be placed in either char (8-bit) types (or any other integer type, for that matter) and Char (16-bit) types. Here are a few examples:

'A'   '0'   '+'

Escape sequences are a little more elaborate and come in a few flavors. Like the character literal form, escape sequences are placed within single quotes. The first character within the quotes is always a backslash [\]. After the backslash will be a character such as the ones shown in Table 2-9, an octal number, or an *x* followed by a hexadecimal number. The octal or hexadecimal numbers are the numeric equivalent of the character you want the literal to represent.

Table 2-9. *Special Escape Sequences*

Escape Sequence	Character
\?	Question mark
\'	Single quote
\"	Double quote
\\	Backslash
\0	Null
\a	Bell or alert
\b	Backspace
\f	Form feed
\n	New line
\r	Carriage return
\t	Tab
\v	Vertical tab

All the character literal types can be prefixed with the letter L to tell the compiler to create a Unicode equivalent of the character literal. Remember that Unicode characters are 16 bits, so they will not fit in the char type; instead, they should be placed in Char types.

Listing 2-12 is a program showing character literals in action.

Listing 2-12. *Character Literals in Action*

```
using namespace System;

// Character Literals in Action
void main()
{
    char a = 'a';         // character 'a'
    Char b = L'b';        // Unicode 'b'

    char t = '\t';        // tab escape
    Char s = L'\\';       // Unicode backslash escape

    char d = '\45';       // octal escape
    Char e = L'\x0045';   // Unicode hexadecimal escape

    Console::WriteLine ( a ); // displays numeric equiv of 'A'
    Console::WriteLine ( b ); // displays the letter 'b'
    Console::WriteLine ( t ); // displays numeric equiv of tab
    Console::WriteLine ( s ); // displays backslash
    Console::WriteLine ( d ); // displays decimal equiv of octal 45
    Console::WriteLine ( e ); // displays the letter 'e'
}
```

Figure 2-13 shows the results of this little program.

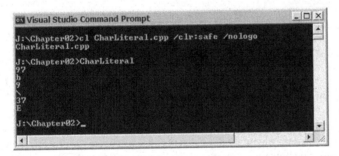

Figure 2-13. *Results of CharLiteral.exe*

String Literals

Managed *string literals* are simply character strings enclosed in double quotes. You can also create literal strings prefixed with the letter L, creating a Unicode string literal.

By the way, the escape sequences shown previously also work within Strings. You must be careful to avoid too many characters after the backslash being taken as the escape sequence. Realistic examples of this are difficult with the Latin alphabet, but this illustrates the point:

```
String ^s1 = "\x61";   // a
String ^s2 = "\x611";  // is NOT a1 but a Unicode hexadecimal escape of 611
```

Listing 2-13 is a program showing string literals in action.

Listing 2-13. *String Literals in Action*

```
using namespace System;

// String Literals in Action
void main()
{
    String^ a = "Managed String";
    String^ b = L"Unicode String";

    Console::WriteLine(a);
    Console::WriteLine(b);
}
```

Figure 2-14 shows the results of this little program.

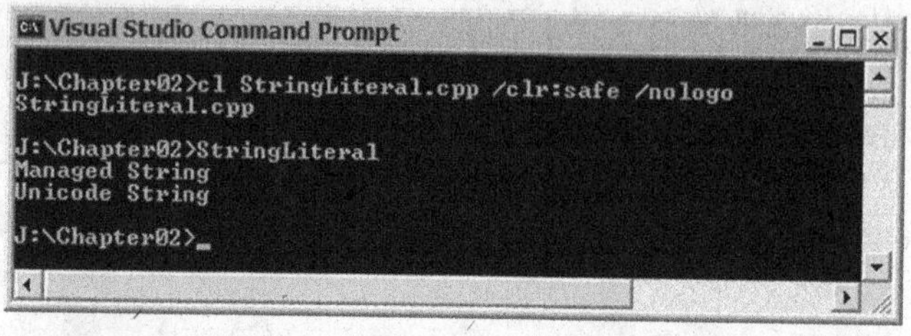

Figure 2-14. *Results of StringLiteral.exe*

Comments

Documenting programs is a very important practice all software developers should do, no matter what programming language they use. Unfortunately, documentation is often the first thing to suffer when a project is crunched for time.

If you are the only developer for a program, you might think that because you wrote the program, you should have no problem remembering how the program works. From experience, leaving a piece of code and coming back to it six months or more later is nearly equivalent to reading someone else's code, unless, of course, it is documented.

C++/CLI, like traditional C++, provides two comment styles: the single-line comment and the multiline comment. There is also a third comment style that allows for the autogeneration of documentation. I'll cover this style in Chapter 6.

The single-line comment begins with a double slash (//). Anything after the double slash is a comment. Depending on where you place the double slash, you can use a single-line comment for an entire line or just part of a line. By the way, you probably noticed the comments in the previous example code, but here are a couple more examples:

```
// This entire line is a comment.
int x = 0;    // This comment uses part of the line.
```

The multiline comment starts with /* and ends with */. You can place multiline comments anywhere in the code, even on different lines. You must use care with this kind of comment, because embedding a multiline comment within a multiline comment will cause errors. Here are some multiline comments:

```
/*****************************************************
* Common comment box. You will see these frequently *
* within programs.                                  *
*****************************************************/

Int32 x = 0;  /* This is a comment on a single line */
Int32 y = 0;  /* This is a comment that stretched for
                More than one line */
/* Embedded comments like this /* do not work
   as you  might expect */ this portion would
   not be commented and will in this case cause errors */
```

Because of the embedded comment problem, many programmers, myself included, prefer to use the double slash comment.

Operators

C++/CLI and traditional C++ are identical, except for one new operator introduced in C++/CLI, the unary % (or reference operator). If you have programmed in C++, then you should find very little new information in this section, but it might serve as a bit of a refresher. For anyone inexperienced in C++, this section is essential because it shows all the basic operations available to a C++/CLI programmer.

Arithmetic Operators

Arithmetic operators are used to perform arithmetic operations on integer, floating-point, and decimal data types. Seven arithmetic operations are available, as shown in Table 2-10.

Table 2-10. *Arithmetic Operators*

Operator	Action
-	Subtraction or unary minus
+	Addition
*	Multiplication
/	Division
%	Modulus
--	Decrement
++	Increment

The -, +, *, and / operators perform exactly as expected. The % operator evaluates to the remainder of a division operation. The -- and ++ operators decrease and increase the operand by 1, respectively. You can place the -- and ++ operators before the operand, and in this way, the operand is incremented or decremented before any other operations take place in the expression. You can also place these operators after the operand, and in this case, the operand is incremented or decremented after all the operations in the expression are done.

When an expression contains more than one arithmetic operator, the arithmetic operators will be evaluated according to the precedence shown in Table 2-11. If two operators of the same precedence occur in the expression, then they are evaluated from left to right.

Table 2-11. *Arithmetic Precedence*

Precedence	Operators
Highest	-- ++ - (unary minus)
	* / %
Lowest	- +

Comparisons and Logical Operators

Comparison operators are used to compare two expressions and then generate a Boolean value (true/false) based on the result of the comparison. There are six comparison operators, as shown in Table 2-12.

Table 2-12. *Comparison Operators*

Operator	Meaning
>	Greater than
>=	Greater than or equal to
<	Less than
<=	Less than or equal to
==	Equal to
!=	Not equal to

Caution Be very careful when using the assignment operator = and the equal to operator ==. If you mistakenly use = for the comparison operator, the left value is overwritten by the right, and if the left value is nonzero, then the comparison will have a true result. This is unlikely to be what you want.

Logical operators are similar to comparison operators except that they compare Boolean values instead of expressions. The three logical operators are shown in Table 2-13.

Table 2-13. *Logical Operators*

Operator	Meaning
!	NOT: If the operand was true, then false is evaluated or vice versa.
&&	AND: If both operands are true, then evaluate to true; otherwise, evaluate to false.
||	OR: If either or both operands are true, then evaluate to true; otherwise, evaluate to false.

Often, you will find both a comparison and a logical operator in the same comparison statement. For grins and giggles, figure out what this means:

```
a < b && c >= d || !e
```

When a statement contains more than one comparison or logical operator, then they will be evaluated according to the precedence shown in Table 2-14. If two operators of the same precedence occur in the expression, then they are evaluated from left to right.

Table 2-14. *Comparison and Logical Operator Precedence*

Highest	!
	> >= < <=
	== !=
	&&
Lowest	||

Bitwise Operators

The bitwise operators are used to manipulate the bits of an integer type value. There are six bitwise operators, as shown in Table 2-15.

Table 2-15. *Bitwise Operators*

Operator	Action
&	Bitwise AND
|	Bitwise OR
^	Bitwise XOR
~	Ones complement
>>	Right shift
<<	Left shift

The bitwise AND operator compares the bit pattern of its two operands. If both the bits at the same offset in the bit pattern are 1s, then the resulting bit pattern will become a 1; otherwise, it will become a 0. For example:

```
0101 & 0011 becomes 0001
```

The bitwise OR operator compares the bit pattern of its two operands. If either or both the bits at the same offset in the bit pattern are 1s, then the resulting bit pattern will become a 1; otherwise, it will become a 0. For example:

```
0101 & 0011 becomes 0111
```

The bitwise XOR operator compares the bit pattern of its two operands. If either, but not both, of the bits at the same offset in the bit pattern is a 1, then the resulting bit pattern will become a 1; otherwise, it will become a 0. For example:

```
0101 & 0011 becomes 0110
```

The ones complement operator simply flips the bits. If it was a 1, then it becomes a 0, and vice versa:

```
0101 becomes 1010
```

The shift operators shift all the bits of the operand per the number of bits specified right (>>) or left (<<). For example:

```
Right shift -  00101100 >> 2 becomes 00001011
Left shift  -  00101100 << 2 becomes 10110000
```

Tip Right-shifting by 1 bit is equivalent to dividing by 2, and left-shifting by 1 bit is equivalent to multiplying by 2. Both shifts are far faster than either dividing or multiplying on a computer. So, if you need a little more speed in your application, and you are working with integer types and dividing or multiplying by factors of 2, you might want to consider shifting instead.

When a statement contains more than one bitwise operator, then the bitwise operators will be evaluated according to the precedence shown in Table 2-16. If two operators of the same precedence occur in the expression, then they are evaluated from left to right.

Table 2-16. *Bitwise Operator Precedence*

Highest	~
	>> <<
	&
	^
Lowest	|

Conditional Operator

The *conditional operator* is the only ternary operator available to C++/CLI programmers. A *ternary* operator uses three expressions.

The conditional operator takes the first expression and sees if it is true (nonzero) or false (zero). If it is true, then the second expression is executed. If it is false, then the third expression is executed. A conditional operator looks like this:

```
expression1 ? expression2 : expression3;
a < b ? "a is less than b" : "a is greater than or equal to b";
```

Comma Operator

The *comma operator* causes a sequence of expressions to act as a single expression, with the last expression ultimately becoming that to which the total expression evaluates. You can place a series of comma-delimited expressions anywhere you can place a normal expression.

You will probably see the comma operator most frequently used in the initialization and increment sections of a for loop, but there is nothing stopping a programmer from using it elsewhere. I discuss for loops later in this chapter.

The following example, though completely contrived, shows the comma operator in action. First, b is incremented, then a is assigned the value of multiplying post incremented a and b, and finally, c is assigned the value of a modulus b:

```
int a = 2;
int b = 3;
int c = (b++, a = b++ * a++, a % b);
```

The values of the variables after this code snippet finishes are

```
a = 9
b = 5
c = 4
```

Assignment Operators

There are 11 assignment operators available to C++/CLI, as shown in Table 2-17.

Table 2-17. *Assignment Operators*

Operator	Action
=	Assign
+=	Add then assign
-=	Subtract then assign
*=	Multiply then assign
/=	Divide then assign
%=	Modulus then assign
>>=	Shift right then assign
<<=	Shift left then assign
&=	AND then assign
^=	XOR then assign
|=	OR then assign

The operator used to assign one value to another is simply the equal sign (=). The expression on the right side of the equal sign is calculated and then assigned to the value on the left side of the equal sign.

You have seen assignment used several times already in this chapter, but here are a few more examples:

```
String ^str = "This is a managed string.";
int num1 = 0x1234;
int num2 = 4321;
num1 = num2;
```

Assigning a common value to several different variables can be accomplished by stringing together several assignments. For example, to assign 42 to the variables a, b, and c, you would write

```
a = b = c = 42;
```

It is a common practice to take a value, do some operation it, and then place the results back into the original operator. For example:

```
a = a + 5;
b = b * 2;
```

So common is this that C++/CLI provides a set of special assignments to handle it:

```
a += 5;
b *= 2;
```

Address of, Reference, and Indirection Operators

Three operators are available to C++/CLI programmers for handling handles and pointers, as shown in Table 2-18.

Table 2-18. *Address of, Reference, and Indirection Operators*

Operator	Action
& (unary)	Address of
% (unary)	Reference
* (unary)	Indirection

The *address of operator* returns the address of the object after it. For example, if x were located at address 1024, then to place the address (1024) in variable y, you would write this:

```
y = &x;     // place the address of x into y
```

Unsafe The address of operator, by its very nature of being a manipulator of pointers, has to be and is an unsafe operation.

The *reference operator* was introduced, by necessity, in C++/CLI as a consequence of a syntactical lack of a safe operator to reference handles. Introduced for the same reason as the handle, the reference operator provides a means to reference only managed data objects (objects on the managed heap). Thus, it provides an obvious syntactical difference between managed and unsafe code (which use the address of operator). The following code shows how to create a reference of an int value type:

```
int intVT = 10;
int %intRef = intVT;        // Assign int value type to a reference.
Console::WriteLine(intRef);  // Print out reference. This should contain 10.
intRef = 20;                // Change value of reference.
Console::WriteLine(intVT);   // Print out value type. This should contain 20.
```

The *indirection operator* has been augmented in C++/CLI from Managed Extensions for C++ and now gets the value from the address or a handle stored within itself. On the one hand, if y contained the address 1024, then to place the value of 50 at the address 1024, you would write

```
*y = 50;  // place the value of 50 at the address y points to
```

On the other hand, if y were a handle to an int, then to place the value of 50 on that handle, you would write:

```
*y = 50;  // place the value of 50 at the int handle y
```

Hmm . . . Looks kind of familiar, don't you think?

Listing 2-14 is a program that shows the reference and indirection operators in action. I'll hold off demonstrating the address of operator until I discuss unsafe code in detail in Chapters 20 and 21.

Listing 2-14. *Reference and Indirection Operators in Action*

```
using namespace System;

ref class RefClass
{
public:
    int X;

    RefClass(int x)
    {
        X = x;
    }
};

// Reference and Indirection in Action
void main()
{
    RefClass rc(10);
    RefClass ^o;

    o = %rc;                 // place a reference of rc in the handle o
    Console::WriteLine(o->X); // print out object. This should contain 10.

    rc.X = 20;               // place 50 at the address y points to
    Console::WriteLine(o->X); // print out object. This should contain 20.

    int %i = rc.X;           // assign rc.X to a reference

    i = 30;                  // change value of reference
    Console::WriteLine(o->X); // print out object. This should contain 30.

    Console::WriteLine();
```

```
    int ^y = gcnew int(100);   // create a handle to an int
    Console::WriteLine(y);     // print out int.

    *y = 110;                  // Assign new value to dereferenced int
    Console::WriteLine(*y);    // print out dereferenced int.
}
```

Figure 2-15 shows the results of this little program.

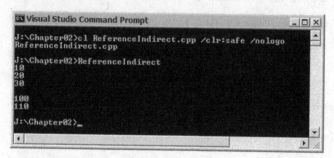

Figure 2-15. *Results of ReferenceIndirect.exe*

Unsafe Code Directly modifying a dereferenced value is unverifiable and therefore is an unsafe operation. Thus, the preceding example cannot be compiled using the /clr:safe option.

Operator Precedence

I have shown operator precedence for each operator in its own section, but what if operators from different sections occur in the same statement? Table 2-19 shows the precedence of all the operators.

Table 2-19. *Operator Precedence*

Precedence	Operators
Highest	() [] ::
	! ~ ++ -- - (unary) * (unary) % (unary) & (unary)
	* / %
	+ -
	<< >>
	< <= > >=
	== !=
	&
	^
	|
	&&

Table 2-19. *Operator Precedence*

Precedence	Operators
	||
	?:
Lowest	= += -= *= /= %= >>= <<= &= ^= |=

Flow Control Constructs

Normally in a C++/CLI program, statements are executed sequentially from beginning to end. There will be times when a program is going to execute a portion of code only if certain conditions are true. To handle conditional execution of code, C++/CLI provides two flow control constructs: if and switch.

if Statement

The if statement enables the conditional execution of code based on the evaluated value of some condition. An if statement in its simplest form is as follows:

```
if ( condition )
{
    statements;
}
```

The condition can be any expression, but to make more sense it should evaluate to a Boolean value of either true or false. It is perfectly valid to evaluate to a zero (false) or nonzero (true) condition, as well.

Obviously, it is possible to execute a block of code when a condition is not true, as shown here:

```
if ( ! condition )
{
    statements;
}
```

What if you want a block of code to execute when a condition is true and some other block of code to execute when the condition is false? You could write two if statements, one for the true condition and one for the false condition, or you could use the if-else statement, which looks like this:

```
if ( condition )
{
    statements;
}
else  // ! condition (the comment is optional)
{
    statements;
}
```

There is one more construct for if statements. What if you want different blocks of code to be executed based on mutually exclusive conditions? You could write a stream of if conditions, one for each condition, but then each condition would have to be checked, which would be a waste of time. Instead, you should use the if-else-if-else construct, also called the nested if construct, which exits the if construct once it matches a condition. The nested if construct looks like this:

```
if ( condition1 )  // first mutually exclusive condition
{
    statements;
}
else if ( condition2 )  // second mutually exclusive condition
{
    statements;
}
else  // optional catch the rest condition
{
    statements;
}
```

This example will display a different string depending on the value of the animal variable:

```
enum Creature : int {Dog, Cat, Eagle};
Creature animal;

// assign a value to animal
animal = Cat;

if ( animal == Dog )
{
    Console::WriteLine ("The animal is a dog");
}
else if ( animal == Cat )
{
    Console::WriteLine ("The animal is a cat");
}
else  // animal is not a dog or cat
{
    Console::WriteLine ("Maybe the animal is a bird");
}
```

switch Statement

The switch statement is a multiple-choice flow-control construct. It functions in a very similar manner to the nested if construct, except that it only works for integer value types or expressions that evaluate to integers. The switch statement works like this: The switch expression is checked against each case constant. If a case constant matches the expression, then its associated statements are executed. If no case constant matches the expression, then the default statements are executed. Finally, the switch statement is exited.

A switch statement looks like this:

```
switch ( expression )
{
    case constant1:
        statements1;
        break;
    case constant2:
        statements2;
        break;
    default:
        statements3;
}
```

You can write the preceding nested if statement as a switch statement, like this:

```
switch ( animal )
{
    case Dog:
        Console::WriteLine ("The animal is a dog");
        break;
    case Cat:
        Console::WriteLine ("The animal is a cat");
        break;
    default:
        Console::WriteLine ("Maybe the animal is a bird");
}
```

The first thing you may notice is that each case ends with a break statement. This break statement tells the switch that it is finished. If you fail to place a break statement at the end of a case, then the following case will also be executed. This may sound like a mistake, but there are times when this falling through to the next case is exactly what you will want. For example, this case statement executes the same code for lower- and uppercase characters:

```
switch ( keypressed )
{
    case 'A':
    case 'a':
        Console::WriteLine ("Pressed the A key");
        break;
    case 'B':
    case 'b':
        Console::WriteLine ("Pressed the B key");
        break;
    default:
        Console::WriteLine ("Pressed some other key");
}
```

■ **Caution** A missing break statement is a very common and difficult error to debug, because often the error caused by it does not occur until later in the program.

Looping Constructs

So far, you have seen that C++/CLI programs are statements that are executed sequentially from beginning to end, except when flow control dictates otherwise. Obviously, there are scenarios in which you would like to be able to repeat a single statement or a block of statements a certain number of times, until a certain condition occurs or for all elements of a collection. C++/CLI provides four looping constructs for this: while, do while, for, and for each.

while Loop

The while loop is the simplest looping construct provided by C++/CLI. It simply repeats a statement or a block of statements while the condition is true (some people prefer to say until the condition is false). The basic format of a while loop is as follows:

```
while ( condition )
{
    statements;
}
```

The condition is checked at the start of each iteration of the loop, including the first. Thus, if the condition evaluates at the start to false, then the statements never are executed. The while loop condition expression is the same as an if statement condition.

In its simplest form, the while loop repeats a statement or a block of statements forever:

```
while ( true )
{
    statements;
}
```

I cover how to break out of this type of loop a little later.

More commonly, you will want the while loop condition to be evaluated. Here is an example of how to display all the numbers from 1 to 6 inclusive:

```
int i = 0;
while ( i < 6 )
{
    i++;
    Console::WriteLine(i);
}
```

do-while Loop

There are scenarios in which you will want or need the loop to always execute at least once. You could do this in one of two ways:

- Duplicate the statement or block of statements before the while loop.
- Use the do while loop.

Obviously, the do while loop is the better of the two solutions.

Like the while loop, the do while loop loops through a statement or a block of statements until a condition becomes false. Where the do while differs is that it always executes the body of the loop at least once. The basic format of a do while loop is as follows:

```
do {
    statements;
} while ( condition );
```

As you can see, the condition is checked at the end of every iteration of the loop. Therefore, the body is guaranteed to execute at least once. The condition is just like the while statement and the if statement.

Like the while statement, the most basic form of the do while loop loops forever, but because this format has no benefit over the while statement, it is seldom used. Here is the same example previously used for the while statement. It displays the numbers 1 to 6 inclusive.

```
int i = 0;
do {
    i++;
    Console::WriteLine(i);
} while ( i  < 6 );
```

for Loop

The for loop is the most complex construct for handling looping and can be used for almost any kind of loop. In its simplest form, the for loop, like the other two loop constructs, simply repeats a statement or a block of statements forever:

```
for ( ; ; )
{
    statements;
}
```

Normally, you will want control of how your program will loop, and that's what the for loop excels at. With the for loop, you can not only check to see if a condition is met as you do in the while loop, but you can also initialize and increment variables on which to base the condition. The basic format for a for loop is this:

```
for (initialization; condition; increment)
{
    statements;
}
```

When the code starts executing a for loop (only the first time), the initialization is executed. The initialization is an expression that initializes variables that will be used in the loop. It is also possible to actually declare and initialize variables that will only exist while they are within the loop construct.

The condition is checked at every iteration through the loop, even the first. This makes it similar to the while loop. In fact, if you don't include the initialization and increment, the for loop acts in an identical fashion to the while loop. You can use almost any type of condition statement, so long as it evaluates to false or zero when you want to exit the loop.

The increment executes at the end of each iteration of the for loop and just before the condition is checked. Usually the code increments (or decrements) the variables that were initialized in the initialization, but this is not a requirement.

Let's look at a simple for loop in action. This for loop creates a counter i, which will iterate so long as it remains less than 6 or, in other words, because you start iterating at zero, this for loop will repeat six times.

```
for (int i = 0; i < 6; i++)
{
    Console::WriteLine ( i );
}
```

The output of this for loop is as follows:

```
0
1
2
3
4
5
```

One thing to note is that the initialization variable is accessible within the for loop, so it is possible to alter it while the loop is executing. For example, this for loop, though identical to the previous example, will only iterate three times:

```
for (int i = 0; i < 6; i++)
{
    i++;
    Console::WriteLine ( i );
}
```

The output of this for loop is as follows:

```
1
3
5
```

for loops are not restricted to integer type. It is possible to use floating-point or even more advanced constructs. Though this might not mean much to some of you, for loops are a handy way of iterating through link lists. (I know it is a little advanced at this point in the book, but I am throwing it in here to show how powerful the for loop can be.) For those of you who want to know what this does, it loops through the elements of a link list to the maximum of ten link list elements:

```
for (int i=0, list *cur=headptr; i<10 && cur->next != 0; i++, cur=cur->next)
{
    statements;
}
```

for each Loop

Although the for each construct has been in Visual Basic for a long time and in C# since its inception, the for each loop is just now making its appearance in C++/CLI. For now, the for each is strictly a C++/CLI construct, as it allows the iteration through all items in a collection deriving from the IEnumerable interface. I will cover in detail collections and the IEnumerable interface in Chapter 7, so at present I will stick to the collection that we already have covered, the array.

You might think that because of the specific nature of this construct it won't be very helpful. Well, you would be wrong—the .NET Framework is filled with collections, and most developers use many different types of collections (not just arrays) within their code. Thanks to the for each construct your code will be considerably simplified.

The basic syntax of the for each loop is

```
for each ( <data declaration> in collection)
{
}
```

Therefore, if you have an array named numbers, this is how you iterate through it:

```
array<int>^ numbers = gcnew array<int> { 1, 2, 3, 4 };
for each ( int i  in numbers )
{
    Console::WriteLine(i);
}
```

There is one *gotcha*, however. With the for each loop, you can't modify the collection itself while iterating through. This doesn't mean you can't change the contents of the elements of the collection. It means you can't add or remove elements to or from the collection. This is not an issue for arrays, given that this is not allowed anyway, but for many other collection types it may be a problem. The worst thing is if the compiler doesn't catch it. It is the CLR that lets you know about it by throwing an exception. I'll cover exceptions in Chapter 4; I show you this gotcha in action when I cover collections in Chapter 7.

Skipping Loop Iterations

Even though you have set up a loop to iterate through multiple iterations of a block of code, there may be times that some of the iteration doesn't need to be executed. In C++/CLI, you can do this with a continue statement.

You usually find the continue statement in some type of condition statement. When the continue statement is executed, the program jumps immediately to the next iteration. In the case of the while and do while loops, the condition is checked, and the loop continues or exits depending on the result of the condition. For a for each loop the next element in the collection is retrieved and then continues, unless there are no more elements, and then the loop exits. If continue is used in a for loop, the increment executes first, and then the condition executes.

Here is a simple and quite contrived example that will print out all the prime numbers under 30:

```
for (Int32 i = 1; i < 30; i++)
{
    if ( i % 2 == 0 && i / 2 > 1)
        continue;
    else if ( i % 3 == 0 && i / 3 > 1)
        continue;
    else if ( i % 5 == 0 && i / 5 > 1)
        continue;
    else if ( i % 7 == 0 && i / 7 > 1)
        continue;
    Console::WriteLine(i);
}
```

Breaking Out of a Loop

Sometimes you need to leave a loop early, maybe because there is an error condition and there is no point in continuing, or in the case of the loops that will loop indefinitely, you simply need a way to exit the loop. In C++/CLI, you do this with a break statement. The break statement in a loop works the same way as the switch statement you saw earlier.

There is not much to the break statement. When it is executed, the loop is terminated, and the flow of the program continues after the loop.

Though this is not really a very good example, the following sample shows how you could implement do while type flow in a for loop. This loop breaks when it gets to 10:

```
for ( int i = 0; ; i++ )
{
    Console::WriteLine(i);

    if (i >= 10)
        break;
}
```

Functions

At the core of all C++/CLI programs is the *function*. It is the source of all activity within a program. Functions also enable programmers to break their programs into manageable chunks. You have already been using a function called main(). Now let's see how you can go about creating a few of your own.

The general format of a function looks like this:

```
return-type function-name ( parameter-list )
{
    statements-of-the-function;
}
```

The return-type of the function is the value type, handle, pointer, or reference that is returned by the function when it finishes. The return type can be any value type, reference, handle, or pointer, even ones that are user defined. If no return type is specified for the function, then C++/CLI defaults the return value to int. If the function does not return a value, then the return value should be set to the keyword void.

The function-name is obviously the name of the function. The rules of naming a function are the same as those for naming a variable.

The parameter-list is a comma-separated list of variable declarations that define the variable, which will be passed to the function when it starts executing. Parameter variables can be any value types, references, handles, or pointers, even ones that are user defined.

Passing Arguments to a Function

There are two different ways of passing arguments to a function: by value and by reference. Syntactically, there is little difference between the two. In fact, the only difference is that passing by reference has an additional reference operator (percent [%]) placed before the value name:

```
void example ( int ByValue, int %ByReference )
{
}
```

The big difference is in how the actual values are passed. When passing by value, a copy of the variable is passed to the function. Because the argument is a copy, the function can't change the original passed argument value. For example, this function takes the value of parameter a and adds 5 to it:

```
void example ( int a )
{
    a = a + 5;
}
```

When the function is called,

```
int a = 5;
example(a);
```

the value of a will still be 5.

What if you want to actually update the value of the parameter passed so that it reflects any changes made to it within the function? You have two ways to handle this. The first is to pass a handle by value. Because you are passing a handle to the value, and not the actual value, any changes that you make to the value within the function will be reflected outside the function. The problem of passing by handle is that now the syntax of the function is more complicated because you have to worry about dereferencing the handles.

```
void example ( int ^a )
{
    *a = *a + 5;
}
```

When the function is called,

```
int ^a = 5;
example(a);
```

the value of a will be 10.

The second approach is to pass the arguments by reference. When passing arguments by reference, the argument value is not copied; instead, the function is accessing an alias of the argument or, in other words, the function is accessing the argument directly.

```
void example ( int %a )
{
    a = a + 5;
}
```

When the function is called,

```
int a = 5;
int b = example(a);
```

the value of a will be 10.

There is a pro and a con to using references. The pro is that it is faster to pass arguments by reference, as there is no copy step involved. The con is that, unlike using handlers, other than %, there is no difference between passing by value or reference. There is a very real possibility that changes can happen to argument variables within a function without the programmer knowing.

The speed benefit is something some programmers don't want to give up, but they still want to feel secure that calling a function will not change argument values. To solve this problem, it is possible to pass const reference values. When these are implemented, the compiler makes sure that nothing within the function will cause the value of the argument to change:

```
void example ( const int %a )
{
//    a = a + 5;      // This line will cause a compiler error because
                      // we are trying to change the const a

    int b = a + 5;
}
```

When the function is called,

```
int a = 5;
example(a);
```

the value of a will still be 5.

Returning Values from a Function

Returning a value from a function is a two-step process. First, specify the type of value the function will return, and second, using the return statement, pass a return value of that type:

```
double example()
{
    double a = 8.05;
    // do some stuff
    return a;
}
```

Returning Handles

You need to take care when you return a handle from a function.

Caution Never return a handle to a variable of local scope to a function, because it will not be a valid handle on exiting the function.

Never do this:

```
ref class RefClass {};

RefClass^ ERRORexample()
{
    RefClass a;
    // do some stuff;
    return %a;     // This variable will disappear when the function ends, so
                   // reference will be invalid
}
```

Instead, you should return the handle a that was passed to the function or the handle b that was created by the gcnew operator in the function:

```
ref class RefClass
{
public:
    int X;
    RefClass(int x) : X(x) {}
};

RefClass^ Okexample(RefClass^ a)
{
    RefClass^ b = gcnew RefClass(8);
    // do some stuff;
    if (a->X > b->X)
        return a;
    else
        return b;
}

void main()
{
    RefClass ^r = gcnew RefClass(7);
    RefClass ^a = Okexample(r);
}
```

In traditional C++, the variable b in the preceding example would be a classic location for a memory leak, because the developer would have to remember to call the delete statement on the returned value b. This is not the case in C++/CLI, because handles are garbage collected automatically when no longer used; thus delete need not be called.

Returning References

You also need to take care when you return a reference from a function.

> **Caution** Never return a reference to a variable of local scope to a function, because it will not be a valid reference on exiting the function.

Never do this:

```
ref class RefClass {};

RefClass% ERRORexample()
{
    RefClass a;
    // do some stuff;
    return a;     // This variable will disappear when the function ends, so
                  // reference will be invalid
}
```

Instead, you should return a reference that was passed to the function, or a pointer or reference to a variable that was created by the gcnew operator within the function:

```
ref class RefClass
{
public:
    int X;
    RefClass(int x) : X(x) {}
};

RefClass% Okexample(RefClass %a)
{
    RefClass^ b = gcnew RefClass(8);
    // do some stuff;
    if (a.X > b->X)
        return a;
    else
        return *b;
}

void main()
{
    RefClass r(9);
    RefClass %a = Okexample(r);
}
```

Something worth noting in this function is the creation of a reference using the gcnew operator. Again, with traditional C++ you would have to delete the reference. Fortunately, because handles get garbage collected in C++/CLI, there is no need for the delete statement and no memory leak occurs.

Prototypes

You can't use a function until it has been defined. Okay, there is nothing stopping you from placing function declarations in every *.cpp file where it is used, but then you would have a lot of redundant code.

The correct approach is to create prototypes of your functions and place them within an include (.h) file. (I cover include files in Chapter 4.) This way, the compiler will have the definition it needs, and the function implementation will be in only one place. A prototype is simply a function without its body followed by a semicolon:

```
int example ( const int %a );
```

Function Overloading

In the dark ages of C, it was a common practice to have many functions with very similar names doing the same functionality for different data types. For example, you would see functions such as PrintInt(int x) to print an integer, PrintChar(char c) to print a character, PrintString(char *s) to print an array of characters, and so on. Having many names doing the same thing became quite a pain. Then, along came C++, and now C++/CLI, with an elegant solution to this annoyance: function overloading.

Function overloading is simply C++/CLI's way of having two or more methods with exactly the same name but with a different number or type of parameter. Usually, the overloaded functions provide the same functionality but use different data types. Sometimes the overloaded functions provide a more customized functionality as a result of having more parameters to more accurately solve the problem. But, in truth, the two overloaded functions could do completely different things. This, however, would probably be an unwise design decision, as most developers would expect similar functionality from functions using the same name.

When a function overloaded call takes place, the version of the method to run is determined at compile time by matching the calling function's signature with those of the overloaded function. A function signature is simply a combination of the function name, number of parameters, and types of parameters. For function overloading, the return type is not significant when it comes to determining the correct method. In fact, it is not possible to overload functions by changing only the return type. If you do this, the compiler will give a bunch of errors, but only the one indicating that a function is duplicated is relevant.

There is nothing special about coding overloaded functions. For example, here is one function overloaded three times for the supersecret Test function:

```
int Test () { /* do stuff */ }
int Test (int x) { /* do stuff */ }
int Test (int x, int y, double z) { /* do stuff */ }
```

Calling an overloaded function is nothing special either. Simply call the function you want with the correct parameters. For example, here is some code to call the third supersecret Test function:

```
Test (0, 1, 2.0);
```

The only thing that C++/CLI programmers need to concern themselves with that traditional C++ programmers do not is that fundamental types and their corresponding runtime value types produce the same signature. Thus, these two functions are the same and will produce an error:

```
Int32 Test (Int32 x) { /* do stuff */ }
int Test (int x) { /* do stuff */ }  // Error Duplicate definition of Test
```

Passing Arguments to the main() Function

So far in every example in this book, the main() function has had no arguments. If you have worked with C++ before, you know that it is possible to retrieve the parameters passed to a program from the command line via the main() function's arguments. (If you haven't, well, now you do.)

C++/CLI has made a rather large change to the main() function, especially if you come from the traditional C++ world or even from the Managed Extensions for C++ world. You now have a choice of main() functions.

int main (int argc, char *argv[])

The first choice is the standard main() function, which counts all the parameters passed to it, including the program that is being run, and places the count in the first argument, traditionally called argc. Next, it takes all the parameters and places them in an unmanaged pointer to char array, with each parameter being a separate element of the array. Finally, it passes a pointer to this array as the second argument, usually called argv.

Unsafe Code Passing arguments to this main() function is unsafe code because it uses pointers to pass the values.

Yep, I said pointer. Alarms should have gone off in your head—yes, passing arguments to the main() function using this choice is unsafe code, as passing arguments in this fashion actually compiles to native code and not MSIL code, so the argv argument is not garbage collected. Fortunately, the cleanup of argv is handled automatically (so, you could say that it is sort of garbage collected). Unfortunately, because it is not garbage collected, it adds a major wrinkle when compiling. You can't use the option /clr:safe. Instead, you can use /clr or /clr:pure.

Listing 2-15 is a little program that reads in all the parameters passed to it and then writes them out.

Listing 2-15. *Parsing a Command Line the Traditional Method*

```
using namespace System;

// Passing parameters to main() traditional method
int main ( int argc, char *argv[] )
{
    Console::WriteLine ( argc.ToString() );
    for (int i = 0; i < argc; i++)
    {
        Console::WriteLine ( gcnew String(argv[i]) );
    }
    return 0;
}
```

Figure 2-16 shows the results of this little program when passed the parameter "This is a test this is only a test".

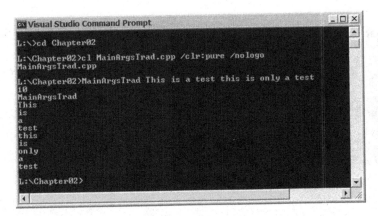

Figure 2-16. *Results of MainArgsTrad.exe*

int main (array<System::String ^> ^args)

The second choice more resembles the static `main()` method of C#. It simply takes all the parameters and places them on a managed array.

One advantage of this type of `main()` function is that it doesn't need to have the number of elements being passed, because the managed array provides the number of the argument in a property called `Length`. By the way, if you process the args array using the `for` each method, you won't even need to know how many arguments are being passed.

Another major advantage of this choice of `main()` function is that it is safe and can be compiled using the `/clr:safe` option.

Caution The first element of the `args` array is *not* the name program being run as you would expect in the traditional `main()` function. Instead, it is the first parameter passed to the program.

Listing 2-16 is a little program that reads in all the parameters passed to it and then writes them out.

Listing 2-16. *Parsing a Command Line the New Method*

```
using namespace System;

// Passing parameters to main() new method
int main(array<System::String ^> ^args)
{
    Console::WriteLine (args->Length);

    for each (String^ s in args)
    {
        Console::WriteLine(s);
    }
    return 0;
}
```

Figure 2-17 shows the results of this little program when passed the parameter "This is a test this is only a test". Notice the number of arguments passed is one less than the traditional `main()` function, as the program name is not passed.

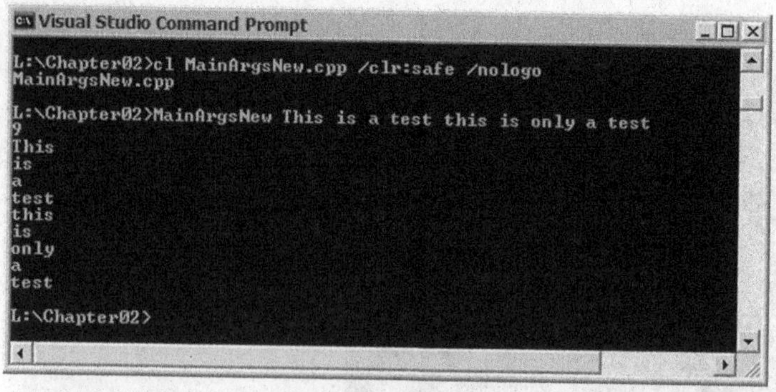

Figure 2-17. *Results of MainArgsNew.exe*

Summary

I covered a lot of ground in this chapter, starting with variables and C++/CLI's fundamental types. Next, you learned about literals and operators. Then you examined two basic C++/CLI constructs: flow control and looping. You finished by exploring functions.

For the traditional C++ programmer, much of this chapter was not new. The areas that you should pay close attention to are .NET Framework class library fundamental data types, Strings, value types, arrays, all the literals (in particular, string literals), and returning pointers and references from functions.

In the next chapter, you will continue to expand on your knowledge of the basics. This time, you will focus on the object-oriented aspects of C++/CLI.

Object-Oriented C++/CLI

In the previous chapter, I covered in detail the basics of C++/CLI, focusing on programming strictly in a procedural style. This chapter explores the real strength of C++/CLI: as an object-oriented language.

The chapter starts with a review of object-oriented programming (OOP) in general. You will then explore C++/CLI's OOP capabilities, focusing primarily on ref classes, which are the cornerstones of C++/CLI OOP. You will do this by breaking ref classes down into their parts and examining each part in detail. Finally, you will learn about interfaces.

Caution Don't skip this chapter, even if you know C++ very well, because several things are different between traditional C++ and C++/CLI. True, some of the changes may not be significant, but recognizing and understanding these changes now may make your life easier in the future.

OOP is more a way of thinking than a programming technique. For those making the transition from procedural programming, you must understand that OOP will involve a paradigm shift for you. But, once you realize this and make the shift, you will wonder why you programmed any other way.

OOP is just an abstraction taken from everyday life and applied to software development. The world is made up of objects. In front of you is a book. It is an object. You are sitting on a chair or a couch, or you might be lying on a bed—all objects. I could go on, but I'm sure you get the point. Almost every aspect of our lives revolves around interacting with, fixing, and improving objects. It should be second nature to do the same thing with software development.

Object-Oriented Concepts

All objects support three specific concepts: encapsulation, inheritance, and polymorphism. Think about the objects around you—no, scratch that; think about yourself. You are an object: You are made up of arms, legs, a torso, and a head, but how they work does not matter to you—this is encapsulation. You are a mammal, human, and male or female—this is inheritance. When greeted, you respond with "Good day," "Bonjour," "Guten Tag," or "Buon giorno"—this is polymorphism.

As you shall see shortly, you can apply the object paradigm to software development as well. C++/CLI does it by using software objects called ref classes and ref structs. But before I get into software objects, let's examine the concepts of an object more generically.

Encapsulation

All objects are made up of a combination of different things or objects. Many of these things are not of any concern to the other objects that interact with them. Going back to you as an example of an object, you are made up of things such as blood, muscles, and bone, but most objects that interact with you don't care about that level of things. Most objects that interact with you only care that you have hands, a mouth, ears, and other features at this level of abstraction.

Encapsulation basically means hiding the parts of an object that do things internally from other objects that interact with it. As you saw in the previous example, the internal workings of hands, a mouth, and ears are irrelevant to other objects that interact with you.

Encapsulation is generally used to simplify the model that other objects have to interact with. It allows other objects to only be concerned with using the right interface and passing the correct input to get the required response. For example, a car is a very complex object. But, to me, a car is simple: A steering wheel, an accelerator, and a brake represent the interface; and turning the steering wheel, stepping on the accelerator, and stepping on the brake represent input.

Encapsulation also allows an object to be fixed, updated, or replaced without having to change the other objects interacting with it. When I trade in my Mustang LX for a Mustang GT, I still only have to worry about turning the steering wheel, stepping on the accelerator, and stepping on the brake.

The most important thing about encapsulation is that because portions of the object are protected from external access, it is possible to maintain the internal integrity of the object. This is because it is possible to allow only indirect access, or no access at all, to private features of the object.

Inheritance

Inheritance is hardly a new concept. We all inherit many traits (good and bad) from both of our parents. We also inherit many traits from being a mammal, such as being born, being nursed, having four limbs, and so on. Being human, we inherit the traits of opposable thumbs, upright stature, capacity for language, and so forth. I'm sure you get the idea. Other objects also inherit from other more generic objects.

You can think of inheritance as a tree of objects starting with the most generic traits and expanding to the most specific. Each level of the tree expands on the definition of the previous level, until finally the object is fully defined. Inheritance allows for the reuse of previously defined objects. For example, when you say that a Mustang is a car, you know that it has four wheels and an engine. In this scenario, the base object definition came for free—you didn't have to define it again.

Notice, though, that a Mustang is always a car, but a car need not be a Mustang. The car could be a Ferrari. The link of inheritance is one way, toward the root.

Polymorphism

The hardest concept to grasp is polymorphism—not that it's difficult, but it's just taken so much for granted that it's almost completely overlooked. *Polymorphism* is simply the ability for different objects derived from a common base object to respond to the same stimuli in completely different ways.

For example, (well-trained) cats, dogs, and birds are all animals, but when asked to speak, they will all respond differently. (I added "well-trained" because normally a cat will look at you as if you are crazy, a dog will be to busy chasing his tail, and a bird will squawk even if you don't ask it to do anything.)

You can't have polymorphism without inheritance, as the stimuli that the object is expected to respond to must be to an interface that all objects have in common. In the preceding example, you are asking an animal to speak. Depending on the type of animal (inheritance), you will get a different response.

A key thing about polymorphism is that you know that you will get a response of a certain type, but the object responding—not the object requesting—determines what the actual response will be.

Applying Objects to Software Development

Okay, you know what objects and their concepts are and how to apply them to software development. With procedural programming, there is no concept of an object, just a continual stream of logic and data. Let me back up a bit on that. It could be argued that, even in procedural programming, objects exist, given that variables, literals, and constants could be considered objects (albeit simple ones). In procedural programming, breaking up the logic into smaller, more manageable pieces is done by way of functions. To group common data elements together, the structure or class is used depending on language.

Before you jump on me, I would like to note that there were (obviously) other object-oriented languages before C++, but this book only covers C++/CLI's history. It wasn't until C++ that computer data and its associated logic was packaged together into the struct and a new construct known as the class. (If you are a purist, there was "C with Classes" first.) With the combination of data and logic associated with this data into a single construct, object-oriented concepts could be applied to programming.

Here, in a nutshell, is how objected-oriented concepts are applied to C++/CLI development. Classes and structures are programming constructs that implement within the C++ language the three key object-oriented concepts: encapsulation, inheritance, and polymorphism.

Encapsulation, or the hiding of complexity, is accomplished by not allowing access to all data and functionality found in a class. Instead, only a simpler and more restricted interface is provided to access the class.

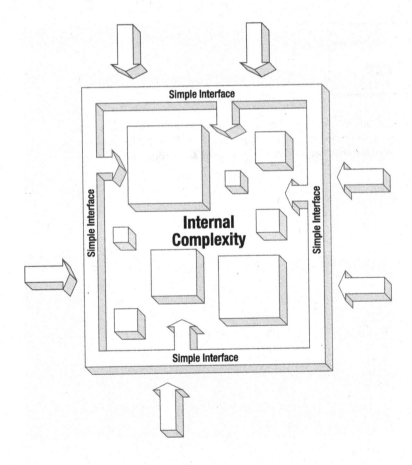

Inheritance is the ability to innately reuse the functionality and data of one class within another derived class.

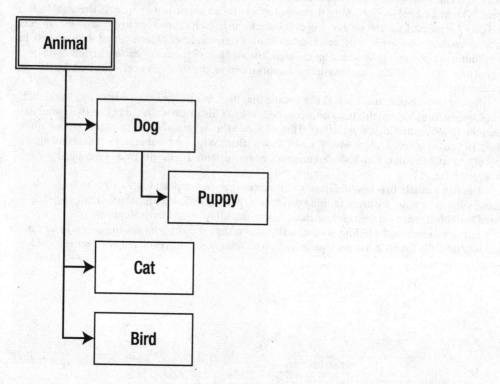

Polymorphism is the ability for different classes to respond to the same request in different ways. Classes provide something called the *virtual method*, or *function*, which allows any class derived from the same parent class to respond differently to the same request.

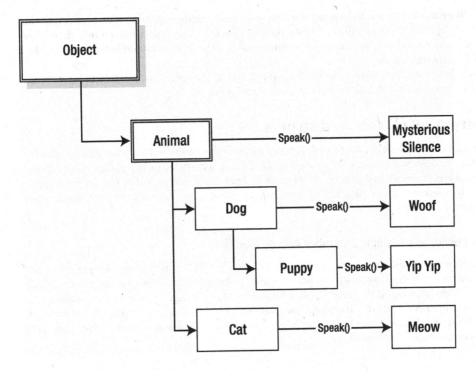

I expand on each of these concepts as the chapter progresses.

Now that you understand OOP conceptually, let's see how it is actually done with C++/CLI.

ref class/struct Basics

First off, there is nothing forcing you to program in an objected-oriented fashion with ref classes or ref structs, and using ref classes and ref structs does not mean you are doing OOP. For example, it is possible to break the code based on function areas instead of objects. It may appear to be OOP, but what you really are doing is just using a ref class as a namespace. Plus, you gain none of the benefits of OOP.

Note I am currently only dealing with the managed data types within C++/CLI (ref class, ref struct, value class, and value struct). In Chapters 20 and 21, I'll cover unmanaged and native data types (class and struct).

It is the organization of code and data into unique objects that distinguishes procedural coding from object-oriented coding.

For those totally new to object programming, you need to understand that each time you create (or instantiate) a ref class definition a new instance of the ref class object will be created. In other words, no matter how many instances you want, they will all be unique instances created from the same ref class definition.

But before you look at objects and OOP, you will look at the ref class and the ref struct and what makes up a ref class and a ref struct in general terms.

Declaring ref classes and structs

The ref class and ref struct are basically an extension of the traditional C++ class and struct. Like traditional C++ classes and structs, ref classes and ref structs are made up of variables and methods. Unlike traditional classes and structs, ref classes and ref structs are created and destroyed in a completely different manner. Also, ref classes and ref structs have an additional construct called the property.

Private, Public, and Protected Member Access Modifiers

There really is no real difference between a ref class and ref struct except for the default access to its members. A ref classes defaults to private access to its members, whereas a ref struct default to public. Notice that I used the term "default." It is possible to change the access level of either the ref class or the ref struct. So, truthfully, the usage of a ref class or a ref struct is just a matter of taste. Most people who code C++ use the keywords ref class when they create objects, and ref struct is very seldom if ever used.

Note Because ref struct is very seldom used, I'm going to use ref class from here on, but you can assume ref struct applies as well.

The way you declare ref classes is very similar to the way you declare traditional classes. Let's look at a ref class declaration. With what you learned in Chapter 2, much of a ref class definition should make sense. First, there is the declaration of the ref class itself and then the declaration of the ref class's variables, properties, and methods.

The following example is the Square ref class, which is made up of a constructor, a method to calculate the square's area, and a dimension variable:

```
ref class Square
{
    // constructor
    Square ( int d)
    {
        Dims = d;
    }

    // method
    int Area()
    {
        return Dims * Dims;
    }

    // variable
    int Dims;
};
```

The first thing to note about this ref class is that because the access to ref classes defaults to private, the constructor, the method, and the variable are not accessible outside the ref class. This is probably not what you want. To make the ref class's members accessible outside of the ref class, you need to add the access modifier public: to the definition:

```
ref class Square
{
public:
    // public constructor
    Square ( int d)
    {
        Dims = d;
    }

    // public method
    int Area()
    {
        return Dims * Dims;
    }

    // public variable
    int Dims;
};
```

With this addition, all the ref class's members are accessible. What if you want some members to be private and some public? For example, what if you want the variable Dims only accessible through the constructor? To do this, you add the private: access modifier:

```
ref class Square
{
public:
    Square ( int d)
    {
        Dims = d;
    }

    int Area()
    {
        return Dims * Dims;
    }
private:
    int Dims;
};
```

Besides public and private, C++/CLI provides one additional member access modifier: protected. Protected access is sort of a combination of public and private; where a protected ref class member has public access when it's inherited but private access (i.e., can't be accessed) by methods that are members of a ref class that don't share inheritance.

Here is a quick recap of the access modifiers for members.

If the member has public access, it is

- Accessible by external functions and methods
- Accessible to derived `ref` classes

If the member has private access, it is

- Not accessible by external functions and methods
- Not accessible to derived `ref` classes

If the member has protected access, it is

- Not accessible by external functions and methods
- Accessible to derived `ref` classes

If you are visually oriented, as I am, maybe Figure 3-1 will help clear up member access modifiers.

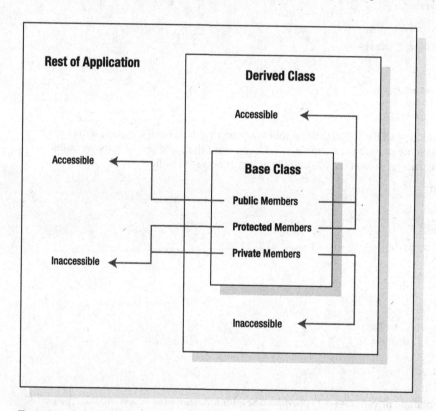

Figure 3-1. *Summary of the three member access modifiers*

The ref Keyword

If you have come from the traditional C++ world, you may have noticed the new keyword `ref` in front of the class's definition. This is one of the biggest and most important changes between traditional C++ and C++/CLI. (It is also a big change from C++/CLI and Managed Extensions for C++, as the keyword was `__gc`.) The use of the `ref` keyword tells the compiler, which in turn tells the common language runtime (CLR), that this class will be a reference object on the managed heap. C++/CLI, to be consistent with traditional C++, defaults to classes being placed on the CRT heap and not the managed heap. It is up to developers to decide if they want the class to be managed and, if so, they must manually place the ref in front of the class.

For this minor inconvenience, you get several benefits:

- Garbage collection
- Inheritance from any .NET Framework base class that is not sealed (I cover sealed classes later in the chapter) or, if no base class is specified, automatic inheritance from the System::Object class
- Ability for the ref class to be used within .NET Framework collections and arrays
- Inheritance from any number of managed interfaces
- Ability to contain properties
- Ability to contain pointers to unmanaged classes

Unsafe Code Because pointers to unmanaged classes is unverifiable, placing these pointers within a ref class is unsafe.

With the good, there is the bad. Traditional C++ programmers might find these items drawbacks with ref classes:

- Only single class inheritance is allowed.
- Inheritance from unmanaged classes is not allowed.
- In addition, ref classes
  - Cannot be a parent class of an unmanaged type
  - Do not support friends
  - Cannot contain an overridden gcnew or delete operator
  - Must use public inheritance
  - Cannot be used with the sizeof or offsetof operator
- Pointer arithmetic on the ref class handles is not allowed.

On the other hand, these drawbacks may not be as bad as you might think. A ref class allows multiple interface inheritance, though, as I will show later, you are forced to implement all the methods for these interfaces within the new ref class. The .NET Framework is quite extensive, so inheritance of unmanaged classes may not be needed as frequently as you might expect. Overriding gcnew and delete seems to defeat the purpose of ref classes. Because pointer arithmetic is not allowed on handles, sizeof and offsetof are kind of useless, anyway, and pointer arithmetic is a very big contributor to memory leaks and programs aborting as a result of illegal memory access.

Inheriting ref classes

Even though writing a stand-alone ref class can provide quite a lot of functionality to an object, it is in the object-oriented nature of ref classes and their capability to inherit from other ref classes that their real strength lays.

As I mentioned earlier, ref classes have the ability to inherit from a single ref class and multiple interfaces. I focus on ref class inheritance now, and later in this chapter, I will look at interface inheritance.

Inheriting from a ref class allows an inheriting ref class (usually known as the *child*) to get access to all the public and protected members of the inherited ref class (usually known as the *parent* or *base class*). You can think of inheritance in one of two ways: It allows the functionality of the base class to expand without the need to duplicate any of the code, or it allows the child class to fix or augment some feature of its parent class without having to know or understand how the parent functions (this is encapsulation, by the way). But, really, they both mean the same thing.

A restriction imposed by C++/CLI on ref classes is that ref classes can only use public inheritance. For example:

```
ref class childClass : public baseClass {};
```

is allowed, but the following will generate compile time errors:

```
ref class childClass : protected baseClass {};  // Error
ref class childClass : private baseClass {};    // Error
```

This means that with the public access to a base class, the child can access any public or protected member of the base class as if it were one of its own members. Private members of the base class, on the other hand, are not accessible by the child class, and trying to access them will generate a compilation error.

Unmanaged classes (also known as *native* and *unsafe* classes) can have public, protected, or private access to their base class. Notice there is no "ref" in front of these classes:

```
class childClass : public baseClass {}
class childClass : protected baseClass {}
class childClass : private baseClass {}
```

Unsafe Code *Unmanaged classes* are not verifiable and thus are an unsafe coding construct.

For private ref class access, all base class members are inherited as private and thus are not accessible. Protected ref class access allows access to public and protected base class members but changes the public access to protected. Personally, I've never used private or protected base class access, as I've simply never had a use for it, but it's available if you ever need it.

Listing 3-1 shows the Cube ref class inheriting from a Square ref class. Notice that because both the member access and the ref class access of the Square ref class are public, the Cube ref class has complete access to the Square ref class and can use all the Square ref class's members as if they were its own.

Listing 3-1. *Inheritance in Action*

```
using namespace System;

// Base class
ref class Square
{
public:
    int Area()
    {
        return Dims * Dims;
    }

    int Dims;
};
```

```
// Child class
ref class Cube : public Square
{
public:
    int Volume()
    {
        return Area() * Dims;
    }
};

// Inheritance in action
void main()
{
    Cube ^cube = gcnew Cube();
    cube->Dims = 3;

    Console::WriteLine(cube->Dims);
    Console::WriteLine(cube->Area());
    Console::WriteLine(cube->Volume());
}
```

Figure 3-2 shows the results of this little program.

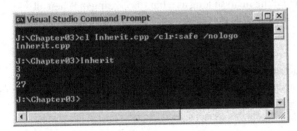

Figure 3-2. *Results of Inherit.exe*

Sealed ref classes

A *sealed* ref class is one that cannot be inherited from. The sealed ref class enables a developer to stop all other developers from inheriting from the defined ref class. I have never had an opportunity to seal any of my ref classes. I have come across it a few times. Almost every time, I was forced to create my own similar ref class because I needed additional functionality that the sealed ref class lacked. Personally, I feel the sealed ref class goes against object-oriented development, because it stops one of the key OOP cornerstones: inheritance. But the tool is available for those who wish to use it.

The code to seal a ref class is simply the addition of the specific location identifier sealed after the ref class name in the ref class definition, like this:

```
ref class sealClass sealed
{
};
```

Using the ref class

Unlike procedural code, the declaration of a ref class is simply that: a declaration. The ref class's methods do nothing on their own and only have meaning within the confines of an object. An object is an instantiated ref class. A neat thing about when a ref class is instantiated is that automatically all the ref classes it is derived from also get instantiated.

The code to instantiate or create an object from the ref class in the previous section is simply this:

```
Square ^sqr = gcnew Square();  // a handle
```

or this:

```
Square sqr;  // a local or stack instance
```

Notice that you can create either a handle or a local or stack instance to the Square object. For those of you coming from a traditional C++ background, the syntax when working with handles is identical to pointers except for the initial declaration just shown. I personally have found the syntax when working with stack instances of an object a little easier but, as you will find out, in many cases you simply can't use them.

Handle to an Object

If you recall from the previous chapter, C++/CLI data types can fall into one of two types: value types and reference types. A ref class is a reference type. What this means is that the ref class, when created using the gcnew operator, allocates itself on the managed heap, and then a handle is placed on the stack indicating the location of the allocated object.

This is only half the story, though. The CLR places the ref class object on the managed heap. The CLR will maintain this ref class object on the heap so long as a handle is using it. When all handles to the object go out of scope or, in other words, no variables are accessing it, the CLR will delete it automatically.

Caution If the ref class object accesses certain unmanaged resources that hold system resources, the CLR will hold the ref class object for an indefinite (not necessarily infinite) period of time. Using COM-based ADO is a classic example of this. This was a major issue in prior versions of C++/CLI (Managed Extensions for C++), but the addition of deterministic destructors has helped alleviate this issue. I cover destructors later in this chapter.

Once you have created an instance of a ref class using the following:

```
Square ^sqr = gcnew Square();  // a handle
```

you now have access to its variables, properties, and methods. The code to access a reference object handle is simply the name of the object you created followed by the arrow [->] operator. For example:

```
sqr->Dims = 5;
int area = sqr->Area();
```

You might be wondering why pointer arithmetic is not allowed on reference object handles. They seem harmless enough. Well, the problem comes from the fact that the location of the object in the managed heap memory can move. The garbage collection process not only deletes unused objects in heap memory, it also compacts it. Thus, it is possible that a ref class object can be relocated during the compacting process.

Local or Stack Objects

I assume that up until now you've been using the member access operator or dot [.] operator on faith that I would explain it later. There really isn't anything special about the dot operator; it's only used for accessing individual member variables, properties, or methods out of a ref class. Its syntax is simply this:

```
class-name . member-data-or-method
int intval;                          // value type
String ^s = intval.ToString();
Square sqr;                          // reference type
int i = sqr.Dims;
```

You have seen both the -> and . operators used when accessing ref class members. What is
the difference? The -> operator is used to access data or methods from a handle or a pointer off a
heap, whereas the dot [.] operator is used to access the object off the stack.

You have already seen one type of stack object the value type. It is also possible to create a stack
object out of a reference type as was just shown.

Listing 3-2 is an example of using a ref class as both a stack and a heap reference.

Listing 3-2. *Stack Reference Object in Action*

```
using namespace System;

ref class Square
{
public:
    int Area()
    {
        return Dims * Dims;
    }
    int Dims;
};

void main()
{
    Square ^sqr1 = gcnew Square();      // Handle
    sqr1->Dims = 2;
    Console::WriteLine( sqr1->Area() );

    Square sqr2;                        // local stack instance
    sqr2.Dims = 3;
    Console::WriteLine( sqr2.Area() );
}
```

Figure 3-3 shows the results of this little program.

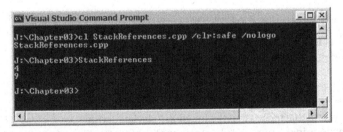

Figure 3-3. *Results of StackReferences.exe*

Member Variables

This fancy name is simply C++/CLI's way of reminding programmers that ref classes are objects.
Member variables are simply variables defined within the definition of a ref class.

The syntax of defining member variables is identical to that of ordinary variables except for one important thing: You cannot initialize a variable in its definition. I explain how to initialize variables later in this chapter when I cover constructors. The definition of a variable is simply a data type and a variable name, or a comma-delimited list of variable names:

```
ref class varExample
{
    int x;
    String ^str1, ^str2;
};
```

In C++/CLI, member variables can be either managed data types or a pointer to an unmanaged data type.

Unsafe Code The pointer to an unmanaged data type causes the entire ref class to become unsafe.

Member variables can be public, protected, or private. With C++/CLI and `ref` classes, public member variables should be handled with care, especially if invalid values in these variables will cause problems in the program's execution. A better solution is to make them private (or protected, so that inherited access can still access them directly), and then make public properties to them for external methods to access. Properties can, if coded correctly, perform validation on the data entered into the variable. Otherwise, they work just like normal member variables. I cover properties later in this chapter.

Static Member Variables

Static member variables are variables that provide `ref` class-wide storage. In other words, the same variable is shared by all instances of a `ref` class. At first glance, you might wonder why you would want a shared member variable across all instances of and `ref` class type. A couple of reasons that you will frequently come across for using static member variable is as a counter of how many instances of the `ref` class have been created and how many of those instances are currently active. Though, I'm sure you will come up with several other reasons to use them.

To define a static member variable in a `ref` class, simply define it as static and assign a value to it in the `ref` class definitions, like this:

```
ref class staticVar
{
    static int staticVar = 3;
};
```

You might be wondering how initializing the variable within the `ref` class can work, as it would appear that the value would be reset for each instance of the `ref` class. Fortunately, this is not the case; only the first time that the `ref` class is instantiated is the variable created and initialized.

Member Methods

A *member method* is simply a fancy term that means that the function is declared within a `ref` class. Everything you learned about functions in the previous chapter is applicable to member methods. You might consider revisiting Chapter 2's section on functions if you are uncertain how they are defined or how they work.

Like all members of a ref class, member methods can be public, protected, or private. Public methods are accessible outside of the ref class and are the workhorse of interclass communication. It is via methods that ref classes pass messages, requesting and being requested to perform some type of functionality. Protected member methods are the same as private member methods except that inherited ref classes have access to them. Private ref classes encapsulate the functionality provided by the ref class, as they are not accessible from outside the ref class except via some public member method that uses it.

Just as a quick recap, Listing 3-3 is a public member method that calls a protected member method that calls a private member method.

Listing 3-3. *Member Methods in Action*

```
using namespace System;

ref class MethodEx
{
public:
    void printPublic(int num)
    {
        for (int i = 0; i < num; i++)
        {
            Console::WriteLine( "Public" );
        }
        printProtected(num/2);
    }
protected:
    void printProtected(int num)
    {
        for (int i = 0; i < num; i++)
        {
            Console::WriteLine( "Protected" );
        }
        printPrivate(num/2);
    }
private:
    void printPrivate(int num)
    {
        for (int i = 0; i < num; i++)
        {
            Console::WriteLine( "Private" );
        }
    }
};

int main()
{
    MethodEx ex;

    ex.printPublic(4);
    // ex.printProtected(4);   // Error cannot access
    // ex.printPrivate(4);     // Error cannot access
}
```

Figure 3-4 shows the results of this little program.

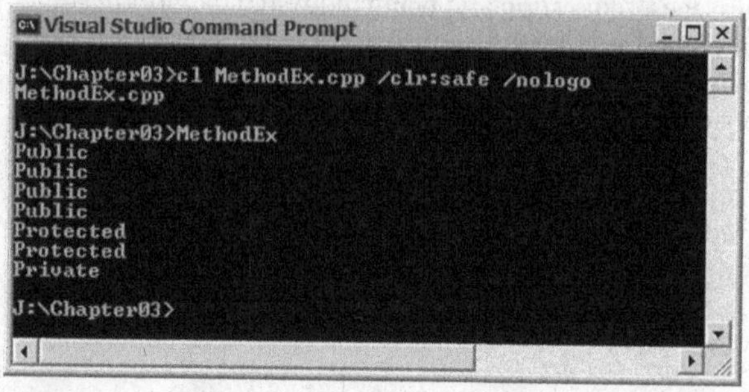

Figure 3-4. *Results of MethodEx.exe*

Static Member Methods

Static member methods are methods that have ref class scope. In other words, they exist without your having to create an instance of the ref class. Because they are not associated with any particular instance of a ref class, they can use only static member variables, which also are not associated with a particular instance. For the same reason, a static member method cannot be a virtual member method, as virtual member methods are also associated with ref class instances.

Coding static member methods is no different from coding normal member methods, except that the function declaration is prefixed with the static keyword.

Listing 3-4 uses a static member method to print out a static member variable. Oh, by the way, WriteLine() is also a static member method.

Listing 3-4. *Static Member Methods and Variables in Action*

```
using namespace System;

ref class StaticTest
{
private:
    static int x = 42;
public:
    static int get_x()
    {
        return x;
    }
};

void main()
{
    Console::WriteLine ( StaticTest::get_x() );
}
```

Figure 3-5 shows the results of this little program.

Figure 3-5. *Results of StaticMethodEx.exe*

You might have noticed that to access the static member method, you use the ref class name and the :: operator instead of the . or -> operator. The reason is because you've not created an object, so you're effectively accessing the namespace tree.

ref class Constructors

The ref class *constructor* is a special ref class method that is different in many ways from the member method. In C++/CLI, a constructor is called whenever a new instance of a ref class is created. Instances of ref classes are created using the operator gcnew. Memory for the instance is allocated on the managed heap that is maintained by the CLR.

The purpose of the constructor is to get the object to an initialized state. There are two ways that the actual initialization process can take place, within the constructor or in a separate method that the constructor calls. Normally, you would use the first method if the ref class instance is only initialized once. The second method would be used if the ref class is reused and needs to be reinitialized at a later time. When this reinitialization takes place the initialization method is called, as you can't call the constructor method directly.

The ref class constructor process differs from the unmanaged class constructor process in that, for ref class constructors, all member variables are initialized to zero before the actual constructor is called. (Although this is helpful, initialization to zero is not always what you need. You might want to initialize to a specific value.) Thus, even if the constructor does nothing, all member variables will still have been initialized to zero or the data type's equivalent. For example, the DateTime data type initializes to 1/1/0001 12:00:00 a.m., which is this data type's equivalent of zero.

A ref class constructor method always has the same name as the ref class itself. A ref class constructor method does not return a value and must not be defined with the void return type. A constructor method can take any number of parameters. Note that a constructor method needs to have public accessibility to be accessible by the gcnew operator.

If no constructor method is defined for a ref class, then a default constructor method is generated. This constructor method does nothing of its own, except it calls the constructor method of its parent and sets all member variables to a zero value. If you define a constructor method, then a default constructor method will not be generated. Thus, if you create a constructor method with parameters and you expect the ref class to be able to be created without parameters, then you must manually create your own default zero-parameter constructor method.

A special construct of a constructor method is the *initializer list*. It's a list of variables that need to be initialized before the constructor method itself is called. You can use it to initialize the ref class's own variables as well; in fact, it's more efficient to do it this way, but it's also much harder to read in this format. The most common use of an initializer list is to initialize a parent ref classes by way of one of the parent's constructors. The syntax for an initializer list involves simply placing a colon (:) and a comma-delimited list of functional notation variable declarations between the constructor method's declaration and the constructor method's implementation:

```
Constructor (int x, int y, int z) : var1(x, y), var2(z) { }
```

A new constructor type has been added in C++/CLI, the copy constructor. The copy constructor initializes a ref class object to be a copy of an existing ref class object of the same type. This type of constructor should not be anything new to developers who have already been coding in C++, except that the syntax has change a little. You now use the % operator instead of the & operator.

Listing 3-5 shows the constructors for a ref class called ChildClass inherited from ParentClass.

Listing 3-5. *Constructors in Action*

```
using namespace System;

// Parent Class
ref class ParentClass
{
public:
    // Default constructor that initializes ParentVal to a default value
    ParentClass() : PVal(10) { }

    // A constructor that initializes ParentVal to a passed value
    ParentClass(int inVal) : PVal(inVal) { }
    // Copy Constructor
    ParentClass(const ParentClass %p) : PVal(p.PVal) {}

    int PVal;
};

// Child class that inherits form ParentClass
ref class ChildClass : public ParentClass
{
public:
    // Default constructor that initializes ChildVal to a default value
    ChildClass () : CVal(20) {};    // default constructor

    // A constructor that initialized CVal to a passed value
    ChildClass(int inVal) : CVal(20) {};

    // A constructor that initialized the parent class with a passed value
    // and initializes ChildVal to a another passed value
    ChildClass (int inVal1, int inVal2) : ParentClass(inVal1), CVal(inVal2) { }

    // copy constructor
    ChildClass(const ChildClass %v) : ParentClass(v.PVal), CVal(v.CVal) { }

    int CVal;
};
```

```
void main()
{
    ParentClass p1(4);     // Constructor
    ParentClass p2 = p1;   // Copy Constructor

    p1.PVal = 2;           // Change original, new unchanged

    Console::WriteLine("p1.PVal=[{0}] p2.PVal=[{1}]", p1.PVal, p2.PVal);

    ChildClass ^c1 = gcnew ChildClass(5,6); // Constructor
    ChildClass  c2 = *c1;                    // Copy Constructor

    c1->CVal = 12;         // Change original, new unchanged

    Console::WriteLine("c1=[{0}/{1}] c2=[{2}/{3}]",
        c1->PVal, c1->CVal, c2.PVal, c2.CVal);
}
```

Figure 3-6 shows the results of this little program.

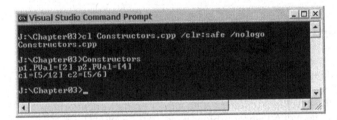

Figure 3-6. *Results of Constructors.exe*

Static ref class Constructors

In traditional C++, the syntax for initializing static member variables was rather cumbersome. It forced you to define it in the ref class and then initialize it outside the ref class before the main() function was called. You saw that with ref classes you could directly assign a value to a static member variable—but what happens if you need something more elaborate than a simple assignment? C++/CLI has provided a new construct for ref classes called the *static* ref class *constructor*.

The static ref class constructor's purpose is to initialize static member variables normally with something more complex than a simple assignment, but not necessarily. Any ref class can have a static ref class constructor, though it only really makes sense if the ref class has static member variables, because the static ref class constructor is not allowed to initialize any nonstatic member variables.

When the static ref class constructor is invoked it is undefined, but it is guaranteed to happen before any instances of the ref class are created or any references are made to any static members of the ref class.

If you recall, it is possible to initialize static member variables directly in the definition of the ref class. If you use the static ref class constructor, then these default values are overwritten by the value specified by the static ref class constructor.

The static `ref class` constructor syntax is identical to the default constructor syntax, except that the `static` keyword is placed in front. This means that a static `ref class` constructor cannot take any parameters.

In the following example, the `ref class Test` is made up of two static member variables initialized to 32 and a static `ref class` constructor that overwrites the first constant with the value of 42:

```
ref class Test
{
public:
    static Test()
    {
        value1 = 42;
    }
    static int value1 = 32;
    static int value2 = 32;
};
```

By the way, you can have both static and nonstatic (normal, I guess) constructor methods in the same `ref class`.

Destructors

Destructors serve two purposes in C++/CLI. The first is the deallocating of memory previously allocated to a heap by either the `new` or `gcnew` operator. The second purpose is the often overlooked releasing of system resources, either managed or unmanaged.

In versions prior to C++/CLI, Managed Extensions for C++ only handled the deallocating of managed memory and managed resources. To handle the releasing of unmanaged memory or unmanaged resources, it forced the developer to inherit from a .NET Framework interface `IDisposable`. If this means nothing to you, don't worry—things have gotten a whole lot easier.

Memory Management Destructors

All objects allocated on the managed heap using `gcnew` need to be deallocated. You have a choice about how to do this. You can call the `delete` operator on the handle of the `ref class` object, and the managed memory will be deallocated immediately in reverse order to which it was allocated. In other words, if the object allocated internal objects, then they would be deallocated first.

To start the deallocation process when a program is finished with the object, you simply call the `delete` operator on the object:

```
delete classname;
```

This is new to C++/CLI and is what is known as *deterministic cleanup*. The programmer now has complete control of when things are finally cleaned up.

The other choice is that the developer does not have to give up the garbage collection functionality of the CLR, if it doesn't matter when the memory is finally deallocated. In this case, the program is not required to call the `delete` operator; it simply has does nothing. It will be the job of the CLR to detect when an object is no longer being accessed and then garbage collect it. In most cases, this choice is the best, and there is really no need to call the `delete` operator because CLR garbage collection works just fine.

The destructor method, which the `delete` operator calls, has the same syntax as the default constructor method except that a tilde (~) is placed before the destructor method's name:

```
~Test() {}   // destructor
```

Note For the delete operator to be able to access the destructor, the destructor needs public access.

Within the destructor, you would call the delete operator for any objects that the ref class needs to clean up. If your ref class doesn't allocate anything while it was running, then there is no need to create a destructor as a default one will be generated for you.

Resource Management Destructors

Cleaning up managed resources like String or an ArrayList is handled just like managed memory resources.

Unmanaged resources, like open handles to files, kernel objects, or database objects, are a little trickier. The reason is if you don't specifically code the closing of these objects, then they don't get closed until the program ends or sometimes not until the machine is rebooted. Yikes!

Surprisingly, the CLR does not even have any explicit runtime support for cleaning up unmanaged resources. Instead, it is up to the programmer to implement a pattern for resource management based on a .NET Framework core interface IDisposable. The pattern is to place all resources that needed to be cleaned up within the Dispose() method exposed by the IDisposable interface and then call the Dispose() method when the resources are no longer needed. A little cumbersome, if you ask me.

With Managed Extensions for C++ version 1.1 and prior, that is exactly how you would have had to code unmanaged resource cleanup. In version C++/CLI, things have become a whole lot easier. With the addition of deterministic cleanup to C++/CLI, the delete operator now implements the IDisposable interface pattern automatically for you. Therefore, all you need to do to clean up your unmanaged resources is to add code to your ref class's destructor and then call the delete operator when the object and the resources it's accessing are no longer needed. Simple, right? Well, there is a catch.

What if you forget to call the delete operator? The answer is, unfortunately, that the destructor and subsequently the IDisposable interface pattern are not called. This means the unmanaged resources are not cleaned up. Ouch! So much for .NET's great ability to clean up after itself, right?

Fortunately, this is not the end of the story. The CLR's garbage collection process has not yet occurred. This process will deallocate all managed objects whenever it gets around to that chore (you have no control of this). As an added bonus, C++/CLI has made things easier by providing an interface directly with the CLR garbage collection process (for when this finally does happen) called the Finalize destructor.

The Finalize destructor method is called by the CLR, when the CLR detects an object that needs to be cleaned up. An elegant solution, don't you think? Well, the elegance doesn't end there. The CLR, before it calls the Finalize destructor, checks to see if the delete operator has been already called on the object and, if so, does not even waste its time on calling the Finalize destructor.

What does this boil down to? You can clean up unmanaged resource yourself, or if you don't care when cleanup finally does occur (or you forget to do it), the CLR will do the cleanup for you. Nice, huh?

The Finalize destructor has the same syntax as the standard destructor, except an exclamation point (!) is used instead of a tilde (~), and it has to have protected access:

```
protected:
    !Test() {}    // Finalize destructor
```

Note The Finalize destructor must have protected access.

Here is how you code destructor logic, if you want all your bases covered for an object that has managed and unmanaged memory and resources to clean up:

```
ref  class ChildClass : public ParentClass
{
public:
    ~Test()
    {
        // free all managed and unmanaged resources and memory
    }
protected:
    !Test()
    {
        // free all unmanaged resources and memory only
    }
}
```

The managed cleanup code is only found in the deterministic cleanup destructor, whereas unmanaged cleanup is found in both the deterministic cleanup and Finalize destructor. One thing you will find is that there is usually duplicate unmanaged memory and resource cleanup code in both of these destructors. Most likely, you will write an additional method, which these destructors call to eliminate this duplication.

Virtual Methods

Virtual methods are the cornerstone of polymorphism, as they allow different child ref classes derived from a common base ref class to respond to the same method call in a way specific to each child ref class. Polymorphism occurs when a virtual method is called through a base ref class handle. For example:

```
BaseClass ^BaseObject = gcnew ChildClass()
BaseObject->DoStuff() // will call the Child class version instead of the Base
                      // class version as long as DoStuff is declared a virtual.
```

This works because when the call is made, it is the type of the actual object pointed to that determines which copy of the virtual method is called.

Technically, when you declare a virtual method, you are telling the compiler that you want dynamic or runtime binding to be done on any method with an identical signature in a derived ref class. To make a method virtual, you simply need to place the keyword virtual in front of the method declaration.

```
virtual void Speak () {}
```

Any method that you declare as virtual will automatically be virtual for any directly or indirectly derived ref class.

Normally, in a standard virtual animal example, you would first declare a base ref class Animal with a virtual method of Speak(). You then create specific animal-type ref classes derived from Animal and override the virtual method Speak(). In the main() function, you would create an array of Animal objects and assign specific animal derived objects to it. Finally, you would loop through the Animal array. Because the Speak() method is virtual, the actual object type assigned to the Animal array determines which Speak() to execute.

There are two methods of overriding a virtual function: implicit and explicit (or named). You can also hide the virtual override sequence and start a new one, or you can simply stop the virtual sequence altogether.

Implicit Virtual Overriding

For implicit overriding, the method signature of the base ref class must be the same as the derived ref class including the prefix virtual. This means that the name of the method and the number of parameters and their types must be identical. The return type of the method need not be identical, but it must at least be derived from the same type as that of the base method's return type. Also, you need to append the new keyword override after the parameters:

```
virtual void Speak () override
{
}
```

Hiding Virtual Overriding

Usually, if a parent defines a method as virtual, there is usually a good reason. I haven't yet had a reason to do this, but if you really want to overrule a parent ref class and hide a method from propagating virtual overriding to its children, you can. To do so, add the keyword new after the method declaration:

```
void Speak() new
{
}
```

You can also hide virtual overriding propagation and start a new one from the current ref class by making the above member method virtual:

```
virtual void Speak() new
{
}
```

To me, both of these method declarations go against proper OOP, but they are available if there is good reason.

Explicit or Named Virtual Overriding

Explicit or named overriding allows you to assign a method with a different name to a virtual function. To do this, you need to declare the overriding method as virtual and then assign the name of the virtual method being overridden:

```
ref class Puppy : public Dog
{
public:
    virtual void Yip () = Dog::Speak
    {
    }
};
```

One handy feature of explicit overriding is that it allows you to overcome a virtual sequence that has been hidden by the new operator, as an explicit overriding does not need to override a direct parent. It can override an indirect parent, occurring before the virtual method sequence hide point, by specifying the ref class name of a grandparent (or great grandparent, or . . .) along with the method being overridden:

```
ref class Tiger : public Cat
{
public:
    virtual void Growl () = Animal::Speak
    {
    }
};
```

An even cooler feature of explicit virtual overriding is that you can actually continue two different virtual method sequences from a single virtual method. You do this by explicitly overriding a sealed sequence, which has been declared virtual to start a new sequence, using the same method name as the new sequence and then adding an explicit virtual override. Explaining it is a bit confusing, but an example should make things clearer:

```
ref class Animal
{
public:
    virtual void Speak ()
    {
        Console::WriteLine("Animal is Mysteriously Silent");
    }
}
```

```
ref class Cat : public Animal
{
public:
    virtual void Speak() new    // sequence hidden and a new one created
    {
        Console::WriteLine("Cat says Meow");
    }
};
```

```
ref class Tiger : public Cat
{
public:
    virtual void Speak() override = Animal::Speak   //both sequences continue here
    {
        Console::WriteLine("Tiger says Growl");
    }
};
```

You can also do the same thing using a comma-delimited list of methods you want to explicitly override with this one method. However, in this case the new virtual method needs a different name, or the compiler will complain a little bit:

```
ref class Tiger : public Cat
{
public:
    virtual void Growl() = Animal::Speak, Cat::Speak
    {
        Console::WriteLine("Tiger says Growl");
    }
};
```

It probably is obvious, but like implicit overriding, explicit overriding requires that the signature of the overriding method must match the virtual method being overwritten.

Listing 3-6 is not your standard virtual animal example. It's a very contrived example, trying to show all the different statements associated with virtual methods.

Listing 3-6. *Virtual Methods in Action*

```
using namespace System;

ref class Animal
{
public:
    virtual void Speak ()
    {
        Console::WriteLine("Animal is Mysteriously Silent");
    }
};

ref class Dog : public Animal
{
public:
    // Standard explicit virtual override
    virtual void Speak() override
    {
        Console::WriteLine("Dog says Woof");
    }
};

ref class Puppy : public Dog
{
public:
    // Yip name overrides dog's virtual speak
    virtual void Yip() = Dog::Speak
    {
        Console::WriteLine("Puppy says Yip Yip");
    }
};

ref class Cat : public Animal
{
public:
    // Start a new speak virtual sequence so animal's virtual speak fails
    virtual void Speak() new
    {
        Console::WriteLine("Cat says Meow");
    }
};

ref class Tiger : public Cat
{
public:
    // Though inherited from cat, Tiger name overrides Animal's speak
    // thus, can speak though animal virtual sequence
    // also this method overrides Cat's virtual Speak method as well
```

```cpp
    virtual void Growl() = Animal::Speak, Cat::Speak
    {
        Console::WriteLine("Tiger says Growl");
    }
};

void main()
{
    // Array of Animal handles
    array<Animal^>^ animals = gcnew array<Animal^>
    {
        gcnew Animal(),
        gcnew Dog(),
        gcnew Puppy(),
        gcnew Cat(),
        gcnew Tiger()
    };

    for each ( Animal ^a in animals)
    {
        a->Speak();
    }

    Console::WriteLine();

    Animal^ cat1 = gcnew Cat();
    Cat^   cat2  = gcnew Cat();
    Cat^   tiger = gcnew Tiger();

    // new cancels virtual sequence of Animal
    cat1->Speak();

    // new speak sequence established for cat
    cat2->Speak();
    tiger->Speak();
}
```

Figure 3-7 shows the results of this little program.

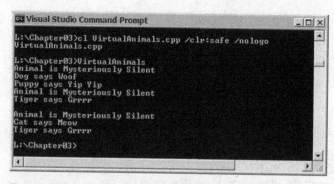

Figure 3-7. *Results of VirtualAnimals.exe*

Pure Virtual Method

When you look at the previous example, you may notice that the base ref class virtual method Speak() really has a nonsense implementation and shouldn't even be included in the ref class. A better way to implement this example and ensure that the virtual method is always overridden is to force the inheriting ref classes to override the virtual method and, if they don't, generate an error. You can do this with a *pure virtual method.*

The big difference between a pure virtual method and a virtual method is that a ref class that contains pure virtual methods cannot be instantiated. In other words, a ref class that has pure virtual methods must be inherited to be used. I cover this in more detail later in the chapter in the section about abstract ref classes.

A pure virtual method is simply a definition of a method without any implementation. When you use it, the compiler checks to make sure that the pure virtual method is overwritten. If it is not, then the compiler generates an error.

A pure virtual method has the same syntax as a regular virtual method, except that instead of a method implementation, a = 0; is appended:

```
virtual void PureVirtualFunction() = 0;
```

Caution You cannot hide a pure virtual method with the new operator.

Method Overriding

Method overriding is defining a method in a derived ref class that has an identical signature to the base ref class. How the derived ref class actually works depends on whether the method is virtual or not. If the method is virtual, it runs as I described previously.

On the other hand, if the method is not virtual, then it works in a completely different way, because polymorphism does not come into effect at all. First, no dynamic binding occurs, only standard static or compile-time binding. What this means is that whatever type the method is called with is executed. For example, in the VirtualAnimal example, if the Speak() method were not virtual, then the Animal ref class's Speak() method would be called every time in the for each loop. This displays "Mysterious Silence" every time as opposed to the assorted messages generated by the virtual version of the example. The reason this happens is because the array is of type Animal.

To get each animal to speak now, you must create instances of each type of animal and call that animal's speak() method directly. Overriding a nonvirtual method simply has the effect of hiding the base ref class's copy of the method.

Method Overloading

There is nothing special about coding overloaded methods, given that they are handled in exactly the same way as function overloading, which I covered in the previous chapter. The only real difference is that they are now methods inside a ref class and not functions out on their own. For example, here is the same supersecret method (this time) overloaded three times in a Secret ref class:

```
ref class Secret
{
    int Test () { /* do stuff */ }
    int Test (int x) { /* do stuff */ }
    int Test (int x, int y, double z) { /* do stuff */ }
};
```

Calling an overloaded method is nothing special either. Simply call the method you want with the correct parameters. For example, here is some code to call the second supersecret Test method from a handle called secret and the third method from a stack object:

```
secret->Test (0, 1, 2.0);   // handle
secret.Test(5);             // local stack
```

For those of you coming from a traditional C++ or Visual Basic background, you might have used default arguments. Unfortunately, with C++/CLI, ref classes do not support default arguments in member methods. In fact, they generate an error.

A suggested solution to this change in syntax is to use overloaded methods. That is, define a method with fewer parameters and then initialize the variable in the method body. For example, here are four methods that when combined are equivalent to one method with three defaulted arguments:

```
ref class NoDefaultArgs
{
    // Invalid method with default values
    // int DefArgs (int x = 1, int y = 2, int z = 3) { /* do stuff */ }

    // Equivalent combination of overloaded methods
    int DefArgs ()
    {
        x = 1;
        y = 2;
        z = 3;
        /* do stuff */
    }
    int DefArgs ( int x )
    {
        y = 2;
        z = 3;
        /* do stuff */
    }
    int DefArgs ( int x, int y )
    {
        z = 3;
        /* do stuff */
    }
    int DefArgs ( int x, int y, int z )
    {
        /* do stuff */
    }
}
```

I'm sure there is a good reason why Microsoft eliminated default arguments, but personally, I hope it puts them back in, because using overloads can get quite cumbersome.

Managed Operator Overloading

Operator overloading is one important feature that most traditional C++ programmers learn to work with early in their careers. It is one of C++'s claims to fame. Operator overloading is the ability to use standard operators and give them meaning in a ref class—for example, adding two strings together to get a new concatenated string.

C++/CLI's ref classes support operator overloading as well, but in a slightly different syntax than traditional C++. The major difference in the syntax revolves round the aspect that to support the .NET Framework's feature of multiple (computer) language support, managed operator overloads must be declared as static. Also as a consequence of this, binary operators must pass both the left- and right-hand sides of the operator as parameters, and unary operators must pass the left-hand side of the operator as a parameter. This contrasts with the traditional operator overloading where the parameters are declared as member variables, and one fewer parameter is passed because the other parameter is an instance variable.

Therefore, traditional operator overloading syntax for the multiplication operator looks like this:

```
OpClass^ operator *(const OpClass ^rhs);
```

whereas managed operator overloading syntax for the multiplication operator looks like this:

```
static OpClass^ operator *(const OpClass ^lhs, const OpClass ^rhs);
```

One thing to keep in mind is that traditional operator overloading syntax is only supported within the C++/CLI language environment, because this syntax does not adhere to the requirements of being static and passing all operands.

A convenient feature of managed operator overloading for veteran C++ developers is that if you will never support multiple languages, then you can still use the traditional syntax that you are accustomed to. Or, if you do plan to support multiple languages, you can use the managed operator overloading syntax only with ref class for which you plan to support multiple languages and use traditional for the rest. Personally, I stick to the managed operator overloading syntax because, you never know, in the future, you might need multilanguage support.

■ **Caution** You cannot use both traditional and managed syntaxes for operator overloading for the same operator within the same ref class.

Not all operators can be overloaded. The most notable missing operators are the open and closed square brackets [ ], open and closed round brackets ( ), gcnew, new, and delete. The Table 3-1 is a list of the operators available to be overloaded.

Table 3-1. *Supported Managed Operators*

Operators				
+	-	*	/	%
^	&	|	~	!
=	<	>	+=	-=
*=	/=	%=	^=	&=
|=	<<	>>	<<=	>>=
==	!=	<=	>=	&&
||	++	--	,	

There are two types of operator overloads: unary and binary. You would have a good case, if you claimed that the increment and decrement operators are a third type of operator. As you will see, the increment and decrement operator syntax is the same as that of a unary operator. It is only the implementation of the operators that makes them different.

Overloading Unary Operators

Unary operators, if you recall from the previous chapter, are operators that take only one operand. With built-in operators, except for the increment and decrement operators, the operand themselves are not changed by the operator. For example, when you place the negative operator in front of a number (operand), the number (operand) does not change and become negative, though the value returned is negative:

```
int i = 1;
int j = -i;   // j = -1 but i = 1
```

With managed operators, unlike their built-in arithmetic equivalent, you have a little more power over how unary operators actually work. You can make the operands mutable if you want, though, this could be dangerous, as most developers would not expect functionality. To ensure that the operand is not mutable, you should use the const operator in the argument of the operator overload method:

```
static OpClass^ operator -(const OpClass ^lhs)
{
    OpClass^ ret = gcnew OpClass();
    ret->i = -(lhs->i);
    return ret;
}
```

With the const operator, the compiler will fail if the lhs argument is changed within the body of the method. On the other hand, if you want the argument to change during the operation then you would leave off the const operator:

```
static OpClass^ operator -(OpClass ^lhs)
{
    lhs->i = -(lhs->i);
    return lhs;
}
```

The preceding is mutability and is probably not what you want but it is available if there is a need. In fact, this mutability was how I thought the increment and decrement was implemented but I found out instead that the compiler generates code specifically for the operators. Here is how you could implement an increment operator. Notice the const operator in the argument:

```
static OpClass^ operator ++(const OpClass ^lhs)
{
    OpClass^ ret = gcnew OpClass();
    ret->i = (lhs->i) + 1;
    return ret;
}
```

Overloading Binary Operators

A binary operator takes two operands; what you do with this operand when it comes to managed operator overloading is totally up to you. For example, you could return a bool for a logical operator, a result object for an arithmetic operator, or return a void and mutate the first argument for an assignment operator.

Here are each of these types of operation using the same operator.

Note You can't place all these overloads in one ref class as there would be method ambiguity, but each is perfectly valid if implemented uniquely in a ref class. On the other hand, the user of these operators would most likely be completely confused by the first two examples as they go against how they are normally used.

- Logical operator (unexpected implementation):

```
static bool operator *=(const OpClass ^lhs, const OpClass ^rhs)
{
    return lhs->i == rhs->i;
}
// ...
bool x = op1 *= op2;
```

- Arithmetic operator (unexpected implementation):

```
static OpClass^ operator *=(const OpClass ^lhs, const OpClass ^rhs)
{
OpClass^ ret = gcnew OpClass();
ret->i = lhs->i * rhs->i;
return ret;
}
// ...
OpClass^ x = y *= z;
```

- Assignment operator (expected implementation):

```
static void operator *=(OpClass ^lhs, const OpClass ^rhs)
{
lhs->i *= rhs->i;
}
// ...
x *= y;
```

By the way, you could even implement these operators a fourth way by having the operator overload return a different type than Boolean or the operator ref class. For example:

```
static int operator *=(const OpClass ^lhs, const OpClass ^rhs) {}
```

Listing 3-7 is an example of assorted managed operator overloads.

Listing 3-7. *Operator Overload in Action*

```
using namespace System;

ref class OpClass
{
public:
    OpClass() : i(0) {}
    OpClass(int x) : i(x) {}

    // x != y
    static bool operator !=(const OpClass ^lhs, const OpClass ^rhs)
    {
        return lhs->i != rhs->i;
    }
```

```cpp
    // x * y
    static OpClass^ operator *(const OpClass ^lhs, const OpClass ^rhs)
    {
        OpClass^ ret = gcnew OpClass();
        ret->i = lhs->i * rhs->i;
        return ret;
    }

    // x *= y
    static void operator *=(OpClass ^lhs, const OpClass ^rhs)
    {
        lhs->i *= rhs->i;
    }

    // -x
    static OpClass^ operator -(const OpClass ^lhs)
    {
        OpClass^ ret = gcnew OpClass();
        ret->i = -(lhs->i);
        return ret;
    }

    // ++x and x++
    static OpClass^ operator ++(const OpClass ^lhs)
    {
        OpClass^ ret = gcnew OpClass();
        ret->i = (lhs->i) + 1;
        return ret;
    }

    virtual String ^ ToString() override
    {
        return i.ToString();
    }
private:
    int i;
};

void main()
{
    OpClass ^op1 = gcnew OpClass(3);
    OpClass ^op2 = gcnew OpClass(5);
    OpClass ^op3 = gcnew OpClass(15);

    if ( op1 * op2 != op3)
        Console::WriteLine("Don't Equal");
    else
        Console::WriteLine("Equal");

    op1 *= op2;
    Console::WriteLine(op1);
```

```
    Console::WriteLine(++op1);  // prints 15 then increments to 16
    Console::WriteLine(op1++);  // increOpClassents to 17 then prints

    Console::WriteLine(-op1);   // Negation of OpClass1
    Console::WriteLine(op1);    // prior Negation op left OpClass1 unchanged
}
```

Figure 3-8 shows the results of this little program.

Figure 3-8. *Results of OperatorOverload.exe*

Both operands don't have to be of the same type as the defining ref class, but at least one of the managed operands must be of the same type as the defining ref class. Defining a managed operands with one argument, something other then the defining ref class, is not automatically associative. You must define the other combination as well. Listing 3-8 compares whether the ref class Number is greater than an int associatively.

Listing 3-8. *Operator Overload for Mixed Data Types in Action*

```
using namespace System;

ref class Number
{
public:
    Number(int x) : i(x) {}

    static bool operator >(Number^ n, int v)  // maps to operator >
    {
        return n->i > v;
    }
    static bool operator >(int v, Number^ n)  // maps to operator >
    {
        return v > n->i;
    }

    virtual String ^ ToString() override
    {
        return i.ToString();
    }
private:
    int i;
};
```

```
int main()
{
    Number^ n = gcnew Number(5);

    if ( n > 6 )
        Console::WriteLine("{0} Greater than 6", n);
    else
        Console::WriteLine("{0} Less than or Equal 6", n);

    if ( 6 > n )
        Console::WriteLine("6 Greater than {0}", n);
    else
        Console::WriteLine("6 Less than or Equal {0}", n);
}
```

Figure 3-9 shows the results of this little program.

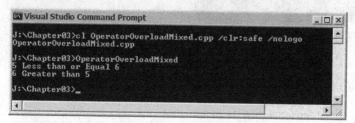

Figure 3-9. *Results of OperatorOverloadMixed.exe*

Member Properties

The purpose of properties is to enrich encapsulation for ref classes by hiding member variables, yet at the same time providing protected access to the values contained in these variables. Properties are successful in doing this, and as an added benefit, they provide an improved and simplified interface to a member variable.

A problem with traditional C++ classes is that there is no simple and standardized way of maintaining member variables. Frequently, programmers will simplify the syntax of interfacing with their class and allow public access to member variables even at the risk of having invalid data placed into them. Seeing the risk of exposing some of the more volatile variables, a programmer then might decide to write "getter and setter" methods. These methods protect the member variables but also complicate the necessary syntax for their access, because you always have to access the variables as a function call instead of using the more intuitive variable access format.

Properties solve this problem by providing direct member variable-like access to member variables, but with the security and flexibility of getter and setter methods. To the programmer accessing the ref class, properties act like member variables. Member properties resemble simple scalar variables, static variables, arrays, and indexes. To the developer of the ref class, properties are simply getter and setter methods with specific rules and syntax. The complexity of these methods is totally up to the ref class creator.

Trivial Properties

Trivial properties are the most common implementation of a property with getter and setter methods accessing a single member variable without any additional actions being done on that member variable. You might consider the trivial property as a placeholder for future enhancement to the ref classes

API as it enables a ref class to maintain binary compatibility when a more elaborate property evolves. If you were to initially code the API as directly accessing the member variable, then in the future, you would lose binary compatibility if you changed the API access to properties.

Coding trivial properties is, as the name suggests, trivial. Simply declare the member variable with a prefix of the keyword property.

```
property type PropertyName;
```

You would then access the property just as you would any other member variable but, under the covers, you are actually accessing the variable as a property.

Scalar Properties

One step up from trivial properties is the scalar property. This form of property allows the ability to provide read-only, write-only, or both read and write access to a member variable. It also allows doing things like validating the property before updating its underlying member variable or logging all changes made to the property.

To create a scalar property with read and write access, you need to extend the trivial property syntax by adding a get() and set() method:

```
property type PropertyName
{
    type get() {};
    void set (type value) {};
}
```

You can make a property write-only by excluding the set method in the property's declaration:

```
property type PropertyName
{
    type get() {};
}
```

Conversely, you can make the property read-only by excluding the get method:

```
property type PropertyName
{
    void set (type value) {};
}
```

The get() method gives you full access to the property to do as you please. The most common thing you will do is validate the parameter and then assign it to a private member variable.

The only real catch you might encounter is that the property name cannot be the same as a member variable. A conversion I use, which is by no means a standard, is to use a lowercase letter as the first letter of the member variable and an uppercase letter as the first letter of the property name.

With the addition of a set() method, you are now free to put any calculation you want within the method, but it must return the type specified. For this type of property, the most common body of the method is a simple return of the member variable storage of the property.

Listing 3-9 shows a trivial property, and scalar properties that are readable, writable, and both readable and writable.

Listing 3-9. *Scalar Properties in Action*

```
using namespace System;

ref class ScalarProp
{
```

```
public:
    // Constructor
    ScalarProp()
    {
        Cost        = 0.0;
        number      = 0;
        name        = "Blank Name";
        description = "Scalar Property";
    }

    // trivial property
    property double Cost;

    // Read & write with validated parameter
    property int Number
    {
        void set(int value)
        {
            if (value < 1)
                value = 1;
            else if (value > 10)
                value = 10;

            number = value;
        }

        int get()
        {
            return number;
        }
    }

    // Write-only property
    property String^ Name
    {
        void set(String^ value)
        {
            name = value;
        }
    }

    // Ready-only property
    property String ^Description
    {
        String^ get()
        {
            return String::Concat(name, " ", description);
        }
    }
private:
    String ^name;
    String ^description;
    int     number;
};
```

```
void main()
{
    ScalarProp sp;

    sp.Name = "The Ref Class";

    Console::WriteLine(sp.Description);

    sp.Cost = 123.45;
    Console::WriteLine(sp.Cost);

    sp.Number = 20;     // Will be changed to 10
    Console::WriteLine(sp.Number);

    sp.Number = -5;     // Will be changed to 1
    Console::WriteLine(sp.Number);

    sp.Number = 6;      // Will not change
    Console::WriteLine(sp.Number);
}
```

Figure 3-10 shows the results of this program.

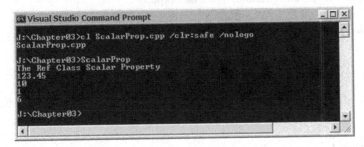

Figure 3-10. *Results of ScalarProp.exe*

Static Properties

As I mentioned previously, ref classes also contain static member variables. Likewise, C++/CLI provides property syntax to support *static properties*, or properties that have ref class-wide storage.

Static properties are nearly identical to scalar properties except that they contain the keyword static in their definition and they can only use static variables for storage. To create a readable and writable static property, simply use this syntax:

```
property static type PropertyName
{
    type get() {};
    void set (type value) {};
}
```

For example:

```
property static String^ Name
{
    void set(String^ value)
    {
        name = value;
    }
    String^ get()
    {
        return name;
    }
}
```

You can optionally place the keyword static in front of the get() and set() method, but I personally find this redundant.

Programmers can access a static property in the same way they would a static member variable, by using ref class name and the :: operator:

```
class::PropertyName
```

For example:

```
StaticProp::Name = "Static Property";
Console::WriteLine(StaticProp::Name);
```

Listing 3-10 shows a simple readable and writable static Name property.

Listing 3-10. *Static Properties in Action*

```
using namespace System;

ref class StaticProp
{
public:
    property static String^ Name
    {
        void set(String^ value)
        {
            name = value;
        }
        String^ get()
        {
            return name;
        }
    }
private:
    static String^ name;
};

int main()
{
    StaticProp::Name = "Static Property";
    Console::WriteLine(StaticProp::Name);
}
```

Figure 3-11 shows the results of this little program.

Figure 3-11. *Results of StaticProp.exe*

Array Properties

C++/CLI provides simple array syntax for properties. This is a big improvement over traditional C++, where getter and setter methods simply don't perform that elegantly.

The syntax for array properties is the same as that for the scalar property, except that the property's type is an array:

```
property array<type>^ NumArray
{
    array<type>^ get() {}
    void set ( array<type>^ value ) {}
}
```

For example:

```
property array<int>^ NumArray
{
    array<int>^ get() {}
    void set ( array<int>^ value ) {}
}
```

Once the get() and set() methods have been created, it is a simple matter to access an array property using normal array syntax. Listing 3-11 shows how to add a readable and writable array property to a ref class.

Listing 3-11. *Array Properties in Action*

```
using namespace System;

ref class ArrayProp
{
public:
    ArrayProp(int size)
    {
        numArray = gcnew array<int>(size);
    }

    property array<int>^ NumArray
    {
        array<int>^ get()
        {
            return numArray;
        }
```

```
            void set ( array<int>^ value )
            {
                numArray = value;
            }
        }
private:
    array<int>^ numArray;
};

void main()
{
    ArrayProp aprop(5);

    for ( int i = 0 ; i < aprop.NumArray->Length ; ++i )
        aprop.NumArray[i] = i;

    for each (int i in aprop.NumArray)
        Console::WriteLine(i);
}
```

Figure 3-12 shows the results of this little program.

Figure 3-12. *Results of ArrayProp.exe*

Indexed Properties

At first glance, *indexed properties* may appear to provide the same functionality as array properties. They allow you to look up a property based on an index. The syntax to allow you to do this is more complex than that of the array property:

```
property type PropertyName [ indexType1, ..., indexTypeN ]
{
    type get(indexType1 index1, ..., indexTypeN indexN) {};
    void set(indexType1 index1, ..., indexTypeN indexN, type value) {};
}
```

Here is an example of two indices being used in an indexed property:

```
property AType^ PropertyName [ int, int ]
{
    AType^ get(String^ index1, int index2) {};
    void    set(String^ index1, int index2, AType^ value) {};
}
```

So why would a programmer go through all of the problems of using indexed properties? It boils down to one thing: The index doesn't have to be numeric. In other words, when you use indexed properties, you get the ability to work with an array index of any type.

In the preceding sample, the index is of type String^. So, when programmers want to access an indexed property, they would access it like this:

```
PropertyName["StringValue", intValue]
```

If the indexed properties are still a little hazy, Listing 3-12 is a more complex example to show them in action. You start by defining a Student ref class with two trivial properties. You then create a Course ref class, which, using a nested ref class (covered next), stores a linked list of students and their grades for the course. You use an indexed property ReportCard to extract the grades from the linked list using the student's name.

Listing 3-12. *Indexed Properties in Action*

```cpp
using namespace System;

ref class Student
{
public:
    Student(String^ s, int g)
    {
        Name  = s;
        Grade = g;
    }

    property String^ Name;
    property int Grade;
};

ref class Course
{
    ref struct StuList
    {
        Student ^stu;
        StuList ^next;
    };
    StuList ^Stu;
    static StuList ^ReportCards = nullptr;

public:
    property Student^ ReportCard [String^]
    {
        Student^ get(String^ n)
        {
            for(Stu = ReportCards; Stu && (Stu->stu->Name != n); Stu = Stu->next)
                ;
            if (Stu != nullptr)
                return Stu->stu;
            else
                return gcnew Student("",0);  // empty student
        }
```

```
        void set(String^ n, Student^ s)
        {
            for(Stu = ReportCards; Stu && (Stu->stu->Name != n); Stu = Stu->next)
                ;
            if (Stu == nullptr)
            {
                StuList ^stuList = gcnew StuList;
                stuList->stu = s;
                stuList->next = ReportCards;
                ReportCards = stuList;
            }
        }
    }
};

void main()
{
    Course  EnglishLit;
    Student Stephen("Stephen", 95);                    // student as stack variable
    Student ^Sarah = gcnew Student("Sarah", 98); // student as heap variable

    EnglishLit.ReportCard[ "Stephen" ] = %Stephen;     // index as String literal
    EnglishLit.ReportCard[ Sarah->Name ] = Sarah;      // index as String^

    Console::WriteLine(EnglishLit.ReportCard[ Stephen.Name ]->Grade);
    Console::WriteLine(EnglishLit.ReportCard[ "Sarah" ]->Grade);
}
```

Figure 3-13 shows the results of this little program.

Figure 3-13. *Results of IndexProps.exe*

Default Indexed Property (Indexer)

Scalar properties provide fieldlike access on an instance of an object. A default indexed property, however, allows arraylike access directly on specific collection within an instance of an object. The default indexed property is a convenience, simplifying the access to a selected (default) collection within a ref class.

The syntax of a default indexed property is identical to an indexed property, except that the keyword default is used in place of the name of the property. That way, when you want to access the default collection within the ref class, you omit the property name and just reference the instance of the object as if it where the default collection itself.

Listing 3-13 is a simple example of a default index property where the default collection called defaultArray is coded to be the default index property.

Listing 3-13. *Indexed Properties in Action*

```
using namespace System;

ref class Numbers
{
public:
    Numbers()
    {
        defaultArray = gcnew array<String^>
        {
            "zero", "one", "two", "three", "four", "five"
        };
    }

    property String^ default [int]
    {
        String^ get(int index)
        {
            if (index < 0)
                index = 0;
            else if (index > defaultArray->Length)
                index = defaultArray->Length - 1;

            return defaultArray[index];
        }
    }
private:
    array<String^>^ defaultArray;
};

void main()
{
    Numbers numbers;

    Console::WriteLine(numbers[-1]);
    Console::WriteLine(numbers[3]);
    Console::WriteLine(numbers[10]);
}
```

Figure 3-14 shows the results of this little program.

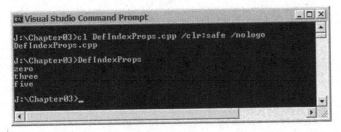

Figure 3-14. *Results of DefIndexProps.exe*

By the way, there is no restriction that the index be an integer. Just like an indexed property, a default indexed property can be any type and number of indexes.

Nested ref classes

As their name suggests, *nested* ref classes are ref classes defined inside another ref class. You might think of them as member ref classes.

Nested classes differ from inherited classes in that inherited classes have an "is a" relationship, whereas nested classes have a "contains a" relationship. In other words, for inheritance class A "is a" class B, and for nested classes, class C "contains a" class D. Of course, you can always use a separate class instead of a nested class to do this. What you gain by using nested classes is context, because a nested class only has context within the class containing it.

I very seldom use nested classes, but they do make sense if the nested class only really has meaning within its container class.

Like all members of a class, a nested class's accessibility is determined by whether it is located within the public, protected, or private area of its class. Unlike member types, a nested class, though limited to the scope of the enclosing class, has its own members, and these members adhere to the accessibility of the nested class. For example, if the nested class has public accessibility, but the accessibility of the nested class's member variable is private, then the member variable is private as far as the surrounding class is concerned, even though the nested class is accessible to external functions and methods.

In Listing 3-14, you can see a surrounding class with a nested class. The nested class has three members: a public, a protected, and a private member variable. The surrounding class has three member variable references to the nested class: public, protected, and private. The surrounding class also has an initializer list constructor for the member variables and a method to access all the nested class instances within the surrounding class. The listing shows an inheriting class to the surrounding class with a method showing how to access the nested class instances of its parent class. Finally, the listing shows a main() function that indicates how to reference the member variable found within the nested class within the surrounding class. The class has no output. Its purpose is to show you a method of accessing nested classes' public members.

Listing 3-14. *Nested Classes in Action*

```
using namespace System;

ref class SurroundClass
{
public:
    ref class NestedClass        // Declaration of the nested class
    {
    public:
        int publicMember;
    protected:
        int protectedMember;
    private:
        int privateMember;
    };

    NestedClass^ protectedNC;    // protected variable reference to NestedClass

private:
    NestedClass^ privateNC;      // private variable reference to NestedClass
```

```
public:
    NestedClass^ publicNC;       // public variable reference to NestedClass

    // Constructor for SurroundClass
    // Notice the initializer list declaration of the reference member variable
    SurroundClass() : publicNC(gcnew NestedClass),
                      protectedNC(gcnew NestedClass),
                      privateNC(gcnew NestedClass)
    {}

    // A member showing how to access NestedClass within SurroundClass
    // Notice only public member variables of the nested class are accessed
    // The private and protected are hidden
    void method()
    {
        int x;

        NestedClass nc1;             // Declared another reference NestedClass

        x = nc1.publicMember;        // Accessing new NestedClass variable

        x = publicNC->publicMember;    // Accessing public NestedClass variable
        x = protectedNC->publicMember;// Accessing protected NestedClass variable
        x = privateNC->publicMember;   // Accessing private NestedClass variable
    }
};

// A inherited class showing how to access NestedClass within a member method
// Notice only public and protected NestedClass are accessed
// The private is hidden
ref class inheritSurroundClass : public SurroundClass
{
public:
    void method()
    {
        int x;

        NestedClass nc1;           // can access because NestedClass
                                   // declaration protected
        x = nc1.publicMember;

        x = publicNC->publicMember;
        x = protectedNC->publicMember;
    }
};

// The main function shows how to access NestedClass from outside SurroundClass
// inheritance tree
// Notice only the public NestedClass reference is accessible
void main()
{
    SurroundClass sc;
    int x = sc.publicNC->publicMember;
}
```

There is a lot of code in Listing 3-14. Figure 3-15 should clear up any confusion.

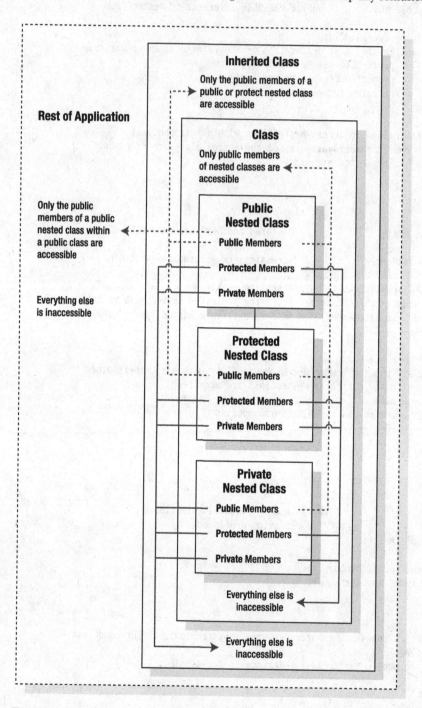

Figure 3-15. *Accessing nested class members*

Only public members are accessible outside of a nested class. For the surrounding class to access the public variable, the nested class can be public, protected, or private. For an inheriting class of the surrounding class, only public or protected access to the nested class will allow access to the nested class's public member variable. Finally, to access the nested class's public member variable outside of the inheritance tree of the surrounding class, both the nested class and the surrounding class must have public access.

Type Casting Between Classes

Type casting is the process of converting from one type to another. I covered type casting of the built-in types in Chapter 2. Now I expand on that discussion to include class and struct types.

C++/CLI provides three different operators for type casting between classes or structs: static_cast, dynamic_cast, and safe_cast. Each performs the process of trying to convert from one class type to another.

Notice that I wrote "trying to convert." To legally convert a class to another, it needs to inherit from or be the class type to which it is being converted. For example, let's say class B inherits from class A, which in turn inherits from the Object class (all ref classes inherit from the Object class). This means that class B can safely be converted to a class A or the Object class. Class A, on the other hand, can safely convert to the Object class, but it would be an invalid conversion to class B, as class A is not inherited from class B.

The static_cast operator is the fastest of the three conversion operators, but it is also the most dangerous, as it assumes that the programmer knows what she is doing, and so it does no validity checks of its own. The syntax for the operator is simply this:

```
static_cast<target_type>(object_to_convert);
```

or

```
static_cast<int>(var);
static_cast<ClassA^>(ClassBvar);
```

■**Unsafe Code** The static_cast operator cannot be verified and thus is classified as unsafe code.

The dynamic_cast operator is slower than the static_cast operator because it verifies that the type casting is valid. If the conversion is allowed, then the dynamic_cast operator completes the conversion. On the other hand, if it's not a valid conversion, then the dynamic_cast operator returns nullptr. The syntax of the dynamic_cast operator is identical to the static_cast operator except that static is replaced with dynamic in the following statement:

```
dynamic_cast<ClassA^>(ClassBvar);
```

A nifty little trick to check if a class is of a certain type can be done using the dynamic_cast operator. If you come from the C# world, then this is equivalent to the is operator:

```
if ( dynamic_cast<ClassA^>(ClassB) != 0)
{
    // ClassB is of type ClassA
}
```

The last conversion operator is the safe_cast. The safe_cast is the closest match the conversion behavior of all other .NET-supported languages and is designed so that you can rely exclusively on it for writing verifiable code. Because of this, C++/CLI uses safe_cast as the premier cast type for C-style casting. Thus, you normally won't even need to use the safe_cast operator at all, just the C-style cast. The syntax of the safe_cast operator is also identical to the static_cast operator, except that static is replaced this time with safe in the following statement:

```
safe_cast<ClassA^>(ClassBvar);
```

The safe_cast operator is similar to the static_cast operator in that it can call user-defined conversions both implicitly and explicitly. It also can reverse standard conversion, like from a base class to an inherited class. The safe_cast is also like the dynamic_cast in that it checks to see if the cast was valid, except that instead of returning a nullptr, it throws an exception of type System::InvalidCastException. I cover exceptions in Chapter 4.

Listing 3-15 doesn't produce any output. I've provided comments on what the result of each statement is. If you want to prove to yourself that I'm right, you can run the code through a debugger and watch the results as you execute each statement.

Listing 3-15. *Type Casting in Action*

```
using namespace System;

ref class A {};
ref class B : public A {};
ref class C {};

void main()
{
    Object ^v1 = gcnew A();
    Object ^v2 = gcnew B();
    Object ^v3 = gcnew C();

    A ^a1 = gcnew A();
    A ^a2 = gcnew B();
    A ^a3 = dynamic_cast<A^>(v1);   // downcast
    A ^a4 = dynamic_cast<A^>(v2);   // downcast
    A ^a5 = static_cast<A^>(v3);    // a5 has invalid value of type C class

    B ^b1 = gcnew B();
    B ^b2 = dynamic_cast<B^>(v2);   // downcast
    B ^b3 = dynamic_cast<B^>(v3);   // Fails b3 = null. Miss match classes
    B ^b4 = dynamic_cast<B^>(a2);   // downcast

    C ^c1 = gcnew C();
    C ^c2 = dynamic_cast<C^>(v1);   // Fails c2 = null. Miss match classes
    C ^c3 = static_cast<C^>(v2);    // c3 has invalid value of type B class
    C ^c4 = safe_cast<C^>(v3);      // downcast

    C ^c5 = (C^)(v3);               // downcast

//  B ^e1 = safe_cast<B^>(c1);      // does not compile as compiler knows these
                                   // are unrelated handles.
}
```

Abstract ref classes

An *abstract* ref class is an incomplete definition of a ref class, and it contains at least one pure virtual member method. It is a binding agreement between the ref class that derives from the abstract ref class and the ref class that calls the methods of that derived ref class.

In every other way, an abstract ref class is the same as a normal ref class. It can have variables, methods, properties, constructors, and destructors. The only thing it can't do is instantiate an object from itself. Though, it is possible to instantiate a derived ref class of the abstract ref class and then access the derived ref class using a handle to the abstract class.

```
AbstractClass ^ac = gcnew DerivedClass();
```

You might be wondering why you would need a constructor if you can't create an abstract class. The constructor of an abstract class serves the same purpose it does in a normal class: to initialize the member variables. There's one catch, though. The only place you can put an abstract class constructor is in the derived class's initializer list. Because the constructor only needs to be accessed by the deriving class, it's safest to declare the constructor as protected.

Any class that derives from an abstract class must implement the pure virtual function, or it will become an abstract class itself.

Any class that has pure virtual methods is abstract. In fact, even though C++/CLI has added the keyword abstract to declare a class as abstract, the keyword is optional and not needed. What it does is simply make the class notation explicit. It also makes your code more readable, as now you can see that a class is abstract from its initial declaration and you do not have to search the class for pure virtual methods.

However, if you do make the class abstract by including the keyword abstract, the class becomes abstract even if it normally would not be abstract. Thus, if a class is declared as abstract, you cannot create an instance of the class. Instead, only inherited classed from it can be instantiated. To make a class explicitly abstract, add the abstract keyword after the class declaration:

```
ref class AbstractExClass abstract
{
};
```

Because an abstract class has to be inherited, obviously a sealed class is not allowed, but it is legal to seal a virtual method, if the abstract class implements it.

To show abstract classes in action, Listing 3-16 shows an abstract class defined with a constructor and two methods, one of which is a pure virtual method. Another class inherits this class and seals Method1, but because it does not implement Method2, it too is abstract. Finally, this second abstract class is called by a third class, which implements the pure virtual function. Because the class now has all classes implemented, it can be instantiated. The example also shows how to pass an abstract class handle as a parameter.

Listing 3-16. *Abstract Classes in Action*

```
using namespace System;

ref class AbstractExClass abstract
{
protected:
    int AbstractVar;
    AbstractExClass(int val): AbstractVar(val) {}
```

```cpp
public:
    virtual void Method1() = 0;   // unimplemented method
    virtual void Method2() = 0;   // unimplemented method
    void Method3()
    {
        Console::WriteLine(AbstractVar.ToString());
    }
};

ref class MidAbstractExClass abstract : public AbstractExClass
{
public:
    virtual void Method1() override sealed
    {
        Console::WriteLine((AbstractVar * 3).ToString());
    }
protected:
    MidAbstractExClass(int val) : AbstractExClass(val) {}
};

ref class DerivedExClass : public MidAbstractExClass
{
public:
    DerivedExClass(int val) : MidAbstractExClass(val) {}
    virtual void Method2() override
    {
        Console::WriteLine((AbstractVar * 2).ToString());
    }
};

void testMethod(AbstractExClass ^aec)
{
    aec->Method1();
    aec->Method2();
    aec->Method3();
}

void main()
{
    AbstractExClass ^Ab1 = gcnew DerivedExClass(5);
    Ab1->Method1();
    Ab1->Method2();
    Ab1->Method3();

    AbstractExClass ^Ab2 = gcnew DerivedExClass(6);
    testMethod(Ab2);

    DerivedExClass ^dc = gcnew DerivedExClass(7);
    testMethod(dc);
}
```

Figure 3-16 shows the results of this little program.

Figure 3-16. *Results of AbstractEx.exe*

Interfaces

An *interface* is similar to an abstract class in that it is a binding agreement between the class that derives from the abstract class and the class that calls the methods of that derived class. The key difference is that an interface only contains public, pure virtual methods. As the name suggests, it defines an interface to a class. But defining is all it does, as it does not contain variables or implementations for any methods.

Though classes can only inherit one class, they are able to inherit as many interfaces as needed to define the interface to the class. It is up to the class to implement all interfaces.

Like an abstract class, you can't instantiate an object from an interface. But, like abstract ref classes, it is possible to instantiate a ref class that implements the interface and then access the implementing ref class using a handle to the interface.

```
AnInterface ^iface = gcnew AnInterfaceImplementer();
```

This allows a developer to write a "generic" class that operates only on the interface. When a developer implements the interface, the base class can use the derived object in place of the interface.

Traditionally, C++ programmers have defined an interface as a ref class that contains only pure virtual methods. With C++/CLI, it has been formalized with the keywords interface class. To create an interface, preface the keyword class with the keyword interface (instead of ref) in the definition and then place in the body of the interface a set of public, pure virtual methods.

Note You can also just place within the interface class method prototypes without the keyword virtual or the "= 0" suffix, because they are assumed.

Because only public access is allowed within an interface, the default logically for interface access is public. This means there is no need to include the public access modifier, as you would if it were a class. Oh, by the way, if you try to use access modifiers in your interface, the compiler slaps your hand and tells you to remove them.

Obviously, because an interface is only made up of pure virtual methods, the sealed keyword has no relevance to interfaces and will generate an error.

One additional note about interfaces: Even though they cannot contain method variables, is it is perfectly legal to define properties within an interface. The definition of the properties cannot have an implementation—like other methods in the interface, the properties need to be implemented in the interface's inheriting class.

Listing 3-17 shows how to create a couple of interfaces, one with pure virtual methods only and another with a combination of methods and property definitions. It then shows how to do multiple inheritances in a ref class (one base class and two interfaces).

Listing 3-17. *Interfaces in Action*

```
using namespace System;

interface class Interface1
{
    void Method1();
    void Method2();
};

interface class Interface2
{
    void Method3();
    property String^ X;
};

ref class Base
{
public:
    void MethodBase()
    {
        Console::WriteLine("MethodBase()");
    }
};

ref class DerivedClass : public Base, public Interface1, public Interface2
{
public:
    virtual property String^ X
    {
        String^ get()
        {
            return x;
        }

        void  set(String^ value)
        {
            x = value;
        }
    }

    virtual void Method1()
    {
        Console::WriteLine("Method1()");
    }
```

```
    virtual void Method2()
    {
        Console::WriteLine("Method2()");
    }

    virtual void Method3()
    {
        Console::WriteLine("Method3()");
    }

    virtual void Print()
    {
        MethodBase();
        Method1();
        Method2();
        Method3();
    }

private:
    String^ x;
};

void main()
{
    DerivedClass dc;

    dc.X = "Start'n Up";
    Console::WriteLine(dc.X);

    dc.Print();
}
```

Figure 3-17 shows the results of this little program. One thing you should note about the code is that the class that implements the interface requires each interface method to be prefixed with the keyword virtual. If you forget, you'll get a sequence of pretty self-explanatory compile time errors telling you to add the keyword.

Figure 3-17. *Results of InterfaceEx.exe*

Summary

This chapter covered the basics of objected-oriented development using C++/CLI. You started with a quick refresher on what objects are and their fundamental concepts. From there, you saw how these concepts fit into the world of C++/CLI. You looked at ref classes in general, and then you broke down a ref class into its parts: member variables, member methods, and member properties. You finished the chapter by looking at abstract ref classes and interfaces.

Unlike the basics, C++/CLI has implemented many changes to traditional C++. Though none of the changes are complex—in fact, many simplify things—this chapter should be read carefully by experienced C++ programmers.

You will continue to examine C++/CLI in the next chapter, but now that you have covered the basics, you can move onto a few more complex and, dare I say, fun topics.

CHAPTER 4

■■■

Advanced C++/CLI

You have learned the basics of C++/CLI and moved on to explore its object-oriented nature. Now it is time to start looking at some of the more advanced features of C++/CLI. Unlike the previous chapters, this one does not have a common thread from start to finish; instead, it consists of an assortment of more advanced topics that didn't fit into the previous two chapters.

This chapter covers the following topics:

- Working with preprocessor directives
- Using multifile libraries and building an assembly from them
- Referencing the custom-built assemblies in your applications
- Templates
- Generics
- Handling errors in C++/CLI using exceptions
- Working with delegates
- Using delegates in events

Preprocessor Directives

Before any actual compiling occurs on a piece of program source code in C++/CLI, it must first go through the preprocessor, just as in traditional C++. The purpose of the preprocessor is to prepare the program source code for compiling using a number of instructions called *preprocessor directives*.

These preprocessor directives enable the programmer to do tasks such as include or exclude code based on conditions, define constants, and so on. All of the directives are prefixed with the # symbol (variously called pound, number sign, and hash), which makes them stand out from the rest of the program source code. Table 4-1 shows a complete set of all preprocessor directives for C++/CLI.

Table 4-1. *C++/CLI Preprocessor Directives*

Directive	Description
#define	Defines or undefines a meaningful name to a constant or macro in your program.
#undef	
#if	Allows for conditional compilation of program source code.
#ifdef	
#ifndef	
#elif	
#else	
#endif	
#error	Intended to allow you to generate a diagnostic error when something goes wrong in the preprocessor stage.
#include	Provides header file insertion.
#line	Redefines the compiler's internally stored line number and filename with the provided line number and filename.
#pragma	Provides machine/operating system–specific features while retaining compatibility with C++. Most likely, the only #pragma directives that you will encounter in C++/CLI are once, which causes an include file to be only included once, and managed and unmanaged, which allow for function-level control of compiling functions as managed or unmanaged.
#using	Imports .NET assembly metadata into program source code using C++/CLI.

The three directives that you'll most likely deal with using C++/CLI are the defining, conditional, and include directives. Other than the #using directive, there's no difference between C++/CLI and traditional C++ when it comes to the available processor directives, though the #import and many #pragma directives don't make sense and won't be used with C++/CLI. This is appropriate, given that C++/CLI wasn't designed to change how C++ works; instead, it's supposed to expand C++ so that it works seamlessly with .NET.

By convention, preprocessor directives are placed near the top of the source code. In actuality, other than a select few exceptions (the #using preprocessor directive comes to mind as it needs global scope) you can place a preprocessor directive on its own line almost anywhere in the code—basically wherever it makes sense. The #define declarative, for instance, just needs to be placed before it is used.

Defining Directives

The #define directive is used to execute a macro substitution of one piece of text for another. Here are the three basic syntaxes for implementing #define:

```
#define identifier
#define identifier token-string
#define identifier(parameter1,..., parameterN) token-string
```

The first syntax defines the existence of a symbol. The second syntax allows for the substitution of text identified by the identifier with the following token-string. The third syntax provides the same functionality as the second, and the passed parameters are placed within the token-string. Listing 4-1 shows the source code before it has been passed through the preprocessor.

Listing 4-1. *Original #defined Code*

```
using namespace System;
#define DISAPPEARS
#define ONE 1
#define TWO 2
#define POW2(x) (x)*(x)

void main ()
{
    Console::Write("The following symbol disappears->" DISAPPEARS);
    Console::WriteLine("<-");

    int x = TWO;
    int y = POW2(x + ONE);

    Console::WriteLine(y);
}
```

Listing 4-2 shows the source code after it has passed through the preprocessor. Notice that all identifiers have been substituted with their token-string, or lack of token-string in the case of the DISAPPEARS identifier.

Listing 4-2. *Processed #defined Code*

```
using namespace System;

void main ()
{
    Console::Write("The following symbol disappears->" );
    Console::WriteLine("<-");

    int x = 2;
    int y = (x + 1)*(x + 1);

    Console::WriteLine(y);
}
```

The #undef directive's purpose is to remove a previously defined symbol. Unlike #define, there is only one syntax:

```
#undef identifier
```

The #undef directive undefines symbols that have been previously defined using the #define directive or the /D compile-time switch. If the symbol was never defined, then the #undef directive will be ignored by the preprocessor. If you forget to #undef a symbol before you #define it again, the compiler will generate a warning but will let you continue. It is probably a good idea whenever you see this warning to #undef the variable just before you #define it again to get rid of the warning, but there is nothing saying you have to.

Another approach that you can use to get rid of the warning for an already assigned symbol is to use the #pragma push_macro() and #pragma pop_macro() directives in conjunction with the #undef and #define directives. With this approach, the value of the symbol is stored so that it can be reassigned later after the application no longer needs the new symbol definition. Here is a simple example:

```
#define MY_SYMBOL "Original"

#pragma push_macro("MY_SYMBOL")
#undef MY_SYMBOL
#define MY_SYMBOL "New Value"
    Console::WriteLine(MY_SYMBOL);

#pragma pop_macro("MY_SYMBOL")
    Console::WriteLine(MY_SYMBOL);
```

Conditional Directives

Conditional directives provide the ability to selectively compile various pieces of a program. They work in a similar manner to the if flow control construct covered in Chapter 2. The big difference is that instead of not executing a particular section of code, now it will not be compiled.

The basic syntax for conditional directives is as follows:

```
#if constant-expression
// code
#elif constant-expression
// code
#else
// code
#endif
```

Similar to the if flow control construct, the first #if or #elif constant-expression that evaluates to nonzero or true will have its body of code compiled. If none of the constant-expressions evaluates to true, then the #else body of code is compiled.

Only one of the blocks of code will be compiled, depending on the result of the constant-expressions. The constant-expressions can be any combination of symbols, integer constants, character constants, and preprocessor operators (see Table 4-2).

Table 4-2. *Preprocessor Operators*

Operator	Description
+	Addition
-	Subtraction
*	Multiplication
/	Division
%	Modulus
&	Bitwise AND
|	Bitwise OR
^	Bitwise XOR
&&	Logical AND
||	Logical OR
<<	Left shift

Table 4-2. *Preprocessor Operators*

Operator	Description
>>	Right shift
==	Equality
!=	Inequality
<	Less than
>	Greater than
<=	Less than or equal to
>=	Greater than or equal to
defined	Symbol is defined
!defined	Symbol is not defined

Though usually quite simple, an expression can become quite complex, as the following example suggests:

```
#define ONE     1
#define TWO     2
#define THREE   3

#if ((ONE & THREE) && (TWO <= 2)) || defined FOUR
    Console::WriteLine("IF");
#else
    Console::WriteLine("ELSE");
#endif
```

The #if directive has two special preprocessor operators called defined and !defined. The first evaluates to true on the existence of the identified symbol. The second, obviously, evaluates to true if the identified symbol does not exist. To simplify the syntax, and because the defined and !defined operators are the most commonly used preprocessor operators with the #if directive, special versions of the directive were created: #ifdef and #ifndef.

These two directives are equivalent:

```
#if defined symbol
#ifdef symbol
```

and so are these two:

```
#if !defined symbol
#ifndef symbol
```

Include Directive

The #include directive causes the compiler to insert a piece of code into another piece of code. The most common usage of the #include directive is to place header files containing type definitions at the top of a piece of source file to ensure that the types are defined before they are used.

There are two different #include directive syntaxes for including a file in a source. The first uses angle brackets (<>) to enclose the file's path, and the second uses double quotes (""):

```
#include <file-path-spec>
#include "file-path-spec"
#include <windows.h>
#include "myclassdef.h"
#include "c:/myincludes/myclassdef.h"
```

Each directive syntax causes the replacement of that directive by the entire contents of its specified file. The difference when processing the two syntaxes is the order that files are searched for when a path is not specified. If the file's path is specified, then no search is done, and the file is expected to be at the location specified by the path. One major drawback is that the path cannot be a network path (per the Universal Naming Convention [UNC]). In a corporate, multideveloper site, this inability could be quite a nuisance or possibly even crippling. Table 4-3 summarizes the differences between the angle bracket and double quote syntax search methods when no path is specified.

Table 4-3. *#include Syntax Search Differences*

Syntax Form	Search Method
#include <...>	Check for files along the path specified by the /I compiler option and then along paths specified by the INCLUDE environment variable.
#include "..."	Check for files in the same directory of the file that contains the #include statement, then along the path specified by the /I compiler option, and finally, along paths specified by the INCLUDE environment variable.

Caution Though the C++/CLI compiler supports the INCLUDE environment variable, Visual Studio 2005 does not.

Using Directive

#using is a preprocessor directive specific to C++/CLI. When compiled, it generates metadata that is used by the common language runtime (CLR) to identify which assemblies to load. If you are an experienced C++ programmer, you can think of this directive as being similar to the #include directive, except that instead of including an .h file, you are now including a compiled .dll assembly file.

The syntax of the #using directive purposely resembles that of the #include directive. This makes sense, as the #using directive's function resembles that of the #include directive. The only difference in the syntax between #using and #include is that you replace "include" with "using":

```
#using <assembly-path-spec>
#using "assembly-path-spec"
#using <mscorlib.dll>
#using "myassembly.dll"
#using <DEBUG/myassembly.dll>
```

There is no difference between using quotes and angle brackets with #using as there is with the #include directive. Because this is the case, you will generally see angle brackets with #using directives. With either the double quote method or the angle bracket method, the compiler searches for the assembly using the following path:

- The path specified by the #using directive
- The current directory
- The .NET Framework system directory
- Directories added with the /AI compiler option
- Directories in the LIBPATH environment variable

Caution The #using directive is only used to help the compiler and the Visual Studio 2005 IDE find the assembly. It does not tell the CLR where to find it. To run the application, you must still place the assembly in a location where the CLR knows to look for it.

It should be noted that the keyword using and the preprocessor directive #using are different. The using keyword enables coding without the need of explicit qualifications. The using keyword says, "Whenever a class or variable does not exist in the current scope, check the scope of the namespace specified by the using statement, and if it is there, use it just like it is part of the current scope."

Okay, now after that nice long explanation, I should tell you that you will probably never use the #using directive if you are developing C++/CLI code within Visual Studio 2005 because in VS .NET the best way to add assembly references is via Solution Explorer.

Multifile Libraries

So far, in every example, you have used only one file as the source of an application. For small example or demonstration programs, this might be okay, but for more complex applications, using multiple source files to break up an application to make it more readable is a much better approach.

Breaking up the source code of an application into its possible many parts can be done in any number of ways. One of the most common approaches is to break off the source into groups of common functionality, better known as *libraries*. Libraries are a powerful means of breaking up an application because they are more conducive to code reuse, and only at the cost of some minor up-front design work.

The first thing that you will confront when building multifile libraries is that all types need to be declared before they are used in C++/CLI. This is not a problem in a single file, because all you have to do is place the declaration of the type before it is used.

With multifile libraries, you run into the problem of how to access a type that is declared in a different file. You could define a whole bunch of classes and then cut and paste all of the class definitions that you need in every file that uses them, but then you are going to be living in maintenance hell for the lifetime of the library. A better solution is to use header files to hold all these definitions and then #include them at the start of any source file that uses these definitions.

Almost all C++/CLI libraries (and applications, for that matter) should be broken up into two types of files: header files and source files. A *header file* is made up of the code needed to describe the types that are used, and a *source file* is made up of all the code that implements these types.

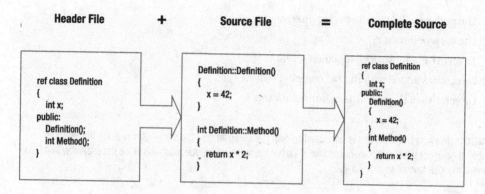

With this split, it is a simple thing to place all needed definitions of types by a source file at its top. You discovered earlier that it is a simple matter to place all the declarations in a header file and then insert the contents of the header into the main source code using the #include directive. Coding this way also ensures that all types will be declared before they are used, just as they need to be, by C++/CLI.

Okay, you know that you can split source code into two parts, and you know how to actually include the definition part of the source. Let's examine the two parts in more detail.

Header Files

Header files look very similar to all the examples that you have seen in this book so far. Instead of ending in .cpp, they usually end in .h, but that is not mandatory—they can actually end with anything. The only real difference between what you have seen in Chapter 3's class definitions and the class definitions found in header files in this chapter is that the header files now only contain the definition portion of functions, member properties, and member methods.

Note Header files are made up of function prototypes and class definitions.

It is legal to place the implementation of a class within a header file. In fact, so far that is how I have been coding every class in the book. To a C++ programmer this is called inline coding.

Here is an example of a header file:

```
//square.h

ref class Square
{
public:
    Square ( int d);
    int Area();
private:
    int Dims;
};
```

Notice that the only difference between this file and what you have seen previously is that there is no main() function, and that the constructor Square() and the member method Area() are only declared and have no implementation. You could, in fact, have implemented both the constructor and the member method, and the header file still would have been valid because classes in C++/CLI are just definitions. What you can't include in header files are function implementations—for example, the main() function. What you can include are only function prototypes.

Source Files

You have seen source files previously in this book. They are C++/CLI files that end with .cpp. With traditional C++ source files, the definition is not found in the source file, unlike all the examples you have seen thus far. Instead, they contain only the implementation of the definitions specified in the header file.

The syntax for implementing member methods in a separate source file from their definitions is similar to that of the function, which was covered in Chapter 2, except that the member method is prefixed with the name of the class it is implementing and the scope resolution (::) operator.

The following example shows the source file for the square.h header file listed previously. Its structure is very typical of all C++/CLI source files. It starts with the standard using namespace System; statement. Next comes the include statement for the header file, which this source file will be defining, and finally, the actual implementations of all the unimplemented member methods.

```
// square.cpp

using namespace System;

#include "square.h"

Square::Square ( int d)
{
    Dims = d;
}

int Square::Area()
{
    return Dims * Dims;
}
```

Namespaces

Adding a namespace to a library is optional but highly recommended. Remember that all identifiers have to be unique in C++/CLI, at least within their own scope. When you develop code on your own, keeping identifiers unique should not be a problem. With careful coordination and a detailed naming convention, a small group of programmers can keep all their identifiers unique. However, with the addition of third-party source code, unique identifiers become increasingly harder to maintain. That is, unless namespaces are used.

Namespaces create a local-scope declarative region for types. In other words, namespaces allow programmers to group code under a unique name. Thus, with a namespace, it is possible for programmers to create all types with any names they like and be secure in the knowledge that the types will be unique within the application if they are placed within a uniquely identified namespace.

The basic syntax of a namespace is simply this:

```
namespace name
{
    // all types to be defined within the namespace
}
```

If you want a namespace called Test to provide local scope to the Square class defined previously, you would simply code it like this:

```
namespace Test
{
    public ref class Square
    {
    public:
        Square (int d);
        int Area();
    private:
        int Dims;
    };
}
```

Those of you with a traditional C++ background may have noticed the additional keyword public placed in front of the class declaration. C++/CLI handles namespaces differently from traditional C++. Types within a namespace have private access. Thus, to make the class accessible outside the namespace, it has to be declared public. In traditional C++, all types are public within a namespace.

Personally, I don't like the new syntax, as it is inconsistent with C++. It should be public: (be careful, this is invalid syntactically), as it is in classes and structures. This syntax resembles C# and Java.

Caution If you fail to make any of the classes within the namespace public, then the namespace will not be accessible and will generate an error when you attempt to use the using statement for the namespace.

The syntax to implement a member method within a namespace does not change much. Simply add the namespace's name in front of the class name, delimited by the scope resolution (::) operator.

```
using namespace System;

#include "square.h"

Test::Square::Square ( int d)
{
    Dims = d;
}

int Test::Square::Area()
{
    return Dims * Dims;
}
```

If you are observant or have a good memory, you might remember that you could use the `using` statement to simplify the preceding code to this:

```
using namespace System;

#include "square.h"
using namespace Test;

Square::Square ( int d)
{
    Dims = d;
}

int Square::Area()
{
    return Dims * Dims;
}
```

Be careful to place the `using` statement after the `#include` directive because the namespace `Test` is defined in the included header file.

Building Assemblies from Multifile Libraries

I don't cover assemblies until Chapter 18, so let's not get bogged down with the details of what an assembly really is until then. For now, think of an assembly as a specially formatted .dll or .exe file that is executed by the CLR.

A key feature that you need to know about assemblies is that they're self-describing. What does that mean to a C++/CLI programmer? Simply put, you don't need header files to use the types placed within an assembly. Or, in other words, all those header files you meticulously created when you built your library are no longer needed once you finish creating your assembly. This is a major change from traditional C++.

Note Header files are not needed with assemblies!

Building Multifile Library Assemblies

You will learn how to actually access an assembly later in this chapter. The common C++ way of creating a library, either static or dynamic, is to create a set of header files to describe all the functionality found within the library. Then, in separate source files, implement all the functionality defined by these header files. All of the source code, along with all the associated header files, is run through the compiler to generate object files. Then all the object files are linked together to create a library file.

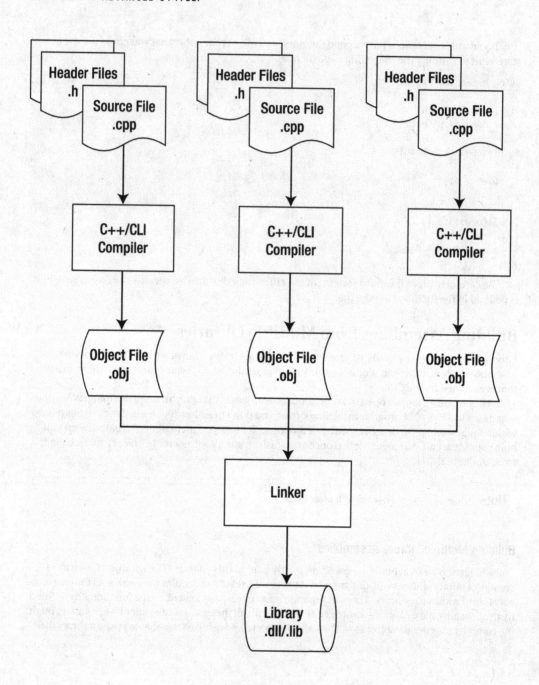

The main reason for all these header files is that when the class is implemented, all the classes, structures, variables, and so on are defined and thus are accessible.

This exact process can be used to generate library assemblies as well. The only difference in the process would be that the C++/CLI flags are turned on for the compiler and linker.

The following example, which consists of Listings 4-3 through 4-6, shows how to create an assembly using the traditional C++ method.

Listing 4-3 shows the header definition to the Card.h file. This file defines an enum of playing card Suits and a Card class within the namespace of Cards. Notice that the keyword public is placed in front of both the enum class and the ref class, as both need to be publicly accessible.

Listing 4-3. *Card.h: Traditional Method*

```
namespace Cards
{
    public enum class Suits { Heart, Diamond, Spade, Club };

    public ref class Card
    {
    private:
        int type;
        Suits suit;

    public:
        Card(int type, Suits suit);

        property int Type
        {
            int get();
            void set(int value);
        }

        property Suits Suit
        {
            Suits get();
            void set(Suits value);
        }

        virtual String^ ToString() override;
    };
}
```

Listing 4-4 shows the implementation of the class's constructor and member methods. There are a couple of things of note in this file. First is how you implement the getter and setter methods. Notice that you must include the class name and the property name before the get or set method declaration. Second is how you can override the virtual method ToString() inherited from the Object class. This allows you to use the class directly within the Console::WriteLine() method. As you can see, there is nothing special to doing either of these. I also do a little magic to get the characters that represent the heart, diamond, spade, and club.

Listing 4-4. *Card.cpp: Traditional Method*

```cpp
using namespace System;

#include "card.h"
using namespace Cards;

Card::Card(int type, Suits suit)
{
    Type = type;
    Suit = suit;
}

int Card::Type::get()
{
    return type;
}

void Card::Type::set(int value)
{
    type = value;
}

Suits Card::Suit::get()
{
    return suit;
}

void Card::Suit::set(Suits value)
{
    suit = value;
}

String^ Card::ToString()
{
    String ^t;

    if (Type > 1 && Type < 11)
        t = Type.ToString();
    else if (Type == 1)
        t = "A";
    else if (Type == 11)
        t = "J";
    else if (Type == 12)
        t = "Q";
    else
        t = "K";

    switch (Suit)
    {
        case Suits::Heart:
            return String::Concat(t, gcnew String((Char)3, 1));
        case Suits::Diamond:
            return String::Concat(t, gcnew String((Char)4, 1));
```

```
        case Suits::Club:
            return String::Concat(t, gcnew String((Char)5, 1));
        default:  //Spade
            return String::Concat(t, gcnew String((Char)6, 1));
    }
}
```

Listing 4-5 defines a second class named Deck. Notice that you use the Card class within the class, yet you never declare it within the header file. The trick to handling this is to remember that header files are pasted wholesale into the source file during compilation. Because this is the case, you simply place the include file of Card.h before Deck.h in the Deck.cpp source file, as you will see in Listing 4-6. Thus, the Card class is pasted in first and, therefore, defined as needed before the Deck class.

Listing 4-5. *Deck.h: Traditional Method*

```
namespace Cards
{
    public ref class Deck
    {
        array<Card^>^  deck;
        int    curCard;

    public:
        Deck(void);

        Card ^Deal();
        void Shuffle();
    };
}
```

Listing 4-6 shows the final source file to the mini library. Notice, as I stated previously, that Card.h is included before Deck.h. If you're observant, you might also notice that the Random class is used. You can find this class within the .NET Framework class library.

Listing 4-6. *Deck.cpp: Traditional Method*

```
using namespace System;

#include "card.h"
#include "deck.h"

using namespace Cards;

Deck::Deck(void)
{
    deck = gcnew array<Card^>(52);

    for (int i = 0; i < 13; i++)
    {
        deck[i]    = gcnew Card(i+1, Suits::Heart);
        deck[i+13] = gcnew Card(i+1, Suits::Club);
        deck[i+26] = gcnew Card(i+1, Suits::Diamond);
        deck[i+39] = gcnew Card(i+1, Suits::Spade);
    }
```

```
        curCard = 0;
}

Card^ Deck::Deal()
{
    if (curCard < deck->Length)
        return deck[curCard++];
    else
        return nullptr;
}

void Deck::Shuffle()
{
    Random ^r = gcnew Random();
    Card ^tmp;
    int j;

    for( int i = 0; i < deck->Length; i++ )
    {
        j       = r->Next(deck->Length);
        tmp     = deck[j];
        deck[j] = deck[i];
        deck[i] = tmp;
    }

    curCard = 0;
}
```

The command you need to execute to build a library assembly from the command line is a little more complex than what you have seen so far, but it is hardly rocket science. The syntax is simply as follows (without the ellipsis):

```
cl source1.cpp source2.cpp...sourceN.cpp /clr:safe /LD /FeOutputName.dll
```

The first change to the command line is that it takes a list of source file names. The next change is the /LD argument, which tells the linker to create a .dll and then, finally, the /Fe argument, which indicates the name of the .dll file to create. Notice that there is no space between the /Fe argument and the name of the file to create.

To compile the previous example, you would use

```
cl card.cpp deck.cpp /clr:safe /LD /FeCards.dll
```

Assembly Referencing

Once you place all of your library logic in an assembly, you are going to want to access it. With C++/CLI, getting access to or referencing an assembly is remarkably easy: one file copy (even this step can be eliminated) and one line of code. In fact, the command to compile the application doesn't even change.

After you have done these two things, you can access the library classes as if they were coded directly within your application. If you are using Visual Studio 2005, then you will even have full access to the type definitions within the assembly using IntelliSense.

You'll learn more about configuring access to library assemblies in Chapter 18, but the simplest method is just to place the assembly in the same directory where the final .exe file is going to be placed. Moving or copying the assembly can be done by using the simple copy.exe command or by just dragging and dropping using Windows Explorer. That's it. There's no registering, unregistering, GUIDs, or variants.

You've already covered the line that needs to be added to the source code: #using. Simply add a #using statement at the top of the source code, and voilá! The library is available as if it were coded right there in your code. You don't even need any header files—the assembly fully describes itself to the compiler, so it doesn't need any headers.

Listing 4-7 shows an application called PlayCards.exe that references the Cards.dll assembly that you just created. Notice that you have access to the namespace and classes, just as you would if you had coded them in the application. You can make references and handles to the classes. In fact, you can even inherit from them. You can use them just as you would any other class in the application.

Listing 4-7. *PlayCards.cpp: Reference a User Assembly*

```
#using <cards.dll>

using namespace System;
using namespace Cards;

void main()
{
    Deck deck;

    deck.Shuffle();

    Card ^card;
    int cnt = 0;
    while ((card = deck.Deal()) != nullptr)
    {
        Console::Write(card->ToString());
        Console::Write("\t");
        cnt++;

        if (cnt > 4)
        {
            Console::WriteLine("");
            cnt = 0;
        }
    }
    Console::WriteLine("");
}
```

To build this application from the command line, simply copy Cards.dll to the same directory as the source of PlayCards.cpp and then execute the same command from the command line as you always have:

```
cl PlayCards.cpp /clr:safe
```

Figure 4-1 shows a sample output of this random program.

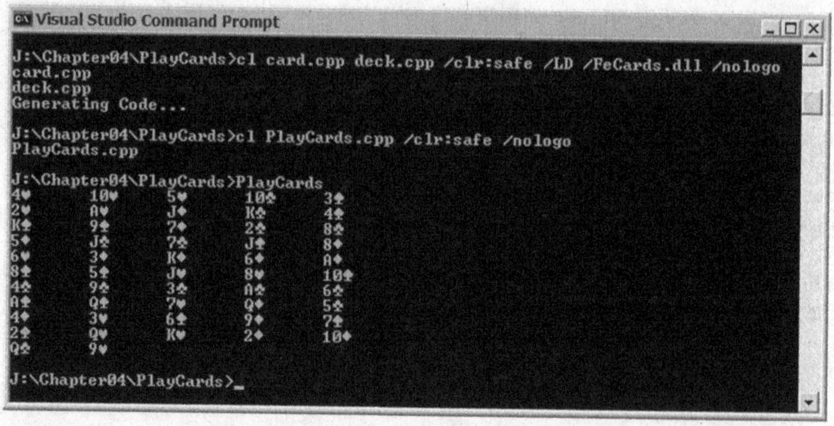

Figure 4-1. *Example results of PlayCards.exe*

Templates

Templates are a welcome addition to C++/CLI. I personally feel that this feature's omission contributed quite a bit to Managed Extensions for C++'s (C++/CLI's predecessor) lackluster adoption and C#'s rapid rise as the number one language for .NET development. Without templates, there was no real difference between the two languages. (The lack of ASP.NET support by C++/CLI may in the future be another major factor. With Managed Extensions for C++, there was at least partial support, but now with C++/CLI, there is no longer even partial support for ASP.NET.)

Though often overlooked by the novice C++ programmer, templates frequently become an often-used feature as a developer's skills in C++ improve. As a consequence of its strong ability to encourage code reusability, I am sure the same will hold true with C++/CLI.

There really isn't much difference between C++ and C++/CLI, so a developer who has experience in templates should feel right at home with the C++/CLI implementation. The important things that an experienced developer should be aware of are that templates are verifiable (safe) and only work within a single assembly. To perform template-like functionality across assemblies requires a .NET Framework 2.0 construct known as generics. I'll cover generics later in this chapter.

Okay, so what are templates? Templates are used as a compile-time technique that enables a programmer to specify, with a single set of code, a complete range of related functions and/or classes. Have you ever taken a piece of code, cut and pasted it somewhere else, and then just changed the data type(s) implemented within this code? Well, that is what templates do, but without the cut and paste.

There are types of C++/CLI templates (just as in standard C++): function templates and class templates. At first glance, both types of templates look quite complicated, but once you build one or two of them, you will see just how easy they actually are.

Function Templates

Function templates provide the ability to implement the same functionality on different data types. In ancient times, developers used to implement this using #define macro directives. Unfortunately, this method was not always type-safe and it was rather complex to write, especially if the macro was large. Function templates, on the other hand, have complete type checking, and the template function is nearly identical to a standard function. Also, compile-time error messages are detailed and noted on the line in the template where the error occurs. The #define macro directives have more cryptic error messages and appear where the macro is implemented but not where it is declared.

To implement a template, you need to create a regular function but replace the data types for which you want to replicate the functionality with a template data type. Then you prefix the function with a template header, within which you declare this template data type:

```
template <class T>
T min ( T a, T b)
{
    return (a < b) ? a : b;
}
```

> **Note** You can use any identifier for the template class, not just T as I do in the examples.

> **Note** Though I only use the class operator within the template statement, you can also use typename. Both are interchangeable.

By the way, here is the same code as a #define macro directive (yes, all the brackets are needed):

```
#define min(a,b) ((a) < (b)) ? (a) : (b)
```

Then you use the template just as you would any other function:

```
int a = 5;
int b = 6;
Console::WriteLine("The min of {0} and {1} is {2}", a, b, min(a,b));
```

The compiler will look at the function min and check to see if the data types are the same. If they are, it will generate an instance of a function to handle the function. For example, if a and b are int values, then code similar to the following will be generated:

```
int min ( int a, int b)
{
    return (a < b) ? a : b;
}
```

Be careful, though, because the template specifies that the data type of both parameters must be the same, given that only one type is specified within the template. If you were to implement the preceding template like this:

```
int a = 5;
double b = 6;
Console::WriteLine("The min of {0} and {1} is {2}", a, b, min(a,b));
```

the compiler would generate an error, as it would not be able to resolve the template type.

Templates allow you to specify multiple template types. You could go wild and instead declare the preceding template to support different data types, like this:

```
template <class T1, class T2>
T1 min ( T1 a, T2 b)
{
    return (T1)((a < b) ? a : b);
}
```

Then if you implemented the template using different data types, you would be fine.

Or would you? What happens if the type data types in the template could not be compared? For example, what would happen if the first data type was an int and the second a handle to String?

```
int a = 5;
String^ b = "Hi";
Console::WriteLine("The min of {0} and {1} is {2}", a, b, min(a,b));
```

The types are compared at compile time and will be found to be incompatible, and a compile-time error will be generated.

All the preceding implementation of the template functions has been implicit. It is also possible to implement the template explicitly. This is done by specifying the data type to use in square brackets after the function name within the function call. Now, because there is no longer any ambiguity of the data type being used, the explicit instantiation of the original min function template would compile.

```
int a = 5;
double b = 6;
Console::WriteLine("The min of {0} and {1} is {2}", a, b, min<double>(a,b));
```

Class Templates

The idea behind class templates is the same as function templates. This time, though, the template creates data type generic classes. Syntactically, the declaration of a class template is the same as a standard class, except that you prefix the class with a template statement and then use the data type specified by the prefix within the class declaration.

```
template <class T>
ref class Point2D
{
public:
    Point2D();
    T X;
    T Y;
    static Point2D^ operator*(const Point2D^ lhs, const T rhs);
};
```

The implementation of the template is a little more involved, as you need to also prefix the methods with the template statement and qualify the method with the class template followed by a template argument list. One thing I find a little odd about the class template implementation is that you don't need a template argument list when you use a template class within a method, but if you return a template class, you do. Take a closer look at the operator* method to see what I mean:

```
template <class T>
Point2D<T>::Point2D() : X((T)0), Y((T)0) {}

template <class T>
Point2D<T>^ Point2D<T>::operator*(const Point2D^ lhs, const T rhs)
{
    Point2D^ ret = gcnew Point2D();
    ret->X = lhs->X * rhs;
    ret->Y = lhs->Y * rhs;
    return ret;
}
```

Creating an instance of a class template is nearly as easy as creating an instance of a class. You simply need to explicitly specify the data type to be used by the template when you create the instance of the template class using a template argument list:

```
Point2D<double>^ TopLeft = gcnew Point2D<double>(10.5, 10.9);
```

That's it. From here on, you will be coding just as you would a standard class. One thing you need to note is that each time you create an instance of a template with different data type, you are creating a new copy of the class template or what is known as a *new generated class*.

Caution The definition and implementation of a class template must reside within the same file (usually a header file). The reason for this is that a generated class is created when an instantiation occurs during the compile and both the definition and implementation have to be available at that time.

Template Specialization and Partial Specialization

There will come a time when you are going to want to perform special actions when a certain data type is used within the class template. This is what is known as *template specialization*. For example, let's say your class will not work properly for a particular data type. By providing a specialization for the generation of that type, you could throw an exception notifying the implementer of the class template of the problem. (I cover exceptions later in this chapter.)

To create a template specialization, you simple create an additional copy of the class template but with an explicit data type in the template argument list:

```
template <>
ref class Point2D<char>
{
public:
    Point2D() { throw gcnew Exception("Data Type is too small"); }
};
```

You create an instance of a template specialization exactly like a class template:

```
Point2D<char>^ TopLeft = gcnew Point2D<char>(10.5, 10.9);
```

Because the compiler finds the specialized data type, it generates the specialization instance instead. A partial specialization is very similar to a specialization except that not all of the template data types are explicitly specified:

```
// template class
template <class T1, class T2>
ref class ACB
{
};

// partial specialization template
template <class T1>
ref class ABC<T1, char>
{
};

void main()
{
    // generates instance of template class
    ABC<int,int>^ templateClass = gcnew ABC<int,int>();

    // generates instance of partial specialization
    ABC<int,char>^ partialSpec = gcnew ABC<int,char>();
}
```

Template Parameters

Class templates have an additional construct that allows you to specify a default parameter to provide to the class. This comes in handy for things like preinitializing an array within the template. All default parameters are treated like const.

```
template <class T, int elements>
ref class X
{
private:
    static array<T>^ iArray = gcnew array<T>(elements);
public:
    X() {}
};
```

To create and instance of a template with a parameter, use the following syntax:

```
X<int,10> x;
// - or -
X<int,10>^ x = gcnew X<int,10>();
```

The managed heap declaration looks like a managed array declaration, doesn't it?

It is also possible to provide default data types and parameters:

```
template <class T = int, int elements = 10>
ref class X
{
};
```

Now, that everything is defaulted, you can declare the template, like this:

```
X<> x;
// - or -
X<>^ x = gcnew X<>();
```

Listing 4-8 is an example of both a function template and a very simple (read: incomplete) Point2D class template. The Point2D class template also has a specialization on the char data type, which throws an exception if implemented.

Listing 4-8. *Templates in Action*

```
using namespace System;

// Function Template  ---------------------------------------

template <class T>
T min ( T a, T b)
{
    return (a < b) ? a : b;
}

// Class Template  -----------------------------------------

template <class T>
ref class Point2D
{
```

```
public:
    Point2D();
    Point2D(T x, T y);

    T X;
    T Y;

    static Point2D^ operator-(const Point2D^ lhs, const Point2D^ rhs);
    static Point2D^ operator*(const Point2D^ lhs, const T rhs);

    virtual String^ ToString() override;
};

template <class T>
Point2D<T>::Point2D() : X((T)0), Y((T)0) {}

template <class T>
Point2D<T>::Point2D(T x, T y) : X(x), Y(y) {}

template <class T>
Point2D<T>^ Point2D<T>::operator-(const Point2D^ lhs, const Point2D^ rhs)
{
    Point2D^ ret = gcnew Point2D();

    ret->X = lhs->X - rhs->X;
    ret->Y = lhs->Y - rhs->Y;

    return ret;
}

template <class T>
Point2D<T>^ Point2D<T>::operator*(const Point2D^ lhs, const T rhs)
{
    Point2D^ ret = gcnew Point2D();

    ret->X = lhs->X * rhs;
    ret->Y = lhs->Y * rhs;

    return ret;
}

template <class T>
String^ Point2D<T>::ToString()
{
    return String::Format("X={0} Y={1}", X, Y);
}

// Class Template Specialization ---------------------------

template <>
ref class Point2D<char>
{
```

```cpp
public:
    Point2D() { throw gcnew Exception("Data Type is too small"); }
    Point2D(char x, char y) { throw gcnew Exception("Data Type is too small"); }
};

// main function  ---------------------------------------------

void main()
{
    int    a = 5;
    int    b = 6;
    double c = 5.1;

    Console::WriteLine("The min of {0} and {1} is {2}", a, b, min(a,b));
    Console::WriteLine("The min of {0} and {1} is {2}", a, c, min<double>(a,c));

    Console::WriteLine("----------------------------");

    Point2D<int>^ TopLeftI = gcnew Point2D<int>(10, 10);
    Point2D<int>^ BottomRightI = gcnew Point2D<int>(15, 20);

    Point2D<int>^ SizeI = BottomRightI - TopLeftI;
    Console::WriteLine(SizeI);

    SizeI = SizeI * 2;
    Console::WriteLine(SizeI);

    Console::WriteLine("----------------------------");

    Point2D<double>^ TopLeft = gcnew Point2D<double>(10.5, 10.9);
    Point2D<double>^ BottomRight = gcnew Point2D<double>(15.2, 20.3);

    Point2D<double>^ SizeD = BottomRight - TopLeft;
    Console::WriteLine(SizeD);

    SizeD = SizeD * 0.5;
    Console::WriteLine(SizeD);

    Console::WriteLine("----------------------------");

    try
    {
        Point2D<char>^ TopLeft = gcnew Point2D<char>(10, 10);
    }
    catch (Exception^ ex)
    {
        Console::WriteLine(ex->Message);
    }
}
```

Figure 4-2 shows the results of this little program.

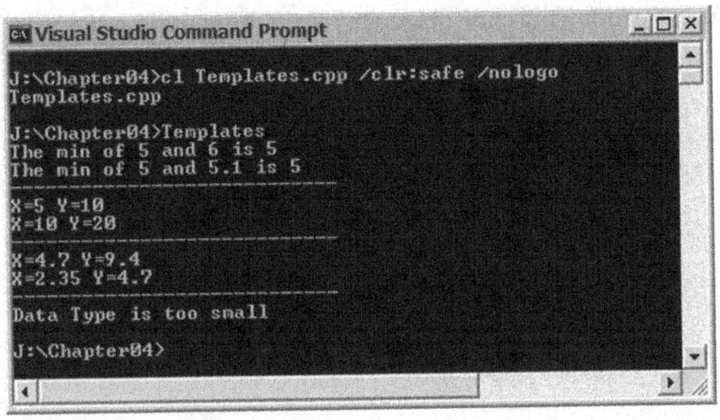

Figure 4-2. *Results of Templates.exe*

Generics

Let's get one thing straight right away. Generics are not .NET templates. Yes, they have a similar syntax to templates and some overlap of functionality, as both templates and generics make it possible to create data type generic types. But that is where the similarities end.

So what are generics? They are runtime, subtype constraint–based, instantiated data type, generic objects that are verifiable and have cross-language support. Okay, perhaps this is not the easiest definition to follow. Maybe it will be easier to understand if I compare and contrast a generic with a template, which it closely resembles.

A generic is syntactically coded in nearly an identical fashion as a template. The big differences are that specializations are not allowed and there are no default parameters. Oh, you also use the keyword generic instead of `template`. In other words, the basic generic is easier to code then a template:

```
generic<class K, class V>
ref class KVClass
{
public:
    property K Key;
    property V Value;
    KVClass(K key, V value);
};

generic<class K, class V>
KVClass<K,V>::KVClass(K key, V value)
{
    Key = key;
    Value = value;
}
```

The preceding code will generate an instance for any key/value data type pair. What happens if the generic will only work for a certain subset of data types? That is where the subtype constraint comes into play. Subtype constraints allow you to specify which base class and/or interfaces that each generic parameter supports.

A subtype constraint cannot be a sealed class or value type, including built-in types such as int or double. The reason is that value types and sealed classes cannot have derived classes; thus, only one class would ever be able to satisfy the subtype constraint—the value type or sealed class itself. If you think about it, you only have to rewrite the generic with the parameter replaced with the value type or sealed class to accomplish the same thing.

To code a subtype constraint, you use the following code placed between the generic statement and the class or method:

```
where type-parameter_1: [class constraint,] [interface constraint list]
//...
where type-parameter_N: [class constraint,] [interface constraint list]
```

or

```
generic<class K, class V>
    where K : IComparable
ref class KVClass
{
};

generic<class K, class V>
    where K : IComparable
V KVClass<K,V>::isGreater(KVClass ^in)
{
}
```

One major difference between generics and templates is when they are instantiated. For templates, it happens at compile time, whereas for generics, it happens at runtime. This difference is significant because instantiation at compile time means that the same template instantiated in two different assemblies results in two different types being generate. The reason is that all types are qualified by the assembly in which they are defined. In other words, the data type DType in assembly 1 is not the same as the data type DType in assembly 2, even if DType is defined exactly the same way in both assemblies. So, assembly 1's myTemplate<T> is a different type from assembly 2's myTemplate<T>. The generic, on the other hand, because it is instantiated at runtime, is able to create one specialization for all references.

Another difference between templates and generics is that only generics provide .NET cross-language support because other languages do not support templates. This means that a generic object created in C++/CLI can be used, for example, by C# or Visual Basic .NET.

Listing 4-9 is an example of a very simple (read: very incomplete) key/value pair generic. You will see in Chapter 7 that the .NET Framework provides a base class for you to inherit to build this type of generic.

Listing 4-9. *Generics in Action*

```
using namespace System;

// Generic Class ----------------------------------------

generic<class K, class V>
    where K : IComparable
ref class KVClass
{
public:
    property K Key;
    property V Value;
    KVClass(K key, V value);

    V isGreater(KVClass ^in);
};
```

```
generic<class K, class V>
KVClass<K,V>::KVClass(K key, V value)
{
    Key = key;
    Value = value;
}

generic<class K, class V>
    where K : IComparable
V KVClass<K,V>::isGreater(KVClass ^in)
{
    if (Key->CompareTo(in->Key) > 0)
        return Value;
    else
        return in->Value;
}

// main function ----------------------------------------

void main()
{
    KVClass<int,String^> ^a = gcnew KVClass<int,String^>(5, "Five");
    KVClass<int,String^> ^b = gcnew KVClass<int,String^>(6, "Six");

    Console::WriteLine(a->isGreater(b));

    KVClass<String^,int> ^t = gcnew KVClass<String^,int>("Tomato", 1);
    KVClass<String^,int> ^c = gcnew KVClass<String^,int>("Carrot", 2);

    Console::WriteLine(t->isGreater(c));
}
```

Figure 4-3 shows the results of this little program.

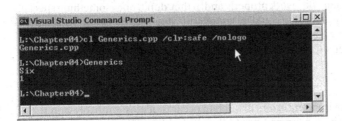

Figure 4-3. *Results of Generics.exe*

typedef

The typedef operator allows you to create new names for existing data types. These operators are extremely handy when it comes to arrays and templates, because they improve readability and simplify coding. For example, a typedef for an array of integers could be declared as

```
typedef array<int> intArray;
```

Now to create an instance of an array of five integers, you would simply code

```
intArray^ x = gcnew intArray(5);
```

Similarly, using `typedef` with class templates can make things easier to read. Instead of

```
Point2D<int>^
Point2D<double>^
```

from the preceding example, you could use the following:

```
typedef Point2D<int> Int2DPoint;
typedef Point2D<double> Double2DPoint;
```

You could then create instances of the templates like this:

```
Int2DPoint^ TopLeftI = gcnew Int2DPoint(10, 10);
Double2DPoint^ TopLeftD = gcnew Double2DPoint(10, 10);
```

The `typedef` operator also has one more important benefit. If the data type defined by the `typedef` were ever to change, you would only have to make the change within the `typedef` statement. If you don't use the `typedef`, you would have to scan through all your code looking for and then changing all instances of the data type.

However, the `typedef` operator can also make your code complicated if not used properly, because there is nothing stopping you from renaming all your date types to meaningless names. For example, you could rename all your data types to animal names. (I'm not sure why you would do this, but you could.)

```
typedef char mouse;
typedef short cat;
typedef int elephant;
// and so on ...
```

Exceptions

Error handling should be nothing new to software developers. All programmers have written code that verifies that the processes in their code work properly and, if they don't, does something special to correct them. Wouldn't it be nice if nothing could go wrong with your programs, and you could write code without having to worry about whether something might go wrong?

Well, you can use exceptions to do that—sort of. Along with the exception's normal role of handling all unforeseen problems, it can actually allow you to code in a manner as if nothing will go wrong and then capture all the possible errors at the end. This separation of error handling from the main code logic can make the program much easier to work with. It eliminates multiple layers of `if` statements with the sole purpose of trapping errors that might occur (but most probably won't).

With C++/CLI, exceptions have been taken one step further than with traditional C++. Exceptions can now be thrown across language boundaries. That means that if, for example, you code a `ref class` in C++/CLI, and the `ref class` is used in some C# code, any exceptions thrown in the C++/CLI class can be caught by the C# code. A major benefit of this is there is that no need for checking the `HResult` for errors any longer (if implemented using exceptions). You just have to code as if things worked correctly, because if they didn't, the error would be caught by the exception handler. I won't go into multilanguage programming in this book, but rest assured it does work.

Basics of Exception Handling

Coding for exceptions is very easy. You break your code up into three parts: the code for successful execution, the errors, and the code to clean up afterward. In C++/CLI, these three parts are known as the try block, the catch block, and the finally block. I will describe the try and catch blocks now and examine the finally block at the end of this section.

The process for handling exceptions is a little tricky for new developers because the linear flow of the code is broken. Whenever an error occurs, the program throws an exception. At this point, normal execution flow of the program ends, and the program goes in search of a handler for the exception that it threw. You'll see how the program searches for exceptions later, in the section "Catching Multiple Exceptions." If it doesn't find an exception, the program terminates. Before C++/CLI, this termination would have left programs without cleaning up after themselves, but if you code with ref classes, you don't have to worry about this.

Exceptions also have to be thrown within a try block, or they will immediately terminate without searching for a handler. The try block is simply a block of code enclosed in curly brackets and prefixed with the keyword try:

```
try
{
    // code body where exception can be thrown
}
```

After the try block are one or more catch blocks. Each catch block handles a different type of error. A catch block looks similar to a function with one parameter, except that the function name is always catch, there is no return type, and the parameter is the exception type to trap.

```
catch (ExceptionType e1)
{
    // code to handle exception
}
// repeat for all specific exception types
catch (ExceptionType eN)
{
    // generic code to handle exception
}
```

Listing 4-10 shows a simple example of an exception. I noted in Chapter 3 that the safe_cast operator throws a System::InvalidCastException when it is unable to convert from one try to another. This coding example shows how to capture this exception so that it can be handled more elegantly than the abrupt termination that would normally happen. The safe_cast operator is actually to smart to be used directly as it knows that class X and class Y are not related, so I had to use the C-cast style type cast, which internally uses the safe_cast operator.

Listing 4-10. *CatchException.exe: Simple Exception Handling Example*

```cpp
using namespace System;

ref class X {};
ref class Y {};

void main()
{
    X ^x = gcnew X;

    try
    {
        Y ^y = (Y^)x;
        Console::WriteLine("No Exception");  // Should not execute
    }
```

```
catch (InvalidCastException ^e)
{
    Console::WriteLine("Invalid Cast Exception");
    Console::WriteLine(e->StackTrace);
}
}
```

Figure 4-4 shows the results of this little program.

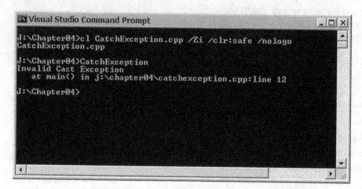

Figure 4-4. *Results of CatchException.exe*

.NET Framework Base Class: Exception Classes

The .NET Framework has an extensive set of exceptions that it may throw. You'll encounter two different types of exceptions while using .NET:

- ApplicationException
- SystemException

System::ApplicationException is the base class of those exceptions that are user-defined or, in other words, the ones that you have defined yourself.

System::SystemException, on the other hand, handles exceptions created within the CLR, for example, exceptions caused by stream I/O, databases, security, threading, XML, and so on. You can be sure that if the program has aborted as a result of a system problem, you can catch it using the generic System::SystemException.

Both of these exceptions derive from the System::Exception class, which is the root of all .NET exceptions. The System::Exception class provides many useful properties (see Table 4-4) to help resolve any exceptions that might occur.

Table 4-4. *Key System::Exception Member Properties*

Property	Description
Helplink	The Uniform Resource Name (URN) or Uniform Resource Locator (URL), if appropriate, to a help file providing more information about the exception.
InnerException	This property gives access to the exception that caused this exception, if any.
Message	A textual description of the error.

Table 4-4. *Key System::Exception Member Properties*

Property	Description
Source	The name of the object, assembly, or application that caused the exception.
StackTrace	A text string of all the method calls on the stack made before triggering the exception.
TargetSite	The name of the method that triggered the exception.

SystemException

You can't begin to explore all the exceptions that the .NET Framework class library provides to developers. Even the following illustration, which displays some of the more common exceptions, shows only the tip of the iceberg.

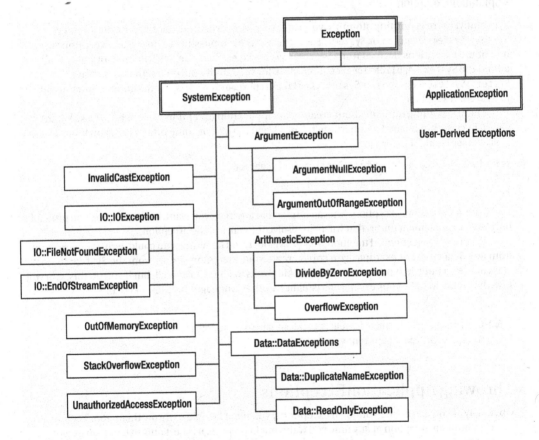

The .NET Framework provides developers with a huge set of classes. If something could go wrong, the .NET Framework class library provides an exception for it. As you can see from the preceding illustration, the names of the exceptions are self-explanatory, and if you add to them the properties mentioned previously, you have a great tool for finding where your application threw its exception and why.

The best resource to use to explore exceptions is the documentation provided by the .NET Framework. You should start your search by looking up System.Exception. From there you should quickly be able to navigate to the exception in question.

There is nothing special about catching exceptions thrown by the system. As long as you place the methods that might throw an exception within a try block, all you have to do is catch the system-thrown exception. Here is an example of exception handling, about as simple as it comes:

```
try
{
    // Methods that throw OutOfMemoryException
}
catch (OutOfMemoryException *oome) // If a method throws an exception
{                                  // Execution will continue here
    // Process exception
}
```

ApplicationException

Truthfully, there is nothing stopping you from throwing exceptions derived from the class System::SystemException or System::Exception. It is even possible to derive an exception from one of the exceptions derived from System::SystemException. The .NET Framework only really added the System::ApplicationException class for readability purposes. In fact, neither System::SystemException nor System::ApplicationException adds any additional functionality to System::Exception.

There is nothing difficult about creating an application exception class. It is just a standard C++/CLI class, but instead of inheriting from System::Object or some other class, you inherit from System::ApplicationException.

```
ref class MyException : public ApplicationException
{
};
```

Within the custom exception, you can implement anything you want, but in practice, you probably only want to implement things that will help resolve the cause of the exception.

If you are an experienced traditional C++ developer, you know that you could derive your exception from any data type. For example, you could create your exception simply from the System::Object class or even a built-in type such as int. This still works in C++/CLI as well, but if you do this, you will lose the ability to have your exceptions caught by other languages besides C++/CLI.

■ **Note** All exceptions you create for your applications should be inherited from System::ApplicationException.

Throwing ApplicationExceptions

Obviously, if you can create your own exceptions, you must be able to throw them, too. Technically, you can throw an exception at any time you want, but in practice, it is best only to throw an exception when something in your program fails unexpectedly and normal process flow can no longer continue. The reason is that the processing of an exception has a lot of overhead, which can slow the program down when executing. Often, it is better to use if statements to process errors.

Syntactically, throwing an exception is very easy. Simply throw a new instance of an exception class. In other words, add code with the following syntax:

```
throw gcnew <Exception-Class>(<constructor-parameters>);
```

or, for example:

```
throw gcnew ApplicationException("Error Message");
```

If you create your own derived exception, just replace ApplicationException with it and pass any parameters to its constructor—if the construct has any parameters, that is.

The actual throw statement does not have to be physically in the try block. It can be located in any method that is executed within the try block or any nested method that is called within a try block.

Listing 4-11 shows how to create a custom exception from the .NET Framework's System::ApplicationException. Notice that because you're using the System namespace, you don't have to prefix the exceptions with System::. This program simply loops through the for loop three times, throwing an exception on the second iteration.

Note that the try block is within the for loop. This is because although you can resolve an exception and allow code to continue processing, the only place you are allowed to start or resume a try block is from its beginning. So, if the for loop was found within the try block, there would be no way of resuming the loop, even if you used the dreaded goto statement to try to jump into the middle of the try block.

Listing 4-11. *ThrowDerived.exe: Throwing an Exception*

```cpp
using namespace System;

ref class MyException : public ApplicationException
{
public:
    MyException( String ^err );
};

MyException::MyException(System::String ^err) : ApplicationException(err)
{
}

void main()
{
    for (int i = 0; i < 3; i++)
    {
        Console::WriteLine("Start Loop");
        try
        {
            if (i == 0)
            {
                Console::WriteLine("\tCounter equal to 0");
            }
            else if (i == 1)
            {
                throw gcnew MyException("\t**Exception** Counter equal to 1");
            }
            else
            {
                Console::WriteLine("\tCounter greater than 1");
            }
        }
```

```
        catch (MyException ^e)
        {
            Console::WriteLine(e->Message);
        }
        Console::WriteLine("End Loop");
    }
}
```

Figure 4-5 shows the results of this little program.

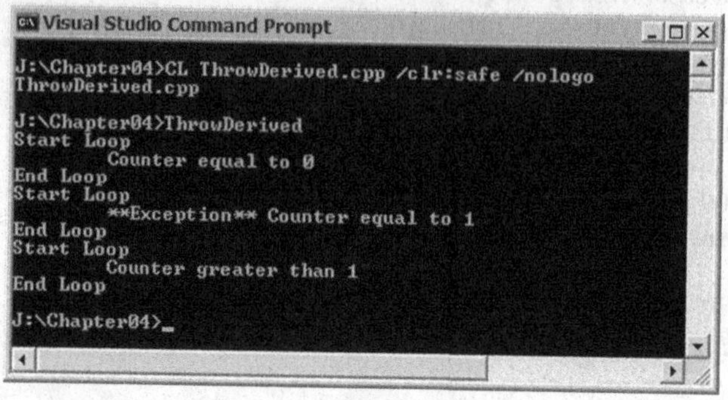

Figure 4-5. *Results of ThrowDerived.exe*

As you can see, there is nothing spectacular about throwing an exception of your own. It is handled exactly the same way as a system exception, except now you are catching an exception class you created instead of one created by the .NET Framework.

Rethrowing Exceptions and Nested try Blocks

Sometimes your program may catch an exception that it cannot completely resolve. In these cases, the program might want to rethrow the exception so that another catch block can resolve the exception.

To rethrow an exception, simply add this statement within the catch block:

```
throw;
```

Once you rethrow the exception, exactly the same exception continues to make its way up the stack, looking for another catch block that matches the exception. Rethrowing an exception only works with nested try blocks. It will not be caught in a catch block at the same level as it was originally caught and thrown but instead will be caught in a catch block at a higher level.

There is no limit on nesting try blocks. In fact, it is a common practice to have one try block that surrounds the entire program within the main() function and to have multiple try blocks surrounding other areas of the code where an exception has a higher probability of occurring. This format allows the program to catch and resolve exceptions close to where the exception occurred, but it still allows the program to catch other unexpected exceptions before the program ends, so that the program may shut down more gracefully.

Listing 4-12 is a contrived example showing an exception being rethrown within nested try blocks. Of course, nesting try blocks immediately together like this doesn't make much sense.

Listing 4-12. *RethrowException.exe: Rethrowing an Exception*

```
using namespace System;

void main()
{
    try
    {
        try
        {
            throw gcnew ApplicationException("\t***Boom***");
            Console::WriteLine("Imbedded Try End");
        }
        catch (ApplicationException ^ie)
        {
            Console::WriteLine("Caught Exception ");
            Console::WriteLine(ie->Message);
            throw;
        }
        Console::WriteLine("Outer Try End");
    }
    catch (ApplicationException ^oe)
    {
        Console::WriteLine("Recaught Exception ");
        Console::WriteLine(oe->Message);
    }
}
```

Figure 4-6 shows the results of this little program.

Figure 4-6. *Results of RethrowException.exe*

Catching Multiple Exceptions

So far, you have only dealt with a single catch block associated with a try block. In reality, you can have as many catch blocks associated with a try block as there are possible exception classes that can be thrown by the try block. (Actually, you can have more, but catching exceptions that are not thrown by the try block is a waste of time and code.)

Using multiple catch blocks can be a little trickier in C++/CLI than in traditional C++ because all exceptions are derived from a single class. The order in which the catch blocks are placed after the try block is important. For catch blocks to work properly in C++/CLI, the most-derived class must appear first and the least-derived class or the base class, System::Exception, must appear last.

For example, System::IO::FileNotFoundException must be caught before
System:IO::IOException is caught, which in turn must be caught before System::SystemException is
caught, which ultimately must be caught before System::Exception. You can find the order of system
exception inheritance in the documentation provided by the .NET Framework.

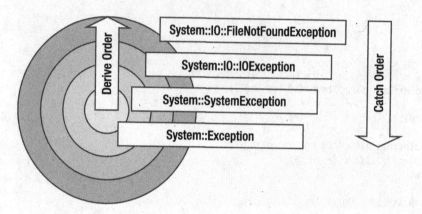

Listing 4-13 shows the correct order of catching exceptions of derived exception class, but this
time they are all derived from the System::ApplicationException class. You might want to change
the order of the catch blocks to see what happens.

Listing 4-13. *MultiException.exe: Catching Multiple Exceptions*

```
using namespace System;

/// <Summary>Base Class</Summary>
ref class LevelOneException : public ApplicationException
{
public:
    LevelOneException( String ^err );
};

LevelOneException::LevelOneException(String ^err) : ApplicationException(err)
{
}


/// <Summary>Inherited Class</Summary>
ref class LevelTwoException : public LevelOneException
{
public:
    LevelTwoException( String ^err );
};

LevelTwoException::LevelTwoException(String ^err) : LevelOneException(err)
{
}

/// <Summary>Catching multiple exceptions</Summary>
void main()
{
```

```
for (int i = 0; i < 4; i++)
{
    Console::WriteLine("Start Loop");
    try
    {
        if (i == 1)
            throw gcnew ApplicationException("\tBase Exception Thrown");
        else if (i == 2)
            throw gcnew LevelOneException("\tLevel 1 Exception Thrown");
        else if (i == 3)
            throw gcnew LevelTwoException("\tLevel 2 Exception Thrown");

        Console::WriteLine("\tNo Exception");
    }
    catch (LevelTwoException ^e2)
    {
        Console::WriteLine(e2->Message);
        Console::WriteLine("\tLevel 2 Exception Caught");
    }
    catch (LevelOneException ^e1)
    {
        Console::WriteLine(e1->Message);
        Console::WriteLine("\tLevel 1 Exception Caught");
    }
    catch (ApplicationException ^e)
    {
        Console::WriteLine(e->Message);
        Console::WriteLine("\tBase Exception Caught");
    }
    Console::WriteLine("End Loop");
}
}
```

Figure 4-7 shows the results of this little program.

Figure 4-7. *Results of MultiException.exe*

Catching All Previously Uncaught Exceptions

If you want to correctly code C++/CLI code, which is used in a multilanguage environment, then the easiest way of catching all exceptions is simply to add the catching of System::Exception to the end of your catch block, because all .NET exceptions—of both system and application origin—are derived from this class.

There is also another way of catching all uncaught exceptions, even those not derived from System::Exception. It is simply a catch block without an exception call. In the class's place is an ellipsis:

```
catch (...)
{
}
```

Unsafe Code The catch(...) block is an unsafe coding construct. You can only throw or catch handles to a ref class with /clr:safe.

This form of catch block doesn't provide much in the way of information to help determine what caused the exception, because it doesn't have as a parameter any type of exception to derive from. Thus, there's no way to print out the stack or messages associated with the exception that's generated. All you actually know is that an exception occurred.

In C++/CLI, this form of catch block should probably only be used as a last resort or during testing, because if this catch block is executed, your code will not work properly in the .NET portable managed multilanguage environment anyway. Of course, if your code is not destined for such an environment, then you may need to use this form of catch block.

The usual reason that this type of exception occurs in C++/CLI is that the developer forgot to derive the exception class from System::ApplicationException. Listing 4-14 shows this occurring.

Listing 4-14. *CatchAll.exe: Catching All Exceptions*

```
using namespace System;

ref class MyDerivedException : public ApplicationException
{
public:
    MyDerivedException( String ^err );
};

MyDerivedException::MyDerivedException(String ^err) : ApplicationException(err)
{
}

ref class MyException  // Not derived from Exception class
{
};
```

```
void main()
{
    for (int i = 0; i < 4; i++)
    {
        Console::WriteLine("Start Loop");
        try
        {
            if (i == 1)
                throw gcnew ApplicationException("\tBase Exception");
            else if (i == 2)
                throw gcnew MyDerivedException("\tMy Derived Exception");
            else if (i == 3)
                throw gcnew MyException();

            Console::WriteLine("\tNo Exception");
        }
        catch (ApplicationException ^e)
        {
            Console::WriteLine(e->Message);
        }
        catch (...)
        {
            Console::WriteLine("\tMy Exception");
        }
        Console::WriteLine("End Loop");
    }
}
```

Figure 4-8 shows the results of this little program.

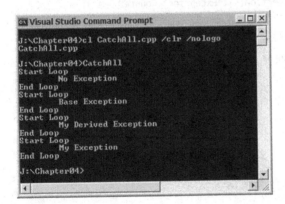

Figure 4-8. *Results of CatchAll.exe*

Executing Code Regardless of an Exception

There are times when code needs to be run at the completion of a try block, whether the try block completed cleanly or threw an exception. For example, you may want to close a file stream or database that has been open in the try block. Up until now, if you threw an exception, there was no way to ensure that such code would always run unless you put the close statement at the end of each of the try and catch blocks.

With C++/CLI, it is now possible to remove this redundant coding by adding a finally block after the last catch block. The syntax for a finally block is the following:

```
finally
{
    // Code to always be executed
}
```

All code within the finally block will always be executed after the completion of the try block or after the completion of the caught catch block.

As you can see in Listing 4-15, the finally block is run both at the successful completion of the try block and after the System::ApplicationException catch block is executed.

Listing 4-15. *Finally.exe: The finally Block*

```
using namespace System;

void main()
{
    for (int i = 0; i < 3; i++)
    {
        Console::WriteLine("Start Loop");
        try
        {
            if (i == 0)
            {
                Console::WriteLine("\tCounter = 0");
            }
            else if (i == 1)
            {
                throw gcnew ApplicationException("\t*Exception* Counter = 1");
            }
            else
            {
                Console::WriteLine("\tCounter greater than 1");
            }
        }
        catch (ApplicationException ^e)
        {
            Console::WriteLine(e->Message);
        }
        finally
        {
            Console::WriteLine("\tDone every time");
        }
        Console::WriteLine("End Loop");
    }
}
```

Figure 4-9 shows the results of this little program.

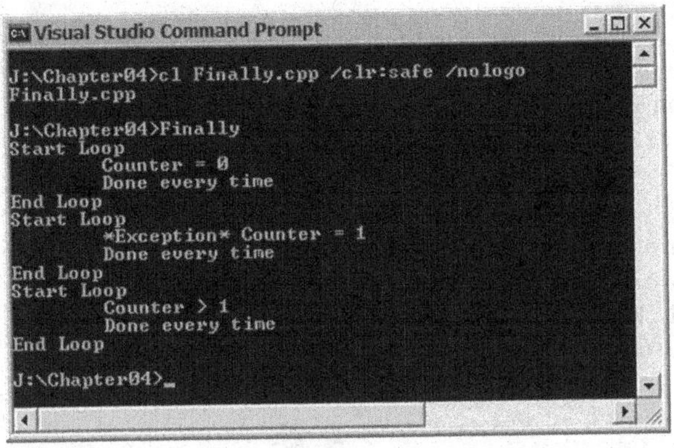

Figure 4-9. *Results of Finally.exe*

Delegates and Events

Delegates and events are completely new concepts to the traditional C++ developer. Truth be told, both provide the same functionality, allowing functions to be manipulated as reference handles. Because a handle can be assigned to more than one value in its lifetime, it is possible to have functions executed based on whichever function was last placed in the handle.

For those of you with a C++ background, you might notice that this object-oriented approach is very similar to function pointers. Where they differ is that delegates and events are ref classes and not pointers, and delegates and events only invoke global functions or member methods of ref classes.

You might be wondering, if they all do the same thing, why introduce the new concepts? Remember that a key aspect of .NET is language independence. Unfortunately, function pointers are strictly a C++ language feature and are not easily implemented in other languages, especially languages that have no pointers. Also, function pointers are far from easy to implement. Delegates and events were designed to overcome these problems.

Delegates

A *delegate* is a ref class that accepts and then invokes one or more methods that share the same signature from global functions or other classes that have methods with this same signature.

The .NET Framework supports two forms of delegates:

- `System::Delegate`: A delegate that accepts and invokes only a single method.

- `System::MulticastDelegate`: A delegate that accepts and invokes a chain of methods. A MulticastDelegate can perform something known as *multicast chaining*, which you can think of as a set of delegates linked together and then later, when called, executed in sequence.

C++/CLI only supports multicast delegates, but this really isn't a problem because there's nothing stopping a multicast delegate from accepting and invoking only one method.

The creating and implementing of delegates is a three-part process with an optional fourth part if multicast chaining is being implemented:

1. Create the delegate.

2. Create the global function(s) or member method(s) to be delegated.

3. Place the method on the delegate.

4. Combine or remove delegates from the multicast chain.

Creating a Delegate

The code involved in creating a delegate is extremely easy. In fact, it is just a method prototype prefixed with the keyword delegate. By convention, a delegate is suffixed with "delegate" but this is not essential, for example:

```
delegate void SayDelegate(String ^name);
```

What happens in the background during the compilation process is a lot more complex. This statement actually is converted to a class with a constructor to accept delegated methods and three member methods to invoke these methods. Figure 4-10 shows the effects of the resulting compilation by running the program ILDASM in Listing 4-16.

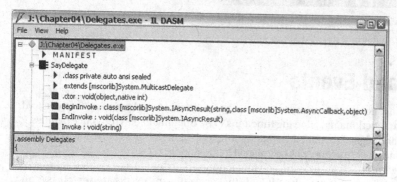

Figure 4-10. *ILDASM snapshot of the generated delegate class*

Creating a Method to Be Delegated

There is nothing special about creating a global function or member method for delegating. The only criteria are that it has the same signature as the delegate and that if it is a member method that it has public scope. The method can be a global function:

```
void SayHello(String ^name)
{
    Console::Write("Hello there ");
    Console::WriteLine(name);
}
```

a static member method:

```
ref class Talkative
{
public:
    static void SayHello(String ^name);
};
```

or an instance member method:

```
ref class Talkative
{
public:
    void SayStuff(String ^name);
};
```

Placing a Method on the Delegate

This is the least obvious part of the delegating process. The reason is that you need to implement the auto-generated constructor of the delegate class. If you were not aware that a delegate was a class, then the syntax would appear quite confusing. But, because you are, it should be obvious that all you are doing is creating a new instance of the delegate class for each method that you want to delegate.

There are two constructors for a delegate. The first takes the address of the method as a parameter. This constructor is used when the method is a global function or a static member method:

```
delegate-name (address-of-method);
```

The other constructor is for instance member methods and takes two parameters, the handle to the instance of the class within which the member method can be found and fully referenced address of the method:

```
delegate-name (handle-of-object, address-of-method);
```

For example, here are delegations of a global function and a static and instance member methods:

```
// Global Function
SayDelegate ^say = gcnew SayDelegate(&SayHello);

// Static member functions
SayDelegate ^hello = gcnew SayDelegate(&Talkative::SayHi);

// Instance member functions
Talkative ^computer = gcnew Talkative();
SayDelegate ^stuff = gcnew SayDelegate(computer, &Talkative::SayStuff);
```

Combining and Removing Delegates from a Multicast Chain

These are the trickiest parts of the delegating process, which doesn't say much. The reason they're tricky is that they require the use of two auto-generated methods or two overloaded operators:

- Combine() method or + operator
- Remove() method or - operator

These methods or operators make sense as you are combining (or adding) and removing (or subtracting) methods from the delegate class.

The syntax for both combining and removing is exactly the same, except for, of course, the operator of the method being called:

```
// create initial delegate
SayDelegate say = gcnew SayDelegate(&SayHello);

// add Static member function
say = say + gcnew SayDelegate(&Talkative::SayHi);
// -or-
say += gcnew SayDelegate(&Talkative::SayHiThere);

// remove delegate
say = say - gcnew SayDelegate(&Talkative::SayHi);
// -or-
say -= gcnew SayDelegate(&Talkative::SayHiThere);
```

The + operator takes the two delegates, chains them together, and then places them on a delegate. The - operator does the opposite of the + operator. It removes the specified delegate from the delegate multicast chain and then places the new chain on a delegate.

I never use the auto-generated methods, because the overloaded operators are so much easier to code. But here they are if you want to use them:

```
SayDelegate ^say =
    (SayDelegate^)(Delegate::Combine(say, gcnew SayDelegate(&SayHello)));

SayDelegate ^say =
    (SayDelegate^)(Delegate::Remove(say, gcnew SayDelegate(&SayHello)));
```

See what I mean? It's a lot more coding, and a type cast is required.

Invoking a Delegate

The process of invoking a delegate is quite simple, but not obvious if you are not aware that a delegate is a class. All you have to do is either call the auto-generated member method Invoke or call the class itself as if it were a method with the parameter list that you specified when you created the delegate:

```
say->Invoke("Mr Fraser");
// -or-
say("Stephen");
```

There is no difference in the syntax, whether you invoke one method or a whole chain of methods. The Invoke method simply starts at the top of the chain and executes methods until it reaches the end. If there is only one method, then it only executes that one method.

Listing 4-16 is a complete example of creating, adding, removing, and invoking delegates. The example simply creates a delegate, adds four different types of methods to the delegate chain, and invokes the delegate. Then it removes two of the methods from the delegate chain and invokes the delegate again, but this time the delegate contains only two methods.

Listing 4-16. *Delegates.exe: Programming Delegates*

```
using namespace System;

/// <summary>A Delegate that talks a lot</summary>
delegate void SayDelegate(String ^name);

/// <summary>A friendly function</summary>
void SayHello(String ^name)
{
    Console::Write("Hello there ");
    Console::WriteLine(name);
}

/// <summary>A talkative class</summary>
ref class Talkative
{
public:
    static void SayHi(String ^name);
    void SayStuff(String ^name);
    void SayBye(String ^name);
};
```

```
void Talkative::SayHi(System::String ^name)
{
    Console::Write("Hi there ");
    Console::WriteLine(name);
}

void Talkative::SayStuff(System::String ^name)
{
    Console::Write("Nice weather we are having. Right, ");
    Console::Write(name);
    Console::WriteLine("?");
}

void Talkative::SayBye(System::String ^name)
{
    Console::Write("Good-bye ");
    Console::WriteLine(name);
}

/// <summary>Delegates in action</summary>
void main()
{
    SayDelegate^ say;

    // Global Function
    say = gcnew SayDelegate(&SayHello);

    // add Static member function
    say += gcnew SayDelegate(&Talkative::SayHi);

    Talkative ^computer = gcnew Talkative();

    // add instance member functions
    say = say + gcnew SayDelegate(computer, &Talkative::SayStuff);
    say += gcnew SayDelegate(computer, &Talkative::SayBye);

    // invoke delegate
    say->Invoke("Stephen");

    Console::WriteLine("-----------------------------");

    // remove a couple of methods
    say = say - gcnew SayDelegate(&Talkative::SayHi);
    say -= gcnew SayDelegate(computer, &Talkative::SayBye);

    // invoke delegate again with two fewer methods
    say("Stephen");
}
```

Figure 4-11 shows the results of this little program.

Figure 4-11. *Results of Delegates.exe*

Events

An *event* is a specific implementation of delegates. You'll see it used quite extensively when I describe Windows Forms in Chapters 9 and 10. For now, you can explore what events are and how they work without worrying about the .NET Framework event model.

In simple terms, events allow one class to trigger the execution of methods found in other classes without knowing anything about these classes or even from which classes it is invoking the method. This allows a class to execute methods and not have to worry about how, or even if, they are implemented. Because events are implemented using multicast delegates, it is possible for a single class to call a chain of methods from multiple classes.

There are always at least two classes involved with events. The first is the source of the event. This class generates an event and then waits for some other class, which has delegated a method to handle the event, to process it. If there are no delegated methods to process the event, then the event is lost. The second and subsequent classes, as was hinted previously, receive the event by delegating methods to handle the event. Truthfully, only one class is needed to handle an event, given that the class that created the event could also delegate a method to process the event. But why would you want to do this, when a direct call to the method could be used, thus avoiding the event altogether? And it would be much more efficient.

Building an Event Source Class

Before you create an event source class, you need to define a delegate class on which the event will process. The delegate syntax is the same as was covered previously. In fact, there is no difference between a standard delegate and one that handles events. To differentiate between these two types of delegates, by convention delegates that handle events have a suffix of "Handler":

```
delegate void SayHandler(String ^name);
```

Once you have the delegate defined, you can then create an event source class. There are basically two pieces that you will find in all event source classes: the event and an event trigger method. Like delegates, events are easy to code but do a little magic in the background. To create an event, include within a ref class in a public scope area a delegate class declaration prefixed by the keyword event:

```
ref class EventSource
{
public:
    event SayHandler^ OnSay;
//...
};
```

Simple enough, but when the compiler encounters this, it is converted into three member methods:

- add_<delegate-name>: A public member method that calls the Delegate::Combine method to add delegated receiver class methods. To simplify the syntax, use the overloaded += operator instead of calling add_<delegate-name> directly.

- remove_<delegate-name>: A public member method that calls the Delegate::Remove method to remove delegated receiver class methods. To simplify the syntax, use the overloaded -= operator instead of calling remove_<delegate-name> directly.

- raise_<delegate-name>: A protected member method that calls the Delegate::Invoke method to call all delegated receiver class methods. This method is protected so that client classes cannot call it. It can only be called through a managed internal process.

Figure 4-12 is an ILDASM snapshot that shows the methods that were created by the event keyword within the event source class in Listing 4-17.

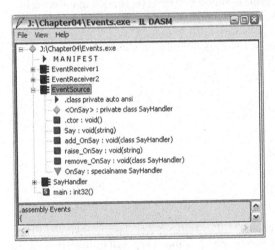

Figure 4-12. *ILDASM snapshot of the generated event member methods*

Finally, now that you have an event, you need a way to trigger it. The triggering event can be almost anything. In Web Forms, the triggering event will be handled by things such as mouse clicks and key presses. In this case, you will simply call the delegate directly:

```
ref class EventSource
{
public:
    event SayHandler^ OnSay;

    void Say(String ^name)
    {
        OnSay(name);
    }
};
```

Notice that I don't have to make sure that the event is not a nullptr. With C++/CLI, the event has a default value that does nothing, so we don't have to make the check. In fact, if you check to see if the event is unassigned by comparing the event to nullptr, you get the compile-time error C3918. This code generates the following error:

```
void Say(String ^name)
{
    if (OnSay != nullptr)  // Error C3918 is generated
        OnSay(name);
}
```

■ **Caution** If you are converting Managed Extensions for C++ code to C++/CLI code, you will have to check that you don't compare an event or delegate to a `nullptr`, because this was how the validation of the event or delegate was originally handled.

Building Event Receiver Class(es)

One or more classes can process an event. The process for delegating a member class to an event is identical for each class. Other than the simplified syntax, you will find that event handling and delegate processing are the same. First, you create the member method to delegate. Then you combine it on the event handler.

The first thing you need to do is create a public `ref class` member method to be delegated to the event handler. Nothing is new here:

```
ref class EventReceiver
{
public:
//...
    void SayBye(String ^name)
    {
        Console::Write("Good-bye ");
        Console::WriteLine(name);
    }
};
```

Then, to combine this method on the event handler, the event receiver class must know with which event source class it will be associated. The easiest way to do this is to pass it through the constructor. To avoid a null handle error, check to make sure that the handle was passed. I could make more thorough validations, such as verifying the type of class, but this is enough to convey the idea.

Now that you have the event source class and a member method to place, it is simply a matter of creating a new instance of a delegate of the event's delegate type and combining it. Or, in this case, using the operator += to combine the new delegate to the event within the source event class:

```
ref class EventReceiver
{
    EventSource ^source;
public:
    EventReceiver(EventSource ^src)
    {
        if (src == nullptr)
            throw gcnew ArgumentNullException("Must pass an Event Source");
        source = src;
        source->OnSay += gcnew SayHandler(this, &EventReceiver::SayBye);
    }
//...
};
```

What if you have a delegated method that you no longer want handled by the event? You would remove it just as you would a standard delegate. The only difference is that you can now use the -= operator:

```
source->OnSay -= gcnew SayHandler(this, &EventReceiver::SayStuff);
```

Implementing the Event

You now have both a source and a receiver class. All you need to do is create instances of each and then call the event trigger method.

```
void main()
{
    EventSource ^source     = gcnew EventSource();
    EventReceiver ^receiver = gcnew EventReceiver(source);

    source->Say("Mr Fraser");
}
```

Listing 4-17 shows all of the code needed to handle an event. This time, the event source class has two event receiver classes. The event is triggered twice. The first time, all delegates are combined and executed. The second time, one of the delegates is removed. You might notice that the member methods are very familiar.

Listing 4-17. *Events.exe: Programming Events*

```
using namespace System;

delegate void SayHandler(String ^name);

ref class EventSource
{
public:
    event SayHandler^ OnSay;

    void Say(String ^name)
    {
        OnSay(name);
    }
};

ref class EventReceiver1
{
    EventSource ^source;
public:

    EventReceiver1(EventSource ^src)
    {
        if (src == nullptr)
            throw gcnew ArgumentNullException("Must pass an Event Source");

        source = src;
```

```
            source->OnSay += gcnew SayHandler(this, &EventReceiver1::SayHello);
            source->OnSay += gcnew SayHandler(this, &EventReceiver1::SayStuff);
        }

        void RemoveStuff()
        {
            source->OnSay -= gcnew SayHandler(this, &EventReceiver1::SayStuff);
        }

        void SayHello(String ^name)
        {
            Console::Write("Hello there ");
            Console::WriteLine(name);
        }

        void SayStuff(String ^name)
        {
            Console::Write("Nice weather we are having. Right, ");
            Console::Write(name);
            Console::WriteLine("?");
        }
    };

    ref class EventReceiver2
    {
        EventSource ^source;
    public:

        EventReceiver2(EventSource ^src)
        {
            if (src == nullptr)
                throw gcnew ArgumentNullException("Must pass an Event Source");

            source = src;

            source->OnSay += gcnew SayHandler(this, &EventReceiver2::SayBye);
        }

        void SayBye(String ^name)
        {
            Console::Write("Good-bye ");
            Console::WriteLine(name);
        }
    };

    void main()
    {
        EventSource ^source = gcnew EventSource();

        EventReceiver1 ^receiver1 = gcnew EventReceiver1(source);
        EventReceiver2 ^receiver2 = gcnew EventReceiver2(source);

        source->Say("Mr Fraser");
```

```
Console::WriteLine("-------------------------------");

receiver1->RemoveStuff();

source->Say("Stephen");
}
```

Figure 4-13 shows the results of this little program.

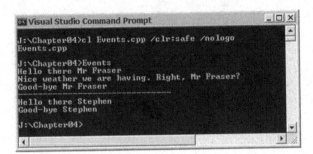

Figure 4-13. *Results of Events.exe*

Summary

In this chapter, you looked at some more advanced C++/CLI language topics. You started with the preprocessor directives, and then you moved on to multifile software development. Next, you covered templates, typedef, and exceptions, and finally, you ended with delegates and events.

This chapter covered a lot of new ground for the traditional C++ developer, though much of it had a very familiar flavor to it. You use much of this chapter later in the book, so a good understanding of these topics is essential.

Okay, you have finally covered C++/CLI as a language. In the next chapter, you make your first real foray into the world of .NET software development by looking at the .NET Framework class library.

PART 2

.NET Framework Development in C++/CLI

CHAPTER 5

∎∎∎

The .NET Framework Class Library

To put it bluntly, the .NET Framework class library is just plain huge. One chapter could never do it justice. There are, in fact, several books devoted solely to describing all the interfaces, structures, enumerations, classes, methods, variables, and so on, that are contained within this library. This chapter's goal is to focus on giving you a head start in learning how to navigate through this massive library.

Even though the library is big, it is well organized and (gasp!) well documented. Once you understand the basics of how the library is organized, it will be easy for you to locate what you are looking for. It should also be quite simple to figure out if what you are looking for is not included in the library.

I just briefly touch upon the contents of the class library here. In the following chapters, I delve deeper into many specific areas in the library.

Library Organizational Structure

The first thing you need to know about the .NET Framework class library is that it is an object-oriented tree derived from a single root: System::Object. The next important characteristic is that the .NET Framework class library strictly follows the rules specified by the common language specification (CLS), covered in Chapter 1. The key rules that you should be aware of are as follows:

- Global functions and variables are not allowed.

- There is no imposed case sensitivity (a consequence of the need to support languages like Visual Basic .NET), so all exposed types differ by more than their case. In other words, all public or protected members differ by more then just case.

- The primitive types allowed as parameters conform to the CLS, namely, Byte, Int16, Int32, Int64, Single, Double, Boolean, Char, Decimal, IntPtr, and String.

- Variable-length parameter lists to methods are not allowed. Fixed-length arrays are used as parameters instead.

- Pointers are not allowed.

- Class types must inherit from a CLS-compliant class.

- Only single class inheritance is allowed, although multiple inheritance of interfaces is permitted.

Another important aspect of the .NET Framework class library is that the current version is broken up into nearly 100 namespaces. Unlike many other libraries, the component identifiers used for the namespaces are self-describing and thus have the benefit of making it easy to understand what functionality resides within a namespace.

You should be aware that even though namespaces in the .NET Framework class library appear to be broken up into a hierarchy, there is, in fact, no actual "class inheritance hierarchy" that corresponds directly to this "namespace hierarchy." Instead, the namespaces are simply a way of organizing classes into common functionality groups. For example, there is a "namespace hierarchy" of System::Collections::Specialized, but many of the classes found in the System::Collections::Specialized namespace don't inherit from System::Collections.

The .NET Framework class library is physically made up of multiple assembly .dlls, which you have to add references to in your code either using the #using statement or in the program's reference properties, if using Visual Studio 2005. An assembly does not necessarily correspond directly to a namespace, as an assembly may contain multiple namespaces. Also, some of the namespaces spread across multiple assemblies. This does complicate things, as there is no one-to-one correlation, but the .NET Framework class library has placed the most commonly used classes into one assembly: mscorlib.dll. Then, it spread out the less common classes into assemblies made up of common functionality.

Unfortunately, I know of no way to easily figure out which assembly contains which classes. I've tried to help you in this regard by pointing out the necessary assemblies to include for each namespace. The only other way I know of to figure out which assembly is needed (other than looking it up in the .NET documentation) is to look for the C1190 error when compiling (I suppose "linking" is more accurate). This error tells you which assembly is missing.

Library Namespaces

It's unlikely that you'll use every namespace in the .NET Framework class library. (That's not to say you won't—it's just unlikely.) Instead, you'll probably work with the subset of namespaces described in the sections that follow.

I will start with the root namespace System and then progress alphabetically through the most common namespaces. This chapter will not provide you everything you need to implement the classes within a namespace. Instead, it will give you an understanding of what functionality resides within it. If you want a deeper understanding of all the details of the classes within a namespace (I do not cover the namespace in the subsequent chapters), then I suggest you peruse the documentation provided with the .NET Framework, as it is remarkably well done.

System

The System namespace is the root of the .NET Framework class library namespace hierarchy. The namespace is defined within the mscorlib.dll assembly.

Unlike the other namespaces of the .NET Framework class library, which focus on a particular area of functionality, the System namespace is more a mishmash of core data types and basic functionality that is needed by the rest of the namespace hierarchy.

The most important class within the System namespace is probably the Object class because it is the root of all other classes found within the class library. When you create C++/CLI ref classes of your own, the Object class is inherited by default if you do not specify a parent class. Remember that because C++/CLI ref classes can only inherit from other C++/CLI ref classes, ultimately your class will inherit the Object class.

Some of the other common functional areas covered by the System namespace are as follows:

- Primitive types, such as Byte, Int32, Double, and String
- Arrays
- Data type conversion

- Attributes
- Delegates
- Enums
- Events
- Exceptions
- Garbage collection
- Math
- Operating system information
- Random numbers

As you can see, you have already covered most of these areas in previous chapters.

Normally, a developer would allow garbage collection to be handled automatically by the CLR, because it's a well-tuned process. For some applications, there might be occasions when garbage collection simply doesn't run often enough or at the times wanted by the developer. For these cases, the .NET Framework class library provides the System::GC class. This class doesn't allow the programmer the ability to change the garbage collection process, but it changes the triggering process and helps determine when memory is garbage collected. As a C++/CLI developer, you will probably have little need for the System::GC class given that you now have deterministic cleanup at your disposal. Other .NET languages are not so lucky.

The Math class is an important class that I haven't yet covered. It's made up of a set of static data type overloaded member methods such as Abs(), Exp(), Max(), and Sin(). These methods are easy to use. For example, to find the square root of a number, simply code the following:

```
double val = 16;
double root = System::Math::Sqrt( val );
```

Another class that can come in handy is System::OperatingSystem. This class provides information such as the version and platform identifier. The System::Version class is used to hold the four-part version (Build, Major, Minor, and Revision) used by the .NET Framework.

Because I am a games program developer at heart, one of the first classes I went in search of was the random-number generator. System::Random provides random numbers in both integer and floating-point formats.

```
System::Random ^rand = gcnew System::Random();
int  intRandomNumber = rand->Next(1, 10);  // between 1 and 10 inclusive
double doubleRandomNumber = rand->NextDouble(); // between 0.0 and 1.0
```

System::Collections

There are, in fact, three sets of collections available to the .NET Framework programmer: System::Collections, System::Collections::Specialized, and System::Collections::Generic. As the namespaces suggest, the first set contains standard collection types, the second contains collection types with a more specific purpose, and the third set contains collections specifically targeting the new generic class introduced in the .NET Framework version 2.0. You will find the more common and frequently used System::Collections in the mscorlib.dll assembly, whereas the System::Collections::Specialized and System::Collections::Generic are in the system.dll assembly.

Because collections are an integral part of most .NET software development, Chapter 7 goes into many of these collections in much greater detail.

Table 5-1 shows you at a glance what collection types are found in the System::Collections namespace.

Table 5-1. *Collection Types Found Within System::Collections*

Collection	Description
ArrayList	An array that grows dynamically
BitArray	An array of bit values (either 1 or 0)
Hashtable	A collection of key/value pairs organized based on a hash code of the key
Queue	A collection of first-in-first-out objects
SortedList	A collection of key/value pairs sorted by key and accessible by either key or index value
Stack	A collection of first-in-last-out objects

Table 5-2 lists all the collection types that you will find in System::Collection::Specialized. As you can see, you will probably use these collections less often, but the .NET Framework class library is nice enough to provide them if you ever end up needing to use one of them.

Table 5-2. *Collection Types Found Within System::Collections::Specialized*

Collection	Description
BitVector32	A small collection that will represent Boolean or small integers within 32 bits of memory
HybridDictionary	A collection that switches from a list dictionary when small to a hash table when larger
ListDictionary	A singular link list recommended for lists of ten objects or less
NameValueCollection	A collection of string key/value pairs organized on the string key and accessible by either string key or index
StringCollection	A collection of strings
StringDictionary	A hash table with the key strongly typed to be a string

Table 5-3 lists all the collections that you will find in System::Collections::Generic. Most likely, as you become more familiar with generics, these collections will become your primary choice.

■ **Note** After claiming that the .NET Framework strictly adheres to the CLS rules, Microsoft goes ahead and makes me a liar. System::Collections::Generic classes are not CLS compliant. Personally, I think the CLS rules will be expanded to include generics, but we shall see.

Table 5-3. *Collection Types Found Within System::Collections::Generic*

Collection	Description
Collection<T>	A base class for generic collections from which users are urged to derive their own specialized container classes.
Dictionary<K,V>	A collection of key/value paired generic objects that are organized based on the key and retrieved as a KeyValuePair<K,V> struct.
KeyedCollection<K,V>	A base class for generic collections using key/value pairs from which users are urged to derive their own specialized container classes.
LinkedList<T>	A doubly (forward and backward) linked list generic objects.
List<T>	An array of generic objects that grows dynamically.
Queue<T>	A collection of first-in-first-out generic objects.
ReadOnlyCollection<T>	A base class for a generic read-only collection from which users are urged to derive their own specialized container classes. A collection that is read-only is simply a collection with a wrapper that prevents modifying the collection.
SortedDictionary<K,V>	A collection of key/value paired generic objects that are sorted based on the key.
Stack<T>	A collection of first-in-last-out generic objects.

System::Data

The System::Data namespace is the root for all ADO.NET classes found in the .NET Framework class library. ADO.NET is the data access technology written for the .NET Framework and replaces the use of ADO where it is important to remain entirely within .NET. Accessing a database is a very common practice in software development, so you might think that it would be included in the mscorlib.dll default assembly, but you would be wrong. You need to reference two different assemblies. The first is the System.Data.dll assembly, which makes sense now that you know that it's a separate assembly. The second is the System.Xml.dll assembly. I go into detail about why this assembly is needed in Chapter 12. A simple reason is that ADO.NET uses a lot of XML and exposes member methods that use XML. To include these assemblies, if you don't recall, simply add these lines to the top of your source:

```
#using <System.data.dll>
#using <System.Xml.dll>
```

The System::Data namespace comprises most of the classes that make up the ADO.NET architecture. The classes that represent the specific databases to which ADO.NET will connect are missing. These classes are known in ADO.NET-speak as *data providers*. Currently, ADO.NET supports multiple data providers. The data providers found in the System::Data namespace are the following:

- System::Data::SqlClient: For Microsoft SQL Server database access
- System::Data::SqlClientCe: For Microsoft SQL Server CE Edition database access
- System::Data::Odbc: For ODBC database access
- System::Data::OleDb: For OLE DB database access
- System::Data::OracleClient: For Oracle database access

Many classes are contained within the System::Data namespace. Depending on your database needs, you may require the use of many of these classes. Most likely, though, you'll only have to rely on a few. Table 5-4 provides a list of the more common classes that you may encounter. But don't despair immediately if the specific database access functionality you require isn't in this table. Chances are that there's a class within this namespace that does what you need because System::Data is quite thorough.

Table 5-4. *Common System::Data Namespace Classes*

Class Name	Description
Constraint	A constraint enforced on a data column—for example, a foreign key constraint or a unique key constraint.
DataColumn	A strong typed column in a data table.
DataRelation	A relationship between two data tables within the data set.
DataRelationCollection	A collection of all the data relations for a data set.
DataRow	A row of data in a data table.
DataSet	An in-memory cache of all retrieved data from the data provider.
DataTable	An in-memory cache of a single data table within the data set.
DataTableCollection	A collection of all data tables within the data set.
DataView	A customized view of a data table used for sorting, filtering, searching, editing, and navigation. This view can be bound to higher-level constructs such as GUI tables and lists.

You will look at the System::Data and its five data provider namespaces when you learn about ADO.NET in great detail in Chapter 12.

System::Deployment

The System::Deployment namespace comprises all of the classes needed to programmatically update an application supporting Microsoft's ClickOnce deployment model. Being a very specialized namespace, it was placed within its own assembly, System.Deployment.dll. To add the namespace, the following code is required at the top of your source:

```
#using <System.Deployment.dll>
```

In a nutshell, you use the class ApplicationDeployment to check for the existence of new updates over the Internet or intranet. If they are available, the class downloads and installs them on the client machine, either synchronously or asynchronously and automatically or user controlled.

System::Diagnostics

Executing a program in the CLR environment has its advantages, one of those being readily available diagnostic information. True, it is possible to code your traditional C++ to capture diagnostic information, but with .NET, you get it virtually free with the classes within the System::Diagnostics namespace. The only catch is that because this namespace is not used that frequently, you need to implement the System.dll assembly:

```
#using <System.dll>
```

The diagnostic functionality available ranges from simply allowing viewing of event log files and performance counters to allowing direct interaction with system processes. An added bonus is that this namespace provides classes to handle debugging and tracing.

Two main classes handle event logs in the System::Diagnostics namespace. EventLog provides the ability to create, read, write, and delete event logs or event sources across a network. EntryWrittenEventHandler provides asynchronous interaction with event logs. Numerous supporting classes provide more detailed control over the event logs.

It is possible to monitor system performance using the class PerformanceCounter. It is also possible to set up your own custom performance counters using the class PerformanceCounterCategory. You can only write to local counters, but the restriction is eased when it comes to reading counters. Of course, you need to have the right to access the remote machine from where you want to read the counter.

The System::Diagnostics namespace provides an amazing amount of power when it comes to processes. For example, the Process class has the ability to start, monitor, and stop processes on your local machine. In fact, the Process class can also monitor processes on remote machines. Added to this are the ProcessThread and ProcessModule classes, which allow you to monitor the process's threads and modules. It is also possible to control how a process runs by having control over things such as arguments and environment variables, and input, output, and error streams using the ProcessStartInfo class.

Almost every programmer uses debug and/or trace statements within his code. So common is the practice that the .NET Framework class library includes the Debug and Trace classes to ease your coding life. Syntactically, the Debug and Trace classes are nearly identical. The difference between them lies in the time of compilation and the current development environment being used. Trace statements are executed no matter what the environment (unless you code otherwise), whereas debug statements are only included and executed while within the Debug environment.

Table 5-5 provides you with a quick lookup table of the classes you might find useful within the System::Diagnostics namespace.

Table 5-5. *Common System::Diagnostics Namespace Classes*

Class Name	Description
Debug	Methods and properties to help debug a program
Debugger	Provides communication to a debugger
DefaultTraceListener	The default output method for Trace
EntryWrittenEventHandler	Handler to provide asynchronous interaction with event logs
EventLog	Provides interaction with event logs
PerformanceCounter	Provides access to system performance counters
PerformanceCounterCategory	Creates and provides access to custom performance counters
Process	Provides access to local and remote processes and the ability to start and stop local processes
ProcessModule	Provides access to process modules
ProcessStartInfo	Provides control over the environment for which a process starts
ProcessThread	Provides access to process threads
Trace	Provides methods and properties to help trace a program

System::DirectoryServices

System::DirectoryServices is a small namespace providing easy access to Active Directory. Not the most commonly used namespace, it has been placed in its own assembly, System.Directoryservices.dll. To add the namespace, you require the following code at the top of your source:

```
#using <System.Directoryservices.dll>
```

It is assumed that you have prior knowledge of Active Directory before you use the class; in a nutshell, here is how to use the class. First, you use the class DirectoryEntry constructor to get access to a node or object within Active Directory. Then, with the DirectoryEntry node and some help classes, you are capable of activities such as creating, deleting, renaming, setting passwords, moving a child node, and enumerating children.

You can use the classes in this namespace with any of the Active Directory service providers. The current providers are

- Internet Information Services (IIS)
- Lightweight Directory Access Protocol (LDAP)
- Novell NetWare Directory Service (NDS)
- Windows NT

Another class that you might find of some use in System::DirectoryServices is the DirectorySearcher class. This class allows you to perform a query against an Active Directory hierarchy. Unfortunately, as of now, only LDAP supports DirectorySearcher.

The book *Pro .NET Directory Services Programming* by Mikael Freidlitz, Ajit Mungale, Erick Sgarbi, Noel Simpson, and Jamie Vachon (Apress, 2003) covers in extreme detail how to use this namespace. Though the book is written for C# and VB .NET developers, I think you can still use it to get the information you need.

System::Drawing

Computer software without some form of graphics is nearly a thing of the past, especially in the PC world. The .NET Framework relies on a technology named GDI+ to handle graphics. GDI+ is easy to use. It is designed to handle the myriad graphic adapters and printers in a device-independent fashion, thus saving you from having to worry about coding for each graphic device on your own. Of course, this is not a new concept; Windows has had a Graphical Device Interface (GDI) since its earliest versions. Those of you from the GDI world should see a considerable simplification of how you now have to code graphics. But you will also find a huge increase in added functionality.

System::Drawing provides the core graphic classes of GDI+, whereas the following four other child namespaces provide more specialized graphics capabilities:

- System::Drawing::Drawing2D: Adds advanced two-dimensional (2D) and vector graphics
- System::Drawing::Imaging: Adds advanced GDI+ imaging
- System::Drawing::Printing: Adds print-related services
- System::Drawing::Text: Adds advanced GDI+ typography

Every System::Drawing namespace requires that you add the System.Draw.dll assembly to the top of your source:

```
#using <System.Drawing.dll>
```

I go into GDI+ software development in detail in Chapter 11, but for those of you who can't wait that long, here's a brief summary of the functionality.

The core of all GDI+ classes can be found in the System::Drawing namespace. This large namespace contains classes to handle things ranging from a point on the graphics device all the way up to loading and displaying a complete image in many graphic file formats, including BMP, GIF, and JPEG.

The key to all graphics development is the aptly named Graphics class. This class basically encapsulates the graphics device—for example, the display adaptor or printer. With it you can draw a point, line, polygon, or even a complete image. When you use the Graphics class with other System::Drawing classes, such as Brush, Color, Font, and Pen, you have the means to create amazing and creative images on your display device.

Though you can do almost any 2D work you want with System::Drawing, the .NET Framework class library provides you with another set of classes found within the System::Drawing::Drawing2D that allows for more fine-tuned 2D work. The basic principle is similar to the "connect-the-dots" pictures that you did as a kid. The image you want to draw is laid out in 2D space by drawing straight and curved lines from one point to another. Images can be left open or closed. They can also be filled. Filling and line drawing can be done using a brush and/or using a color gradient.

The System::Drawing namespace can handle most imaging functionality. With the System::Drawing::Imaging namespace, you can add new image formats that GDI+ does not support. You can also define a graphic metafile that describes a sequence of graphics operations that can be recorded and then played back.

GDI+ can display (or, more accurately, print) to a printer. To do so is very similar to displaying to a monitor. The difference is that a printer has many different controls that you will not find on a monitor—for example, a paper source or page feed. All these differences were encapsulated and placed into the System::Drawing::Printing namespace.

Nearly all the functionality to handle text is located within the System::Drawing namespace. The only thing left out and placed in the System::Drawing::Text namespace is the ability to allow users to create and use collections of fonts.

System::EnterpriseServices

The System::EnterpriseServices namespace provides the ability for .NET Framework objects to interface with COM+ objects. COM+ objects are a key component of Microsoft's enterprise-wide application architecture. You can think of COM+ as an extension of COM into the enterprise environment.

With the System::EnterpriseServices namespace, it is fairly easy to use .NET Framework objects within enterprise applications. Table 5-6 shows some of the more common classes and attributes within the System::EnterpriseServices namespace.

Every System::EnterpriseServices namespace requires that you add the System. Enterpriseservices.dll assembly to the top of your source:

```
#using <System.Enterpriseservices.dll>
```

Table 5-6. *Common System::EnterpriseServices Namespace Classes and Attributes*

Class Name	Description
ApplicationActivationAttribute	An attribute that enables you to specify whether components in the assembly run in the creator's process (Library) or in a system process (Server)
ContextUtil	A class made up several static members from which you retrieve contextual information about the COM+ object
EventClassAttribute	An attribute that specifies that the object is an Event class
JustInTimeActivationAttribute	An attribute that turns just-in-time (JIT) activation on or off
SecurityIdentity	A class that contains information regarding the identity assumed by a COM+ object
SecurityRoleAttribute	An attribute that configures a role of an application or component
ServicedComponent	A base class for all classes using COM+ services
SharedProperty	A class that provides access to a shared property
SharedPropertyGroup	A class that provides access to a collection of shared properties
SharedPropertyGroupManager	A class that controls the access to shared properties
TransactionAttribute	An attribute that specifies the type of transaction that is available to the attributed object (Disabled, NotSupported, Required, RequiredNew, and Supported)

System::Globalization

The System::Globalization namespace contains classes that define culture-related information, such as language, currency, numbers, and calendar. Because globalization is a key aspect of .NET, the namespace was included within the mscorlib.dll assembly.

I cover globalization in Chapter 18, when I go into assembly programming. The CultureInfo class contains information about a specific culture, such as the associated language, the country or region where the culture is located, and even the culture's calendar. Within the CultureInfo class, you will also find reference to the date, time, and number formats the culture uses. Table 5-7 shows some of the more common classes within the System::Globalization namespace.

Table 5-7. *Common System::Globalization Namespace Classes*

Class Name	Description
Calendar	Specifies how to divide time into pieces (e.g., weeks, months, and years)
CultureInfo	Contains specific information about a culture
DateTimeFormatInfo	Specifies how dates and times are formatted
NumberFormatInfo	Specifies how numbers are formatted

Table 5-7. *Common System::Globalization Namespace Classes*

Class Name	Description
RegionInfo	Contains information about the country and region
SortKey	Maps a string to its sort key
TextInfo	Specifies the properties and behaviors of the writing system

System::IO

If you are not using sockets or a database to retrieve and store data, then you are most likely using file and/or stream input and output (I/O). Of course, it is completely possible that you are using sockets, a database, and file and stream I/O within the same application. As you can guess by the name System::IO, it handles the .NET Framework library class's file and stream I/O. To access System::IO, you need to reference the mscorlib.dll assembly:

```
#using <mscorlib.dll>
```

Typically when you deal with the System::IO namespace's classes, you are working with files and directories on your local machine and network, or streams of data probably via the Internet. These, however, are not the only uses of the classes found within the System::IO namespace. For example, it is possible to read data from and write data to computer memory, usually either a string buffer or a specific memory location.

You learn about the .NET Framework class library's I/O capabilities in some detail in Chapter 8. For now, Table 5-8 shows some of the more common classes that you might come across in the System::IO namespace.

Table 5-8. *Common System::IO Namespace Classes*

Class Name	Description
BinaryReader	Reads in .NET primitive types from a binary stream.
BinaryWriter	Writes out .NET primitive types to a binary stream.
Directory	A collection of static methods for creating, moving, and enumerating directories.
DirectoryInfo	A collection of instance methods for creating, moving, and enumerating directories.
File	A collection of static methods for creating, copying, deleting, moving, and opening files. It also can be used in the creation of a FileStream.
FileInfo	A collection of instance methods for creating, copying, deleting, moving, and opening files. It also can be used in the creation of a FileStream.
FileNotFoundException	An exception that is thrown when a file on a disk is not found.
FileStream	Provides support for both synchronous and asynchronous read and write operations to a stream.
FileSystemWatcher	Monitors and then raises events for file system changes.
IOException	An exception that is thrown when an I/O exception occurs.

Table 5-8. *Common System::IO Namespace Classes (Continued)*

Class Name	Description
MemoryStream	Provides support for reading and writing a stream of bytes to memory.
Path	Provides support for operations on a String that contains a file or directory.
StreamReader	Reads a UTF-8 encoded byte stream from a TextReader.
StreamWriter	Writes a UTF-8 encoded byte stream to a TextWriter.
StringReader	Reads a String using a TextReader.
StringWriter	Writes a String using a TextWriter.
TextReader	An abstract reader class that can represent a sequence of characters.
TextWriter	An abstract writer class that can represent a sequence of characters.

System::IO::Ports

The System::IO::Ports namespace provides the developer complete access to the computer's serial port. System::IO::Ports is primarily made up of the one class SerialPort, which presents assorted functionality like synchronous and event-driven I/O, and access to serial driver properties. The SerialPort class also provides a method to allow stream access to the serial ports of the computer.

To access System::IO::Ports, you need to reference the System.dll assembly near the top of your code:

```
#using <System.dll>
```

This was not added until .NET Framework version 2.0, which is a surprising oversight by Microsoft.

System::Management

The System::Management namespace provides access to a large amount of information about the system, devices, and applications maintained within the Windows Management Instrumentation (WMI) infrastructure. The System::Management allows you to query for information like the free space remaining on the disk, CPU utilization, shared device names, and so forth.

You will predominately use classes derived from ManagementObjectSearcher, ManagementQuery, and ManagementEventWatcher to get information for both managed and unmanaged components maintained within the WMI infrastructure.

Though the System::Management namespace appears to be simple, it is actually deceptively tricky to use. In fact, *.NET System Management Services* by Alexander Golomshtok (Apress, 2003) covers how to use this namespace in great detail, to help you over the learning curve. Though the book is written for C# developers, I think you can still use it to get the information you need.

To access System::Management, you need to reference the System.Management.dll assembly near the top of your code:

```
#using <System.Management.dll>
```

Table 5-9 shows some of the more common classes that you might come across in the `System::Management` namespace.

Table 5-9. *Common System::Management Namespace Classes*

Class Name	Description
EventQuery	Represents a WMI event query. Instances of this class or derived classes from it are used in `ManagementEventWatcher` to subscribe to WMI events
ManagementClass	Represents a management class
ManagementEventWatcher	Used to temporarily subscribe to event notifications based on a specified `EventQuery`
ManagementNamedValueCollection	Represents a collection of key/value pairs containing contextual information to WMI operations
ManagementObject	Represents a data management class
ManagementObjectCollection	Represents a collection data management class retrieved from WMI
ManagementObjectSearcher	This collection retrieves a `ManagementObjectCollection` based on a specific query
ManagementPath	Used to build and parse paths to a specific WMI object
ManagementQuery	An abstract class used to build all management query objects
PropertyData	Represents a specific WMI object property
PropertyDataCollection	Represents a collection of properties about a WMI object
QualifierData	Represents a specific WMI object qualifier
QualifierDataCollection	Represents a collection of qualifiers about a WMI object

System::Net

This namespace will be hidden from most Web developers using .NET, because they will most likely use ASP.NET's higher-level extraction of Internet communication. For those of you who are more familiar with the networks, the .NET Framework class library has provided several namespaces.

To access both the `System::Net` hierarchy of namespaces, you need to reference the System.dll assembly near the top of your code:

```
#using <system.dll>
```

The `System::Net` namespace provides a simple programming interface for many of today's network protocols. It enables you to do things such as manage cookies, make DSN lookups, and communicate with HTTP and FTP servers. If that is not intimate enough for you, then the `System::Net::Sockets` namespace provides you with the ability to program at the sockets level. I cover network programming in detail in Chapter 17.

For those of you who want to program your network at this lower level, Table 5-10 provides a list of all the namespaces that make up the System::Net hierarchy.

Table 5-10. *System::Net Hierarchy Namespaces*

Namespace	Description
System::Net	A simple programming interface for many of the protocols used on networks today
System::Net::Cache	A set of types used to define cache policies for resources obtained using the WebRequest and HttpWebRequest
System::Net::Configuration	A set of types used to access and update configuration settings for the System::Net namespace hierarchy
System::Net::Mail	A simple programming interface for sending electronic mail to a Simple Mail Transfer Protocol (SMTP) server for delivery
System::Net::Mime	A set of types used to define Multipurpose Internet Mail Exchange (MIME) headers
System::Net::NetworkInformation	A simple programming interface for retrieving information about your network like network traffic data, statistics, and address change information
System::Net::Security	A simple programming interface for secured data transfer
System::Net::Sockets	A simple programming interface for Windows Sockets (Winsock)

System::Reflection

Most of the time when you develop code, it will involve static loading of assemblies and the data types found within. You will know that, to execute properly, application X requires class Y's method Z. This is pretty standard and most programmers do it without thinking.

This is the normal way of developing with the .NET Framework class library as well. There are times, though, that a developer may not know which class, method, or other data type is needed for successful execution until the time that the application is running. What is needed is dynamic instance creation of data types. With the .NET Framework class library, this is handled by the classes within the System::Reflection namespace found within the mscorlib.dll assembly:

```
#using <mscorlib.dll>
```

The System::Reflection namespace provides a class that encapsulates assemblies, modules, and types. With this encapsulation, you can now examine and load classes, structures, methods, and so forth. You can also create dynamically an instance of a type and then invoke one of its methods, or access its properties or member variables.

I explore `System::Reflection` in more detail when you examine assembly programming in Chapter 18. Table 5-11 shows some of the more common classes that you might use within the `System::Reflection` namespace.

Table 5-11. *Common System::Reflection Namespace Classes*

Class Name	Description
Assembly	Defines an assembly
AssemblyName	Provides access to all the parts of an assembly's name
AssemblyNameProxy	A remotable version of `AssemblyName`
Binder	Selects a method, property, and so forth, and converts its actual argument list to a generic formal argument list
ConstructorInfo	Provides access to the constructor's attributes and metadata
EventInfo	Provides access to the event's attributes and metadata
FieldInfo	Provides access to the field's attributes and metadata
MemberInfo	Provides access to the member's attributes and metadata
MethodInfo	Provides access to the method's attributes and metadata
Module	Defines a module
ParameterInfo	Provides access to the parameter's attributes and metadata
Pointer	Provides a wrapper class for a pointer
PropertyInfo	Provides access to the property's attributes and metadata
TypeDelegator	Provides a wrapper for an object and then delegates all methods to that object

System::Resources

The .NET Framework can handle resources in several different ways: in an assembly, in a satellite assembly, or as external resource files and streams. The handling of resources within the .NET Framework class library for any of these three ways lies in the classes of the `System::Resources` namespace. Handling resources is a very common task, so it was placed within the mscorlib.dll assembly:

```
#using <mscorlib.dll>
```

Resources can be fixed for an application divided by culture. I examine resources programming with assembly programming in Chapter 18. You will be dealing mostly with three classes within the `System::Resources` namespace, as shown in Table 5-12.

Table 5-12. *Common System::Resources Namespace Classes*

Class Name	Description
ResourceManager	Provides the ability to access culture-specific resources from an assembly or satellite assembly. It can also read from a specified resource file or stream.
ResourceReader	Provides the ability to read from a specified resource file or stream.
ResourceWriter	Provides the ability to write to a specified resource file or stream.

System::Runtime::InteropServices

The System::Runtime::InteropServices namespace provides a wide variety of members that support COM interoperability and platform invoke services.

.NET has not exposed the entire Win32. But all is not lost, because the System::Runtime::InteropServices namespace provides the DLLImportAttribute and some helper attributes to call into these APIs or any other C DLL API.

Developers have made a huge investment in developing COM objects, and it would be quite a waste of effort to rewrite the objects into .NET object. Because of this, the System::Runtime::InteropServices namespace was created to provide types to make interfacing with COM objects extremely easy.

Interfacing with C DLLs and COM objects is explored in more detail with advanced unsafe programming in Chapter 21. Table 5-13 shows some of the more common classes that you might use within the System::Runtime::InteropServices namespace.

To access System::Runtime::InteropServices, you need to reference the mscorlib.dll assembly:

```
#using <mscorlib.dll>
```

Table 5-13. *Common System::Runtime::InteropServices Namespace Classes*

Class Name	Description
ClassInterfaceAttribute	Used to indicate the type of interface that will be generated for the public member types exposed by a managed type to a COM
ComDefaultInterfaceAttribute	Used to specify a default interface exposed to the COM
ComRegisterFunctionAttribute	Used to specify the custom method to call when you register an assembly for use with the COM
ComSourceInterfacesAttribute	Used to identify a list of interfaces that are exposed as COM event sources for the class
ComUnregisterFunctionAttribute	Used to specify the custom method to call when you unregister an assembly for use with the COM
DispIdAttribute	Used to specify the COM dispatch identifier (DISPID) of a method, field, or property

Table 5-13. *Common System::Runtime::InteropServices Namespace Classes*

Class Name	Description
DllImportAttribute	Used to indicate that the method is exposed by an unmanaged dynamic-link library (C DLL) as a static entry point and thus can be called by the platform invoke services (PInvoke)
GuidAttribute	Used to supply an explicit System::Guid to a class interface or type library when an automatic GUID is undesirable
IDispatchImplAttribute	Used to indicate which IDispatch implementation the CLR uses when exposing dual interfaces and dispinterfaces to COM
InAttribute	Used to indicate that data should be marshaled only from the caller to the callee
InterfaceTypeAttribute	Used to indicate how a managed interface is exposed to COM (dual, dispatch-only, or IUnknown)
Marshal	A collection of methods for allocating unmanaged memory, copying unmanaged memory, and converting managed to unmanaged types, as well as an assortment of methods for interacting with unmanaged code
OutAttribute	Indicates that data should be marshaled only from the callee back to the caller
ProgIdAttribute	An attribute that allows the assigning of a ProgID to a class
RegistrationServices	A collection of services for registering and unregistering managed assemblies for use from COM

System::Runtime::Remoting

System::Runtime::Remoting is a hierarchy of namespaces providing classes and interfaces that allow developers the ability to create and configure distributed applications. For those of you who are pre-.NET developers, this namespace hierarchy replaces (or is possibly equivalent to) DCOM.

A distributed application is an application where its parts are distributed among multiple machines allowing improved performance, scalability, and maintainability. Development using System::Runtime::Remoting hierarchy of namespaces is a large topic and well beyond the scope of this book. Fortunately, *Advanced .NET Remoting, Second Edition* by Ingo Rammer (Apress, 2005) covers in depth how to develop applications using this namespace hierarchy. Although the book is written for C# developers, I think you can still use it to get the information you need.

To access System::Runtime::Remoting, you need to reference the mscorlib.dll assembly:

```
#using <mscorlib.dll>
```

Table 5-14 provides a list of all the namespaces that make up the System::Runtime::Remoting hierarchy.

Table 5-14. *System::Runtime::Remoting Hierarchy Namespaces*

Namespace	Description
System::Runtime::Remoting	Provides classes and interfaces that allow developers to create and configure distributed applications. Some of the more important classes of the namespace are RemotingConfiguration, RemotingServices, and ObjRef.
System::Runtime::Remoting::Activation	Provides classes that support server and client activation of remote objects.
System::Runtime::Remoting::Channels	Provides classes that support and handle channels (objects that transport messages between applications across remoting boundaries) and channel sinks.
System::Runtime::Remoting::Channels::Http	Provides classes that support and handle channels and channel sinks using the HTTP protocol.
System::Runtime::Remoting::Channels::Ipc	Provides classes that support and handle channels and channel sinks using the IPC protocol.
System::Runtime::Remoting::Channels::Tcp	Provides classes that support and handle channels and channel sinks using the TCP protocol.
System::Runtime::Remoting::Contexts	Provides classes that define the contexts (ordered sequence of properties that defines an environment for the class) for all objects that reside within.
System::Runtime::Remoting::Lifetime	Provides classes that manage the lifetime of remote objects.
System::Runtime::Remoting::Messaging	Provides classes that are used to create and transmit messages.
System::Runtime::Remoting::Metadata	Provides classes and attributes that can be used to customize generation and processing of SOAP for objects and fields.
System::Runtime::Remoting::Metadata::W3cXsd2001	Provides classes that contains the XML Schema Definition (XSD) defined by the World Wide Web Consortium (W3C) in 2001.
System::Runtime::Remoting::MetadataServices	Provides classes that contain the classes used to convert metadata to and from XML schema for the remoting infrastructure.
System::Runtime::Remoting::Proxies	Provides classes that control and provide functionality for proxies.
System::Runtime::Remoting::Services	Provides classes that contain service classes that provide functionality to the .NET Framework.

System::Runtime::Serialization

System::Runtime::Serialization contains all the classes used to serialize and deserialize objects. *Serialization* is the process of converting an object, most likely an instance of a class to a linear sequence of bytes appropriate for things like storage or transmission over a stream. *Deserialization* is the conversion of a linear sequence of bytes back into an object.

The .NET Framework provides two formats for the linear sequence: SOAP and binary. You can also create your own format as well. The choice of which format is determined by which formatter namespace is chosen.

I cover serialization and deserialization of class objects in Chapter 8. Table 5-15 shows some of the common classes that you might use within the System::Runtime::Serialization namespace.

To access System::Runtime::Serialization, you need to reference the mscorlib.dll assembly:

```
#using <mscorlib.dll>
```

Table 5-15. *Common System::Runtime::Serialization Namespace Classes*

Class Name	Description
Formatter	The base functionality for the CLR serialization formatters
Formatters::Binary::BinaryFormatter	A class used to serialize and deserialize objects into a binary format
Formatters::Soap::SoapFormatter	A class used to serialize and deserialize objects into a SOAP format
FormatterServices	A class containing static methods which help in the implementing of a Formatter for serialization
SerializationInfo	A class that contains all the data needed to serialize or deserialize an object

System::Security

The System::Security namespace and the hierarchy of namespaces below it make up a major portion of .NET's security functionality. System::Web::Security makes up most of the rest. You can break up .NET security primarily into three different areas: role-based security, code access security, and cryptography.

Role-based security determines what programs may be run based on the role of the user. Code access security adds granularity to .NET security by allowing the CLR to determine what code block within a program can be executed based on evidence of who the user is and the permissions that user may have. Cryptography provides the ability to allow only the users with appropriate keys the ability to read data and code.

I cover .NET security in Chapter 19. Table 5-16 shows all the namespaces within the System::Security namespace hierarchy.

Table 5-16. *System::Security Hierarchy Namespaces*

Namespace	Description
System::Security	Provides the underlying structure of the CLR security system.
System::Security::AccessControl	Provides all the security access information on objects like Active Directory, Files, Registry, Mutex, and Semaphores.
System::Security::Authentication	Provides a set of enumerations that describe the security of a connection.
System::Security::Cryptography	Provides cryptographic services, including secure encoding and decoding of data. This namespace also contains functions, such as hashing, random number generation, and message authentication.
System::Security::Permissions	Defines classes that control access to operations and resources based on policy.
System::Security::Policy	Contains code groups, membership conditions, and evidence.
System::Security::Principal	Defines a principal object that represents the security context under which code is running.

System::Threading

Multithread programming can be a very powerful feature, because when coded properly, it allows for more optimal CPU usage and a better perception of response time. Very seldom is a computer at 100 percent usage, and running more than one thread concurrently can help you get more out of your CPU.

The .NET Framework has built-in multithreading. In fact, an important feature of .NET, garbage collection, is handled using multithreading. The .NET Framework exposes its multithreading capabilities with the classes found in the System::Threading namespace. Multithreading, as an important and frequently used feature of the .NET Framework, is found in the mscorlib.dll assembly:

```
#using <mscorlib.dll>
```

The System::Threading namespace provides a class to manage groups of threads, a thread scheduler, a class to synchronize mutually exclusive threads, and an assortment of other functionalities to handle multithreading. I cover multithreading in Chapter 16. For now, Table 5-17 lists all the common classes in the System::Threading namespace that you might use.

Table 5-17. *Common System::Threading Namespace Classes*

Class Name	Description
Interlocked	Provides atomic operations for a shared variable across multiple threads
Monitor	Provides a lock for critical sections of a thread, allowing for synchronized access
Mutex	Provides synchronized access to shared resources across mutually exclusive threads

Table 5-17. *Common System::Threading Namespace Classes*

Class Name	Description
ReaderWriterLock	Provides a lock that allows a single writer for many readers
Thread	Creates and controls threads
ThreadPool	Provides a pool of efficient worker threads that are managed by the system
Timer	Provides the ability for threads to execute at discrete intervals

System::Web

The System::Web namespace and the hierarchy of namespaces below it make up a major portion of the .NET Framework class library. This makes sense, as .NET came into being because of the Internet and the World Wide Web.

The System::Web hierarchy is too massive to cover fully here, and given that C++/CLI only supports a small portion of the namespaces, those relating to Web services, I only give these namespaces cursory coverage and leave it to the .NET Framework documentation to provide any detailed explanations you need of any particular class. The .NET Framework breaks Web development into two pieces: Web applications and Web services. I only cover Web services (in Chapter 15) because C++/CLI does not support Web applications, although even this chapter really just scratches the surface of the functionality available to you.

Table 5-18 helps you navigate through the myriad classes provided by the System::Web namespace hierarchy by providing you with a list of some of the more common namespaces that you might use.

Table 5-18. *Common System::Web Hierarchy Namespaces*

Namespace	Description
System::Web	Contains classes to handle browser–server communications. This namespace contains HttpRequest and HttpResponse to handle the HTTP dialog between the browser and the Web server.
System::Web::Caching	Contains the cache class used to provide caching of frequently used data on the Web server.
System::Web::Configuration	Contains classes to help set up the ASP.NET configuration.
System::Web::Hosting	Provides the ability to host managed applications that reside outside of the Microsoft Internet Information Services (IIS).
System::Web::Mail	Contains classes to create and send e-mail using either the SMTP mail service built into Microsoft Windows 2000 or an arbitrary SMTP server.
System::Web::Security	Contains classes to handle ASP.NET security in Web applications.
System::Web::Services	Contains classes to create and implement Web services using ASP.NET and XML Web service clients.
System::Web::SessionState	Contains classes to store the data specific to a client within a Web application, giving to the user the appearance of a persistent connection.

Table 5-18. *Common System::Web Hierarchy Namespaces (Continued)*

Namespace	Description
System::Web::UI	Contains classes and interfaces to create server controls and pages for Web applications.
System::Web::UI::HtmlControls	Contains classes to create HTML server controls on Web Form pages of Web applications.
System::Web::UI::Imaging	Contains classes to create dynamic images and custom image generation services.
System::Web::UI::WebControls	Contains classes to create Web server controls on Web pages of Web applications.

System::Windows::Forms

Visual Basic has been using forms for many versions, and Windows Forms is modeled on Visual Basic's form technology, but with a much finer grain of control. Normally you will create Windows Forms using a drag-and-drop tool, but you also have full access to all aspects of the Win form within your code.

As of the current release, Windows Forms and Windows-based GUI applications are pretty much synonymous. However, if the .NET Framework starts to get ported to other platforms, as it can be, then a Windows Form will be more equivalent to a GUI application.

First off, all the classes that make up the .NET Windows Forms environment are actually found within the System::Windows::Forms namespace. This namespace is large, containing several hundred different types (classes, structures, enumerations, and delegates). You probably will not use every type within the namespace, but there is a good chance that you may use a large number of them, especially if your Windows Form has any complexity involved.

You will cover Windows Forms in detail in Chapters 9 and 10, but you will also see them used many times in subsequent chapters. For those of you who want a head start, Table 5-19 shows a good number of common classes that you will become quite familiar with if you plan to build Windows Forms.

Table 5-19. *Common System::Windows::Forms Namespace Classes*

Class Name	Description
Application	Provides static methods and properties for managing an application
Button	Represents a Windows Forms Button control
CheckBox	Represents a Windows Forms CheckBox control
CheckListBox	Represents a Windows Forms CheckListBox control
Clipboard	Provides methods to placé data in and retrieve data from the system clipboard
ComboBox	Represents a Windows Forms ComboBox control
Control	Represents the base class of all controls in the Windows Forms environment

Table 5-19. *Common System::Windows::Forms Namespace Classes*

Class Name	Description
Cursor	Represents a Windows Forms cursor
Form	Represents a window or dialog box, which makes up part of the application's user interface
Label	Represents a Windows Forms Label control
LinkLabel	Represents a Windows Forms label control that can display a hyperlink
ListBox	Represents a Windows Forms ListBox control
Menu	Represents the base functionality of all Windows Forms menus
PictureBox	Represents a Windows Forms PictureBox control
RadioButton	Represents a Windows Forms RadioButton control
RichTextBox	Represents a Windows Forms RichTextBox control
ScrollBar	Represents a Windows Forms ScrollBar control
StatusBar	Represents a Windows Forms StatusBar control
TextBox	Represents a Windows Forms TextBox control
ToolBar	Represents a Windows Forms ToolBar
TreeView	Represents a hierarchical display list of TreeNodes

System::Xml

XML is a key component of the .NET Framework. Much of the underlying technological architecture of .NET revolves around XML. No matter what type of application you plan on developing, be it for the Web or a local machine, there is a good chance that somewhere in your application XML is being used. You just might not be aware of it. Because of this, there are a lot of specialized XML classes available to a .NET developer.

To provide XML support to your .NET applications requires the addition of the System.Xml.dll assembly to the top of your source code:

```
#using <System.Xml.dll>
```

The .NET Framework provides a developer two different methods of processing XML data: a fast, noncaching, forward-only stream, and a random access in-memory Document Object Model (DOM) tree. You will cover both methods in Chapter 13. You will also see a little bit of XML in Chapter 15.

Table 5-20 shows all of the .NET Framework class library's XML-related classes that fall within the System::Xml namespace hierarchy.

Table 5-20. *Common System::Xml Namespace Classes*

Class Name	Description
System::Xml	All the core classes needed to create, read, write, and update XML
System::Xml::Schema	Provides XML schema support
System::Xml::Serialization	Provides the ability to serialize .NET managed objects to and from XML
System::Xml::Xpath	Provides support for the XPath and evaluation engine
System::Xml::Xsl	Provides support for Extensible Stylesheet Transformations (XSLT)

Microsoft::Win32

One namespace within the .NET Framework that I find very helpful at times that does not fall directly under the System namespace hierarchy is the Microsoft::Win32 namespace. There are other namespaces within the Microsoft hierarchy, but they are very specialized, and most likely you will not use them.

To access Microsoft::Win32, you need to reference the mscorlib.dll assembly:

```
#using <mscorlib.dll>
```

What makes Microsoft::Win32 unique is that two of its classes, Registry and RegistryKey, provide access to the Windows registry. Although the Windows registry is being used less and less because of .NET's web.config and application.config files, I still find the registry helpful on some occasions.

Summary

In this chapter, you took a high-level look at the core library provided to .NET developers: the .NET Framework class library. You started by learning the basic structure of the .NET Framework class library. You then moved on to examine many of the namespaces that make up the class library. You will see many of these namespaces in later chapters. You should now have an appreciation of how large the library is and a good idea of how to navigate through it.

In the next chapter, you will look at the very helpful C++/CLI-integrated XML documentation. With this addition, you will be able to make your own documentation that is easy to read, write, and maintain.

■ ■ ■

CHAPTER 6

Integrated XML Documentation

An important and necessary evil of all software development is documentation. As a programmer I can vouch for the fact that I hate writing documentation—even more so if I have to write both inline and external documentation. If I could remove the necessity to do only one set of documentation, I'd be a much happier camper. With Visual Studio 2005 my wish has finally come true.

What I am referring to is integrated XML documentation.

Integrated XML documentation is a new commenting style introduced in Visual Studio 2005 but new to C++/CLI in that it allows the developer to add documentation internally to the program and then, with a compile switch, to generate external documentation from these new comments. The generated documentation is in the form of XML, which with several third-party tools on the market can be used to build impressive-looking documentation in multiple formats. (I use the de facto standard NDoc, and all generated documentation in this chapter is created using NDoc. You can get more information and download NDoc from `http://ndoc.sourceforge.net`.)

Integrated XML documentation has always been a part of C#, and I have often wondered why it was excluded from Managed Extensions for C++ as I saw no real reason that it should be left out. I'm sure Visual Basic .NET developers thought the same thing as well. Yes, there are third-party add-ons that added the functionality, but it has taken Microsoft until now to see the light and now it is available to all C++/CLI programmers.

In this chapter I discuss the basics of the new documentation tool, then I show some of the documentation tags available, and finally I present an example that uses all the standard tags provided by the C++/CLI compiler.

The Basics

I have to be one of the first people to admit, I hate documenting my code. It seems like such a waste of time as the code seems so self-explanatory at the time you write it. Of course the function `GetDate()` gets a date and `BuildDataTree()` builds a data tree. Isn't it obvious? Then six months rolls around and the project leader asks you to make a change to your code. You look at the code you wrote and wonder who was the dimwit who wrote this code without documentation? What date is the `GetDate()` getting and which data tree is the `BuildDataTree()` building? Then you remember the dimwit is yourself for being too lazy to write reasonable documentation for your code.

The key to documentation as far as I'm concerned is determining what a reasonable amount of documentation is. I've seen both extremes on this. I had a colleague who came from an RPG II background and literally commented every line of his COBOL program. If you don't know COBOL (lucky you!), it is one of the most self-documenting computer languages around, obviously if written properly. Commenting every line is like repeating every sentence in a book.

As you read this book you will see that I am at the other extreme: I only document stuff that I think is unusual or coded in such a way that might cause confusion. This is a very bad habit!

Don't follow my lead on this. I have the luxury in this book to have another 800 or so pages of documentation surrounding my code, and duplicating the text in my book within the code would make the book even longer. An unfortunate side effect is that the downloaded code is virtually commentless.

A reasonable number of comments fall somewhere in between these two extremes, and it is up to the developer to find this documentation sweet spot.

So what is reasonable? Oh, there are hundreds, if not thousands, of pages written on the topic, but I personally consider a reasonable amount of commenting as enough documentation to allow you, and by proxy someone else, to understand your code six months after you have written it. I feel that after approximately six months you will be looking at the code in nearly the same perspective as any other programmer with a basic overall understanding of the software being developed. Remember, this is just my personal standard. If you don't like it or think it too simplistic, then be my guest and read up on the topic.

You should try to establish documentation standards and a definition of what is reasonable documentation early in the project when you are developing in a team environment. I find early code reviews to be the best place to solidify the standards set during the design phase.

One aspect of software development that I like even less than commenting my code is writing the same documentation twice: once in the code itself and then again in an external reference document. Not liking it doesn't mean I don't see the need for it. In fact, I have to admit, it is more or less essential, especially for projects in which multiple developers are going to share the code. And let's not even get started discussing how both internal and external documentation is indispensable for maintenance programmers.

That said, wouldn't it be nice to have to write documentation in only one place and then generate the other needed forms of documentation from it? Guess what, you can. (Duh?! or I wouldn't be writing this chapter.)

Although I'm sure other languages provide the facility, C# was my first exposure to a language that provided a built-in tool to allow me to tackle both of my areas of least pleasure at one time. This tool is integrated XML documentation, or, as I like to call it, the *triple slash comment*. (This feature was one of the many that first attracted me to code C# over Managed Extensions for C++ when I first started developing for .NET.) Now, with Visual Studio 2005 and C++/CLI, the playing field has been leveled in this area, because triple slash comments have been added.

The Triple Slash Comment

So what are triple slash comments? They are a new commenting syntax added to C++/CLI that allows XML documentation to be generated from them. There really is nothing special about them. You just write three forward slashes (///) and then write an XML-formatted comment associated with the next class, method, property, or variable.

One common error that you will find when using the triple slash comment is associating them with variables and functions outside of classes; this is not allowed (nor can you use them with namespaces).

Caution You can use triple slash comments only with classes and their members.

In addition to this error, triple slash comments can be used only in the code declaration (within the class itself) and not in external implementations either within the .h or .cpp file.

Caution Triple slash comments are valid only within the class declaration itself.

Another common error is not having well-formed XML within your triple slash comments, as this results in a compile-time warning being thrown.

Caution Triple slash comments must use well-formed XML.

The third most common mistake (it's really not an error) is expecting the formatting that you place within your triple slash comments to be maintained in your generated XML documents. There are tags that allow you to format your generated XML.

Caution White space is ignored within triple slash comments by the compiler.

Adding Triple Slash Comment to Your Code

Okay, let's look at the simple triple slash comment example in Listing 6-1. I provide more advanced examples a little later.

Listing 6-1. *Simple Triple Slash Comments*

```
using namespace System;

namespace SimpleTripleSlash
{
    /// <summary>
    ///    This is a summary comment for Class1
    /// </summary>
    public ref class Class1
    {
    public:
        /// <summary>This is a summary comment for Method1</summary>
        void Method1() {}

        /// <summary>This is a summary comment for Variable1</summary>
        int Variable1;
    };
}
```

Not much of a difference between a triple slash comment and a standard C++/CLI comment, is there? In fact, if you were not paying attention, you probably wouldn't have noticed anything different about these comments.

But believe me, there is a world of difference. First off, the actual comments are enclosed in the XML tags, in this case the <summary>. The <summary> tag is one of the many tags available to you for generating integrated XML documentation from triple slash comments. The biggest difference, however, occurs when you compile this class (with the addition of a compile switch or of a simple project property change—I cover both next), as compiling the class causes an XML file to be generated. These generated XML files contain the <summary> XML tag, as well as a few other auto-generated tags and attributes. It is with these XML files that you can generate very impressive external code documentation.

The triple slash comments are single-line comments, but as shown in Listing 6-1, you can stretch your comments within a tag over multiple lines. Remember, however, that white space is removed by the compiler, so don't spend your time lining up everything and expect it to line up in the generated XML documentation. But don't panic, I will show you later how you can do some formatting to make your comments look impressive.

Generating XML Documentation Files

It is really a no-brainer when it comes to generating XML documentation files from triple slash comments.

If you are developing your code with Visual Studio 2005, you simply need to set the Generate XML Documentation Files property of the project to yes. To do this, follow these steps:

1. Right-click the project in the Solution Explorer.

2. Select the Properties menu item. This will display the project's property page, as shown in Figure 6-1.

3. Select All Configurations from the Configuration drop-down list (if you want documentation generated for all configuration) or select the appropriate option to suit your needs.

4. Expand the Configuration Properties and C/C++ branches.

5. Select Output Files.

6. Select Yes (/doc) within the Generate XML Documentation Files property.

7. Click the OK button.

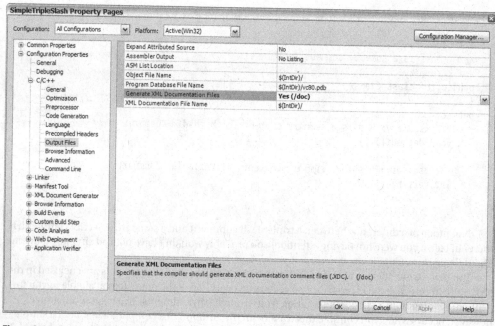

Figure 6-1. *The project property page*

If, on the other hand, you are developing your code using some other development editor, you need to add the /doc argument to the cl compile command:

```
cl SimpleTripleSlash.cpp /clr:safe /doc
```

With either scenario, the same XML documentation file is generated (see Listing 6-2).

Listing 6-2. *Generated XML Documentation*

```xml
<?xml version="1.0"?>
<doc>
    <assembly>
        SimpleTripleSlash
    </assembly>
    <members>
        <member name="T:SimpleTripleSlash.Class1">
            <summary>
  This is a summary comment for Class1
</summary>
        </member>
        <member name="M:SimpleTripleSlash.Class1.Method1">
            <summary>This is a summary comment for Method1</summary>
        </member>
        <member name="F:SimpleTripleSlash.Class1.Variable1">
            <summary>This is a summary comment for Variable1</summary>
        </member>
    </members>
</doc>
```

Not what you expected, is it? It's definitely not the beautiful MSDN documentation that you have become accustomed to. Believe it or not, IntelliSense and NDoc (as you can see in Figure 6-2) can take this document and work wonders with it, as it actually contains a lot of information.

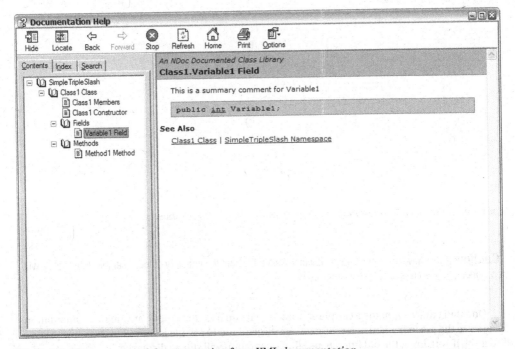

Figure 6-2. *NDoc-generated documentation from XML documentation*

First, it tells the assembly name that the document is associated with within the <assembly> tag. Next it contains, with a <members> tag, all the member types (T:), methods (M:), and fields (F:) found in the assembly and fully clarified within `<member>` tags. Finally, also within the member tags, are your triple slash comments (without the triple slash).

In this simple example there are only `<summary>` tags but, as you will see later in the chapter, a number of tags can be added. Plus, you can also add your own custom tags.

Note The actual compile process, which is normally hidden from you (and usually irrelevant to you), is that the cl.exe command generates an .xdc file, which then gets converted to an .xml file by the xdcmake.exe command. That is why there is an .xdc file in your project's Debug directory.

Viewing Integrated XML Documentation in IntelliSense

One very cool feature of integrated XML documentation is that you can use it to provide IntelliSense for your class libraries. All you need to do is copy the generated XML documentation file to the same directory as your class library assembly and then auto-*magically* the triple slash documentation of the summary and param tags that you added to the class becomes part of the information IntelliSense displays. You can see this in action in Figure 6-3.

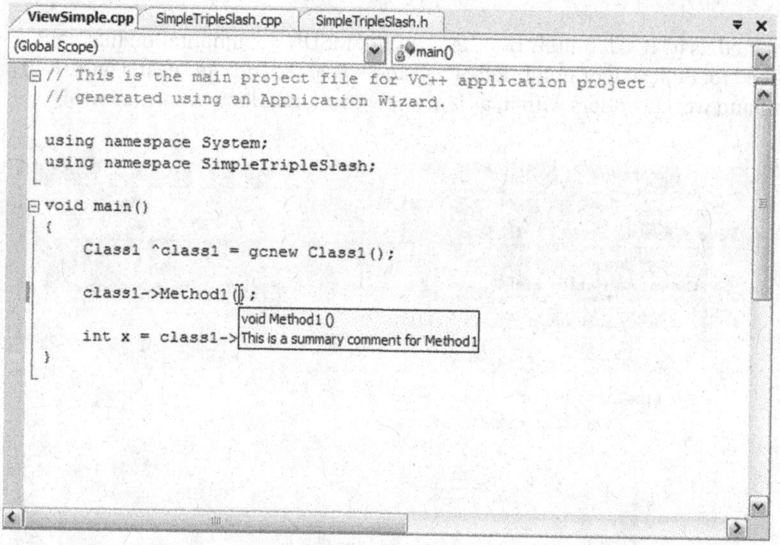

Figure 6-3. *Automatically generated IntelliSense from triple slash comments*

Caution If you move or delete the XML documentation file from the directory of the assembly, IntelliSense will stop working for the classes of that assembly.

One thing that caught me a couple of times is that you have to compile any new documentation changes to the assembly and make sure the newly generated XML file is moved to the appropriate directory. If you don't, the old IntelliSense documentation will still be displayed.

What if you place your assembly in some nonstandard place—does this mean you have to manually copy the XML documentation file to this same location? The answer is yes you can, but you don't have to because you can append the directory you want the XML file written to after the /doc argument:

```
cl SimpleTripleSlash.cpp /clr:safe /doc"C:\some\special\place\"
```

You can also rename the XML file by appending a file name instead of a path, although I'm not sure why you would want to do this.

Visual Studio 2005 also provides a method for specifying an XML file's name or path:

1. Right-click the project in the Solution Explorer.

2. Select the Properties menu item.

3. Select All Configurations from the Configuration drop-down list (if you want documentation generated for all configurations) or select the option that suits your needs.

4. Expand the Configuration Properties and C/C++ branches.

5. Select Output Files.

6. Update the filename or path within the XML Documentation File Name property.

7. Click the OK button.

Documentation Tags

Although the compiler will process any tag that is valid XML, most likely you will restrict yourself to the 16 tags described in this section. These 16 tags make up the most commonly used set of tags implemented by most documenting systems that use the compiler's auto-generated XML documentation. They also happen to cover all the documentation you normally need to fulfill the "reasonable amount" requirement I discussed previously.

Notice that I said the compiler will process any valid XML. You have to be careful here, as it is possible to create what looks like great documentation, only to have your compiler throw out garbage. The biggest culprit of breaking valid XML rules is the use of the less-than [<] symbol in implementation code examples. Instead of your comments saying something is less than something else, it says that a new tag has started. Not quite what you are expecting, I am sure. To get around this, you need to replace the [<] symbol with the < XML code.

The common integrated XML documentation tags available to the C++/CLI developer fall into three different categories. The first kind of tag describes the functionality of the subsequent type, member, or field. The second kind helps provide formatting to the tags and is used within the functionality tags. The third tag type provides ways of referencing other documentation sources.

The order that you place the functionality tags (and include tag) is not relevant, but it is probably a good thing to use the tags in the same order because shifting the order may lead to confusion or tags being forgotten. Formatting tags and reference tags must be placed inside functionality tags (except the include tag as just noted). Be careful, though: you cannot embed functionality tags within each other. Finally, not every tag is applicable to every type being documented. In most cases it is fairly obvious which tag(s) to use.

Note All example figures of documentation are generated by NDoc. The code for each was generated from the documentation example at the end of this section.

Functionality Tags

As I noted previously, the order in which you add the functionality tags to your source is irrelevant; however, I'm going to cover them in the order that I personally place them in my programs.

Something you might want to note is all of the tags can be repeated except `<summary>`, `<remarks>`, and `<returns>`. This makes sense to me, as you are only going to need one instance of these three tags. (I could make a case, however, that multiple `<remarks>` tags come in handy.)

`<summary>`

You will probably use the `<summary>` tag (see Figure 6-4) every time you triple slash comment your code. You should probably treat this tag as mandatory.

Its basic purpose is to provide an overall summary of the type, method, or field being documented. The `<summary>` tag is used by most development tools as the primary source of the description of the object being described. IntelliSense and the Object Browser in Visual Studio 2005 rely on it to provide the functionality summary displayed.

The basic syntax is

```
/// <summary> The summary text </summary>
```

But most likely you will split the `<summary>` tag on multiple lines, something like this:

```
/// <summary>
///    The summary text
/// </summary>
```

Remember that white space is not significant, unless one of the formatting tags is embedded within the `<summary>` tag. I cover formatting tags later in the chapter.

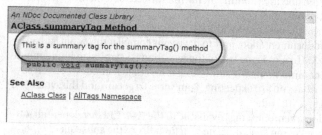

Figure 6-4. *NDoc-generated `<summary>` tag*

`<param>`

You will only use the `<param>` tag (see Figure 6-5) if the object you are documenting is a method, as it describes one of the parameters being passed to a method. Of course, if the method has no parameters, using this tag is quite useless.

The syntax is

```
/// <param name="parameterName"> Description of the parameter </param>
```

The name attribute must match the name of the parameter exactly. If not, the compiler will warn you of the discrepancy and IntelliSense will be unable to provide you information about the parameter as you pass your cursor over the parameter within your code.

Personally, I like to mention the data type of the parameter using a `<see>` tag (I cover the `<see>` tag a little later); that way, if the documentation is being viewed online, it enables the reader to quickly click the data type to get more information about what is being passed.

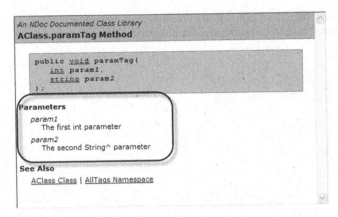

Figure 6-5. *NDoc-generated <param> tag*

<returns>

Like the <param> tag, you will only use the <returns> tag (see Figure 6-6) when documenting methods. The purpose of the <returns> tag is to describe what gets returned by a method. Obviously, if the method does not return a value, a <returns> tag should not be included for the method. You might think this tag would be useful for properties, but you should use a <value> tag for that instead.

The syntax is

```
/// <returns> Description of the value returned </returns>
```

Like the <param> tag, I find it useful to add the data type returned with the <see> tag. This provides a quick link for online documentation created from the generated XML documentation.

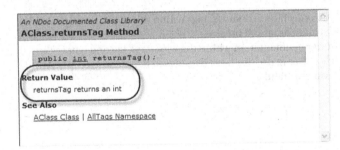

Figure 6-6. *NDoc-generated <returns> tag*

<value>

The <value> tag documents the value of a property (see Figure 6-7). You should probably consider it as a mandatory tag for all public properties.

You need to put the <value> tag outside of the property and not within it. In other words, don't place the tag next to the get or set declarations; instead, place it outside above the property's grouping declaration. For a trivial property, you don't have much choice.

The syntax is

```
/// <value> Description of the property's value </value>
```

Just like the `<returns>` and `<param>` tags, I like to mention the data type of the property value using a `<see>` tag, so that online documentation can provide quick links to the values data type for more details.

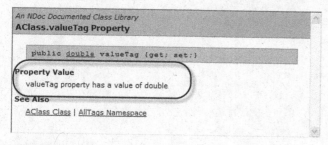

Figure 6-7. *NDoc-generated <value> tag*

<remarks>

The `<remarks>` tag's purpose is to provide supplemental information about the object being documented (see Figure 6-8).

The basic syntax is

```
/// <remarks> The remark text </remarks>
```

But most often you will split the `<remarks>` tag on multiple lines, like you did with the `<summary>` tag, something like this:

```
/// <remarks>
///     The remark text
/// </remarks>
```

Most likely you will extensively use one of the formatting tags within this tag, as it will probably contain things like lists, code snippets, and paragraph breaks.

You could potentially place all your documentation within the `<summary>` tag and ignore the `<remarks>` tag altogether. I feel that it is better to use the `<remarks>` tags to point out special information that you think is important and want to stand out.

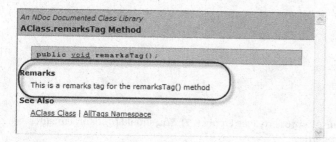

Figure 6-8. *NDoc-generated <remarks> tag*

<example>

As I'm sure you can figure out, the purpose of the `<example>` tag is to supply examples, most likely coding examples, for the object being documented (see Figure 6-9). This tag is extremely helpful if you are creating a class library API because it shows how to implement the object.

Unfortunately, I find that most developers don't use this tag as much as they should (sometimes even me; hey, I never claimed to be a perfect software developer!). In a perfect world, every method in a class should have an implementation example, but instead most developers just put one catchall example at the class level.

The basic syntax is

```
/// <example> The example </example>
```

You will probably never use the <example> tag without embedding within it a formatting tag of some sort—most examples require some form of formatting, especially if the example is code.

The following is the syntax of the example you will more than likely use. (Sorry about the chicken and egg scenario; the formatting tags are covered later in the chapter.)

```
/// <example>
///     <para> Example summary </para>
///     <para>[Visual Basic]</para>
///     <code>
///         Visual Basic .NET code example
///     </code>
///     <para>[C#]</para>
///     <code>
///         C# code example
///     </code>
///     <para>[C++]</para>
///     <code>
///         C++ code example
///     </code>
/// </example>
```

The <example> tag shown in this sample code first gives a basic outline of what the example contains and then provides implementation examples for each language.

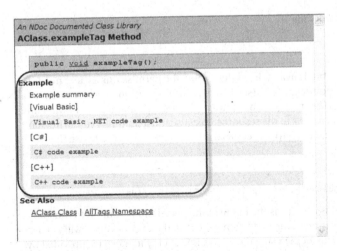

Figure 6-9. *NDoc-generated* <example> *tag*

<exception>

The often overlooked `<exception>` tag is used to describe one exception that a method may throw (see Figure 6-10). If your method throws more than one exception type, you should provide one `<exception>` tag for each exception thrown.

Fortunately, the .NET Framework documentation uses this tag quite extensively. However, I have worked with fairly well-documented class libraries that failed to use it, and when an exception occurs I have no clue why the exception happened or how to proceed.

The basic syntax is

```
/// <exception cref="ExceptionClass">
///    Description of exception and how to resolve it
/// </exception>
```

The cref attribute of the `<exception>` tag is the class name of the exception being thrown and must match exactly the exception thrown in the code. In some cases if the exception isn't defined within the same namespace, you will have to fully qualify the cref, for example:

```
/// <exception cref="System::OverflowException"> ... </exception>
```

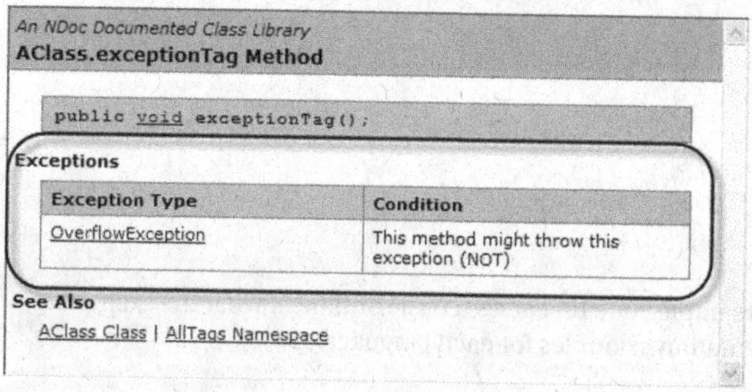

Figure 6-10. *NDoc-generated <exception> tag*

<permission>

The `<permission>` tag is seldom used but is available for describing the permissions a caller needs to be able to call and execute the method successfully (see Figure 6-11). Usually you restrict access to a method when it is providing an interface to a system resource of some type and it doesn't want any Tom, Dick, or Harry program to have access to the resource. Because most methods you write don't access such resources, there is no need to restrict access permission, thus, no need to use the `<permission>` tag.

The basic syntax is

```
/// <permission cref="PermissionClass"> Description of permission </permission>
```

The cref attribute of the `<permission>` tag is the name of the permission required to run and must match exactly the permissions used in the code. In most cases, the cref attribute will need to be fully qualified as you will most liking being using the System::Security namespace provided by the .NET Framework. In fact, it will probably be the System::Security::PermissionSet class.

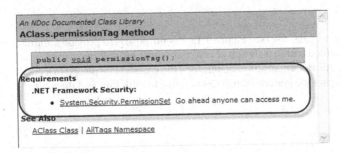

Figure 6-11. *NDoc-generated <permission> tag*

Formatting Tags

If you could only generate documentation as one continuous stream without paragraphs, formatting, or lists, I could safely say it would not be used. Documentation needs to be user-friendly and easy to read or it isn't likely to be used, although there have been some exceptions in the past, mostly out of sheer necessity.

You might be thinking that because the documentation generated from triple slash comments is based on XML, and its white space is not significant, auto-generated documentation will be unformatted and awfully bland. This is not the case, however, as integrated XML documentation has predefined tags to provide formatting.

One thing to remember is that formatting tags are, in fact, just tags. It is up to the document generation tool to provide the actual formatting associated with these tags. You might find different tools handle these tags differently, but their basic underlying results should be similar.

Another thing to remember is that formatting tags are placed within other tags and are not used as stand-alone comments.

<c>

The `<c>` tag is the first of two formatting tags used to provide code formatting (see Figure 6-12). The other is the `<code>` tag. In most cases, code formatting means the use of a fixed-width font and white space is significant.

You use the `<c>` tag to embed code directly within the current line of text and the code contains no line breaks. The basic syntax is

```
<c>Some Code</c>
```

You can use this tag within all of the other tags (except another `<c>` or `<code>` tag, as that would be redundant).

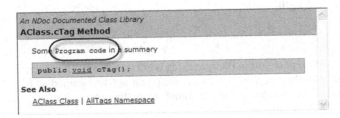

Figure 6-12. *NDoc-generated <c> tag*

<code>

The second code formatting tag is the <code> tag (see Figure 6-13). Its purpose is to provide a stand-alone block of code. So, when embedded within a stream of text, the <code> tag will cause a line break on both ends of the tag. For some documentation generators, the code will be placed in a gray box. Just like the <c> tag, you can expect the generated text to use a fixed-width font and the white space to be significant.

The basic syntax is

```
/// <code>
/// A code statement
/// Another code statement;
/// </code>
```

Remember that with the <code> tag white space is significant, so adding tabs, spaces, and return characters will be reflected in the generated code. White space significance starts after the last slash of the triple slash comment.

Caution Be careful of tabs, as they can make your code formatting look—how should I say it?—ugly.

You will most likely use this tag within the <example> tag, but there is nothing stopping you from using it within other tags.

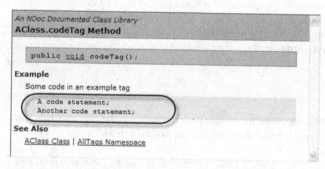

Figure 6-13. *NDoc-generated <code> tag*

<para>

You will often find that your functionality tags contain text that needs to be split into multiple paragraphs (see Figure 6-14). This is where the <para> tag comes in handy. You use the <para></para> pair to delimit the start and end of a paragraph.

The basic syntax is

```
<para> The paragraph </para>
```

One thing to be aware of is that white space within the <para> tag is not significant. Therefore, you can place the <para> end to end or on their own lines and have the paragraph text immediately follow the tag or start on a new line and have the document generated create the same result.

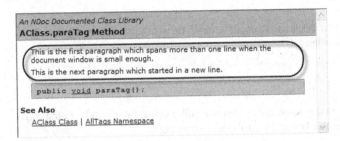

Figure 6-14. *NDoc-generated <para> tag*

<list>

The <list> tag (see Figure 6-15) is one of the most complex tags available to you, as it allows you to create a bulleted list, numbered list, a table, and a definition of a term. (The reason for not designing four different tags escapes me.) Just to make things easier, I'll cover each format individually.

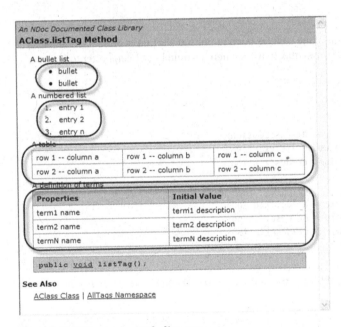

Figure 6-15. *NDoc-generated <list> tag*

Bulleted List

The bulleted list's basic syntax is quite simple. Create a <list> tag with a type of bullet and then list all the bullets as <item> tags:

```
/// <list type="bullet">
///    <item> bullet </item>
///    <item> bullet </item>
/// </list>
```

You will most likely use this tag within the <summary> and <remarks> tags, but there is nothing stopping you from using it within other tags.

Note The documentation states that you should use a `<description>` tag within each `<item>` tag, but I don't see any need for it; it seems to work fine without it.

Numbered List

The numbered list's basic syntax is nearly the same as that of a bulleted list. Create a `<list>` tag with a type of `number` and then list all the numbered list entries as `<item>` tags:

```
/// <list type="number">
///    <item> entry 1 </item>
///    <item> entry 2 </item>
///    <item> entry n </item>
/// </list>
```

You will most likely use this tag within the `<summary>` and `<remarks>` tags, but there is nothing stopping you from using it within other tags.

Table

Personally, I don't like the basic syntax of the table, as I don't think it really makes sense. I feel whoever developed this is just trying to force the syntax to work when it would have been better to create a new tag.

Here is the table's basic syntax:

```
/// <list type="table">
///    <item>
///       <description>row 1 -- column a</description>
///       <description>row 1 -- column b</description>
///       <description>row 1 -- column c</description>
///    </item>
///    <item>
///       <description>row 2 -- column a</description>
///       <description>row 2 -- column b</description>
///       <description>row 2 -- column c</description>
///    </item>
/// </list>
```

Create a `<list>` tag with a type of `table` and then create rows using the `<item>` tag and columns using the `<description>` tag.

Definition of Terms

On the other hand, I think the basic syntax of terms makes perfect sense, except I would have added another type, instead of duplicating the `table` type.

Here is the definition of terms' basic syntax:

```
/// <list type="table">
///    <listheader>
///       <term>Properties</term>
///       <description>Initial Value</description>
```

```
///    </listheader>
///    <item>
///       <term>term1 name</term>
///       <description>term1 description</description>
///    </item>
///    <item>
///       <term>term2 name</term>
///       <description>term2 description</description>
///    </item>
///    <item>
///       <term>termN name</term>
///       <description>termN description</description>
///    </item>
/// </list>
```

First, just like all of the other lists, create a `<list>` but this time with a type of `table` (why not `terms`?), and then create a `<listheader>` section containing two subsection headers, `<term>` and `<description>`. These headers are used in the header section of the definition of terms table. Finally, add `<item>` tags for each `<term>` and `<description>` pair contained in the table.

Reference Tags

The last four tags, for lack of a better word, I call "reference" tags as each references something—although I will admit I'm stretching it a bit with the `<include>` tag. They are especially helpful because they keep you from having to write the same documentation repeatedly.

<include>

The `<include>` tag (see Figure 6-16) provides the ability to include documentation from an external XML file. You should be comfortable with the concept of include files, as you use them all the time in C++ programming. The only difference here is that you are including documentation instead of code.

The basic syntax is

```
/// <include file='DocumentationFile' path='XPathToComment' />
```

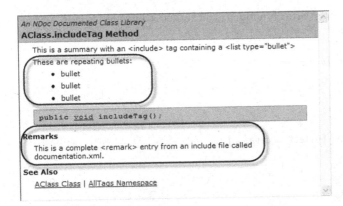

Figure 6-16. *NDoc-generated <include> tag*

The `<include>` tag is useful, but only in specific conditions; it should not be abused. For example, the `<include>` tag is handy when you have a repeating set of documentation that you don't want to type over and over again. With the <include> tag, you can write it once in an external XML file and then include it repeatedly within your triple slash comments.

A neat thing about the <include> tag is that you can include a complete tag like <remarks>. That way, if you have a repeating remark, you only have to write it once in an include XML file and then just put the <include> tag in the triple slash comment.

There is one gotcha that keeps getting me when I use the <include> tag: changes made to the include documentation XML file do not force a build to occur. In other words, a build when you have only changed the include documentation XML does nothing.

■ **Caution** A build of a class library will not occur if you only make changes in the included documentation XML file. You need to either specify a rebuild or make a change to the class library code.

The big problem with the <include> tag is, because the documentation is now in a separate file, you lose the benefit of triple slash's internal documentation capability. Let's look at some examples in Listings 6-3 and 6-4 so you can see what I mean.

Listing 6-3. *Included Comments*

```
using namespace System;

namespace AllTags
{
    public ref class AClass
    {
    public:
        /// <summary> This is a summary with an &lt;include&gt; tag containing
        ///     a &lt;list type="bullet"&gt;
        ///     <include file='document.xml' path='AllDoc/Entry[@num="1"]/*' />
        /// </summary>
        /// <include file='document.xml' path='AllDoc/Entry[@num="2"]/*' />
        void includeTag() {}
    };
}
```

As you can see, the comments mean virtually nothing to the reader of the code. Listing 6-4 is the actual XML documentation XML file.

Listing 6-4. *An Include XML Documentation File*

```
<?xml version="1.0" encoding="utf-8"?>
<AllDoc>

    <Entry num="1">
        <para>These are repeating bullets:</para>
        <list type="bullet">
            <item> bullet </item>
            <item> bullet </item>
            <item> bullet </item>
        </list>
    </Entry>
```

```
<Entry num="2">
    <remarks>
        This is a complete &lt;remark&gt; entry from an include
        file called documentation.xml.
    </remarks>
</Entry>
```

```
</AllDoc>
```

Notice you have to use the < XML code in both of these listings because, if you don't, invalid XML will be created in the triple slash comment.

One thing of note about <include> tags (and the main reason I don't use them very often) is that not only are they not very helpful in documenting the code itself, but they cause you to lose the context of the comment within the include XML documentation file because it is not directly associated with the code it is documenting.

I guess what I am saying is, I don't like the <include> tag. I'd rather cut and paste the repeated code, but it's your code and your documentation standards.

<paramref>

The <paramref> tag (see Figure 6-17) is similar to the <param> tag in that they both reference a parameter of the method being documented. The difference is that the <paramref> tag gets embedded in the comment text, while the <param> tag creates its own section in the documentation.

The basic syntax is

```
<paramref name="parameterName"/>
```

This tag really doesn't do much more than provide a way to let the document generated know this is a parameter name and provide a unique format style. For example, in the case of NDoc, it simply gets italicized.

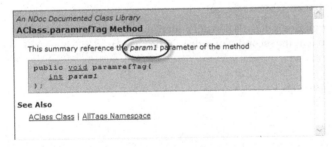

Figure 6-17. *NDoc-generated <paramref> tag*

<see>

The <see> tag (see Figure 6-18) is one of the most powerful tags in your triple slash comment arsenal. It allows you to reference other documentation in your documentation environment. Most important, it allows you to reference all of the .NET Framework. Thus, you can provide references (as I noted previously) to the data types you are using within the <param>, <returns>, <value>, <exception>, and <permission> tags. This enables the documentation's users to quickly jump to the documentation of the referenced data type if they are uncertain about its functionality.

The basic syntax is

```
<see cref="datatype"/>
```

What is generated is a link to the specified data type embedded in the text of your comments. One problem (or not, depending on how you look at it) is that the link text will not be fully qualified even if the cref is fully qualified. Sometimes you will want to have the qualifiers show up in the link text (or any other text for that matter), so this tag provides additional syntax:

```
<see cref="datatype"> link text </see>
```

With this syntax, whatever text you place within the <see></see> pair gets used as the link text.

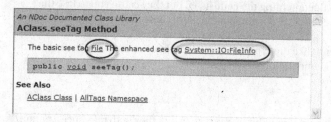

Figure 6-18. *NDoc-generated <see> tag*

<seealso>

The <seealso> tag is similar to the <see> tag except instead of placing the link to the reference data type directly in the comment text, it gets placed in the "See Also" section of the documentation (see Figure 6-19).

Like the <see> tag, the <seealso> tag has two syntaxes:

```
<seealso cref="datatype"/>
<seealso cref="datatype"> embedded text </seealso>
```

The difference between the two syntaxes is that the first does not place any text in the comment where the <seealso> tag is placed, whereas the second syntax does. (The text placed is just normal text and not a link.)

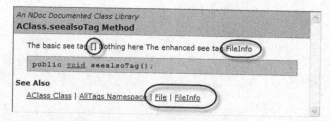

Figure 6-19. *NDoc-generated <seealso> tag*

Documentation Example

Listing 6-5 is a nonsense example demonstrating all the common tags provided by the C++/CLI compiler. You can see the NDoc results of this example in Figures 6-4 through 6-19.

Note When I first started using triple slash comments, I found that they looked simple enough to use, but I always seemed to mess up on which got embedded into which. Hopefully this long-winded example will help you get over this hurdle I experienced.

Listing 6-5. *All the Documentation Tags in Action*

```
using namespace System;
using namespace System::IO;

namespace AllTags
{
    public ref class AClass
    {
    public:

        /// <summary>
        /// This is a summary tag for the summaryTag() method
        /// </summary>
        void summaryTag() {}

        /// <param name="param1">The first int parameter</param>
        /// <param name="param2">The second String^ parameter</param>
        void paramTag(int param1, String ^param2) {}

        /// <returns> returnsTag returns an int </returns>
        int returnsTag() {return 0;}

        /// <value> valueTag property has a value of double</value>
        property double valueTag
        {
            double get() {return 0.0;}
            void set(double val) {}
        }

        /// <remarks>
        /// This is a remarks tag for the remarksTag() method
        /// </remarks>
        void remarksTag() {}

        /// <example>
        ///    <para> Example summary </para>
        ///    <para>[Visual Basic]</para>
        ///    <code>
        ///    Visual Basic .NET code example
        ///    </code>
        ///    <para>[C#]</para>
        ///    <code>
        ///    C# code example
        ///    </code>
        ///    <para>[C++]</para>
        ///    <code>
        ///    C++ code example
```

```
///    </code>
/// </example>
void exampleTag() {}


/// <exception cref="System::OverflowException">
/// This method might throw this exception (NOT)
/// </exception>
void exceptionTag() {}


/// <permission cref="System::Security::PermissionSet">
///    Go ahead anyone can access me.
/// </permission>
void permissionTag() {}


/// <summary>
/// Some <c>Program code</c> in a summary
/// </summary>
void cTag() {}


/// <example>
/// Some code in an example tag
/// <code>
///    A code statement;
///    Another code statement;
/// </code>
/// </example>
void codeTag() {}


/// <summary>
/// <para>This is the first paragraph which spans more than one line
/// When the document window is small enough.</para><para>This is the
/// next paragraph which started in a new line.</para>
/// </summary>
void paraTag() {}


/// <summary>
/// A bullet list
/// <list type="bullet">
///    <item> bullet </item>
///    <item> bullet </item>
/// </list>
/// A numbered list
/// <list type="number">
///    <item> entry 1 </item>
///    <item> entry 2 </item>
///    <item> entry n </item>
/// </list>
/// A table
/// <list type="table">
///    <item>
///       <description>row 1 -- column a</description>
///       <description>row 1 -- column b</description>
///       <description>row 1 -- column c</description>
///    </item>
```

```
///    <item>
///       <description>row 2 -- column a</description>
///       <description>row 2 -- column b</description>
///       <description>row 2 -- column c</description>
///    </item>
/// </list>
/// A definition of terms
/// <list type="table">
///    <listheader>
///       <term>Properties</term>
///       <description>Initial Value</description>
///    </listheader>
///    <item>
///       <term>term1 name</term>
///       <description>term1 description</description>
///    </item>
///    <item>
///       <term>term2 name</term>
///       <description>term2 description</description>
///    </item>
///    <item>
///       <term>termN name</term>
///       <description>termN description</description>
///    </item>
/// </list>
/// </summary>
void listTag() {}

/// <summary> This is a summary with an &lt;include&gt; tag containing
///     a &lt;list type="bullet"&gt;
///     <include file='document.xml' path='AllDoc/Entry[@num="1"]/*' />
/// </summary>
/// <include file='document.xml' path='AllDoc/Entry[@num="2"]/*' />
void includeTag() {}

/// <summary> This summary references the <paramref name="param1"/>
/// parameter of the method
/// </summary>
void paramrefTag(int param1) {}

/// <summary>
/// The basic see tag <see cref="File" />
/// The enhanced see tag <see cref="FileInfo">System::IO:FileInfo</see>
/// </summary>
void seeTag() {}

/// <summary>
/// The basic see tag [<seealso cref="File" />] Nothing here
/// The enhanced see tag <seealso cref="FileInfo">FileInfo</seealso>
/// </summary>
void seealsoTag() {}
};
}
```

Summary

This chapter described in detail the integrated XML documentation provided by the C++/CLI compiler, beginning with the basics of documentation and the triple slash comment provided by the compiler, followed by each of the standard tags available to the C++/CLI developer. The chapter ended with an examination of the triple slash comment in action in an example that featured every common documentation tag.

In the next chapter, you'll begin exploring the .NET development and, in particular, the collection functionality provided by the .NET Framework class library.

CHAPTER 7

■■■

Collections

Anyone who has been around the coding world for any length of time has more than likely written his or her own collection routine—probably a simply linked list. Newer programmers may not have written one of their own, but instead, in the case of C++ programmers, used the Standard Template Library (STL) version of a linked list. Either way, most programmers have found a need to work with collections. The .NET Framework uses collections as well. Because collections are so common, the .NET Framework class library provides a large number of different types.

There are, in fact, three primary sets of collections available to the .NET Framework programmer: System::Collections, System::Collections::Specialized, and System::Collections::Generic. As the names of these namespaces suggest, the first set contains standard collection types, the second contains collection types with a more specific purpose, and the third set contains collections specifically targeting the new generic type introduced in the .NET Framework version 2.0.

Something to be aware of is that the names of the three namespaces just mentioned seem to imply that the specialized collections and generic collections are inherited from the standard collections, but in fact there is no such relationship. The namespaces are just groupings of different types of collections.

This chapter focuses on the standard collection set shown in Table 7-1 and the generic collection set shown in Table 7-2. However, the .NET Framework class library has many other specific collections scattered throughout the many namespaces—for example, System::Text::RegularExpressions::Group, System::Security::PermissionSet, System::Web::UI::WebControls::DataKeyCollection, and even System::Array.

Table 7-1. *.NET Standard Collection Classes*

Collection	Description
ArrayList	An array that grows dynamically
BitArray	An array of bit values (either 1 or 0)
BitVector32	A small collection that will represent Boolean or small integers within 32 bits of memory
CollectionBase	An abstract base class for deriving strongly typed collections
DictionaryBase	An abstract base class for deriving strongly typed collections of key/value pairs
Hashtable	A collection of key/value pairs organized based on a hash code of the key
HybridDictionary	A collection that switches from a ListDictionary when small to a Hashtable when large

Table 7-1. *.NET Standard Collection Classes (Continued)*

Collection	Description
ListDictionary	A singular linked list recommended for lists of ten objects or less
NameValueCollection	A collection string of key/value pairs organized on the string key and accessible by either string key or index
Queue	A collection of first-in-first-out objects
SortedList	A collection of key/value pairs sorted by key and accessible by either key or index value
Stack	A collection of first-in-last-out objects
StringCollection	A collection of strings
StringDictionary	A Hashtable with the key strong typed to be a string

Table 7-2. *.NET Generic Collection Classes*

Collection	Description
Collection<T>	A base class for generic collections from which users are urged to derive their own specialized container classes.
Dictionary<K,V>	A collection of key/value paired generic objects that are organized based on the key and retrieved as a KeyValuePair<K,V> struct.
KeyedCollection<K,V>	A base class for generic collections using key/value pairs from which users are urged to derive their own specialized container classes.
LinkedList<T>	A doubly (forward and backward) linked list generic object.
List<T>	An array of generic objects that grows dynamically.
Queue<T>	A collection of first-in-first-out generic objects.
ReadOnlyCollection<T>	A base class for a generic read-only collection from which users are urged to derive their own specialized container classes. A collection that is read-only is simply a collection with a wrapper that prevents modifying the collection.
SortedDictionary<K,V>	A collection of key/value paired generic objects that are sorted based on the key.
Stack<T>	A collection of first-in-last-out generic objects.

To make things easier for the developer, the .NET Framework class library provides several interfaces (see Table 7-3 for standard and Table 7-4 for generic) that help provide some commonality between the collections. Learning collections is simplified because many of the collections share these interfaces, and once you learn an interface in one collection, it requires little effort to learn it in a second one.

Table 7-3. *.NET Standard Collection Interfaces*

Interface	Description
ICollection	Defines methods to determine the size, and provide synchronization and enumeration through all nongeneric collections
IComparer	Exposes a method to compare objects of the collection
IDictionary	Defines methods to allow access to key/value pairs within the collection
IDictionaryEnumerator	Exposes methods to access keys and values while enumerating a collection
IEnumerable	Exposes a method to retrieve an object that implements the IEnumerator interface
IEnumerator	Exposes a method to enumerate through a collection
IHashCodeProvider	Exposes a method to provide a custom hash algorithm
IList	Defines methods to add, insert, delete, and access objects using an index

■**Note** Default implementations of collections in System::Collections::Generic are not synchronized (thread-safe).

Table 7-4. *.NET Generic Collection Interfaces*

Interface	Description
ICollection<T>	Defines properties to determine the size of the collection and methods to add, remove, copy, and clear elements, as well as check for the existence of elements
IComparer<T>	Exposes a method to compare objects of the collection
IDictionary<K,V>	Defines properties to allow access to key/value pairs within the collection and methods to add and remove elements, as well as check for the existence of elements
IEnumerable<T>	Exposes a method to retrieve an object that implements the IEnumerator<T> interface
IEnumerator<T>	Exposes a method to enumerate through a collection
IList<T>	Defines methods to add, insert, delete, and access objects using an index

IEnumerable, IEnumerator, and for each

Even though each of the collections in Tables 7-1 and 7-2 is implemented differently internally, all except BitVector32 implement either the IEnumerable or IEnumerable<T> interface. These interfaces expose one member method, GetEnumerator(). This method returns a handle to an object that implements either the IEnumerator or IEnumerator<T> interface. And both the IEnumerator and IEnumerator<T> interfaces expose member methods that allow all collections to be handled the exact same way if there is a need.

The IEnumerator and IEnumerator<T> interfaces are fairly simple. You call the method MoveNext() to advance the enumerator to the next item in the collection, and then you grab the item out of the Current property. You know you have reached the end of the collection when MoveNext() returns false.

The IEnumerator interface contains one more method called Reset(), which the implementing class should define, that moves the enumerator back to the start of the collection.

Sound simple enough? There is an even easier way to iterate through a collection. Remember the for each statement? It implements all this IEnumerator and IEnumerator<T> stuff for you.

The following code shows equivalent implementation, first using the IEnumerable and IEnumerator interfaces, and then for each. Both are implemented on the same array (which also implements the IEnumerable interface even though it is not a member of System::Collections):

```
using namespace System;
using namespace System::Collections;

void main()
{
    array<int>^ IntList = gcnew array<int> { 1, 2, 3, 4, 5 };


    IEnumerable ^collection = (IEnumerable^)IntList;  //Not really needed
    IEnumerator ^enumerator = collection->GetEnumerator();

    Console::WriteLine("IEnumerator\n-----------");

    while (enumerator->MoveNext())
    {
        int i = (int)enumerator->Current;
        Console::WriteLine(i);
    }

    Console::WriteLine("\nfor each\n--------");

    for each (int i in IntList)
        Console::WriteLine(i);
}
```

Figure 7-1 shows the results of the IEnum_foreach.exe program.

The choice of which to use is entirely up to you. There are a few occasions when your only choice is to use IEnumerable/IEnumerator. I show an example in HashSortList.cpp later in the chapter. I find for each to be easier to use, and I try to use it whenever possible.

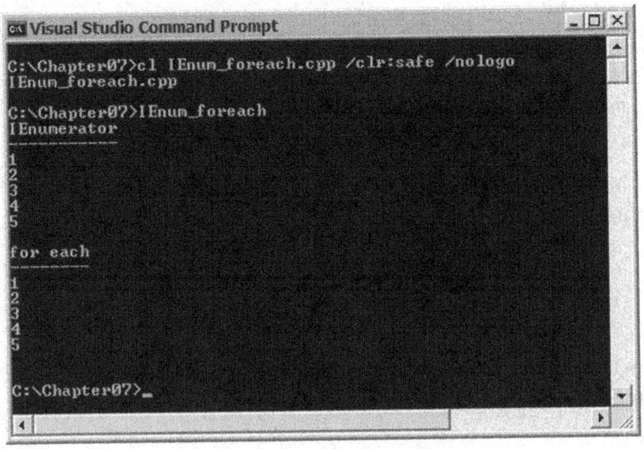

Figure 7-1. *Results of IEnum_foreach.exe*

Standard Collections

Now that you've looked at the major similarity among the .NET Framework class library collections, you'll take a look at how they differ. You'll start with the standard, or more common, collections of the class library. There's nothing new about these collection types, as they've been around for quite a long time. What's different is how the .NET Framework class library implements them and what interfaces the library provides.

ArrayList

If you've never coded an array, then you probably haven't been coding very long. Arrays, with their simple syntax, are the easiest of all collections to work with, especially when you know exactly how much data you're working with. Unfortunately, they quickly lose their usefulness when the number of data elements is unknown.

The ArrayList is a solution to the shortcomings of the simple array. You get the simple syntax of an array without having to worry about the number of data elements. Well, that's not quite accurate: you actually get a slightly more complex array syntax, but only after the array is already loaded. Loading the ArrayList requires member method calls—simple ones, but method calls just the same. Once the ArrayList is loaded, though, you can treat it almost exactly as you would a simple array.

There is nothing difficult about creating an ArrayList; it is simply a standard class. It does have three different constructors. The default takes no parameters. This constructor creates an ArrayList with a starting Capacity of 16:

```
ArrayList ^alist = gcnew ArrayList();
```

That doesn't mean that the ArrayList is restricted to 16; it just means that the first internal array contains space for 16 elements. If the number of elements, also known as the Count, exceeds the Capacity, then the Capacity is doubled or, in other words, the internal array of the ArrayList doubles and the original array is copied to the new, expanded array.

> **Caution** When the size of the `ArrayList` exceeds its capacity, the capacity is doubled. This could cause the `ArrayList` to be larger than is useful. For example, if your capacity is 20,000 and you add a 20,001st element, then the capacity becomes 40,000, which might not be what you want.

The second constructor allows you to set the initial `Capacity`. This allows you to optimize the loading of the `ArrayList`, as no doubling of the `Capacity` need occur if you can restrict the size of the `ArrayList` to less than the `Capacity`.

```
ArrayList ^alist = gcnew ArrayList(300);
```

The last constructor allows you to create an `ArrayList` from another specified collection. This constructor copies the elements from the originating collection and then sets the `Capacity` and `Count` to the number of elements copied.

```
ArrayList ^org = gcnew ArrayList();
//...populate org
ArrayList ^alist = gcnew ArrayList(org);
```

It is possible to get the `Count` or `Capacity`.

```
int count = alist->Count;
int capacity = alist->Capacity;
```

It is also possible to change the `Capacity` of an `ArrayList` at runtime by changing the `Capacity` property. If you change the `Capacity` to 0, the `Capacity` changes to the default `Capacity` of 16. Here is how you would code the setting of the capacity to 123:

```
alist->Capacity = 123;
```

> **Caution** Setting the `Capacity` to a value less than the `Count` of the `ArrayList` will result in an `ArgumentOutOfRangeException` being thrown.

Loading an `ArrayList` requires the use of member methods. All of the member methods are quite simple to use and self-explanatory. You can append or insert one or a range of elements to an `ArrayList`. You can also remove a specific element either by index or by specific content, or you can remove a range of elements by index.

```
alist->Add("One");

array<String^>^ morenums1 = gcnew array<String^> {"Three", "Six"};
alist->AddRange(morenums1);

alist->Insert(1, "Two");

array<String^>^ morenums2 = gcnew array<String^> {"Four", "Five"};
alist->InsertRange(3, morenums2);

alist->Remove("Six");
alist->RemoveAt(1);
alist->RemoveRange(0,4); // Index, Count
```

Once the `ArrayList` is loaded, it is possible to access the `ArrayList` in nearly the same way as a simple array. The only difference is that you are accessing a default index property into the `ArrayList`, instead of accessing the array element directly.

```
alist[1] = "Three";

for (int i = 0; i < alist->Count; i++)
{
    Console::Write("{0} ", alist[i]);
}
```

Caution Trying to access an ArrayList element that does not exist via the default index property will throw an ArgumentOutOfRangeException.

Note The default index property index starts at 0, just like any other array in C++.

The ArrayList provides a few useful methods that might make your coding life a little easier. For example, it is possible to reverse the order of all the elements of the ArrayList with Reverse().

```
alist->Reverse();
```

Another useful method is the Sort() method, which allows you to sort the ListArray.

```
Alist->Sort();
```

It is also possible to do a binary search of a sorted ArrayList to search for a specific element. With this method, the element's index is returned. If the element is not found, then the search method returns a negative number that indicates the index of the next largest object in the ArrayList.

```
int indx = alist->BinarySearch("Four");
```

Similar to the binary search, you can do a linear search to check if the ArrayList contains an element. If the search finds the element, it returns true. If not, it returns false.

```
bool fnd = alist->Contains("One");
```

Listing 7-1 shows the ArrayList in action and demonstrates many of the functionalities described previously.

Listing 7-1. *Working with ArrayLists*

```
using namespace System;
using namespace System::Collections;

void main()
{
    ArrayList ^alist = gcnew ArrayList(4); // will double to 8
    alist->Add("One");
    alist->Add("-");
    alist[1] = "Three";

    alist->Insert(1, "Two");

    array<String^>^ morenums = gcnew array<String^> {"Four", "Five"};

    alist->AddRange(morenums);
```

```
    alist->Reverse();

    Console::WriteLine("*** The ArrayList ***");
    for (int i = 0; i < alist->Count; i++)
    {
        Console::Write("{0} ", alist[i]);
    }

    Console::WriteLine("\n\nCapacity is: {0}", alist->Capacity.ToString());

    alist->Capacity = 10;
    Console::WriteLine("New capacity is: {0}", alist->Capacity.ToString());

    Console::WriteLine("Count is: {0}", alist->Count.ToString());

    alist->Sort();

    int indx = alist->BinarySearch("Four");
    Console::WriteLine("Four found at index: {0}", indx.ToString());

    bool fnd = alist->Contains("One");
    Console::WriteLine("ArrayList contains a 'One': {0}", fnd.ToString());

    Console::WriteLine();
}
```

Figure 7-2 shows the results of the ArrayList.exe program.

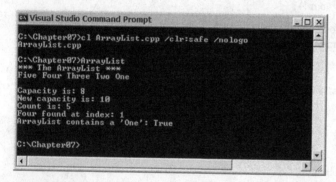

Figure 7-2. *Results of ArrayList.exe*

BitArray

This is a neat little collection that stores an array containing only true and false values. Unlike the ArrayList, the length of the BitArray is fixed at creation. It can, on the other hand, be set to any length (memory permitting, of course).

There are several constructors for creating a BitArray. You can divide them into three different types. The first type simply sets a predetermined array length of bools to either true or false.

```
BitArray ^barray1 = gcnew BitArray( 8 );    // Sets to false
BitArray ^barray2 = gcnew BitArray( 32, false );
BitArray ^barray3 = gcnew BitArray( 256, true );
```

The second type takes an array of bools, unsigned chars, or ints and moves their bit values into the BitArray, where, in the case of unsigned chars and ints, bits of 1 are true and bits of 0 are false.

```
array<bool>^ bools = gcnew array<bool> { true, false, true, true, false };
BitArray ^barray1 = gcnew BitArray( bools );

array<unsigned char>^ chars = gcnew array<unsigned char> { 0x55, 0xAA };
BitArray ^barray2 = gcnew BitArray( chars );

array<int>^ ints = gcnew array<int> { 0x55555555, 0xAAAAAAAA };
BitArray ^barray3 = gcnew BitArray( ints );
```

The last constructor type takes one BitArray and copies it to another BitArray.

```
BitArray ^barray1 = gcnew BitArray( 8 );
BitArray ^barray2 = gcnew BitArray(barray1);
```

A convenient feature of BitArrays is that they can be treated as arrays of Booleans. The array is manipulated in the same way as an ArrayList—that is, using the default index property—but this time the array items are only bools.

```
barray1[1] = false;
barray1[4] = true;

Console::WriteLine("Item[0]={0}", barray1[0]);
Console::WriteLine("Item[7]={0}", barray1[7]);
```

The functionality associated with BitArrays is obviously related to bit manipulation or, more specifically, AND, OR, XOR, and NOT. The basic idea around these bit manipulation methods is to take the original BitArray, and then take another and apply a bitwise operation on the two BitArrays.

```
BitArray ^barray1 = gcnew BitArray( 8 );
//...Manipulate bits for barray1
BitArray ^barray2 = gcnew BitArray( 8 );
//...Manipulate bits for barray2

barray2->And(barray1);
barray2->Or(barray1);
barray2->Xor(barray1);
```

The NOT method is a little different in that it only works on its own BitArray.

```
barray1->Not();
```

One last method that could come in handy is SetAll(). This method returns all the values in the BitArray back to either true or false depending on the value passed to it.

```
barray2->SetAll(true);
barray2->SetAll(false);
```

Listing 7-2 shows the BitArray in action and demonstrates many of the functionalities described previously.

Listing 7-2. *Working with BitArrays*

```
using namespace System;
using namespace System::Collections;

void Print( BitArray ^barray, String ^desc)
{
    Console::WriteLine(desc);

    int i = 0;
    for each( bool^ val in barray )
    {
        Console::Write("{0} ", val);

        if (++i > 7)
        {
            Console::WriteLine();
            i = 0;
        }
    }
    Console::WriteLine();
}

void main()
{
    BitArray ^barray1 = gcnew BitArray( 8, true );
    Print(barray1, "BitArray( 8, true );");

    barray1[1] = false;
    barray1[4] = false;
    barray1->Not();
    Print(barray1, "Modified bit 1&4 then Not");

    BitArray ^barray2 = gcnew BitArray( 8, true );
    barray2->And(barray1);
    Print(barray2, "And with BitArray( 8, true )");

    barray2->SetAll(true);
    barray2->Or(barray1);
    Print(barray2, "Or with BitArray( 8, true )");

    barray2->SetAll(true);
    barray2->Xor(barray1);
    Print(barray2, "Xor with BitArray( 8, true )");

    array<unsigned char>^ chars = gcnew array<unsigned char> { 0x55, 0xAA };
    BitArray ^barray3 = gcnew BitArray( chars );
    Print(barray3, "BitArray(0x55, 0xAA);");

    Console::WriteLine("Item[0]={0}", barray3[0]);
    Console::WriteLine("Item[8]={0}", barray3[8]);

    Console::WriteLine();
}
```

Figure 7-3 shows the results of the BitArray.exe program.

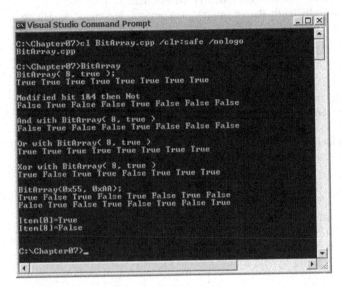

Figure 7-3. *Results of BitArray.exe*

Hashtable and SortedList

The Hashtable is a powerful method for storing data. The Hashtable works by storing its values in memory and then uses its key to later look up these values. What makes the Hashtable so powerful is that it doesn't search through all the keys to find a match; instead, it takes the key and analyzes it to figure out the index to the key's value. It then retrieves the value using this index.

The SortedList is a combination of a Hashtable and an Array. Depending on how you access the SortedList, it will respond like a Hashtable or an Array. For example, if you access the SortedList using the default index property, it works like a Hashtable. On the other hand, if you use the GetByIndex() method, the SortedList works like an Array.

A SortedList can do everything that a Hashtable can do and more. To access the values out of a Hashtable, you use the key. With a SortedList, on the other hand, you can use the key or access the data in a sorted manner directly using an index, making retrieval very fast. The cost of this added functionality is that the SortedList is slower for deletes, updates, and inserts.

The reason the SortedList is slower is that both the keys and the values must be accessible in a sorted manner. This means that when data is added to or removed from the SortedList, the values may be inserted into or removed from the internal value array. This requires memory manipulation. For the Hashtable, the values do not normally require this manipulation. (I had to add the "normally" qualifier in the previous sentence, because as those of you who understand the internal workings of the Hashtable know, a Hashtable can have the same bad performance if multiple keys hash to the same bucket.)

Both the Hashtable and SortedList have numerous constructors, but in most cases, you will probably simply use the default constructor.

```
Hashtable ^hashtable  = gcnew Hashtable();
SortedList ^sortedlist = gcnew SortedList();
```

On the other hand, all the other constructors provide parameters to help with the efficiency of the collection.

A major factor both the Hashtable and SortedList have in common is Capacity. If many entries are to be made into these collection types, then creating them with a sufficiently large capacity allows the entries to be inserted more efficiently than if you let them perform automatic rehashing as needed to grow the collections.

```
Hashtable ^hashtable  = gcnew Hashtable(300);
SortedList ^sortedlist = gcnew SortedList(300);
```

A Hashtable constructor provides another parameter to further refine the collection's efficiency: the load factor. The *load factor* is the ratio of the number of filled buckets to the total number of buckets available. A bucket is full when it points to or contains a data element. The load factor is a value between 0.1 and 1.0. A smaller load factor means faster lookup at the cost of increased memory consumption. Conversely, a larger load factor uses memory more efficiently at the cost of longer expected time per lookup. The default load factor of 1.0 generally provides the best balance between speed and size.

```
Hashtable ^hashtable  = gcnew Hashtable(300, 0.75);
```

You use the Add() method to load these collections. Neither the Hashtable nor the SortedList have an insert method. If you think about it, an insert really doesn't make sense, because the Hashtable analyzes the key and doesn't care where the values are located, and the SortedList is sorted whenever the Add() method is invoked.

```
hashtable->Add(nullptr, "zero");
sortedlist->Add("A", "two");
```

Note Database programmers, take note that in the preceding example, null is a valid key.

Unloading individual elements in the Hashtable and SortedList requires the use of the Remove() method and the specific key. The SortedList also allows elements of the collection to be removed by index value using the RemoveAt() method. It is also possible to remove all the elements of the collections using the Clear() method.

```
hashtable->Remove(nullptr);
hashtable->Clear();
sortedlist->Remove( "A" );
sortedlist->RemoveAt( 2 );
sortedlist->Clear();
```

Now that you can put key/value pairs into a Hashtable and a SortedList, you need to be able to get them out. Both of these collection types provide a plethora of methods to do just that. One of the easiest methods is to use the default index property. Be careful: this is not an array property like you have seen in the previous collection types. A default index property, if you recall from Chapter 3, takes an Object instead of an integer value type between the square brackets, which you normally associate with an array. In this case, the object you would use is the key of the value you wish to retrieve.

```
Console::WriteLine("key="A" value={1}", hash["A"]);
Console::WriteLine("key="A" value={1}", sort["A"]);
```

If you don't know the keys or you simply want all the data and, in the case of a Hashtable, don't care about the order, then you can enumerate through the collections. It's possible to enumerate by key, by value, or by both key and value at the same time. To get the enumerator, you need to use the Keys property, the Values property, or the GetEnumerator() method.

```
IDictionaryEnumerator ^enum1 = hash->GetEnumerator();
IDictionaryEnumerator ^enum2 = sort->GetEnumerator();
IEnumerator ^keys1 = hash->Keys->GetEnumerator();
IEnumerator ^keys2 = sort->Keys->GetEnumerator();
IEnumerator ^vals1 = hash->Values->GetEnumerator();
IEnumerator ^vals2 = sort->Values->GetEnumerator();
```

Enumerating by both key and value at the same time is a little different from what you have seen so far. You need to use the IDictionaryEnumerator interface instead of IEnumerator. Also, to retrieve the key and value from the collection, you use the Key and Value properties and not the Current property (see Listing 7-3 for an example).

The code to enumerate keys and values on their own, though, is no different than any other collection.

If you are not sure, but you want a quick way to see if a Hashtable or SortedList contains a key or a value, you would use the ContainsKey() (or Contains()) method and the ContainsValue() method. Simply use the key or value you are searching for as a parameter. The methods will return true or false.

```
bool b1 = hash->Contains("A");
bool b2 = sort->Contains("A");
bool b3 = hash->ContainsKey("Z");
bool b4 = sort->ContainsKey("Z");
bool b5 = hash->ContainsValue("cat");
bool b6 = sort->ContainsValue("cat");
```

Three methods specific to SortedList are based on indexes to values. Because a Hashtable doesn't have an index to its values, these methods wouldn't make sense, so they aren't included. You can get a value by index or you can get the index of a key or a value.

```
Console::WriteLine("Index {0} contains: {1}", i, sort->GetByIndex(i));
Console::WriteLine("Index key 'B': {0}", sort->IndexOfKey("B"));
Console::WriteLine("Index val 'cat': {0}", sort->IndexOfValue("cat"));
```

Listing 7-3 shows the Hashtable and SortedList in action and demonstrates the functionality described previously.

Listing 7-3. *Working with Hashtables and SortedLists*

```
using namespace System;
using namespace System::Collections;

void main()
{
    Hashtable ^hash  = gcnew Hashtable();
    SortedList ^sort = gcnew SortedList();

    array<String^>^ keys = gcnew array<String^> {"B", "A", "C", "D"};
    array<String^>^ skeys = gcnew array<String^>{"A", "B", "C", "D"};
    array<String^>^ values = gcnew array<String^> {"moose", "zebra",
                                                    "horse", "frog" };

    for (int i = 0; i < keys->Length; i++)
    {
        hash->Add(keys[i], values[i]);
        sort->Add(keys[i], values[i]);
    }
```

```
    Console::WriteLine("Hashtable\tSortedList");

    Console::WriteLine("By indexed property");
    for (int i = 0; i < hash->Count; i++)
    {
        Console::WriteLine("{0} {1}\t\t{2} {3}", skeys[i],
            hash[skeys[i]], skeys[i], sort[skeys[i]]);
    }

    Console::WriteLine("\nBy index");
    for (int i = 0; i < sort->Count; i++)
    {
        Console::WriteLine("N/A\t\t{0} {1}", i, sort->GetByIndex(i));
    }

    Console::WriteLine("\nBy enumerator");
    IDictionaryEnumerator ^enum1 = hash->GetEnumerator();
    IDictionaryEnumerator ^enum2 = sort->GetEnumerator();
    while ( enum1->MoveNext() && enum2->MoveNext())
    {
        Console::Write("{0} {1}\t\t", enum1->Key, enum1->Value);
        Console::WriteLine("{0} {1}", enum2->Key, enum2->Value);
    }

    Console::WriteLine("\nEnumerate Key");
    IEnumerator ^keys1 = hash->Keys->GetEnumerator();
    IEnumerator ^keys2 = sort->Keys->GetEnumerator();
    while ( keys1->MoveNext() && keys2->MoveNext())
    {
        Console::Write("{0}\t\t", keys1->Current);
        Console::WriteLine("{0}", keys2->Current);
    }

    Console::WriteLine("\nEnumerate Value");
    IEnumerator ^vals1 = hash->Values->GetEnumerator();
    IEnumerator ^vals2 = sort->Values->GetEnumerator();
    while ( vals1->MoveNext() && vals2->MoveNext())
    {
        Console::Write("{0}\t\t", vals1->Current);
        Console::WriteLine("{0}", vals2->Current);
    }

    Console::WriteLine("\nContains a Key 'A' and 'Z'");
    Console::WriteLine("{0}\t\t{1}", hash->Contains("A"),
                                      sort->Contains("A"));
    Console::WriteLine("{0}\t\t{1}", hash->ContainsKey("Z"),
                                      sort->ContainsKey("Z"));

    Console::WriteLine("\nContains a Value 'frog' and 'cow'");
    Console::WriteLine("{0}\t\t{1}", hash->ContainsValue("frog"),
                                      sort->ContainsValue("frog"));
    Console::WriteLine("{0}\t\t{1}", hash->ContainsValue("cow"),
                                      sort->ContainsValue("cow"));
```

```
Console::WriteLine("\n\t\t'B' key index: {0}",
    sort->IndexOfKey("B"));

Console::WriteLine("\t\t'frog' value index: {0}",
    sort->IndexOfValue("frog"));
}
```

Figure 7-4 shows the results of the HashSortList.exe program.

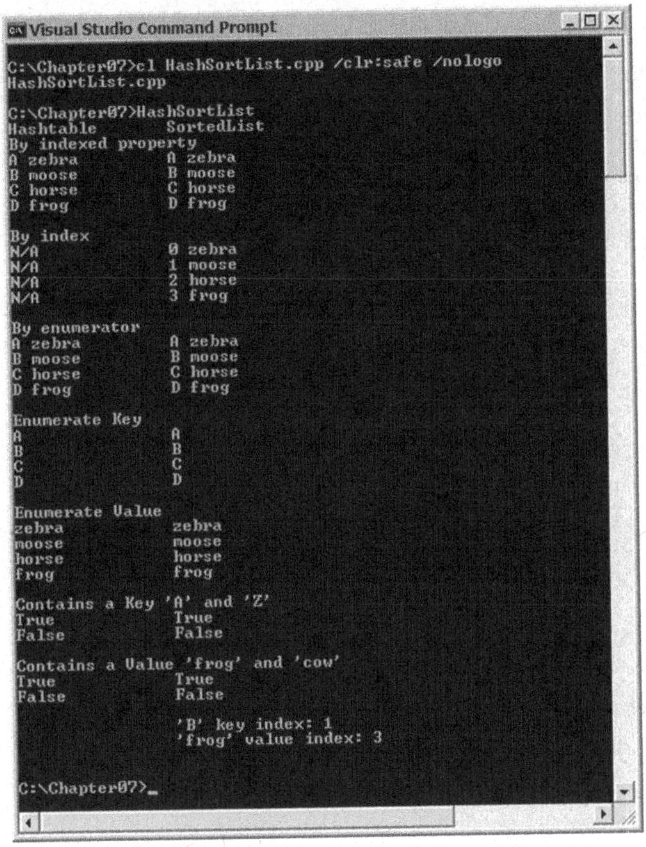

Figure 7-4. *Results of HashSortList.exe*

Queue and Stack

The Queue and Stack collections are simple but handy. If you have ever been to an amusement park and waited to get on a ride, then you should be very familiar with a queue. Basically, the order you go in is the order you come out. A Queue is often known as a *first-in-first-out* (FIFO) collection. The best real-world example that I know of a stack is a plate dispenser at an all-you-can-eat buffet. Here, the last plate placed in is the first one out. A Stack is often known as a *last-in-first-out* (LIFO) collection.

The Queue and Stack collections don't provide a vast array of methods, as many of the other collections do. They do both contain the standard Count property, and the GetEnumerator() and Contains() methods.

Even the constructors of a Queue and a Stack are quite simple. You can create them from another collection, specifying their initial size or taking the default size.

```
Queue ^que1 = gcnew Queue();
Stack ^stk1 = gcnew Stack();
Queue ^que2 = gcnew Queue(8);
Stack ^stk2 = gcnew Stack(8);
Queue ^que3 = gcnew Queue(stk1);
Stack ^stk3 = gcnew Stack(que1);
```

Both the Queue and Stack have one more method in common: the Peek() method. This method allows the program to see the next element that is going to come off the Queue or Stack but does not actually remove it.

```
Console::WriteLine( que->Peek() );
Console::WriteLine( stk->Peek() );
```

Both the Queue and Stack collections have the same process of placing elements on and off. However, they use different method names that more closely resemble the type of collection they are. To place an element onto a Queue, you use the Enqueue() method, and to take an element off the Queue, you use the Dequeue() method. (I know, neither of these method names is actually an English word, but hey, we're programmers, not authors. Wait a minute—I am!)

```
que->Enqueue("First");
que->Dequeue();
```

To place an element onto a Stack, you use the Push() method, and to take it off, you use the Pop() method.

```
stk->Push("First");
stk->Pop();
```

There are occasions when you want to Dequeue or Pop all elements of the Queue or Stack. You can do this with the single method Clear().

Listing 7-4 shows the Queue and Stack in action and demonstrates the functionality described previously.

Listing 7-4. *Working with Queues and Stacks*

```
using namespace System;
using namespace System::Collections;

void main()
{
    Queue ^que = gcnew Queue();
    Stack ^stk = gcnew Stack();

    array<String^>^ entry = gcnew array<String^> {
        "First", "Second", "Third", "Fourth"
    };

    Console::WriteLine("Queue\t\tStack");

    Console::WriteLine("** ON **");
    for (int i = 0; i < entry->Length; i++)
    {
        que->Enqueue(entry[i]);
        stk->Push(entry[i]);
```

```
        Console::WriteLine("{0}\t\t{1}", entry[i], entry[i]);
    }

    Console::WriteLine("\n** OFF **");
    while ((que->Count > 0) && (stk->Count > 0))
    {
        Console::WriteLine("{0}\t\t{1}", que->Dequeue(), stk->Pop());
    }

    que->Clear();
    stk->Clear();

    Console::WriteLine("\n");
}
```

Figure 7-5 shows the results of the QueueStack.exe program.

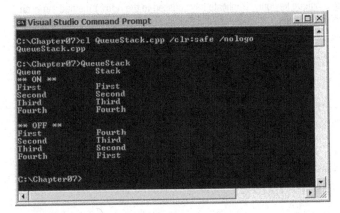

Figure 7-5. *Results of QueueStack.exe*

Specialized Collections

Now that you have covered all of the standard collections, you'll take a look at a few of the more commonly used specialized collections provided by the .NET Framework class library. Unlike the standard set of collections that I discussed previously, these specialized collections require the referencing of the System.dll assembly and use the System::Collections::Specialized namespace.

```
#using <system.dll>
using System::Collections::Specialized;
```

ListDictionary

If you require quick access to a short list of elements, a ListDictionary might just be what you need. It has very little overhead. It is just a singular linked list, which makes it very fast for one-way access in the creation order, if you plan on restricting the number of data elements.

> **Note** Microsoft in the documentation states that the `ListDictionary` is faster than a `Hashtable` if you restrict the size to ten or less. My take on this is that when you plan on having more than ten elements, it is probably better to use a `Hashtable`.

In fact, the .NET Framework class library provides a specialized collection called the `HybridDictionary` that starts off as a `ListDictionary` when the number of entries is small and automatically changes to a `Hashtable` when the number of elements increases.

The `ListDictionary` has few methods, all of which you learned about earlier in this chapter. A feature that the `ListDictionary` shares with the `Hashtable` (and the `SortedList`), which you haven't covered already, is the capability to add key/value pairs using the default index property. As you might expect, when the key passes, the value is changed because the default index property already exists. (What you might not expect is that if the key is unique, then the key/value pair is added.)

> **Caution** `Add()` works when adding a unique key only. Duplicate keys passed to the `Add()` method throw an `ArgumentException` instead of replacing the value.

Listing 7-5 shows the `ListDictionary` in action and demonstrates the functionality described previously.

Listing 7-5. *Working with ListDictionary*

```
#using <system.dll>

using namespace System;
using namespace System::Collections;
using namespace System::Collections::Specialized;

void main()
{
    ListDictionary ^ldict = gcnew ListDictionary();

    ldict->Add("A", "First");
    ldict->Add("B", "Second");
    ldict->Add("C", "Third");
    ldict["D"] = "Fourth";

    try {
        ldict->Add("C", "Third Replaced");
    }
    catch (ArgumentException ^e)
    {
        Console::WriteLine("ldict->Add(\"C\", \"Third Replaced\");");
        Console::WriteLine("Throws exception: {0}", e->Message);
    }
    ldict["B"] = "Second Replaced";
```

```
Console::WriteLine("\nEnumerate");
IEnumerator ^keys = ldict->Keys->GetEnumerator();
IEnumerator ^vals = ldict->Values->GetEnumerator();
while ( keys->MoveNext() && vals->MoveNext())
{
    Console::WriteLine("{0}\t\t{1}", keys->Current, vals->Current);
}

Console::WriteLine();
}
```

Figure 7-6 shows the results of the ListDict.exe program.

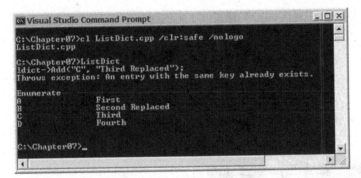

Figure 7-6. *Results of ListDict.exe*

StringCollection

When you plan to maintain many strings, it might be more advantageous to use a StringCollection than any of the other collection types (unless you want key/value access), as a StringCollection is designed to specifically handle strings. A StringCollection resembles a simplified ArrayList in many ways, except that it lacks a few of its methods and uses the StringEnumerator instead of the IEnumerator.

Listing 7-6 shows the StringCollection in action. As you can see, it has many of the same methods as an ArrayList and is strongly typed to strings.

Listing 7-6. *Working with StringCollection*

```
#using <system.dll>

using namespace System;
using namespace System::Collections;
using namespace System::Collections::Specialized;

void main()
{
    StringCollection ^strcol = gcnew StringCollection();

    strcol->Add("The first String");
```

```
array<String^>^ tmpstr = gcnew array<String^> {"Third", "Fourth" };
strcol->AddRange(tmpstr);

strcol->Insert(1, "Second");

strcol[0] = "First";

StringEnumerator ^strenum = strcol->GetEnumerator();
while ( strenum->MoveNext())
{
    Console::WriteLine(strenum->Current);
}

Console::WriteLine("\n'for each' works as well");

for each (String^ s in strcol)
    Console::WriteLine(s);

Console::WriteLine();
}
```

Figure 7-7 shows the results of the StringColl.exe program.

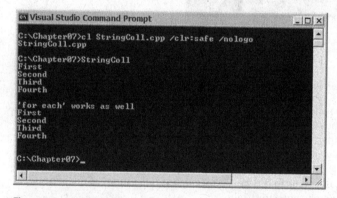

Figure 7-7. *Results of StringColl.exe*

StringDictionary

The StringDictionary sounds impressive, don't you think? It's really just a Hashtable strongly typed and designed specifically for strings. There's nothing new here, other than pretty well all methods expect the String type instead of the Object type.

Listing 7-7 shows the StringDictionary in action. This example shows one of the many ways of displaying the StringDictionary in alphabetical order, as a StringDictionary does not sort its entries. If you recall, a Hashtable works by simply looking up the key to find its value, and no sorting occurs. In the example, you get a copy of all the keys and place them into an ArrayList. Then, you use the ArrayList's built-in Sort() method.

Listing 7-7. *Working with StringDictionary*

```
#using <system.dll>

using namespace System;
using namespace System::Collections;
using namespace System::Collections::Specialized;

void main()
{
    StringDictionary ^strdict = gcnew StringDictionary();

    strdict->Add("Dog", "Four leg, hydrant loving, barking, mammal");
    strdict->Add("Frog", "Green, jumping, croaking, amphibian");

    strdict["Crocodile"] = "Ugly, boot origin, snapping, reptile";

    ArrayList ^alist = gcnew ArrayList();
    alist->AddRange(strdict->Keys);
    alist->Sort();

    for (int i = 0; i < alist->Count; i++)
    {
        Console::WriteLine("{0,10}:\t{1}", alist[i],
            strdict[(String^)alist[i]]);
    }

    Console::WriteLine();
}
```

Figure 7-8 shows the results of the StringDict.exe program.

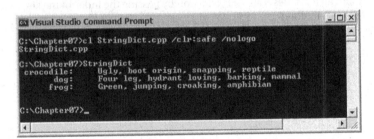

Figure 7-8. *Results of StringDict.exe*

NameValueCollection

Let's finish off the standard collections with one final type: NameValueCollection. This collection is similar in many ways to the StringDictionary. It uses a Hashtable internally and is optimized for handling string. Where it differs is in its ability to have multiple values for a single key.

You can add a key/value pair to a NameValueCollection using the Add() or Set() method, or the default index property. However, only the Add() method allows multiple values to be assigned to a single key:

```
nvCol->Set("Flower", "Rose");
nvCol->Add("Animal", "Dog");
nvCol["Fruit"] = "Plum";
```

You can update the value of a key using either the default index property or the Set() method, but in both cases only a single value can be assigned to a key.

■ **Caution** The default index property and the Set() method will overwrite a key with multiple values with a single value. In other words, you will lose all values assigned to the key and they will be replaced with the new single value.

To get all the keys in the collection, you use the AllKeys property. This property returns an array, which has been cached for better performance and is automatically refreshed when the collection changes.

```
array<String^>^ keys = nvCol.AllKeys;
```

There are two different ways of getting the values using a key: either as an array of strings using the GetValues() method or as a comma-delimited list using the Get() method.

```
array<String^>^ vals = nvCol.GetValues("Flower");
String ^vals = nvCol.Get("Flower");
```

It is also possible to manipulate the collection using indexes. To get a key at a specific index, use the GetKey() method.

```
String ^key = nvCol.GetKey(1);
```

To get the values at a specific index, you use the default index property, but this time passing a numeric index. Using the default index property this way returns a comma-delimited list of values.

```
String ^vals = nvCol[3];
```

You remove a specific key and all its values from the collection by passing the index of the key you want to remove into the Remove() method.

Listing 7-8 shows the NameValueCollection in action.

Listing 7-8. *Working with NameValueCollection*

```
#using <system.dll>

using namespace System;
using namespace System::Collections::Specialized;

void main()
{
    NameValueCollection^ nvCol = gcnew NameValueCollection();

    nvCol->Add(nullptr, "void");

    nvCol->Set("Flower", "Rose");
```

```
nvCol->Add("Animal", "Dog");
nvCol->Add("Animal", "Cat");
nvCol->Add("Animal", "Cow");

nvCol->Add("Fruit", "Apple");
nvCol->Add("Fruit", "Pear");
nvCol->Add("Fruit", "Peach");


array<String^>^ keys = nvCol->AllKeys;

Console::WriteLine("Key\t\tValue");
for (int i = 0; i < keys->Count; i++)
{
    array<String^>^ vals = nvCol->GetValues(keys[i]);

    Console::WriteLine("{0}:\t\t{1}", keys[i], vals[0]);
    for (int j = 1; j < vals->Count; j++)
    {
        Console::WriteLine("\t\t{0}", vals[j]);
    }
}
Console::WriteLine("------ Index Lookups ------");
Console::WriteLine("Key @[1]:\t{0}", nvCol->GetKey(1));
Console::WriteLine("Values @[3]:\t{0}", nvCol[3]);


nvCol->Remove(nullptr);

nvCol["Fruit"] = "Plum";

nvCol->Set("Animal", "Deer");
nvCol->Add("Animal", "Ape");

keys = nvCol->AllKeys;

Console::WriteLine("--------- Updated ---------");
for (int i = 0; i < keys->Count; i++)
{
    Console::WriteLine("{0}:\t\t{1}", keys[i],
                        nvCol->Get(keys[i]));
}

Console::WriteLine();
}
```

Figure 7-9 shows the results of the NameValue.exe program.

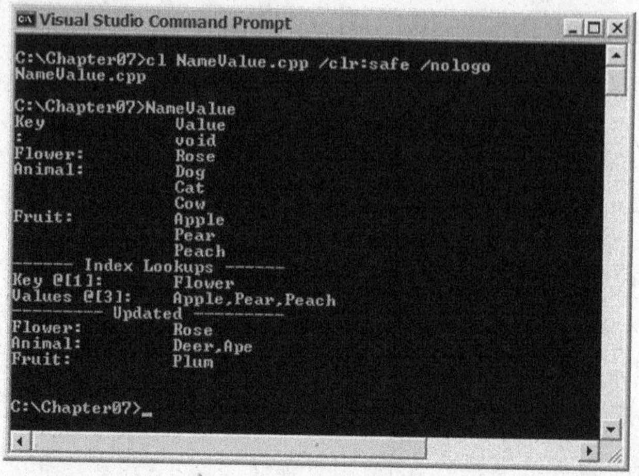

Figure 7-9. *Results of NameValue.exe*

Generic Collections

Originally, I was expecting to write a lot about this set of collections. As I started to work with them, I realized that I'd already covered most of what you need to know earlier in the chapter. The reason for this—the only big difference between generic collections and the standard ones—is the initial code to create the collection and the collection once defined only allows the data type defined in the collection's declaration (or one inherited from it) as an element of the collection. This differs from the standard collection since standard collections don't care which managed types you add to the collection.

Most of the collection types within the generic collection set have standard collection equivalents. The one noticeable and, I think, welcome addition is the LinkedList<T>. I'm not sure I know why it does not have a standard set equivalent, especially since it is many C++ programmers' second choice when it comes to collections (array being the first).

The use of the generic collection set requires either mscorlib.dll:

- List<T>
- Queue<T>
- Stack<T>
- Dictionary<K,V>
- SortedDictionary<K,V>

or System.dll:

- LinkedList<T>
- Collection<T>
- ReadOnlyCollection<T>
- KeyedCollection<K,V>

They all, on the other hand, use the namespace System::Collections::Generic.

One thing that you need to know about generic collections is that none of them support the IsSynchronized or SyncRoot properties and the Synchronized() method (unless you add the functionality yourself). Thus, there is no way to make the default generic collections thread-safe.

Caution The default generic collections cannot be made thread-safe.

List<T>

The List<T> collection is the generic equivalent to the ArrayList. There are some differences, however. List<T> provides most of the functionality of ArrayList; the only notable exception is ArrayList's ability to fix its length. List<T>, on the other hand, has added some functionality: performing a common operation on all elements using an Action<T> delegate, finding elements based on a Predicate<T> delegate, and determining if all have something in common, again using the Predicate<T> delegate.

I'm not going to cover the features that List<T> and ArrayList have in common; just look them up in the earlier ArrayList section, as they are almost always coded the same way.

The List<T> has three constructors. The first is the default constructor, which has no parameters:

```
List<T> ^list = gcnew List<T>();        // T is the data type of the list.
```

You should use this constructor when you have no ballpark idea of how many elements are going to be in the list. If you do know, or have an idea of, how many elements the list contains, then you should use the second constructor, which has a capacity parameter:

```
List<T> ^list = gcnew List<T>(capacity); // T is the data type of the list.
```

The reason this constructor is better is because the capacity is already correct (or almost correct) and the collection doesn't have to perform numerous resizing operations. Remember, though, the caution I mentioned earlier: the collection doubles in size when it needs to perform a resize operation. So if you make the capacity a large number like 32000, and the actual count is 32001, then you'll get a collection of size 64000 elements. That would be a big waste of memory, though you could perform a TrimToSize() or set the Capacity property directly to get the memory back.

The last constructor takes as a parameter another List<T> from which it makes a copy. The initial capacity is the size of the copied List<T>:

```
List<T> ^listOrig = gcnew List<T>();
// ... initialize listOrig wth some elements
List<T> ^listCopy = gcnew List<T>(listOrig);
```

Most of List<T>'s new functionally is available because all the data elements within the collection are the same type or inherited from the same type. Therefore, it is safe to perform common operations on each element without having to worry if the element will abort due to type incompatibility. For the List<T> collection, these operations fall onto two delegates: Action<T> and Predicate<T>.

Action<T>

The Action<T> delegate represents the method that performs an action on the specified element of a collection. Its declaration is

```
public delegate void Action<T>(T obj) sealed;
```

The parameter obj is the object on which the action is being performed.

When you implement the Action<T> delegate, you can make it either a stand-alone function or a static method within a class. Most likely, you will make it a static member of the class of the type of the obj parameter:

```
ref class datatype
{
public:
    static void ActionDelegate(datatype obj);
};

void datatype::ActionDelegate(datatype obj)
{
    // do some operations on obj
}
```

Predicate<T>

The Predicate<T> delegate represents the method that defines a set of conditions and determines whether the specified object meets those conditions. Its declaration is

```
public delegate bool Predicate<T>(T obj) sealed;
```

The parameter obj is the object to which the conditions are being compared.

Just like the Action<T> delegate, when you implement the Predicate<T> delegate, you can make it either a stand-alone function or a static method within a class. Most likely, you will make it a static member of the class of the type of the obj parameter:

```
ref class datatype
{
public:
    static void PredicateDelegate(datatype obj);
};

void datatype::PredicateDelegate(datatype obj)
{
    // compare conditions on obj
}
```

Using Action<T> and Predicate<T>

The Action<T> delegate is used with the List<T>'s ForEach() method. This method allows you to perform specific actions on each element of a List<T> based on the type of List<T>. This differs from the for each statement, because the for each statement performs the same operations on the List<T> no matter what its type. The syntax of the ForEach method is simply

```
list->ForEach(gcnew Action<datatype>(datatype::ActionDelegate));
```

Upon completion of this method, every element of the list will have had the ActionDelegate performed upon it.

The Predicate<T> delegate is used by several methods within the List<T> class:

- Exists(): Determines if elements match the criteria of the Predicate<T>
- Find(): Returns the first element that matches the criteria of the Predicate<T>
- FindAll(): Returns all elements that match the criteria of the Predicate<T>

- FindIndex() Returns a zero-based index to the first element that matches the criteria of the Predicate<T>

- FindList(): Returns the last element that matches the criteria of the Predicate<T>

- FindLastIndex(): Returns a zero-based index to the last element that matches the criteria of the Predicate<T>

- TrueForAll(): Returns true if all elements match the criteria of the Predicate<T>

All of these functions have basically the same syntax. Here is FindAll():

```
List<datatype>^ ret =
    list->FindAll(gcnew Predicate<datatype>(datatype::PredicateDelegate));
```

Some have overloaded methods with additional parameters to limit the number of elements to work on.

Listing 7-9 shows List<T>, Action<T>, and Predicate<T> in action.

Listing 7-9. *Working with List<T>, Action<T>, and Predicate<T>*

```
using namespace System;
using namespace System::Collections::Generic;

// -------- StringEx class -----------------------------------

ref class StringEx
{
public:
    String^ Value;

    StringEx(String^ in);
    virtual String^ ToString() override;

    static bool With_e_Predicate(StringEx^ val);
    static void SurroundInStars(StringEx^ val);
};

StringEx::StringEx(String^ in) : Value(in) {}

String^ StringEx::ToString() { return Value; }

bool StringEx::With_e_Predicate(StringEx^ val)
{
    return val->Value->ToUpper()->IndexOf("E") > 0;
}

void StringEx::SurroundInStars(StringEx^ val)
{
    val->Value = String::Format("** {0} **", val->Value);
}
```

```
// ---------- Main function ----------------------------------------

void main()
{
    List<StringEx^>^ alist = gcnew List<StringEx^>();

    alist->Add(gcnew StringEx("One"));
    alist->Add(gcnew StringEx("-"));
    alist[1] = gcnew StringEx("Three");

    alist->Insert(1, gcnew StringEx("Two"));

    List<StringEx^>^ morenums = gcnew List<StringEx^>();
    morenums->Add(gcnew StringEx("Four"));
    morenums->Add(gcnew StringEx("Five"));

    alist->AddRange(morenums);

//  alist[0] = "Six";      // Compile time error not a StringEx
//  alist->Add("Six");     // Compile time error not a StringEx

    Console::WriteLine("*** The List<StringEx^> ***");
    for (int i = 0; i < alist->Count; i++)
        Console::WriteLine("{0} ", alist[i]);

    // Find all words in list that contain an 'e'
    List<StringEx^>^ With_e =
        alist->FindAll(gcnew Predicate<StringEx^>(StringEx::With_e_Predicate));

    Console::WriteLine("\n\n*** The List<StringEx^> containing an 'e' ***");

    for each(StringEx^ str in With_e)
        Console::WriteLine("{0} ", str);

    // Surround all elements with stars
    alist->ForEach(gcnew Action<StringEx^>(StringEx::SurroundInStars));

    Console::WriteLine("\n\n*** The List<StringEx^> surrounded by stars ***");

    for each(StringEx^ str in alist)
        Console::WriteLine("{0} ", str);

    Console::WriteLine("\n");
}
```

Figure 7-10 shows the results of the ListGeneric.exe program.

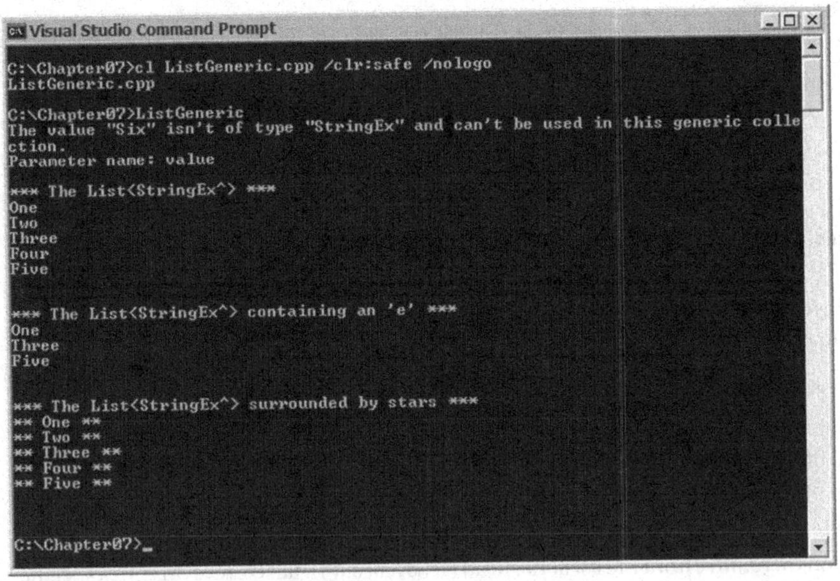

Figure 7-10. *Results of ListGeneric.exe*

LinkedList<T>

A linked list is probably one of the simplest types of collections available, second only to an array. Linked lists store arbitrarily located data in such a way as to make the data sequentially accessible. Specifically, the programmer writes a struct or class containing a handle pointing to the next (and, for a doubly linked list, to the previous) struct or class in the sequence.

A linked list has some advantages even over the array; the most notable advantage being that you can quickly insert and delete items in the sorted linked list. When you insert and delete items in a sorted array, you need to either make room for the new items or fill the hole left by deleting an item. These operations both require all elements after the insertion point to be copied up to the next element in the array in the case of insertion, or down in the case of a delete. The biggest disadvantage to a linked list is that you cannot immediately locate any particular element. Instead, you must traverse the list until you reach the element.

Now, with .NET version 2.0, you have a linked list built into the framework so you don't have to write your own. You might argue that there are plenty of other, more powerful collections available. However, I think there is something to be said for the simplicity of the linked list and its lack of overhead requirements as compared to the other collection types.

The LinkedList<T> has two public constructors. The first is the default constructor, which takes no parameters and creates an empty link list:

```
LinkedList<datatype>^ list = gcnew LinkedList<datatype>();
```

The second takes an object implementing the IEnumerable<T> interface as a parameter. This allows the linked list to start with some existing data:

```
LinkedList<datatype>^ list =
    gcnew LinkedList<datatype>((IEnumerable<datatype>^)existingList);
```

By the way, the array supports the IEnumerable<T> interface, so you can use it to initialize a LinkedList<T>:

```
array<String^>^ arrList = gcnew array<String^> {"One", "Two", "Three"};

LinkedList<String^>^ list =
    gcnew LinkedList<String^>((IEnumerable<String^>^)arrList);
```

The LinkedList<T> is very simple and limited. It is designed to be fast and have little overhead. If you want more features, then you have many more feature-rich collections from which to choose. The features you will most likely use are as follows:

- The LinkedListNode<T> properties to the Head and Tail of the list
- The Find() and FindList() methods, which return a LinkedListNode<T> to the first or last matching node in the list
- The methods to add a new node to the list at the head (AddHead()), tail (AddTail()), before another node (AddBefore()), or after another node (AddAfter())
- The methods to remove from the list at the head (RemoveHead()), tail (RemoveTail()), a specific node (Remove()), or all nodes (Clear())

To reference specific nodes within or to navigate through your LinkedList<T>, you need to use the LinkedListNode<T> class. (You can also use the for each statement to walk (only) forward through the LinkedList<T> as well.

Navigation using LinkedListNode<T> is rather easy. All you do is get the next or previous node from LinkedList<T> via the handle property, pointing to the Next and Previous node on the accessed LinkedListNode<T> object. You know you have reached the beginning or end of the linked list when the Next or Previous property on the LinkedListNode<T> is a nullptr. The Value property contains the actual data being stored by the linked list.

Listing 7-10 shows a plethora of properties and methods of the List<T> and LinkedListNode<T> in action.

Listing 7-10. *Working with Linked Lists*

```
using namespace System;
using namespace System::Collections::Generic;

int main()
{
    array<String^>^ arrList = gcnew array<String^> {"Two", "Three", "Four"};

    LinkedList<String^>^ list =
        gcnew LinkedList<String^>((IEnumerable<String^>^)arrList);

    list->AddTail("Six");
    list->AddHead("Zero");
    list->AddAfter(list->Head, "One");
    list->AddBefore(list->Tail, "5");

    Console::WriteLine("Write with error");

    LinkedListNode<String^>^ current = list->Tail;
```

```
    while (current != nullptr)
    {
        Console::WriteLine(current->Value);
        current = current->Previous;
    }

    Console::WriteLine("\nNumber of elements = {0}", list->Count);

    LinkedListNode<String^>^ node = list->Find("5");

    list->AddBefore(node, "Five");
    list->Remove(node);

    list->RemoveHead();

    Console::WriteLine("\nWrite with corrections");
    for each (String^ str in list)
        Console::WriteLine(str);

    Console::WriteLine("\nNumber of elements = {0}\n", list->Count);

//  list->Add(4);     // Compile time error as type is not a String^
}
```

Figure 7-11 shows the results of the LinkListGeneric.exe program.

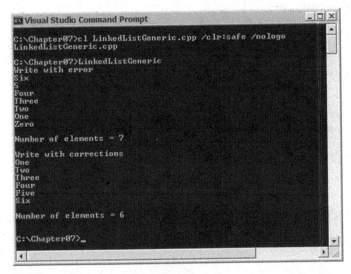

Figure 7-11. *Results of LinkedListGeneric.exe*

Queue<T> and Stack<T>

Other than the syntax of the constructors, there is really no difference between the generic and standard versions. In fact, they contain nearly exactly the same methods and properties. A noticeable exception is the thread-safe properties and methods, which the generic collections lack.

Since there is nothing really new, I'll just provide Listing 7-11, which is a conversion of the earlier standard Queue and Stack example to Queue<T> and Stack<T>. Notice that the only two lines that changed from QueueStack.cpp are

```
Queue<String^>^ que = gcnew Queue<String^>();
Stack<String^>^ stk = gcnew Stack<String^>();
```

Listing 7-11. *Working with Queue<T>s and Stack<T>s*

```
#using <system.dll>

using namespace System;
using namespace System::Collections::Generic;

void main()
{
    Queue<String^>^ que = gcnew Queue<String^>();
    Stack<String^>^ stk = gcnew Stack<String^>();

    array<String^>^ entry = gcnew array<String^> {
        "First", "Second", "Third", "Fourth"
    };

    Console::WriteLine("Queue\t\tStack");

    Console::WriteLine("** ON **");
    for (int i = 0; i < entry->Length; i++)
    {
        que->Enqueue(entry[i]);
        stk->Push(entry[i]);

        Console::WriteLine("{0}\t\t{1}", entry[i], entry[i]);
    }

    Console::WriteLine("\n** OFF **");
    while ((que->Count > 0) && (stk->Count > 0))
    {
        Console::WriteLine("{0}\t\t{1}", que->Dequeue(), stk->Pop());
    }

    que->Clear();
    stk->Clear();

    Console::WriteLine("\n");
}
```

Figure 7-12 shows the results of the QueueStackGeneric.exe program.

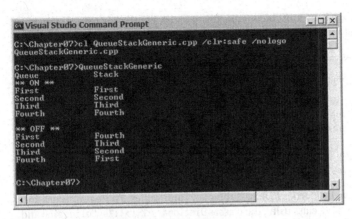

Figure 7-12. *Results of QueueStackGeneric.exe*

Dictionary<K,V>, SortedDictionary<K,V>

The Dictionary<K,V> and SortedDictionary<K,V> are extremely handy key/value pair collections. With the addition of generics, you are now provided an elegant way to control your key/value pair type storage. Each allows you to define the data types of both the key and the value, and then ensure that those data types are the only ones used when implementing the collection.

The Dictionary<K,V> and SortedDictionary<K,V> are very similar in many respects. Obviously, as the collection names suggest, their biggest difference is that the SortedDictionary<K,V> is sorted. (Why do I want to write "Duh!" here?) You also have greater control over the elements when working with the SortedDictionary<K,V>, mainly because it is sorted.

Both dictionary collections have six constructors. The first three are pretty standard: default with no parameters, a parameter of capacity, and a parameter of IDictionary for preloading.

```
Dictionary<K,V>^ dict1 = gcnew Dictionary<K,V>();
SortedDictionary<K,V>^ dict2 = gcnew SortedDictionary<K,V>();

Dictionary<K,V>^ dict3 = gcnew SortedDictionary<K,V>(100);
SortedDictionary<K,V>^ dict4 = gcnew SortedDictionary<K,V>(100);

Dictionary<K,V>^ dict5 = gcnew SortedDictionary<K,V>(inDictionary);
SortedDictionary<K,V>^ dict6 = gcnew SortedDictionary<K,V>(inDictionary);
```

One thing that you might note is that since both the Dictionary<K,V> and SortedDictionary<K,V> inherit from the IDictionary interface, you can interchangeably load from either dictionary type.

One requirement of both these dictionary types is that the key's data type needs to implement IComparable<K> or System::IComparable. If it doesn't, then you need to use one of the three remaining constructors that take the additional parameter of IComparer<K>, thus adding the ability to compare the keys.

One cool feature is that you can implement your own version of IComparer<K> for the dictionary. This allows, in the case of SortedDictionary<K,V>, a way of sorting the elements as you wish.

You can load either of these dictionaries using either the Add() method or the default index property. The default index property takes as its index the key of the value.

```
dict->Add("Key1", "One");
dict["Key2"] = "Two";
```

All keys for either type of dictionary must be unique. If you try to repeat a key using the Add() method, the dictionary is going to throw the exception

```
System.ArgumentException: An item with the same key has already been added.
```

On the other hand, if you repeat a key using the default index property, the value is just replaced:

```
dict->Add("Key3", "3");
dict["Key3"] = "Three";    // replaces value
dict->Add("Key3", "3");    // throws exception
```

To access the value for a key, simply call the default index property with the index of the key:

```
String^ value = dict["Key3"];
```

Both dictionaries contain two properties to access their keys and values. These properties are implemented for the Dictionary<K,V> class using the classes Dictionary<K,V>::KeyCollection and Dictionary<K,V>::ValueCollection, and for the SortedDictionary<K,V> class using the classes SortedDictionary<K,V>::KeyCollection and SortedDictionary<K,V>::ValueCollection. From these classes, you grab an enumerator to the keys and values with the GetEnumerator() method:

```
Dictionary<K,V>::KeyCollection::Enumerator ^k = dict->Keys->GetEnumerator();
Dictionary<K,V>::ValueCollection::Enumerator ^v =dict->Values->GetEnumerator();

while ( k->MoveNext() && v->MoveNext())
{
    Console::WriteLine("Key = [{0}]\tValue = [{1}]", k->Current, v->Current);
}
```

and

```
SortedDictionary<K,V>::KeyCollection::Enumerator ^k =
    dict->Keys->GetEnumerator();
SortedDictionary<K,V>::ValueCollection::Enumerator ^v =
    dict->Values->GetEnumerator();

while ( k->MoveNext() && v->MoveNext())
{
    Console::WriteLine("Key = [{0}]\tValue = [{1}]", k->Current, v->Current);
}
```

Both dictionary types allow you to remove key/value pairs from the collection using the Remove() method, which takes as a parameter the key.

Okay, here is one last note before moving on to an example. A for each statement requires, as the first part of the statement, the type of each element in the collection. Since each element of the dictionaries is a key/value pair, the element type is not the type of the key or the type of the value. Instead, the element type is KeyValuePair<K,V>. Therefore, to use the for each statement to iterate through the collection, you need to code something similar to this:

```
for each (KeyValuePair<K,T> pair in dictionary)
{
    Console::WriteLine("Key = [{0}]\tValue = [{1}]", pair->Key, pair->Value);
}
```

Listing 7-12 shows the Dictionary<K,V> and SortedDictionary<K,V> in action.

Listing 7-12. *Working with Generic Dictionaries*

```cpp
#using <system.dll>

using namespace System;
using namespace System::Collections::Generic;

// Make the dictionary sort in reverse
ref class Reverse : public IComparer<int>
{
public:
    virtual int Compare(int x, int y) { return y - x; }
    virtual bool Equals(int x, int y) { return x == y; }
    virtual int GetHashCode(int obj) { return obj.GetHashCode(); }
};

Dictionary<int,String^>^ DictionaryExample()
{
    Dictionary<int,String^>^ dict = gcnew Dictionary<int,String^>();

    dict->Add(1,  "One");
    dict->Add(6,  "Six");
    dict->Add(5,  "Five");

    dict->Add(3,  "3");
//  dict->Add(3,  "3");  // throws an exception
    dict[3] = "Three";

    dict[7] = "Seven";

    String^ t = dict[3];
    Console::WriteLine("dict[3] = {0}\n", t);

    for each (KeyValuePair<int,String^>^ pair in dict)
    {
        Console::WriteLine("Key = [{0}]\tValue = [{1}]",
            pair->Key, pair->Value);
    }

    Console::WriteLine("\nDictionary contains 6? [{0}]",
        dict->ContainsKey(6));

    dict->Remove(6);

    Console::WriteLine("\nDictionary had 6 removed? [{0}]\n",
        !dict->ContainsKey(6));

    Dictionary<int,String^>::KeyCollection::Enumerator ^key =
        dict->Keys->GetEnumerator();
    Dictionary<int,String^>::ValueCollection::Enumerator ^value =
        dict->Values->GetEnumerator();
```

```
    while ( key->MoveNext() && value->MoveNext())
    {
        Console::WriteLine("Key = [{0}]\tValue = [{1}]",
            key->Current, value->Current);
    }

    return dict;
}

void SortedDictionaryExample(Dictionary<int,String^>^ inDict)
{
    SortedDictionary<int,String^>^ dict =
        gcnew SortedDictionary<int,String^>(inDict, gcnew Reverse());

    dict->Add(6,  "Six");

    String^ t = dict[3];
    Console::WriteLine("dict[3] = {0}\n", t);

    Console::WriteLine("Sorted Values:");
    for each (String ^s in dict->Values)
        Console::WriteLine("\t{0}",s);

    Console::WriteLine();

    for each (KeyValuePair<int,String^>^ pair in dict)
    {
        Console::WriteLine("Key = [{0}]\tValue = [{1}]",
            pair->Key, pair->Value);
    }

    Console::WriteLine("\nSortedDictionary contains 'Six'? [{0}]",
        dict->ContainsValue("Six"));

    dict->Remove(6);

    Console::WriteLine("\nSortedDictionary had 'Six' removed? [{0}]\n",
        !dict->ContainsValue("Six"));

    SortedDictionary<int,String^>::KeyCollection::Enumerator ^key =
        dict->Keys->GetEnumerator();
    SortedDictionary<int,String^>::ValueCollection::Enumerator ^value =
        dict->Values->GetEnumerator();

    while ( key->MoveNext() && value->MoveNext())
    {
        Console::WriteLine("Key = [{0}]\tValue = [{1}]",
            key->Current, value->Current);
    }
}
```

```
void main()
{
    Console::WriteLine("Dictionary\n----------");
    Dictionary<int,String^>^ dict = DictionaryExample();

    Console::WriteLine();

    Console::WriteLine("\nReverse SortedDictionary\n----------------");
    SortedDictionaryExample(dict);

    Console::WriteLine();
}
```

Figure 7-13 shows the results of the DictionaryGeneric.exe program.

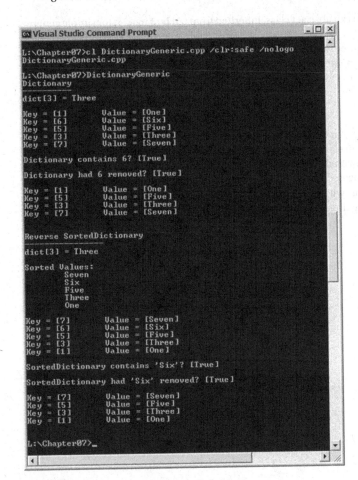

Figure 7-13. *Results of DictionaryGeneric.exe*

Collection<T> and ReadOnlyCollection<T>

Since exposing collections from an object is such a common activity in .NET development, the .NET Framework has provided three base classes to do this: Collection<T>, ReadOnlyCollection<T>, and KeyedCollection<K,V>. There is really nothing new to learn about these collections. All they implement is the minimum functionality required for accessing collections, which we have already gone over in detail.

The Collection<T> class is the base class for simple generic collections and provides implementations for the IList<T>, ICollection<T>, IEnumerable<T>, IList, ICollection, and IEnumerable interfaces.

The ReadOnlyCollection<T> class is the base class for simple generic read-only collections and provides implementations for the IList<T>, ICollection<T>, IEnumerable<T>, IList, ICollection, and IEnumerable interfaces. Unlike Collection<T> class, there are no properties or methods to update the collection.

The KeyedCollection<K,V> is an abstract class, inherited from Collection<T>, for simple generic key/value collections.

Microsoft suggests that you return one of these three types of collections from your objects if you want to provide a standard, plain-vanilla collection API.

Summary

In this chapter, you took a somewhat detailed look at some of the collections made available by the .NET Framework class library. You started by looking at the IEnumerable interface, which is common to most collections. Next, you covered all the common collections. You then examined a few of the more specialized collections provided by the .NET Framework class library. You finished by examining the generic type collections, which are new to .NET version 2.0.

In the next chapter, you're going to look at how the .NET Framework addresses the important areas of file I/O.

CHAPTER 8

■ ■ ■

Input, Output, and Serialization

Most programs are of little use if there is no way of retrieving input from some source and outputting it to the same or another source. You have several options available for handling input/output (I/O). In this chapter, you will examine file and directory I/O, I/O manipulation, and finally, serialization or the process of storing the state of an object or member to a permanent medium.

There are other I/O mechanisms. For example, this book covers databases, XML, and GUI interfaces in later chapters. Before you get to these more complex I/O systems, you'll start with simple files. Files are the core of most I/O-related activities in a program.

The first thing you need to look at is the file system. Anybody who plays (oops, I mean *works*) on a computer sees the file system as an uncomplicated means of placing files wherever he wants them. Usually, the file system is taken for granted. Truthfully, the file system is anything but simple and, without the .NET Framework class library, a developer would see just how complicated it really is.

Once you have the file system under your belt, you will end this chapter with serialization. *Serialization* is the process of storing a class to the file system for later retrieval. You will see how unbelievably easy this is to do with the .NET Framework class library.

File System Input and Output

When you think of the file system, you need to consider its two parts: files and directories. The .NET Framework class library tries to treat files and directories in a very similar way. But, obviously, there are things that you can do with one that you can't do with the other. Because of this, the .NET Framework class library has split the functionality of files and directories into two. Well, that is not actually correct, the functionality was split into four: two classes for files and two for directories.

The reason files and directories were split into two classes each is because of the two different ways programmers tend to work with them: either one-time access or over the lifetime of a method, a class, or even an application. One-time access operations on a file or directory really don't need the overhead of creating an instance of a class to handle the operation. Instead, the use of static methods seems more appropriate. On the other hand, if the file handle or directory handle is going to be around for a while, it makes sense to create a class instance to hold the file handle or directory handle.

The two classes that make up file access are `File` and `FileInfo`. The `File` class contains static methods to access files, whereas you need to create an instance of a `FileInfo` class to access files. They have much of the same functionality, so selecting one over the other based on functionality does not normally make sense. Instead, you should choose one class over the other based on the number of times the file will be accessed and whether the information being accessed needs to be cached to increase performance. If it will be accessed one time only, then `File` makes sense. If you need repeated cached access to the file, you should use the `FileInfo` class.

Managing the File System

As someone who has coded before, you know that you can open, read, and write to files. The .NET Framework class library takes files and the file system in general a step further. It treats files and directories like the objects they are. It provides not only the standard I/O features you have come to expect in a framework, but also ways of dealing with files and directories as a whole. For example, it is possible to copy, move, get information about, and delete complete file and directory objects. With these functions, you now have a way of providing for the maintenance of the file system as a whole and not just the files that make up the system.

FileSystemInfo

You will look at files and directories separately, but you could almost cover them as one, because they have numerous methods and properties in common. In fact, both DirectoryInfo and FileInfo are derived from the same abstract class, FileSystemInfo.

The FileSystemInfo class provides the numerous properties and methods that the DirectoryInfo and FileInfo classes have in common (see Table 8-1).

Table 8-1. *Commonly Used FileSystemInfo Class Members*

Property/Method	Description
Attributes	Gets or sets attributes associated with the current file system object.
CreationTime	Gets or sets creation date and time of current file system object.
Exists	Determines whether the file system object exists.
Extension	Gets the string extension associated with the current file system object.
FullName	Gets full name of the current file system object. This will include the file or directories path.
LastAccessTime	Gets or sets last access date and time of current file system object.
LastWriteTime	Gets or sets last date and time current file system object was updated.
Name	Gets the name of the file or the last directory of current file system object.
Delete()	Deletes the current file system object.

As you can see, other than the Delete() method, each of the FileSystemInfo class members in Table 8-1 provides information about the file or directory of the current instance. Some even provide you with update abilities.

Directory and DirectoryInfo

The Directory and DirectoryInfo classes provide you with a means of maintaining the directory structure under which your program has control. If you've ever worked directly with the directory structure without the aid of some form of framework, then you'll quickly come to appreciate the ease with which you can maintain the directory system using the .NET Framework class library. To prove that it's simple to work with directories in the .NET Framework class library, let's examine a few of the more common methods and properties.

Whether you are using the static methods provided by Directory or the properties and member method of DirectoryInfo will determine if you need to call a constructor. Obviously, calling static member methods does not require you to instantiate a class, and thus there is no need for a constructor.

The constructor for the DirectoryInfo class simply takes the full path to the directory you wish to manipulate as a parameter, though the directory doesn't need to exist if you're creating it. As you continue, you'll see that the Directory static member calls have this same full path as the member's first parameter.

```
DirectoryInfo ^dir = gcnew DirectoryInfo("C:\\WinNT\\Temp");
```

To examine the details of a directory using the DirectoryInfo class, you need to implement the inherited properties of the FileSystemInfo class. On the other hand, if you are implementing the Directory class, the static member methods are a bit different.

```
// DirectoryInfo implementation:
String^        Name       = dir->FullName;
DateTime       Created    = dir->CreationTime;
DateTime       Accessed   = dir->LastAccessTime;
DateTime       Updated    = dir->LastWriteTime;
FileAttributes Attributes = dir->Attributes;


// Directory implementation
// No equivalent for dir->FullName
DateTime Created  = Directory::GetCreationTime("C:\\WinNT\\Temp");
DateTime Accessed = Directory::GetLastAccessTime("C:\\WinNT\\Temp");
DateTime Updated  = Directory::GetLastWriteTime("C:\\WinNT\\Temp");
// No equivalent for dir->Attributes
```

Commonly, you are going to want to list all the files and directories that are contained within the current directory. Both Directory and DirectoryInfo provide methods to get all the files and subdirectories separately in two method calls or together in one method call. Notice, though, that the DirectoryInfo implementation returns an Object, whereas the Directory implementation returns complete directory strings.

```
// DirectoryInfo implementation:
array<DirectoryInfo^>^  subDirs   = dir->GetDirectories();
array<FileInfo^>^       files     = dir->GetFiles();
array<FileSystemInfo^>^ dirsFiles = dir->GetFileSystemInfos();


// Directory implementation
array<String^>^ subDirs   = Directory::GetDirectories("C:\\WinNT\\Temp");
array<String^>^ files     = Directory::GetFiles("C:\\WinNT\\Temp");
array<String^>^ dirsFiles = Directory::GetFileSystemEntries("C:\\WinNT\\Temp");
```

Three useful methods that Directory has that DirectoryInfo doesn't are as follows:

```
String ^currentDirectory = Directory::GetCurrentDirectory();
Directory::SetCurrentDirectory(currentDirectory);
array<String^>^ logicalDrives = Directory::GetLogicalDrives();
```

These methods get and set the current working directory and get all current logical drives on the system.

A handy auxiliary class that you can use to manipulate the complete directory strings is the Path class. This class contains several static methods to combine, extract, and manipulate path strings. Table 8-2 shows some of the more useful static methods.

Table 8-2. *Commonly Used Path Class Members*

Method	Description
ChangeExtension()	Changes the extension of the path string.
GetDirectoryName()	Extracts the directory name out of the path string. Notice that for a directory, this method extracts the parent path.
GetExtension()	Gets the extension from the filename contained in the path string.
GetFileName()	Gets the filename or the directory name.
GetFileNameWithoutExtension()	Gets the extension from the filename contained in the path string.
GetFullPath()	Gets the absolute path of the path string.

To extract the filename out of a complete directory string, you would use the following GetFileName() method of the Path class:

```
array<String^>^ files = Directory::GetFileSystemEntries(path);
for each (String^ file in files)
{
    Console::WriteLine(Path::GetFileName(file));
}
```

The activities that you will probably do most with directories are checking whether the directory exists, creating a directory, moving or renaming an existing directory, and deleting a directory.

```
// DirectoryInfo implementation:
if (dir->Exists) {}
dir->Create();  // Notice it creates the directory specified by constructor
dir->CreateSubdirectory("SubDir");
dir->MoveTo("C:\\WinNT\\TempXXX"); // Move or rename the current directory tree
dir->Delete();  // Will fail if directory is not empty
dir->Delete(true);  // Deletes the entire directory tree (security permitting)

// Directory implementation
if (Directory::Exists("C:\\WinNT\\Temp")) {}
Directory::CreateDirectory("C:\\WinNT\\TempXXX");
Directory::Move("C:\\WinNT\\Temp", "C:\\WinNT\\TempXXX");
Directory::Delete("C:\\WinNT\\TempXXX");
Directory::Delete("C:\\WinNT\\TempXXX", true);
```

Listing 8-1 shows the DirectoryInfo class in action and demonstrates many of the functionalities described previously.

Listing 8-1. *Working with DirectoryInfo*

```
using namespace System;
using namespace System::IO;
using namespace System::Text;

int main(array<System::String ^> ^args)
{
    if (args->Length == 0)
    {
        Console::WriteLine("Usage: DirInfo <Directory>");
        return -1;
    }

    StringBuilder ^tmppath = gcnew StringBuilder();

    for each (String^ s in args)
    {
        tmppath->Append(s);
        tmppath->Append(" ");
    }

    String ^path = tmppath->ToString()->Trim();

    DirectoryInfo ^dir = gcnew DirectoryInfo(path);

    if (!dir->Exists)
    {
        Console::WriteLine("Directory Not Found");
        return -1;
    }

    Console::WriteLine("Name:        {0}", dir->FullName);

    Console::WriteLine("Created:    {0} {1}",
        dir->CreationTime.ToShortDateString(),
        dir->CreationTime.ToLongTimeString());

    Console::WriteLine("Accessed:    {0} {1}",
        dir->LastAccessTime.ToShortDateString(),
        dir->LastAccessTime.ToLongTimeString());

    Console::WriteLine("Updated:    {0} {1}",
        dir->LastWriteTime.ToShortDateString(),
        dir->LastWriteTime.ToLongTimeString());

    Console::WriteLine("Attributes: {0}",
        dir->Attributes);

    Console::WriteLine("Sub-Directories:");
```

```
    array<DirectoryInfo^>^ subDirs = dir->GetDirectories();
    if (subDirs->Length == 0)
        Console::WriteLine("\tNone.");
    else
    {
        for each (DirectoryInfo^ dinfo in subDirs)
        {
            Console::WriteLine("\t{0}", dinfo->Name);
        }
    }

    Console::WriteLine("Files:");

    array<FileInfo^>^ files = dir->GetFiles();
    if (files->Length == 0)
        Console::WriteLine("\tNone.");
    else
    {
        for each (FileInfo^ finfo in files)
        {
            Console::WriteLine("\t{0}", finfo->Name);
        }
    }

    return 0;
}
```

Figure 8-1 shows the results of the DirInfo.exe program.

Figure 8-1. *Results of DirInfo.exe*

File and FileInfo

Once you understand how to manage directories, it's not a big leap to manage files. Most of the properties and methods you use to manage files are identical to those you use to manage directories. The big difference, obviously, is that the class names have changed to `File` and `FileInfo`. In addition, there are a few additional file-specific methods added and a couple of directory-specific methods removed. There are also several methods to open up files in different ways. You will learn more about those a little later in the chapter.

Just like directories, having a constructor depends on whether you are using the static methods of `File` or the instance member methods of `FileInfo`.

```
FileInfo ^fileinfo = gcnew FileInfo("C:\\WinNT\\Temp\\file.dat");
```

■ **Note** You could also have coded the previous line as

```
FileInfo ^fileinfo = gcnew FileInfo("file.dat");
```

So long as the current directory is C:\WinNT\Temp. You can get and set the current directory with the Directory class's `GetCurrentDirectory()` and `SetCurrentDirectory()` methods.

Examining the details of a file while implementing the `FileInfo` class requires the use of the inherited properties of the `FileSystemInfo` class. You will see very little difference between the file methods and the directory methods. The `File` class's static methods are also the same as the directory equivalent, but this time there is a static method to retrieve attributes (see Table 8-3). There is an additional property to get the length of the file out of a `FileInfo` class but, oddly enough, there is no static method in the `File` class.

```
// FileInfo implementation:
String^          Name       = fileinfo->FullName;
DateTime         Created    = fileinfo->CreationTime;
DateTime         Accessed   = fileinfo->LastAccessTime;
DateTime         Updated    = fileinfo->LastWriteTime;
FileAttributes Attributes = fileinfo->Attributes;
Int64            Length     = fileinfo->Length; // Physical, uncompressed, and
                                                //  unclustered size


// File implementation
// No equivalent for file->FullName
DateTime         Created    = File::GetCreationTime("C:\\WinNT\\Temp\\file.dat");
DateTime         Accessed   = File::GetLastAccessTime("file.dat");
DateTime         Updated    = File::GetLastWriteTime("file.dat");
FileAttributes Attributes = File::GetAttributes("file.dat");
// No equivalent for file->Length;
```

Table 8-3. *Common File Attributes*

Attribute	Description
Archive	This attribute marks a file for archive or backup.
Directory	The file is a directory.
Encrypted	For a file, it means it is encrypted. For a directory, it means that all newly created files in the directory will be encrypted.
Hidden	The file is hidden from normal directory display.
Normal	The file is normal and has no other attributes set. (Note: This attribute is only valid if it is the only attribute set.)
ReadOnly	The file is read-only.
System	The file is part of the operating system.

Other than open files, which I cover next, the most likely activities you will do with files are check whether a file exists, copy or move an existing file, or simply delete a file. You will find that the methods closely resemble those of the directory.

```
// FileInfo implementation:
if (fileinfo->Exists) {}
fileinfo->CopyTo("C:\\WinNT\\Temp\\file.dat");
fileinfo->CopyTo("file.dat", true);  // Overwrite existing
fileinfo->MoveTo("C:\\WinNT\\Temp\\file.dat"); // Target file can't exist
fileinfo->Delete(); // delete the file

// File implementation:
if (File::Exists("C:\\WinNT\\Temp\\file.dat")) {}
File::Copy("C:\\WinNT\\Temp\\file1.dat", "C:\\WinNT\\Temp\\file2.dat");
File::Copy("file1.dat", "file2.dat", true); //overwrite existing
File::Move("C:\\WinNT\\Temp\\file1.dat", "file2.dat");
File::Delete("file1.dat");
```

■**Caution** Even though the documentation sort of suggests otherwise, the destination of the Move() and MoveTo() methods cannot be a directory. The destination must be a nonexistent filename or a complete path including the filename.

Listing 8-2 shows the FileInfo class in action and demonstrates many of the functionalities described previously.

Listing 8-2. *Working with FileInfo*

```
using namespace System;
using namespace System::IO;
using namespace System::Text;

int main(array<System::String ^> ^args)
{
    if (args->Length == 0)
    {
        Console::WriteLine("Usage: FileInfo <File>");
        return -1;
    }

    StringBuilder ^tmpfile = gcnew StringBuilder();

    for each (String^ s in args)
    {
        tmpfile->Append(s);
        tmpfile->Append(" ");
    }

    String ^strfile = tmpfile->ToString()->Trim();

    FileInfo ^fileinfo = gcnew FileInfo(strfile);

    if (!fileinfo->Exists)
    {
        Console::WriteLine("File Not Found");
        return -1;
    }

    Console::WriteLine("Name:       {0}", fileinfo->FullName);

    Console::WriteLine("Created:    {0} {1}",
        fileinfo->CreationTime.ToShortDateString(),
        fileinfo->CreationTime.ToLongTimeString());

    Console::WriteLine("Accessed:   {0} {1}",
        fileinfo->LastAccessTime.ToShortDateString(),
        fileinfo->LastAccessTime.ToLongTimeString());

    Console::WriteLine("Updated:    {0} {1}",
        fileinfo->LastWriteTime.ToShortDateString(),
        fileinfo->LastWriteTime.ToLongTimeString());

    Console::WriteLine("Length:     {0}", fileinfo->Length);

    Console::WriteLine("Attributes: {0}", fileinfo->Attributes);

    return 0;
}
```

Figure 8-2 shows the results of the FileInfo.exe program.

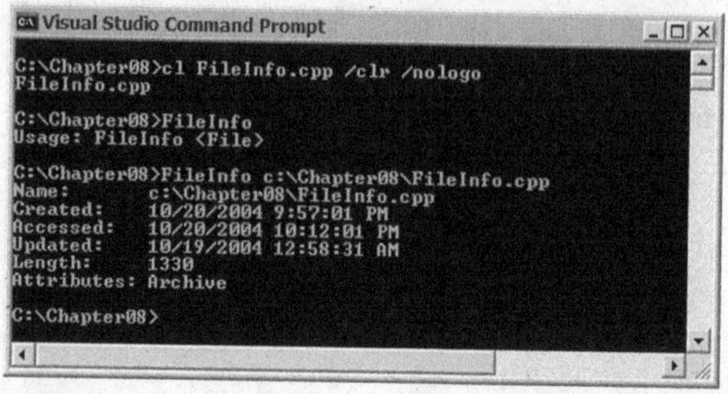

Figure 8-2. *Results of FileInfo.exe*

Opening Files

There is no shortage of ways that you can open a file using the .NET Framework class library. There are 14 methods combined in the File and FileInfo class (see Table 8-4). Many of these methods have numerous parameter combinations. Both File and FileInfo use the same 7 method names, and each of the methods with the same name do the same thing. Though the methods have the same name, the parameters passed differ, or at least the first parameter differs.

There always seems to be one exception. The File::Create() has an overloaded method that has a buffer size parameter that the FileInfo class's Create() method lacks.

Table 8-4. *Opening a File Using the File and FileInfo Classes*

Method	Description
Open()	Creates a FileStream to a file providing a plethora of read/write and share privilege options
Create()	Creates a FileStream providing full read and write privileges to a file
OpenRead()	Creates a read-only FileStream to an existing file
OpenWrite()	Creates a write-only unshared FileStream to a file
AppendText()	Creates a StreamWriter that appends text to the end of an existing file
CreateText()	Creates a StreamWriter that writes a new text file
OpenText()	Creates a StreamReader that reads from an existing file

You will see FileStream, StreamWriter, and StreamReader later in this chapter.

Of these 14 (7×2) methods, only 2 actually take any parameters (other than the name of the file you wish to open for the static methods). Basically, the .NET Framework class library provides 2 equivalent file open methods and 12 shortcuts.

The Open Methods

There are only two root open methods in the .NET Framework class library: `File::Open()` and `FileInfo::Open()`. These methods are virtually the same, except the `File::Open()` method has one additional parameter: the path to the file you want to open. The `FileInfo::Open()` method gets this information from its constructor.

The `Open()` method is made up of three overloaded methods. Each overload provides progressively more information about how you want the file opened. The first overload takes as a parameter the file mode with which you wish to open the file (see Table 8-5). Because the other two parameters are not specified, the file will open by default with read/write access and as unshared.

```
FileInfo  ^fileinfo = gcnew FileInfo("file.dat");
FileStream ^fs = fileinfo.Open(FileMode::Truncate);
// or
FileStream ^fs = File::Open("file.dat", FileMode::CreateNew);
```

Table 8-5. *FileMode Enumeration Values*

FileMode	Description
Append	Opens a file if it exists and sets the next write point to the end of the file. If the file does not exist, it creates a new one. You can only use `FileMode::Append` with a file access of write-only, as any attempt to read throws an `ArgumentException`.
Create	Creates a new file. If the file already exists, it will be overwritten.
CreateNew	Creates a new file. If the file already exists, an `IOException` is thrown.
Open	Opens an existing file. If the file does not exist, a `FileNotFoundException` is thrown.
OpenOrCreate	Opens an existing file. If the file does not exist, it creates a new file.
Truncate	Opens an existing file and truncates it to a length of 0 bytes. If the file does not exist, a `FileNotFoundException` is thrown.

The second overload takes the additional parameter of the file access you require the file to have (see Table 8-6). The file will also be opened by default as unshared.

```
FileInfo  ^fileinfo = gcnew FileInfo("file.dat");
FileStream ^fs = fileinfo->Open(FileMode::Truncate, FileAccess::ReadWrite);
// or
FileStream ^fs = File::Open("file.dat", FileMode::Append, FileAccess::Write);
```

Table 8-6. *FileAccess Enumeration Values*

FileAccess	Description
Read	Allows data only to be read from the file
ReadWrite	Allows data to be read from and written to the file
Write	Allows data only to be written to the file

The final overload has one more parameter. It specifies how the file is shared with others trying to access it concurrently (see Table 8-7).

```
FileInfo  ^fileinfo = gcnew FileInfo("file.dat");
FileStream ^fs = fileinfo->Open(FileMode::Truncate, FileAccess::ReadWrite,
                        FileShare::Read);
// or
FileStream ^fs = File::Open("file.dat", FileMode::Append, FileAccess::Write,
                            FileShare::None);
```

Table 8-7. *FileShare Enumeration Values*

FileShare	Description
None	Specifies exclusive access to the current file. Subsequent openings of the file by a process, including the current one, will fail until the file closes.
Read	Specifies that subsequent openings of the file by a process, including the current one, will succeed only if it is for a FileMode of Read.
ReadWrite	Specifies that subsequent openings of the file by a process, including the current one, will succeed for either reading or writing.
Write	Specifies that subsequent openings of the file by a process, including the current one, will succeed only if it is for a FileMode of Write.

All those parameters make the file open process very configurable, but also a little tedious. This is especially true if you just want to open the file in a very generic and standard way. The .NET Framework class library provides you with a way to simplify file opening if the way you want to open a file happens to fall in one of six standard open configurations.

```
FileInfo    ^fileinfo       = gcnew FileInfo("file.dat");
FileStream  ^CreateFile     = fileinfo.Create();
FileStream  ^OpenReadFile   = fileinfo.OpenRead();
FileStream  ^OpenWriteFile  = fileinfo.OpenWrite();
StreamWriter ^AppendTextFile = fileinfo.AppendText();
StreamWriter ^CreateTextFile = fileinfo.CreateText();
StreamReader ^OpenTextFile   = fileinfo.OpenText();
// or
FileStream  ^CreateFile     = File::Create("file.dat");
FileStream  ^OpenReadFile   = File::OpenRead("file.dat");
FileStream  ^OpenWriteFile  = File::OpenWrite("file.dat");
StreamWriter ^AppendTextFile = File::AppendText("file.dat");
StreamWriter ^CreateTextFile = File::CreateText("file.dat");
StreamReader ^OpenTextFile   = File::OpenText("file.dat");
```

Notice that none of the preceding file opening methods takes any parameters, except the file path in the case of the static method of the File class. Personally, I think the names of the methods make them pretty self-explanatory.

I/O Manipulation

Okay, you now have a file open and it is time to actually do something with it. Oops, did I say "file"? Files are only one thing that you can do I/O manipulation with. You can also do I/O manipulation in and out of memory using the MemoryStream and BufferedStream classes and in and out of network sockets using NetworkStream. You will look at the MemoryStream class a little later to see how it differs from a FileStream.

There are several different means to accomplish I/O manipulation. You will examine the three most common: using Streams, using TextReaders and TextWriters, and using BinaryReaders and BinaryWriters. Figure 8-3 shows the class hierarchy for manipulating files.

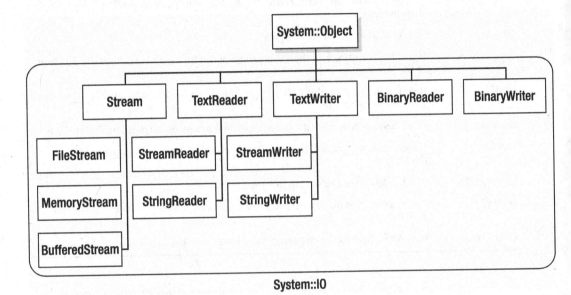

Figure 8-3. *The class hierarchy for I/O manipulation*

Using Streams

In the computer world, streams are a method of transferring a sequential stream of data to and from one source to another in either a synchronous or asynchronous manner. The .NET Framework class library sends this data as a stream of bytes. A stream can also transfer these blocks of data starting from any location in one source to any location in another source.

What does this mean to you? Basically, you can read data, write data, and adjust the current location where you access the data. Not much to it, is there?

All stream-based I/O in the .NET Framework class library derives from the abstract base class Stream. The Stream class contains several virtual methods, which the inheriting class must define (see Table 8-8). Basically, these virtual methods define core Stream functionality and thus ensure that the inheriting class satisfies the definition of a stream as stated previously.

Table 8-8. *The Virtual Methods and Properties of the Stream Class*

Member	Description
CanRead	A Boolean value specifying whether reading is supported.
CanSeek	A Boolean value specifying whether seeking is supported.
CanWrite	A Boolean value specifying whether writing is supported.
Close()	A method that closes the file and releases resources associated with the stream.
Flush()	This method moves the data from the source buffer to its destination source and then clears the buffer. If the stream does not support a buffer, this method does nothing.
Length	The length of the stream in bytes.
Position	If seeking is supported, then this property can be used to get or set the position in the stream.
Read()	Reads a specified number of bytes from the stream and then advances the position after the last read byte.
ReadByte()	Reads a single byte from the stream and then advances the position after the byte.
Seek()	If seeking is supported, then this method can be used to set the position in the stream.
SetLength()	Sets the length of the stream in bytes.
Write()	Writes a specified number of bytes to the stream and then advances the position after the last written byte.
WriteByte()	Writes one byte to the stream and then advances the position after the byte.

You will see some of these properties and methods implemented in the following stream implementations.

FileStreams

One of the most common implementations of a Stream is the FileStream class. This class provides implementations for the abstract Stream class so that it can perform file-based streaming. Or, in other words, it allows you to read from and write to a file.

You have already seen several ways to open a FileStream. It is also possible to open a FileStream directly without using File or FileInfo. To do this, you use one of the FileStream's many constructors. The most common parameters passed to the constructor are identical to those passed to the static File::Open() method.

```
FileStream ^fs = gcnew FileStream("file.dat", FileMode::CreateNew);
FileStream ^fs = gcnew FileStream("file.dat", FileMode::Append,
                            FileAccess::Write);
FileStream ^fs = gcnew FileStream("file.dat", FileMode::Create,
                            FileAccess::Write, FileShare::None);
```

Once you finally have the FileStream open, you can start to read and/or write Bytes of data from or to it. As you saw from the virtual methods defined by the Stream class in Table 8-8, there are two ways of reading and writing to a stream. You can do it either by individual unsigned chars or by arrays of unsigned chars.

```
array<unsigned char>^ data = { 'A', 'p', 'p', 'l', 'e' };
fso->Write(data, 0, 4);
fso->WriteByte(data[4]);

array<unsigned char>^ ca = gcnew array<unsigned char>(5);
ca[0] = fsi->ReadByte();
fsi->Read(ca, 1, 4);
```

Simply placing the location in the `Position` property sets the location of the next place to read from or write to the file.

```
fsi->Position = 0;
```

You can also set the location of the next read or write by the `Seek()` method. This method allows you to use offsets from the beginning of the file (same as the `Position` property), the current location, or the end of the file.

```
fsi->Seek(0, SeekOrigin::Begin);
```

If you desire further access but want the data available in the file (for another operation or just for safety), flush the file buffer.

```
fso->Flush();
```

You should always close your files after you are done with them.

```
fso->Close();
```

Listing 8-3 shows the `FileStream` class in action and demonstrates many of the functionalities described previously.

Listing 8-3. *Working with a FileStream*

```
using namespace System;
using namespace System::IO;

void main()
{
    FileStream ^fso = gcnew FileStream("file.dat", FileMode::Create,
                                  FileAccess::Write, FileShare::None);

    array<unsigned char>^ data = gcnew array<unsigned char> { 'T', 'h', 'i',
                        's', ' ', 'i', 's', ' ', 'a', ' ', 't', 'e',
                        's', 't', '!', '\r', '\n', 'T', 'h', 'i', 's',
                        ' ', 'i', 's', ' ', 'o', 'n', 'l', 'y', ' ',
                        'a', ' ', 't', 'e', 's', 't', '.','\r', '\n' };

    for (int i = 0; i < data->Length-5; i += 5)
    {
        fso->Write(data, i, 5);
    }

    for (int i = data->Length -4; i < data->Length; i++)
    {
        fso->WriteByte(data[i]);
    }
```

```
        fso->Close();

        FileInfo ^fi = gcnew FileInfo("file.dat");
        FileStream ^fsi = fi->OpenRead();

        int b;
        while ((b = fsi->ReadByte()) != -1)
        {
            Console::Write((Char)b);
        }

        fsi->Position = 0;

        array<unsigned char>^ ca = gcnew array<unsigned char>(17);
        fsi->Read(ca, 0, 17);
        for (int i = 0; i < ca->Length; i++)
        {
            Console::Write((Char)ca[i]);
        }

        Console::WriteLine();

        fsi->Close();

        fi->Delete();   // If you want to get rid of it
}
```

Figure 8-4 shows the file output generated by the FileStream.exe program.

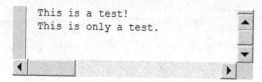

Figure 8-4. *File output of FileStream.exe*

MemoryStreams

Programming with a MemoryStream is not much different from working with a FileStream. Obviously, what's happening behind the scenes, on the other hand, is completely different. You're no longer dealing with files; instead, you're dealing with computer memory.

There are only a few differences from a coding perspective when you deal with a MemoryStream. Obviously, the constructor is different.

```
MemoryStream ^fs = gcnew MemoryStream();
```

A MemoryStream has an additional property and a couple of unique methods (see Table 8-9).

Table 8-9. *Additional MemoryStream Property and Methods*

Member	Description
Capacity	This property gets or sets the number of bytes allocated to the stream.
GetBuffer()	This method returns an unsigned array of bytes that the stream created.
WriteTo()	This method writes the contents of the MemoryStream to another stream, which comes in handy if you want to write the stream out to a FileStream.

Listing 8-4 shows the MemoryStream class in action and demonstrates many of the functionalities described previously.

Listing 8-4. *Working with a MemoryStream*

```
using namespace System;
using namespace System::IO;

void main()
{
    array<unsigned char>^ data = gcnew array<unsigned char> { 'T', 'h', 'i',
                  's', ' ', 'i', 's', ' ', 'a', ' ', 't', 'e', 's', 't',
                  '!', '\r', '\n', 'T', 'h', 'i', 's', ' ', 'i', 's', ' ',
                  'o', 'n', 'l', 'y', ' ', 'a', ' ', 't', 'e', 's', 't',
                  '.', '\r', '\n' };

    MemoryStream ^ms = gcnew MemoryStream();
    ms->Capacity = 40;

    for (int i = 0; i < data->Length-5; i += 5)
    {
        ms->Write(data, i, 5);
    }

    for (int i = data->Length -4; i < data->Length; i++)
    {
        ms->WriteByte(data[i]);
    }

    array<unsigned char>^ ca = ms->GetBuffer();
    for each (unsigned char c in ca)
    {
        Console::Write((Char)c);
    }
    Console::WriteLine();

    FileStream ^fs = File::OpenWrite("file.dat");

    ms->WriteTo(fs);

    fs->Close();
    ms->Close();
}
```

Figure 8-5 shows a display of the buffer contained within the MemoryStream. Figure 8-6 shows the results displayed to the console. Figure 8-7 shows the resulting file output generated by the MemoryStream.exe program. Notice that Figures 8-5 through 8-7 all have the same results, as expected.

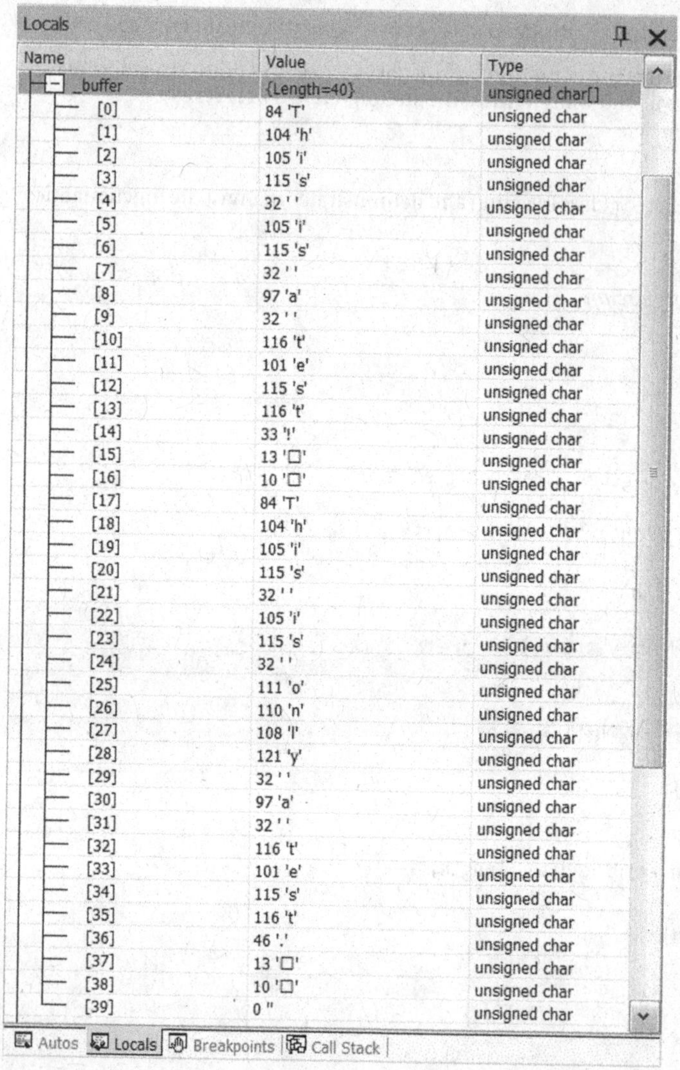

Locals		🗗 ✕
Name	Value	Type
⊟ _buffer	{Length=40}	unsigned char[]
[0]	84 'T'	unsigned char
[1]	104 'h'	unsigned char
[2]	105 'i'	unsigned char
[3]	115 's'	unsigned char
[4]	32 ' '	unsigned char
[5]	105 'i'	unsigned char
[6]	115 's'	unsigned char
[7]	32 ' '	unsigned char
[8]	97 'a'	unsigned char
[9]	32 ' '	unsigned char
[10]	116 't'	unsigned char
[11]	101 'e'	unsigned char
[12]	115 's'	unsigned char
[13]	116 't'	unsigned char
[14]	33 '!'	unsigned char
[15]	13 '□'	unsigned char
[16]	10 '□'	unsigned char
[17]	84 'T'	unsigned char
[18]	104 'h'	unsigned char
[19]	105 'i'	unsigned char
[20]	115 's'	unsigned char
[21]	32 ' '	unsigned char
[22]	105 'i'	unsigned char
[23]	115 's'	unsigned char
[24]	32 ' '	unsigned char
[25]	111 'o'	unsigned char
[26]	110 'n'	unsigned char
[27]	108 'l'	unsigned char
[28]	121 'y'	unsigned char
[29]	32 ' '	unsigned char
[30]	97 'a'	unsigned char
[31]	32 ' '	unsigned char
[32]	116 't'	unsigned char
[33]	101 'e'	unsigned char
[34]	115 's'	unsigned char
[35]	116 't'	unsigned char
[36]	46 '.'	unsigned char
[37]	13 '□'	unsigned char
[38]	10 '□'	unsigned char
[39]	0 ''	unsigned char

🔲 Autos 🔲 Locals 🔲 Breakpoints 🔲 Call Stack

Figure 8-5. *Display of the buffer of the MemoryStream created by MemoryStream.exe*

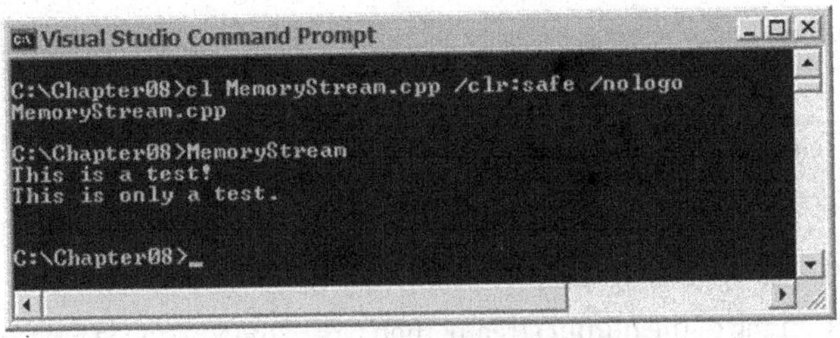

```
Visual Studio Command Prompt                                    _ □ X
C:\Chapter08>cl MemoryStream.cpp /clr:safe /nologo
MemoryStream.cpp

C:\Chapter08>MemoryStream
This is a test!
This is only a test.

C:\Chapter08>_
```

Figure 8-6. *Console results of MemoryStream.exe*

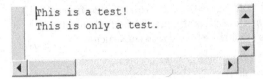
```
This is a test!
This is only a test.
```

Figure 8-7. *File output of MemoryStream.exe*

Using StreamReaders and StreamWriters

A drawback when using a FileStream is that it isn't very String- or character-friendly. Because what you often want to store are Strings and characters, it only makes sense that methods be made to optimize and simplify the process of writing these to a stream. This is where the StreamReader and StreamWriter classes become helpful.

Just like the Stream class, the abstract StreamReader and StreamWriter classes define all the functionality that needs to be implemented to support String and character reading and writing (see Tables 8-10 and 8-11).

Table 8-10. *Common StreamReader Members*

Method	Description
Close()	Closes the file and releases any resources
Peek()	Reads the next character without advancing the stream pointer
Read()	Reads data from the input stream
ReadBlock()	Reads a specified number of characters from the stream to a specified starting location in an input buffer
ReadLine()	Reads a line of data from the input stream and returns it as a String
ReadToEnd()	Reads the rest of the data from the current file location to the end and returns it as a single String

Table 8-11. *Common StreamWriter Members*

Method	Description
Close()	Closes the file and releases any resources
Flush()	Forces the writing of the current buffer and then clears it
Write()	Writes the specified String to the output stream
WriteLine()	Writes the specified String to the output stream, then writes the NewLine String

There are many ways to create a StreamReader and a StreamWriter. You can start from the File or FileInfo class and create one directly from its methods. It is also possible to build one from a FileStream, again using the File or FileInfo class or with the FileStream constructor.

```
StreamReader ^sr1 = File::OpenText("file.dat");
StreamWriter ^sw1 = fileinfo->CreateText("file.dat");

StreamReader ^sr2 = gcnew StreamReader(File::Open("file.dat",
                    FileMode::Open, FileAccess::Read, FileShare::None));
StreamWriter ^sw2 = gcnew StreamWriter(gcnew FileStream("file.dat",
                    FileMode::Create, FileAccess::Write, FileShare::None));
```

Writing to the StreamWriter, after you have created it, is no different than writing to the console. You should be very familiar with the Write() and WriteLine() methods. Reading is a little trickier, as you can read one character, an array of characters, or the rest of the characters in the stream. In most cases, you will most likely be using the StreamReader methods ReadLine() and ReadToEnd(). The first reads a single line of text, while the second reads all the text remaining on the stream. Both return their results as a String.

```
String ^in1 = sr->ReadLine();
String ^in2 = sr->ReadToEnd();
```

Listing 8-5 shows the StreamWriter and StreamReader classes in action and demonstrates many of the functionalities described previously. It also resembles the previous examples but, as you can see, the code is much simpler.

Listing 8-5. *Working with a StreamWriter and a StreamReader*

```
using namespace System;
using namespace System::IO;

void main()
{
    array<String^>^ data = gcnew array<String^> {
        "This is ", "a test!", "This is only a test." };

    StreamWriter ^sw = gcnew StreamWriter(gcnew FileStream("file.dat",
                    FileMode::Create, FileAccess::Write, FileShare::None));

    for (int i = 0; i < data->Length-1; i++)
    {
        sw->Write(data[i]);
    }
```

```
    sw->WriteLine();

    sw->WriteLine(data[2]);

    sw->Close();

    StreamReader ^sr = File::OpenText("file.dat");

    String^ in = sr->ReadLine();
    Console::WriteLine(in);

    Console::WriteLine(sr->ReadToEnd());

    sw->Close();
}
```

Figure 8-8 shows the results of StreamRW.exe displayed to the console. Figure 8-9 shows the resulting file output generated by the StreamRW.exe program. Notice that Figures 8-8 and 8-9 have the same results, as expected.

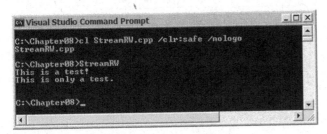

Figure 8-8. *Console results of StreamRW.exe*

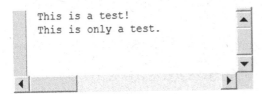

Figure 8-9. *File output of StreamRW.exe*

Using BinaryReader and BinaryWriter

You have looked at I/O for Bytes and Strings. What if you want to store all the other data types, such as Booleans, integers, and floating points? This is where the BinaryReader and BinaryWriter come into play. These classes were designed specifically to handle all the .NET Framework's built-in data types (including Byte and String).

To create a BinaryReader or BinaryWriter class, you need to use its constructor and pass it a Stream. This means, by the way, that BinaryReaders and BinaryWriters can take as a parameter a FileStream, MemoryStream, NetworkStream, and so on.

```
FileStream ^fs = File::OpenRead(fname);
BinaryReader ^br = gcnew BinaryReader(fs);

MemoryStream ^ms = gcnew MemoryStream();
BinaryWriter ^br = gcnew BinaryWriter(ms);
```

The process of writing with the BinaryWriter is very simple. After you create your BinaryWriter, you only need to use two more methods, Write() and Close(). The Write() method takes care of all the hard work by being made up of numerous overloaded versions of itself (one for each supported data type).

The BinaryReader class is a little harder to work with. This time, you need to work with many different read methods (one for each supported type). They all have the same syntax: Readxxx(), where xxx is the data type. Examples of read methods are ReadInt32(), ReadBoolean(), and ReadSingle().

A drawback of the BinaryReader is that you need to know the data type you are reading in before you actually do the read, so that you can make the correct call.

Listing 8-6 shows the BinaryWriter and BinaryReader classes in action and demonstrates many of the functionalities described previously. You might want to notice the special coding you need to do to handle DateTime classes.

Listing 8-6. *Working with a BinaryWriter and a BinaryReader*

```
using namespace System;
using namespace System::IO;
using namespace System::Runtime::Serialization::Formatters::Binary;

// ------ Player class ----------------------------------------------

ref class Player
{
    String ^Name;
    Int32   Strength;
    Boolean IsMale;
    DateTime CreateDate;

public:
    Player();
    Player (String ^Name, int Str, bool IsMale);

    void Print();
    void Save(String ^fname);
    void Load(String ^fname);
};

Player::Player()
{
}

Player::Player (String ^Name, int Str, bool IsMale)
{
    this->Name      = Name;
    this->Strength  = Str;
    this->IsMale    = IsMale;
    this->CreateDate = DateTime::Now;
}
```

```
void Player::Print()
{
    Console::WriteLine("Name: {0} ({1})", Name, (IsMale ? "M" : "F"));
    Console::WriteLine("Str:  {0}", Strength);
    Console::WriteLine("Date: {0}", CreateDate.ToString());
}

void Player::Save(String ^fname)
{
    FileStream   ^fs = File::OpenWrite(fname);
    BinaryWriter ^bw = gcnew BinaryWriter(fs);

    bw->Write(Name);
    bw->Write(Strength);
    bw->Write(IsMale);

    // Due to multicultures this is a safe way of storing DateTimes
    bw->Write(CreateDate.Ticks);

    bw->Close();
    fs->Close();
}

void Player::Load(String ^fname)
{
    FileStream   ^fs = File::OpenRead(fname);
    BinaryReader ^br = gcnew BinaryReader(fs);

    Name     = br->ReadString();
    Strength = br->ReadInt32();
    IsMale   = br->ReadBoolean();

    // Due to multicultures this is a safe way of retrieving DateTimes
    CreateDate = DateTime( br->ReadInt64() );

    br->Close();
    fs->Close();
}

// ------- Main Function ---------------------------------------------

void main()
{
    Player ^Joe = gcnew Player("Joe", 10, true);
    Joe->Save("Player.dat");

    Console::WriteLine("Original Joe");
    Joe->Print();

    Player ^JoeClone = gcnew Player();
    JoeClone->Load("Player.dat");

    Console::WriteLine("\nCloned Joe");
    JoeClone->Print();
}
```

Figure 8-10 shows the results of BinaryRW.exe displayed to the console. Figure 8-11 shows the resulting file output generated by the BinaryRW.exe program. Notice that Figure 8-11 is pretty unreadable unless you know the format in which it was stored. The fact that Figure 8-10 and Figure 8-11 represent the same data is not obvious.

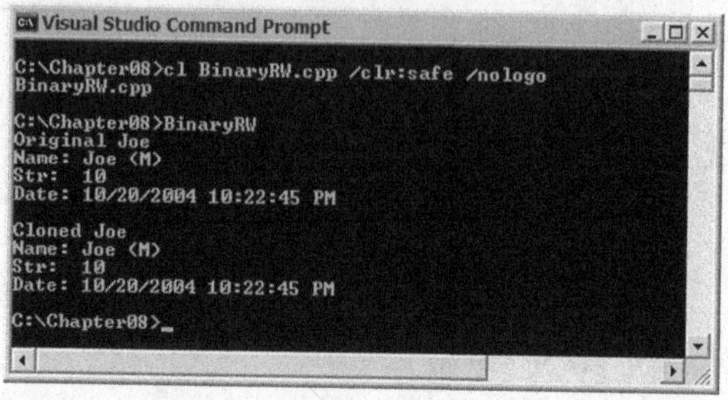

Figure 8-10. *Console results of BinaryRW.exe*

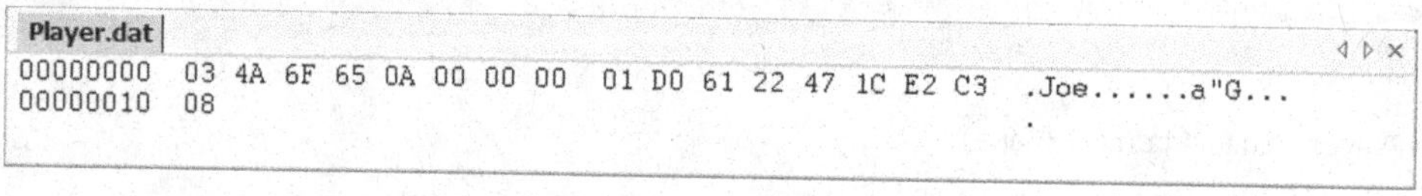

Figure 8-11. *File output of BinaryRW.exe*

Serialization of Managed Objects

The BinaryReader and BinaryWriter classes are okay when it comes to storing small classes to disk and retrieving them later, as you saw in the last section. But classes can become quite complicated. What happens when your class has numerous member variables and/or linked objects? How do you figure out which data type belongs with which class? In what order were they saved? It can become quite a mess very quickly. Wouldn't it be nice if you didn't have to worry about the details and could just say, "Here's the file I want the class saved to. Now, save it." I'm sure you know where I'm going with this; this is the job of serialization.

Serialization is the process of storing the state of an object or member to a permanent medium, most probably to disk for later retrieval or to be transported over the network for some remote process to use, but there are many other uses for serialization. *Deserialization* is the process of restoring an object or member from disk, network, or wherever you serialized it to. Sounds tough, but the .NET Framework class library actually makes it quite simple to do.

Setting Up Classes for Serialization

The process of setting a class up for serialization is probably one of the easiest things that you can do in C++/CLI. You simply place the [Serializable] attribute in front of the managed object you want to serialize. Yep, that is it!

```
[Serializable]
ref class ClassName
{
//...
};
```

The reason this is possible is because all the class's information is stored in its metadata. This metadata is so detailed that all the information regarding serializing and deserializing the class is available at runtime for the CLR to process the serialization or deserialization request.

Listing 8-7 shows the entire process of setting up the Player class for serialization. To make things interesting, I split PlayerAttr off into its own class. As you will see, even the serialization of a linked object like this only requires placing the [Serializable] attribute in front of it.

Listing 8-7. *Making a Class Ready for Serialization*

```
// --------- Player Attribute class -----------------------------------

[Serializable]
ref class PlayerAttr
{
public:
    property int Strength;
    property int Dexterity;
    property int Constitution;
    property int Intelligence;
    property int Wisdom;
    property int Charisma;

    PlayerAttr(int Str, int Dex, int Con, int Int, int Wis, int Cha);
    void Print();
};

PlayerAttr::PlayerAttr(int Str, int Dex, int Con, int Int, int Wis, int Cha)
{
    this->Strength     = Str;
    this->Dexterity    = Dex;
    this->Constitution = Con;
    this->Intelligence = Int;
    this->Wisdom       = Wis;
    this->Charisma     = Cha;
}

void PlayerAttr::Print()
{
    Console::WriteLine("Str: {0}, Dex: {1}, Con {2}",
        Strength, Dexterity, Constitution);
    Console::WriteLine("Int: {0}, Wis: {1}, Cha {2}",
        Intelligence, Wisdom, Charisma);
}

// -------- Player class ---------------------------------------

[Serializable]
ref class Player
{
public:
    property String ^Name;
    property String ^Race;
    property String ^Class;
    property PlayerAttr ^pattr;
```

```
    Player (String ^Name, String ^Race, String ^Class,
        int Str, int Dex, int Con, int Int, int Wis, int Cha);
    void Print();
};

Player::Player (String ^Name, String ^Race, String ^Class,
    int Str, int Dex, int Con, int Int, int Wis, int Cha)
{
    this->Name  = Name;
    this->Race  = Race;
    this->Class = Class;
    this->pattr = gcnew PlayerAttr(Str, Dex, Con, Int, Wis, Cha);
}

void Player::Print()
{
    Console::WriteLine("Name:  {0}", Name);
    Console::WriteLine("Race:  {0}", Race);
    Console::WriteLine("Class: {0}", Class);
    pattr->Print();
}
```

If you can't tell, I play Dungeons and Dragons (D&D). These classes are a very simplified player character. Of course, you would probably want to use enums and check minimums and maximums and so forth, but I didn't want to get too complicated.

BinaryFormatter vs. SoapFormatter

Before you actually serialize a class, you have to make a choice. In what format do you want to store the serialized data? Right now, the .NET Framework class library supplies you with two choices. You can store the serialized class data in a binary format or in an XML format or, more specifically, in a Simple Object Access Protocol (SOAP) format.

The choice is up to you. Binary is more compact, faster, and works well with the CLR. SOAP, on the other hand, is a self-describing readable text format that can be used with a system that doesn't support the CLR. Which formatter type you should use depends on how you plan to use the serialized data.

It is also possible to create your own formatter. This book does not cover how to do this, because this book is about .NET, and the main reason that you might want to create your own formatter is if you are interfacing with a non-CLR (non-.NET) system that has its own serialization format. You should check the .NET Framework documentation for details on how to do this.

Serialization Using BinaryFormatter

As I hinted at previously, the process of serializing a class is remarkably easy. First off, all the code to handle serialization is found in the mscorlib.dll assembly. This means you don't have to worry about loading any special assemblies. The hardest thing about serialization is that you have to remember that the BinaryFormatter is located in the namespace System::Runtime::Serialization:: Formatters::Binary. You have the option of using the fully qualified version of the formatter every time, but I prefer to add a using statement and save my fingers for typing more important code.

```
using namespace System::Runtime::Serialization::Formatters::Binary;
```

The simplest constructor for the BinaryFormatter is just the standard default, which takes no parameters.

```
BinaryFormatter ^bf = gcnew BinaryFormatter();
```

To actually serialize a class, you need to call the BinaryFormatter's Serialize() method. This method takes a Stream and a class handle. Make sure you open the Stream for writing. You also need to truncate the Stream or create a new copy each time. And don't forget to close the Stream when you're done.

```
BinaryFormatter ^bf = gcnew BinaryFormatter();

FileStream ^plStream = File::Create("Player.dat");
bf->Serialize(plStream, Joe);
plStream->Close();
```

The process of deserializing is only slightly more complicated. This time, you need to use the deserialize() method. This method only takes one parameter, a handle to a Stream open for reading. Again, don't forget to close the Stream after you're finished with it. The tricky part of deserialization is that the deserialize() method returns a generic Object class. Therefore, you need to typecast it to the class of the original serialized class.

```
plStream = File::OpenRead("Player.dat");
Player ^JoeClone = (Player^)(bf->Deserialize(plStream));
plStream->Close();
```

Listing 8-8 shows the entire process of serializing and deserializing the Player class.

Listing 8-8. *Serializing and Deserializing the Player Class*

```
using namespace System;
using namespace System::IO;
using namespace System::Runtime::Serialization::Formatters::Binary;

void main()
{
    Player ^Joe =
        gcnew Player("Joe", "Human", "Thief", 10, 18, 9, 13,10, 11);

    Console::WriteLine("Original Joe");
    Joe->Print();

    FileStream ^plStream = File::Create("Player.dat");

    BinaryFormatter ^bf = gcnew BinaryFormatter();
    bf->Serialize(plStream, Joe);
    plStream->Close();

    plStream = File::OpenRead("Player.dat");

    Player ^JoeClone = (Player^)bf->Deserialize(plStream);
    plStream->Close();

    Console::WriteLine("\nCloned Joe");
    JoeClone->Print();
}
```

Figure 8-12 shows the results of BinFormSerial.exe displayed to the console. Figure 8-13 shows the resulting binary-formatted serialization output file generated.

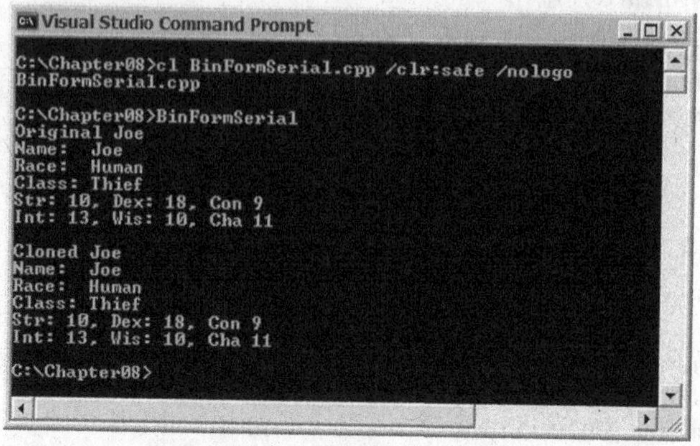

Figure 8-12. *Console results of BinFormSerial.exe*

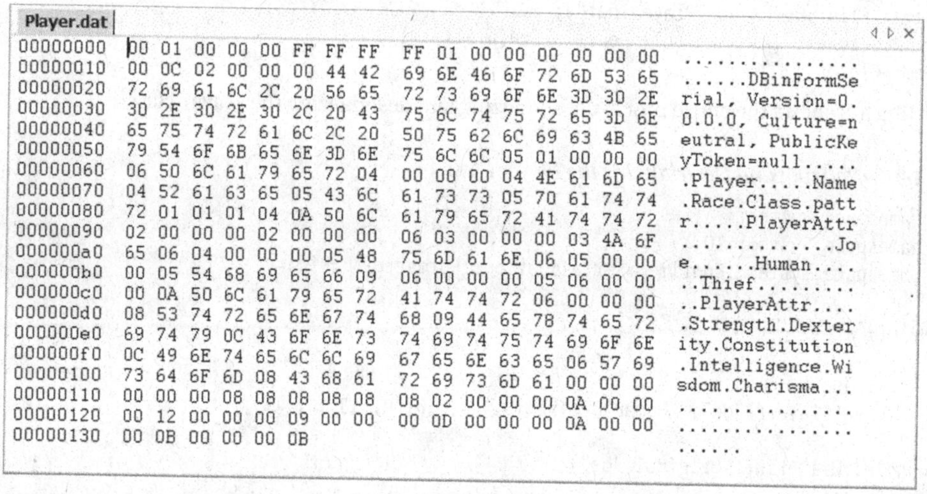

Figure 8-13. *Binary-formatted file output of the serialization of the Player class*

Serialization Using SoapFormatter

There is very little difference in the code required to serialize using the SoapFormatter when compared with the BinaryFormatter. One obvious difference is that you use the SoapFormatter object instead of a BinaryFormatter object. There is also one other major difference, but you have to be paying attention to notice it, at least until you finally try to compile the serializing application. The SoapFormatter is not part of the mscorlib.dll assembly. To use the SoapFormatter, you need to reference the .NET assembly system.runtime.serialization.formatters.soap.dll. You will also find the SoapFormatter class in the namespace System::Runtime::Serialization::Formatters::Soap, which also differs from the BinaryFormatter.

```
#using <system.runtime.serialization.formatters.soap.dll>
using namespace System::Runtime::Serialization::Formatters::Soap;
```

The biggest difference is one that doesn't occur in the code. Instead, it's the serialized file generated. BinaryFormatted serialization files are in an unreadable binary format, whereas SoapFormatted serialization files are in a readable XML text format.

Listing 8-9 shows the entire process of serializing and deserializing the Player class using the SoapFormatter. Notice that the only differences between SOAP and binary are the #using and using statements and the use of SoapFormatter instead of BinaryFormatter.

Listing 8-9. *Serializing and Deserializing the Player Class Using SoapFormatter*

```
#using <system.runtime.serialization.formatters.soap.dll>

using namespace System;
using namespace System::IO;
using namespace System::Runtime::Serialization::Formatters::Soap;

int main(void)
{
    Player ^Joe = gcnew Player("Joe", "Human", "Thief", 10, 18, 9, 13,10, 11);

    Console::WriteLine("Original Joe");
    Joe->Print();

    FileStream ^plStream = File::Create("Player.xml");

    SoapFormatter ^sf = gcnew SoapFormatter();
    sf->Serialize(plStream, Joe);
    plStream->Close();

    plStream = File::OpenRead("Player.xml");

    Player ^JoeClone = (Player^)sf->Deserialize(plStream);
    plStream->Close();

    Console::WriteLine("\nCloned Joe");
    JoeClone->Print();
}
```

Figure 8-14 shows the resulting SOAP-formatted serialization output file generated by SoapFormSerial.exe.

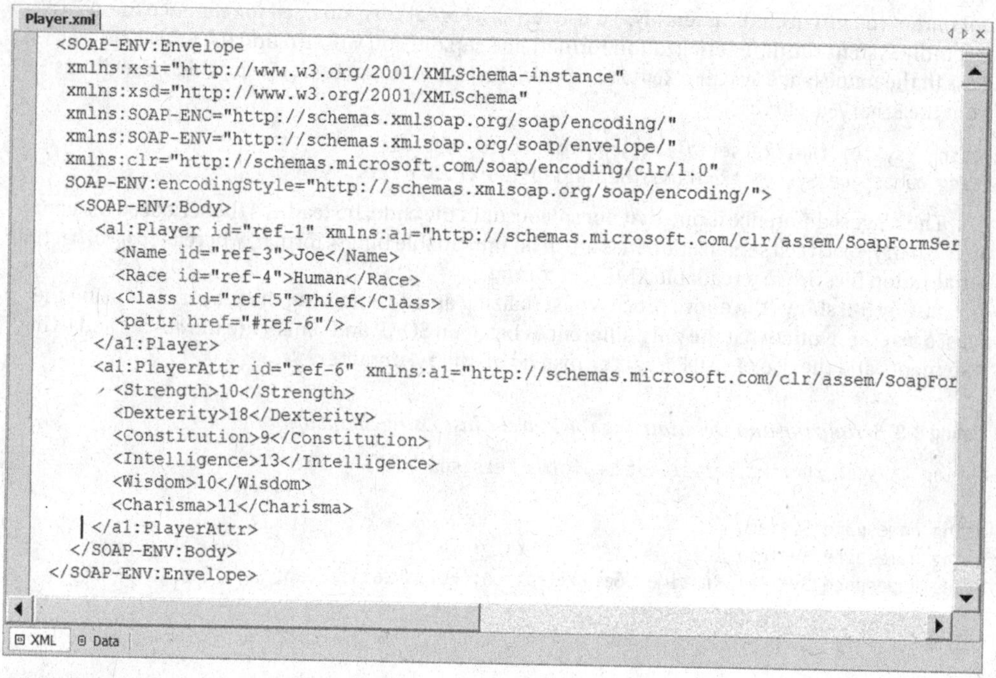

```xml
<SOAP-ENV:Envelope
 xmlns:xsi="http://www.w3.org/2001/XMLSchema-instance"
 xmlns:xsd="http://www.w3.org/2001/XMLSchema"
 xmlns:SOAP-ENC="http://schemas.xmlsoap.org/soap/encoding/"
 xmlns:SOAP-ENV="http://schemas.xmlsoap.org/soap/envelope/"
 xmlns:clr="http://schemas.microsoft.com/soap/encoding/clr/1.0"
 SOAP-ENV:encodingStyle="http://schemas.xmlsoap.org/soap/encoding/">
  <SOAP-ENV:Body>
    <a1:Player id="ref-1" xmlns:a1="http://schemas.microsoft.com/clr/assem/SoapFormSer
      <Name id="ref-3">Joe</Name>
      <Race id="ref-4">Human</Race>
      <Class id="ref-5">Thief</Class>
      <pattr href="#ref-6"/>
    </a1:Player>
    <a1:PlayerAttr id="ref-6" xmlns:a1="http://schemas.microsoft.com/clr/assem/SoapFor
      <Strength>10</Strength>
      <Dexterity>18</Dexterity>
      <Constitution>9</Constitution>
      <Intelligence>13</Intelligence>
      <Wisdom>10</Wisdom>
      <Charisma>11</Charisma>
    </a1:PlayerAttr>
  </SOAP-ENV:Body>
</SOAP-ENV:Envelope>
```

□ XML   □ Data

Figure 8-14. *SOAP-formatted file output of the serialization of the Player class*

Summary

In this chapter, you explored a major component of software development: I/O. You started by looking at how the .NET Framework class library provides an object-style approach to the Windows file system, covering files and directories. You then moved on to look at how to open files for I/O manipulation. Next, you learned how to perform many different methods of reading, writing, and seeking to not only files, but also memory streams. You finished by looking at a specialized I/O system known as serialization.

Though none of the concepts in this chapter should be new to anyone who has worked with file I/O before, how it is done with the .NET Framework class library is new. And, as you should suspect, I/O manipulation can be accomplished in many different ways.

In the next chapter, you will move away from the humdrum of the console and start playing with one of Windows's claims to fame: the graphical user interface (GUI).

CHAPTER 9

■■■

Basic Windows Forms Applications

Console applications are fine for quick utilities and testing functionality, but Windows applications really shine when they present a graphical user interface (GUI) to the world. With the release of Visual Studio 2005, Microsoft is continuing to extend its "easy-to-build" initiative for C++/CLI windows applications. It is effortless to drag and drop your complete user interface using the built-in design tool provided by Visual Studio 2005. Adding event handling to these GUI components is a breeze as well—all it requires is a double-click at design time on the component.

The available GUI options in the .NET Framework are quite staggering, and no one chapter can do them justice. As this is the case, I have broken up the topic into two parts. In this chapter I cover the more basic areas of .NET Framework Windows GUI development, better known as *Windows Forms* (or *Win Forms*). On completing this chapter, you should have a firm background on how to develop (albeit bland) Win Forms on your own. You will have to wait for the next chapter to learn more of the bells and whistles.

In this chapter you will learn how to use the design tool, but that is not the only focus of the chapter. You will also learn how to build your Win Forms without the design tool. The reason I cover both approaches is that I feel the intimate knowledge of the Win Form components that you gain by manual development will allow you to build better interfaces. Once you know both methods, you can combine the two to create the optimal interface to your Windows application.

Win Forms Are Not MFC

The first thing you need to know about Win Forms is that they are not an upgrade, enhancement, new version, or anything else of the Microsoft Foundation Classes (MFC). They are a brand-new, truly object-oriented Windows GUI implementation. A few classes have the same names and support the same functionalities, but that is where the similarities end.

Win Forms have a much stronger resemblance to Visual Basic's (pre-.NET) forms from an implementation standpoint. In fact, Microsoft has taken the Visual Basic GUI development model of forms, controls, and properties and created a language-neutral equivalent for the .NET Framework.

When you create Windows applications with the .NET Framework, you will be working with Win Forms. It is possible to still use MFC within Visual Studio 2005; in fact the line between MFC and Win Forms is becoming quite blurry as you are now able to work with components of both with a single Windows GUI application. However, once you have worked with Win Forms for a while, you will see that it is a much easier-to-code, cleaner, more object-oriented, and more complete implementation of the Windows GUI. More than likely you will start to phase out your MFC development altogether.

This book will completely ignore MFC and focus entirely on Win Forms.

"Hello World!" Win Form Style

Okay, you did the obligatory "Hello World!" for a console application, so now you'll do it again for a Win Form application. The first thing you need to do is create a project using the Windows Forms Application (.NET) template, exactly as you did for the console application (see Figure 9-1).

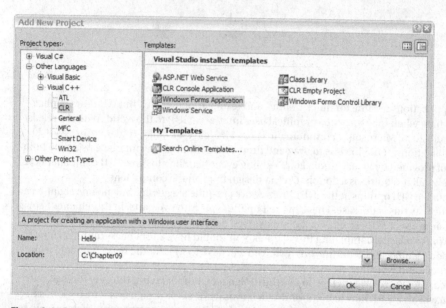

Figure 9-1. *Creating a Win Form "Hello World!" application project*

Once the project template is finished being built, you have a complete Windows application. Okay, on to the next chapter . . . Just kidding!

The process of building the "Hello World!" application involves the following steps:

1. Expand the GUI Toolbox view.

2. Click the required GUI component in the Toolbox view.

3. Drag the component to the design form.

4. Change the component's properties in the Properties view.

5. Double-click the component to create the event handler for the component. This will bring up the IDE editor.

6. Enter the code in the IDE editor to handle the event for the component.

This is very straightforward. If this level of simplicity gives you the willies, as it did me, be comforted by the fact that you can go in and code everything by hand if you want. After a while, you will come to realize that you do not have to code much in the way of the GUI interface manually.

So what code is provided? Listing 9-1 shows Hello.cpp. It doesn't look as if much is going on, but looks can be deceiving.

Listing 9-1. *The Default Hello.cpp*

```
// Hello.cpp : main project file.

#include "stdafx.h"
#include "Form1.h"

using namespace Hello;

[STAThreadAttribute]
int main(array<System::String ^> ^args)
{
    // Enabling Windows XP visual effects before any controls are created
    Application::EnableVisualStyles();
    Application::SetCompatibleTextRenderingDefault(false);

    // Create the main window and run it
    Application::Run(gcnew Form1());
    return 0;
}
```

The first thing you notice is that the wizard includes the stdafx.h header file. Within the header file is nothing but a #pragma once directive. This handy file, which has been preconfigured to be precompiled, can be used in the future when you need to include common header (.h) files across all your source (.cpp) files.

Make sure you keep the #include "Form1.h" line, which, as you'll see, contains the definition of the form.

The next thing the code does is add metadata, using [STAThreadAttribute], which will let the Win Form know to use *single-threaded apartment* (STA), if needed. If you don't know what an *apartment state* is, don't worry about it—it's a process threading thing for COM, and this book doesn't look at COM until Chapter 21. The .NET Framework normally doesn't use apartment threads, but just to be safe, the apartment state is set to a single-threaded apartment in case a COM object is wrapped and used later in the application.

Next, the template sets up the default look and feel for the Win Form application by adding the Application::EnableVisualStyles() method to give the application an Windows XP look. You can do what you like with this method; I normally just leave it.

The template then adds the SetCompatibleTextRenderingDefault() method, which you use to specify backward compatibility on rendering of text with .NET 1.1. When this method is passed a value of true, text rendering is compatible with .NET 1.1; when passed a value of false, this method provides richer GDI rendering capabilities that are not backward compatible. You can leave this set to false unless you are using rendering methods from .NET 1.1 assemblies and you find that things don't render as expected.

Finally, the program uses the Application::Run() method to start up Form1. As you will see, the Application class is a fairly powerful class containing several static methods and properties to manage an application. The most common tasks you will use it for are starting and stopping your applications, processing Windows messages, and processing the previously noted template defaulted EnableVisualStyles() and SetCompatibleTextRenderingDefault() static methods. You may also find it useful for getting information about an application via its properties.

Not much there, was there? Okay, maybe all the magic is in the Form1.h file (see Listing 9-2). To access the source code of Form1.h, you need to right-click Form1.h within Solution Explorer (or within the form designer window) and select View Code.

Notice that the template makes extensive use of inline coding. My guess is that the Microsoft development team stole a lot of GUI design code from the C# version and doing it this way simplified development. (Also, I had to slightly change the Form1 class <Summary> comment to fit the dimensions of the book.)

Listing 9-2. *The Default Form1.h*

```cpp
#pragma once

namespace Hello
{
    using namespace System;
    using namespace System::ComponentModel;
    using namespace System::Collections;
    using namespace System::Windows::Forms;
    using namespace System::Data;
    using namespace System::Drawing;

    /// <summary>
    /// Summary for Form1
    ///
    /// WARNING: If you change the name of this class, you will need to change
    ///          the 'Resource File Name' property for the managed resource
    ///          compiler tool associated with all .resx files this class
    ///          depends on.  Otherwise, the designers will not be able to
    ///          interact properly with localized resources associated with
    ///          this form.
    /// </summary>
    public ref class Form1 : public System::Windows::Forms::Form
    {
    public:
        Form1(void)
        {
            InitializeComponent();
            //
            //TODO: Add the constructor code here
            //
        }

    protected:
        /// <summary>
        /// Clean up any resources being used.
        /// </summary>
        ~Form1()
        {
            if (components)
            {
                delete components;
            }
        }
```

```
    private:
        /// <summary>
        /// Required designer variable.
        /// </summary>
        System::ComponentModel::Container ^components;

#pragma region Windows Form Designer generated code
        /// <summary>
        /// Required method for Designer support - do not modify
        /// the contents of this method with the code editor.
        /// </summary>
        void InitializeComponent(void)
        {
            this->components = gcnew System::ComponentModel::Container();
            this->Size = System::Drawing::Size(300,300);
            this->Text = L"Form1";
            this->Padding = System::Windows::Forms::Padding(0);
            this->AutoScaleMode = System::Windows::Forms::AutoScaleMode::Font;
        }
#pragma endregion
    };
}
```

Believe it or not, Form1.h, along with Hello.cpp, is a complete Win Forms application. You want to know something else? If you code Form1.h by hand, all you need is this:

```
#pragma once

using namespace System;
using namespace System::Windows::Forms;

namespace Hello
{
    public ref class Form1 : public Form
    {
    protected:
        ~Form1()
        {
            if (components)
            {
                delete components;
            }
        }

    public:
        Form1()
        {
            this->Size = Drawing::Size(300,300);
            this->Text = L"Form1";
        }
    };
}
```

All the rest of the code is for the design tool. Now this is simple! All the code does is specify the form's size and title. The rest is handled within the .NET Framework.

Okay, now for grins and giggles, let's change the title of the form to Hello World!. To do this, just change the form's Text property. You can do this in a couple of ways. First, you can just type Hello World! in the source code, replacing the String Text property value Form1. Second, you can change the Text text box within the Properties view. Notice that if you change the property in one place, the other automatically gets updated as well.

As a thought, I guess the developers of the .NET Framework could have made things easier by calling this the Title property, but as you will soon see, the Text property is found in all Win Forms controls and is used for the default text-based property of the control.

When you finally finish staring in disbelief, go ahead and try compiling and running hello.exe. (Pressing Ctrl-F5 is the fastest way of doing this.) Rather unexciting, as you can see in Figure 9-2, but hey, what do you expect from a one-line code change?

Figure 9-2. *The "Hello World!" form*

Customizing the Form Class

The Form class by itself is not the most exciting thing, but before you move on and give it some functionality, let's look at what you'll be getting in the default Form class. Then let's see what else you can customize.

So what do you get for free with a Form class? Among many things, you get the following:

- Sized
- Minimized
- Maximized
- Moved
- Closed

It displays an icon, provides a control box, and does a lot of stuff in the background such as change the cursor when appropriate and take Windows messages and convert them into .NET events.

The Form class is also very customizable. By manipulating a few of the Form class's properties you can get a completely different look from the default, along with some additional functionality that was disabled in the default form configuration. Some of the more common properties are as follows:

- AutoScroll is a Boolean that specifies whether the form should automatically display scroll bars if sizing the window obscures a displayable area. The default value is true.

- ClientSize is a System::Drawing::Size that specifies the size of the client area. The *client area* is the size of the window within the border and caption bar. You use this control to adjust the size of the window to your liking or to get the dimensions of it for GDI+ drawing. You will examine GDI+ in Chapter 11.

- Cursor is a Cursor control that you use to specify the cursor to display when over the Win Form. The default is conveniently named Cursors::Default.

- FormBorder is a FormBorderStyle enum class that specifies the style of the border. You use this control to change the look of the form. Common styles are FixedDialog, FixedToolWindow, and SizableToolWindow, but the style you will see most often is the default Sizable.

- Icon is a System::Drawing::Icon that you use to specify the icon associated with the form.

- MaximizeBox is a Boolean that specifies whether the maximize button should be displayed on the caption bar. The default is true.

- Menu is a MainMenu control you use as the menu displayed on the form. The default is null, which signifies that there is no menu.

- MinimizeBox is a Boolean that specifies whether the minimize button should be displayed on the caption bar. The default is true.

- Size is a System::Drawing::Size that specifies the size of the form. The size of the window includes the borders and caption bar. You use this control to set the size of the Win Form.

- WindowState is a FormWindowState enum class that allows you to find out or specify whether the Win Form is displayed as Normal, Minimized, or Maximized. The default window state is FormWindowState::Normal.

There's nothing special about working with Form class properties. You can either change them using the Properties view, as shown in Figure 9-3, or directly in code, as Listing 9-3 points out. The choice is yours. Frequently you'll start off by making general changes using the Properties window and then go into the code's InitializeComponent() method (which you can find in the Form1.h file for all the examples in the book) to fine-tune the changes. It doesn't matter if you make the changes in the code or in the Properties window, as any changes you make in one will immediately be reflected in the other.

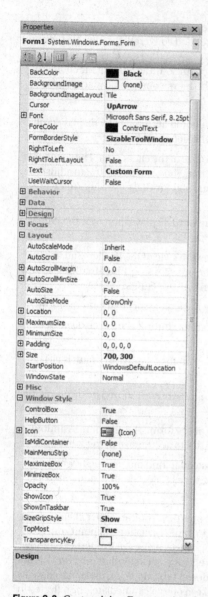

Figure 9-3. *Customizing Form1 using the Properties view*

Caution Be careful when you make changes within the InitializeComponent() method. The changes have to be made in exactly the same manner as the code generator or you may cause Visual Studio 2005's GUI design tool to stop functioning. Also, if you add code to this section it may be deleted if you modify the form by adding or removing components.

To customize a form (or any other control, for that matter), you just assign the appropriate types and values you want to the properties and let the form handle the rest. The example in Figure 9-3 and Listing 9-3 shows a hodgepodge of different form customizations just to see what the form will look like when it's done. The biggest change happened when I modified FormBorderStyle.

Tip Properties that differ from the default appear in boldface in the Properties view.

Listing 9-3. *Customizing Form1.h*

```
#pragma once

namespace CustomHello
{
    using namespace System;
    using namespace System::ComponentModel;
    using namespace System::Collections;
    using namespace System::Windows::Forms;
    using namespace System::Data;
    using namespace System::Drawing;

    public ref class Form1 : public System::Windows::Forms::Form
    {
    public:
        Form1(void)
        {
            InitializeComponent();
        }

    protected:
        ~Form1()
        {
            if (components)
            {
                delete components;
            }
        }

    private:
        System::ComponentModel::Container ^components;

#pragma region Windows Form Designer generated code
```

```
void InitializeComponent(void)
{
    this->SuspendLayout();
    //
    // Form1
    //
    this->AutoScaleMode = System::Windows::Forms::AutoScaleMode::Font;
    this->BackColor = System::Drawing::Color::Black;
    this->ClientSize = System::Drawing::Size(692, 274);
    this->Cursor = System::Windows::Forms::Cursors::UpArrow;
    this->FormBorderStyle =
        System::Windows::Forms::FormBorderStyle::SizableToolWindow;
    this->Name = L"Form1";
    this->SizeGripStyle = System::Windows::Forms::SizeGripStyle::Show;
    this->Text = L"Custom Form";
    this->TopMost = true;
    this->ResumeLayout(false);
}

#pragma endregion
};
}
```

The running of CustomHello.exe results in the display in Figure 9-4. Notice that this form is quite a bit different from the default form generated by the previous example, Hello.exe. For instance, this form has no control box and no minimize or maximize button, and in the bottom right there is a form-sizing grip and an up-arrow cursor.

Figure 9-4. *A very customized form*

■**Note** For the rest of the chapter I will not list the .cpp file, as it is the same for every example. I will also remove compiler-generated comments and directives, unless they aid in the reading of the code, just to save a tree or two when printing this book.

Handling Win Form Delegates and Events

Remember back in Chapter 4 when I discussed delegates and events and you thought to yourself, "That would be a great way to handle an event-driven GUI application!" You know what? You were right. This is exactly how the Win Form handles its user- and system-generated events.

Win Forms uses the .NET Framework's event model to handle all the events that take place within the form. This requires a delegate, an event source class, and an event receiver class. (You might want to revisit Chapter 4 if this means nothing to you.) Fortunately, many of the delegates and event source classes you need to worry about are already part of the .NET Framework class library. You need to define the event receiver class.

For the following example, you'll use the MouseDown event that's defined in the event source class System::Windows::Forms::Control:

```
event MouseEventHandler ^MouseDown;
```

This event uses the MouseEventHandler delegate, which is defined in the System::Windows::Forms namespace:

```
public delegate void MouseEventHandler(Object^ sender, MouseEventArgs^ e);
```

For those of you who are curious, the class MouseEventArgs provides five properties that you can use to figure out information about the MouseDown event:

- Button: An enum class specifying which mouse button was pressed down.
- Clicks: The number of times the mouse was pressed and released.
- Delta: The number of detents the mouse wheel was rotated. A *detent* is one notch of the mouse wheel.
- X: The horizontal location of the mouse where it was clicked.
- Y: The vertical location of the mouse where it was clicked.

The first step in creating an event receiver class is to create the event handler that will handle the event generated by the event source class. So, in the case of MouseDown, you need to create a method with the same signature as MouseEventHandler. Notice also that you make the handler private. You don't want any outside method calling this event by accident, as it's only intended to be called within the event receiver class.

```
private:
    void Mouse_Clicked(System::Object^ sender,
                       System::Windows::Forms::MouseEventArgs^ e)
    {
    }
```

Once you have the handler, all you need to do is delegate it onto the MouseDown event. As you may recall from Chapter 4, C++/CLI uses multicast delegates; therefore, you can chain as many handler methods as you need to complete the MouseDown event.

```
MouseDown += gcnew MouseEventHandler(this, Mouse_Clicked);
```

If at a later time you no longer want this handler to handle the MouseDown event, all you need to do is remove the delegated method.

```
MouseDown -= gcnew MouseEventHandler(this, Mouse_Clicked);
```

After describing all this, I'll now tell you that you can create and delegate event handlers automatically using the design tool and you don't have to worry about syntax or coding errors for the declarations. All you have to code is the functionality that handles the event. To add event handlers to a control or (in this case) a form, follow these steps:

1. In the Properties window, click the icon that looks like a lightning bolt. This will change the view from properties to events (see Figure 9-5).

Figure 9-5. *Properties view of event handlers*

2. Double-click the event you want to add to the control or form. This will create all the appropriate code in the form using the default name.

or

Enter the name of the new method in the text box next to the event handler you are creating.

or

If you have already written the method, select the method from the drop-down list next to the event that you want it to handle.

Listing 9-4 is a fun little program that jumps your Win Form around the screen depending on where your mouse pointer is and which mouse button you press within the client area of the form. As you can see, event handling is hardly challenging. Most of the logic of this program is designed just to determine where to place the form on a MouseDown event.

Listing 9-4. *Mouse Jump: Press a Mouse Button and See the Form Jump*

```cpp
#pragma once

namespace MouseJump
{
    using namespace System;
    using namespace System::ComponentModel;
    using namespace System::Collections;
    using namespace System::Windows::Forms;
    using namespace System::Data;
    using namespace System::Drawing;

    public ref class Form1 : public System::Windows::Forms::Form
    {
    public:
        Form1(void)
        {
            InitializeComponent();
        }

    protected:
        ~Form1()
        {
            if (components)
            {
                delete components;
            }
        }

    private:
        System::ComponentModel::Container ^components;

#pragma region Windows Form Designer generated code

        void InitializeComponent(void)
        {
            this->SuspendLayout();
            //
            // Form1
            //
```

```cpp
            this->AutoScaleDimensions = System::Drawing::SizeF(6, 13);
            this->AutoScaleMode = System::Windows::Forms::AutoScaleMode::Font;
            this->ClientSize = System::Drawing::Size(450, 300);
            this->Name = L"Form1";
            this->Text = L"Mouse Jump";
            this->MouseDown +=
                gcnew System::Windows::Forms::MouseEventHandler(this,
                                                    &Form1::Form1_MouseDown);
            this->ResumeLayout(false);
        }

#pragma endregion

    private:
        System::Void Form1_MouseDown(System::Object^  sender,
                                System::Windows::Forms::MouseEventArgs^ e)
        {
            // Get mouse x and y coordinates
            int x = e->X;
            int y = e->Y;

            // Get Forms upper left location
            Point loc = DesktopLocation;

            // Handle left button mouse click
            if (e->Button == Windows::Forms::MouseButtons::Left)
            {
                Text = String::Format("Mouse Jump - Left Button at {0},{1}",
                                x, y);

                DesktopLocation = Drawing::Point(loc.X + x, loc.Y +y);
            }
            // Handle right button mouse click
            else if (e->Button == Windows::Forms::MouseButtons::Right)
            {
                Text = String::Format("Mouse Jump - Right Button at {0},{1}",
                                x, y);

                DesktopLocation = Point((loc.X+1) - (ClientSize.Width - x),
                                (loc.Y+1) - (ClientSize.Height - y));
            }
            // Handle middle button mouse click
            else
            {
                Text = String::Format("Mouse Jump - Middle Button at {0},{1}",
                                x, y);
                DesktopLocation = Point((loc.X+1) - ((ClientSize.Width/2) - x),
                                (loc.Y+1) - ((ClientSize.Height/2) - y));
            }
        }
    };
}
```

The MouseJump.exe application shown in Figure 9-6 is hardly exciting, because you can't see the jumping of the form in a still image. Notice that the coordinates at which the mouse was last clicked are displayed in the title bar.

Figure 9-6. *The form after a mouse jump*

Adding Controls

Okay, now that you have covered the basics of a form and how to handle events from a form, you'll go ahead and make the form do something constructive. To do this, you need to add what the .NET Framework class library calls *controls*.

Controls give you the ability to build an interface by breaking it down into smaller components. Each control provides a specific type of input and/or output functionality to your Win Form. For example, there are controls to place a label on the screen, display and input text data, select a data item from a list, and display and (if you want) update a tree of data. There is even a control to display a calendar.

All controls inherit from the Component and Control classes, with each class providing a number of standard methods and properties. Each control will have a few methods and properties of its own that make it unique. Also, all controls have events, for which you can create handlers. You can find all controls provided by the .NET Framework class library within the System::Windows::Forms namespace.

You can add controls to a Win Form in one of two ways, just like almost any other process when it comes to Win Forms. You can use Visual Studio 2005 GUI tool to drop and drag the controls to the Win Form, or you can code the controls by hand using Visual Studio 2005's IDE editor (or almost any other editor for that matter).

Let's look at how to drag and drop controls onto a Win Form, as this is essentially what you're going to mimic when you code by hand. The steps are as follows:

1. Resize the form to the size you want by dragging the borders of the form in the design window. Make it a little bigger than you think you'll need. Don't worry—you can change the size later to enclose the controls better. I've learned from past experience that having the extra real estate makes things easier when designing.

2. Bring the cursor over the Toolbox tab (if you don't have it tacked open). This will expand the Toolbox.

3. Click, hold, and then drag the control you want from the Toolbox to the form. (If you don't have the Toolbox tacked open, you may need to drag the control to an open location on the form and release it there. This will cause the Toolbox to close so that you can click again and drag the control to the desired location on the form.)

4. Alter the properties of the controls as you wish by changing them in the Properties view. I recommend changing the Name property at a minimum, but there is nothing stopping you from using the default name for the control.

5. Add event handlers as desired. You might consider holding off on this step until you have the entire Win Form laid out.

6. Repeat steps 1 through 5 for all other required controls.

Behind the scenes, these steps add a definition of the control to the class and then create an instance of it. Each property that is changed adds a line of code that updates one of the control's properties. Each event handler added adds a delegation statement and then creates an event handler.

As a developer, you can rely solely on the drag-and-drop functionality of Visual Studio 2005 or you can do as I do and use the tool to build the basic design but then fine-tune it within the code itself. You could also be a glutton for punishment and do it all by hand. But why bother? The tool is there, so why not use it?

Okay, now that you know how to add a control to the Win Form, you'll take a look at an assortment of the more common controls provided by the .NET Framework class library, starting with one of the easiest: Label.

The Label Control

The name of this control is a little misleading. It gives you the impression that its only purpose is to display static text in the form. Nothing could be further from the truth. The Label control is also great for displaying dynamic text to the form. Heck, the Label control can even trigger an event when clicked.

In general, though, you'll normally use a Label control to statically label something else. The usual process of creating a label is simply to create the Label control and then set its properties so that the control looks the way you want it to. Here are some of the more common properties used by the Label control:

- BackColor is a System::Drawing::Color that represents the background color of the label and defaults to the DefaultBackColor property.

- Font is a System::Drawing::Font that represents the font used by the label and defaults to the DefaultFont property.

- ForeColor is a System::Drawing::Color that represents the foreground color (or the actual color of the text) of the label and defaults to the DefaultForeColor property.

- Image is a System::Drawing::Image that represents the image displayed within the label. The default is null, which signifies that no image is to be displayed.

- ImageAlign is a ContentAlignment enum class that represents the alignment of the image within the label. I like to visualize the different alignments by picturing a tic-tac-toe game in my head, with each box a possible alignment. The default alignment is the center box of the tic-tac-toe game or ContentAlignment::MiddleCenter.

- Text is a String containing the actual text to be displayed.

- TextAlign is a ContentAlignment enum class that represents the alignment of the image within the label. The default is based on the culture of the computer. Because my computer has a culture of en-us, the default alignment is the top-left corner, or ContentAlignment::TopLeft.

- UseMnemonic is a Boolean that specifies whether or not the ampersand (&) character should be interpreted as an access-key prefix character. The default is true.

Now that you have seen the more common properties, for grins and giggles you'll implement a Label control using some of its less common properties (see Listing 9-5).

Listing 9-5. *The MightyLabel, an Implementation of the Uncommon Properties*

```cpp
#pragma once

namespace MightyLabel
{
    using namespace System;
    using namespace System::ComponentModel;
    using namespace System::Collections;
    using namespace System::Windows::Forms;
    using namespace System::Data;
    using namespace System::Drawing;

    public ref class Form1 : public System::Windows::Forms::Form
    {
    public:
        Form1(void)
        {
            labelSwitch = true;
            InitializeComponent();
        }

    protected:
        ~Form1()
        {
            if (components)
            {
                delete components;
            }
        }

    private:
        System::Windows::Forms::Label^  MightyLabel;
        bool labelSwitch;

        System::ComponentModel::Container ^components;

#pragma region Windows Form Designer generated code

        void InitializeComponent(void)
        {
            this->MightyLabel = (gcnew System::Windows::Forms::Label());
            this->SuspendLayout();
            //
            // MightyLabel
            //
            this->MightyLabel->BorderStyle =
                System::Windows::Forms::BorderStyle::FixedSingle;
```

```cpp
        this->MightyLabel->Cursor = System::Windows::Forms::Cursors::Hand;
        this->MightyLabel->Location = System::Drawing::Point(63, 91);
        this->MightyLabel->Name = L"MightyLabel";
        this->MightyLabel->Size = System::Drawing::Size(150, 35);
        this->MightyLabel->TabIndex = 1;
        this->MightyLabel->Text =
            L"This is the mighty label! It will change when you click it";
        this->MightyLabel->TextAlign =
            System::Drawing::ContentAlignment::MiddleCenter;
        this->MightyLabel->Click +=
            gcnew System::EventHandler(this, &Form1::MightyLabel_Click);
        //
        // Form1
        //
        this->AutoScaleDimensions = System::Drawing::SizeF(6, 13);
        this->AutoScaleMode = System::Windows::Forms::AutoScaleMode::Font;
        this->ClientSize = System::Drawing::Size(292, 273);
        this->Controls->Add(this->MightyLabel);
        this->Name = L"Form1";
        this->Text = L"The Mighty Label";
        this->ResumeLayout(false);
    }

#pragma endregion

    private:
        System::Void MightyLabel_Click(System::Object^ sender,
                                       System::EventArgs^ e)
        {
            if (labelSwitch)
                MightyLabel->Text = L"Ouchie!!!  That hurt.";
            else
                MightyLabel->Text = L"Ooo!!!  That tickled.";
            labelSwitch = !labelSwitch;
        }
    };
}
```

As you can see, dragging and dropping can save you a lot of time when you're designing a form, even in such a straightforward case. But even this simple program shows that a programmer is still needed. A designer can drag and drop the label to where it's needed, and can even change the control's properties, but a programmer is still needed to give the controls life or, in other words, to handle events.

Notice that a Form class is like any other C++/CLI class in that you can add your own member variables, methods, and properties. In this example, I add a bool member variable called labelSwitch to hold the current state of the label. I initialize it in the constructor just as I would in any other class and then use it within the Click event handler. Basically, as long as you don't code within the areas that the generated code says to avoid, you're safe to use the Form class as you see fit.

Figure 9-7 shows what MightyLabel.exe looks like when you execute it. Be sure to click the label a couple of times.

Figure 9-7. *The MightyLabel example*

The Button Controls

Buttons are one of the most commonly used controls for getting user input found in any Win Forms application, basically because the average user finds buttons easy to use and understand. And yet they are quite versatile for the software developer.

The .NET Framework class library provides three different types of buttons: Button, CheckBox, and RadioButton. All three inherit from the abstract ButtonBase class, which provides common functionality across all three. Here are some of the common properties provided by ButtonBase:

- FlatStyle is a FlatStyle enum class that represents the appearance of the button. The default is FlatStyle::Standard, but other options are Flat and Popup.

- Image is a System::Drawing::Image that represents the image displayed on the button. The default is null, meaning no image is to be displayed.

- IsDefault is a protected Boolean that specifies whether the button is the default for the form. In other words, it indicates whether the button's Click event gets triggered when the Enter key is pressed. The default is false.

- Text is a String that represents the text that will be displayed on the button.

Remember, you also get all the properties of Control and Component. Thus, you have a plethora of properties and methods to work with.

Button

The Button control does not give much functionality beyond what is defined by the abstract ButtonBase class. You might think of the Button control as the lowest-level implementation of the abstract base class.

Most people think of Button as a static control that you place on the Win Form at design time. As the example in Listing 9-6 points out (over and over again), this is not the case. Yes, you can statically place a Button control, but you can also dynamically place it on the Win Form.

Listing 9-6. *The Code for "Way Too Many Buttons!"*

```
#pragma once

namespace TooManyButtons
{
    using namespace System;
    using namespace System::ComponentModel;
    using namespace System::Collections;
    using namespace System::Windows::Forms;
    using namespace System::Data;
    using namespace System::Drawing;

    public ref class Form1 : public System::Windows::Forms::Form
    {
    public:
        Form1(void)
        {
            InitializeComponent();
        }

    protected:
        ~Form1()
        {
            if (components)
            {
                delete components;
            }
        }
    private:
        System::Windows::Forms::Button^  TooMany;

        System::ComponentModel::Container ^components;

#pragma region Windows Form Designer generated code

        void InitializeComponent(void)
        {
            this->TooMany = (gcnew System::Windows::Forms::Button());
            this->SuspendLayout();
            //
            // TooMany
            //
            this->TooMany->Location = System::Drawing::Point(12, 12);
            this->TooMany->Name = L"TooMany";
            this->TooMany->Size = System::Drawing::Size(75, 23);
            this->TooMany->TabIndex = 1;
            this->TooMany->Text = L"Click Me!";
            this->TooMany->Click +=
                gcnew System::EventHandler(this, &Form1::TooMany_Click);
```

```
        //
        // Form1
        //
        this->AutoScaleDimensions = System::Drawing::SizeF(6, 13);
        this->AutoScaleMode = System::Windows::Forms::AutoScaleMode::Font;
        this->AutoScroll = true;
        this->ClientSize = System::Drawing::Size(292, 273);
        this->Controls->Add(this->TooMany);
        this->Name = L"Form1";
        this->Text = L"Too Many Buttons";
        this->ResumeLayout(false);
    }

#pragma endregion

    private:
        System::Void TooMany_Click(System::Object^ sender,
                                    System::EventArgs^ e)
    {
        // Grab the location of the button that was clicked
        Point p = ((Button^)sender)->Location;

        // Create a dynamic button
        Button ^Many = gcnew Button();
        Many->Location = Drawing::Point(p.X + 36, p.Y + 26);
        Many->Text = L"Click Me!";
        Many->Click += gcnew System::EventHandler(this,
                                            &Form1::TooMany_Click);

        // Add dynamic button to Form
        Controls->Add(Many);
    }
};
}
```

There really isn't much difference between adding a Label control and a Button statically, as you can see in the InitializeComponent() method. The fun code in Listing 9-6 is in the TooMany_Click() event handler method. The first thing this method does is grab the location of the button that was clicked and place it into a Point struct so that you can manipulate it. You'll examine System::Drawing::Point in Chapter 11. You could have grabbed the whole button but you only need its location. Next, you build a button. There's nothing tricky here, except the button is declared within the event handler. Those of you from a traditional C++ background are probably jumping up and down, screaming *Memory leak!* Sorry to disappoint you, but this is C++/CLI and the memory will be collected when it's no longer referenced, so this code is perfectly legal. And finally, the last step in placing the button dynamically on the Win Form is adding it.

Figure 9-8 shows what TooManyButtons.exe looks like when you execute it. Be sure to click a few of the newly created buttons.

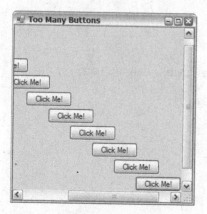

Figure 9-8. *Way too many buttons*

CheckBox

The CheckBox control is also an extension of the ButtonBase class. It's similar to a normal Button control in many ways. The two major differences are that it looks different on the Win Form and that it retains its check state when clicked. Well, the first difference isn't always true—there's a property to make a CheckBox look like a Button.

The CheckBox control, if configured to do so, can have three states: checked, unchecked, and indeterminate. I'm sure you understand checked and unchecked states, but what is this *indeterminate* state? Visually, in this state, the check boxes are shaded. Most likely you saw this type of check box when you installed Visual Studio 2005 on your machine. Remember when you set which parts to install and some of the checkmarks were gray? When you selected the gray box, you found that some of the subparts were not checked. Basically, the indeterminate state of the parent resulted from the fact that not all the child boxes were checked.

In addition to supporting the properties provided by ButtonBase, the CheckBox control supports some properties unique to itself:

- Appearance is an Appearance enum class that specifies whether the check box looks like a button or a standard check box. The default, Appearance::Normal, is a standard check box.

- CheckAlign is a ContentAlignment enum class that represents the alignment of the check box within the CheckBox control. The default alignment is centered and to the left: ContentAlignment::MiddleLeft.

- Checked is a Boolean that represents whether or not the check box is checked. This property returns true if the check box is in an indeterminate state as well. The default is false.

- CheckState is a CheckState enum class that represents the current state of the check box: Checked, Unchecked, or Indeterminate. The default is CheckState::Unchecked.

- ThreeState is a Boolean that specifies whether the check box can have an indeterminate state. The default is false.

In our next example (see Listing 9-7), you'll have a little fun with the CheckBox control, in particular the Visibility property. Enter the code from the listing and have some fun.

Listing 9-7. *The Code for "You Can't Check Me!"*

```
#pragma once

namespace CheckMe
{
    using namespace System;
    using namespace System::ComponentModel;
    using namespace System::Collections;
    using namespace System::Windows::Forms;
    using namespace System::Data;
    using namespace System::Drawing;

    public ref class Form1 : public System::Windows::Forms::Form
    {
    public:
        Form1(void)
        {
            InitializeComponent();
        }

    protected:
        ~Form1()
        {
            if (components)
            {
                delete components;
            }
        }

    private:
        System::Windows::Forms::CheckBox^  BottomCheck;
        System::Windows::Forms::CheckBox^  checkBox2;
        System::Windows::Forms::CheckBox^  checkBox1;
        System::Windows::Forms::CheckBox^  TopCheck;

        System::ComponentModel::Container ^components;

#pragma region Windows Form Designer generated code

        void InitializeComponent(void)
        {
            this->BottomCheck = (gcnew System::Windows::Forms::CheckBox());
            this->checkBox2 = (gcnew System::Windows::Forms::CheckBox());
            this->checkBox1 = (gcnew System::Windows::Forms::CheckBox());
            this->TopCheck = (gcnew System::Windows::Forms::CheckBox());
            this->SuspendLayout();
            //
            // BottomCheck
```

```
//
this->BottomCheck->AutoSize = true;
this->BottomCheck->Enabled = false;
this->BottomCheck->Location = System::Drawing::Point(52, 167);
this->BottomCheck->Name = L"BottomCheck";
this->BottomCheck->Size = System::Drawing::Size(127, 17);
this->BottomCheck->TabIndex = 4;
this->BottomCheck->TabStop = false;
this->BottomCheck->Text = L"You Can\'t Check Me!";
this->BottomCheck->Visible = false;
this->BottomCheck->Enter +=
    gcnew System::EventHandler(this, &Form1::BottomCheck_Enter);
this->BottomCheck->MouseEnter +=
    gcnew System::EventHandler(this, &Form1::BottomCheck_Enter);
//
// checkBox2
//
this->checkBox2->AutoSize = true;
this->checkBox2->Location = System::Drawing::Point(52, 130);
this->checkBox2->Name = L"checkBox2";
this->checkBox2->Size = System::Drawing::Size(106, 17);
this->checkBox2->TabIndex = 5;
this->checkBox2->Text = L"Don\'t Forget ME!";
//
// checkBox1
//
this->checkBox1->AutoSize = true;
this->checkBox1->Checked = true;
this->checkBox1->CheckState =
    System::Windows::Forms::CheckState::Indeterminate;
this->checkBox1->Location = System::Drawing::Point(52, 90);
this->checkBox1->Name = L"checkBox1";
this->checkBox1->Size = System::Drawing::Size(133, 17);
this->checkBox1->TabIndex = 2;
this->checkBox1->Text = L"Check Me! Check Me!";
this->checkBox1->ThreeState = true;
//
// TopCheck
//
this->TopCheck->AutoSize = true;
this->TopCheck->Location = System::Drawing::Point(52, 49);
this->TopCheck->Name = L"TopCheck";
this->TopCheck->Size = System::Drawing::Size(127, 17);
this->TopCheck->TabIndex = 3;
this->TopCheck->TabStop = false;
this->TopCheck->Text = L"You Can\'t Check Me!";
this->TopCheck->Enter +=
    gcnew System::EventHandler(this, &Form1::TopCheck_Enter);
this->TopCheck->MouseEnter +=
    gcnew System::EventHandler(this, &Form1::TopCheck_Enter);
```

```
        //
        // Form1
        //
        this->AutoScaleDimensions = System::Drawing::SizeF(6, 13);
        this->AutoScaleMode = System::Windows::Forms::AutoScaleMode::Font;
        this->ClientSize = System::Drawing::Size(242, 273);
        this->Controls->Add(this->BottomCheck);
        this->Controls->Add(this->checkBox2);
        this->Controls->Add(this->checkBox1);
        this->Controls->Add(this->TopCheck);
        this->Name = L"Form1";
        this->Text = L"Can\'t Check Me";
        this->ResumeLayout(false);
        this->PerformLayout();
    }
#pragma endregion

    private:
        System::Void TopCheck_Enter(System::Object^ sender,
                             System::EventArgs^ e)
        {
            // Hide Top checkbox and display bottom
            TopCheck->Enabled = false;
            TopCheck->Visible = false;
            BottomCheck->Enabled = true;
            BottomCheck->Visible = true;
        }

    private:
        System::Void BottomCheck_Enter(System::Object^ sender,
                               System::EventArgs^ e)
        {
            // Hide Bottom checkbox and display top
            BottomCheck->Enabled = false;
            BottomCheck->Visible = false;
            TopCheck->Enabled = true;
            TopCheck->Visible = true;
        }
    };
}
```

You may have noticed that I threw in the indeterminate state in the first/second/first... (whichever) check box, just so you can see what it looks like.

An important thing to take from this example is that it shows you can delegate the same event handler to more than one event. Doing this in the Visual Studio 2005 Properties view requires that you use the drop-down list to select the event handler that you want to re-delegate.

The example also shows how to enable/disable and show/hide both in the Properties view and at runtime.

Figure 9-9 shows what CheckMe.exe looks like when you execute it. Who says programmers don't have a sense of humor!

Figure 9-9. *You can't check me!*

RadioButton

From a coding perspective, there isn't much to say about the RadioButton control other than you code it in exactly the same way you code a CheckBox control. The only difference between the RadioButton and CheckBox controls is that with the RadioButton you lose the CheckState property and its associated CheckStateChanged event.

The RadioButton control works a little differently than the CheckBox control. Only one RadioButton can be checked at a time within a given container, which at this point is the Win Form. (You will see that you can have multiple containers placed on a Win Form later in this chapter in the section "The GroupBox Control.") If you have ever played with a car radio, you should understand exactly how a RadioButton works.

Listing 9-8 shows a neat little trick that the GUI design tool can't do—it shows how to create an array of radio buttons. Having unique names for what amounts to a single entity with multiple values seems a little silly in most cases, and at worst the code goes on forever. I think developing a set of radio buttons, as shown in Listing 9-8, makes good sense.

Listing 9-8. *The Code for an Array of Radio Buttons*

```
#pragma once

namespace ArrayOfRadios
{
    using namespace System;
    using namespace System::ComponentModel;
    using namespace System::Collections;
    using namespace System::Windows::Forms;
    using namespace System::Data;
    using namespace System::Drawing;

    public ref class Form1 : public System::Windows::Forms::Form
    {
    public:
        Form1(void)
        {
            InitializeComponent();
```

```cpp
            array<String^>^ rbText = gcnew array<String^> {
                L"Can", L"You", L"Click", L"More", L"Than", L"One"
            };
            radios = gcnew array<RadioButton^>(6);
            label  = gcnew Label();

            for (int i = 0; i < radios->Length; i++)
            {
                int j = 50*i;
                radios[i] = gcnew RadioButton();
                radios[i]->BackColor = Color::FromArgb(255,j+5,j+5,j+5);
                radios[i]->ForeColor = Color::FromArgb(255,250-j,250-j,250-j);
                radios[i]->Location = Drawing::Point(90, 10+(40*i));
                radios[i]->TabIndex = i;
                radios[i]->TabStop = true;
                radios[i]->Text = rbText[i];
                radios[i]->CheckedChanged +=
                    gcnew EventHandler(this, &Form1::radioCheckedChanged);
            }
            Controls->AddRange(radios);

            label->Location = Drawing::Point(90, 10+(40*radios->Length));
            Controls->Add(label);
        }

    protected:
        ~Form1()
        {
            if (components)
            {
                delete components;
            }
        }

    private:
        array<RadioButton^>^ radios;
        Label       ^label;
        System::ComponentModel::Container ^components;

#pragma region Windows Form Designer generated code

        void InitializeComponent(void)
        {
            this->SuspendLayout();
            //
            // Form1
            //
            this->AutoScaleDimensions = System::Drawing::SizeF(6, 13);
            this->AutoScaleMode = System::Windows::Forms::AutoScaleMode::Font;
            this->ClientSize = System::Drawing::Size(292, 273);
            this->Name = L"Form1";
            this->Text = L"An Array Of Radios";
            this->ResumeLayout(false);

        }
```

```
#pragma endregion

    private:
        void radioCheckedChanged(Object ^sender, EventArgs ^e)
        {
            RadioButton ^rb = (RadioButton^)sender;

            if (rb->Checked == true)
                label->Text = rb->Text;
        }
    };
}
```

The code in Listing 9-8 is pretty straightforward. (This example doesn't include the design tool–specific code as it was written by hand.) First, you create an array of RadioButton controls, and then you populate the array. I also threw in a Label control to show how to extract the currently checked RadioButton control.

You should notice a couple of things going on in this listing. First, only one event handler method is needed, as the sender parameter will tell you which RadioButton sent the event. Second, you need to check for a true Checked value because the CheckedChanged event is also triggered on the unchecking event, which also always occurs when a different RadioButton is checked. And the final thing you might want to notice is that you can use the AddRange() method instead of the Add() method to add controls to the form because there is a ready-made array using this method, as the array of RadioButtons is also an array of controls.

I also play with colors a bit, but you look at colors in detail in Chapter 11, so I will hold off the explanation until then.

Figure 9-10 shows what ArrayOfRadios.exe looks like when you execute it.

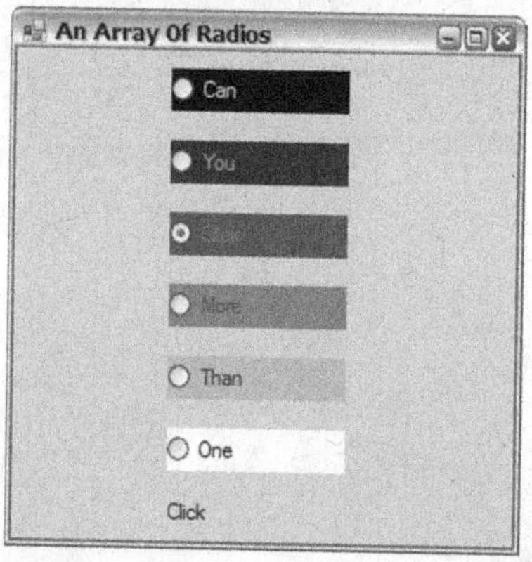

Figure 9-10. *An array of radio buttons*

The GroupBox Control

The GroupBox control does basically what its name suggests: It groups controls into a box. Not only does the GroupBox group controls visually, but it also binds the controls so that they act as a group.

The GroupBox control is predominately used for RadioButton controls, but that isn't a requirement. The requirement is that everything it groups is a control. Grouping random control types is usually done just for cosmetic reasons. Grouping RadioButton controls, on the other hand, provides the RadioButton control with additional functionality. Instead of being able to select only a single RadioButton on the form, you now can select a unique RadioButton for each GroupBox.

The next example (see Listing 9-9) shows how it is now possible to select more than one RadioButton—in this case, one of the RadioButton controls attached to the form and one from each of the GroupBoxes. Notice I use three arrays of RadioButtons. If you were to create a unique RadioButton each time instead of the array, as is the case for the generated GUI-designed code, you would then be declaring and implementing 12 different RadioButtons. I think this is a good example of why knowing how to code Win Forms by hand improves the code.

Listing 9-9. *The Code for Grouping RadioButtons*

```
#pragma once

namespace GroupingRadios
{
    using namespace System;
    using namespace System::ComponentModel;
    using namespace System::Collections;
    using namespace System::Windows::Forms;
    using namespace System::Data;
    using namespace System::Drawing;

    public ref class Form1 : public System::Windows::Forms::Form
    {
    public:
        Form1(void)
        {
            InitializeComponent();
            BuildRadios();
        }

    protected:
        ~Form1()
        {
            if (components)
            {
                delete components;
            }
        }

    private:
        System::Windows::Forms::GroupBox^   groupBox2;
        System::Windows::Forms::GroupBox^   groupBox1;

        array<System::Windows::Forms::RadioButton^>^ radio1;
        array<System::Windows::Forms::RadioButton^>^ radio2;
        array<System::Windows::Forms::RadioButton^>^ radio3;

        System::ComponentModel::Container ^components;
```

```cpp
#pragma region Windows Form Designer generated code

        void InitializeComponent(void)
        {
            this->groupBox2 = (gcnew System::Windows::Forms::GroupBox());
            this->groupBox1 = (gcnew System::Windows::Forms::GroupBox());
            this->SuspendLayout();
            //
            // groupBox2
            //
            this->groupBox2->Location = System::Drawing::Point(125, 153);
            this->groupBox2->Name = L"groupBox2";
            this->groupBox2->Size = System::Drawing::Size(152, 134);
            this->groupBox2->TabIndex = 3;
            this->groupBox2->TabStop = false;
            this->groupBox2->Text = L"Use";
            //
            // groupBox1
            //
            this->groupBox1->Location = System::Drawing::Point(125, 12);
            this->groupBox1->Name = L"groupBox1";
            this->groupBox1->Size = System::Drawing::Size(152, 135);
            this->groupBox1->TabIndex = 2;
            this->groupBox1->TabStop = false;
            this->groupBox1->Text = L"You";
            //
            // Form1
            //
            this->AutoScaleDimensions = System::Drawing::SizeF(6, 13);
            this->AutoScaleMode = System::Windows::Forms::AutoScaleMode::Font;
            this->ClientSize = System::Drawing::Size(352, 330);
            this->Controls->Add(this->groupBox2);
            this->Controls->Add(this->groupBox1);
            this->Name = L"Form1";
            this->Text = L"Using Group Boxes";
            this->ResumeLayout(false);
        }

#pragma endregion

        void BuildRadios()
        {
            this->SuspendLayout();

            // Text for RadioButton places on Form directly
            array<String^>^ rbText1 = gcnew array<String^> {
                L"Can", L"You", L"Click", L"More", L"Than", L"One"
            };

            // Build a RadioButton for each rbText1
            radio1 = gcnew array<RadioButton^>(6);
            for (int i = 0; i < radio1->Length; i++)
            {
                radio1[i] = gcnew RadioButton();
```

```
        radio1[i]->Location = Drawing::Point(20, 20+(40*i));
        radio1[i]->Text = rbText1[i];
    }
    // Add RadioButtons to Form
    Controls->AddRange(radio1);

    // Text for RadioButton places in first GroupBox
    array<String^>^ rbText2 = gcnew array<String^> {
        L"Can", L"If", L"You"
    };

    // Build a RadioButton for each rbText2
    radio2 = gcnew array<RadioButton^>(3);
    for (int i = 0; i < radio2->Length; i++)
    {
        radio2[i] = gcnew RadioButton();
        radio2[i]->Location = Drawing::Point(40, 30+(35*i));
        radio2[i]->Text = rbText2[i];
    }
    // Add RadioButtons to GroupBox
    groupBox1->Controls->AddRange(radio2);

    // Text for RadioButton places in second GroupBox
    array<String^>^ rbText3 = gcnew array<String^> {
        L"Different", L"Group", L"Boxes"
    };

    // Build a RadioButton for each rbText3
    radio3 = gcnew array<RadioButton^>(3);
    for (int i = 0; i < radio3->Length; i++)
    {
        radio3[i] = gcnew RadioButton();
        radio3[i]->Location = Drawing::Point(40, 30+(35*i));
        radio3[i]->Text = rbText3[i];
    }
    // Add RadioButtons to GroupBox2
    groupBox2->Controls->AddRange(radio3);

    this->ResumeLayout(false);
    }
};
}
```

Only a couple of things are new here. First, notice now that you add the GroupBox to the form and then add the RadioButtons to the GroupBox, as opposed to adding the RadioButtons to the form. You can also add the RadioButtons to the GroupBox and then add the GroupBox to the form. Which of the previous methods you choose is not important, as long as the controls are defined and instantiated before being added.

The second new thing is the location where you put the RadioButtons. The location is relative to the GroupBox and not the form. Notice that the same code is used to specify the location of the RadioButtons for both GroupBoxes.

As you can see, you can combine the auto-generated GUI tool code and the hand-coded code together, but you have to be careful. You can't add your code within the InitializeComponent() method, because the GUI design tool will overwrite it any time you change the form using the design tool. Because this is the case, I had to create the BuildRadios() method to add my hand-designed code instead of embedding it directly within the InitializeComponent() method.

Figure 9-11 shows what GroupingRadios.exe looks like when you execute it. Try to click the radio buttons. Now you are able to select three different ones.

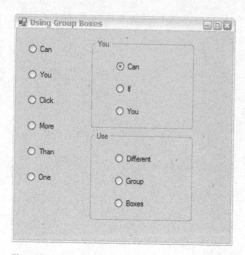

Figure 9-11. *Groups of radio buttons*

The Panel Control

The Panel control is similar in many ways to the GroupBox control. It also groups controls visually into a box and binds them so that they act as a group. It differs in that you can enable it to support scrolling, thus letting the Panel control contain more controls than its area would normally allow.

A feature that both the Panel and GroupBox controls share is that when you disable the Panel, all the controls within the Panel are also disabled. You do this by setting the Enable property to false. Another feature I particularly like is that you can make the Panel invisible by setting the Visible property to false. Using this feature, you can make the form less cluttered by hiding Panels that are not currently relevant.

Listing 9-10 shows how it is now possible to enable, disable, and make Panels reappear. It also highlights how to enable autoscrolling within a Panel.

Listing 9-10. *The Code for Disabling and Hiding Panels*

```
#pragma once

namespace Panels
{
    using namespace System;
    using namespace System::ComponentModel;
    using namespace System::Collections;
    using namespace System::Windows::Forms;
    using namespace System::Data;
    using namespace System::Drawing;
```

```cpp
public ref class Form1 : public System::Windows::Forms::Form
{
public:
    Form1(void)
    {
        InitializeComponent();
    }

protected:
    ~Form1()
    {
        if (components)
        {
            delete components;
        }
    }

private:
    System::Windows::Forms::Panel^  Rightpanel;
    System::Windows::Forms::Button^  button2;
    System::Windows::Forms::Button^  button1;
    System::Windows::Forms::Panel^  Leftpanel;
    System::Windows::Forms::Button^  bnHide;
    System::Windows::Forms::Button^  bnDisable;

    System::ComponentModel::Container ^components;

#pragma region Windows Form Designer generated code

    void InitializeComponent(void)
    {
        this->Rightpanel = (gcnew System::Windows::Forms::Panel());
        this->button2 = (gcnew System::Windows::Forms::Button());
        this->button1 = (gcnew System::Windows::Forms::Button());
        this->Leftpanel = (gcnew System::Windows::Forms::Panel());
        this->bnHide = (gcnew System::Windows::Forms::Button());
        this->bnDisable = (gcnew System::Windows::Forms::Button());
        this->Rightpanel->SuspendLayout();
        this->Leftpanel->SuspendLayout();
        this->SuspendLayout();
        //
        // Rightpanel
        //
        this->Rightpanel->AutoScroll = true;
        this->Rightpanel->BorderStyle =
            System::Windows::Forms::BorderStyle::Fixed3D;
        this->Rightpanel->Controls->Add(this->button2);
        this->Rightpanel->Controls->Add(this->button1);
        this->Rightpanel->Location = System::Drawing::Point(161, 22);
        this->Rightpanel->Name = L"Rightpanel";
        this->Rightpanel->Size = System::Drawing::Size(121, 60);
        this->Rightpanel->TabIndex = 3;
```

```cpp
//
// button2
//
this->button2->Location = System::Drawing::Point(20, 62);
this->button2->Name = L"button2";
this->button2->Size = System::Drawing::Size(75, 23);
this->button2->TabIndex = 1;
this->button2->Text = L"button 2";
//
// button1
//
this->button1->Location = System::Drawing::Point(20, 7);
this->button1->Name = L"button1";
this->button1->Size = System::Drawing::Size(75, 23);
this->button1->TabIndex = 0;
this->button1->Text = L"button 1";
//
// Leftpanel
//
this->Leftpanel->BorderStyle =
    System::Windows::Forms::BorderStyle::FixedSingle;
this->Leftpanel->Controls->Add(this->bnHide);
this->Leftpanel->Controls->Add(this->bnDisable);
this->Leftpanel->Location = System::Drawing::Point(28, 22);
this->Leftpanel->Name = L"Leftpanel";
this->Leftpanel->Size = System::Drawing::Size(120, 95);
this->Leftpanel->TabIndex = 2;
//
// bnHide
//
this->bnHide->Location = System::Drawing::Point(17, 62);
this->bnHide->Name = L"bnHide";
this->bnHide->Size = System::Drawing::Size(75, 23);
this->bnHide->TabIndex = 1;
this->bnHide->Text = L"Hide";
this->bnHide->Click +=
    gcnew System::EventHandler(this, &Form1::bnHide_Click);
//
// bnDisable
//
this->bnDisable->Location = System::Drawing::Point(17, 7);
this->bnDisable->Name = L"bnDisable";
this->bnDisable->Size = System::Drawing::Size(75, 23);
this->bnDisable->TabIndex = 0;
this->bnDisable->Text = L"Disable";
this->bnDisable->Click +=
    gcnew System::EventHandler(this, &Form1::bnDisable_Click);
//
// Form1
//
this->AutoScaleDimensions = System::Drawing::SizeF(6, 13);
this->AutoScaleMode = System::Windows::Forms::AutoScaleMode::Font;
this->ClientSize = System::Drawing::Size(310, 139);
this->Controls->Add(this->Rightpanel);
```

```
        this->Controls->Add(this->Leftpanel);
        this->Name = L"Form1";
        this->Text = L"A hidden fourth button";
        this->Rightpanel->ResumeLayout(false);
        this->Leftpanel->ResumeLayout(false);
        this->ResumeLayout(false);
    }

#pragma endregion

    private:
        System::Void bnDisable_Click(System::Object^ sender,
                                     System::EventArgs^ e)
        {
            Rightpanel->Enabled = !Rightpanel->Enabled;
        }

    private:
        System::Void bnHide_Click(System::Object^ sender, System::EventArgs^ e)
        {
            Rightpanel->Visible = !Rightpanel->Visible;
        }
    };
}
```

What's interesting in this form is the ability to use a button to disable and hide Panels. Another neat feature is that you can use the Enable and Visible properties as toggles:

```
Rightpanel->Enabled = !Rightpanel->Enabled;
Rightpanel->Visible = !Rightpanel->Visible;
```

To get RightPanel to scroll, you have to set its client size smaller than the visual area needed to view all controls. Basically, because a control is going to be obscured, the Panel automatically creates the appropriate scroll bar (either vertical or horizontal) so that the control can be exposed.

Figure 9-12 shows what Panels.exe looks like when you execute it and click the Disable Panel button. I guess I could have also clicked the Hide Panel button, but then the RightPanel would have disappeared and you wouldn't be able to tell that it was disabled.

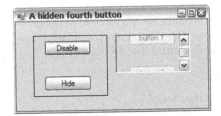

Figure 9-12. *Disabling and hiding panels*

The Text Controls

There is obviously a need to enter text into most Win Forms applications. To handle this, the .NET Framework provides three highly configurable text controls: TextBox, MaskedTextBox, and RichTextBox. All three text controls are very powerful. In fact, the simplest of the three, the TextBox control, has so much functionality that you will probably use it most, if not all, of the time. A few possible exceptions are when you want a specifically formatted sequence of characters, in which case you would select MaskedTextBox, or if you require font styles such as boldface, italic, or underline within the text being entered, in which case you would choose RichTextBox.

As is the common theme in the .NET Framework class library, the text controls derive from a common abstract base class, TextBoxBase. This class provides a common set of functionality that you can use for all three text controls, and it's also a great starting point for those programmers who need to write a text control to meet specific needs.

The abstract TextBoxBase class is composed of numerous properties and methods that can handle text input from the user. Being that TextBoxBase is an abstract class, you can't instantiate from it; instead, you need to use one of its child classes. Here are some common TextBoxBase-specific properties:

- AcceptsTab is a Boolean that represents, in a multiline text control, whether the Tab key will be used as a control character or as a means to move to the next control. The default is false.

- CanUndo is a Boolean that represents whether the control can undo the previous operation that occurred. The default is false.

- MaxLength is an Int32 that represents the maximum number of characters allowed to be entered into the control. The default is 0, which means the allowable number of characters enterable is only restricted by the memory of the computer.

- Modified is a Boolean that represents whether the content of the control has been modified since the control was created or the contents were set. The default is false.

- Multiline is a Boolean that represents whether the control is made up of more than one line. The default is false.

- ReadOnly is a Boolean that represents whether the control is read-only. The default is false.

- SelectedText is a String containing selected text from the control. The default is a zero-length String (not null).

- SelectionLength is an Int32 that represents the length of the selected text. If the SelectionLength property is set to a value larger than the length of text within the control, it's automatically set to the number of characters in the control minus the SelectionStart property.

- SelectionStart is an Int32 that represents the starting location of the selected text within the control. If the SelectionStart property is set to a value larger than the number of characters within the control, it's automatically set to the value after the last character in the control.

- Text is a String that represents the text of the control.

- WordWrap is a Boolean that represents, in a multiline text control, whether a word wraps automatically to the beginning of a line when necessary. If the value is false, the control will scroll horizontally when text is entered beyond the width of the control. The default is true.

Here are some common TextBoxBase-specific methods:

- AppendText() adds text to the end of the current text of the control.
- Clear() sets the text in the control to be empty.
- ClearUndo() removes the last undo operation from the undo buffer.
- Copy() takes the selected text and places it on the Clipboard. The control is unaffected.
- Cut() removes the selected text from the control and places it on the Clipboard.
- Paste() copies the text in the Clipboard to the current location of the cursor in the control.
- Select() selects text within the control using a start location and a length.

- `SelectAll()` selects all the text within the control.
- `Undo()` restores the contents in the text control back to the previous state before the last operation.

TextBox

As stated earlier, you can configure the `TextBox` control in many ways, ranging from long to short, normal to password hidden, and single to multilined. If you enable this control, you have a built-in undo buffer. You can cut and paste to it. The functionality this control has is simply amazing.

Along with the properties provided by `TextBoxBase`, the `TextBox` control adds a few properties of its own:

- `AcceptReturn` is a Boolean that represents, in a multiline control, whether pressing the Enter key creates a new line of text or passes control to the default button of the form. If this property is set to false, then Ctrl-Enter must be pressed to create a new line of text. The default is true.
- `CharacterCasing` is a `CharacterCasing` enum class that notifies the control as characters are entered into the control that it should convert the character to uppercase, lowercase, or leave the character as typed. The default is `CharacterCasing::Normal` or to leave the characters as they are typed.
- `PasswordChar` is a Char that represents the character to be used to replace all the characters typed in, thus hiding the password from view. The default is the value 0, meaning do not use `PasswordChar`.
- `TextAlign` is a `HorizontalAlignment` enum class that represents whether the text should be right justified, left justified, or centered when entered. The default is `HorizontalAlignment::Left`, or left justified.

MaskedTextBox

The basic idea behind the `MaskedTextBox` is it provides a mask by which to enter text data. Then, using an assortment of properties and methods, it ensures that the user is adhering to the specified mask.

Here are some common properties and an event that you would use to ensure the data entered matches the mask:

- `BeepOnError` is a Boolean property that enables or disables the system beep when an invalid character is entered onto the mask entry. If this property is set to true, then invalid keystrokes will beep. The default is false.
- `MaskCompleted` is a Boolean property that becomes true when all required mask entries have been populated.
- `MaskFull` is a Boolean property that becomes true when all mask entries are populated.
- `MaskInputRejected` is an event that provides a way for you to customize the handling of invalid keystroke entries onto the mask.

Having valid characters entered onto the mask does not necessarily mean that you have a valid value to match the given type of the data entry field. In other words, you can enter numbers into a date field, as is required by the mask, and still enter an invalid date. To ensure that a valid data type will result from the entry in the `MaskedTextBox`, you must assign an instance of the data type expected to be entered to the `ValidatingType` property:

```
mtbDoB->ValidatingType = DateTime::typeid;
```

I will cover the `typeid` operator in detail in Chapter 18.

Then to see if the input data of the control matches the data type assigned, you add a handler to the TypeValidationCompleted event, which triggers when the control loses focus. Finally, you examine the IsValidInput property of TypeValidationEventArgs argument passed by the event. If the value is true, then the data entered into the control parses to the data type assign by the ValidatingType property, and the value is placed in TypeValidationEventArgs' ReturnValue property.

Note If you are implementing your own data type, you need to implement the static Parse() method before assigning an instance of it to the ValidatingType property.

If you just want the text value returned from the MaskedTextBox and not a specific data type, then the control provides a number of properties to provide the value in the format you require:

- Text is a String property that returns what the user currently sees in the control.

- OutputText is a String property that returns a value based on the values specified in the IncludeLiteral and IncludePrompt properties. The IncludeLiteral property specifies whether the literals specified in the mask are included, while the IncludePrompt specifies whether the prompt characters are included. Both of these properties default to true.

- InputText is a String property that returns only what the user actually entered in the control.

The MaskedTextBox control's mask must be made up of one or more of the characters defined in Table 9-1. The characters used by MaskedTextBox are based on those used by the Masked Edit Control in Visual Basic 6.0.

Table 9-1. *MaskedTextBox Masking Characters*

Masking Character	Description
0	A mandatory digit between 0 and 9.
9	An optional digit between 0 and 9.
#	An optional digit between 0 and 9 or a +, - or space. If the position of this mask entry is left blank, then the value is space.
L	A mandatory letter between a–z and A–Z.
?	An optional letter between a–z and A–Z.
&	A mandatory letter. If the AsciiOnly property is set, then this mask behaves the same as L.
C	An optional letter. If the AsciiOnly property is set, then this mask behaves the same as ?.
A	A mandatory alphanumeric. If the AsciiOnly property is set, then the only characters allowed are a–z and A–Z.
a	An optional alphanumeric. If the AsciiOnly property is set, then the only characters allowed are a–z and A–Z.
.	A decimal placeholder. The UI culture will determine the actual decimal placeholder used.
,	A thousands placeholder. The UI culture will determine the actual thousands placeholder used.

Table 9-1. *MaskedTextBox Masking Characters*

Masking Character	Description
:	A time separator. The UI culture will determine the actual time separator used.
/	A date separator. The UI culture will determine the actual date separator used.
$	A currency symbol. The UI culture will determine the actual currency symbol used.
<	Converts all subsequent characters to lowercase.
>	Converts all subsequent characters to uppercase.
|	Disables previous > or < masks.
\	Turns a mask character into a literal. A [\\] will turn into a \ literal.
All other characters	A literal that will appear in a static location within the control. The user will not be able to move or delete the literal.

The next example (see Listing 9-11) demonstrates some features of the TextBox and MaskedTextBox control. First it creates a TextBox and a MaskedTextBox to handle input. When the user clicks the Submit button, the text gets inserted into the front of the read-only, multiline text box. This multiline text box can be made editable if you enter "**Editable**" in the bottom password text box.

You should notice the following thing about this example. I set the multiline text box properties AcceptTab and AcceptReturn to true. This causes the pressing of the Tab key to create a tab character in the multiline text box (when editable, obviously) and causes the Enter key to create a new line of text. This differs from the default functionality of the remaining controls, which jump to the next control on the Tab key and causes the AcceptButton to be triggered when the Enter key is pressed.

Listing 9-11. *Some TextBox and MaskedTextBox Code*

```
#pragma once

namespace TextEntry
{
    using namespace System;
    using namespace System::ComponentModel;
    using namespace System::Collections;
    using namespace System::Windows::Forms;
    using namespace System::Data;
    using namespace System::Drawing;

    public ref class Form1 : public System::Windows::Forms::Form
    {
    public:
        Form1(void)
        {
            InitializeComponent();

            DoB = DateTime::MinValue;
```

```cpp
            // setting validating type to DateTime
            mtbDoB->ValidatingType = DateTime::typeid;
        }

    protected:
        ~Form1()
        {
            if (components)
            {
                delete components;
            }
        }

    private:
        System::Windows::Forms::Button^  bnSubmit;
        System::Windows::Forms::Label^  label3;
        System::Windows::Forms::TextBox^  tbPassword;
        System::Windows::Forms::TextBox^  tbOutput;
        System::Windows::Forms::Label^  label2;
        System::Windows::Forms::MaskedTextBox^  mtbDoB;
        System::Windows::Forms::Label^  label1;
        System::Windows::Forms::TextBox^  tbName;

        DateTime^ DoB;

        System::ComponentModel::Container ^components;

#pragma region Windows Form Designer generated code

        void InitializeComponent(void)
        {
            this->bnSubmit = (gcnew System::Windows::Forms::Button());
            this->label3 = (gcnew System::Windows::Forms::Label());
            this->tbPassword = (gcnew System::Windows::Forms::TextBox());
            this->tbOutput = (gcnew System::Windows::Forms::TextBox());
            this->label2 = (gcnew System::Windows::Forms::Label());
            this->mtbDoB = (gcnew System::Windows::Forms::MaskedTextBox());
            this->label1 = (gcnew System::Windows::Forms::Label());
            this->tbName = (gcnew System::Windows::Forms::TextBox());
            this->SuspendLayout();
            //
            // bnSubmit
            //
            this->bnSubmit->Location = System::Drawing::Point(260, 36);
            this->bnSubmit->Margin = System::Windows::Forms::Padding(1,3,3,3);
            this->bnSubmit->Name = L"bnSubmit";
            this->bnSubmit->Size = System::Drawing::Size(56, 20);
            this->bnSubmit->TabIndex = 10;
            this->bnSubmit->Text = L" Submit";
            this->bnSubmit->Click +=
                gcnew System::EventHandler(this, &Form1::bnSubmit_Click);
            //
            // label3
```

```
//
this->label3->AutoSize = true;
this->label3->Location = System::Drawing::Point(14, 232);
this->label3->Name = L"label3";
this->label3->Size = System::Drawing::Size(56, 13);
this->label3->TabIndex = 14;
this->label3->Text = L"Password:";
//
// tbPassword
//
this->tbPassword->CausesValidation = false;
this->tbPassword->Location = System::Drawing::Point(78, 226);
this->tbPassword->MaxLength = 16;
this->tbPassword->Name = L"tbPassword";
this->tbPassword->PasswordChar = '?';
this->tbPassword->Size = System::Drawing::Size(238, 20);
this->tbPassword->TabIndex = 13;
this->tbPassword->UseSystemPasswordChar = true;
this->tbPassword->WordWrap = false;
this->tbPassword->TextChanged +=
    gcnew System::EventHandler(this,&Form1::tbPassword_TextChanged);
//
// tbOutput
//
this->tbOutput->Location = System::Drawing::Point(14, 63);
this->tbOutput->Multiline = true;
this->tbOutput->Name = L"tbOutput";
this->tbOutput->ReadOnly = true;
this->tbOutput->ScrollBars =
    System::Windows::Forms::ScrollBars::Vertical;
this->tbOutput->Size = System::Drawing::Size(302, 156);
this->tbOutput->TabIndex = 12;
this->tbOutput->TabStop = false;
//
// label2
//
this->label2->AutoSize = true;
this->label2->Location = System::Drawing::Point(168, 15);
this->label2->Name = L"label2";
this->label2->Size = System::Drawing::Size(69, 13);
this->label2->TabIndex = 11;
this->label2->Text = L"Date of Birth:";
//
// mtbDoB
//
this->mtbDoB->AllowPromptAsInput = false;
this->mtbDoB->BeepOnError = true;
this->mtbDoB->Location = System::Drawing::Point(168, 36);
this->mtbDoB->Margin = System::Windows::Forms::Padding(3,3,1,3);
this->mtbDoB->Mask = L"00/00/0000";
this->mtbDoB->Name = L"mtbDoB";
this->mtbDoB->Size = System::Drawing::Size(89, 20);
this->mtbDoB->TabIndex = 8;
this->mtbDoB->TypeValidationCompleted +=
```

```
                    gcnew System::Windows::Forms::TypeValidationEventHandler(this,
                                    &Form1::mtbDoB_TypeValidationCompleted);
            //
            // label1
            //
            this->label1->AutoSize = true;
            this->label1->Location = System::Drawing::Point(14, 15);
            this->label1->Name = L"label1";
            this->label1->Size = System::Drawing::Size(38, 13);
            this->label1->TabIndex = 9;
            this->label1->Text = L"Name:";
            //
            // tbName
            //
            this->tbName->Location = System::Drawing::Point(14, 36);
            this->tbName->Name = L"tbName";
            this->tbName->Size = System::Drawing::Size(147, 20);
            this->tbName->TabIndex = 7;
            this->tbName->Validating +=
                gcnew System::ComponentModel::CancelEventHandler(this,
                                            &Form1::tbName_Validating);
            //
            // Form1
            //
            this->AutoScaleDimensions = System::Drawing::SizeF(6, 13);
            this->AutoScaleMode = System::Windows::Forms::AutoScaleMode::Font;
            this->ClientSize = System::Drawing::Size(331, 261);
            this->Controls->Add(this->bnSubmit);
            this->Controls->Add(this->label3);
            this->Controls->Add(this->tbPassword);
            this->Controls->Add(this->tbOutput);
            this->Controls->Add(this->label2);
            this->Controls->Add(this->mtbDoB);
            this->Controls->Add(this->label1);
            this->Controls->Add(this->tbName);
            this->Name = L"Form1";
            this->Text = L"Simple entry data entry";
            this->ResumeLayout(false);
            this->PerformLayout();
        }

#pragma endregion

    private:
        System::Void bnSubmit_Click(System::Object^ sender,
                                    System::EventArgs^ e)
        {
            if (tbName->Text->Length <= 0)          // Blank name bad!
                tbName->Focus();
            else if (*DoB == DateTime::MinValue)    // Bad date bad!
                mtbDoB->Focus();
```

```cpp
    else                                    // Good!
    {
        // Concatinate name and date of birth and add to output
        tbOutput->Text = String::Format("{0} - {1}\r\n{2}",
            tbName->Text, mtbDoB->Text, tbOutput->Text);
        tbName->Clear();
        mtbDoB->Clear();
        DoB = DateTime::MinValue;
    }
}


System::Void tbPassword_TextChanged(System::Object^ sender,
                                    System::EventArgs^ e)
{

    // if the Password TextBox Text equals "Editable" then make
    // the multiline TextBox editable and have a tab stop
    if (tbPassword->Text->Equals("Editable"))
    {
        tbOutput->TabStop = true;
        tbOutput->ReadOnly = false;
    }
    else
    {
        tbOutput->TabStop = false;
        tbOutput->ReadOnly = true;
    }
}


System::Void mtbDoB_TypeValidationCompleted(System::Object^ sender,
                System::Windows::Forms::TypeValidationEventArgs^ e)
{
    // Check to see if the date was valid and less than or equals
    // todays date. When false make the MaskedTextBox yellow
    // and make DoB MinValue. otherwise set it to normal and make
    // DoB the value within MaskedTextBox
    if (e->IsValidInput &&
        (*(DateTime^)e->ReturnValue) <= DateTime::Now)
    {
        DoB = (DateTime^)e->ReturnValue;
        mtbDoB->BackColor = SystemColors::Window;
    }
    else
    {
        mtbDoB->BackColor = Color::Yellow;
        DoB = DateTime::MinValue;
    }
}
```

```
System::Void tbName_Validating(System::Object^ sender,
                        System::ComponentModel::CancelEventArgs^ e)
{
    // Check to make sure there is a name. When false make the
    // TextBox yellow. Otherwise set it to normal as all is okay
    if (tbName->Text->Length <= 0)
        tbName->BackColor = Color::Yellow;
    else
        tbName->BackColor = SystemColors::Window;
}
};
}
```

One thing to note about the code in Listing 9-11 is the use of the Control class's Validating event. This event is triggered when a control loses focus and allows the value within the control to be validated. In the previous example, I use the Validating event to turn the control yellow when no name is entered in the control.

By the way, if you set the Cancel property to true within the CancelEventArgs argument, then the focus will remain within the current control.

Data validation is well beyond the scope of this book, but *Data Entry and Validation with C# and VB .NET Windows Forms* by Nick Symmonds (Apress, 2003) covers the topic in great detail. Again, the book is not written for C++/CLI, but you should be able to follow it well enough to implement its contents.

Figure 9-13 shows what TextEntry.exe looks like when you execute it.

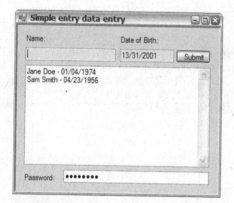

Figure 9-13. *Assorted text boxes*

RichTextBox

Plain and simple, the RichTextBox control is overkill, for most cases, when you need text input. This control provides advanced formatting features, such as boldface, italics, underline, color, and different fonts. It is also possible to format paragraphs. You can assign text directly to the control using the Text property, or you can load it from a Rich Text Format (RTF) or plain text file using the LoadFile() method.

The RichTextBox control is a little tricky to use, as most of the added functionality over the TextBox control requires the handling of events or other controls, such as buttons, to implement. For example, implementing boldfacing of text within a RichTextBox requires implementing the SelectionFont property, which needs to be referenced somehow. In the following example, I do this by pressing the F1 key, but you could do it any number of other ways.

The RichTextBox control provides a number of additional properties to handle the formatting features it provides. Here are some of the more common properties:

- BulletIndent is an Int32 that represents the number of pixels inserted as the indentation after a bullet. The default is 0.

- CanRedo is a Boolean that represents whether undone operations can be reapplied.

- RedoActionName is a String that represents the name of the next redo action to be applied. If the return String is empty (a zero-length String, not a null), then there are no more actions that can be redone.

- RightMargin is an Int32 that represents the number of pixels from the left side of the control where the nonvisible right margin is placed.

- Rtf is a String that represents the RTF-formatted data in the control. The content of the Rtf property differs from that of the Text property in that the Rtf property is in Rich Text Format, whereas the Text property is in just plain text.

- Scrollbars is a RichTextScrollbars enum class that represents which (if any) scroll bars will be visible within the control. The default is RichTextScrollbars::Both, which will display both vertical and horizontal scroll bars if needed. I prefer to use ForceVertical instead because it stops the control from having to readjust itself when the content extends beyond the vertical height of the control. It now simply enables the already visible vertical scroll bar.

- SelectedRtf is a String containing selected RTF-formatted text from the control. The default is a zero-length String (not null).

- SelectionBullet is a Boolean that represents whether the bullet style should be applied to the current selected text or insertion point. The default is false.

- SelectionColor is a System::Drawing::Color that represents the color of the selected text. If more than one color falls within the selected text, then Color::Empty is returned.

- SelectionFont is a System::Drawing::Font that represents the font of the selected text. If more than one font falls within the selected text, then null is returned.

- SelectionHangingIndent is an Int32 that represents the distance in pixels between the left edge of the first line of text in the selected paragraph and the left edge of subsequent lines in the same paragraph.

- SelectionIndent is an Int32 that represents the distance in pixels between the left edge of the control window and the left edge of the current selected text or text added after the insertion point.

- SelectionRightIndent is an Int32 that represents the distance in pixels between the right edge of the text and the right edge of the control.

- SelectionTabs is an array of Int32 that represents a set of absolute tab locations in pixels.

- ShowSelectionMargin is a Boolean that represents whether the selection margin on the left side of the control is expanded for easier access. Clicking the margin highlights the entire row. The default is false.

- UndoActionName is a String that represents the name of the next undo action to be applied. If the return String is empty (a zero-length String, not a null), then there are no more actions that can be undone.

The RichTextBox control provides a number of additional methods as well:

- Find() searches for the specified text within the control.

- LoadFile() loads a text or RTF-formatted file into the control.

- Redo() will redo the last undo operation done on the control.
- SaveFile() saves a text or RTF-formatted file to the specified path/file location.
- Undo() will undo the last operation done on the control.

The next example (see Listing 9-12) is an extremely simple and limited use of the functionality of the RichTextBox. It lacks many of the features that are available, but it is a good starting point and gives you some ideas about how to implement your own RTF editor, if you are so inclined.

In the example, pressing the F9 key loads a couple of pages from a novel I am writing. You can save the file back by pressing F10. To test out the special features of this RichTextBox, select some text with the mouse and then press one of the remaining function keys (F1–F8).

Listing 9-12. *Implementing a Simple RTF Editor*

```
#pragma once

namespace RichText
{
    using namespace System;
    using namespace System::ComponentModel;
    using namespace System::Collections;
    using namespace System::Windows::Forms;
    using namespace System::Data;
    using namespace System::Drawing;

    public ref class Form1 : public System::Windows::Forms::Form
    {
    public:
        Form1(void)
        {
            InitializeComponent();
            BuildLabels();
        }

    protected:
        ~Form1()
        {
            if (components)
            {
                delete components;
            }
        }
    private:
        System::Windows::Forms::RichTextBox^  rtBox;

        array<System::Windows::Forms::Label^>^ labels;

        System::ComponentModel::Container ^components;
```

```cpp
#pragma region Windows Form Designer generated code

        void InitializeComponent(void)
        {
            this->rtBox = (gcnew System::Windows::Forms::RichTextBox());
            this->SuspendLayout();
            //
            // rtBox
            //
            this->rtBox->Anchor =
                static_cast<System::Windows::Forms::AnchorStyles>
                (System::Windows::Forms::AnchorStyles::Top
                | System::Windows::Forms::AnchorStyles::Bottom
                | System::Windows::Forms::AnchorStyles::Left
                | System::Windows::Forms::AnchorStyles::Right);
            this->rtBox->Location = System::Drawing::Point(0, 32);
            this->rtBox->Name = L"rtBox";
            this->rtBox->RightMargin = 900;
            this->rtBox->ScrollBars =
                System::Windows::Forms::RichTextBoxScrollBars::ForcedVertical;
            this->rtBox->ShowSelectionMargin = true;
            this->rtBox->Size = System::Drawing::Size(950, 488);
            this->rtBox->TabIndex = 1;
            this->rtBox->Text = L"";
            this->rtBox->KeyDown +=
                gcnew System::Windows::Forms::KeyEventHandler(this,
                                                &Form1::rtBox_KeyDown);

            //
            // Form1
            //
            this->AutoScaleDimensions = System::Drawing::SizeF(6, 13);
            this->AutoScaleMode = System::Windows::Forms::AutoScaleMode::Font;
            this->ClientSize = System::Drawing::Size(950, 520);
            this->Controls->Add(this->rtBox);
            this->Name = L"Form1";
            this->Text = L"(Very Simple Rich Text Editor)";
            this->ResumeLayout(false);
        }

#pragma endregion

        void BuildLabels()
        {
            array<String^>^ rtLabel = gcnew array<String^> {
                L"F1-Bold",   L"F2-Italics", L"F3-Underline",
                L"F4-Normal", L"F5-Red",     L"F6-Blue",
                L"F7-Green",  L"F8-Black",   L"F9-Load",
                L"F10-Save"
            };
            labels = gcnew array<System::Windows::Forms::Label^>(10);
```

```cpp
    // Build the labels
    for (int i = 0; i < labels->Length; i++)
    {
        labels[i] = gcnew Label();
        labels[i]->BackColor = SystemColors::ControlDark;
        labels[i]->BorderStyle = BorderStyle::FixedSingle;
        labels[i]->Location = Drawing::Point(5+(95*i), 8);
        labels[i]->Size = Drawing::Size(85, 16);
        labels[i]->Text = rtLabel[i];
        labels[i]->TextAlign = ContentAlignment::MiddleCenter;
    }
    // Place labels on the Form
    Controls->AddRange(labels);
}


System::Void rtBox_KeyDown(System::Object^ sender,
                           System::Windows::Forms::KeyEventArgs^ e)
{
    try
    {
        if (rtBox->SelectionLength > 0)
        {
            // Change selected text style
            FontStyle fs;
            switch (e->KeyCode)
            {
                case Keys::F1:
                    fs = FontStyle::Bold;
                    break;
                case Keys::F2:
                    fs = FontStyle::Italic;
                    break;
                case Keys::F3:
                    fs = FontStyle::Underline;
                    break;
                case Keys::F4:
                    fs = FontStyle::Regular;
                    break;
            // Change selected text color
                case Keys::F5:
                    rtBox->SelectionColor = Color::Red;
                    break;
                case Keys::F6:
                    rtBox->SelectionColor = Color::Blue;
                    break;
                case Keys::F7:
                    rtBox->SelectionColor = Color::Green;
                    break;
                case Keys::F8:
                    rtBox->SelectionColor = Color::Black;
                    break;
            }
```

```
        // Do the actual change of the selected text style
        if (e->KeyCode >= Keys::F1 && e->KeyCode <= Keys::F4)
        {
            rtBox->SelectionFont = gcnew Drawing::Font(
                rtBox->SelectionFont->FontFamily,
                rtBox->SelectionFont->Size,
                fs
            );
        }
    }
    // Load hard coded Chapter01.rtf file
    else if (e->KeyCode == Keys::F9)
    {
        rtBox->LoadFile("Chapter01.rtf");
    }
    // Save hard coded Chapter01.rtf file
    else if (e->KeyCode == Keys::F10)
    {
        rtBox->SaveFile("Chapter01.rtf",
                        RichTextBoxStreamType::RichText);
    }
}
// Capture any blowups
catch (Exception ^e)
{
    MessageBox::Show(String::Format("Error: {0}", e->Message));
}
        }
    };
}
```

As you can see, implementing the functionality of the RichTextBox is done externally to the control itself. You need some way of updating the properties. I took the easy way out by capturing simple function keystroke events and updating the selected RichTextBox text as appropriate. You will probably want to use a combination of keystrokes, button clicks, and so on to make the editing process as easy as possible.

Another interesting bit of code in this example is the use of the Anchor property:

```
this->rtBox->Anchor = static_cast<System::Windows::Forms::AnchorStyles>
                    (System::Windows::Forms::AnchorStyles::Top |
                    System::Windows::Forms::AnchorStyles::Bottom |
                    System::Windows::Forms::AnchorStyles::Left |
                    System::Windows::Forms::AnchorStyles::Right);
```

This property allows you to have a control anchor itself to any or all (as shown in the previous code) sides of the parent window. Thus, when the parent window is resized, so is the control. (I removed all the extra, and unneeded, code added by the code generator to make it more readable.)

Be careful when you run this program, as it is dependent on where it is executed. To make things easier, I hard-coded the program to load and save to the current working directory. When you run this program within Visual Studio 2005, the current working directory is located where your source code is. Thus, the Chapter01.rtf file is located in the same directory as the source code. If you run this program on its own out of Windows Explorer, for example, then it will not find the RTF file. In this scenario, you need to copy the file to the same directory as the executable. Obviously, if you wanted to make the program more robust, you would allow a user to specify where the RTF file is, so this dependency would not be an issue.

Figure 9-14 shows what RichText.exe looks like when you execute it.

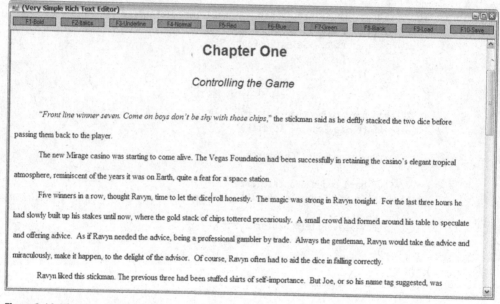

Figure 9-14. *The simple RTF editor in action*

The Selection Controls

The three common selection controls, ListBox, ComboBox, and CheckedListBox, are the last of the more basic controls provided by the .NET Framework class library that you will cover in this chapter. Each of the controls represents a selectable scrolling list of items.

When you create a selection control, you provide it with a collection of values for it to display. Each value within the collection has a unique index. The control keeps track of these indices for you, along with their associated values. All you have to do is handle selection events sent by the selection controls or query the control for which a value or values have been selected, either by value or index.

Selection controls are helpful when you want to select from a list of items of a "reasonable" size. "Reasonable," though, is a very relative term and it depends on what the user is selecting and where the data is coming from (fetching 300 rows from a local hard disk is different than fetching them from a mainframe in another country). For example, a list of 50 items may seem excessive in a selection control if there is no rhyme or reason to it, but it is just right when you are looking for a state in America.

All of the selection controls inherit from the abstract class ListControl. This provides a common set of properties and methods from which to build upon. Selection controls have the capability to display lists originating from sources that implement the IList interface. The functionality is provided by the ListControl's property, DataSource. You will see an example of this when you cover ADO.NET in Chapter 12.

Here is a list of some of the most common properties found in the ListControl class and thus inherited by the ListBox, ComboBox, and CheckListBox controls:

- DataSource is an Object that implements the IList interface, frequently an Array or DataSet, which represents the items that make up the control. The default is null, which means no DataSource is being used.

- `SelectedIndex` is an `Int32` that represents the zero-based index of the currently selected item. If no index is selected, then –1 will be returned.

- `SelectedValue` is an `Object` that represents the value of the currently selected item as specified by the control data source's `ValueMember`. If the `ValueMember` is not specified, then the `ToString()` value is returned.

- `ValueMember` is a `String` that represents the property of the control's data source to use as the value. The default is an empty `String` (and not `null`), meaning that it uses the `ToString()` value.

The `ListBox` is truly just a selection list, whereas the `ComboBox` is a combination of a `ListBox` and a `TextBox`. The `CheckListBox`, on the other hand, is a combination of a `ListBox` and a `CheckBox`. In fact, the `CheckListBox` inherits directly from `ListBox` and thus only indirectly from `ListControl`.

ListBox

The `ListBox` control is a simple scrollable list of items from which a user can select one or more items, depending on the `SelectionMode` of the `ListBox`. Four modes are available:

- `SelectionMode::None`: No items can be selected.

- `SelectionMode::One`: Only one item can be selected at a time.

- `SelectionMode::MultiSimple`: More than one item can be selected.

- `SelectionMode::MultiExtended`: More than one item can be selected. The method of selecting the multiple items uses the Shift and Ctrl keys to allow for swifter selection of items.

The `ListBox` control provides a number of additional properties from the `ListControl` to configure the control and organize, find, and select the data within:

- `Items` is a `ListBox::ObjectCollection` that represents the collection of items within the control. The `ObjectCollection` allows you to do things such as add and remove items from the `ListBox`. Note that this method of providing items to the `ListBox` is not the same as using a `DataSource`. If you use a `DataSource`, you cannot manipulate the items in the `ListBox` using the `ObjectCollection`.

- `MultiColumn` is a `Boolean` that represents whether the control can be broken into multiple columns. The default is `false`.

- `SelectedIndices` is a `ListBox::SelectedIndexCollection` that represents the collection of zero-based indices of currently selected items within the control.

- `SelectedItems` is a `ListBox::SelectedObjectCollection` that represents the collection of currently selected items within the control.

- `Sorted` is a `Boolean` that represents whether the control is automatically sorted. The default is `false`.

- `Text` is a `String` that represents the value of the currently selected item. If you set the value of the `Text` property, then the `ListBox` searches itself for an item that matches the `Text` property and selects that item.

The `ListBox` control also provides a number of additional methods:

- `ClearSelected()` deselects all selected items in the control.

- `FindString()` finds the first item that starts with a given `String`.

- `FindStringExact()` finds the first item that exactly matches a given `String`.

- GetSelected() determines if a given item is currently selected.
- SetSelected() selects the items at the given index.
- Sort() sorts the items in the control.

Listing 9-13 shows how to transfer selected items between two different lists. The ListBox on the left is sorted and is a MultiExtended list, whereas the one on the right is not sorted and is a MultiSimple list.

Listing 9-13. *Transferring Items Between ListBoxes*

```
#pragma once

namespace ListTransfers
{
    using namespace System;
    using namespace System::ComponentModel;
    using namespace System::Collections;
    using namespace System::Windows::Forms;
    using namespace System::Data;
    using namespace System::Drawing;

    public ref class Form1 : public System::Windows::Forms::Form
    {
    public:
        Form1(void)
        {
            InitializeComponent();
        }

    protected:
        ~Form1()
        {
            if (components)
            {
                delete components;
            }
        }

    private:
        System::Windows::Forms::ListBox^  LBDest;
        System::Windows::Forms::Button^  bnR2L;
        System::Windows::Forms::Button^  bnL2R;
        System::Windows::Forms::ListBox^  LBOrg;
        System::Windows::Forms::Label^  label2;
        System::Windows::Forms::Label^  label1;

        System::ComponentModel::Container ^components;
```

```
#pragma region Windows Form Designer generated code

        void InitializeComponent(void)
        {
            this->LBDest = (gcnew System::Windows::Forms::ListBox());
            this->bnR2L = (gcnew System::Windows::Forms::Button());
            this->bnL2R = (gcnew System::Windows::Forms::Button());
            this->LBOrg = (gcnew System::Windows::Forms::ListBox());
            this->label2 = (gcnew System::Windows::Forms::Label());
            this->label1 = (gcnew System::Windows::Forms::Label());
            this->SuspendLayout();
            //
            // LBDest
            //
            this->LBDest->FormattingEnabled = true;
            this->LBDest->Location = System::Drawing::Point(213, 46);
            this->LBDest->Name = L"LBDest";
            this->LBDest->SelectionMode =
                System::Windows::Forms::SelectionMode::MultiSimple;
            this->LBDest->Size = System::Drawing::Size(134, 134);
            this->LBDest->TabIndex = 10;
            this->LBDest->DoubleClick +=
                gcnew System::EventHandler(this, &Form1::LBDest_DoubleClick);
            //
            // bnR2L
            //
            this->bnR2L->Location = System::Drawing::Point(167, 108);
            this->bnR2L->Name = L"bnR2L";
            this->bnR2L->Size = System::Drawing::Size(33, 20);
            this->bnR2L->TabIndex = 9;
            this->bnR2L->Text = L"<==";
            this->bnR2L->Click +=
                gcnew System::EventHandler(this, &Form1::bnR2L_Click);
            //
            // bnL2R
            //
            this->bnL2R->Location = System::Drawing::Point(167, 80);
            this->bnL2R->Name = L"bnL2R";
            this->bnL2R->Size = System::Drawing::Size(33, 20);
            this->bnL2R->TabIndex = 8;
            this->bnL2R->Text = L"==>";
            this->bnL2R->Click +=
                gcnew System::EventHandler(this, &Form1::bnL2R_Click);
            //
            // LBOrg
            //
            this->LBOrg->FormattingEnabled = true;
            this->LBOrg->Items->AddRange(gcnew cli::array< System::Object^>(10)
                {L"System", L"System::Collections", L"System::Data",
                 L"System::Drawing", L"System::IO", L"System::Net",
                 L"System::Threading", L"System::Web",
                 L"System::Windows::Forms", L"System::Xml"});
```

```cpp
            this->LBOrg->Location = System::Drawing::Point(20, 46);
            this->LBOrg->Name = L"LBOrg";
            this->LBOrg->SelectionMode =
                System::Windows::Forms::SelectionMode::MultiExtended;
            this->LBOrg->Size = System::Drawing::Size(133, 134);
            this->LBOrg->Sorted = true;
            this->LBOrg->TabIndex = 6;
            this->LBOrg->DoubleClick +=
                gcnew System::EventHandler(this, &Form1::LBOrg_DoubleClick);
            //
            // label2
            //
            this->label2->AutoSize = true;
            this->label2->Location = System::Drawing::Point(213, 17);
            this->label2->Name = L"label2";
            this->label2->Size = System::Drawing::Size(104, 13);
            this->label2->TabIndex = 7;
            this->label2->Text = L"Unsorted Multisimple";
            //
            // label1
            //
            this->label1->AutoSize = true;
            this->label1->Location = System::Drawing::Point(20, 17);
            this->label1->Name = L"label1";
            this->label1->Size = System::Drawing::Size(107, 13);
            this->label1->TabIndex = 5;
            this->label1->Text = L"Sorted Multiextended";
            //
            // Form1
            //
            this->AutoScaleDimensions = System::Drawing::SizeF(6, 13);
            this->AutoScaleMode = System::Windows::Forms::AutoScaleMode::Font;
            this->ClientSize = System::Drawing::Size(367, 196);
            this->Controls->Add(this->LBDest);
            this->Controls->Add(this->bnR2L);
            this->Controls->Add(this->bnL2R);
            this->Controls->Add(this->LBOrg);
            this->Controls->Add(this->label2);
            this->Controls->Add(this->label1);
            this->Name = L"Form1";
            this->Text = L"List Box Transfers";
            this->ResumeLayout(false);
            this->PerformLayout();
        }

#pragma endregion

    private:
        System::Void LBOrg_DoubleClick(System::Object^ sender,
                                       System::EventArgs^ e)
        {
```

```
        // Add Selected item to other ListBox
        // Then remove item from original
        if (LBOrg->SelectedItem != nullptr)
        {
            LBDest->Items->Add(LBOrg->SelectedItem);
            LBOrg->Items->Remove(LBOrg->SelectedItem);
        }
    }

    System::Void LBDest_DoubleClick(System::Object^ sender,
                                    System::EventArgs^ e)
    {
        // Add Selected item to other ListBox
        // Then remove item from original
        if (LBDest->SelectedItem != nullptr)
        {
            LBOrg->Items->Add(LBDest->SelectedItem);
            LBDest->Items->Remove(LBDest->SelectedItem);
        }
    }

    System::Void bnL2R_Click(System::Object^ sender, System::EventArgs^ e)
    {
        // Add all Selected items to other ListBox
        // Then remove all the items from original
        array<Object^>^ tmp =
            gcnew array<Object^>(LBOrg->SelectedItems->Count);
        LBOrg->SelectedItems->CopyTo(tmp, 0);
        LBDest->Items->AddRange(tmp);
        for (int i = 0; i < tmp->Length; i++)
            LBOrg->Items->Remove(tmp[i]);
    }

    System::Void bnR2L_Click(System::Object^ sender, System::EventArgs^ e)
    {
        // Add all Selected items to other ListBox
        // Then remove all the items from original
        array<Object^>^ tmp =
            gcnew array<Object^>(LBDest->SelectedItems->Count);
        LBDest->SelectedItems->CopyTo(tmp, 0);
        LBOrg->Items->AddRange(tmp);
        for (int i = 0; i < tmp->Length; i++)
            LBDest->Items->Remove(tmp[i]);
    }
};
}
```

The code is pretty straightforward. It creates two ListBoxes and configures them using their properties. There are a couple of things you need to pay attention to in Listing 9-13. First, when handling the double-click event for a list, make sure that an item is actually selected by checking the SelectedItem for a nullptr value before trying to work with the SelectedItem. This is because double-clicking an area of the list that is not an item generates an event with no selection.

The second thing to watch out for is removing items from a list using the SelectedItems property. The SelectedItems property does not create a copy of the items selected; instead, it uses the original items. Thus, if you try to remove items from a list such as the following:

```
// This code DOES NOT work
for (Int32 i = 0; i < LBDest->SelectedItems->Count; i++)
{
    LBDest->Items->Remove(LBDest->SelectedItems->Item[i]);
}
```

not all the selected items get removed—in fact, only half do. What is happening is that LBDest->SelectedItems->Count decreases when you call LBDest->Items->Remove() because the SelectedItems enumeration is decreasing in size at the same time as the ListBox entries are. My solution was to create a copy of the SelectedItems and then use that instead of SelectedItems directly:

```
// This DOES work
array<Object^>^ tmp = gcnew array<Object^>(LBDest->SelectedItems->Count);
LBDest->SelectedItems->CopyTo(tmp, 0);
for (int i = 0; i < tmp->Count; i++)
    LBDest->Items->Remove(tmp[i]);
```

Figure 9-15 shows what ListTransfers.exe looks like when you execute it.

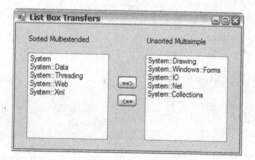

Figure 9-15. *Transferring items between list boxes*

ComboBox

The ComboBox control is a combination of a ListBox control with a TextBox control attached to the top. The ListBox control provides a quick click response, and the TextBox control allows the user to type in an answer.

There are three different DropDownStyles of ComboBox:

- ComboBoxStyle::Simple: The list is always expanded and the text field can be edited.
- ComboBoxStyle::DropDown: The list starts collapsed but can be expanded and the text field can be edited.
- ComboBoxStyle::DropDownList: The list starts collapsed but can be expanded and the text field only accepts Strings that are part of the selection list. (This style of ComboBox does not allow responses that are not part of the list.)

Like all other controls, the ComboBox provides several properties and methods to support the functionality of the control. You will probably recognize that these members are half TextBox and half ListBox in nature. Some of the common members unique to the ComboBox are as follows:

- DroppedDown is a Boolean that represents whether the list portion of the control has been expanded.
- MaxDropDownItems is an Int32 that represents the maximum number of items that can be visually displayed in the list portion of the control. This number can range from 1 to 100. Note that this is not the same as the total items in the control, which is limited to the memory of the computer, though I doubt you will ever create a list that large (unless of course you accidentally create an infinite loop).
- MaxLength is an Int32 that represents the maximum length of the text box portion of the control.
- Select() is a method that selects a specified range of text within the text box portion of the control.
- SelectAll() is a method that selects all the text in the text box portion of the control.
- SelectionLength is an Int32 that represents the length of the selected text within the text box portion of the control.
- SelectionStart is an Int32 that represents the zero-based starting position of the selected text within the text box portion of the control.

Listing 9-14 shows that you can keep all three ComboBox style controls in sync. Selecting an item in one control will automatically update the other two. If you type an entry in the text box area, the other two controls are updated appropriately. Note that if you type in a value that is not on the selection list, then the DropDownList style control does not update.

Listing 9-14. *Synchronizing ComboBoxes*

```
#pragma once

namespace SyncCombos
{
    using namespace System;
    using namespace System::ComponentModel;
    using namespace System::Collections;
    using namespace System::Windows::Forms;
    using namespace System::Data;
    using namespace System::Drawing;

    public ref class Form1 : public System::Windows::Forms::Form
    {
    public:
        Form1(void)
        {
            InitializeComponent();
            PopulateLists();
        }

    protected:
        ~Form1()
        {
            if (components)
            {
                delete components;
            }
        }
```

```cpp
    private:
        System::Windows::Forms::ComboBox^  ddlist;
        System::Windows::Forms::ComboBox^  simple;
        System::Windows::Forms::ComboBox^  ddown;

        System::ComponentModel::Container ^components;

#pragma region Windows Form Designer generated code

        void InitializeComponent(void)
        {
            this->ddlist = (gcnew System::Windows::Forms::ComboBox());
            this->simple = (gcnew System::Windows::Forms::ComboBox());
            this->ddown = (gcnew System::Windows::Forms::ComboBox());
            this->SuspendLayout();
            //
            // ddlist
            //
            this->ddlist->DropDownStyle =
                System::Windows::Forms::ComboBoxStyle::DropDownList;
            this->ddlist->FormattingEnabled = true;
            this->ddlist->Location = System::Drawing::Point(300, 14);
            this->ddlist->Name = L"ddlist";
            this->ddlist->Size = System::Drawing::Size(121, 21);
            this->ddlist->TabIndex = 5;
            this->ddlist->SelectedIndexChanged +=
                gcnew System::EventHandler(this, &Form1::ddlist_Change);
            //
            // simple
            //
            this->simple->DropDownStyle =
                System::Windows::Forms::ComboBoxStyle::Simple;
            this->simple->FormattingEnabled = true;
            this->simple->Location = System::Drawing::Point(154, 11);
            this->simple->Name = L"simple";
            this->simple->Size = System::Drawing::Size(122, 117);
            this->simple->TabIndex = 4;
            this->simple->SelectedIndexChanged +=
                gcnew System::EventHandler(this, &Form1::simple_Change);
            this->simple->TextChanged +=
                gcnew System::EventHandler(this, &Form1::simple_Change);
            //
            // ddown
            //
            this->ddown->FormattingEnabled = true;
            this->ddown->Location = System::Drawing::Point(12, 14);
            this->ddown->MaxDropDownItems = 3;
            this->ddown->MaxLength = 10;
            this->ddown->Name = L"ddown";
            this->ddown->Size = System::Drawing::Size(121, 21);
            this->ddown->TabIndex = 3;
            this->ddown->SelectedIndexChanged +=
                gcnew System::EventHandler(this, &Form1::ddown_Change);
```

```cpp
            this->ddown->TextChanged +=
                gcnew System::EventHandler(this, &Form1::ddown_Change);
            //
            // Form1
            //
            this->AutoScaleDimensions = System::Drawing::SizeF(6, 13);
            this->AutoScaleMode = System::Windows::Forms::AutoScaleMode::Font;
            this->ClientSize = System::Drawing::Size(433, 138);
            this->Controls->Add(this->ddlist);
            this->Controls->Add(this->simple);
            this->Controls->Add(this->ddown);
            this->Name = L"Form1";
            this->Text = L"Synchronized Combo boxing";
            this->ResumeLayout(false);
        }

#pragma endregion

    private:
        void PopulateLists()
        {
            // Item to be placed in all ComboBoxes
            array<Object^>^ ddItems = gcnew array<Object^> {
                L"oranges", L"cherries", L"apples",
                L"lemons",  L"bananas",  L"grapes"
            };
            ddown->Items->AddRange(ddItems);
            simple->Items->AddRange(ddItems);
            ddlist->Items->AddRange(ddItems);
        }

        System::Void ddown_Change(System::Object^ sender, System::EventArgs^ e)
        {
            // Update simple and dropdownlist with dropdown text
            simple->Text = ddown->Text;
            ddlist->SelectedItem = ddown->Text;
        }

        System::Void simple_Change(System::Object^ sender, System::EventArgs^ e)
        {
            // Update dropdown and dropdownlist with simple text
            ddown->Text = simple->Text;
            ddlist->SelectedItem = simple->Text;
        }

        System::Void ddlist_Change(System::Object^ sender, System::EventArgs^ e)
        {
            // Update simple and dropdown with dropdownlist SelectedText
            ddown->SelectedItem = ddlist->SelectedItem;
            simple->SelectedItem = ddlist->SelectedItem;
        }
    };
}
```

When you are working with Simple or DropDown ComboBoxes, all you usually need to worry about is what is currently in the Text property. This property tells you what the current value is in the ComboBox, and placing the value in it automatically changes the SelectedItem property. On the other hand, when you are working with the DropDownList, it is better to work with the SelectedItem property, because it is more efficient for the control as the editing overhead of the text field goes unused.

Figure 9-16 shows what SyncCombos.exe looks like when you execute it.

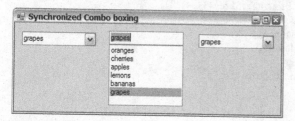

Figure 9-16. *Synchronized combo boxes*

CheckedListBox

The CheckedListBox control provides you a way to group related check boxes in a scrollable and selectable ListBox control. In other words, this control provides the functionality of an array of check boxes and at the same time the functionality of a ListBox, allowing the selection of a checkable item without actually checking the item off.

The CheckedListBox control directly inherits from the ListBox control, so in addition to the functionality provided by the ListBox, the CheckedListBox provides numerous other properties. Some of the more common are as follows:

- CheckedIndices is a CheckedListBox::CheckedIndexCollection that represents the collection of zero-based indices of currently checked or indeterminate state items within the control.

- CheckedItems is a CheckedListBox::CheckedItemCollection that represents the collection of currently checked or indeterminate state items within the control.

- CheckOnClick is a Boolean that represents whether the check box is toggled immediately on the selection of the check box item. The default is false.

- ThreeDCheckBoxes is a Boolean that represents if 3D or flat check boxes are used. The default is false or a flat appearance.

Along with the preceding properties, the CheckListBox control provides several methods. The following methods get access to the checked status of the CheckListBox's items:

- GetItemChecked() checks (using a specified index) whether an item is checked.

- GetItemCheckState() checks (using a specified index) what the check state of the item is.

- SetItemChecked() checks or unchecks an item at a specified index.

- SetItemCheckState() sets the check status of an item at a specified index.

Working with the CheckedListBox can be a little confusing, as selected and checked items are not the same thing. You can have an item that does not check or uncheck when selected.

To get the selected item (you can only have one, unless you select SelectionMode::None), you use the properties prefixed by "Selected". Even though there are properties that suggest more than one item can be selected, these properties return a collection of one item. Basically, the difference between SelectedIndex and SelectedIndices, and SelectedItem and SelectedItems, is that the first returns a single item and the second returns a collection of one item.

To get the checked items from the control, you need to use the properties and methods that contain "Check(ed)" within their name. Note that there are two common ways of getting all the checked items in the CheckedListBox. The first method is to use the default index property of CheckIndices and CheckItems:

```
for (int i = 0; i < checkedlistbox->CheckedItems->Count; i++)
{
    //...do what you want with:
    //     checkedlistbox->CheckedItems[i];
}
```

The second approach is to use the methods GetItemChecked() and GetItemCheckState():

```
for (int i = 0; i < checkedlistbox->Items->Count; i++)
{
    if (checkedlistbox->GetItemChecked(i))
    {
        //...do what you want with:
        //     checkedlistbox->Items[i];
    }
}
```

The main difference between the two is that the first approach provides only a list of checked items, whereas the second requires an iteration through all the items and verifies the check status of each.

The example in Listing 9-15 shows how closely the CheckListBox is to an array of Checkboxes and a ListBox. It does this by synchronizing input using these controls.

Listing 9-15. *Splitting the CheckedListBox*

```
#pragma once

namespace SplitCLB
{
    using namespace System;
    using namespace System::ComponentModel;
    using namespace System::Collections;
    using namespace System::Windows::Forms;
    using namespace System::Data;
    using namespace System::Drawing;

    public ref class Form1 : public System::Windows::Forms::Form
    {
    public:
        Form1(void)
        {
            InitializeComponent();

            array<Object^>^ Items = gcnew array<Object^> {
                "Appleman", "Challa",    "Chand",    "Cornell",
                "Fraser",   "Gunnerson", "Harris",   "Rammer",
                "Symmonds", "Thomsen",   "Troelsen", "Vaughn"
            };
```

```
            clBox->Items->AddRange(Items);
            lBox->Items->AddRange(Items);

            // Create a Check box for each entry in Items array.
            cBox = gcnew array<CheckBox^>(Items->Length);

            int j = cBox->Length/2;
            for (int i = 0; i < j; i++)
            {
                // Build Left Column
                cBox[i] = gcnew CheckBox();
                cBox[i]->Location = Drawing::Point(50, 160+(30*i));
                cBox[i]->TabIndex = i+2;
                cBox[i]->Text = Items[i]->ToString();
                cBox[i]->CheckStateChanged +=
                    gcnew EventHandler(this, &Form1::cBox_CheckStateChanged);

                // Build Right Column
                cBox[i+j] = gcnew CheckBox();
                cBox[i+j]->Location = Drawing::Point(180, 160+(30*i));
                cBox[i+j]->TabIndex = i+j+2;
                cBox[i+j]->Text = Items[i+j]->ToString();
                cBox[i+j]->CheckStateChanged +=
                    gcnew EventHandler(this, &Form1::cBox_CheckStateChanged);
            }
            // Add all CheckBoxes to Form
            Controls->AddRange(cBox);
        }

    protected:
        ~Form1()
        {
            if (components)
            {
                delete components;
            }
        }

    private:
        System::Windows::Forms::ListBox^  lBox;
        System::Windows::Forms::CheckedListBox^  clBox;

        array<CheckBox^>^ cBox;

        System::ComponentModel::Container ^components;
```

```
#pragma region Windows Form Designer generated code

        void InitializeComponent(void)
        {
            this->lBox = (gcnew System::Windows::Forms::ListBox());
            this->clBox = (gcnew System::Windows::Forms::CheckedListBox());
            this->SuspendLayout();
            //
            // lBox
            //
            this->lBox->FormattingEnabled = true;
            this->lBox->Location = System::Drawing::Point(356, 32);
            this->lBox->Name = L"lBox";
            this->lBox->Size = System::Drawing::Size(120, 264);
            this->lBox->TabIndex = 3;
            this->lBox->SelectedIndexChanged +=
                gcnew System::EventHandler(this,
                                        &Form1::lBox_SelectedIndexChanged);
            //
            // clBox
            //
            this->clBox->FormattingEnabled = true;
            this->clBox->Location = System::Drawing::Point(12, 32);
            this->clBox->MultiColumn = true;
            this->clBox->Name = L"clBox";
            this->clBox->Size = System::Drawing::Size(323, 79);
            this->clBox->TabIndex = 2;
            this->clBox->ThreeDCheckBoxes = true;
            this->clBox->SelectedIndexChanged +=
                gcnew System::EventHandler(this,
                                        &Form1::clBox_SelectedIndexChanged);
            this->clBox->ItemCheck +=
                gcnew System::Windows::Forms::ItemCheckEventHandler(this,
                                                &Form1::clBox_ItemCheck);
            //
            // Form1
            //
            this->AutoScaleDimensions = System::Drawing::SizeF(6, 13);
            this->AutoScaleMode = System::Windows::Forms::AutoScaleMode::Font;
            this->ClientSize = System::Drawing::Size(494, 392);
            this->Controls->Add(this->lBox);
            this->Controls->Add(this->clBox);
            this->Name = L"Form1";
            this->Text = L"Splitting The Check List Box";
            this->ResumeLayout(false);
        }
```

```
#pragma endregion

    private:
        System::Void clBox_ItemCheck(System::Object^ sender,
                            System::Windows::Forms::ItemCheckEventArgs^ e)
        {
         // update state of CheckBox with same index as checked CheckedListBox
            cBox[e->Index]->CheckState = e->NewValue;
        }

        System::Void clBox_SelectedIndexChanged(System::Object^ sender,
                                            System::EventArgs^ e)
        {
         // update ListBox with same selected item in the CheckedListBox
            lBox->SelectedItem = clBox->SelectedItem->ToString();
        }

        System::Void lBox_SelectedIndexChanged(System::Object^ sender,
                                            System::EventArgs^ e)
        {
         // update CheckedListBox with same selected item in the ListBox
            clBox->SelectedItem = lBox->SelectedItem;
        }

        void cBox_CheckStateChanged(Object^ sender, EventArgs^ e)
        {
         // update state of CheckedListBox with same index as checked CheckBox
            CheckBox^ cb = (CheckBox^)sender;
            clBox->SetItemCheckState(Array::IndexOf(cBox, cb), cb->CheckState);
        }
    };
}
```

The CheckedListBox provides an event to handle the checking of a box within the control. To handle this event, you need to create a method with the template:

```
ItemCheck(System::Object^ sender, System::Windows::Forms::ItemCheckEventArgs^ e)
```

Conveniently, the handler provides the parameter of type ItemCheckEventArgs, which among other things provides the index of the box being checked and the current and previous state of the box. I use this information to update the external array of check boxes.

```
cBox[e->Index]->CheckState = e->NewValue;
```

One other thing of note in the code is the trick I used to get the index of the CheckBox, which triggered the state change event out of the CheckBox array. The Array class has a neat little static method, Array::IndexOf(), which you pass as arguments to the array containing an entry and the entry itself, with the result being the index to that entry. I used this method by passing it the array of CheckBoxes along with the dynamically cast sender Object.

Figure 9-17 shows what SplitCLB.exe looks like when you execute it.

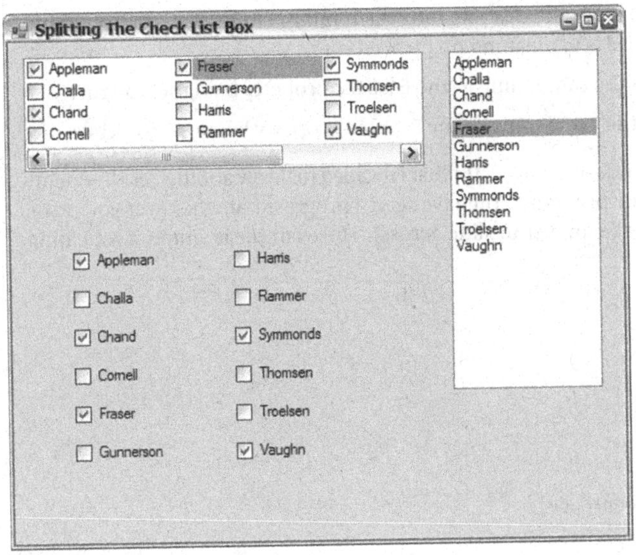

Figure 9-17. *Splitting the checklist box*

Timers

A few timers are sprinkled throughout the .NET Framework class library. One relevant to this chapter is found in the System::Windows::Forms namespace. Though not a GUI control, the Timer is an important component for scheduling events that occur at discrete user-defined intervals.

Notice I called Timer a "component" and not a "control," as it inherits from the Component class but not the Control class. This fact is apparent when you implement a Timer in Visual Studio 2005, because when you drag the component to the Win Form it does not get placed on the form. Instead, it gets placed in its own area at the bottom of the designer window. Even though it is placed there, you still work with the Timer the same way you do with a control. You use the Properties view to update the Timer's properties and events.

The Timer component is easy to use. Just instantiate it in your program:

```
Timer^ timer = gcnew Timer();
```

Create an event handler to accept Tick events:

```
void timer_Tick(Object^ sender, System::EventArgs^ e)
{
    //...Process the Tick event
}
```

And then delegate that event handler:

```
timer->Tick += gcnew EventHandler(this, &Form1::timer_Tick);
```

The Timer component provides a few properties to configure and methods to implement the functionality of the control:

- Enabled is a Boolean that represents whether the Timer is enabled or disabled. When enabled, the Timer will trigger Tick events at an interval specified by the Interval property. The default is false, or disabled.

- Interval is an Int32 that represents the discrete interval in milliseconds between triggering Tick events. The default interval is 0, meaning no interval is set.

- Start() is a method that does the same thing as the Enabled property being set to true.

- Stop() is a method that does the same thing as the Enabled property being set to false.

The Timer is such a simple example (see Listing 9-16) that I decided to throw another less frequently used control, the ProgressBar, into the program. You have seen a progress bar whenever you install software (it's that bar that seems to take forever to slide across). The example is simply a repeating one-minute timer.

Listing 9-16. *The One-Minute Timer*

```cpp
#pragma once

namespace MinuteTimer
{
    using namespace System;
    using namespace System::ComponentModel;
    using namespace System::Collections;
    using namespace System::Windows::Forms;
    using namespace System::Data;
    using namespace System::Drawing;

    public ref class Form1 : public System::Windows::Forms::Form
    {
    public:
        Form1(void)
        {
            InitializeComponent();
            seconds = 0;
        }

    protected:
        ~Form1()
        {
            if (components)
            {
                delete components;
            }
        }

    private:
        System::Windows::Forms::ProgressBar^  progressBar;
        System::Windows::Forms::Label^  lbsecs;
        System::Windows::Forms::Timer^  timer;

        int seconds;

        System::ComponentModel::IContainer^  components;
```

```
#pragma region Windows Form Designer generated code

    void InitializeComponent(void)
    {
        this->components = (gcnew System::ComponentModel::Container());
        this->progressBar = (gcnew System::Windows::Forms::ProgressBar());
        this->lbsecs = (gcnew System::Windows::Forms::Label());
        this->timer =
            (gcnew System::Windows::Forms::Timer(this->components));
        this->SuspendLayout();
        //
        // progressBar
        //
        this->progressBar->Location = System::Drawing::Point(61, 16);
        this->progressBar->Maximum = 60;
        this->progressBar->Name = L"progressBar";
        this->progressBar->Size = System::Drawing::Size(326, 23);
        this->progressBar->TabIndex = 3;
        //
        // lbsecs
        //
        this->lbsecs->AutoSize = true;
        this->lbsecs->Location = System::Drawing::Point(19, 25);
        this->lbsecs->Name = L"lbsecs";
        this->lbsecs->Size = System::Drawing::Size(13, 13);
        this->lbsecs->TabIndex = 2;
        this->lbsecs->Text = L"0";
        this->lbsecs->TextAlign =
            System::Drawing::ContentAlignment::MiddleRight;
        //
        // timer
        //
        this->timer->Enabled = true;
        this->timer->Tick +=
            gcnew System::EventHandler(this, &Form1::timer_Tick);
        //
        // Form1
        //
        this->AutoScaleDimensions = System::Drawing::SizeF(6, 13);
        this->AutoScaleMode = System::Windows::Forms::AutoScaleMode::Font;
        this->ClientSize = System::Drawing::Size(407, 55);
        this->Controls->Add(this->progressBar);
        this->Controls->Add(this->lbsecs);
        this->Name = L"Form1";
        this->Text = L"One minute timer";
        this->ResumeLayout(false);
        this->PerformLayout();
    }
```

```
#pragma endregion

    private:
        System::Void timer_Tick(System::Object^ sender, System::EventArgs^ e)
        {
            // Write current tick count (int 10th of second) to label
            seconds++;
            seconds %= 600;
            lbsecs->Text = String::Format("{0}.{1}", (seconds/10).ToString(),
                                                     (seconds%10).ToString());
            // Update ProgressBar
            progressBar->Value = seconds/10;
        }
    };
}
```

The ProgressBar simply shows the amount completed of some activity. You specify the starting point (Minimum) and the end point (Maximum) for which you want to monitor the progress, and then you simply update the value of the ProgressBar between these two points. The default start and end values are 0 to 100, representing progress from 0 percent to 100 percent, which is the most common use for the ProgressBar. In this example, because I am representing seconds in a minute, it made more sense to go from 0 to 60. Updating the ProgressBar itself is very simple, as it will move over automatically when the value exceeds the specified step factor.

Figure 9-18 shows what MinuteTimer.exe looks like when you execute it.

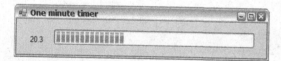

Figure 9-18. *The one-minute timer*

Summary

You covered a lot in this chapter. You started with the lowly "Hello World!" form and worked your way up to building fully functional Win Forms. Along the way, you explored a number (most, actually) of the more common simple GUI controls provided by the .NET Framework class library. You should now be able to build a simple Win Form with a high level of confidence.

In the next chapter, you will continue to look at the GUI interface provided by the .NET Framework class library, but this time you look at some of the more advanced Win Form topics such as views, menus, and dialog boxes.

■ ■ ■

CHAPTER 10

Advanced Windows Forms Applications

In the previous chapter, you got all the basics of Windows Forms applications squared away. It is now time to look at some of the more exciting controls and features provided by the .NET Framework. Even though this chapter covers more advanced Win Forms applications, this does not mean they are more complex or difficult to develop. The main reason is that the .NET Framework uses encapsulation quite extensively in its classes and hides much of the complexities of Win Forms from you. On the other hand, you can still access these complexities if you really want to.

In this chapter, I continue using the approach of covering both manual development and development using the GUI design tool. As I pointed out in the previous chapter, I feel the intimate knowledge of Win Form components, attained by building Win Forms manually, will allow you to build better GUI interfaces to your Windows application.

This chapter covers some of the more powerful GUI controls provided by the .NET Framework. It also looks at three other Win Form development areas: menus, dialog boxes, and the MDI interface.

In Chapter 9, I covered most of the more commonly used data entry controls. Nothing is stopping you from using these controls in a simple form every time you need data from the user. However, doing so is not always the best way to interact with or present information to the user.

Let's now start a whirlwind tour of some of the remaining controls provided by the .NET Framework class library.

ImageList

Before I can go very much further into the discussions about Windows Forms, I have to make a minor detour. As I'm sure you are aware, Windows applications are fairly graphics intensive. In fact, most of the controls I'm going to cover in this chapter have some graphics capabilities.

Though some of the controls allow you to access image files or image resources directly, usually a Win Form control requires you to place all the images you are using within an `ImageList` component. (An `ImageList` inherits from `Component` but not `Control`.) Then, using an index to each image in the `ImageList`, you place the appropriate image in the control's image type property.

The process of creating an `ImageList` is extremely easy with Visual Studio 2005, though behind the scenes a lot is taking place. The steps to create an `ImageList` are as follows:

1. Drag and drop an `ImageList` to the form you want to place images on.

2. Within the `ImageList` property, click the ellipses button next to the `Images` property. This will bring up a dialog box similar to the one shown in Figure 10-1.

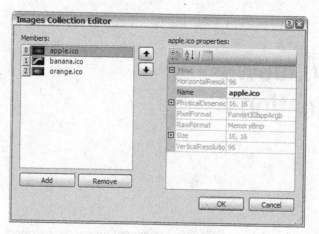

Figure 10-1. *The Images Collection Editor dialog box*

3. Click the Add button, and then navigate to and open the image file within the present Open File dialog box.

4. Repeat step 3 for all desired images.

5. Click the OK button.

Once you have added the images to the ImageList, you may need to configure these three ImageList properties:

- ColorDepth is a ColorDepth object that represents the color depth of the icon. The default is 8-bit color, so most likely you will not need to change this property.

- ImageSize is a Size object that represents the size of the images contained in the list. The default is 16×16 but the maximum is 256×256. Note that all images in the list are the same size.

- TransparentColor is a Color object that represents the transparent color. You probably will be able to ignore this property, as the default is Transparent.

Now that the ImageList is available, it will be selectable from the properties list of all controls within the form that use ImageLists. For a control to get access to the ImageList, simply select the ImageList from this property list.

The final step differs from control to control, but usually to select the specific image to use out of the ImageList, you update an image index property within the control with the corresponding index to the image within the ImageList.

What happens behind the scenes is not quite as easy, and it's fortunate that you don't have to worry about it. First, the ImageList that you created is added to the Form1.resx file. At the same time, code is also added to the Form1.h file for a control to access the ImageList. Next, when the program is compiled, the ImageList is serialized and placed within a resource file. The resource file then gets embedded in the executable assembly.

If you examine the code added to the Form1.h file to get access to the ImageList, you will notice that program actually gets the ImageList from the executable assembly:

```
System::ComponentModel::ComponentResourceManager^ resources =
    gcnew System::ComponentModel::ComponentResourceManager(typeid<Form1>);
// ...
this->imFruitSmall->ImageStream =
    (stdcli::language::safe_cast<System::Windows::Forms::ImageListStreamer^ >
        (resources->GetObject(L"imageList.ImageStream")));
```

You will examine resources and how the preceding code works in much more detail in Chapter 18.

Views

Now that our detour is over, it is finally time to continue on with some advanced, and I think more fun, Window Form controls. Let's start off with two of the views provided by the .NET Framework: ListView and TreeView. There is a third view, DataGridView, but since this view is so closely integrated with database development, I'll hold off discussing it until we tackle database development in Chapter 12. If you have used Windows for any amount of time, then you have seen ListView and TreeView, quite extensively, maybe without knowing it. The reason is that these views, when used correctly, provide a better way of displaying data to the user. Because of this, Microsoft uses them within a large portion of the applications and tools they provide.

A point that may not be readily apparent about views, because of all the underlying functionality they provide, is that they are also controls. This means that they are inheritable and derive from components and then the control class. Thus, any place that you could use a simple control from the previous chapter, you could also use one of these feature rich views. What this means, for example, is that instead of displaying data using rows and rows of Label and TextBox controls, you could plug in one of these views instead.

ListView

The ListView is a powerful (but slightly complicated) control that displays a list of items. You can see what a ListView control looks like by opening up Windows Explorer. The ListView is the right-hand panel if two panels are being displayed. The items can consist of a combination of a record (array) of text, a large icon, and/or a small icon.

You can display a ListView in one of four different View property modes:

- View::LargeIcon displays a large icon with text underneath in a grid layout.
- View::SmallIcon displays a small icon with text along the side in columns.
- View::List displays the root text associated with the item in a single column.
- View::Details displays the root text and subtext in multiple columns.

Providing the functionality of the ListView requires a number of properties, many of which you have seen before. Here are some of the common ones unique to the ListView:

- Activation is an ItemActivation enum that represents whether one or two clicks are required to activate an item. The default is two clicks or ItemActivation::Standard.
- AllowColumnReorder is a Boolean that represents whether the headings can be dragged to reorder the columns. The default is false.

- AutoArrange is a Boolean that represents whether the icons are automatically arranged. The default is true.

- Columns is a ListView::ColumnHeaderCollection that represents a collection of column headers to be used if the View property mode is set to View::Details.

- FocusItem is a ListViewItem that represents the item that currently has focus. If no item has focus, null is returned.

- FullRowSelect is a Boolean that represents whether clicking an item selects all its subitems as well. The default is false.

- GridLines is a Boolean that represents whether grid lines are displayed. The default is false.

- HeaderStyle is a ColumnHeaderStyle enum that represents whether the header is displayed and if it is clickable. The default is displayed and clickable: ColumnHeaderStyle::Clickable.

- HoverSelection is a Boolean that represents whether the item is automatically selected when the cursor hovers over it for a few seconds. The default is false.

- LabelEdit is a Boolean that represents whether the label of an item can be edited. The default is false.

- LabelWrap is a Boolean that represents whether the label wraps when displayed. The default is true.

- LargeImageList is an ImageList of the large icons to be used if the View property is set to View::LargeIcon.

- SmallImageList is an ImageList of the small icons to be used if the View property is set to View::SmallIcon.

Along with these properties, the ListView provides a number of methods. These are some of the common methods unique to ListView:

- ArrangeIcons() arranges the icons in large and small icon views.

- EnsureVisible() ensures that an item is visible even if the ListView must scroll to make it visible.

- GetItemAt() gets an item at a specified x and y location.

Listing 10-1 shows a ListView of fruit, their price, and the month when they are available for harvest. (The data was derived using a high-tech research facility. Okay, you caught me—I made it up.) When an item is selected, its price is displayed in a label. The example also shows how you can switch to any of the four ListView views based on the check value of radio buttons.

Listing 10-1. *A ListView of Fruit*

```
#pragma once

namespace ListViewEx
{
    using namespace System;
    using namespace System::ComponentModel;
    using namespace System::Collections;
    using namespace System::Windows::Forms;
    using namespace System::Data;
    using namespace System::Drawing;

    public ref class Form1 : public System::Windows::Forms::Form
    {
```

```cpp
public:
    Form1(void)
    {
        InitializeComponent();
        FillListView();
    }

protected:
    ~Form1()
    {
        if (components)
        {
            delete components;
        }
    }

private:
    System::Windows::Forms::ImageList^  imFruitSmall;
    System::Windows::Forms::ImageList^  ilFruitLarge;
    System::Windows::Forms::RadioButton^  rbDetails;
    System::Windows::Forms::RadioButton^  rbList;
    System::Windows::Forms::RadioButton^  rbSmallIcon;
    System::Windows::Forms::RadioButton^  rbLargeIcon;
    System::Windows::Forms::Label^  label;
    System::Windows::Forms::ListView^  lView;
    System::Windows::Forms::ColumnHeader^  Fruit;
    System::Windows::Forms::ColumnHeader^  Price;
    System::Windows::Forms::ColumnHeader^  Available;
    System::ComponentModel::IContainer^  components;

#pragma region Windows Form Designer generated code
    /// <summary>
    /// Required method for Designer support - do not modify
    /// the contents of this method with the code editor.
    /// </summary>
    void InitializeComponent(void)
    {
        this->components = (gcnew System::ComponentModel::Container());
        System::ComponentModel::ComponentResourceManager^ resources =
    (gcnew System::ComponentModel::ComponentResourceManager(Form1::typeid));
        this->imFruitSmall =
            (gcnew System::Windows::Forms::ImageList(this->components));
        this->ilFruitLarge =
            (gcnew System::Windows::Forms::ImageList(this->components));
        this->rbDetails = (gcnew System::Windows::Forms::RadioButton());
        this->rbList = (gcnew System::Windows::Forms::RadioButton());
        this->rbSmallIcon = (gcnew System::Windows::Forms::RadioButton());
        this->rbLargeIcon = (gcnew System::Windows::Forms::RadioButton());
        this->label = (gcnew System::Windows::Forms::Label());
        this->lView = (gcnew System::Windows::Forms::ListView());
        this->Fruit = (gcnew System::Windows::Forms::ColumnHeader());
        this->Price = (gcnew System::Windows::Forms::ColumnHeader());
        this->Available = (gcnew System::Windows::Forms::ColumnHeader());
        this->SuspendLayout();
```

```cpp
//
// imFruitSmall
//
this->imFruitSmall->ImageStream =
    (cli::safe_cast<System::Windows::Forms::ImageListStreamer^>
    (resources->GetObject(L"imFruitSmall.ImageStream")));
this->imFruitSmall->Images->SetKeyName(0, L"apple.ico");
this->imFruitSmall->Images->SetKeyName(1, L"banana.ico");
this->imFruitSmall->Images->SetKeyName(2, L"orange.ico");
//
// ilFruitLarge
//
this->ilFruitLarge->ImageStream =
    (cli::safe_cast<System::Windows::Forms::ImageListStreamer^>
    (resources->GetObject(L"ilFruitLarge.ImageStream")));
this->ilFruitLarge->Images->SetKeyName(0, L"apple.ico");
this->ilFruitLarge->Images->SetKeyName(1, L"banana.ico");
this->ilFruitLarge->Images->SetKeyName(2, L"orange.ico");
//
// rbDetails
//
this->rbDetails->Anchor =
    static_cast<System::Windows::Forms::AnchorStyles>
    ((System::Windows::Forms::AnchorStyles::Bottom |
      System::Windows::Forms::AnchorStyles::Right));
this->rbDetails->AutoSize = true;
this->rbDetails->Checked = true;
this->rbDetails->Location = System::Drawing::Point(154, 201);
this->rbDetails->Name = L"rbDetails";
this->rbDetails->Size = System::Drawing::Size(53, 17);
this->rbDetails->TabIndex = 17;
this->rbDetails->Text = L"Details";
this->rbDetails->CheckedChanged +=
    gcnew System::EventHandler(this, &Form1::rbType_CheckedChanged);
//
// rbList
//
this->rbList->Anchor =
    static_cast<System::Windows::Forms::AnchorStyles>
    ((System::Windows::Forms::AnchorStyles::Bottom |
      System::Windows::Forms::AnchorStyles::Right));
this->rbList->AutoSize = true;
this->rbList->Location = System::Drawing::Point(154, 177);
this->rbList->Name = L"rbList";
this->rbList->Size = System::Drawing::Size(37, 17);
this->rbList->TabIndex = 16;
this->rbList->Text = L"List";
this->rbList->CheckedChanged +=
    gcnew System::EventHandler(this, &Form1::rbType_CheckedChanged);
//
// rbSmallIcon
//
this->rbSmallIcon->Anchor =
    static_cast<System::Windows::Forms::AnchorStyles>
```

```
        ((System::Windows::Forms::AnchorStyles::Bottom |
          System::Windows::Forms::AnchorStyles::Right));
this->rbSmallIcon->AutoSize = true;
this->rbSmallIcon->Location = System::Drawing::Point(154, 153);
this->rbSmallIcon->Name = L"rbSmallIcon";
this->rbSmallIcon->Size = System::Drawing::Size(70, 17);
this->rbSmallIcon->TabIndex = 15;
this->rbSmallIcon->Text = L"Small Icon";
this->rbSmallIcon->CheckedChanged +=
    gcnew System::EventHandler(this, &Form1::rbType_CheckedChanged);
//
// rbLargeIcon
//
this->rbLargeIcon->Anchor =
    static_cast<System::Windows::Forms::AnchorStyles>
    ((System::Windows::Forms::AnchorStyles::Bottom |
      System::Windows::Forms::AnchorStyles::Right));
this->rbLargeIcon->AutoSize = true;
this->rbLargeIcon->Location = System::Drawing::Point(154, 129);
this->rbLargeIcon->Name = L"rbLargeIcon";
this->rbLargeIcon->Size = System::Drawing::Size(72, 17);
this->rbLargeIcon->TabIndex = 14;
this->rbLargeIcon->Text = L"Large Icon";
this->rbLargeIcon->CheckedChanged +=
    gcnew System::EventHandler(this, &Form1::rbType_CheckedChanged);
//
// label
//
this->label->Anchor =
    static_cast<System::Windows::Forms::AnchorStyles>
    ((System::Windows::Forms::AnchorStyles::Bottom |
      System::Windows::Forms::AnchorStyles::Left));
this->label->BorderStyle =
    System::Windows::Forms::BorderStyle::FixedSingle;
this->label->Location = System::Drawing::Point(19, 162);
this->label->Name = L"label";
this->label->Size = System::Drawing::Size(64, 21);
this->label->TabIndex = 13;
this->label->TextAlign =
    System::Drawing::ContentAlignment::MiddleCenter;
//
// lView
//
this->lView->Anchor =
    static_cast<System::Windows::Forms::AnchorStyles>
    ((((System::Windows::Forms::AnchorStyles::Top |
        System::Windows::Forms::AnchorStyles::Bottom) |
        System::Windows::Forms::AnchorStyles::Left) |
        System::Windows::Forms::AnchorStyles::Right));
this->lView->Columns->AddRange(
    gcnew cli::array< System::Windows::Forms::ColumnHeader^>(3)
    {
        this->Fruit, this->Price, this->Available
    });
```

```
            this->lView->FullRowSelect = true;
            this->lView->GridLines = true;
            this->lView->LabelEdit = true;
            this->lView->LargeImageList = this->ilFruitLarge;
            this->lView->Location = System::Drawing::Point(0, 0);
            this->lView->MultiSelect = false;
            this->lView->Name = L"lView";
            this->lView->Size = System::Drawing::Size(270, 109);
            this->lView->SmallImageList = this->imFruitSmall;
            this->lView->TabIndex = 12;
            this->lView->View = System::Windows::Forms::View::Details;
            this->lView->SelectedIndexChanged +=
                gcnew System::EventHandler(this,
                                        &Form1::lView_SelectedIndexChanged);
            //
            // Fruit
            //
            this->Fruit->Text = L"Fruit";
            this->Fruit->Width = 115;
            //
            // Price
            //
            this->Price->Text = L"Price";
            this->Price->Width = 50;
            //
            // Available
            //
            this->Available->Text = L"Available";
            this->Available->Width = 100;
            //
            // Form1
            //
            this->AutoScaleDimensions = System::Drawing::SizeF(6, 13);
            this->AutoScaleMode = System::Windows::Forms::AutoScaleMode::Font;
            this->ClientSize = System::Drawing::Size(269, 229);
            this->Controls->Add(this->rbDetails);
            this->Controls->Add(this->rbList);
            this->Controls->Add(this->rbSmallIcon);
            this->Controls->Add(this->rbLargeIcon);
            this->Controls->Add(this->label);
            this->Controls->Add(this->lView);
            this->Name = L"Form1";
            this->Text = L"List View Example";
            this->ResumeLayout(false);
            this->PerformLayout();
        }
#pragma endregion

    private:
        void FillListView()
        {
            array<String^>^ itemRec1 = gcnew array<String^> {
                "Apple", "1.50", "September"
            };
```

```cpp
    lView->Items->Add(gcnew ListViewItem(itemRec1, 0));

    array<String^>^ itemRec2 = gcnew array<String^> {
        "Banana", "3.95", "November"
    };
    lView->Items->Add(gcnew ListViewItem(itemRec2, 1));

    array<String^>^ itemRec3 = gcnew array<String^> {
        "Orange", "2.50", "March"
    };
    lView->Items->Add(gcnew ListViewItem(itemRec3, 2));
}

System::Void lView_SelectedIndexChanged(System::Object^ sender,
                                        System::EventArgs^ e)
{
    if (lView->FocusedItem != nullptr)
        label->Text = lView->FocusedItem->SubItems[1]->Text;
}

System::Void rbType_CheckedChanged(System::Object^ sender,
                                   System::EventArgs^ e)
{
    if (rbLargeIcon->Checked)
        lView->View = View::LargeIcon;
    else if (rbSmallIcon->Checked)
        lView->View = View::SmallIcon;
    else if (rbList->Checked)
        lView->View = View::List;
    else if (rbDetails->Checked)
        lView->View = View::Details;
}
    };
}
```

Working with the ListView is a little tricky because the GUI designer doesn't place things in the code where you expect them (or at least I don't think so). So I'll group the code together so that you can see what's happening more clearly.

First, like any control, you create the ListView and then configure it using its properties. The example ListView is anchored and uses full row selection, display gridlines, no multiple selections, editable labels, large image list, small image list, and is preset to the detailed view.

```cpp
private: System::Windows::Forms::ListView^  lView;
//...
this->lView = gcnew System::Windows::Forms::ListView();

this->lView->Anchor = System::Windows::Forms::AnchorStyles::Top |
                      System::Windows::Forms::AnchorStyles::Bottom |
                      System::Windows::Forms::AnchorStyles::Left |
                      System::Windows::Forms::AnchorStyles::Right;
this->lView->FullRowSelect = true;
this->lView->GridLines = true;
this->lView->LabelEdit = true;
this->lView->LargeImageList = this->ilFruitLarge;
this->lView->Location = System::Drawing::Point(0, 0);
```

```
this->lView->MultiSelect = false;
this->lView->Size = System::Drawing::Size(270, 109);
this->lView->SmallImageList = this->imFruitSmall;
this->lView->View = System::Windows::Forms::View::Details;
this->lView->SelectedIndexChanged +=
    gcnew System::EventHandler(this, &Form1::lView_SelectedIndexChanged);

this->Controls->Add(this->lView);
```

Next, because the detailed view is available, you need to create headers for the ListView's items. Notice that you add the headers to the ListView control's Column property.

```
// Fruit
System::Windows::Forms::ColumnHeader^  Fruit;
this->Fruit = gcnew (gcnew System::Windows::Forms::ColumnHeader());
this->Fruit->Text = L"Fruit";
this->Fruit->Width = 115;

// Price
System::Windows::Forms::ColumnHeader^  Price;
this->Price = (gcnew System::Windows::Forms::ColumnHeader());
this->Price->Text = L"Price";
this->Price->Width = 50;

// Available
System::Windows::Forms::ColumnHeader^  Available;
this->Available = (gcnew System::Windows::Forms::ColumnHeader());
this->Available->Text = L"Available";
this->Available->Width = 100;

// Add header to ListView
this->lView->Columns->AddRange (
    gcnew array<System::Windows::Forms::ColumnHeader^ >(3) {
        this->Fruit, this->Price, this->Available
    }
);
```

Finally, once the ListView is ready for the world to see, you add the list items to the view. I showed this being done manually, but you could also use the designer to add list items. Notice the last parameter of the ListViewItem constructor is an integer index to the image within both image lists (large and small) assigned to the ListView.

```
// Add an Apple to the listview
array<String^>^ itemRec1 = gcnew array<String^> {
    "Apple", "1.50", "September"
};
lView->Items->Add(gcnew ListViewItem(itemRec1, 0));
```

Figure 10-2 shows what ListViewEx.exe looks like when you execute it.

Figure 10-2. *A ListView of fruit*

TreeView

If you have worked with Visual Studio 2005, then you should be familiar with the TreeView control. It is used in numerous places—Solution Explorer, Server Explorer, and Class View, just to name a few. It is a control that displays a hierarchy of items in a tree format.

The TreeView, like the ListView just covered, can be a little complicated when you first try to develop code for it. Once you get the hang of it, though, you will realize that it is worth the effort of learning. The TreeView is a powerful tool that you will probably use several times in your coding career.

Configuring the TreeView control requires setting properties, just as with every other control. Here are the common properties you will likely use:

- CheckBoxes is a Boolean that represents whether check boxes are displayed next to each node in the tree. The default is false.

- ImageIndex is a zero-based Int32 index to the ImageList that represents the position of the default image used by all nodes of the tree. The default is 0. A value of –1 specifies that no image will be used.

- ImageList is a collection of bitmaps, icons, and metafiles that will be used to display the images on the tree control. If the Image list is nullptr, which is the default, no images are displayed on the tree.

- Indent is an Int32 that represents the distance in pixels to indent for each tree hierarchy level. The default is 19.

- LabelEdit is a Boolean that represents whether the label is editable. The default is false.

- Nodes is a TreeNodeCollection that represents all the TreeNodes that make up the tree. You will always have to populate this property and there is no default.

- SelectedImageIndex is a zero-based Int32 index to the ImageList that represents the position of the default selected image used by the tree. The default is 0. A value of –1 specifies that no image will be used.

- SelectedNode is a TreeNode that represents the currently selected node. The default is null, which means no node has been selected.

- ShowLines is a Boolean that represents whether lines will be displayed between nodes. The default is true, which means that lines will be displayed.

- ShowPlusMinus is a Boolean that represents whether the expand (+) and contract (–) buttons are displayed for nodes that have child nodes. The default is true, which means that they will be displayed.

- ShowRootLines is a Boolean that represents whether lines will be displayed between nodes that are at the root of the tree. The default is true, which means that lines will be displayed.

The key to working with the TreeView, like any other control, is to know which event to handle (see Table 10-1). All the events of the TreeView have default handlers, but if you want the control to do anything other than expand and contract, you need to handle the events yourself.

Table 10-1. *Common TreeView Events*

Event	Description
AfterCheck	Occurs after a check box is checked
AfterCollapse	Occurs after a node is collapsed
AfterExpand	Occurs after a node is expanded
AfterLabelEdit	Occurs after a label is edited
AfterSelect	Occurs after a node is selected
BeforeCheck	Occurs before a check box is checked
BeforeCollapse	Occurs before a node is collapsed
BeforeExpand	Occurs before a node is expanded
BeforeLabelEdit	Occurs before a label is edited
BeforeSelect	Occurs before a node is selected

The basic building block of a tree hierarchy is the TreeNode. There is always at least one root node and from it sprouts (possibly many) subnodes. A subnode in turn is also a TreeNode, which can sprout its own TreeNodes.

There are several constructors for the TreeNode, but you'll probably deal with two of them at any one time, unless you create the tree at design time (then you won't have to deal with them at all). Which two you use will depend on whether you have images associated with the tree nodes.

If you are not using images, then the first constructor of the pair takes as a parameter a String as the label for the TreeNode, and the second constructor takes a String label as well as an array of child TreeNodes. The second constructor allows for a node to have one or more child nodes. To make a node with only one child, you need to assign to the second parameter an array of child TreeNodes containing only one node.

```
// Constructor for a node with no children or images
TreeNode^ rtnA = gcnew TreeNode("Root Node A");
// Constructor for a node with children but no images
array<TreeNode^>^ tnodes= gcnew array<TreeNode^> {
    gcnew TreeNode("Node A"),
    gcnew TreeNode("Node B")
};
TreeNode^ rtnB = gcnew TreeNode("Root Node A", tnodes);
```

If you are using images, on the other hand, then the first constructor of the pair takes a String parameter and an integer value representing indexes into the ImageList that you assigned to the TreeView. The second constructor takes these three parameters but also an array of child TreeNodes. Just like the constructor that didn't take image indexes, the second constructor allows for a node to have one or more child nodes.

```
// Constructor for a node with no children but with images
TreeNode^ rtnA = gcnew TreeNode("Root Node A", 0, 1);
// Constructor for a node with children and images
array<TreeNode^>^ tnodes= gcnew array<TreeNode^> {
    gcnew TreeNode("Node A", 2, 3),
    gcnew TreeNode("Node B", 2, 3)
};
TreeNode^ rtnB = gcnew TreeNode("Root Node A", 0, 1, tnodes);
```

The TreeNode has a number of properties to handle its functionality. Many of the properties are used in navigating the tree. Here are some of the more common TreeNode properties:

- Checked is a Boolean that represents whether the current node is checked. The default is false.

- FirstNode is the first TreeNode in the Nodes collection of the current node in the TreeView. If the current node has no child nodes, then the property returns a null value.

- FullPath is a String containing the entire path from the root to the current node delimited by backslashes (\). The path is all the nodes that need to be navigated to get to the current node.

- ImageIndex is a zero-based Int32 index to the TreeView::ImageList associated with the current node that represents the position of the unselected image for the node. The default is the same value as is specified in the TreeView::ImageIndex associated with the current node.

- Index is a zero-based Int32 index that represents the index of the current node within the TreeView's Nodes collection.

- LastNode is the last TreeNode in the Nodes collection of the current node in the TreeView. If the current node has no child nodes, then the property returns a nullptr value.

- NextNode is the next sibling TreeNode in the Nodes collection of the current node in the TreeView. If the current node has no next sibling node, then the property returns a nullptr value.

- Nodes is a TreeNodeCollection that represents all the children nodes that make up the current tree node.

- Parent is a TreeNode that represents the parent node of the current tree node.

- PrevNode is the previous sibling TreeNode in the Nodes collection of the current node in the TreeView. If the current node has no previous sibling node, then the property returns a nullptr value.

- SelectedImageIndex is a zero-based Int32 index to the TreeView::ImageList associated with the current node that represents the position of the selected image for the node. The default is the same value as is specified in the TreeView::ImageIndex associated with the current node.

- Text is a String that represents the text label of the current tree node.

- TreeView is the parent TreeView object that the TreeNode is a member of.

Listing 10-2 shows how to build a tree hierarchy at runtime as opposed to prebuilding it statically. This example builds a new tree hierarchy every time it runs as it generates its node information randomly.

Listing 10-2. *Random Tree Builder*

```
#pragma once

namespace TreeViewEx
{
    using namespace System;
    using namespace System::ComponentModel;
    using namespace System::Collections;
    using namespace System::Windows::Forms;
    using namespace System::Data;
    using namespace System::Drawing;

    public ref class Form1 : public System::Windows::Forms::Form
    {
    public:
        Form1(void)
        {
            InitializeComponent();
        }

    protected:
        ~Form1()
        {
            if (components)
            {
                delete components;
            }
        }

    private:
        System::Windows::Forms::TreeView^  tView;
        System::Windows::Forms::ImageList^  imFolders;
        System::ComponentModel::IContainer^  components;

#pragma region Windows Form Designer generated code
        /// <summary>
        /// Required method for Designer support - do not modify
        /// the contents of this method with the code editor.
        /// </summary>
        void InitializeComponent(void)
        {
            this->components = (gcnew System::ComponentModel::Container());
            System::Windows::Forms::TreeNode^ treeNode1 =
                (gcnew System::Windows::Forms::TreeNode(L"<holder>"));
            System::Windows::Forms::TreeNode^ treeNode2 =
                (gcnew System::Windows::Forms::TreeNode(
                    L"Root Node A", 0, 1,
                    gcnew cli::array< System::Windows::Forms::TreeNode^ >(1)
                    {treeNode1}));
            System::Windows::Forms::TreeNode^ treeNode3 =
                (gcnew System::Windows::Forms::TreeNode(L"<holder>"));
```

```cpp
System::Windows::Forms::TreeNode^ treeNode4 =
    (gcnew System::Windows::Forms::TreeNode(
        L"Root Node B", 0, 1,
        gcnew cli::array< System::Windows::Forms::TreeNode^ >(1)
        {treeNode3}));
    System::ComponentModel::ComponentResourceManager^ resources =
(gcnew System::ComponentModel::ComponentResourceManager(Form1::typeid));
    this->tView = (gcnew System::Windows::Forms::TreeView());
    this->imFolders =
        (gcnew System::Windows::Forms::ImageList(this->components));
    this->SuspendLayout();
    //
    // tView
    //
    this->tView->Dock = System::Windows::Forms::DockStyle::Fill;
    this->tView->ImageIndex = 0;
    this->tView->ImageList = this->imFolders;
    this->tView->LabelEdit = true;
    this->tView->Location = System::Drawing::Point(0, 0);
    this->tView->Name = L"tView";
    treeNode1->Name = L"Node1";
    treeNode1->Text = L"<holder>";
    treeNode2->ImageIndex = 0;
    treeNode2->Name = L"Node0";
    treeNode2->SelectedImageIndex = 1;
    treeNode2->Text = L"Root Node A";
    treeNode3->Name = L"Node3";
    treeNode3->Text = L"<holder>";
    treeNode4->ImageIndex = 0;
    treeNode4->Name = L"Node2";
    treeNode4->SelectedImageIndex = 1;
    treeNode4->Text = L"Root Node B";
    this->tView->Nodes->AddRange(
        gcnew cli::array< System::Windows::Forms::TreeNode^ >(2)
            {treeNode2, treeNode4});
    this->tView->SelectedImageIndex = 1;
    this->tView->Size = System::Drawing::Size(194, 481);
    this->tView->TabIndex = 0;
    this->tView->BeforeExpand +=
        gcnew System::Windows::Forms::TreeViewCancelEventHandler(this,
                                        &Form1::tView_BeforeExpand);
    //
    // imFolders
    //
    this->imFolders->ImageStream =
        (cli::safe_cast<System::Windows::Forms::ImageListStreamer^ >
        (resources->GetObject(L"imFolders.ImageStream")));
    this->imFolders->Images->SetKeyName(0, L"CLSDFOLD.ICO");
    this->imFolders->Images->SetKeyName(1, L"OPENFOLD.ICO");
    //
    // Form1
```

```
                    //
                    this->AutoScaleDimensions = System::Drawing::SizeF(6, 13);
                    this->AutoScaleMode = System::Windows::Forms::AutoScaleMode::Font;
                    this->ClientSize = System::Drawing::Size(194, 481);
                    this->Controls->Add(this->tView);
                    this->Name = L"Form1";
                    this->Text = L"Tree View Example";
                    this->ResumeLayout(false);

            }
    #pragma endregion
        private:
            System::Void tView_BeforeExpand(System::Object^ sender,
                            System::Windows::Forms::TreeViewCancelEventArgs^ e)
            {
                // Already expanded before?
                if (e->Node->Nodes->Count > 1)
                    return;  // Already expanded
                else if (e->Node->Nodes->Count == 1)
                {
                    if (e->Node->Nodes[0]->Text->Equals("<holder>"))
                        e->Node->Nodes->RemoveAt(0); // Node ready for expanding
                    else
                        return; // Already expanded but only one sub node
                }
                // Randomly expand the node
                Random ^rand = gcnew Random();
                int rnd = rand->Next(1,5);
                for (int i = 0; i < rnd; i++) // Randon number of subnodes
                {
                    TreeNode ^stn =
                        gcnew TreeNode(String::Format("Sub Node {0}", i+1), 0, 1);
                    e->Node->Nodes->Add(stn);

                    if (rand->Next(2) == 1)  // Has sub sub-nodes
                        stn->Nodes->Add(gcnew TreeNode("<holder>", 0, 1));
                }
            }
        };
    }
```

The first steps, as with every other control, are to create the TreeView, configure it using properties, and then add it to the Form.

```
this->tView = gcnew TreeView();
this->tView->Dock = System::Windows::Forms::DockStyle::Fill;
this->tView->LabelEdit = true;
this->tView->Size = System::Drawing::Size(200, 450);
this->tView->BeforeExpand +=
    gcnew TreeViewCancelEventHandler(this, &Form1::tView_BeforeExpand);
this->Controls->Add(this->tView);
```

Because in this example you're building a tree hierarchy on the fly, you need to handle an event that occurs just before the tree node is expanded. The BeforeExpand event fits the bill. The BeforeExpand event takes as a handler TreeViewCancelEventHandler. You might note that the handler has the word "Cancel" in it, which means that it's triggered before the expansion of the node and it's possible to have the code cancel the expansion.

Now that you have a tree, you need to add one or more root TreeNodes. You also have to add a holder sub-TreeNode or the expansion box will not be generated. The following code was auto-generated (I added the comments for readability, but be aware that comments and code in the Visual Studio 2005–generated areas will be deleted on recompile or when new components are added by the design tool):

```
// holder node
System::Windows::Forms::TreeNode^ treeNode1 =
    gcnew System::Windows::Forms::TreeNode(L"<holder>");

// root node which take the above holder node as a child
System::Windows::Forms::TreeNode^ treeNode2 =
    gcnew System::Windows::Forms::TreeNode(L"Root Node A", 0, 1,
    gcnew array<System::Windows::Forms::TreeNode^>(1) {treeNode1});
```

At this point, if you were to execute the program (assuming you created a stub for the BeforeExpand event handler), you would get a TreeView with a root TreeNode and a sub-TreeNode. The sub-TreeNode would have the label <holder>.

The last thing you need to do is replace the holder TreeNode when the expansion box is clicked with its own, randomly generated TreeNode hierarchy. Before you replace the holder TreeNode, you need to make sure that this is the first time the node has been expanded. You do this by looking for the holder TreeNode in the first child (and it should be the only child) of the selected expanded TreeNode. You can find all child nodes in the Nodes property in the Node property. (Look at the code—this is easier to code than explain.)

```
if (e->Node->Nodes->Count > 1)
    return;  // Already expanded
else if (e->Node->Nodes->Count == 1)
{
    if (e->Node->Nodes[0]->Text->Equals(S"<holder>"))
        e->Node->Nodes->RemoveAt(0); // Holder node ready for expanding
    else
        return; // Already expanded but only one subnode
}
```

If the node has been expanded previously, just jump out of the handler and let the TreeView reexpand the node with its original tree. If this is the first time the node has been expanded, then remove the holder and randomly create a new sub-TreeNode. The code to create the sub-TreeNode is virtually the same as that of the root TreeNode, except now you add it to the selected to-be-expanded TreeNode.

```
Random ^rand = gcnew Random();
int rnd = rand->Next(1,5);
for (int i = 0; i < rnd; i++) // Random number of subnodes
{
    TreeNode ^stn = gcnew TreeNode(String::Format("Sub Node {0}", i+1), 0, 1);
    e->Node->Nodes->Add(stn);

    if (rand->Next(2) == 1)  // Has sub subnodes
        stn->Nodes->Add(gcnew TreeNode("<holder>"));
}
```

Figure 10-3 shows a sample of what TreeViewEx.exe looks like when you execute it.

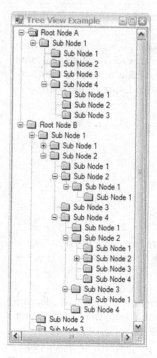

Figure 10-3. *Randomly generated and editable TreeView*

Container Controls

You saw two container controls, GroupBox and Panel, in the previous chapter. These controls simply group controls together. In this chapter, you will look at two more powerful controls: SplitContainer and TabControl.

SplitContainer and TabControl provide for a much better use of Windows Forms real estate. You already saw an improved use of real estate with the Panel control, in that it allowed more controls to be placed in a smaller area of the screen by implementing scroll bars. In this section, you'll see how the TabControl and SplitContainer controls improve on this paradigm.

TabControl

You can think of the TabControl control as several forms or, more accurately, TabPages layered on top of each other. The actual TabPage displayed is determined by which TabPage's tab is selected. It's a neat tool to conserve desktop real estate and group common but stand-alone functionality together.

Several properties are associated with the TabControl control, but in most cases you will simply configure the control, assign the appropriate controls to each tab panel, and then forget about it. The internal default functionality of the TabControl is usually good enough that you will not have to interfere with how it works.

The following are some TabControl properties that you might actually work with:

- Alignment is a TagAlignment enum that represents which side (Top, Left, Right, or Bottom) of the control the tabs of the TabPages will be displayed. The default is Top.

- Appearance is a TabAppearance enum that represents the appearance of the control's tabs. Possible appearances are Buttons, FlatButtons, and Normal. The default is the standard tab appearance of Normal.

- HotTrack is a Boolean that represents whether the tab changes color when the mouse passes over it. The default is false, which means that the tab's color will not change when passed over.
- ImageList is a collection of bitmaps, icons, and metafiles that will be used to display the images on the tab control. If the Image list is null, which is the default, no images are displayed on the control.
- Multiline is a Boolean that represents whether the tabs can be displayed on multiple lines. The default is false, which forces all tabs to be placed on one line.
- SelectedTab is a TabPage that represents the currently selected tab. If no page is selected, null is returned.
- ShowToolTips is a Boolean that represents whether ToolTips are displayed when the mouse passes over the control's tabs. The default is false, meaning no ToolTips are displayed.
- TabCount is an Int32 that represents the number of tabs found on the control.
- TabPages is a TabPageCollection that represents all the TabPages that make up the control.

You work with a TabPage class in almost the exact same way you do a Form class, as it has many of the same properties. Really the only difference between a Form and a TabPage is that the TabPage provides a few properties to configure how the actual tab of the TabPage is displayed. Here are those properties:

- ImageIndex is a zero-based Int32 index to the TabControl::ImageList associated with the current TabPage that represents the position of the image for the tab.
- Text is a String that represents the text found on the tab.
- ToolTip is a String that represents the text found in the ToolTip for the tab.

Listing 10-3 is a simple two-page TabControl that displays each tab along the left side of the Form, and has HotTrack and ShowToolTips set on. The tab pages themselves have a different color background, and each has a different label displayed within it. I could have used any control(s) I wanted within each tab page, but I didn't want to cloud the issue of building the TabControl.

Listing 10-3. *A Simple TabControl*

```
#pragma once

namespace TabControlEx
{
    using namespace System;
    using namespace System::ComponentModel;
    using namespace System::Collections;
    using namespace System::Windows::Forms;
    using namespace System::Data;
    using namespace System::Drawing;

    public ref class Form1 : public System::Windows::Forms::Form
    {
    public:
        Form1(void)
        {
            InitializeComponent();
        }
```

```cpp
    protected:
        ~Form1()
        {
            if (components)
            {
                delete components;
            }
        }

    private:
        System::Windows::Forms::TabControl^  tabControl1;
        System::Windows::Forms::TabPage^  tabPage1;
        System::Windows::Forms::Label^  label2;
        System::Windows::Forms::TabPage^  tabPage2;
        System::Windows::Forms::Label^  label1;

        System::ComponentModel::Container ^components;

#pragma region Windows Form Designer generated code

        void InitializeComponent(void)
        {
            this->tabControl1 = (gcnew System::Windows::Forms::TabControl());
            this->tabPage1 = (gcnew System::Windows::Forms::TabPage());
            this->label2 = (gcnew System::Windows::Forms::Label());
            this->tabPage2 = (gcnew System::Windows::Forms::TabPage());
            this->label1 = (gcnew System::Windows::Forms::Label());
            this->tabControl1->SuspendLayout();
            this->tabPage1->SuspendLayout();
            this->tabPage2->SuspendLayout();
            this->SuspendLayout();
            //
            // tabControl1
            //
            this->tabControl1->Alignment =
                System::Windows::Forms::TabAlignment::Bottom;
            this->tabControl1->Controls->Add(this->tabPage1);
            this->tabControl1->Controls->Add(this->tabPage2);
            this->tabControl1->Dock = System::Windows::Forms::DockStyle::Fill;
            this->tabControl1->HotTrack = true;
            this->tabControl1->Location = System::Drawing::Point(0, 0);
            this->tabControl1->Multiline = true;
            this->tabControl1->Name = L"tabControl1";
            this->tabControl1->SelectedIndex = 0;
            this->tabControl1->ShowToolTips = true;
            this->tabControl1->Size = System::Drawing::Size(215, 129);
            this->tabControl1->TabIndex = 1;
            //
            // tabPage1
            //
            this->tabPage1->BackColor = System::Drawing::Color::PaleGreen;
            this->tabPage1->Controls->Add(this->label2);
            this->tabPage1->Location = System::Drawing::Point(4, 4);
            this->tabPage1->Name = L"tabPage1";
```

```cpp
this->tabPage1->Padding = System::Windows::Forms::Padding(3);
this->tabPage1->Size = System::Drawing::Size(207, 103);
this->tabPage1->TabIndex = 0;
this->tabPage1->Text = L"Tab One";
this->tabPage1->ToolTipText = L"This is tab one";
this->tabPage1->UseVisualStyleBackColor = false;
//
// label2
//
this->label2->AutoSize = true;
this->label2->Location = System::Drawing::Point(61, 44);
this->label2->Name = L"label2";
this->label2->Size = System::Drawing::Size(78, 13);
this->label2->TabIndex = 1;
this->label2->Text = L"This is Tab One";
//
// tabPage2
//
this->tabPage2->BackColor = System::Drawing::Color::Plum;
this->tabPage2->Controls->Add(this->label1);
this->tabPage2->Location = System::Drawing::Point(4, 4);
this->tabPage2->Name = L"tabPage2";
this->tabPage2->Padding = System::Windows::Forms::Padding(3);
this->tabPage2->Size = System::Drawing::Size(207, 103);
this->tabPage2->TabIndex = 1;
this->tabPage2->Text = L"Tab Two";
this->tabPage2->ToolTipText = L"This is tab two";
this->tabPage2->UseVisualStyleBackColor = false;
//
// label1
//
this->label1->AutoSize = true;
this->label1->Location = System::Drawing::Point(61, 44);
this->label1->Name = L"label1";
this->label1->Size = System::Drawing::Size(79, 13);
this->label1->TabIndex = 0;
this->label1->Text = L"This is Tab Two";
//
// Form1
//
this->AutoScaleDimensions = System::Drawing::SizeF(6, 13);
this->AutoScaleMode = System::Windows::Forms::AutoScaleMode::Font;
this->ClientSize = System::Drawing::Size(215, 129);
this->Controls->Add(this->tabControl1);
this->Name = L"Form1";
this->Text = L"Tab Control Example";
this->tabControl1->ResumeLayout(false);
this->tabPage1->ResumeLayout(false);
this->tabPage1->PerformLayout();
this->tabPage2->ResumeLayout(false);
this->tabPage2->PerformLayout();
this->ResumeLayout(false);
}
```

```
#pragma endregion
    };
}
```

The best part about TabControls is that you don't have to know anything about them because Visual Studio 2005's design GUI tool can handle everything for you. The only real issue about TabControls is that there is no TabPage control in the Toolbox view to drag to the TabControl. Instead, to add a TabPage, you need to add it to the TabPages collection property within the TabControl's Properties view.

I think the generated code is pretty self-explanatory. You add the TabPage to the TabControl, add the Label to a TabPage, and finally add the TabControl to the Form.

Figure 10-4 shows what TabControlEx.exe looks like when you execute it. Unfortunately, you can't see it in action in this still image.

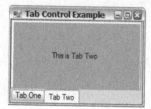

Figure 10-4. *A simple TabControl*

SplitContainer

The SplitContainer is a simple little control that takes two panels and allows you to resize them at runtime using a little area located between the panels known as the splitter. You can spot this area between the panels not only because the area is (normally) a different color than the panels, but also because the cursor changes automatically into what Windows calls a VSplit or HSplit cursor, depending on whether you use a vertical or horizontal SplitContainer.

The SplitContainer is a vast improvement over its predecessor, the Splitter control. The largest improvement in my mind is that with the Splitter you were required to do several elaborate steps to get it configured. Now, with the SplitContainer, you simply drag the control onto the Design view, and then using the Orientation property, you specify whether the container will be split vertically or horizontally. Most likely you will also use the dock property to fill the Window Form or the container control that you place it in, but you don't have to, as Listing 10-4 points out.

The following are some SplitContainer properties that you might work with:

- FixedPanel specifies that a panel stays a fixed size when a resize event occurs. The default is none, which causes the two panels that make up the control to stay proportionally the same.

- Panel1 is the left or top Panel control depending on the type of split.

- Panel1Collapsed is a Boolean value that allows you to make the Panel1 completely collapse when set to true. When collapsed, there is no way to resize the control; you must programmatically set the value back to false to allow the control to resize again.

- Panel2 is the right or bottom Panel control depending on the type of split.

- Panel2Collapsed is a Boolean value that allows you to make the Panel2 completely collapse when set to true. When collapsed, there is no way to resize the control; you must programmatically set the value back to false to allow the control to resize again.

- SplitterDistance is an Int32 value of the number of pixels from the left or top where the split occurs.

- SplitterWidth is an Int32 value of the size between the two panels.

In the example, I fill the SplitContainer control's Panel1 and Panel2 properties with TextBox controls, though this is not necessary. You can use the SplitContainer control's Panel properties just like you would a standard Panel control.

Listing 10-4 shows the SplitContainer being used twice. The first time I split the entire Window Form vertically using a green background. The second time I split horizontally a small portion of the Right panel using a red background.

Listing 10-4. *The SplitContainer Control*

```
#pragma once

namespace SplitContainerEx
{
    using namespace System;
    using namespace System::ComponentModel;
    using namespace System::Collections;
    using namespace System::Windows::Forms;
    using namespace System::Data;
    using namespace System::Drawing;

    public ref class Form1 : public System::Windows::Forms::Form
    {
    public:
        Form1(void)
        {
            InitializeComponent();
        }

    protected:
        ~Form1()
        {
            if (components)
            {
                delete components;
            }
        }
    private:
        System::Windows::Forms::SplitContainer^  splitContainer1;
        System::Windows::Forms::TextBox^  textBox1;
        System::Windows::Forms::SplitContainer^  splitContainer2;
        System::Windows::Forms::TextBox^  textBox2;
        System::Windows::Forms::TextBox^  textBox3;

        System::ComponentModel::Container ^components;
```

```cpp
#pragma region Windows Form Designer generated code

    void InitializeComponent(void)
    {
        this->splitContainer1 =
            (gcnew System::Windows::Forms::SplitContainer());
        this->textBox1 = (gcnew System::Windows::Forms::TextBox());
        this->splitContainer2 =
            (gcnew System::Windows::Forms::SplitContainer());
        this->textBox2 = (gcnew System::Windows::Forms::TextBox());
        this->textBox3 = (gcnew System::Windows::Forms::TextBox());
        this->splitContainer1->Panel1->SuspendLayout();
        this->splitContainer1->Panel2->SuspendLayout();
        this->splitContainer1->SuspendLayout();
        this->splitContainer2->Panel1->SuspendLayout();
        this->splitContainer2->Panel2->SuspendLayout();
        this->splitContainer2->SuspendLayout();
        this->SuspendLayout();
        //
        // splitContainer1
        //
        this->splitContainer1->BackColor = System::Drawing::Color::Green;
        this->splitContainer1->Dock =
            System::Windows::Forms::DockStyle::Fill;
        this->splitContainer1->Location = System::Drawing::Point(0, 0);
        this->splitContainer1->Name = L"splitContainer1";
        //
        // splitContainer1.Panel1
        //
        this->splitContainer1->Panel1->Controls->Add(this->textBox1);
        //
        // splitContainer1.Panel2
        //
        this->splitContainer1->Panel2->Controls->Add(this->splitContainer2);
        this->splitContainer1->Size = System::Drawing::Size(292, 273);
        this->splitContainer1->SplitterDistance = 116;
        this->splitContainer1->TabIndex = 1;
        this->splitContainer1->Text = L"splitContainer1";
        //
        // textBox1
        //
        this->textBox1->AutoSize = false;
        this->textBox1->BorderStyle =
            System::Windows::Forms::BorderStyle::None;
        this->textBox1->Dock = System::Windows::Forms::DockStyle::Fill;
        this->textBox1->Location = System::Drawing::Point(0, 0);
        this->textBox1->Name = L"textBox1";
        this->textBox1->Size = System::Drawing::Size(116, 273);
        this->textBox1->TabIndex = 0;
        this->textBox1->Text = L"Left Textbox";
        this->textBox1->TextAlign =
            System::Windows::Forms::HorizontalAlignment::Center;
```

```
//
// splitContainer2
//
this->splitContainer2->BackColor = System::Drawing::Color::Red;
this->splitContainer2->Location = System::Drawing::Point(18, 82);
this->splitContainer2->Name = L"splitContainer2";
this->splitContainer2->Orientation =
    System::Windows::Forms::Orientation::Horizontal;
//
// splitContainer2.Panel1
//
this->splitContainer2->Panel1->Controls->Add(this->textBox2);
//
// splitContainer2.Panel2
//
this->splitContainer2->Panel2->Controls->Add(this->textBox3);
this->splitContainer2->Size = System::Drawing::Size(132, 102);
this->splitContainer2->SplitterDistance = 42;
this->splitContainer2->TabIndex = 0;
this->splitContainer2->Text = L"splitContainer2";
//
// textBox2
//
this->textBox2->AutoSize = false;
this->textBox2->BorderStyle =
    System::Windows::Forms::BorderStyle::None;
this->textBox2->Dock = System::Windows::Forms::DockStyle::Fill;
this->textBox2->Location = System::Drawing::Point(0, 0);
this->textBox2->Name = L"textBox2";
this->textBox2->Size = System::Drawing::Size(132, 42);
this->textBox2->TabIndex = 0;
this->textBox2->Text = L"Top Right Textbox";
this->textBox2->TextAlign =
    System::Windows::Forms::HorizontalAlignment::Center;
//
// textBox3
//
this->textBox3->AutoSize = false;
this->textBox3->BorderStyle =
    System::Windows::Forms::BorderStyle::None;
this->textBox3->Dock = System::Windows::Forms::DockStyle::Fill;
this->textBox3->Location = System::Drawing::Point(0, 0);
this->textBox3->Name = L"textBox3";
this->textBox3->Size = System::Drawing::Size(132, 56);
this->textBox3->TabIndex = 0;
this->textBox3->Text = L"Bottom Right Textbox";
this->textBox3->TextAlign =
    System::Windows::Forms::HorizontalAlignment::Center;
//
// Form1
//
this->AutoScaleDimensions = System::Drawing::SizeF(6, 13);
this->AutoScaleMode = System::Windows::Forms::AutoScaleMode::Font;
this->ClientSize = System::Drawing::Size(292, 273);
```

```
                    this->Controls->Add(this->splitContainer1);
                    this->Name = L"Form1";
                    this->Text = L"Form1";
                    this->splitContainer1->Panel1->ResumeLayout(false);
                    this->splitContainer1->Panel2->ResumeLayout(false);
                    this->splitContainer1->ResumeLayout(false);
                    this->splitContainer2->Panel1->ResumeLayout(false);
                    this->splitContainer2->Panel2->ResumeLayout(false);
                    this->splitContainer2->ResumeLayout(false);
                    this->ResumeLayout(false);
            }
#pragma endregion
        };
}
```

Figure 10-5 shows what SplitControlEx.exe looks like when you execute it.

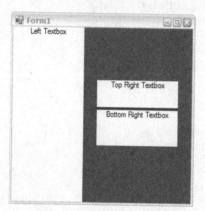

Figure 10-5. *A simple pair of SplitContainer controls*

Strips

If you have worked with prior versions of Windows Forms, you may have noticed that your toolbars, status bar, and menus bore little resemblance to and lacked much of the functionality of those you found on many of Microsoft's applications and tools. To fix this (oversight?), several third-party controls were developed. However, with .NET version 2.0 Web Forms, many of these third-party controls may have become obsolete due to the new strip controls—ToolStrip, StatusStrip, and MenuStrip.

ToolStripContainer and ToolStripPanel

In previous versions of Windows Forms, there was little flexibility to how and where you displayed your main menu, status bar, and toolbars (I'll just call them strip controls from here on). You had no options to drag your strip controls to different sides of your form or display multiple strip controls together. This has now been changed with the addition of the ToolStripContainer control.

The ToolStripContainer control is where you place your strip controls if you want them aligned along the border. More accurately, any one of the following (aptly named) four ToolStripPanel properties is where you place your strip controls:

- TopToolStripPanel
- BottomToolStripPanel
- LeftToolStripPanel
- RightToolStripPanel

A fifth panel, the ContentPanel, fills the center area between all the ToolStripPanels. You use this area as the home for all the content of your form.

Before you add your strip control within Visual Studio 2005, you first add a ToolStripContainer just like you would any other control. Once added, you dock fill it to the form so that the four ToolStripPanels align with the sides of the form. Next, you expand the ToolStripPanel where you want to place your strip. Finally, you drag and drop your strip to the expanded ToolStripPanel.

One nice feature that the ToolStripPanel control provides is the ability to display multiple strip controls together. The ToolStripPanel is a container control that provides flow layout functionality. As you add strip controls to the ToolStripPanel control, they are arranged from left to right in the case of a ToolStripPanel control docked to the top or bottom, and from top to bottom in the case of a ToolStripPanel control docked to the left or right side. When you reach the edge of the ToolStripPanel, additional controls flow to the next row.

There's not much to the coding of ToolStripContainer controls. You declare it as follows:

```
System::Windows::Forms::ToolStripContainer^ toolStripContainer1;
```

You create instances of it like so:

```
this->toolStripContainer1 = gcnew system::Windows::Forms::ToolStripContainer();
```

You use the following to dock it to a Windows Form border (and optionally set a few of its properties):

```
this->toolStripContainer1->Dock = System::Windows::Forms::DockStyle::Fill;
```

To add it to the Windows Form:

```
this->Controls->Add(this->toolStripContainer1);
```

And finally, to add strip controls to the appropriate ToolStripPanel using any combination of the following statements:

```
this->toolStripContainer1->TopToolStripPanel->Controls->Add(this->Strip1);
this->toolStripContainer1->BottomToolStripPanel->Controls->Add(this->Strip1);
this->toolStripContainer1->LeftToolStripPanel->Controls->Add(this->Strip1);
this->toolStripContainer1->RightToolStripPanel->Controls->Add(this->Strip1);
```

By the way, you can add strips without using the ToolStripContainer, but then you lose the ability to move the strips around.

ToolStripManager

The ToolStripManager class is made up of several static properties and methods that you use to control the arrangement, rendering, and display style of strip controls. You can, in most cases, just use the defaults and ignore the ToolStripManager class completely, but if you find you have the need, the following three properties are available to specify a renderer and display styles:

- Renderer is a ToolStripRenderer object that specifies the default painting styles for the Windows Form.

- RenderMode is a ToolStripManagerRenderMode enum specifying whether the System (flat style with system colors) or Professional (custom palette and a streamlined style) mode will be used.

- VisualStylesEnabled is a Boolean that represents whether rendered is done using themes.

The main reason I use the ToolStripManager class is to merge two strip controls together and then later, when I no longer need the controls to be merged, undo the merge. The merging of two strip controls is done with the aptly named method Merge(), while you undo or revert the merge using the RevertMerge() method.

ToolStrip

Most Windows applications have a tool strip. Many like Microsoft Word have more than one, often all visible at the same time. In this section, you'll learn how to implement ToolStrip controls using the .NET Framework class library.

The ToolStrip has improved considerably over its predecessor the ToolBar. It provides a lot more functionality with a much cleaner interface. With all this extra functionality, the ToolStrip control is a little more complex than the ToolBar, but the design tool is intuitive, which evens things out.

I guess I could have placed this ToolStrip discussion in with the "Container Controls" section as the ToolStrip is in fact a container. However, unlike the other containers, it can contain only controls derived from the ToolStripItem class. This isn't really an issue, as you can place standard controls within the ToolStripControlHost control and then place them on the ToolStrip. The .NET Framework supports several ToolStripItems out of the box. The following are the most common ones you might use:

- ToolStripButton is a selectable button that can contain text and images.

- ToolStripComboBox is a combo box.

- ToolStripSplitButton is a combination of a standard button on the left and a drop-down button on the right.

- ToolStripLabel is a nonselectable item that displays text, images, and hyperlinks.

- ToolStripSeparator is a separator.

- ToolStripDropDownButton is a control that, when clicked, displays an associated list of buttons from which the user can select a single item.

- ToolStripTextBox is a text box.

The ToolStrip control has a few overall tool strip configuration properties. These properties work in conjunction with the preceding ToolStripItems to get the final look and feel of the tool strip. Here are some of the more commonly used ToolStrip properties:

- AllowItemReorder is a Boolean value indicating whether the ToolStrip will allow and handle by itself drag-and-drop and item reordering. The default value is false.

- AllowMerge is a Boolean value indicating whether multiple MenuStrip, ToolStripDropDownMenu, ToolStripMenuItem, and other types can be combined. The default is false.

- CanOverflow is a Boolean value indicating whether items in the ToolStrip can be sent to an overflow menu. The default is true.

- GripStyle is a ToolStripGripStyle enum value of either Visible or Hidden. The default is Visible.

- `ImageList` is a collection of bitmaps, icons, and metafiles that will be used to display the images on the `ToolStrip`. The default is `nullptr` or no image list.

- `OverflowButton` is the `ToolStripItem` that is the overflow button for a `ToolStrip` with `CanOverflow` equal to true.

- `RenderMode` is a `ToolStripRenderMode` enum that specifies the tool strip renderer to use. You will most likely use `ManagerRenderMode`, which uses the renderer specified by the `ToolStripManager`, but you can also specifically select `System` (flat style with system colors) or `Professional` (custom palette and a streamlined style).

- `ShowItemToolTips` is a `Boolean` that represents whether tool tips are displayed for all `ToolStripItems` when the mouse passes over them. The default is `false`.

The `ToolStripItem` class provides a number of common properties used to configure the tool strip items themselves. Here are some of the more common properties:

- `AutoToolTip` is a `Boolean` value indicating whether to use the `Text` property or the `ToolTipText` property for the `ToolStripItem` tool tip. The default is `true`, meaning the `Text` property is used.

- `DisplayStyle` is a `ToolStripGripStyle` enum value indicating whether `Image`, `ImageAndText`, `None`, or `Text` is displayed. The default is `ImageAndText`.

- `ImageIndex` is a zero-based `Int32` index to the `ToolStrip::ImageList` associated with the current `ToolStripItem` that represents the position of the image for the button. The default is –1, or no image will appear on the button.

- `ImageScaling` is a `Boolean` value indicating whether the image automatically resizes to fit in a container.

- `Pressed` is a `Boolean` that represents whether the item is pressed.

- `Selected` is a `Boolean` that represents whether the item is selected.

- `Text` is a `String` that represents the text displayed on the button.

- `TextImageRelation` is a `TextImageRelation` enum value indicating the relationship between its text and image. Possible values are `ImageAboveText`, `ImageBeforeText`, `Overlay`, `TextAboveImage`, or `TextBeforeImage`. The default is `ImageBeforeText`.

- `ToolTipText` is a `String` that appears in the `ToolTip` control associated with the item.

The code in Listing 10-5 builds a tool strip with two `ToolStripButtons`: a happy face and a sad face, `ToolStripLabel` and a `ToolStripTextBox`. When you click either of the buttons, the label in the body of the form is updated with a combination of the `ToolStripTextBox`'s `Text` property and `ToolTipText` of the `ToolStripButton` inherited from the `ToolStripItem`.

Listing 10-5. *An Emotional Tool Strip*

```
namespace ToolStripEx
{
    using namespace System;
    using namespace System::ComponentModel;
    using namespace System::Collections;
    using namespace System::Windows::Forms;
    using namespace System::Data;
    using namespace System::Drawing;
```

```cpp
public ref class Form1 : public System::Windows::Forms::Form
{
public:
    Form1(void)
    {
        InitializeComponent();
    }

protected:
    ~Form1()
    {
        if (components)
        {
            delete components;
        }
    }

private:
    System::Windows::Forms::Label^  lbOutput;
    System::Windows::Forms::ToolStrip^  toolStrip;
    System::Windows::Forms::ToolStripButton^  tsbnHappy;
    System::Windows::Forms::ToolStripButton^  tsbnSad;
    System::Windows::Forms::ToolStripSeparator^  Sep1;
    System::Windows::Forms::ToolStripLabel^  Label;
    System::Windows::Forms::ToolStripTextBox^  tstbName;
    System::Windows::Forms::ToolStripContainer^  toolStripContainer1;

    System::ComponentModel::Container ^components;

#pragma region Windows Form Designer generated code

    void InitializeComponent(void)
    {
        System::ComponentModel::ComponentResourceManager^ Resources =
        (gcnew System::ComponentModel::ComponentResourceManager(Form1::typeid));
        this->lbOutput = (gcnew System::Windows::Forms::Label());
        this->toolStrip = (gcnew System::Windows::Forms::ToolStrip());
        this->tsbnHappy = (gcnew System::Windows::Forms::ToolStripButton());
        this->tsbnSad = (gcnew System::Windows::Forms::ToolStripButton());
        this->Sep1 = (gcnew System::Windows::Forms::ToolStripSeparator());
        this->Label = (gcnew System::Windows::Forms::ToolStripLabel());
        this->tstbName = (gcnew System::Windows::Forms::ToolStripTextBox());
        this->toolStripContainer1 =
            (gcnew System::Windows::Forms::ToolStripContainer());
        this->toolStrip->SuspendLayout();
        this->toolStripContainer1->ContentPanel->SuspendLayout();
        this->toolStripContainer1->TopToolStripPanel->SuspendLayout();
        this->toolStripContainer1->SuspendLayout();
        this->SuspendLayout();
        //
        // lbOutput
```

```
//
this->lbOutput->AutoSize = true;
this->lbOutput->Font =
    (gcnew System::Drawing::Font(L"Microsoft Sans Serif", 8.25F,
        System::Drawing::FontStyle::Bold,
        System::Drawing::GraphicsUnit::Point,
        static_cast<System::Byte>(0)));
this->lbOutput->Location = System::Drawing::Point(47, 42);
this->lbOutput->Name = L"lbOutput";
this->lbOutput->Size = System::Drawing::Size(208, 13);
this->lbOutput->TabIndex = 7;
this->lbOutput->Text = L"Enter a name then click an emotion";
//
// toolStrip
//
this->toolStrip->Dock = System::Windows::Forms::DockStyle::None;
this->toolStrip->Items->AddRange(
    gcnew cli::array< System::Windows::Forms::ToolStripItem^ >(5)
    { this->tsbnHappy, this->tsbnSad,
      this->Sep1, this->Label, this->tstbName});
this->toolStrip->Location = System::Drawing::Point(0, 0);
this->toolStrip->Name = L"toolStrip";
this->toolStrip->Size = System::Drawing::Size(300, 25);
this->toolStrip->Stretch = true;
this->toolStrip->TabIndex = 6;
this->toolStrip->Text = L"toolStrip1";
//
// tsbnHappy
//
this->tsbnHappy->Image =
    (cli::safe_cast<System::Drawing::Image^>
      (resources->GetObject(L"tsbnHappy.Image")));
this->tsbnHappy->Name = L"tsbnHappy";
this->tsbnHappy->Size = System::Drawing::Size(58, 22);
this->tsbnHappy->Text = L"Happy";
this->tsbnHappy->ToolTipText = L"a happy camper";
this->tsbnHappy->Click +=
    gcnew System::EventHandler(this, &Form1::tsbn_Click);
//
// tsbnSad
//
this->tsbnSad->Image =
    (cli::safe_cast<System::Drawing::Image^>
      (resources->GetObject(L"tsbnSad.Image")));
this->tsbnSad->Name = L"tsbnSad";
this->tsbnSad->Size = System::Drawing::Size(45, 22);
this->tsbnSad->Text = L"Sad";
this->tsbnSad->ToolTipText = L"major gloomy";
this->tsbnSad->Click +=
    gcnew System::EventHandler(this, &Form1::tsbn_Click);
//
// Sep1
```

```
            //
            this->Sep1->Name = L"Sep1";
            this->Sep1->Size = System::Drawing::Size(6, 25);
            //
            // Label
            //
            this->Label->Name = L"Label";
            this->Label->Size = System::Drawing::Size(34, 22);
            this->Label->Text = L"Name";
            //
            // tstbName
            //
            this->tstbName->Name = L"tstbName";
            this->tstbName->Size = System::Drawing::Size(92, 25);
            this->tstbName->Text = L"Computer";
            //
            // toolStripContainer1
            //
            this->toolStripContainer1->ContentPanel->Controls->Add(
                this->lbOutput);
            this->toolStripContainer1->ContentPanel->Size =
                System::Drawing::Size(300, 105);
            this->toolStripContainer1->Location = System::Drawing::Point(0, 0);
            this->toolStripContainer1->Name = L"toolStripContainer1";
            this->toolStripContainer1->Size = System::Drawing::Size(300, 130);
            this->toolStripContainer1->TabIndex = 8;
            this->toolStripContainer1->Text = L"toolStripContainer1";
            //
            // toolStripContainer1.TopToolStripPanel
            //
            this->toolStripContainer1->TopToolStripPanel->Controls->Add(
                this->toolStrip);
            //
            // Form1
            //
            this->AutoScaleMode =
                System::Windows::Forms::AutoScaleMode::Inherit;
            this->ClientSize = System::Drawing::Size(300, 129);
            this->Controls->Add(this->toolStripContainer1);
            this->Name = L"Form1";
            this->Text = L"Emotional Tool Strip";
            this->toolStrip->ResumeLayout(false);
            this->toolStrip->PerformLayout();
            this->toolStripContainer1->ContentPanel->ResumeLayout(false);
            this->toolStripContainer1->ContentPanel->PerformLayout();
            this->toolStripContainer1->TopToolStripPanel->ResumeLayout(false);
            this->toolStripContainer1->TopToolStripPanel->PerformLayout();
            this->toolStripContainer1->ResumeLayout(false);
            this->toolStripContainer1->PerformLayout();
            this->ResumeLayout(false);
        }
```

```
#pragma endregion

    private:
        System::Void tsbn_Click(System::Object^ sender, System::EventArgs^ e)
        {
            this->lbOutput->Text = String::Format("{0} is {1}!",
                tstbName->Text, ((ToolStripButton^)sender)->ToolTipText);
        }
    };
}
```

The process for creating a ToolStrip within Visual Studio 2005 is relatively straightforward, once you know how to do it. The steps are as follows:

1. Add a ToolStripContainer as outlined earlier.

2. Drag and drop the ToolStrip from the Toolbox to the ToolStripPanel of choice within the Design view.

3. Within the ToolStrip's Properties dialog box, click the ellipses button next to the Items property. This will bring up a dialog box similar to the one shown in Figure 10-6.

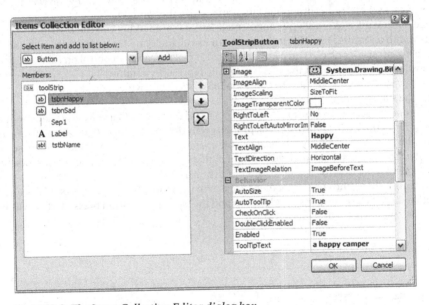

Figure 10-6. *The Items Collection Editor dialog box*

4. Select the appropriate ToolStrip item type from the drop-down list.

5. Click the Add button and then update the ToolStrip item's properties as appropriate.

6. Repeat step 4 for all the items.

7. Click the OK button.

Figure 10-7 shows what ToolStripEx.exe looks like when you execute it.

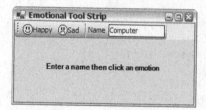

Figure 10-7. *The emotional toolbar*

StatusStrip

The StatusStrip is an easy-to-use control whose purpose is to display status information to the user. You will find the status strip at the bottom of many Windows applications. The truth is, the placement of the status strip is only a well-accepted convention, as the StatusStrip supports being placed anywhere on the Windows Form.

I have already covered almost everything you need to know about the StatusStrip, as the StatusStrip is a child of the ToolStrip. The only difference that you probably have to worry about is that the StatusStrip provides the Boolean property SizeGrip, which the ToolStrip doesn't. If you set SizeGrip to false, the SizeGrip disappears. The default is true. The SizeGrip, by the way, is that dotted triangle in the bottom corner that you use to resize the window.

Since the StatusStrip is a slightly augmented ToolStrip, anything you can do with a ToolStrip you can do with a StatusStrip. This means you can use all the same ToolStripItems, plus the ToolStripProgressBar control. (You can use the ToolStripProgressBar control on the ToolStrip as well, but you rarely, if ever, see it there as it normally represents a status.)

In most cases, you will probably use only the ToolStripLabel, which allows you to place text and images in the status strip.

One property that you will use on a StatusStrip's ToolStripLabel that you don't use as frequently on a ToolStrip is the Spring property. This property tells the ToolStripLabel to fill up all unused spaces on the StatusStrip, in effect causing all other controls to be left or right justified based on whether the ToolStripLabel is on the left or right of that control. In the example that follows, that is how I right justify the two mouse coordinate ToolStripLabels.

Listing 10-6 shows the creation of the StatusStrip with three ToolStripLabels. The status information displayed is the mouse *x, y* location and the last mouse button pressed while within the ContentPanel area of the ToolStripContainer.

Listing 10-6. *Status Bar Display of x, y Coordinates*

```
namespace StatusStripEx {

    using namespace System;
    using namespace System::ComponentModel;
    using namespace System::Collections;
    using namespace System::Windows::Forms;
    using namespace System::Data;
    using namespace System::Drawing;

    public ref class Form1 : public System::Windows::Forms::Form
    {
    public:
        Form1(void)
        {
            InitializeComponent();
        }
```

```
    protected:
        ~Form1()
        {
            if (components)
            {
                delete components;
            }
        }

    private:
        System::Windows::Forms::ToolStripContainer^  tsContainer;
        System::Windows::Forms::StatusStrip^ statusStrip1;
        System::Windows::Forms::ToolStripStatusLabel^  statusButtons;
        System::Windows::Forms::ToolStripStatusLabel^  statusXCoord;
        System::Windows::Forms::ToolStripStatusLabel^  statusYCoord;

        System::ComponentModel::Container ^components;

#pragma region Windows Form Designer generated code

        void InitializeComponent(void)
        {
            this->tsContainer =
                (gcnew System::Windows::Forms::ToolStripContainer());
            this->statusStrip1 =
                (gcnew System::Windows::Forms::StatusStrip());
            this->statusButtons =
                (gcnew System::Windows::Forms::ToolStripStatusLabel());
            this->statusXCoord =
                (gcnew System::Windows::Forms::ToolStripStatusLabel());
            this->statusYCoord =
                (gcnew System::Windows::Forms::ToolStripStatusLabel());
            this->tsContainer->BottomToolStripPanel->SuspendLayout();
            this->tsContainer->SuspendLayout();
            this->statusStrip1->SuspendLayout();
            this->SuspendLayout();
            //
            // tsContainer
            //
            //
            // tsContainer.BottomToolStripPanel
            //
            this->tsContainer->BottomToolStripPanel->Controls->Add(
                this->statusStrip1);
            //
            // tsContainer.ContentPanel
            //
            this->tsContainer->ContentPanel->Size =
                System::Drawing::Size(292, 251);
            this->tsContainer->ContentPanel->MouseDown +=
                gcnew System::Windows::Forms::MouseEventHandler(this,
                &Form1::tsContainer_ContentPanel_MouseDown);
```

```
this->tsContainer->ContentPanel->MouseMove +=
    gcnew System::Windows::Forms::MouseEventHandler(this,
    &Form1::tsContainer1_ContentPanel_MouseMove);
this->tsContainer->Dock = System::Windows::Forms::DockStyle::Fill;
this->tsContainer->Location = System::Drawing::Point(0, 0);
this->tsContainer->Name = L"tsContainer";
this->tsContainer->Size = System::Drawing::Size(292, 273);
this->tsContainer->TabIndex = 0;
this->tsContainer->Text = L"toolStripContainer1";
//
// statusStrip1
//
this->statusStrip1->Dock = System::Windows::Forms::DockStyle::None;
this->statusStrip1->Items->AddRange(
    gcnew cli::array< System::Windows::Forms::ToolStripItem^>(3)
    {this->statusButtons, this->statusXCoord, this->statusYCoord});
this->statusStrip1->Location = System::Drawing::Point(0, 0);
this->statusStrip1->Name = L"statusStrip1";
this->statusStrip1->Size = System::Drawing::Size(292, 22);
this->statusStrip1->TabIndex = 0;
//
// statusButtons
//
this->statusButtons->Name = L"statusButtons";
this->statusButtons->Size = System::Drawing::Size(177, 17);
this->statusButtons->Spring = true;
this->statusButtons->TextAlign =
    System::Drawing::ContentAlignment::MiddleLeft;
//
// statusXCoord
//
this->statusXCoord->AutoSize = false;
this->statusXCoord->BorderSides =
static_cast<System::Windows::Forms::ToolStripStatusLabelBorderSides>
((((System::Windows::Forms::ToolStripStatusLabelBorderSides::Left
| System::Windows::Forms::ToolStripStatusLabelBorderSides::Top)
| System::Windows::Forms::ToolStripStatusLabelBorderSides::Right)
| System::Windows::Forms::ToolStripStatusLabelBorderSides::Bottom));
this->statusXCoord->BorderStyle =
    System::Windows::Forms::Border3DStyle::Sunken;
this->statusXCoord->Name = L"statusXCoord";
this->statusXCoord->Size = System::Drawing::Size(50, 17);
//
// statusYCoord
//
this->statusYCoord->AutoSize = false;
this->statusYCoord->BorderSides =
static_cast<System::Windows::Forms::ToolStripStatusLabelBorderSides>
((((System::Windows::Forms::ToolStripStatusLabelBorderSides::Left
| System::Windows::Forms::ToolStripStatusLabelBorderSides::Top)
| System::Windows::Forms::ToolStripStatusLabelBorderSides::Right)
| System::Windows::Forms::ToolStripStatusLabelBorderSides::Bottom));
```

```cpp
        this->statusYCoord->BorderStyle =
            System::Windows::Forms::Border3DStyle::Sunken;
        this->statusYCoord->Name = L"statusYCoord";
        this->statusYCoord->Size = System::Drawing::Size(50, 17);
        //
        // Form1
        //
        this->AutoScaleDimensions = System::Drawing::SizeF(6, 13);
        this->AutoScaleMode = System::Windows::Forms::AutoScaleMode::Font;
        this->ClientSize = System::Drawing::Size(292, 273);
        this->Controls->Add(this->tsContainer);
        this->Name = L"Form1";
        this->Text = L"Status Strip Mouse Tracking";
        this->tsContainer->BottomToolStripPanel->ResumeLayout(false);
        this->tsContainer->BottomToolStripPanel->PerformLayout();
        this->tsContainer->ResumeLayout(false);
        this->tsContainer->PerformLayout();
        this->statusStrip1->ResumeLayout(false);
        this->statusStrip1->PerformLayout();
        this->ResumeLayout(false);


    }
#pragma endregion

private:
        System::Void tsContainer_ContentPanel_MouseDown(System::Object^ sender,
                                    System::Windows::Forms::MouseEventArgs^ e)
        {
            // clicked mouse button in first status bar panel
            if (e->Button == System::Windows::Forms::MouseButtons::Right)
                statusButtons->Text = "Right";
            else if (e->Button == System::Windows::Forms::MouseButtons::Left)
                statusButtons->Text = "Left";
            else
                statusButtons->Text = "Middle";
        }

        System::Void tsContainer1_ContentPanel_MouseMove(System::Object^ sender,
                                    System::Windows::Forms::MouseEventArgs^  e)
        {
            // x,y coords in second and third status bar panels
            statusXCoord->Text = String::Format("X={0}", e->X);
            statusYCoord->Text = String::Format("Y={0}", e->Y);
        }
    };
}
```

Figure 10-8 shows what StatusBar.exe looks like when you execute it.

Figure 10-8. *A three-panel status bar*

MenuStrip and ContextMenuStrip

There are two types of Windows Forms menus in the .NET Framework, the MenuStrip or the main menu that you find (almost always at the very top of the Windows Form) on most applications and the ContextMenuStrip or a menu that pops up within the context of some other control, for example, when you right-click an item in the Solution Explorer in Visual Studio 2005.

There is very little difference between either of these menus, especially while developing them. Simply drag either the MenuStrip or ContextMenuStrip to the Design view from the Toolbox window and then build the menu the exact same way. The only two differences are that they use different constructors, and you need to assign a ContextMenuStrip to a control's ContextMenuStrip property, while a MenuStrip is added to a RaftingContainer control.

Believe it or not, you have almost already learned everything you need to know about a MenuStrip or a ContextMenuStrip, as they are, like the StatusStrip, slightly enhanced ToolStrips. So slightly enhanced that I found no methods or properties worth mentioning.

Since the MenuStrip and the ContextMenuStrip are slightly augmented ToolStrips, anything you can do with a ToolStrip you can do with either the MenuStrip or the ContextMenuStrip. This means you can use all the same ToolStripItems, plus the ToolStripMenuItem. (You can use the ToolStripMenuItem control on the ToolStrip as well, but you rarely, if ever, see it there as it normally represents a menu item.)

By convention and in most cases because it only makes visual or logical sense, you use the following ToolStripItems on a MenuStrip or ContextMenuStrip:

- ToolStripMenuItem is a menu item.
- ToolStripComboBox is a combo box.
- ToolStripSeparator is a separator.
- ToolStripTextBox is a textbox.

Building a menu is very straightforward. Add ToolStripMenuItems to the MenuStrip or ContextMenuStrip. If you want a submenu for the current ToolStripMenuItem, then add ToolStripMenuItems to its DropDownItems collection property. If you want a different ToolStripItem type, then add that ToolStripItem type instead of the ToolStripMenuItem.

The ToolStripMenuItem is well suited for menu development as it includes probably every property or method you will need to add a menu item. Here is a list of the properties that you will most likely use:

- Checked is a Boolean that represents whether a check mark appears next to the menu item. The default is false, which means it won't display the check mark.

- CheckOnClick a Boolean that represents whether the ToolStripMenuItem should automatically appear checked/unchecked when clicked.

- CheckState is a CheckState enum indicating whether a ToolStripMenuItem is in the Checked, Unchecked, or Indeterminate state. The default is Unchecked.

- DropDownItems is a ToolStripItemCollection of submenu items for the current ToolStripMenuItem.

- Enabled is a Boolean that represents whether the menu item is enabled. The default is true, which means it can be accessed.

- Image is an Image object that represents the image to display for the menu item.

- ShortcutKeys is a Keys enum that represents the shortcut keystroke associated with the menu item. The default is Keys::None, which associates no shortcut.

- ShowShortcutKeys is a Boolean that represents whether the shortcut key is displayed. The default is true.

- Text is a String that represents the text to display for the menu item.

The ToolStripItem that first surprised me when I first saw it as a standard item for a menu was the ToolStripComboBox, but then once I thought about it, I came to realize it made sense. Real estate on a menu is pretty scarce, and the use of multiple mutually exclusive radio button menu items to select a single item can be quite a waste of space. With a ToolStripComboBox, you can select an appropriate mutually exclusive item from a large list and at the same time only use up one line on the menu. My conclusion was reinforced when I found out that there is a radio button check in the ToolStripMenuItem.

Listing 10-7 shows the creation of a MenuStrip with an assortment of ToolStripMenuItems with different properties set. It also includes a ToolStripComboBox to show how you can use it to retrieve a single value from a mutually exclusive list.

Listing 10-7. *Simple Assorted Menu*

```
namespace SimpleMenu
{
    using namespace System;
    using namespace System::ComponentModel;
    using namespace System::Collections;
    using namespace System::Windows::Forms;
    using namespace System::Data;
    using namespace System::Drawing;

    public ref class Form1 : public System::Windows::Forms::Form
    {
    public:
        Form1(void)
        {
            InitializeComponent();
        }
```

```cpp
    protected:
        ~Form1()
        {
            if (components)
            {
                delete components;
            }
        }

    private:
        System::Windows::Forms::ToolStripContainer^ toolStripContainer1;
        System::Windows::Forms::MenuStrip^ mainMenuStrip;
        System::Windows::Forms::ToolStripMenuItem^ miFile;
        System::Windows::Forms::ToolStripMenuItem^ miFileSub;
        System::Windows::Forms::ToolStripComboBox^ miFileSubThis;
        System::Windows::Forms::ToolStripMenuItem^ miFileExit;
        System::Windows::Forms::ToolStripMenuItem^ miFileSubCheck;
        System::Windows::Forms::ToolStripMenuItem^ miFileSubImage;
        System::Windows::Forms::ToolStripMenuItem^ miFileSubSayBoo;
        System::Windows::Forms::ToolStripMenuItem^ miHelp;
        System::Windows::Forms::ToolStripMenuItem^ miHelpAbout;
        System::Windows::Forms::ToolStripSeparator^ miFileSep1;
        System::ComponentModel::IContainer^ components;

#pragma region Windows Form Designer generated code
        void InitializeComponent(void)
        {
            System::ComponentModel::ComponentResourceManager^ resources =
        (gcnew System::ComponentModel::ComponentResourceManager(Form1::typeid));
            this->toolStripContainer1 =
                (gcnew System::Windows::Forms::ToolStripContainer());
            this->mainMenuStrip = (gcnew System::Windows::Forms::MenuStrip());
            this->miFile = (gcnew System::Windows::Forms::ToolStripMenuItem());
            this->miFileSub =
                (gcnew System::Windows::Forms::ToolStripMenuItem());
            this->miFileSubThis =
                (gcnew System::Windows::Forms::ToolStripComboBox());
            this->miFileSubCheck =
                (gcnew System::Windows::Forms::ToolStripMenuItem());
            this->miFileSubImage =
                (gcnew System::Windows::Forms::ToolStripMenuItem());
            this->miFileSubSayBoo =
                (gcnew System::Windows::Forms::ToolStripMenuItem());
            this->miFileSep1 =
                (gcnew System::Windows::Forms::ToolStripSeparator());
            this->miFileExit =
                (gcnew System::Windows::Forms::ToolStripMenuItem());
            this->miHelp =
                (gcnew System::Windows::Forms::ToolStripMenuItem());
            this->miHelpAbout =
                (gcnew System::Windows::Forms::ToolStripMenuItem());
            this->toolStripContainer1->TopToolStripPanel->SuspendLayout();
```

```
this->toolStripContainer1->SuspendLayout();
this->mainMenuStrip->SuspendLayout();
this->SuspendLayout();
//
// toolStripContainer1
//
// toolStripContainer1.ContentPanel
//
this->toolStripContainer1->ContentPanel->Size =
    System::Drawing::Size(292, 249);
this->toolStripContainer1->Dock =
    System::Windows::Forms::DockStyle::Fill;
this->toolStripContainer1->Location = System::Drawing::Point(0, 0);
this->toolStripContainer1->Name = L"toolStripContainer1";
this->toolStripContainer1->Size = System::Drawing::Size(292, 273);
this->toolStripContainer1->TabIndex = 0;
this->toolStripContainer1->Text = L"toolStripContainer1";
//
// toolStripContainer1.TopToolStripPanel
//
this->toolStripContainer1->TopToolStripPanel->Controls->Add(
    this->mainMenuStrip);
//
// mainMenuStrip
//
this->mainMenuStrip->Dock =System::Windows::Forms::DockStyle::None;
this->mainMenuStrip->Items->AddRange(
    gcnew cli::array< System::Windows::Forms::ToolStripItem^>(2)
    {this->miFile, this->miHelp});
this->mainMenuStrip->Location = System::Drawing::Point(0, 0);
this->mainMenuStrip->Name = L"mainMenuStrip";
this->mainMenuStrip->Size = System::Drawing::Size(292, 24);
this->mainMenuStrip->TabIndex = 0;
this->mainMenuStrip->Text = L"menuStrip1";
//
// miFile
//
this->miFile->DropDownItems->AddRange(
    gcnew cli::array< System::Windows::Forms::ToolStripItem^>(3)
    {this->miFileSub, this->miFileSep1, this->miFileExit});
this->miFile->Name = L"miFile";
this->miFile->Size = System::Drawing::Size(35, 20);
this->miFile->Text = L"&File";
//
// miFileSub
//
this->miFileSub->DropDownItems->AddRange(
    gcnew cli::array< System::Windows::Forms::ToolStripItem^>(4)
    {this->miFileSubThis, this->miFileSubCheck,
     this->miFileSubImage, this->miFileSubSayBoo});
this->miFileSub->Name = L"miFileSub";
this->miFileSub->Size = System::Drawing::Size(152, 22);
this->miFileSub->Text = L"&Sub";
//
```

```
// miFileSubThis
//
this->miFileSubThis->Items->AddRange(
    gcnew cli::array< System::Object^>(3)
    {L"This", L"That", L"Other Thing"});
this->miFileSubThis->Name = L"miFileSubThis";
this->miFileSubThis->Size = System::Drawing::Size(121, 21);
//
// miFileSubCheck
//
this->miFileSubCheck->Checked = true;
this->miFileSubCheck->CheckOnClick = true;
this->miFileSubCheck->CheckState =
    System::Windows::Forms::CheckState::Checked;
this->miFileSubCheck->Name = L"miFileSubCheck";
this->miFileSubCheck->Size = System::Drawing::Size(181, 22);
this->miFileSubCheck->Text = L"Check Me";
//
// miFileSubImage
//
this->miFileSubImage->Image =
    (cli::safe_cast<System::Drawing::Image^>
    (resources->GetObject(L"miFileSubImage.Image")));
this->miFileSubImage->Name = L"miFileSubImage";
this->miFileSubImage->Size = System::Drawing::Size(181, 22);
this->miFileSubImage->Text = L"I have an image";
//
// miFileSubSayBoo
//
this->miFileSubSayBoo->Name = L"miFileSubSayBoo";
this->miFileSubSayBoo->ShortcutKeys =
    static_cast<System::Windows::Forms::Keys>
    ((System::Windows::Forms::Keys::Control |
      System::Windows::Forms::Keys::S));
this->miFileSubSayBoo->Size = System::Drawing::Size(181, 22);
this->miFileSubSayBoo->Text = L"Say Boo";
this->miFileSubSayBoo->Click +=
    gcnew System::EventHandler(this,&Form1::miFileSubSayBoo_Click);
//
// miFileSep1
//
this->miFileSep1->Name = L"miFileSep1";
this->miFileSep1->Size = System::Drawing::Size(149, 6);
//
// miFileExit
//
this->miFileExit->Name = L"miFileExit";
this->miFileExit->Size = System::Drawing::Size(152, 22);
this->miFileExit->Text = L"E&xit";
this->miFileExit->Click +=
    gcnew System::EventHandler(this, &Form1::miFileExit_Click);
//
// miHelp
//
```

```cpp
            this->miHelp->DropDownItems->AddRange(
                gcnew cli::array< System::Windows::Forms::ToolStripItem^>(1)
                {this->miHelpAbout});
            this->miHelp->Name = L"miHelp";
            this->miHelp->Size = System::Drawing::Size(40, 20);
            this->miHelp->Text = L"&Help";
            //
            // miHelpAbout
            //
            this->miHelpAbout->Name = L"miHelpAbout";
            this->miHelpAbout->Size = System::Drawing::Size(152, 22);
            this->miHelpAbout->Text = L"About";
            this->miHelpAbout->Click +=
                gcnew System::EventHandler(this, &Form1::miHelpAbout_Click);
            //
            // Form1
            //
            this->AutoScaleDimensions = System::Drawing::SizeF(6, 13);
            this->AutoScaleMode = System::Windows::Forms::AutoScaleMode::Font;
            this->ClientSize = System::Drawing::Size(292, 273);
            this->Controls->Add(this->toolStripContainer1);
            this->MainMenuStrip = this->mainMenuStrip;
            this->Name = L"Form1";
            this->Text = L"Simple Menu";
            this->toolStripContainer1->TopToolStripPanel->ResumeLayout(false);
            this->toolStripContainer1->TopToolStripPanel->PerformLayout();
            this->toolStripContainer1->ResumeLayout(false);
            this->toolStripContainer1->PerformLayout();
            this->mainMenuStrip->ResumeLayout(false);
            this->mainMenuStrip->PerformLayout();
            this->ResumeLayout(false);
        }
#pragma endregion

    private:
        System::Void miFileExit_Click(System::Object^ sender,
                                      System::EventArgs^ e)
        {
            Application::Exit();
        }

        System::Void miHelpAbout_Click(System::Object^ sender,
                                       System::EventArgs^ e)
        {
            MessageBox::Show("Simple Menu v.1.0.0.0");
        }

        System::Void miFileSubSayBoo_Click(System::Object^ sender,
                                           System::EventArgs^ e)
        {
            MessageBox::Show("BOO");
        }
    };
}
```

Figure 10-9 shows what SimpleMenu.exe looks like when you execute it.

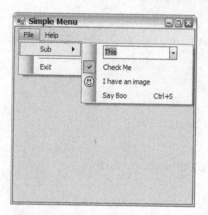

Figure 10-9. *A simple menu*

Bells and Whistles Controls

You'll finish off looking at Win Form controls by exploring some fun controls that you may not use that often, but that can occasionally come in handy.

PictureBox

The PictureBox is a handy little control for displaying an existing image file. What makes it really cool is that it has built-in support for bitmaps, metafiles, and icons, and .jpg, .gif, and .png files. You implement all of them the same way:

1. Drag and drop the PictureBox to your Win Form.

2. Update the Image property in the PictureBox's Properties view with the location of your file using the provided Open dialog box.

Like all controls, PictureBox provides properties to manipulate itself. In most cases you will only have to worry about the following:

*   BorderStyle is a BorderStyle enum that represents the border to surround your image. Three borders are available: Fixed3D, FixedSingle, and the default None.

*   Image is an Image object that represents the image to be displayed. The Image object supports bitmaps, metafiles, and icons, and .jpg, .gif, and .png files.

*   Size is a Size object that represents the height and width of the control. If the SizeMode is set to StretchImage, then the images inside will stretch or shrink to fit this size.

*   SizeMode is a PictureBoxSizeMode that represents how the image will be displayed. The four modes are AutoSize, which forces the control to be the same size as the image; CenterImage, which centers the image within the control (the image will be clipped if the control is too small); the default Normal, which aligns the picture with the upper-left corner; and StretchImage, which makes the image the same size as the control.

The code in Listing 10-8 shows a picture of my daughter in a StretchImage mode PictureBox.

Listing 10-8. *PictureBox of Shaina*

```
namespace PictureBoxEx
{
    using namespace System;
    using namespace System::ComponentModel;
    using namespace System::Collections;
    using namespace System::Windows::Forms;
    using namespace System::Data;
    using namespace System::Drawing;

    public ref class Form1 : public System::Windows::Forms::Form
    {
    public:
        Form1(void)
        {
            InitializeComponent();
        }

    protected:
        ~Form1()
        {
            if (components)
            {
                delete components;
            }
        }
    private:
        System::Windows::Forms::PictureBox^  pictureBox1;
        System::ComponentModel::Container ^components;

#pragma region Windows Form Designer generated code

        void InitializeComponent(void)
        {
            System::ComponentModel::ComponentResourceManager^ resources =
        (gcnew System::ComponentModel::ComponentResourceManager(Form1::typeid));
            this->pictureBox1 = (gcnew System::Windows::Forms::PictureBox());
            (cli::safe_cast<System::ComponentModel::ISupportInitialize^>
                (this->pictureBox1))->BeginInit();
            this->SuspendLayout();
            //
            // pictureBox1
            //
            this->pictureBox1->Anchor =
                static_cast<System::Windows::Forms::AnchorStyles>
                ((((System::Windows::Forms::AnchorStyles::Top
                | System::Windows::Forms::AnchorStyles::Bottom)
                | System::Windows::Forms::AnchorStyles::Left)
                | System::Windows::Forms::AnchorStyles::Right));
            this->pictureBox1->Image = (cli::safe_cast<System::Drawing::Image^>
                (resources->GetObject(L"pictureBox1.Image")));
            this->pictureBox1->Location = System::Drawing::Point(12, 12);
            this->pictureBox1->Name = L"pictureBox1";
```

```
        this->pictureBox1->Size = System::Drawing::Size(369, 287);
        this->pictureBox1->SizeMode =
            System::Windows::Forms::PictureBoxSizeMode::StretchImage;
        this->pictureBox1->TabIndex = 0;
        this->pictureBox1->TabStop = false;
        //
        // Form1
        //
        this->AutoScaleDimensions = System::Drawing::SizeF(6, 13);
        this->AutoScaleMode = System::Windows::Forms::AutoScaleMode::Font;
        this->ClientSize = System::Drawing::Size(393, 311);
        this->Controls->Add(this->pictureBox1);
        this->Name = L"Form1";
        this->Text = L"Shaina Shoshana";
        (cli::safe_cast<System::ComponentModel::ISupportInitialize^>
            (this->pictureBox1))->EndInit();
        this->ResumeLayout(false);
    }
#pragma endregion
    };
}
```

You might want to note in the preceding code that Visual Studio 2005 creates a resource of the PictureBox's image and places it within the assembly in a similar fashion to the ImageList, instead of referencing the file. If you don't want the image placed in the assembly for some reason, then you'll have to code the updating of the Image property manually with code similar to this:

```
this->pictureBox->Image = new Drawing::Bitmap(S"ShainaOk.jpg");
```

Figure 10-10 shows what PictureBoxEx.exe looks like when you execute it.

Figure 10-10. *A PictureBox of Shaina*

MonthCalendar

The MonthCalendar is a neat little control that provides the ability to display a month to the user and then allow the user to do things such as navigate from month to month and select a year, month, day, or range of days. Another feature of the MonthCalendar control is it allows the user to highlight specific dates on the control, either on an annual, monthly, or specific single-day basis.

Like all controls, you configure MonthCalendar using properties. Here are some of the most commonly used properties:

- AnnuallyBoldedDates is an array of DateTime objects that represents which dates to bold every year.

- BoldedDates is an array of DateTime objects that represents which specific dates to bold.

- CalendarDimensions is a System::Drawing::Size that represents the number of rows and columns of months to be displayed within the control. The maximum number of months that can be displayed is 12.

- MaxDate is a DateTime that represents the maximum date that can be shown in the control. The default is 12/31/9998.

- MaxSelectionCount is an Int32 that represents the maximum number of dates that can be selected at one time. The default is 7.

- MinDate is a DateTime that represents the minimum date that can be shown in the control. The default is 01/01/1753.

- MonthlyBoldedDates is an array of DateTime objects that represents which dates to bold every month.

- SelectionEnd is a DateTime that represents the end date of the selected date range. The default is SelectionEnd (equaling SelectionStart).

- SelectionRange is a SelectionRange object that represents the selected range of dates within the control.

- SelectionStart is a DateTime that represents the start date of the selected date range.

- ShowToday is a Boolean that represents whether the date specified in the TodayDate property is shown at the bottom of the control.

- ShowTodayCircle is a Boolean that represents whether the date specified in the TodayDate property is circled.

- ShowWeekNumbers is a Boolean that represents whether the week number is displayed for each week.

- TodayDate is a DateTime representing any date that you want to be set as today's date. The default is the current system date.

- TodayDateSet is a Boolean that represents whether the TodayDate property was explicitly set.

Something you might want to note about the MonthCalendar control is that you can't select dates at random intervals. You can only select individual days or a range of days sequentially.

Listing 10-9 presents the MonthCalendar in action. The code simply shows a two-by-two MonthCalendar control that generates DateChanged events when clicked. It also has two additional labels to display the selected day or ranges of days.

Listing 10-9. *The MonthCalendar Control*

```
namespace MonthCalendarEx
{
    using namespace System;
    using namespace System::ComponentModel;
    using namespace System::Collections;
    using namespace System::Windows::Forms;
    using namespace System::Data;
    using namespace System::Drawing;

    public ref class Form1 : public System::Windows::Forms::Form
    {
    public:
        Form1(void)
        {
            InitializeComponent();
        }

    protected:
        ~Form1()
        {
            if (components)
            {
                delete components;
            }
        }
    private:
        System::Windows::Forms::Label^  End;
        System::Windows::Forms::Label^  Start;
        System::Windows::Forms::MonthCalendar^  monthCal;
        System::ComponentModel::Container ^components;

#pragma region Windows Form Designer generated code
        void InitializeComponent(void)
        {
            this->End = (gcnew System::Windows::Forms::Label());
            this->Start = (gcnew System::Windows::Forms::Label());
            this->monthCal = (gcnew System::Windows::Forms::MonthCalendar());
            this->SuspendLayout();
            //
            // End
            //
            this->End->BorderStyle =
                System::Windows::Forms::BorderStyle::FixedSingle;
            this->End->Location = System::Drawing::Point(230, 323);
            this->End->Name = L"End";
            this->End->Size = System::Drawing::Size(83, 20);
            this->End->TabIndex = 5;
            //
            // Start
            //
            this->Start->BorderStyle =
                System::Windows::Forms::BorderStyle::FixedSingle;
```

```cpp
            this->Start->Location = System::Drawing::Point(122, 323);
            this->Start->Name = L"Start";
            this->Start->Size = System::Drawing::Size(83, 20);
            this->Start->TabIndex = 4;
            //
            // monthCal
            //
            this->monthCal->AnnuallyBoldedDates =
                gcnew cli::array< System::DateTime >(1)
                {System::DateTime(2004, 12, 31, 0, 0, 0, 0)};
            this->monthCal->CalendarDimensions = System::Drawing::Size(2, 2);
            this->monthCal->Location = System::Drawing::Point(13, 11);
            this->monthCal->MaxSelectionCount = 365;
            this->monthCal->MonthlyBoldedDates =
                gcnew cli::array< System::DateTime >(2)
                {System::DateTime(2004, 10, 1, 0, 0, 0, 0),
                 System::DateTime(2004, 10, 15, 0, 0, 0, 0)};
            this->monthCal->Name = L"monthCal";
            this->monthCal->ShowWeekNumbers = true;
            this->monthCal->Size = System::Drawing::Size(410, 297);
            this->monthCal->TabIndex = 3;
            this->monthCal->DateChanged +=
                gcnew System::Windows::Forms::DateRangeEventHandler(this,
                                                &Form1::monthCal_DateChanged);

            //
            // Form1
            //
            this->AutoScaleDimensions = System::Drawing::SizeF(6, 13);
            this->AutoScaleMode = System::Windows::Forms::AutoScaleMode::Font;
            this->ClientSize = System::Drawing::Size(436, 355);
            this->Controls->Add(this->End);
            this->Controls->Add(this->Start);
            this->Controls->Add(this->monthCal);
            this->Name = L"Form1";
            this->Text = L"Month Calendar";
            this->ResumeLayout(false);

        }
#pragma endregion
    private:
        System::Void monthCal_DateChanged(System::Object^ sender,
                            System::Windows::Forms::DateRangeEventArgs^ e)
        {
            // Update start and end range labels when date changes
            Start->Text = e->Start.Date.ToShortDateString();
            End->Text   = e->End.Date.ToShortDateString();
        }
    };
}
```

The only thing unusual about the preceding code is that you need to remember that System::DateTime is a value type structure, and thus you don't create it on the stack with the gcnew statement. Also, when you use System::DateTime in a statement, you use the operator . and not ->.

Figure 10-11 shows what MonthCalendarEx.exe looks like when you execute it.

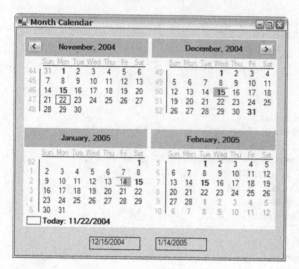

Figure 10-11. *The MonthCalendar control*

ErrorProvider

The ErrorProvider control is a nice piece of eye candy, especially when it comes to form validation, as you can use it to provide visual attention to data entry errors on the form. It has the additional bonus of being able to tell the user the reason for the data entry error. It provides this functionality by placing an icon next to the control in error and then providing a ToolTip-like pop-up displaying the reason for the error when the mouse pauses over the icon. Actually, it displays any text that you provide to it. In theory, this text should be the reason for the error.

Another interesting feature of the ErrorProvider control is that you need only one for your entire form. Yet, at the same time, it provides a specific error message for each control in error.

To implement the ErrorProvider control, drag and drop it to your Design view from the Toolbox view. Then, when an error occurs in your validation process, place an error message along with a pointer to the control in error into the ErrorProvider.

To customize the look and feel of the ErrorProvider control, a few members are provided. These are the properties that you will most likely change:

- BlinkRate is an Int32 that represents the flash rate of the icon in milliseconds. The default is 250 milliseconds.

- BlinkStyle is an ErrorBlinkStyle enum that represents the style that the icon blinks. The possible values are AlwaysBlink, NeverBlink, and the default BlinkIfDifferentError.

- Icon is an Icon object that represents the icon to be displayed on error. The default is a red circle with a white exclamation point inside.

- SetError() is a method that sets the error for a specified control to display when the mouse pauses over the icon. When the message is an empty string, no icon or error is displayed.

- SetIconAlignment() is a method that sets the icon's location relative to a specified control. The default is MiddleRight.

- SetIconIconPadding() is a method that specifies the number of pixels of padding to add between an icon and a specified control. Because many controls have white space surrounding them, this control is not used too often.

Listing 10-10 shows the ErrorProvider control in action. The code is the start of a login form that validates that a name and password have been entered. When either of these fields is blank, the ErrorProvider control is added after the control on the form. Just for grins and giggles, I show how to place the icon on the left side of the control when validating on the Button control.

Listing 10-10. *The ErrorProvider Control*

```
namespace ErrorProviderEx
{
    using namespace System;
    using namespace System::ComponentModel;
    using namespace System::Collections;
    using namespace System::Windows::Forms;
    using namespace System::Data;
    using namespace System::Drawing;

    public ref class Form1 : public System::Windows::Forms::Form
    {
    public:
        Form1(void)
        {
            InitializeComponent();
        }

    protected:
        ~Form1()
        {
            if (components)
            {
                delete components;
            }
        }

    private:
        System::Windows::Forms::TextBox^  tbPword;
        System::Windows::Forms::Label^  lbPword;
        System::Windows::Forms::Button^   bnLogin;
        System::Windows::Forms::TextBox^  tbName;
        System::Windows::Forms::Label^  lbName;
        System::Windows::Forms::ErrorProvider^  eProvider;
        System::ComponentModel::IContainer^  components;

#pragma region Windows Form Designer generated code
        void InitializeComponent(void)
        {
            this->components = (gcnew System::ComponentModel::Container());
            this->tbPword = (gcnew System::Windows::Forms::TextBox());
            this->lbPword = (gcnew System::Windows::Forms::Label());
            this->bnLogin = (gcnew System::Windows::Forms::Button());
            this->tbName = (gcnew System::Windows::Forms::TextBox());
            this->lbName = (gcnew System::Windows::Forms::Label());
            this->eProvider =
                (gcnew System::Windows::Forms::ErrorProvider(this->components));
```

```
(cli::safe_cast<System::ComponentModel::ISupportInitialize^>
    (this->eProvider))->BeginInit();
this->SuspendLayout();
//
// tbPword
//
this->tbPword->Location = System::Drawing::Point(103, 83);
this->tbPword->Name = L"tbPword";
this->tbPword->PasswordChar = '*';
this->tbPword->Size = System::Drawing::Size(100, 20);
this->tbPword->TabIndex = 9;
this->tbPword->Validating +=
    gcnew System::ComponentModel::CancelEventHandler(this,
                                    &Form1::textbox_Validating);
//
// lbPword
//
this->lbPword->AutoSize = true;
this->lbPword->Location = System::Drawing::Point(34, 83);
this->lbPword->Name = L"lbPword";
this->lbPword->Size = System::Drawing::Size(53, 13);
this->lbPword->TabIndex = 8;
this->lbPword->Text = L"&Password";
//
// bnLogin
//
this->bnLogin->Location = System::Drawing::Point(75, 131);
this->bnLogin->Name = L"bnLogin";
this->bnLogin->Size = System::Drawing::Size(75, 23);
this->bnLogin->TabIndex = 7;
this->bnLogin->Text = L"&Login";
this->bnLogin->Click +=
    gcnew System::EventHandler(this, &Form1::login_Click);
//
// tbName
//
this->tbName->Location = System::Drawing::Point(103, 31);
this->tbName->Name = L"tbName";
this->tbName->Size = System::Drawing::Size(100, 20);
this->tbName->TabIndex = 6;
this->tbName->Validating +=
    gcnew System::ComponentModel::CancelEventHandler(this,
                                    &Form1::textbox_Validating);
//
// lbName
//
this->lbName->AutoSize = true;
this->lbName->Location = System::Drawing::Point(34, 31);
this->lbName->Name = L"lbName";
this->lbName->Size = System::Drawing::Size(35, 13);
this->lbName->TabIndex = 5;
this->lbName->Text = L"&Name";
```

```
            //
            // eProvider
            //
            this->eProvider->ContainerControl = this;
            //
            // Form1
            //
            this->AutoScaleDimensions = System::Drawing::SizeF(6, 13);
            this->AutoScaleMode = System::Windows::Forms::AutoScaleMode::Font;
            this->ClientSize = System::Drawing::Size(237, 185);
            this->Controls->Add(this->tbPword);
            this->Controls->Add(this->lbPword);
            this->Controls->Add(this->bnLogin);
            this->Controls->Add(this->tbName);
            this->Controls->Add(this->lbName);
            this->Name = L"Form1";
            this->Text = L"System Login";
            (cli::safe_cast<System::ComponentModel::ISupportInitialize^>
                (this->eProvider))->EndInit();
            this->ResumeLayout(false);
            this->PerformLayout();

        }
#pragma endregion

    private:
        System::Void textbox_Validating(System::Object^ sender,
                                   System::ComponentModel::CancelEventArgs^ e)
        {
            try
            {
                TextBox ^tb = (TextBox^)(sender);

                if (tb->Text->Equals(""))
                    eProvider->SetError(tb, "**Error** Missing Entry!");
                else
                    eProvider->SetError(tb, "");
            }
            catch (Exception^)
            {
                // Not TextBox
            }
        }

        System::Void login_Click(System::Object^ sender, System::EventArgs^ e)
        {
            if (tbName->Text->Equals(""))
                eProvider->SetError(tbName, "**Error** Missing Entry!");
            else
                eProvider->SetError(tbName, "");
```

```
            if (tbPword->Text->Equals(""))
            {
                // Place the icon left side of control
                eProvider->SetIconAlignment(tbPword,
                                            ErrorIconAlignment::MiddleLeft);
                eProvider->SetError(tbPword, "**Error** Missing Entry!");
            }
            else
                eProvider->SetError(tbPword, "");
        }
    };
}
```

Figure 10-12 shows what ErrorProviderEx.exe looks like when you execute it.

Figure 10-12. *The ErrorProvider control*

NotifyIcon

If you've tried to add an icon to the notification area in your past life, you know that it wasn't a simple task. Well, with the .NET Framework, it is. All it takes is a drag and drop of the NotifyIcon control from the Toolbox view to the Design view.

The NotifyIcon control also provides four properties that you'll probably change:

- Icon is an Icon object that represents the icon to display on the notification area. The default is null, which causes no icon to be displayed. (Why someone would do this, I'm not sure.)

- Text is a String that represents the ToolTip text to be displayed when the mouse pauses over the icon in the notification area. The default is null, which causes no text to be displayed.

- ContextMenu is a ContentMenu object that represents a pop-up menu displayed when the icon is right-clicked. The default is null, which causes no menu to be displayed. (I cover ContentMenus earlier in this chapter.)

- Visible is a Boolean that represents whether the icon is displayed in the notification area. The default is true, which displays the icon.

Listing 10-11 shows the NotifyIcon control in action. To give the example some life, I added two buttons. The first toggles the icon in the notification area, and the second toggles the program display in the taskbar. When you write your own program, you may want to display either in the notification area or in the taskbar, but not in both. I also added a context menu so that you can exit the application if you happen to minimize the application while the taskbar icon is turned off.

Listing 10-11. *The NotifyIcon Control*

```
namespace NotifyIconEx
{
    using namespace System;
    using namespace System::ComponentModel;
    using namespace System::Collections;
    using namespace System::Windows::Forms;
    using namespace System::Data;
    using namespace System::Drawing;

    public ref class Form1 : public System::Windows::Forms::Form
    {
    public:
        Form1(void)
        {
            InitializeComponent();
        }

    protected:
        ~Form1()
        {
            if (components)
            {
                delete components;
            }
        }

    private:
        System::Windows::Forms::Button^  bnTaskBar;
        System::Windows::Forms::Button^  bnNotify;
        System::Windows::Forms::NotifyIcon^  notifyIcon;
        System::Windows::Forms::ContextMenuStrip^  menuExit;
        System::Windows::Forms::ToolStripMenuItem^  miExit;
        System::ComponentModel::IContainer^  components;

#pragma region Windows Form Designer generated code

        void InitializeComponent(void)
        {
            this->components = (gcnew System::ComponentModel::Container());
            System::ComponentModel::ComponentResourceManager^ resources =
        (gcnew System::ComponentModel::ComponentResourceManager(Form1::typeid));
            this->bnTaskBar = (gcnew System::Windows::Forms::Button());
            this->bnNotify = (gcnew System::Windows::Forms::Button());
            this->notifyIcon =
                (gcnew System::Windows::Forms::NotifyIcon(this->components));
            this->menuExit =
            (gcnew System::Windows::Forms::ContextMenuStrip(this->components));
            this->miExit = (gcnew System::Windows::Forms::ToolStripMenuItem());
            this->menuExit->SuspendLayout();
            this->SuspendLayout();
```

```
//
// bnTaskBar
//
this->bnTaskBar->Location = System::Drawing::Point(28, 59);
this->bnTaskBar->Name = L"bnTaskBar";
this->bnTaskBar->Size = System::Drawing::Size(131, 23);
this->bnTaskBar->TabIndex = 3;
this->bnTaskBar->Text = L"Toggle TaskBar Icon";
this->bnTaskBar->Click +=
    gcnew System::EventHandler(this, &Form1::bnTaskBar_Click);
//
// bnNotify
//
this->bnNotify->Location = System::Drawing::Point(28, 12);
this->bnNotify->Name = L"bnNotify";
this->bnNotify->Size = System::Drawing::Size(131, 23);
this->bnNotify->TabIndex = 2;
this->bnNotify->Text = L"Toggle Notify Icon";
this->bnNotify->Click +=
    gcnew System::EventHandler(this, &Form1::bnNotify_Click);
//
// notifyIcon
//
this->notifyIcon->ContextMenuStrip = this->menuExit;
this->notifyIcon->Icon = (cli::safe_cast<System::Drawing::Icon^>
    (resources->GetObject(L"notifyIcon.Icon"))));
this->notifyIcon->Text = L"Notify Icon Example";
this->notifyIcon->Visible = true;
//
// menuExit
//
this->menuExit->Items->AddRange(
    gcnew cli::array< System::Windows::Forms::ToolStripItem^>(1)
    {this->miExit});
this->menuExit->Name = L"miExit";
this->menuExit->RightToLeft =
    System::Windows::Forms::RightToLeft::No;
this->menuExit->Size = System::Drawing::Size(153, 48);
//
// miExit
//
this->miExit->Name = L"miExit";
this->miExit->Size = System::Drawing::Size(152, 22);
this->miExit->Text = L"E&xit";
this->miExit->Click +=
    gcnew System::EventHandler(this, &Form1::miExit_Click);
//
// Form1
//
```

```cpp
            this->AutoScaleDimensions = System::Drawing::SizeF(6, 13);
            this->AutoScaleMode = System::Windows::Forms::AutoScaleMode::Font;
            this->ClientSize = System::Drawing::Size(192, 106);
            this->Controls->Add(this->bnTaskBar);
            this->Controls->Add(this->bnNotify);
            this->Icon = (cli::safe_cast<System::Drawing::Icon^>
                (resources->GetObject(L"$this.Icon")));
            this->Name = L"Form1";
            this->Text = L"Notify Icon";
            this->menuExit->ResumeLayout(false);
            this->ResumeLayout(false);

        }
#pragma endregion

    private:
        System::Void bnNotify_Click(System::Object^ sender,
                                    System::EventArgs^ e)
        {
            notifyIcon->Visible = !notifyIcon->Visible;
        }

        System::Void bnTaskBar_Click(System::Object^ sender,
                                     System::EventArgs^ e)
        {
            this->ShowInTaskbar = ! this->ShowInTaskbar;
        }

        System::Void miExit_Click(System::Object^ sender,
                                  System::EventArgs^  e)
        {
            Application::Exit();
        }
    };
}
```

There really isn't much to the preceding code, and building it is a snap (or a few drags and drops, to be more accurate). You simply drag the NotifyIcon and two buttons to the form and change a few properties. Then you add the events to toggle the icon and taskbar entry.

Coding the context menu is only slightly more complex, but I covered that earlier.

You change the program's icon and the NotifyIcon's icon in the exact same way. Just double-click the app.ico in the Resource folder of Solution Explorer. This brings up a paint editor on which you can draw your icon.

Tip Within an icon file are multiple icons of different sizes. Remember to change all the different sizes or you will get mismatching icons when the system uses icons of different sizes. (To switch to an icon of a different size, right-click in the graphic Design view, outside of your icon drawing area, and select the Current Icon Image Types menu item. Then select the submenu item for the icon size you want to edit.)

Figure 10-13 shows what NotifyIconEx.exe looks like when you execute it.

Figure 10-13. *The NotifyIcon control*

Dialog Boxes

First things first: Dialog boxes are just Forms that are called or started differently and can, if you want, pass and/or return data and return a DialogResult. That's it! Forget what you once knew about dialog boxes (if you were a classic Visual C++ MFC programmer)—things have gotten a lot easier.

Everything that you've learned so far in this chapter works the same for dialog boxes. All you need to do is learn a couple of optional features and how to call the dialog box itself, and then you'll know all you need to develop dialog boxes.

Custom Dialog Boxes

Building a custom dialog box is almost exactly the same as creating the main Win Form, except it requires two additional steps. Here are the steps you follow to create a custom dialog box:

1. Right-click the project folder within Solution Explorer.
2. Select Add New Item from the drop-down menu item Add. A dialog box similar to the one in Figure 10-14 appears.

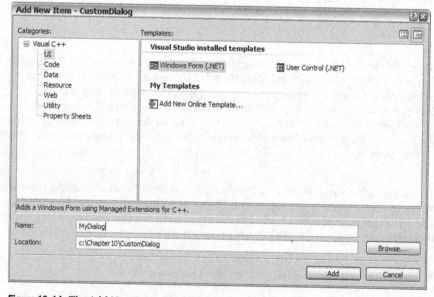

Figure 10-14. *The Add New Item dialog box*

3. Select the Windows Form (.NET) icon from the Templates panel and give the dialog box a name. I used **MyDialog**.

4. Click Open. This will provide you with an empty form in the Design view.

5. Build the form exactly as you do the main form.

You can now work with this form in exactly the same way as you do with the application's main form, except for a couple of minor things.

The first minor difference is that if you want to pass information to the dialog box or get information back from the dialog box, you need to add properties to your form to get and set the information:

```
public:
    property String^ PassedValue1;  // Trival

// or

    Property String^ PassedValue2
    {
        void set(String^ value)
        {
            tbPassedValue->Text = value;
        }
        String^ get()
        {
            return tbPassedValue->Text;
        }
    }
```

Another method of doing this would be to change the constructor to send data to the dialog box, but I prefer properties. Plus, if you use the constructor to pass data to the dialog box, you still need to create properties or methods to send data back, so why not bite the bullet and use properties in both cases? This method is clean and safe (because you can verify the validity of the passed data) and it's easy to use.

The second change that you can make, which is totally optional, is to change the style of the dialog box to look more like a dialog box and less like a form:

```
this->FormBorderStyle =
    System::Windows::Forms::FormBorderStyle::FixedToolWindow;
// Or
this->FormBorderStyle =
    System::Windows::Forms::FormBorderStyle::SizableToolWindow;
```

The third difference is that you want to have any buttons that close your dialog box return a DialogResult. The .NET Framework class library provides a number of possible DialogResults (see Table 10-2).

Table 10-2. *DialogResults*

Type	Description
Abort	Returns the value Abort. Usually you will have a button labeled Abort to handle this.
Cancel	Returns the value Cancel. This is the value returned when the Esc key is pressed (if enabled) or the close dialog box button is clicked. Also, you will have a button on the form labeled Cancel.

Table 10-2. *DialogResults (Continued)*

Type	Description
Ignore	Returns the value Ignore. Usually you will have a button labeled Ignore to handle this.
No	Returns the value No. Usually you will have a button labeled No to handle this.
None	Returns nothing. You will use this with a modal dialog box, which is discussed later in this section.
OK	Returns the value OK. This is the value returned when the Enter key is pressed (if enabled). Also, you will have a button on the form labeled OK.
Retry	Returns the value Retry. Usually you will have a button labeled Retry to handle this.
Yes	Returns the value Yes. Usually you will have a button labeled Yes to handle this.

To return a DialogResult value to the calling form, you need to assign to the button that will end the dialog the desired DialogResult value:

```
bnOK->DialogResult = DialogResult::OK;
```

When the button is clicked, it will automatically return the DialogResult it was set to (DialogResult::OK is set in the preceding code). By the way, you can still handle the Click event, if you need to, for the button. (You can even change its DialogResult in the handler if you really want to. For example, you could turn DialogResult::OK into DialogResult::Cancel if no text is entered in the dialog box.)

The final change you are probably going to want to make is to assign default buttons to respond to the Accept and Cancel conditions. You do this by assigning a button to the form's AcceptButton and CancelButton properties:

```
AcceptButton = bnOK;
CancelButton = bnCancel;
```

Once you have performed the preceding additional steps, you have a complete custom dialog box. Listing 10-12 shows the code of a custom dialog box that takes in some text, places it in a text box, allows it to be updated, and then returns the updated text to the calling form. The dialog box also allows the user to abort or cancel the dialog box.

Listing 10-12. *The MyDialog.h File*

```
using namespace System;
using namespace System::ComponentModel;
using namespace System::Collections;
using namespace System::Windows::Forms;
using namespace System::Data;
using namespace System::Drawing;
```

```
namespace CustomDialog
{
    public ref class MyDialog : public System::Windows::Forms::Form
    {
    public:
        MyDialog(void)
        {
            InitializeComponent();
        }

    protected:
        ~MyDialog()
        {
            if (components)
            {
                delete components;
            }
        }

    public:
        property String^ PassedValue   // PassedValue property
        {
            void set(String ^value)
            {
                tbPassedValue->Text = value;
            }
            String ^get()
            {
            return tbPassedValue->Text;
            }
        }

    private:
        System::Windows::Forms::Button^  bnCancel;
        System::Windows::Forms::Button^  bnAbort;
        System::Windows::Forms::Button^  bnOK;
        System::Windows::Forms::TextBox^  tbPassedValue;
        System::ComponentModel::Container ^components;

#pragma region Windows Form Designer generated code

        void InitializeComponent(void)
        {
            this->bnCancel = (gcnew System::Windows::Forms::Button());
            this->bnAbort = (gcnew System::Windows::Forms::Button());
            this->bnOK = (gcnew System::Windows::Forms::Button());
            this->tbPassedValue = (gcnew System::Windows::Forms::TextBox());
            this->SuspendLayout();
```

```
            //
            // bnCancel
            //
            this->bnCancel->DialogResult =
                System::Windows::Forms::DialogResult::Cancel;
            this->bnCancel->Location = System::Drawing::Point(205, 60);
            this->bnCancel->Name = L"bnCancel";
            this->bnCancel->Size = System::Drawing::Size(75, 23);
            this->bnCancel->TabIndex = 7;
            this->bnCancel->Text = L"Cancel";
            //
            // bnAbort
            //
            this->bnAbort->DialogResult =
                System::Windows::Forms::DialogResult::Abort;
            this->bnAbort->Location = System::Drawing::Point(110, 60);
            this->bnAbort->Name = L"bnAbort";
            this->bnAbort->Size = System::Drawing::Size(75, 23);
            this->bnAbort->TabIndex = 6;
            this->bnAbort->Text = L"Abort";
            //
            // bnOK
            //
            this->bnOK->DialogResult = System::Windows::Forms::DialogResult::OK;
            this->bnOK->Location = System::Drawing::Point(13, 60);
            this->bnOK->Name = L"bnOK";
            this->bnOK->Size = System::Drawing::Size(75, 23);
            this->bnOK->TabIndex = 5;
            this->bnOK->Text = L"OK";
            //
            // tbPassedValue
            //
            this->tbPassedValue->Location = System::Drawing::Point(13, 20);
            this->tbPassedValue->Name = L"tbPassedValue";
            this->tbPassedValue->Size = System::Drawing::Size(267, 20);
            this->tbPassedValue->TabIndex = 4;
            //
            // myDialog
            //
            this->AutoScaleDimensions = System::Drawing::SizeF(6, 13);
            this->AutoScaleMode = System::Windows::Forms::AutoScaleMode::Font;
            this->ClientSize = System::Drawing::Size(292, 102);
            this->Controls->Add(this->bnCancel);
            this->Controls->Add(this->bnAbort);
            this->Controls->Add(this->bnOK);
            this->Controls->Add(this->tbPassedValue);
            this->Name = L"myDialog";
            this->Text = L"My Custom Dialog";
            this->ResumeLayout(false);
            this->PerformLayout();
        }
#pragma endregion
    };
}
```

Figure 10-15 shows what the preceding example looks like when you execute it.

Figure 10-15. *A custom dialog box*

Now let's take a look at the code to implement a custom dialog box (see Listing 10-13). The example calls the dialog box by clicking anywhere in the form.

Listing 10-13. *Implementing a Custom Dialog Box*

```
#include "MyDialog.h"

namespace CustomDialog
{
    using namespace System;
    using namespace System::ComponentModel;
    using namespace System::Collections;
    using namespace System::Windows::Forms;
    using namespace System::Data;
    using namespace System::Drawing;

    public ref class Form1 : public System::Windows::Forms::Form
    {
    public:
        Form1(void)
        {
            InitializeComponent();
        }

    protected:
        ~Form1()
        {
            if (components)
            {
                delete components;
            }
        }

    private:
        System::Windows::Forms::Label^  lbRetString;
        System::Windows::Forms::Label^  lbRetVal;
        System::ComponentModel::Container ^components;
```

```cpp
#pragma region Windows Form Designer generated code

        void InitializeComponent(void)
        {
            this->lbRetString = (gcnew System::Windows::Forms::Label());
            this->lbRetVal = (gcnew System::Windows::Forms::Label());
            this->SuspendLayout();
            //
            // lbRetString
            //
            this->lbRetString->Location = System::Drawing::Point(34, 119);
            this->lbRetString->Name = L"lbRetString";
            this->lbRetString->Size = System::Drawing::Size(225, 19);
            this->lbRetString->TabIndex = 3;
            //
            // lbRetVal
            //
            this->lbRetVal->Location = System::Drawing::Point(34, 77);
            this->lbRetVal->Name = L"lbRetVal";
            this->lbRetVal->Size = System::Drawing::Size(225, 19);
            this->lbRetVal->TabIndex = 2;
            //
            // Form1
            //
            this->AutoScaleDimensions = System::Drawing::SizeF(6, 13);
            this->AutoScaleMode = System::Windows::Forms::AutoScaleMode::Font;
            this->ClientSize = System::Drawing::Size(292, 273);
            this->Controls->Add(this->lbRetString);
            this->Controls->Add(this->lbRetVal);
            this->Name = L"Form1";
            this->Text = L"Click Form to get dialog";
            this->Click +=
                gcnew System::EventHandler(this, &Form1::Form1_Click);
            this->ResumeLayout(false);
        }

#pragma endregion

    private:
        System::Void Form1_Click(System::Object^ sender, System::EventArgs^ e)
        {
            MyDialog ^mydialog = gcnew MyDialog();
            mydialog->PassedValue = "This has been passed from Form1";

            if (mydialog->ShowDialog() ==
                System::Windows::Forms::DialogResult::OK)
                lbRetVal->Text = "OK";
            else if (mydialog->DialogResult ==
                System::Windows::Forms::DialogResult::Abort)
                lbRetVal->Text = "Abort";
            else
                lbRetVal->Text = "Cancel";
```

```
            lbRetString->Text = mydialog->PassedValue;
        }
    };
}
```

Figure 10-16 shows what the preceding example looks like when you execute it.

Figure 10-16. *Calling a custom dialog box*

Not much of a change, is there? First, you include the include file for the definition of the MyDialog class using the standard include statement:

```
#include "MyDialog.h"
```

You need to do this because C++/CLI requires (like standard C++) that classes be defined before you use them. Next, you create an instance of the dialog box:

```
MyDialog ^mydialog = gcnew MyDialog();
```

Optionally, you can pass all the data you want to the dialog box:

```
mydialog->PassedValue = "This has been passed from Form1";
```

Then you call the dialog box in one of two ways:

- ShowDialog()
- Show()

The first mode, ShowDialog(), is modal. In this mode, you wait for the dialog box to finish before you continue processing. Normally, you would check the DialogResult upon exit, as you do in the example, but that is not necessary:

```
if (mydialog->ShowDialog() == System::Windows::Forms::DialogResult::OK)
    lbRetVal->Text = "OK";
else if (mydialog->DialogResult == System::Windows::Forms::DialogResult::Abort)
    lbRetVal->Text = "Abort";
else
    lbRetVal->Text = "Cancel";
```

The second mode, Show(), is modeless. In this mode, the dialog box opens and then returns control immediately back to its caller. You now have two threads of execution running. (I cover threads in Chapter 16.) I usually use modeless dialog boxes for displaying information and not retrieving information. A classic example is the about box:

```
AboutBox->Show();
```

This is not to say that you can't use a modeless dialog box to retrieve information, but you just need to be aware that the code that opens the dialog box is still executing, and it will not be waiting for a result from the dialog box. If this confuses you, you might want to consult Chapter 16 on how to code for two (or more) threads of execution.

The final thing you might do (again, this is optional) is grab the changed data out of the dialog box:

```
lbRetString->Text = mydialog->PassedValue;
```

By the way, I have been using Strings to pass data back and forth between the dialog box and the main application. This is not a restriction, though—you can use any data type you want.

Common .NET Framework–Provided Dialog Boxes

When you've worked with Windows for any length of time, you soon come to recognize some common dialog boxes that many applications use. The .NET Framework class library provides you easy access to using these same Windows dialog boxes in your programs. Table 10-3 shows a list of the available common dialog boxes.

Table 10-3. *The Common Dialog Boxes*

Dialog Box	Description
ColorDialog	A dialog box to select a color
FolderBrowserDialog	A dialog box that allows the user to choose a folder
FontDialog	A dialog box to select a font
OpenFileDialog	A common Open File dialog box
PageSetupDialog	A dialog box that manipulates page settings, such as margins
PrintDialog	A dialog box to select a printer and the portion of the document you want to print
SaveFileDialog	A common File Save dialog box

You call the common dialog boxes in the same way you do the custom dialog box you just built. Listing 10-14 shows just how simple it is to call the ColorDialog. Calling all the other custom dialog boxes is done the same way.

Listing 10-14. *Calling a Common ColorDialog*

```
namespace ColorDialogEx
{
    using namespace System;
    using namespace System::ComponentModel;
    using namespace System::Collections;
    using namespace System::Windows::Forms;
    using namespace System::Data;
    using namespace System::Drawing;
```

```cpp
    public ref class Form1 : public System::Windows::Forms::Form
    {
    public:
        Form1(void)
        {
            InitializeComponent();
        }

    protected:
        ~Form1()
        {
            if (components)
            {
                delete components;
            }
        }

    private:
        System::ComponentModel::Container ^components;

#pragma region Windows Form Designer generated code

        void InitializeComponent(void)
        {
            this->SuspendLayout();
            //
            // Form1
            //
            this->AutoScaleDimensions = System::Drawing::SizeF(6, 13);
            this->AutoScaleMode = System::Windows::Forms::AutoScaleMode::Font;
            this->ClientSize = System::Drawing::Size(292, 273);
            this->Name = L"Form1";
            this->Text = L"Common Color Dialog - Click Form";
            this->Click +=
                gcnew System::EventHandler(this, &Form1::Form1_Click);
            this->ResumeLayout(false);

        }
#pragma endregion

    private:
        System::Void Form1_Click(System::Object^ sender, System::EventArgs^ e)
        {
            ColorDialog^ colordialog = gcnew ColorDialog();

            if (colordialog->ShowDialog() ==
                System::Windows::Forms::DialogResult::OK)
            {
                BackColor = colordialog->Color;
            }
        }
    };
}
```

There is nothing new or special here. First, check to make sure that the dialog box exited with the DialogResult of OK, and then set the color of the object you want changed with the value in the Color property of the ColorDialog.

Figure 10-17 shows what the example looks like when you execute it.

Figure 10-17. *Calling a common ColorDialog*

Summary

In this chapter, you've encountered many of the more powerful controls available to the Win Forms developer. You started off with a couple of views and then moved on to container controls. Next, you looked at the strip controls ToolStrip, StatusStrip, and MenuStrip. Then, to finish off the coverage of controls, you took a look at some of the more fun controls available. After your whirlwind tour of controls, you ended Windows Form development with examining dialog boxes.

You should now be able to build a commercial-grade GUI interface that will impress all of your peers.

In the next chapter, you'll continue to examine the GUI interface provided by the .NET Framework class library, but this time you'll look at working with things such as fonts and prebuilt images, and drawing your own images from scratch.

CHAPTER 11

■ ■ ■

Graphics Using GDI+

Using the .NET Framework class library's Windows Form controls is not the only way to graphically present data to the user. There is no doubt that Win Form controls are powerful, but occasionally you may want more control over what exactly is displayed by the computer than these controls can provide. This chapter covers another major method of displaying data to Windows applications: GDI+.

Unlike in a Win Forms application, when you write GDI+ code, you do it from scratch. There are no GUI drag-and-drop tools available to ease development, though you still lay out the form on which you plan to use GDI+ with the GUI design tool. The entire form does not need to be the target of the GDI+ images. Instead, GDI+ images can be painted on any control. Thus, you can develop a complex form and designate only a small portion of the form to working with GDI+.

In this chapter you will see just how easy it is to develop applications using GDI+. You will start with a high-level overview of GDI+ by looking at what it is and what it consists of. You will then look in detail at some of its functionality, such as fonts, pens, colors, and lines. Once you have covered the basics of GDI+, you will then look at more advanced topics, such as scrolling, optimization, and double buffering. Finally, to round off the discussion, you will discover that GDI+ is not just for displaying data to your monitor—you can also use it on printers.

At first glance, you might think this chapter is solely for the graphics guru. This is somewhat true, but many of the topics presented in this chapter are used by other areas of the .NET Framework class library such as Win Forms and Web Forms. For example, the Font class and the Color, Size, and Position structures are used frequently in Win Forms and Web Forms. Graphics gurus will want to read this chapter, and the average Win Forms or Web Forms developer should probably skim this chapter as well.

What Is GDI+?

In the simplest terms, GDI+ is a set of namespaces that provides for the rendering of 2D graphics. For example, GDI+ provides support for colors, pens, fonts, image transformations, and anti-aliasing. GDI+ contains none of the advanced animation and 3D rendering features found in DirectX.

Notice that I didn't include the phrase "render to the video adapter" in the preceding paragraph, because the device GDI+ renders to is immaterial. Well, almost immaterial—some differences have to be accounted for between some devices. For example, video adapters don't have to worry about form feeds, whereas printers obviously do. GDI+ is designed to support almost any graphical display device.

GDI+ originated from the Windows Graphical Device Interface (GDI), which has been around since Microsoft Windows 3.0. GDI+ shares many of the features of its predecessor, but with the .NET Framework class library there have been several improvements, thus the new name of GDI+.

A Quick Look at the GDI+ Namespaces

You can find the core functionality of GDI+ in the .NET Framework class library namespaces listed in Table 11-1.

Table 11-1. *GDI+ Core Namespaces*

Namespace	Description
System::Drawing	This namespace is the core of GDI+. It consists of numerous classes to handle basic 2D rendering. It is also the location of the Graphics class from which all GDI+ functionality springs.
System::Drawing::Drawing2D	This namespace extends the 2D rendering capabilities of GDI+ by providing more advanced 2D rendering and vector graphics.
System::Drawing::Imaging	This namespace provides classes that allow direct manipulation of graphical images.
System::Drawing::Printing	This namespace provides classes that allow printing to a printer. It also provides classes to interact with the printer.
System::Drawing::Text	This namespace provides advanced font and font family functionality.

Primarily, most of the functionality that you'll be working with is found in the classes and structures in the System::Drawing namespace (see Table 11-2).

Table 11-2. *Key System::Drawing Namespace Classes and Structures*

Class/Structure	Description
Bitmap	A class that represents and provides limited manipulation capabilities for an image file with formats such as .bmp, .gif, and .jpg
Brush	A class used to specify the color and pattern to fill the interior of a shape such as a rectangle, ellipsis, or polygon
Brushes	A class made up of several static properties of predefined brushes
Color	A structure that represents a color
Font	A class that represents a font
FontFamily	A class that defines a group of fonts with the same basic design
Graphics	The core class of GDI+ that represents a drawing surface where you will place your text, shapes, and images
Icon	A class that represents a Windows icon
Image	An abstract base class used in all image type classes such as bitmaps and icons
Pen	A class used to specify the color, thickness, and pattern used to outline shapes
Pens	A class made up of several static properties of predefined pens

Table 11-2. *Key System::Drawing Namespace Classes and Structures*

Class/Structure	Description
Point, PointF	A structure that represents an *x, y* coordinate as either a pair of Int32s or Singles
Rectangle, RectangleF	A structure that represents the size and location of a rectangle using either Int32 or Single values
Region	A sealed class that describes a geometric shape using rectangles
Size, SizeF	A structure that represents a size as either a pair of Int32s or Singles
SolidBrushes	A class that defines a Brush that fills a shape with a solid color
StringFormat	A sealed class that specifies the layout information such as alignment, formatting, and line spacing for a set of text
SystemBrushes	A class made up of several static properties of SolidBrushes using system colors
SystemColors	A class made up of several static properties of system colors
SystemFonts	A class made up of several static properties of system fonts
SystemIcons	A class made up of several static properties of Windows system icons
SystemPens	A class made up of several static properties of Pens using system colors
TextureBrush	A class that represents a Brush that uses an image to fill a shape interior

All of the functionality of GDI+ is located within the System.Drawing.dll assembly. Thus, you need to reference it at the top of your source code with the following #using statement:

```
#using <System.Drawing.dll>
```

Note If you are using Visual Studio 2005 to do your Win Forms development, System.Drawing.dll is automatically added as a reference.

"Hello World!" GDI+ Style

Why break a trend I've set in the book? Here's "Hello World!" again (see Listing 11-1). This time it's using GDI+ to render the "Hello World" text.

Listing 11-1. *"Hello World!" GDI+ Style*

```
namespace HelloGDI
{
    using namespace System;
    using namespace System::ComponentModel;
    using namespace System::Collections;
    using namespace System::Windows::Forms;
    using namespace System::Data;
    using namespace System::Drawing;
```

```cpp
        public ref class Form1 : public System::Windows::Forms::Form
        {
        public:
            Form1(void)
            {
                InitializeComponent();
            }

        protected:
            ~Form1()
            {
                if (components)
                {
                    delete components;
                }
            }

        private:
            System::ComponentModel::Container ^components;

#pragma region Windows Form Designer generated code
            void InitializeComponent(void)
            {
                this->SuspendLayout();
                this->AutoScaleDimensions = System::Drawing::SizeF(6, 13);
                this->AutoScaleMode = System::Windows::Forms::AutoScaleMode::Font;
                this->ClientSize = System::Drawing::Size(292, 273);
                this->Name = L"Form1";
                this->Text = L"Hello GDI+";
                this->Paint +=
                    gcnew System::Windows::Forms::PaintEventHandler(this,
                                                        &Form1::Form1_Paint);
                this->ResumeLayout(false);
            }
#pragma endregion
        private:
            System::Void Form1_Paint(System::Object^ sender,
                                    System::Windows::Forms::PaintEventArgs^ e)
            {
                Graphics ^g = e->Graphics;
                g->DrawString("Hello World!",
                    gcnew Drawing::Font("Arial", 16), Brushes::Black, 75.0, 110.0);
            }
        };
}
```

Figure 11-1 shows the results of the program HelloGDI.exe.

Figure 11-1. *Results of "Hello World!" GDI+ style*

As you can see, not much is new here. The big differences are the addition of the PaintEventHandler event handler and the using of an instance of the Graphics class. The rest of the code is identical to that of any program you looked at in the previous two chapters.

All controls generate a Paint event when they determine that it needs to be updated. The Form class happens to also be a child of the Control class. A Paint event is triggered whenever the control is created, resized, or restored, or when another control that had overlaid it is moved, re-exposing a portion or all of the overlaid control.

As was pointed out previously, this "Hello World!" example differs from the previous two chapters in that it implements an event handler, PaintEventHandler, and uses a Graphics class. PaintEventHandler has two parameters. The first parameter is the sender of the Paint event. In this case, it is the form, but it can be almost any control. The second parameter is a pointer to the PaintEventArgs class. It is from the PaintEventArgs class that you will get two important pieces of information: the Graphics class and the ClipRectangle or the area that needs to be updated on the form. You will learn about the ClipRectangle later in the chapter when you look at optimization.

The Graphics class is the key to GDI+, but I delay exploration of the class until its own section a little later in the chapter. For the example, all you need to know is that the Graphics class has a member method, DrawString(), that you will use to draw the string to the display device. To get access to the Graphics class, you usually extract its pointer from the PaintEventHandler parameter:

```
System::Void Form1_Paint(System::Object^ sender,
                         System::Windows::Forms::PaintEventArgs^ e)
{
    Graphics ^g = e->Graphics;
```

The final piece of this "Hello World!" program is to actually render the "Hello World" string to the display device. The DrawString method takes a few parameters. This example shows rendering on the drawing surface, at location x equals 75 and y equals 100, in black, 16-point Arial font:

```
g->DrawString("Hello World!",
    gcnew Drawing::Font("Arial", 16), Brushes::Black, 75.0, 110.0);
```

Something to note about rendering with GDI+ is that the location coordinates are based on the client area of the form or, more accurately, the control. Rendering to a location outside of the control will be clipped and won't be visible. Don't panic; you'll see how to add a scroll bar so you can scroll over and make hidden renderings visible.

OnPaint vs. PaintEventHandler

There's a second way of processing Paint events: the protected virtual OnPaint() method. Unlike what you've seen before, you don't call the OnPaint() method. Instead, you need to override it and then let the system handle it when it's called. Listing 11-2 shows the "Hello World!" program again, this time using the virtual OnPaint() method.

Listing 11-2. *"Hello World!" Using OnPaint()*

```
namespace HelloGDI_OnPaint
{
    using namespace System;
    using namespace System::ComponentModel;
    using namespace System::Collections;
    using namespace System::Windows::Forms;
    using namespace System::Data;
    using namespace System::Drawing;

    public ref class Form1 : public System::Windows::Forms::Form
    {
    public:
        Form1(void)
        {
            InitializeComponent();
        }

    protected:
        ~Form1()
        {
            if (components)
            {
                delete components;
            }
        }

    private:
        System::ComponentModel::Container ^components;

#pragma region Windows Form Designer generated code
        void InitializeComponent(void)
        {
            this->components = gcnew System::ComponentModel::Container();
            this->Size = System::Drawing::Size(300,300);
            this->Text = L"Hello GDI+";
            this->Padding = System::Windows::Forms::Padding(0);
            this->AutoScaleMode = System::Windows::Forms::AutoScaleMode::Font;
        }
#pragma endregion
```

```
protected:
    virtual void OnPaint(System::Windows::Forms::PaintEventArgs ^e) override
    {
        Form::OnPaint(e);

        Graphics ^g = e->Graphics;
        g->DrawString("Hello World!",
            gcnew Drawing::Font("Arial", 16), Brushes::Black, 75.0, 110.0);
    }
};
}
```

The results of HelloGDI_OnPaint.exe when run are identical to the PaintEventHandler version. Most of the code is the same as well. The first difference is that there's no handling of the Paint event within the InitializeComponent() method. It isn't needed because the OnPaint() method will handle the Paint events for you. That isn't to say that you can't have the handler. I see a possibility where a static set of graphic rendering activities are placed within the OnPaint() method and then a set of other graphic rendering activities are placed in multiple Paint event handlers and, based on conditions, dynamically delegated to the appropriate handler. However, you could do the same thing using an OnPaint() or a Paint event handler alone.

So what's the difference (if any) between the OnPaint() method and the handler PaintEventHandler? Isn't the OnPaint() method just a prepackaged PaintEventHandler? I thought so, like many other people (I assume), but I was wrong. The fact is that the Control class's OnPaint() method is actually in charge of executing all the delegated Paint event handlers. This means the only way you can be assured that a Paint event happens is by overriding the OnPaint() method, because it's possible to disable the Paint event handlers from actually firing within the OnPaint() method. It's a very simple thing to do—you just have to not call the base class Form::OnPaint() within the OnPaint() method.

As you can see, the first statement within the OnPaint() method is to call the base class version of itself:

```
virtual void OnPaint(System::Windows::Forms::PaintEventArgs ^e) override
{
    Form::OnPaint(e);
    //...Do stuff
}
```

Placing the OnPaint() method first was a conscious decision on my part, as it can make a difference where the base method call is placed within the implementation of the method. Placing it first, as shown in the preceding code, indicates that you must handle all the other delegated Paint events first or, in other words, do the rendering specified within this OnPaint() method last. Now if you place the base method call after doing the rendering of the method:

```
virtual void OnPaint(System::Windows::Forms::PaintEventArgs ^e) override
{
    //...Do stuff
    Form::OnPaint(e);
}
```

this indicates render first what is in this method, and then handle all other delegated Paint events. Both might be legitimate depending on what you want to do. Try the code in Listing 11-3 first by placing Form::OnPaint() as the first line in the overloaded method and then as the last.

Listing 11-3. *Placing the OnPaint Base Class Method*

```
namespace OnPaintWhere
{
    using namespace System;
    using namespace System::ComponentModel;
    using namespace System::Collections;
    using namespace System::Windows::Forms;
    using namespace System::Data;
    using namespace System::Drawing;

    public ref class Form1 : public System::Windows::Forms::Form
    {
    public:
        Form1(void)
        {
            InitializeComponent();
        }

    protected:
        ~Form1()
        {
            if (components)
            {
                delete components;
            }
        }

    private:
        System::ComponentModel::Container ^components;

#pragma region Windows Form Designer generated code
        void InitializeComponent(void)
        {
            this->SuspendLayout();
            this->AutoScaleDimensions = System::Drawing::SizeF(6, 13);
            this->AutoScaleMode = System::Windows::Forms::AutoScaleMode::Font;
            this->ClientSize = System::Drawing::Size(292, 273);
            this->Name = L"Form1";
            this->Text = L"Form1";
            this->Paint +=
                gcnew System::Windows::Forms::PaintEventHandler(this,
                                                    &Form1::Form1_Paint);
            this->ResumeLayout(false);
        }
#pragma endregion

    protected:
        virtual void OnPaint(System::Windows::Forms::PaintEventArgs ^e) override
        {
//          Form::OnPaint(e);

            e->Graphics->DrawString("Hello GDI+",
                gcnew Drawing::Font("Arial", 16), Brushes::Black, 75.0, 110.0);
```

```
            Form::OnPaint(e);
        }

    private:
        System::Void Form1_Paint(System::Object^ sender,
                                 System::Windows::Forms::PaintEventArgs^ e)
        {
            e->Graphics->DrawString("Hello GDI+",
                gcnew Drawing::Font("Arial", 16), Brushes::Purple, 75.0, 110.0);
        }
    };
}
```

Figure 11-2 shows OnPaintWhere.exe in action where the text "Hello GDI+" is in purple in this black-and-white image. Guess you'll have to take my word for it.

Figure 11-2. *The rendering results if the base OnPaint is placed last in the method*

When `Form::OnPaint()` is placed on the first line, the text turns out black, as the `OnPaint()` method's version of the `DrawString()` method is handled last. When `Form::OnPaint()` is placed at the end, on the other hand, the text is purple because the `PaintEventHandler` version of the `DrawString()` method is handled last. By the way, if you remove all the logic within the `OnPaint()` method, no text is displayed, because the `PaintEventHandler` is never triggered as `Form::OnPaint()` was not called to execute the delegated `Paint` events.

Now after saying all this, does it really matter if your `OnPaint()` method calls its base class version? The usual answer to this is "Not really." If you don't plan on using the `Paint` event handler yourself and the form that you created is never inherited (both normally being the case), then calling `OnPaint()` makes no difference. In fact, it might speed things up minutely if you don't call it because it isn't doing any unneeded method calls. (This is my take on it, though. The .NET Framework documentation says you should always call the base class method, so maybe you should take Microsoft's word, as there might be some hidden reason that I'm unaware of. That said, so far I haven't come across any problems.)

Which should you use: the `OnPaint()` method or the `Paint` event handler? I think the `OnPaint()` method, as it doesn't have the event delegate implementation overhead. But because it's easier to use than the `Paint` event (you only have to double-click the event handler in the Properties dialog box to add it) and the cost of the overhead is so minute, I use the `Paint` handler from this point on.

The Graphics Class

So what is this magical Graphics class? It's the heart of all rendering activity of GDI+. It's a device-independent representation of the drawing surface that you plan to render graphics on. It can represent a monochrome display device like many PDAs or cell phones, a true-color display device like those supported on a good number of computers used today, or anything in between. It can also be used for printers, from plotter to dot matrix to color laser.

Graphics Class Members

The Graphics class provides developers with a large number of rendering methods (see Table 11-3) from which they can choose to render their images. The rendering methods of the Graphics class can be divided into two groups: lines/outlines (draws) and fills. (The Clear() method is technically a fill.) Draws are used to outline open-ended and closed shapes or, in other words, they draw lines and outline shapes. Fills . . . well, they fill shapes.

Table 11-3. *Common Graphics Class Rendering Methods*

Method	Description
Clear()	Clears the entire client area to the background color
DrawArc()	Draws a part of an ellipse
DrawClosedCurve()	Draws a closed curve defined by an array of points
DrawCurve()	Draws an open curve defined by an array of points
DrawEllipse()	Draws an ellipse
DrawIcon()	Draws an icon
DrawImage()	Draws an image
DrawImageUnscaled()	Draws an image without scaling
DrawLine()	Draws a line
DrawLines()	Draws a series of connected lines
DrawPie()	Draws a pie segment
DrawPolygon()	Draws a polygon defined by an array of points
DrawRectangle()	Draws a rectangle
DrawRectangles()	Draws a series of rectangles
DrawString()	Draws a text string
FillClosedCurve()	Fills a closed curve defined by an array of points
FillEllipse()	Fills an ellipse
FillPie()	Fills a pie segment
FillPolygon()	Fills a polygon defined by an array of points
FillRectangle()	Fills a rectangle
FillRectangles()	Fills a series of rectangles

Something that might disturb you a little bit is that there is no Graphics constructor. The main way of getting an instance of a Graphics class is by grabbing from

- A PaintEventArgs's Graphics property
- A control using its CreateGraphics() method
- An image using the Graphics static FromImage() method
- A handle to a window using the Graphics static FromHwnd() method

Usually you will only use PaintEventArgs's Graphics property or, as you will see in the "Double Buffering" section, the FromImage() method.

Disposing of Resources with Deterministic Cleanup

The Graphics object uses a lot of system resources. Some examples of Graphics objects are System::Drawing::Graphics, System::Drawing::Brush, and System::Drawing::Pen. It's important that if you create a Graphics object, you release it as soon as you've finished with it. You do this by calling the destructor for the object once you're done with it. This allows the system resources associated with the Graphics object to be reallocated for other purposes.

You're probably thinking, "Won't the garbage collector handle all this?" Yes, it will, but because you have no control over when the garbage collector will run on the object and because graphics resources are precious, it's better to use deterministic cleanup and call the destructor yourself.

Be careful to call the destructor only on objects you create. For example, you don't call the destructor for the Graphics object you extracted from PaintEventArg, as you're just accessing an existing object and not creating your own. Listing 11-4 presents an example where you need to call the destructor for a Graphics object.

Rendering Outside of the Paint Event

Now you'll examine CreateGraphics() in an example (see Listing 11-4) and see what happens when you minimize and then restore the window after clicking a few coordinates onto the form.

Listing 11-4. *The Problem with Using CreateGraphics*

```
\namespace DisappearingCoords
{
    using namespace System;
    using namespace System::ComponentModel;
    using namespace System::Collections;
    using namespace System::Windows::Forms;
    using namespace System::Data;
    using namespace System::Drawing;

    public ref class Form1 : public System::Windows::Forms::Form
    {
    public:
        Form1(void)
        {
            InitializeComponent();
        }
```

```cpp
    protected:
        ~Form1()
        {
            if (components)
            {
                delete components;
            }
        }

    private:
        System::ComponentModel::Container ^components;

#pragma region Windows Form Designer generated code
        void InitializeComponent(void)
        {
            this->SuspendLayout();
            this->AutoScaleDimensions = System::Drawing::SizeF(6, 13);
            this->AutoScaleMode = System::Windows::Forms::AutoScaleMode::Font;
            this->ClientSize = System::Drawing::Size(292, 273);
            this->Name = L"Form1";
            this->Text = L"Click and see coords";
            this->MouseDown +=
                gcnew System::Windows::Forms::MouseEventHandler(this,
                                                &Form1::Form1_MouseDown);
            this->ResumeLayout(false);

        }
#pragma endregion

    private:
        System::Void Form1_MouseDown(System::Object^ sender,
                                        System::Windows::Forms::MouseEventArgs^ e)
        {
            Graphics ^g = this->CreateGraphics();
            g->DrawString(String::Format("({0},{1})", e->X, e->Y),
                gcnew Drawing::Font("Courier New", 8),
                Brushes::Black, (Single)e->X, (Single)e->Y);

            delete g;        // we delete the Graphics object because we
                             // created it with the CreateGraphics() method.
        }
    };
}
```

Figure 11-3 shows the program DisappearingCoords.exe with the coordinate strings clipped after resizing the form.

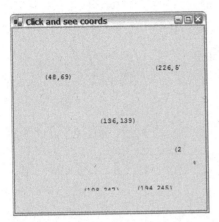

Figure 11-3. *Clipped rendered coordinate strings*

The coordinates disappear! What's happening here? When you minimize a window or overlay it with another window, its graphics device memory is released back to the system resource pool. Thus, everything that was displayed on the graphics device is lost, along with all the coordinates that you clicked onto the drawing surface.

With the preceding logic, the only time that a coordinate string is drawn to the graphics device is during a mouse click. Because this is the case, there is no way of restoring the coordinates without at least one mouse click occurring. This is why you want to use the Paint event; it is automatically triggered whenever more of the drawing surface area is exposed, either because it was restored, resized, or something that was obscuring it was removed.

Added to this, because none of the information about what was displayed on the drawing surface is stored anywhere when the surface area is reduced, you need to store the coordinates that you previously clicked so they can all be restored. Listing 11-5 shows how to fix the shortcomings of the previous example.

Listing 11-5. *Corrected Clipping Problem*

```cpp
namespace CorrectingCoords
{
    using namespace System;
    using namespace System::ComponentModel;
    using namespace System::Collections;
    using namespace System::Windows::Forms;
    using namespace System::Data;
    using namespace System::Drawing;

    public ref class Form1 : public System::Windows::Forms::Form
    {
    public:
        Form1(void)
        {
            InitializeComponent();
            coords = gcnew ArrayList();  // Instantiate coords array
        }
```

```cpp
    protected:
        ~Form1()
        {
            if (components)
            {
                delete components;
            }
        }

    private:
        System::ComponentModel::Container ^components;
        ArrayList ^coords;

#pragma region Windows Form Designer generated code
        void InitializeComponent(void)
        {
            this->SuspendLayout();
            this->AutoScaleDimensions = System::Drawing::SizeF(6, 13);
            this->AutoScaleMode = System::Windows::Forms::AutoScaleMode::Font;
            this->ClientSize = System::Drawing::Size(292, 273);
            this->Name = L"Form1";
            this->Text = L"Click and see coords";
            this->Paint +=
                gcnew System::Windows::Forms::PaintEventHandler(this,
                                                    &Form1::Form1_Paint);
            this->MouseDown +=
                gcnew System::Windows::Forms::MouseEventHandler(this,
                                                    &Form1::Form1_MouseDown);
            this->ResumeLayout(false);
        }
#pragma endregion

    private:
        System::Void Form1_MouseDown(System::Object^ sender,
                                    System::Windows::Forms::MouseEventArgs^ e)
        {
            coords->Add(Point(e->X, e->Y));
            Invalidate();
        }

    private:
        System::Void Form1_Paint(System::Object^ sender,
                                 System::Windows::Forms::PaintEventArgs^ e)
        {
            for each (Point^ p in coords)
            {
                e->Graphics->DrawString(String::Format("({0},{1})",p->X,p->Y),
                    gcnew Drawing::Font("Courier New", 8),
                    Brushes::Black, (Single)p->X, (Single)p->Y);
            }
        }
    };
}
```

Figure 11-4 shows CorrectingCoords.exe, though it's hard to tell after it has been minimized, resized, and overlaid. Notice the rendered string still appears as expected.

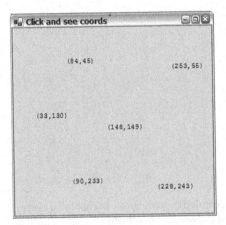

Figure 11-4. *Correctly rendered coordinate strings*

Now the MouseDown event handles the adding of the click coordinates to an array for safekeeping, and the responsibility of rendering the coordinates is back where it should be: in the Paint event handler (Form1_Paint()). Notice that every time the drawing surface is painted, every coordinate is rewritten, which is hardly efficient. You will look at optimizing this later.

How does the control know when to trigger a Paint event when the mouse clicks it on? That is the job of the Invalidate() method.

The Invalidate Method

What is this Invalidate() method and why was it called? The Invalidate() method is the manual way of triggering a Paint event. Thus, in the previous example, because you no longer draw the coordinate information to the screen in the MouseDown handler, you need to trigger the Paint event using the Invalidate() method.

Calling the Invalidate() method without any parameters, as shown in the preceding example, tells the form that its entire client area needs updating. The Invalidate() method also can take parameters. These parameters allow the Invalidate() method to specify that only a piece of the client area within the control needs to be updated. You will look at this type of the Invalidate() method in GDI+ optimization later in the chapter.

GDI+ Coordinate Systems

When you rendered the strings earlier, you placed them where they were supposed to be on the screen by specifying pixel distances from the top-left corner, increasing the X-axis when moving to the right and increasing the Y-axis when moving down to the bottom (see Figure 11-5).

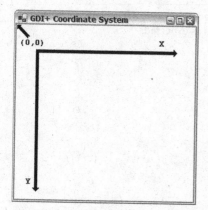

Figure 11-5. *The default GDI coordinate system*

A key aspect of GDI+ is that it is supposed to be device independent. How can that be, if everything is rendered based on a pixel standard? Pixels are only one of several coordinate systems supported by GDI+ (see Table 11-4). For example, instead of coordinate (100, 100), meaning 100 pixels to the right and 100 pixels down, the meaning could be 100 millimeters to the right and 100 millimeters down. To change the coordinate system to be based on a different unit of measure, you need to change the PageUnit property of the Graphics class to a different GraphicsUnit.

Table 11-4. *GDI+-Supported GraphicsUnits*

System	Description
Display	Specifies 1/75 of an inch as a unit of measure
Document	Specifies 1/300 of an inch as a unit of measure
Inch	Specifies 1 inch as a unit of measure
Millimeter	Specifies 1 millimeter as a unit of measure
Pixel	Specifies 1 pixel as a unit of measure
Point	Specifies a printer's point or 1/72 of an inch as a unit of measure

It is also possible to move the origin (0, 0) away from the top-left corner to somewhere else on the drawing surface. This requires you to translate the origin (0, 0) to where you want it located using the Graphics class's TranslateTransform() method.

The example in Listing 11-6 changes the unit of measure to millimeter and shifts the origin to (20, 20).

Listing 11-6. *Changing the Unit of Measure and the Origin*

```
namespace CorrectingCoords
{
    using namespace System;
    using namespace System::ComponentModel;
    using namespace System::Collections;
    using namespace System::Windows::Forms;
```

```cpp
using namespace System::Data;
using namespace System::Drawing;

public ref class Form1 : public System::Windows::Forms::Form
{
public:
    Form1(void)
    {
        InitializeComponent();
        coords = gcnew ArrayList();   // Instantiate coords array
    }

protected:
    ~Form1()
    {
        if (components)
        {
            delete components;
        }
    }

private:
    System::ComponentModel::Container ^components;
    ArrayList ^coords;

#pragma region Windows Form Designer generated code
    void InitializeComponent(void)
    {
        this->SuspendLayout();
        this->AutoScaleDimensions = System::Drawing::SizeF(6, 13);
        this->AutoScaleMode = System::Windows::Forms::AutoScaleMode::Font;
        this->ClientSize = System::Drawing::Size(292, 273);
        this->Name = L"Form1";
        this->Text = L"Click and see coords";
        this->Paint +=
            gcnew System::Windows::Forms::PaintEventHandler(this,
                                                &Form1::Form1_Paint);

        this->MouseDown +=
            gcnew System::Windows::Forms::MouseEventHandler(this,
                                                &Form1::Form1_MouseDown);

        this->ResumeLayout(false);
    }
#pragma endregion

private:
    System::Void Form1_MouseDown(System::Object^ sender,
                            System::Windows::Forms::MouseEventArgs^ e)
    {
        coords->Add(Point(e->X, e->Y));
        Invalidate();
    }
```

```
    private:
        System::Void Form1_Paint(System::Object^ sender,
                                 System::Windows::Forms::PaintEventArgs^ e)
        {
            for each (Point^ p in coords)
            {
                e->Graphics->DrawString(String::Format("({0},{1})",p->X,p->Y),
                    gcnew Drawing::Font("Courier New", 8),
                    Brushes::Black, (Single)p->X, (Single)p->Y);
            }
        }
    };
}
```

As you can see in NewUnitsOrigin.exe, it is possible to use multiple types of units of measure and origins within the same Paint event handler. Figure 11-6 displays a small rectangle, which was generated by the default pixel unit of measure and origin. The larger and thicker lined rectangle is what was generated when the unit of measure was changed to millimeter and origin was moved to (20, 20).

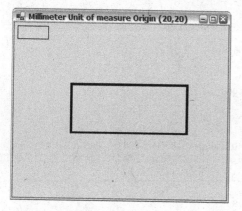

Figure 11-6. *Changing the unit of measure and the origin*

You should notice a couple of things in this example. First, the client size still uses pixel width and height. There is no PageUnit property for a form. Second, when you change the PageUnit of the Graphics class, all rendering from that point is changed to the new unit of measure. This is true even for the width of lines. Pens::Black creates lines 1 unit thick. When the unit is millimeters, Pens::Black will end up creating a line 1 millimeter thick.

Common Utility Structures

When you render your own text, shape, or image, you need to be able to tell the Graphics class where to place it and how big it is. It is not surprising that the .NET Framework class library provides a small assortment of structures and a class to do just that. Here they are in brief:

- Point/PointF is used to specify location.
- Size/SizeF is used to specify size.
- Rectangle/RectangleF is used to specify both location and size at the same time.
- Region is used to specify combinations of rectangles and regions.

All of these types use units of measure configured by the property PageUnit within the Graphics class. You need to take care that you always configure PageUnit consistently, or you might find that even though the same values are placed in these structures, they in fact represent different locations and sizes.

All the structures have int and float versions. Both provide the same functionality. The only real difference is the level of granularity that is supported in numeric values stored within the structures. In most cases, the int version will be good enough, but if you want finer granularity, you might want to choose the float version. Just remember that ultimately, the resolution of the drawing surface will decide how the shape, image, or text is displayed.

Point and PointF

As the name of this structure suggests, Point/PointF is an (x, y) location in units. Remember that units do not necessarily mean pixels. Pixels are only the default. The Point/PointF structure provides a few members (see Table 11-5) to aid in their manipulation.

Table 11-5. *Common Point/PointF Members*

Member	Description
+ operator	Translates a Point/PointF by a Size/SizeF.
- operator	Translates a Point/PointF by the negative of a Size/SizeF.
== operator	Compares the equality of two points. Both Xs and Ys must equal for the point to equal.
!= operator	Compares the inequality of two points. If either the Xs or Ys don't equal, then the points don't equal.
IsEmpty	Specifies if the point is empty.
Ceiling()	Static member that returns next higher integer Point from a PointF.
Offset()	Translates the point by the specified *x* and *y* amounts.
Round()	Static member that returns a rounded Point from a PointF.
Truncate()	Static member that returns a truncated Point from a PointF.
X	Specifies the *x* coordinate of the point.
Y	Specifies the *y* coordinate of the point.

To access the X or Y values within the Point/PointF structure, you simply need to access the X or Y property:

```
Drawing::Point a = Drawing::Point(10,15);
int x = a.X;
int y = a.Y;
```

Casting from Point to PointF is implicit, but to convert from PointF, you need to use one of two static methods: Round() or Truncate(). The Round() method rounds to the nearest integer, and the Truncate() method simply truncates the number to just its integer value.

```
Drawing::Point  a = Drawing::Point(10,15);
Drawing::PointF b = a;
Drawing::Point  c = Drawing::Point::Round(b);
Drawing::Point  d = Drawing::Point::Truncate(b);
```

The Offset() method is only found in Point, and it translates the point by the x and y coordinates passed to it.

```
a.Offset(2, -3);
```

The method is cumbersome as it returns void. I think it should return a Point type. I think it should also be a member of PointF.

Size and SizeF

Mathematically, Size/SizeF and Point/PointF are virtually the same. How they differ is really just conceptually. Point/PointF specifies where something is, whereas Size/SizeF specifies how big it is. Point/PointF and Size/SizeF even have many of the same members (see Table 11-6). The biggest difference is that sizes have widths and heights, whereas the points have x and y coordinates.

Table 11-6. *Common Size/SizeF Members*

Member	Description
+ operator	Adds two sizes together.
- operator	Subtracts one size from another.
== operator	Compares the equality of two sizes. Both Widths and Heights must equal for the points to equal.
!= operator	Compares the inequality of two sizes. If either Widths or Heights don't equal, then the points don't equal.
IsEmpty	Specifies whether the size is empty.
Ceiling()	Static member that returns the next higher integer Size from a SizeF.
Round()	Static member that returns a rounded Size from a SizeF.
Truncate()	Static member that returns a truncated Size from a SizeF.
Height	Specifies the height of the size.
Width	Specifies the width of the size.

It is possible to add or subtract two sizes and get a size in return. It is also possible to subtract a size from a point that returns another point. Adding or subtracting points generates a compiler error.

```
Drawing::Size sizeA = Drawing::Size(100, 100);
Drawing::Size sizeB = Drawing::Size(50, 50);
Drawing::Size sizeC = sizeA + sizeB;
Drawing::Size sizeD = sizeC - sizeB;

Drawing::Point pointA = Drawing::Point(10, 10) + sizeD;
Drawing::Point pointB = pointA - sizeC;
```

You can cast Point/PointF to Size/SizeF. What happens is the value of X becomes Width and the value of Y becomes Height, and vice versa. The following code shows how to implement all the combinations. It also shows the Size to SizeF combinations:

```
size   = point;
point  = size;
sizeF  = pointF;
pointF = (Drawing::PointF)sizeF;

sizeF  = (Drawing::Size)point;
pointF = (Drawing::Point)size;
sizeF  = size;

size   = Drawing::Size::Round(pointF);
size   = Drawing::Size::Truncate(pointF);
point  = Drawing::Point::Round((Drawing::PointF)sizeF);
point  = Drawing::Point::Truncate((Drawing::PointF)sizeF);
size   = Drawing::Size::Round(sizeF);
size   = Drawing::Size::Truncate(sizeF);
```

Rectangle and RectangleF

As I'm sure you can guess, the Rectangle/RectangleF structure represents the information that makes up a rectangle. It's really nothing more than a combination of a Point structure and a Size structure. The Point specifies the starting upper-left corner and the Size specifies the size of the enclosed rectangular area starting at the point. There is, in fact, a Rectangle/RectangleF constructor that takes as its parameters a Point and a Size.

The Rectangle structure provides many properties and methods (see Table 11-7), a few of which are redundant. For example, there are properties called Top and Left that return the exact same thing as the properties X and Y.

Table 11-7. *Common Rectangle/RectangleF Members*

Member	Description
==	Returns whether the rectangle has the same location and size
!=	Returns whether the rectangle has different location or size
Bottom	Returns the y coordinate of the bottom edge
Ceiling()	Static member that returns the next higher integer Rectangle from a RectangleF
Contains	Returns whether a point falls within the rectangle
Height	Specifies the height of the rectangle
Intersect()	Returns a Rectangle/RectangleF that represents the intersection of two rectangles
IsEmpty	Specifies whether all the numeric properties are zero
Left	Returns the x coordinate of the left edge
Location	A Point structure that specifies the top-left corner
Offset()	Relocates a rectangle by a specified amount

Table 11-7. *Common Rectangle/RectangleF Members (Continued)*

Member	Description
Right	Returns the *x* coordinate of the right edge
Round()	Static member that returns a rounded Rectangle from a RectangleF
Size	A Size structure that specifies the size of the rectangle
Top	Returns the *y* coordinate of the top edge
Truncate()	Static member that returns a truncated Rectangle from a RectangleF
Union()	Returns a Rectangle/RectangleF that represents the smallest possible rectangle that can contain the two rectangles
Width	Specifies the width of the rectangle
X	Specifies the *x* coordinate of the top-left corner
Y	Specifies the *y* coordinate of the top-left corner

The rectangle provides three interesting methods. The first is the Intersection() method, which can take two rectangles and generate a third rectangle that represents the rectangle that the two others have in common. The second is the Union() method. This method does not really produce the union of two rectangles as the method's name suggests. Instead, it generates the smallest rectangle that can enclose the other two. The third interesting method is Contains(), which specifies whether a point falls within a rectangle. This method could come in handy if you want to see if a mouse click falls inside a rectangle.

The example in Listing 11-7 uses these three methods. This program checks whether a point falls within an intersection of the two rectangles or within the union of two rectangles. (Obviously, if the point falls within the intersection, it also falls within the union.)

Listing 11-7. *Intersection, Union, or Neither*

```
namespace InterOrUnion
{
    using namespace System;
    using namespace System::ComponentModel;
    using namespace System::Collections;
    using namespace System::Windows::Forms;
    using namespace System::Data;
    using namespace System::Drawing;

    public ref class Form1 : public System::Windows::Forms::Form
    {
    public:
        Form1(void)
        {
            InitializeComponent();
```

```
            // Build the rectangles from points and size
            Drawing::Point point1 = Drawing::Point(25,25);
            Drawing::Point point2 = Drawing::Point(100,100);
            Drawing::Size size    = Drawing::Size(200, 150);
            rect1 = Drawing::Rectangle(point1, size);
            rect2 = Drawing::Rectangle(point2, size);
        }

    protected:
        ~Form1()
        {
            if (components)
            {
                delete components;
            }
        }

    private:
        System::ComponentModel::Container ^components;

        // intersecting and unions rectangles
        Drawing::Rectangle rect1;
        Drawing::Rectangle rect2;

#pragma region Windows Form Designer generated code
        void InitializeComponent(void)
        {
            this->SuspendLayout();
            this->AutoScaleDimensions = System::Drawing::SizeF(6, 13);
            this->AutoScaleMode = System::Windows::Forms::AutoScaleMode::Font;
            this->ClientSize = System::Drawing::Size(330, 300);
            this->Name = L"Form1";
            this->Text = L"Click in Window";
            this->Paint +=
                gcnew System::Windows::Forms::PaintEventHandler(this,
                                                    &Form1::Form1_Paint);

            this->MouseDown +=
                gcnew System::Windows::Forms::MouseEventHandler(this,
                                                    &Form1::Form1_MouseDown);

            this->ResumeLayout(false);
        }
#pragma endregion

    private:
        System::Void Form1_Paint(System::Object^ sender,
                                System::Windows::Forms::PaintEventArgs^ e)
        {
            // Draw a couple of rectangles
            e->Graphics->DrawRectangle(Pens::Black, rect1);
            e->Graphics->DrawRectangle(Pens::Black, rect2);
        }
```

```
private:
    System::Void Form1_MouseDown(System::Object^ sender,
                                 System::Windows::Forms::MouseEventArgs^ e)
    {
        // build a point from x,y coords of mouse click
        Point p = Point(e->X, e->Y);

        // did we click in the intersection?
        if (Rectangle::Intersect(rect1, rect2).Contains(p))
            Text = "Intersection and Union";
        // did we click in the union?
        else if (Rectangle::Union(rect1, rect2).Contains(p))
            Text = "Union";
        // did we miss altogether
        else
            Text = "Outside of Both";
    }
};
}
```

The first thing you need to do is declare and build two rectangles that you will make the mouse check against:

```
Drawing::Rectangle rect1;
Drawing::Rectangle rect2;
//...
// Build the rectangles from points and size
Drawing::Point point1 = Drawing::Point(25,25);
Drawing::Point point2 = Drawing::Point(100,100);
Drawing::Size size    = Drawing::Size(200, 150);

rect1 = Drawing::Rectangle(point1, size);
rect2 = Drawing::Rectangle(point2, size);
```

You will learn about the DrawRectangle() method later, but as you can see in the code, it takes a Pen to draw with and then the Rectangle to draw:

```
g->DrawRectangle(Pens::Black, rect1);
```

Finally, in the MouseDown event, you check to see where the mouse was clicked and place the results in the title:

```
// build a point from x,y coords of mouse click
Point p = Point(e->X, e->Y);

// did we click in the intersection?
if (Rectangle::Intersect(rect1, rect2).Contains(p))
    Text = "Intersection and Union";
// did we click in the union?
else if (Rectangle::Union(rect1, rect2).Contains(p))
    Text = "Union";
// did we miss altogether?
else
    Text = "Outside of Both";
```

Figure 11-7 shows the mouse being clicked in the intersection of the two rectangles in InterOrUnion.exe.

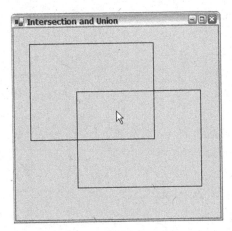

Figure 11-7. *It's an intersection.*

Region

The last of the utility types is the only class in the bunch. Region is a neat little class in that it alters itself with the help of other rectangles and regions into a more complex region. The alterations that the Region class does are things such as unions, intersections, exclusive or, and complements. A Region class has no properties of its own; instead, it is made up of a number of methods (see Table 11-8) that it uses to alter itself.

Table 11-8. *Common Region Members*

Member	Description
Complement()	Alters itself to become the complement of itself. The region of the complement is restricted by a specified rectangle.
Exclude()	Alters itself to become the portion of the region that does not intersect with the given rectangle or region.
GetBounds()	Specifies the smallest rectangle that the region can be contained within.
Intersect()	Alters itself to become the intersection of itself and a specified rectangle or region.
IsEmpty()	Specifies whether the region is made up of an empty area.
IsInfinite()	Specifies whether the region is infinite in size.
MakeEmpty()	Sets the region to empty.
MakeInfinite()	Sets the region to infinite.
Transform()	Transforms itself using a matrix.
Translate()	Translates itself by a specified amount.
Union()	Alters itself to become the union of itself and a specified rectangle or region.
Xor()	Alters itself to become the exclusive or (the union minus the intersection) of itself and a specified rectangle or region.

Listing 11-8 shows some of these methods in action.

Listing 11-8. *Displaying a Region*

```
namespace RegionEx
{
    using namespace System;
    using namespace System::ComponentModel;
    using namespace System::Collections;
    using namespace System::Windows::Forms;
    using namespace System::Data;
    using namespace System::Drawing;

    public ref class Form1 : public System::Windows::Forms::Form
    {
    public:
        Form1(void)
        {
            InitializeComponent();

            Drawing::Point point1 = Drawing::Point(25,25);
            Drawing::Point point2 = Drawing::Point(100,100);
            Drawing::Size size     = Drawing::Size(200, 150);
            Rectangle rect1        = Drawing::Rectangle(point1, size);
            Rectangle rect2        = Drawing::Rectangle(point2, size);

            region = gcnew Drawing::Region(rect1);
            region->Xor(rect2);
        }

    protected:
        ~Form1()
        {
            if (components)
            {
                delete components;
            }
        }

    private:
        System::ComponentModel::Container ^components;
        Drawing::Region ^region;

#pragma region Windows Form Designer generated code
        void InitializeComponent(void)
        {
            this->SuspendLayout();
            this->AutoScaleDimensions = System::Drawing::SizeF(6, 13);
            this->AutoScaleMode = System::Windows::Forms::AutoScaleMode::Font;
            this->ClientSize = System::Drawing::Size(322, 273);
            this->Name = L"Form1";
            this->Text = L"Filling A Region";
```

```
        this->Paint +=
            gcnew System::Windows::Forms::PaintEventHandler(this,
                                                &Form1::Form1_Paint);

        this->ResumeLayout(false);
    }
#pragma endregion

    private:
        System::Void Form1_Paint(System::Object^ sender,
                            System::Windows::Forms::PaintEventArgs^ e)
        {
            e->Graphics->FillRegion(Brushes::Blue, region);
        }
    };
}
```

To save typing, I decided to cut and paste the code to build the rectangle from the previous example.

To build a Region class, you start with an empty Region and then add a rectangle or a Region to it:

```
Drawing::Region ^region;
region = gcnew Drawing::Region(rect1);
```

Now you can start to alter the Region. Notice that the Region methods return void. In other words, the Region actually gets changed with each method call to itself. To Xor it with another rectangle, call the Xor() method:

```
region->Xor(rect2);
```

You will cover filling regions later, but so that you know, the FillRegion() method takes a Brush to specify the color to fill it with and then the Region to fill.

Figure 11-8 shows the area that makes up the region that you built with RegionEx.exe from two rectangles.

Figure 11-8. *Displaying a region*

Drawing Strings

Drawing strings almost doesn't require a section of its own—all it involves is a single call to the DrawString() method found in the Graphics class. The more difficult part of drawing strings is setting up the font and color you want to print with. (I cover both topics later.)

Now you'll take a quick peek at the DrawString() method. If you were to look at the .NET Framework documentation, you'd find a plethora of overloads. When you examine them more closely, you'll discover that they all start with the parameters String, Font, and Brush. From there, it gets a little tricky because you have to decide if you just want to specify the starting upper-left corner of where you want the string displayed, using either (x, y) coordinates or a Point, or specify the entire rectangle that you want to restrict the string to.

```
g->DrawString(string, font, brush, xF, yF);
g->DrawString(string, font, brush, pointF);
g->DrawString(string, font, brush, rectangleF);
```

When you restrict the string to a rectangle, the text automatically word-wraps, as Listing 11-9 shows. It unfortunately will also show half of a line of text if the vertical height is not enough.

Listing 11-9. *Drawing a String to a Rectangle*

```
namespace StringRect
{
    using namespace System;
    using namespace System::ComponentModel;
    using namespace System::Collections;
    using namespace System::Windows::Forms;
    using namespace System::Data;
    using namespace System::Drawing;

    public ref class Form1 : public System::Windows::Forms::Form
    {
    public:
        Form1(void)
        {
            InitializeComponent();
        }

    protected:
        ~Form1()
        {
            if (components)
            {
                delete components;
            }
        }

    private:
        System::ComponentModel::Container ^components;
```

```
#pragma region Windows Form Designer generated code
        void InitializeComponent(void)
        {
            this->SuspendLayout();
            this->AutoScaleDimensions = System::Drawing::SizeF(6, 13);
            this->AutoScaleMode = System::Windows::Forms::AutoScaleMode::Font;
            this->ClientSize = System::Drawing::Size(292, 273);
            this->Name = L"Form1";
            this->Text = L"String in a Rectangle";
            this->Paint +=
                gcnew System::Windows::Forms::PaintEventHandler(this,
                                                        &Form1::Form1_Paint);

            this->ResumeLayout(false);
        }
#pragma endregion

    private:
        System::Void Form1_Paint(System::Object^ sender,
                              System::Windows::Forms::PaintEventArgs^ e)
        {
            // Draw the string
            e->Graphics->DrawString(
                "Let's draw a string to a rectangle and go a little "
                    "overboard on the size of the string that we place "
                    "inside of it",
                gcnew Drawing::Font(gcnew FontFamily("Arial"), 12),
                Brushes::Black, Drawing::RectangleF(20.0, 40.0, 260.0, 50.0));
        }
    };
}
```

Figure 11-9 shows that StringRect.exe draws a string to a rectangle that is too small.

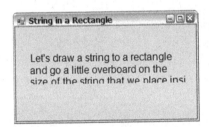

Figure 11-9. *A string restricted to a too-small rectangle*

In reality, each of the overloads for the DrawString() method listed previously has one more parameter of type StringFormat, which has been defaulted to GenericDefault.

```
g.DrawString(string, font, brush, xF, yF, stringformat);
g.DrawString(string, font, brush, pointF, stringformat);
g.DrawString(string, font, brush, rectangleF, stringformat);
```

StringFormat is a class containing several properties (see Table 11-9) that allow the DrawString() method to do things such as draw the text vertically and left-, right-, or center-align it.

Table 11-9. *Common StringFormat Properties*

Property	Description
Alignment	Specifies alignment of the text
FormatFlags	Specifies StringFormatFlags such as DirectionVertical and NoWrap
GenericDefault	A static method that gets the generic default StringFormat object
GenericTypographic	A static method that gets the generic typographic StringFormat object
LineAlignment	Specifies line alignment
Trimming	Specifies how to trim a string that doesn't fit completely within a display area

Listing 11-10 shows the same text as shown earlier, but this time it is written in a downward direction and centered on each line.

Listing 11-10. *Drawing Strings Downward in a Rectangle*

```
namespace DownwardStringRect
{
    using namespace System;
    using namespace System::ComponentModel;
    using namespace System::Collections;
    using namespace System::Windows::Forms;
    using namespace System::Data;
    using namespace System::Drawing;

    public ref class Form1 : public System::Windows::Forms::Form
    {
    public:
        Form1(void)
        {
            InitializeComponent();
        }

    protected:
        ~Form1()
        {
            if (components)
            {
                delete components;
            }
        }

    private:
        System::ComponentModel::Container ^components;
```

```
#pragma region Windows Form Designer generated code
        void InitializeComponent(void)
        {
            this->SuspendLayout();
            this->AutoScaleDimensions = System::Drawing::SizeF(6, 13);
            this->AutoScaleMode = System::Windows::Forms::AutoScaleMode::Font;
            this->ClientSize = System::Drawing::Size(300, 145);
            this->Name = L"Form1";
            this->Text = L"Downward String in a Rectangle";
            this->Paint +=
                gcnew System::Windows::Forms::PaintEventHandler(this,
                                                      &Form1::Form1_Paint);

            this->ResumeLayout(false);
        }
#pragma endregion

    private:
        System::Void Form1_Paint(System::Object^ sender,
                            System::Windows::Forms::PaintEventArgs^ e)
        {
            // create and configure the StringFormat object
            StringFormat ^stringformat = gcnew StringFormat();
            stringformat->FormatFlags  = StringFormatFlags::DirectionVertical;
            stringformat->Alignment    = StringAlignment::Center;

            // Draw the string
            e->Graphics->DrawString(
                "Let's draw a string to a rectangle and go a little "
                    "overboard on the size of the string that we place "
                    "inside of it",
                gcnew Drawing::Font(gcnew FontFamily("Arial"), 13),
                Brushes::Black, Drawing::RectangleF(20.0, 40.0, 250.0, 80.0),
                stringformat);
        }
    };
}
```

Figure 11-10 shows that DownwardStringRect.exe draws a string in a downward direction and centers it in a rectangle that is too small. This causes the string to be clipped on the final line.

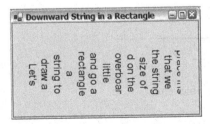

Figure 11-10. *A string drawn downward and restricted to a too-small rectangle*

Fonts

It seems that many people seem overly concerned about the differences between GDI+'s Font class and FontFamily class. Here's my take on it: A Font class represents a single font and a FontFamily class represents a group of fonts that share many characteristics. You might think of a font family as "Arial" and a font as "Arial, 10-point, italic."

When you draw strings with GDI+, you don't have much of a choice. You have to build a Font class. You can't draw a string with a FontFamily class.

When you build a Font class, you have the choice of starting with a FontFamily class or a String containing the name of a font family. You'll probably use a String if you're planning on building a Font class from one of the standard fonts found on a computer (e.g., Arial, Courier, and Times New Roman). On the other hand, if your font is a little less common, you probably will search the computer for a list of font families currently loaded on your computer. If you find the FontFamily class in the list of font families, then it's a simple matter of using the FontFamily class instead of the String containing the font family's name. In general, I don't find the FontFamily class that useful as I tend to use the more common fonts in my programs, but you might have more exotic tastes. Basically, to use the FontFamily class, just replace the String in the first parameter of the Font constructor with the FontFamily class.

The process of building a font is quite easy. You do it using the Font constructors. You will use three constructors most often. They are really the same except that parameters are defaulted for two of them.

The first constructor has no defaulted values and takes the name of the font family and the unit size, the font style, and the graphics unit:

```
Font ^f = gcnew Drawing::Font("Arial", 16, FontStyle::Bold,GraphicsUnit::Point);
```

In most cases, fonts default to a graphics unit of pixels. Therefore, Font provides a constructor with the graphics unit defaulted to pixels:

```
Font ^f = gcnew Drawing::Font("Arial", 16, FontStyle::Bold);
```

In addition, most of the time you are going to work with the font in the regular font style (not boldface, italic, or underline). So, again, Font provides a default for this:

```
Font ^f = gcnew Drawing::Font("Arial", 16);
```

Even though the Font class has several properties (see Table 11-10), they are all read-only. In other words, you can't change a font once you have constructed it.

Table 11-10. *Common Font Properties*

Property	Description
Bold	true if the font is boldface
FontFamily	Gets the font family
Height	Gets the height of the font in the current graphics unit
Italic	true if font is italicized
Name	Gets the name of the font
Size	Gets the size of the font in the current graphics unit
SizeInPoints	Gets the size of the font in points (1/72 inch)

Table 11-10. *Common Font Properties*

Property	Description
Strikeout	true if the font is struck out
Style	Gets the style information
Underline	true if the font is underlined
Unit	Gets the graphics unit

The code in Listing 11-11 creates ten random fonts and then displays them.

Listing 11-11. *Generating Random Fonts·*

```
namespace FontsGalore
{
    using namespace System;
    using namespace System::ComponentModel;
    using namespace System::Collections;
    using namespace System::Windows::Forms;
    using namespace System::Data;
    using namespace System::Drawing;
    using namespace System::Drawing::Text;

    public ref class Form1 : public System::Windows::Forms::Form
    {
    public:
        Form1(void)
        {
            InitializeComponent();

            fonts = gcnew array<Drawing::Font^>(10);
            fontstr = gcnew array<String^>(10);

            // Used to generate random fonts
            array<float>^ sizes = gcnew array<float> {
                10.0, 12.5, 16.0
            };

            array<FontStyle>^ fontstyles = gcnew array<FontStyle> {
                FontStyle::Regular, FontStyle::Bold,
                FontStyle::Italic,
            (FontStyle)(FontStyle::Underline|FontStyle::Bold|FontStyle::Italic)
            };

            array<GraphicsUnit>^ units = gcnew array<GraphicsUnit> {
                GraphicsUnit::Point, GraphicsUnit::Pixel
            };

            // Get all fonts on computer
            InstalledFontCollection ^availFonts =
                gcnew InstalledFontCollection();
```

```cpp
            array<FontFamily^>^ fontfamilies = availFonts->Families;

            Random ^rand = gcnew Random();
            int ff, s, fs, u;

            for (int i = 0; i < fonts->Length; i++)
            {
                s  = rand->Next(0,3);
                fs = rand->Next(0,3);
                u  = rand->Next(0,2);

                // Not all fonts support every style
                do {
                    ff = rand->Next(0,fontfamilies->Length);
                }
                while (!fontfamilies[ff]->IsStyleAvailable(
                    (FontStyle)fontstyles[fs]));

                // Display string of font
                fontstr[i] = String::Format("{0} {1} {2}",
                    fontfamilies[ff]->Name,
                    sizes[s],
                    String::Concat(fontstyles[fs], " ",
                                   units[u]));

                // Create the font
                fonts[i] = gcnew Drawing::Font(fontfamilies[ff], sizes[s],
                                        (FontStyle)fontstyles[fs],
                                        (GraphicsUnit)units[u]);
            }
        }

    protected:
        ~Form1()
        {
            if (components)
            {
                delete components;
            }
        }

    private:
        System::ComponentModel::Container ^components;
        array<Drawing::Font^>^ fonts;
        array<String^>^ fontstr;

#pragma region Windows Form Designer generated code

        void InitializeComponent(void)
        {
            this->SuspendLayout();
            this->AutoScaleDimensions = System::Drawing::SizeF(6, 13);
            this->AutoScaleMode = System::Windows::Forms::AutoScaleMode::Font;
            this->ClientSize = System::Drawing::Size(292, 273);
```

```
            this->Name = L"Form1";
            this->Text = L"Many Fonts";
            this->Paint +=
                gcnew System::Windows::Forms::PaintEventHandler(this,
                                                    &Form1::Form1_Paint);

            this->ResumeLayout(false);
        }
#pragma endregion

    private:
        System::Void Form1_Paint(System::Object^ sender,
                                 System::Windows::Forms::PaintEventArgs^ e)
        {
            float lineloc = 0;
            for (int i = 0; i < fonts->Length; i++)
            {
                // Display font
                e->Graphics->DrawString(fontstr[i], fonts[i], Brushes::Black,
                    10, lineloc);

                // Calculate the top of the next line
                lineloc += fonts[i]->Height;
            }
        }
    };
}
```

Deep within the code is the routine to get a list of all the font families on your system:

```
InstalledFontCollection ^availFonts = gcnew InstalledFontCollection();
array<FontFamily^>^ fontfamilies = availFonts->Families;
```

After these two lines are run, you have an array of all FontFamilies on your computer. It is pretty easy, no? The only hard part is remembering to add the namespace System::Drawing::Text, which you need to get access to the InstalledFontCollection class.

Something you might want to notice is how I figured out where to start the next line of String. I did this by adding the height of the font to the current line y coordinate after I finished drawing with it:

```
lineloc += fonts[i]->Height;
```

Figure 11-11 shows one instance of FontsGalore.exe running. I doubt you will ever see the same combination of fonts displayed twice.

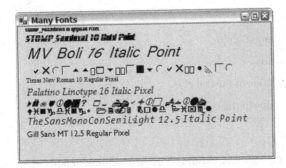

Figure 11-11. *Displaying random fonts*

Colors

Most current display device technology defines colors by breaking them up into their three basic components: red, green, and blue. Depending on the configuration of the display device, these components usually will have a value that ranges from 0 to 255. The principle is that by combining different amounts of red, green, and blue, you can generate any color. Thus, many of today's display devices can display up to 16,777,216 (256 cubed) unique colors.

But the story doesn't end there. Colors also provide an alpha component. This component represents how transparent the color is. If the alpha value is 0, then the color is completely transparent (a kind of useless color), and a value of 255 is completely opaque. In between these two points are varying degrees of transparency that will, when drawn to the screen, merge with any color already existing at that location. You see this effect used most often in computer games.

Many of the Graphics class's Drawing methods need a System::Drawing::Color structure containing one of the colors built from the values described previously before they can be used. The Color class has a number of members (see Table 11-11) available to get color information from. You can use only three common methods to place color information into a Color structure:

- FromArgb() returns a Color class based on the alpha, red, green, and blue values passed to it.
- FromKnownColor() returns a Color class based on a predefined color.
- FromName() returns a Color class based on the string color name passed.

You must use one of these three methods to create your color because there is no Color constructor.

Table 11-11. *Common Color Members*

Member	Description
A	Gets the alpha component
B	Gets the blue component
G	Gets the green component
GetBrightness()	Gets the brightness of the color based on the hue-saturation-brightness (HSB) value of the color
GetHue()	Gets the hue of the color, based on the HSB value of the color
GetSaturation()	Gets the saturation of the color, based on the HSB value of the color
IsKnownColor()	true if it is a known color
IsNamedColor()	true if it is a named color
IsSystemColor()	true if it is a system color
Name	Gets the name of a "named" color
R	Gets the red component
ToArgb()	Gets the 32-bit ARGB value of the color
ToKnownColor()	Gets the KnownColor value of the color

There are two basic methods of defining a Color class: defining it using a combination of red, green, blue, and alpha component values or selecting the color from a list of predefined colors.

Custom Colors

To build your own custom color, you need to use the `Color` class's `FromArgb()` method. There are several overloads of the method, but you will most likely use two of them. The first method takes only the red, green, and blue components and defaults the alpha component to opaque (255). The second method allows you to specify the alpha component.

```
// Pure red
Color red1 = Color::FromArgb(255, 0, 0);
Color red2 = Color:: FromArgb(255, 255, 0, 0);
//Pure green
Color green1 = Color::FromArgb(0, 255, 0);
Color green2 = Color::FromArgb(255, 0, 255, 0);
//Pure blue
Color blue1 = Color::FromArgb(0, 0, 255);
Color blue2 = Color::FromArgb(255, 0, 0, 255);
```

You can make transparent or semitransparent colors by adjusting the alpha component passed to the `FromArgb()` method:

```
Color transparentgray = Color::FromArgb(127, 127, 127, 127);
```

Named Colors

The `Color` class provides a large number of predefined, or named, colors. There are two types of named colors. The first is a name that describes the color. These types of colors range (alphabetically) from AliceBlue to YellowGreen. The second type of color uses a name that describes its role in the Windows standard interface, such as ControlText, ScrollBar, and Window.

The three ways of creating named colors are using the `FromKnownColor()` method, using the static named color method directly, or using the string name of the color.

```
Color c1 = Color::FromKnownColor(KnownColor::AliceBlue);
Color c2 = Color::AliceBlue;
Color c3 = Color::FromName("AliceBlue");
```

Pens and Brushes

When you render images to a drawing surface, you need an object to actually do the drawing. GDI+ provides two objects: the `Pen` and the `Brush`. The `Pen` type is used to draw the outline of a shape, and the `Brush` type fills in an enclosed shape. (Makes sense, don't you think?)

Pens

You've all worked with a pen, so the idea of what a pen does shouldn't be hard to visualize. Normally, you use a pen to draw the outline of the object. Most likely, you draw a solid line, but sometimes you might use a sequence of a bunch of dots and dashes. When you're drawing a line between two objects, you probably will put an arrow on one or both ends. If you like variety, you might even use a red or blue pen along with your black one.

The `Pen` type provided by GDI+ provides basically the same functionality.

Custom Pens

You use the Pen constructor to create a Pen object, and then you use its properties (see Table 11-12) to indicate how you want the Pen used. There are several constructors to create a Pen, but in most cases the simple color and width constructors do the trick:

```
Pen^ pen1 = gcnew Pen(Color::Blue, 3.0);
```

Or if you want the Pen to be only 1 graphics unit thick, you could use this even easier code:

```
Pen^ pen2 = gcnew Pen(Color::Blue);
```

Notice I used the term "graphics unit." The Pen type's thickness is based on the graphics unit, not pixels, though the default is pixels.

Table 11-12. *Common Pen Properties*

Property	Description
Color	Specifies the color of the Pen
CompoundArray	Specifies the splitting of the width of a line into multiple parallel lines
CustomEndCap	Specifies a custom cap for the end of the line
CustomStartCap	Specifies a custom cap for the start of the line
DashCap	Specifies the dash-dot-space pattern used at the cap of a line
DashOffset	Specifies the distance from the start of the line to the beginning of the dash-dot-space pattern
DashPattern	Specifies a predefined dash-dot-space pattern to be used for a line
DashStyle	Specifies the style of the dash lines
EndCap	Specifies a predefined cap to be used for the end of the line
LineJoin	Specifies the style of the join between two consecutive lines
PenType	Specifies the style of the line generated by the Pen
StartCap	Specifies a predefined cap to be used for the start of the line
Width	Specifies the width of the Pen

Named Pens

If you are creating a pen that is only 1 graphics unit thick and uses a named color, then you can use one of the pens found in the Pens class. The name of the pen is the same as the name of the named color it is using:

```
Pen^ pen = Pens::AliceBlue;
```

System Pens

System pens are virtually the same as named pens, except that instead of a pen being named after a color, it is named after the role that the Pen would use on the Windows GUI interface. Also, you will find system pens in the SystemPens class and not in the Pens class:

```
Pen^ pen = SystemPens::MenuText;
```

Listing 11-12 presents an example program that draws a few lines using the CompoundArray, DashStyle, StartCap, and EndCap properties.

Listing 11-12. *Creating Some Random Lines*

```
namespace DrawingLines
{
    using namespace System;
    using namespace System::ComponentModel;
    using namespace System::Collections;
    using namespace System::Windows::Forms;
    using namespace System::Data;
    using namespace System::Drawing;
    using namespace System::Drawing::Drawing2D;

    public ref class Form1 : public System::Windows::Forms::Form
    {
    public:
        Form1(void)
        {
            InitializeComponent();

            pen = gcnew array<Pen^>(5);

            // a one unit width black pen
            pen[0] = Pens::Black;

            // a one unit with purple pen broken with dashes
            pen[1] = gcnew Pen(Color::Purple);
            pen[1]->DashStyle = DashStyle::Dash;

            // a 4 unit width chocolate pen
            pen[2] = gcnew Pen(Color::Chocolate, 4);

            // An 8 width royalblue pen made of three lines narrow wide narrow
            pen[3] = gcnew Pen(Color::RoyalBlue, 10);
            array<float>^ cArray = gcnew array<float> {
                0.0f, 0.1f, 0.3f, 0.7f, 0.9f, 1.0f
            };
            pen[3]->CompoundArray = cArray;

            // a 5 width tomato pen with diamond start and round end anchors
            pen[4] = gcnew Pen(Color::Tomato, 5);
            pen[4]->StartCap = LineCap::DiamondAnchor;
            pen[4]->EndCap = LineCap::RoundAnchor;
        }
    }
}
```

```
    protected:
        ~Form1()
        {
            if (components)
            {
                delete components;
            }
        }

    private:
        System::ComponentModel::Container ^components;
        array<Pen^>^ pen;

#pragma region Windows Form Designer generated code

        void InitializeComponent(void)
        {
            this->SuspendLayout();
            this->AutoScaleDimensions = System::Drawing::SizeF(6, 13);
            this->AutoScaleMode = System::Windows::Forms::AutoScaleMode::Font;
            this->ClientSize = System::Drawing::Size(292, 273);
            this->Name = L"Form1";
            this->Text = L"Drawing Some lines";
            this->Paint +=
                gcnew System::Windows::Forms::PaintEventHandler(this,
                                                    &Form1::Form1_Paint);
            this->ResumeLayout(false);

        }
#pragma endregion

    private:
        System::Void Form1_Paint(System::Object^ sender,
                            System::Windows::Forms::PaintEventArgs^ e)
        {
            Random ^rand = gcnew Random();

            for (int i = 0; i < 10; i++)
            {
                e->Graphics->DrawLine(pen[i%5], rand->Next(0,299),
                    rand->Next(0,299), rand->Next(0,299), rand->Next(0,299));
            }
        }
    };
}
```

Figure 11-12 shows one instance of DrawingLines.exe running. I doubt you will ever see the same combination of lines being displayed twice.

The preceding code is pretty self-explanatory, with the help of the embedded comments, except for two things. The first is that you need to add the System::Drawing::Drawing2D namespace. This namespace defines both the DashStyle and LineCap classes.

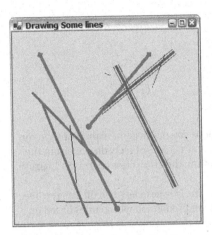

Figure 11-12. *Displaying random lines*

The second is the code that implements the `CompoundArray` property. This property splits a single line into multiple parallel lines. It does this by taking the width of a line and defining some portions as visible and other portions as not visible. The basic idea is, starting at 0 percent, find the first percent value that the line will be visible and write that into a `Single` area, and then find the percent where it becomes invisible again and write that value into the area. Repeat the process for all the parallel sublines that make up the full area, stopping at 100 percent.

If you want to define the entire line width as being visible (a waste of time, by the way), the array will look like this:

```
array<float>^ cArray = gcnew array<float> { 0.0f, 1.0f };
```

If you want to define the top half of the line as visible and the bottom as invisible (again, a waste of time), the array will look like this:

```
array<float>^ cArray = gcnew array<float> { 0.0f, 0.5f };
```

If you want the top 10 percent and the bottom 10 percent only to be visible, the array will look like this:

```
array<float>^ cArray = gcnew array<float> { 0.0f, 0.1f, 0.9f, 1.0f };
```

Notice that the compound array always has an even number of elements.
The preceding example breaks the line like this:

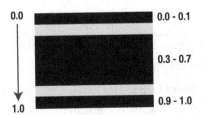

So the code ends up looking like this:

```
pen[3] = gcnew Pen(Color::RoyalBlue, 10);
array<float>^ cArray = gcnew array<float> {
    0.0f, 0.1f, 0.3f, 0.7f, 0.9f, 1.0f
};
pen[3]->CompoundArray = cArray;
```

Brushes

You use brushes to fill in the objects that you drew with the pens you defined in the previous section. Unlike the Pen class, the Brush class is an abstract class. You don't create objects directly from the Brush class; instead, brushes are created from classes derived from the Brush class such as SolidBrush, HatchBrush, and TextureBrush.

You can also create named brushes and SystemBrushes. The Brushes class will fill a shape like the SolidBrush class. The only difference is that the brushes are predefined with names based on named colors.

```
Brush^ brush = Brushes::AliceBlue;
```

SystemBrushes are like the Brushes class, but instead of colors, the SystemBrushes are named based on the Windows role they would represent.

```
Brush^ brush = SystemBrushes:: ActiveBorder;
```

SolidBrush, HatchBrush, and TextureBrush are not the only brushes available, but I cover only them to give you some ideas on how to work with brushes.

Solid Brushes

The SolidBrush class is the easiest of the brushes. All it takes in its constructor is the color that you want to fill the shape with. Its only property with any relevance is the color you used in the constructor:

```
SolidBrush^ brush = gcnew SolidBrush(Color::Black);
```

Hatch Brushes

The HatchBrush class is a little more complicated than the SolidBrush class. First, you need to add the namespace System::Drawing::Drawing2D so that you can access the both the HatchBrush class and the HatchStyle enumeration. The HatchBrush uses the HatchStyle enumeration (see Table 11-13) to define the look of the brush. GDI+ provides numerous hatch styles.

Table 11-13. *Ten of the Many HatchStyle Enumerations*

Enumeration	Description
BackwardDiagonal	Specifies a pattern of diagonal lines from the upper right to lower left
Cross	Specifies a pattern of vertical and horizontal lines
DiagonalBrick	Specifies a pattern that looks like slanted bricks
Divots	Specifies a pattern that looks like divots (a golfer's nightmare)
Horizontal	Specifies a pattern of horizontal lines
Plaid	Specifies a pattern that looks like plaid
SmallConfetti	Specifies a pattern that looks like small confetti

Table 11-13. *Ten of the Many HatchStyle Enumerations*

Enumeration	Description
Sphere	Specifies a pattern of spheres laid adjacent to each other
Vertical	Specifies a pattern of vertical lines
ZigZag	Specifies a pattern of horizontal lines that looks like zigzags

The constructor is a little more complicated too, as you need to pass the HatchStyle and two colors, the first being the foreground hatch color and the second being the background color.

```
using namespace System::Drawing::Drawing2D;

HatchBrush^ b = gcnew HatchBrush(HatchStyle::Divots,
                           Color::Brown, Color::Green);
```

Textured Brushes

A TextureBrush class allows you to place an image in the brush and then use it to fill in shapes. The best part of TextureBrush is how little code is needed to get it to work. The basic tasks behind the creation of a TextureBrush are loading the image and then placing it in the brush:

```
Image^ brushimage = gcnew Bitmap("MyImage.bmp");
TextureBrush^ tbrush = gcnew TextureBrush(brushimage);
```

Because I haven't covered images yet, I defer their explanation until later in the chapter. But as you can see in the preceding constructor, once you have an image available, it is a simple process to place it into a TextureBrush.

But that is not where the story ends. What happens if the brush is smaller than the shape it is trying to fill? The TextureBrush provides a WrapMode parameter (see Table 11-14) in the constructor (and also a property) to determine what to do—either clamp it or tile it. Clamping means that only one copy of the image is drawn, and tiling means that the image is repeatedly drawn until the area is filled.

Table 11-14. *WrapModes Enumeration*

Enumeration	Description
Clamp	Clamp the image to the object boundary
Tile	Tile the shape
TileFlipX	Tile the shape, flipping horizontally on each column
TileFlipXY	Tile the shape, flipping horizontally and vertically
TileFlipY	Tile the shape, flipping vertically on each row

There is one more piece of the puzzle. The first brush starts in the upper-left corner of the control you are drawing in. Thus, if you are filling a rectangle, for instance, and you want the brush to start in the upper-left corner of the rectangle, then you need to call the Brush class's TranslateTransform() method to translate the brush to start at that location:

```
// Translate brush to same start location as rectangle
tbrush->TranslateTransform(25,25);
// Fill rectangle with brush
g->FillRectangle(tbrush, 25, 25, 250, 250);
```

Listing 11-13 shows the tiling of the TextureBrush using WrapMode::TileFlipXY. It also shows how to translate the starting point of the tiling to the upper-left corner of the shape you are trying to fill.

Listing 11-13. *Filling with a TextureBrush*

```cpp
namespace TextureBrushEx
{
    using namespace System;
    using namespace System::ComponentModel;
    using namespace System::Collections;
    using namespace System::Windows::Forms;
    using namespace System::Data;
    using namespace System::Drawing;
    using namespace System::Drawing::Drawing2D;

    public ref class Form1 : public System::Windows::Forms::Form
    {
    public:
        Form1(void)
        {
            InitializeComponent();
        }

    protected:
        ~Form1()
        {
            if (components)
            {
                delete components;
            }
        }

    private:
        System::ComponentModel::Container ^components;

#pragma region Windows Form Designer generated code

        void InitializeComponent(void)
        {
            this->SuspendLayout();
            this->AutoScaleDimensions = System::Drawing::SizeF(6, 13);
            this->AutoScaleMode = System::Windows::Forms::AutoScaleMode::Font;
            this->ClientSize = System::Drawing::Size(292, 273);
            this->Name = L"Form1";
            this->Text = L"Texture Brush";
            this->Paint +=
                gcnew System::Windows::Forms::PaintEventHandler(this,
                                                &Form1::Form1_Paint);
            this->ResumeLayout(false);

        }
```

```
#pragma endregion

    private:
        System::Void Form1_Paint(System::Object^ sender,
                                  System::Windows::Forms::PaintEventArgs^ e)
        {
            // Load Image
            Image^ bimage = gcnew Bitmap("Images\\CLICppCover.gif");
            // Create brush
            TextureBrush^ tbsh = gcnew TextureBrush(bimage,
                                                    WrapMode::TileFlipXY);

            // Translate brush to same start location as rectangle
            tbsh->TranslateTransform(25,25);
            // Fill rectangle with brush
            e->Graphics->FillRectangle(tbsh, 25, 25, 250, 250);
        }
    };
}
```

Figure 11-13 shows TextureBrushEx.exe in action. Remember to make sure that the bitmap file is in the Images directory off the current executable starting directory so the program can find it. If it is not, then the program will abort.

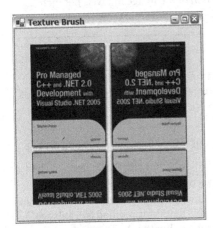

Figure 11-13. *Displaying the tiled TextureBrush*

Rendering Prebuilt Images

If you are implementing GDI+, you are probably planning to do one of two things: Render an existing image or draw your own image. You will cover rendering an existing image first, as it is the easier of the two processes.

Here's the process in a nutshell. Load the image. Draw the image. That's it. And it can be done in one line, too!

```
g->DrawImageUnscaled(Image::FromFile("Images\\CLICppCover.jpg"), 0.0, 0.0);
```

Of course, if you want a little more control, there is another DrawImage() method that you can work with. The Image class has a few members (see Table 11-15) with which you can manipulate the image.

Table 11-15. *Common Image Class Members*

Member	Description
FromFile()	Static method to load an image from a file
FromHbitmap()	Static method to load a bitmap from a Windows handle
FromStream()	Static method to load an image from a stream
GetBounds()	Returns a bounding rectangle for the image
Height	Specifies the height of the image
HorizontalResolution	Specifies the horizontal resolution of the image in pixels per inch
PhysicalDimensions	Specifies the size of the image
RotateFlip()	Rotates, flips, or rotates and flips the image
Save()	Saves the file to a stream
Size	Specifies the size of the image
VerticalResolution	Specifies the vertical resolution of the image in pixels per inch
Width	Specifies the width of the image

Before you can render an image, you need to load it from some source, either from a file as shown previously or a data stream (maybe the Internet?). Once the image is loaded, the Image class provides you the ability to flip and rotate the image.

Note The Image class doesn't use the GraphicsUnit, as you might expect. Instead, it uses pixels per inch.

Once you have an image, you're ready to render it. You've seen the Graphics class's DrawImageUnscaled() method. That is about the extent of the functionality it provides. It can take an image and the location where you want to place it. A more flexible rendering method is DrawImage(). It takes myriad overloads (you can examine them at your leisure within the .NET Framework documentation), but the most useful overload takes the image and stretches it to the size you want (see Listing 11-14).

Listing 11-14. *Stretching an Image*

```
namespace DrawImageEx
{
    using namespace System;
    using namespace System::ComponentModel;
    using namespace System::Collections;
    using namespace System::Windows::Forms;
    using namespace System::Data;
    using namespace System::Drawing;
```

```cpp
public ref class Form1 : public System::Windows::Forms::Form
{
public:
    Form1(void)
    {
        InitializeComponent();
    }

protected:
    ~Form1()
    {
        if (components)
        {
            delete components;
        }
    }

private:
    System::ComponentModel::Container ^components;

#pragma region Windows Form Designer generated code

    void InitializeComponent(void)
    {
        this->SuspendLayout();
        this->AutoScaleDimensions = System::Drawing::SizeF(6, 13);
        this->AutoScaleMode = System::Windows::Forms::AutoScaleMode::Font;
        this->ClientSize = System::Drawing::Size(292, 273);
        this->Name = L"Form1";
        this->Text = L"Draw Image";
        this->Paint +=
            gcnew System::Windows::Forms::PaintEventHandler(this,
                                                  &Form1::Form1_Paint);

        this->ResumeLayout(false);
    }
#pragma endregion

private:
    System::Void Form1_Paint(System::Object^ sender,
                             System::Windows::Forms::PaintEventArgs^ e)
    {
        Image^ img = Image::FromFile("Images\\CLICppCover.gif");
        e->Graphics->DrawImage(img, 0, 0, img->Width*2, img->Height*2);
    }
};
}
```

Figure 11-14 shows the end result of DrawImageEx.exe, which doubles the image with the
DrawImage() method. It is a little blurry but not too bad.

Figure 11-14. *Doubling an image's size*

One last note about rendering images. So far you have only loaded images from files of type .gif, but you can actually load .bmp, .jpg, .png, and .tif image files without having to change a single line of code other than the name of the file.

Drawing Your Own Shapes and Lines

Now you can finally get to the fun part of GDI+: drawing your own images. You saw some of this in action earlier in the chapter. The steps involved are quite easy: Grab the Graphics class and then draw or fill the objects you want using the appropriate method. I listed all the methods you will likely use back in Table 11-3, so you might want to take a quick peek back there to refresh your memory.

Because all it really takes to draw an image is calling methods, let's create a simple piece of artwork with the example in Listing 11-15.

Listing 11-15. *A Piece of Art*

```
namespace HappyFace
{
    using namespace System;
    using namespace System::ComponentModel;
    using namespace System::Collections;
    using namespace System::Windows::Forms;
    using namespace System::Data;
    using namespace System::Drawing;

    public ref class Form1 : public System::Windows::Forms::Form
    {
    public:
        Form1(void)
        {
            InitializeComponent();
        }
```

```
    protected:
        ~Form1()
        {
            if (components)
            {
                delete components;
            }
        }

    private:
        System::ComponentModel::Container ^components;

#pragma region Windows Form Designer generated code

        void InitializeComponent(void)
        {
            this->SuspendLayout();
            this->AutoScaleDimensions = System::Drawing::SizeF(6, 13);
            this->AutoScaleMode = System::Windows::Forms::AutoScaleMode::Font;
            this->ClientSize = System::Drawing::Size(300, 300);
            this->Name = L"Form1";
            this->Text = L"Happy Face";
            this->Paint +=
                gcnew System::Windows::Forms::PaintEventHandler(this,
                                                    &Form1::Form1_Paint);

            this->ResumeLayout(false);
        }
#pragma endregion

    private:
        System::Void Form1_Paint(System::Object^ sender,
                            System::Windows::Forms::PaintEventArgs^ e)
        {
            Graphics^ g = e->Graphics;
            Pen^ b4pen = gcnew Pen(Color::Black, 4);

            // Head
            Rectangle rect = Drawing::Rectangle(25, 25, 250, 250);
            g->FillEllipse(Brushes::Yellow, rect);
            g->DrawEllipse(b4pen, rect);

            // Mouth
            g->FillPie(Brushes::White, 100, 175, 100, 50, 0, 180);
            g->DrawPie(b4pen, 100, 175, 100, 50, 0, 180);

            // Left Eye
            rect = Drawing::Rectangle(100, 100, 25, 25);
            g->FillEllipse(Brushes::White, rect);
            g->DrawEllipse(b4pen, rect);
```

```
        // Right Eye
        rect = Drawing::Rectangle(175, 100, 25, 25);
        g->FillEllipse(Brushes::White, rect);
        g->DrawEllipse(b4pen, rect);

        // Get rid of pen Created
        delete b4pen;
    }
};
}
```

Figure 11-15 shows the results of HappyFace.exe, which is about the limit of my artistic abilities.

Figure 11-15. *A happy face*

Advanced GDI+

I kind of like the happy face I created in the last section, so I'll get a little more mileage out of it by using it to demonstrate a few more advanced GDI+ topics: scrollable windows, optimizing, and double buffering. By "advanced," I don't mean difficult—rather, I mean less obvious in how to implement. All three topics aren't that hard to implement.

Scrollable Windows

In the previous chapter on Win Forms, you didn't have to worry about a scrolling window as the Win Form handled it itself. With GDI+, on the other hand, it's up to you to add the necessary two lines in your code to get the scrollable window to work. Yep, you read correctly: two lines of code.

For those of you who aren't sure what a scrollable window is, it's a window that automatically attaches scroll bars to itself when the display information extends beyond its width. You use the scroll bar to shift the display area over so you can view this obscured displayed information.

To enable automatic scroll bars in a form, you need to update the AutoScrollMinSize property for the form:

```
this->AutoScrollMinSize = System::Drawing::Size(400, 400);
```

The size that you need to specify is the smallest area needed to display all the information. In my case, I was a little overzealous on the size so that you can see the scrolling better.

When you add the preceding line to your previous happy face example, you get scroll bars as shown in Figure 11-16, and everything seems hunky-dory.

Figure 11-16. *A happy face in a scrollable window*

Or is it? When you try to scroll the window, you get nothing but garbage, as you can see in Figure 11-17.

Figure 11-17. *A not-so-happy happy face in a scrollable window*

What's happening here? Believe it or not, the program is functioning perfectly—just not how you want it to. You can find the problem in the Paint event handler. The following steps show how the current program is working:

1. You click the scroll bar.

2. The window scrolls.

3. The Invalidate event is triggered for the clip area of the newly exposed window.

4. The Paint event handler executes.

5. The newly exposed window is replaced with any display data that belongs in it.

Sounds like it's working correctly to me, except for one minor detail. How does the program know what belongs in the newly exposed clip area? Notice that all the points in each of the drawing routines haven't been notified that the scroll took place. They're still drawing the same information at the same locations. Thus, the window is just repainting the newly exposed clip area with the original and wrong display information.

You have two (at least) ways of solving this problem. You might try adjusting each of the drawing routines by the amount of the scroll so that when they're called they render correctly. This solution isn't so bad when you're dealing with a handful of drawing and filling routines, but it's not good for a large number of routines.

An easier solution is to translate the origin of the Graphics class using the TranslateTransform() method (which I discussed earlier) to reflect the scroll. This solution has the same effect as the previous solution. The best part is that you have to add only one line of code, instead of changing every draw and fill routine. (Told you it would take two lines of code!)

```
g->TranslateTransform((float)AutoScrollPosition.X,(float)AutoScrollPosition.Y);
```

It's also fortunate that the Form class provides a property, AutoScrollPosition, which indicates how much was scrolled.

Listing 11-16 shows the happy face program modified to handle scroll bars.

Listing 11-16. *A Scrolling Happy Face*

```cpp
namespace ScrollingHappyFace
{
    using namespace System;
    using namespace System::ComponentModel;
    using namespace System::Collections;
    using namespace System::Windows::Forms;
    using namespace System::Data;
    using namespace System::Drawing;

    public ref class Form1 : public System::Windows::Forms::Form
    {
    public:
        Form1(void)
        {
            InitializeComponent();
        }

    protected:
        ~Form1()
        {
            if (components)
            {
                delete components;
            }
        }

    private:
        System::ComponentModel::Container ^components;

#pragma region Windows Form Designer generated code
        void InitializeComponent(void)
        {
            this->SuspendLayout();
```

```cpp
        this->AutoScrollMinSize = System::Drawing::Size(400,400);

        this->AutoScaleDimensions = System::Drawing::SizeF(6, 13);
        this->AutoScaleMode = System::Windows::Forms::AutoScaleMode::Font;
        this->ClientSize = System::Drawing::Size(292, 273);
        this->Name = L"Form1";
        this->Text = L"Scrolling Happy Face";
        this->Paint +=
            gcnew System::Windows::Forms::PaintEventHandler(this,
                                                &Form1::Form1_Paint);

        this->ResumeLayout(false);

    }
#pragma endregion

    private:
        System::Void Form1_Paint(System::Object^ sender,
                            System::Windows::Forms::PaintEventArgs^  e)
        {
            Graphics^ g = e->Graphics;
            g->TranslateTransform((float)AutoScrollPosition.X,
                            (float)AutoScrollPosition.Y);

            Pen^ b4pen = gcnew Pen(Color::Black, 4);

            // Head
            Rectangle rect = Drawing::Rectangle(25, 25, 250, 250);
            g->FillEllipse(Brushes::Yellow, rect);
            g->DrawEllipse(b4pen, rect);

            // Mouth
            g->FillPie(Brushes::White, 100, 175, 100, 50, 0, 180);
            g->DrawPie(b4pen, 100, 175, 100, 50, 0, 180);

            // Left Eye
            rect = Drawing::Rectangle(100, 100, 25, 25);
            g->FillEllipse(Brushes::White, rect);
            g->DrawEllipse(b4pen, rect);

            // Right Eye
            rect = Drawing::Rectangle(175, 100, 25, 25);
            g->FillEllipse(Brushes::White, rect);
            g->DrawEllipse(b4pen, rect);

            // Get rid of pen Created
            delete b4pen;
        }
    };
}
```

Figure 11-18 shows a happily scrolled happy face.

Figure 11-18. *The right side of a happy face*

Optimizing GDI+

You have many ways to optimize GDI+. This section describes the most obvious and easiest-to-implement methods.

Did you notice something about your Paint event handler method in the previous example? It executed every line in itself even if it was only repainting a small sliver of the graphic display. Wouldn't it be better and faster if only the parts of the Paint event handler method that need executing were executed? Let's see how you can do this.

The first thing you have to figure out is how to let a draw or fill method know that it needs to be executed.

What do all the draw and fill routines have in common in the preceding example? They all have a bounding rectangle. This rectangle indicates the area that it is supposed to update. Okay, so you know the area each draw or fill method needs to update.

```
Rectangle Head = Drawing::Rectangle(125, 25, 250, 250);
g->FillEllipse(Brushes::Yellow, Head);
```

Next, you want to know if this area is the same as what needs to be updated on the drawing surface. Remember way back near the beginning of the chapter where I wrote that the PaintEventArgs parameter provides two pieces of information: the Graphics and the ClipRectangle? This clip rectangle is the area that needs to be updated.

```
Drawing::Rectangle ClipRect = pea->ClipRectangle;
```

You now have two rectangles: one that specifies where it will update and another that specifies where it needs to be updated. So by intersecting these two rectangles, you can figure out if the draw routine needs to be executed, because when the intersection is not empty you know that the draw or fill needs to be executed.

```
if (!(Rectangle::Intersect(ClipRect, Head)).IsEmpty)
{
    //...Execute draw or fill method
}
```

The neat thing about this is that if you surround every draw and fill method with this comparison, when the Paint event handler is executed, only the draw or fill methods that need to be executed are.

There is one more wrinkle, though. The clip area is based on the client area and not the scroll area. This sounds familiar, doesn't it? So you have to adjust the clip area by the negative of AutoScrollPosition.

```
ClipRect.Offset(-AutoScrollPosition.X, -AutoScrollPosition.Y);
```

Why negative? You're doing the exact opposite of what you did in the previous example. This time you're moving the object on the drawing surface and keeping the drawing surface still. In the previous example, you kept the objects still and moved the drawing surface (well, it's not really doing this but it's easier to picture this way).

Listing 11-17 shows the scrollable happy face program with this optimization.

Listing 11-17. *An Optimized Scrollable Happy Face*

```
namespace OptimizedHappyFace
{
    using namespace System;
    using namespace System::ComponentModel;
    using namespace System::Collections;
    using namespace System::Windows::Forms;
    using namespace System::Data;
    using namespace System::Drawing;

    public ref class Form1 : public System::Windows::Forms::Form
    {
    public:
        Form1(void)
        {
            InitializeComponent();

            Head  = Drawing::Rectangle(125, 25, 250, 250);
            Mouth = Drawing::Rectangle(200, 175, 100, 50);
            LEye  = Drawing::Rectangle(200, 100, 25, 25);
            REye  = Drawing::Rectangle(275, 100, 25, 25);

            b4pen = gcnew Pen(Color::Black, 4);
        }

    protected:
        ~Form1()
        {
            if (components)
            {
                delete components;
            }
        }

    private:
        System::ComponentModel::Container ^components;

        System::Drawing::Rectangle Head;
        System::Drawing::Rectangle Mouth;
        System::Drawing::Rectangle LEye;
        System::Drawing::Rectangle REye;
        Pen^ b4pen;
```

```cpp
#pragma region Windows Form Designer generated code
        void InitializeComponent(void)
        {
            this->SuspendLayout();

            this->AutoScrollMinSize = System::Drawing::Size(400,400);

            this->AutoScaleDimensions = System::Drawing::SizeF(6, 13);
            this->AutoScaleMode = System::Windows::Forms::AutoScaleMode::Font;
            this->ClientSize = System::Drawing::Size(292, 273);
            this->Name = L"Form1";
            this->Text = L"Optimized Happy Face";
            this->Paint +=
                gcnew System::Windows::Forms::PaintEventHandler(this,
                                                    &Form1::Form1_Paint);
            this->ResumeLayout(false);
        }
#pragma endregion

    private:
        System::Void Form1_Paint(System::Object^ sender,
                            System::Windows::Forms::PaintEventArgs^ e)
        {

            Graphics^ g = e->Graphics;

            Drawing::Rectangle ClipRect = e->ClipRectangle;
            ClipRect.Offset(-AutoScrollPosition.X, -AutoScrollPosition.Y);

            g->TranslateTransform((float)AutoScrollPosition.X,
                            (float)AutoScrollPosition.Y);

            if (!(Rectangle::Intersect(ClipRect, Head)).IsEmpty)
            {
                g->FillEllipse(Brushes::Yellow, Head);
                g->DrawEllipse(b4pen, Head);

                if (!(Rectangle::Intersect(ClipRect, Mouth)).IsEmpty)
                {
                    g->FillPie(Brushes::White, Mouth, 0, 180);
                    g->DrawPie(b4pen, Mouth, 0, 180);
                }
                if (!(Rectangle::Intersect(ClipRect, LEye)).IsEmpty)
                {
                    g->FillEllipse(Brushes::White, LEye);
                    g->DrawEllipse(b4pen, LEye);
                }
                if (!(Rectangle::Intersect(ClipRect, REye)).IsEmpty)
                {
                    g->FillEllipse(Brushes::White, REye);
                    g->DrawEllipse(b4pen, REye);
                }
            }
        }
    };
}
```

Notice that in the code I threw in one more optimization in OptimizedHappyFace.exe. The Paint event handler method doesn't draw the mouth or eyes if the head doesn't need to be painted. I can do this because the mouth and eyes are completely enclosed within the head, so if the head doesn't need painting, there's no way that the mouth or eyes will either.

Double Buffering

Double buffering is the technique of using a secondary off-screen buffer to render your entire screen image. Then, in one quick blast, you move the completed secondary buffer onto your primary on-screen form or control.

The use of double buffering speeds up the rendering process and makes image movement much smoother by reducing flickering. Let's give the happy face some life and let it slide repeatedly across the form.

Unbuffer Method

The first example in Listing 11-18 shows how you can implement this without double buffering. (There are other ways of doing this—some of them are probably more efficient.) There is nothing new in the code. You start by creating a Timer and telling it to invalidate the form each time it is triggered. Then you render the happy face repeatedly, shifting it over to the right and slowing it by changing the origin with the TranslateTransform() method. When the happy face reaches the end of the screen, you reset the happy face back to the left and start again.

Listing 11-18. *Sliding the Happy Face the Ugly Way*

```
namespace SingleBuffering
{
    using namespace System;
    using namespace System::ComponentModel;
    using namespace System::Collections;
    using namespace System::Windows::Forms;
    using namespace System::Data;
    using namespace System::Drawing;

    public ref class Form1 : public System::Windows::Forms::Form_
    {
    public:
        Form1(void)
        {
            InitializeComponent();
            X = -250;  // Preset to be just left of window
        }

    protected:
        ~Form1()
        {
            if (components)
            {
                delete components;
            }
        }
```

```cpp
    private:
        System::Windows::Forms::Timer^ timer1;
        System::ComponentModel::IContainer^ components;

        float X;            // Actual x coordinate of Happy face

#pragma region Windows Form Designer generated code

        void InitializeComponent(void)
        {
            this->components = (gcnew System::ComponentModel::Container());
            this->timer1 =
                (gcnew System::Windows::Forms::Timer(this->components));
            this->SuspendLayout();
            //
            // timer1
            //
            this->timer1->Enabled = true;
            this->timer1->Interval = 10;
            this->timer1->Tick +=
                gcnew System::EventHandler(this, &Form1::timer1_Tick);
            //
            // Form1
            //
            this->AutoScaleDimensions = System::Drawing::SizeF(6, 13);
            this->AutoScaleMode = System::Windows::Forms::AutoScaleMode::Font;
            this->ClientSize = System::Drawing::Size(500, 300);
            this->Name = L"Form1";
            this->Text = L"Form1";
            this->Paint +=
                gcnew System::Windows::Forms::PaintEventHandler(this,
                                                        &Form1::Form1_Paint);
            this->ResumeLayout(false);
        }
#pragma endregion
    private:
        System::Void Form1_Paint(System::Object^ sender,
                            System::Windows::Forms::PaintEventArgs^ e)
        {
            Graphics^ g = e->Graphics;

            // Move image at end of line start from beginning
            if (X < ClientRectangle.Width)
                X += 1.0;
            else
                X = -250.0;

            g->TranslateTransform(X, 25.0);

            // redraw images from scratch
            Pen^ b4pen = gcnew Pen(Color::Black, 4);
```

```
        Drawing::Rectangle Head  = Drawing::Rectangle(0, 0, 250, 250);
        g->FillEllipse(Brushes::Yellow, Head);
        g->DrawEllipse(b4pen, Head);

        Drawing::Rectangle Mouth = Drawing::Rectangle(75, 150, 100, 50);
        g->FillPie(Brushes::White, Mouth,0,180);
        g->DrawPie(b4pen, Mouth, 0, 180);

        Drawing::Rectangle LEye  = Drawing::Rectangle(75, 75, 25, 25);
        g->FillEllipse(Brushes::White, LEye);
        g->DrawEllipse(b4pen, LEye);

        Drawing::Rectangle REye  = Drawing::Rectangle(150, 75, 25, 25);
        g->FillEllipse(Brushes::White, REye);
        g->DrawEllipse(b4pen, REye);

        delete b4pen;
    }

    System::Void timer1_Tick(System::Object^ sender, System::EventArgs^ e)
    {
        // Move the image
        Invalidate();
    }
  };
}
```

When you run SingleBuffering.exe, you will see a rather ugly, flickering happy face sort of sliding across the screen. If you have a superpowered computer with a great graphics card, then the flickering may not be that bad, or it may be nonexistent. My computer is actually on the high end graphically, and it still looks kind of pathetic.

Double Buffer Method

I change as little of the original code as possible in the double buffering example in Listing 11-19, which should enable you to focus on only what is needed to implement double buffering.

As the technique's name suggests, you need an extra buffer. Creating one is simple enough:

```
dbBitmap = gcnew Bitmap(ClientRectangle.Width, ClientRectangle.Height);
```

We have not covered the Bitmap class. But for the purposes of double buffering, all you need to know is that you create a bitmap by specifying its width and height. If you want to know more about the Bitmap class, the .NET Framework documentation is quite thorough.

If you recall, though, you don't call draw and fill methods from a bitmap—you need a Graphics class. Fortunately, it's also easy to extract the Graphics class out of a bitmap:

```
dbGraphics = Graphics::FromImage(dbBitmap);
```

Now that you have a Graphics class, you can clear, draw, and fill it just like you would a form-originated Graphics class:

```
dbGraphics->FillEllipse(Brushes::Yellow, Head);
dbGraphics->DrawEllipse(b4pen, Head);
```

So how do you implement a double buffer? The process is pretty much the same as for a single buffer, except that instead of drawing to the display device directly, you draw to the buffer. Once the image is complete, you copy the completed image to the display device. Notice you copy the image or buffer and not the graphic.

```
e->Graphics->DrawImageUnscaled(dbBitmap, 0, 0);
```

The reason double buffering is faster than single buffering is because writing to memory is faster than writing to the display device. Flickering is not an issue because the image is placed in its complete state onto the screen. There is no momentary delay, as the image is being built in front of your eyes.

Listing 11-19 shows the changes needed to implement double buffering. I don't claim this is the best way to do it. The goal is to show you what you can do using GDI+.

Listing 11-19. *Sliding a Happy Face Double Buffer Style*

```
namespace DoubleBuffering
{
    using namespace System;
    using namespace System::ComponentModel;
    using namespace System::Collections;
    using namespace System::Windows::Forms;
    using namespace System::Data;
    using namespace System::Drawing;

    public ref class Form1 : public System::Windows::Forms::Form
    {
    public:
        Form1(void)
        {
            InitializeComponent();
            this->SetStyle(ControlStyles::Opaque, true);

            dbBitmap = nullptr;
            dbGraphics = nullptr;
            X = -250;  // Preset to be just left of window

            Form1_Resize(nullptr, EventArgs::Empty);
        }

    protected:
        ~Form1()
        {
            if (components)
            {
                delete components;
            }
        }
    private:
        System::Windows::Forms::Timer^  timer1;
        System::ComponentModel::IContainer^  components;

        Bitmap^    dbBitmap;
        Graphics^  dbGraphics;
        int X;          // Actual x coordinate of Happy face
```

```
#pragma region Windows Form Designer generated code

        void InitializeComponent(void)
        {
            this->components = (gcnew System::ComponentModel::Container());
            this->timer1 =
                (gcnew System::Windows::Forms::Timer(this->components));
            this->SuspendLayout();
            //
            // timer1
            //
            this->timer1->Enabled = true;
            this->timer1->Interval = 10;
            this->timer1->Tick +=
                gcnew System::EventHandler(this, &Form1::timer1_Tick);
            //
            // Form1
            //
            this->AutoScaleDimensions = System::Drawing::SizeF(6, 13);
            this->AutoScaleMode = System::Windows::Forms::AutoScaleMode::Font;
            this->ClientSize = System::Drawing::Size(500, 300);
            this->Name = L"Form1";
            this->Text = L"Sliding Happy Face";
            this->Paint +=
                gcnew System::Windows::Forms::PaintEventHandler(this,
                                                    &Form1::Form1_Paint);

            this->Resize +=
                gcnew System::EventHandler(this, &Form1::Form1_Resize);
            this->ResumeLayout(false);


        }
#pragma endregion

    private:
        System::Void Form1_Paint(System::Object^ sender,
                            System::Windows::Forms::PaintEventArgs^ e)
        {
            // Move image at end of line start from beginning
            if (X < ClientRectangle.Width)
            {
                X ++;
                dbGraphics->TranslateTransform(1.0, 0.0);
            }
            else
            {
                X = -250;
                dbGraphics->TranslateTransform(
                    (float)-(ClientRectangle.Width+250), 0.0);
            }

            // Clear background
            dbGraphics->Clear(Color::White);
```

```cpp
        // redraw image from scratch
        Pen^ b4pen = gcnew Pen(Color::Black, 4);

        Drawing::Rectangle Head  = Drawing::Rectangle(0, 0, 250, 250);
        dbGraphics->FillEllipse(Brushes::Yellow, Head);
        dbGraphics->DrawEllipse(b4pen, Head);

        Drawing::Rectangle Mouth = Drawing::Rectangle(75, 150, 100, 50);
        dbGraphics->FillPie(Brushes::White, Mouth,0,180);
        dbGraphics->DrawPie(b4pen, Mouth, 0, 180);

        Drawing::Rectangle LEye  = Drawing::Rectangle(75, 75, 25, 25);
        dbGraphics->FillEllipse(Brushes::White, LEye);
        dbGraphics->DrawEllipse(b4pen, LEye);

        Drawing::Rectangle REye  = Drawing::Rectangle(150, 75, 25, 25);
        dbGraphics->FillEllipse(Brushes::White, REye);
        dbGraphics->DrawEllipse(b4pen, REye);

        // Make the buffer visible
        e->Graphics->DrawImageUnscaled(dbBitmap, 0, 0);

        delete b4pen;
    }

System::Void Form1_Resize(System::Object^ sender, System::EventArgs^ e)
{
    // Get rid of old stuff
    if (dbGraphics != nullptr)
    {
        delete dbGraphics;
    }

    if (dbBitmap != nullptr)
    {
        delete dbBitmap;
    }

    if (ClientRectangle.Width > 0 && ClientRectangle.Height > 0)
    {
        // Create a bitmap
        dbBitmap = gcnew Bitmap(ClientRectangle.Width,
                                ClientRectangle.Height);

        // Grab its Graphics
        dbGraphics = Graphics::FromImage(dbBitmap);

        // Set up initial translation after resize (also at start)
        dbGraphics->TranslateTransform((float)X, 25.0);
    }
}
```

```
        System::Void timer1_Tick(System::Object^ sender, System::EventArgs^ e)
        {
            // Move the image
            Invalidate();
        }
    };
}
```

Let's take a look at some of the changes that were needed. I already mentioned the building of a bitmap, so I'll skip that.

The first difference is that you have to handle the resizing of the form. The reason you must do this is because the secondary off-screen buffer needs to have the same dimensions as the primary on-screen buffer. When a form is resized, the primary buffer changes size; therefore you need to change the secondary buffer.

Notice also that you delete the Graphics class and the Bitmap class. Both of these classes use a lot of resources between them, and disposing of the old one before the new releases those resources. You need to check to make sure they have been initialized, because the first time this method is run they have not been initialized. Also, when the form is minimized you get rid of the buffer, so when the form is expanded you need to build the buffer again.

```
this->Resize += gcnew System::EventHandler(this, &Form1::Form1_Resize);
//...
System::Void Form1_Resize(System::Object^ sender, System::EventArgs^ e)
{
    // Get rid of old stuff
    if (dbGraphics != nullptr)
    {
        delete dbGraphics;
    }
    if (dbBitmap != nullptr)
    {
        delete dbBitmap;
    }
    if (ClientRectangle.Width > 0 && ClientRectangle.Height > 0)
    {
        // Create a bitmap
        dbBitmap = gcnew Bitmap(ClientRectangle.Width,ClientRectangle.Height);
        // Grab its Graphics
        dbGraphics = Graphics::FromImage(dbBitmap);
        // Set up initial translation after resize (also at start)
        dbGraphics->TranslateTransform((float)X, 25.0);
    }
}
```

You need to call the Resize event handler yourself (or write some duplicate code) before the Paint event is called the first time, in order to initialize dbBitmap and dbGraphics. I call the method in the constructor:

```
Form1_Resize(nullptr, EventArgs::Empty);
```

If you don't, the Paint event handler will throw a System.NullReferenceException when it first encounters dbGraphics.

The next difference is an important one. It is the setting of the style of the form to opaque. What this does is stop the form from clearing itself when it receives Invalidate().

```
SetStyle(ControlStyles::Opaque, true);
```

There is no need to clear the on-screen buffer because the off-screen buffer will overwrite everything on the on-screen buffer. All the clearing of the on-screen buffer does is momentarily leave the screen empty before the off-screen buffer writes to it, which produces a flicker.

Caution If you forget to set the style to opaque, your image will flicker.

The last difference that I haven't already discussed is the TranslateTransform() changes. Notice that you translate by one each time and not by "X". The reason for this is that the same Graphics class stays active the entire time this program is running (unless the screen is resized). The same translation matrix is being used, so you only need to increment by one. When you reach the end of the screen, you need to translate all the way back in one big jump.

```
if (X < ClientRectangle.Width)
{
    X++;
    dbGraphics->TranslateTransform(1.0, 0.0);
}
else
{
    X = -250;
    dbGraphics->TranslateTransform((float)-(ClientRectangle.Width+250), 0.0);
}
```

Figure 11-19 shows DoubleBuffering.exe sliding a happy face across the form. Unfortunately, this still image doesn't show much of the sliding.

Figure 11-19. *The sliding happy face*

Printing

I'll finish off this discussion of GDI+ by showing that you aren't restricted to the display adapter when it comes to GDI+. As I've been suggesting throughout the chapter, GDI+ is device independent, so in theory you should be able to draw using GDI+ to the printer. You know what? You can.

The printer is not as closely linked to the computer as the display adapter is, so to get GDI+ to work, you need to somehow provide for this link between your system and the printer. GDI+ does this through the PrintDocument class, which you can find in the System::Drawing::Printer namespace.

You can configure the PrintDocument class using its members (see Table 11-16), but letting the PrintDialog handle this is much easier.

Table 11-16. *Common PrintDocument Members*

Member	Description
DefaultPageSettings	Specifies the default settings to be used on all pages printed
DocumentName	Specifies the name of the document being printed
Print()	A method to start the printing process of a PrintDocument
PrintController	Specifies the print controller that maintains the print process
PrinterSettings	Specifies the printer that prints the document

In the example in Listing 11-20, you'll print the happy face I'm so proud of. First, you'll bring up the happy face using the normal Paint event handler method. Then you'll right-click to bring up the PrintDialog to print the happy face to the printer of your choice.

Just to prove that the same GDI+ code works for both the screen and the printer, I separated the code that generates the happy face into a method of its own that both the screen and print processes access.

First, look at the code as a whole and then I'll walk you through the highlights.

Listing 11-20. *Printing a Happy Face*

```
namespace PrintHappyFace
{
    using namespace System;
    using namespace System::ComponentModel;
    using namespace System::Collections;
    using namespace System::Windows::Forms;
    using namespace System::Data;
    using namespace System::Drawing;

    public ref class Form1 : public System::Windows::Forms::Form
    {
    public:
        Form1(void)
        {
            InitializeComponent();
        }

    protected:
        ~Form1()
        {
            if (components)
            {
                delete components;
            }
        }
```

```cpp
    private:
        System::Drawing::Printing::PrintDocument^  printDocument;
        System::Windows::Forms::PrintDialog^  printDialog;
        System::ComponentModel::Container ^components;

#pragma region Windows Form Designer generated code

        void InitializeComponent(void)
        {
            this->printDocument =
                (gcnew System::Drawing::Printing::PrintDocument());
            this->printDialog = (gcnew System::Windows::Forms::PrintDialog());
            this->SuspendLayout();
            //
            // printDocument
            //
            this->printDocument->PrintPage +=
                gcnew System::Drawing::Printing::PrintPageEventHandler(this,
                                        &Form1::printDocument_PrintPage);
            //
            // printDialog
            //
            this->printDialog->Document = this->printDocument;
            //
            // Form1
            //
            this->AutoScaleDimensions = System::Drawing::SizeF(6, 13);
            this->AutoScaleMode = System::Windows::Forms::AutoScaleMode::Font;
            this->ClientSize = System::Drawing::Size(300, 300);
            this->Name = L"Form1";
            this->Text = L"Click to Print";
            this->Paint +=
                gcnew System::Windows::Forms::PaintEventHandler(this,
                                            &Form1::Form1_Paint);
            this->Click +=
                gcnew System::EventHandler(this, &Form1::Form1_Click);
            this->ResumeLayout(false);
        }
#pragma endregion

    private:
        System::Void Form1_Click(System::Object^ sender, System::EventArgs^ e)
        {
            // Display Print dialog when mouse pressed
            if (printDialog->ShowDialog() == Windows::Forms::DialogResult::OK)
            {
                printDocument->Print();
            }
        }
```

```
System::Void printDocument_PrintPage(System::Object^ sender,
                      System::Drawing::Printing::PrintPageEventArgs^ e)
{
    CreateHappyFace(e->Graphics); //Same call as Form1_Paint
    e->HasMorePages = false;
}

System::Void Form1_Paint(System::Object^ sender,
                      System::Windows::Forms::PaintEventArgs^ e)
{
    CreateHappyFace(e->Graphics);//Same call as printDocument_PrintPage
}

// Generic Happy Face Creator
void CreateHappyFace(Graphics ^g)
{
    Pen^ b4pen = gcnew Pen(Color::Black, 4);

    Rectangle rect = Drawing::Rectangle(25, 25, 250, 250);
    g->FillEllipse(Brushes::Yellow, rect);
    g->DrawEllipse(b4pen, rect);

    g->FillPie(Brushes::White, 100, 175, 100, 50, 0, 180);
    g->DrawPie(b4pen, 100, 175, 100, 50, 0, 180);

    rect = Drawing::Rectangle(100, 100, 25, 25);
    g->FillEllipse(Brushes::White, rect);
    g->DrawEllipse(b4pen, rect);

    rect = Drawing::Rectangle(175, 100, 25, 25);
    g->FillEllipse(Brushes::White, rect);
    g->DrawEllipse(b4pen, rect);

    delete b4pen;
    }
};
}
```

The first thing I did when I created PrintHappyFace was drag and drop a PrintDocument and a PrintDialog control to the form and then set the Document property of the PrintDialog to the newly created PrintDocument. (It will show up in the Document property drop-down box.) Then I added a PrintPage event handler to the PrintDocument. I examine the handler below.

This auto-generates all the code needed to create a PrintDialog and a PrintDocument and then links them together. I need to link the PrintDialog to the PrintDocument so that any configuration changes made to the printers through the PrintDialog get reflected in the PrintDocument.

Next, I added an event handler for the Click event of Form1, which displays the PrintDialog (see Figure 11-20) and gathers the user's input on configuring the printer.

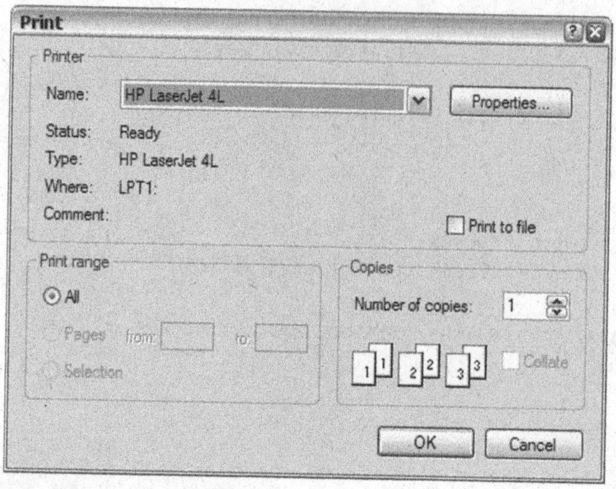

Figure 11-20. *The Print dialog box*

If the user is happy and wants to complete the print process, he or she will click the OK button, which will return DialogResult::OK. If the user doesn't want to complete the print process, he or she will click the Cancel button and DialogResult::Cancel will be returned. I ignore this result in the example, but you might want to acknowledge the cancel. Printers are frequently on the opposite end of the office (I don't know how this is possible, but it seems to be always true), and walking to the printer and waiting for something cancelled could be aggravating to users.

```
if (pdialog->ShowDialog() == System::Windows::Forms::DialogResult::OK)
```

When the DialogResult::OK is received, you call the documents Print() method, which then triggers a PrintPage event:

```
printdoc->Print();
```

The last thing to notice about the preceding example is the PrintPage event handler. The PrintPage event handler handles the printing of only one page at a time. If you want to print more than one page, you need to set the HasMorePages property of the PrintPageEventArgs parameter passed to the PrintPage event handler to true. You must also keep track of where you left off printing, and when the next PrintPage event is triggered you then continue where you left off:

```
System::Void printDocument_PrintPage(System::Object^ sender,
                        System::Drawing::Printing::PrintPageEventArgs^ e)
{
    CreateHappyFace(e->Graphics);
    e->HasMorePages = false;   // false means only one page will be printed.
}
```

Notice that the exact same GDI+ code found in the CreateHappyFace() method is used for displaying to the screen and printing to the printer.

Summary

This has been another long chapter in which you covered a lot of ground. You started off with the basics of what GDI+ is. You created your third "Hello World" program—this time with a GDI+ flavor. You then moved on and examined many of the GDI+ classes, the most important being the Graphics class, from which all GDI+ functionality derives. You played with strings, fonts, and pre-drawn images and ended up with the basics of drawing your own image. Next, you covered the advanced topics: scrollable windows, optimizing, and double buffering. You ended the chapter by demonstrating that you can also use GDI+ to print to printers.

You should now have all the information you need to display your own images and no longer be restricted to drawing with the controls provided by Win Forms.

In the next chapter, you get to play with databases using ADO.NET. Along the way, you will look at some of the tools Visual Studio 2005 provides to work with databases.

CHAPTER 12

■ ■ ■

ADO.NET and
Database Development

You've already looked at two of the four common methods of getting input into and out of your .NET Windows applications: streams and controls. ADO.NET, which you'll examine in detail in this chapter, is the third. In the next chapter, you'll round it out with XML, the fourth and final common method. ADO.NET is a huge topic. In this chapter, you'll learn about some of the more commonly used aspects of it.

When you're implementing with ADO.NET, you're dealing with data stores or, to use the better-known term, databases. Most developers are going to have to deal with the database. If that thought frightens you, it shouldn't, as ADO.NET has made the database an easy and, dare I say, fun thing to work with. The hard part now is no longer interfacing with the database, be it a 2-tier, 3-tier, or even n-tier architecture, but instead designing a good database. Hey—Visual Studio 2005 even works with you there!

The language of relational databases is still SQL. That doesn't change with ADO.NET. If you don't know SQL, then you might need to read up on it a little bit. However, for those of you who don't know SQL, I made this chapter's SQL code rudimentary, to say the least. SQL is a very powerful language, and most programmers should have at least some SQL knowledge. But don't fret if you don't, as the SQL you'll find in this chapter isn't important in your understanding of ADO.NET. What I'm basically trying to say in a roundabout way is that this chapter is about ADO.NET and not SQL.

This chapter starts by covering the basic concepts of ADO.NET. You'll then move on to building, from scratch, a (very simple) database using Visual Studio 2005. Then, using this database, you'll examine in detail the two methods provided by ADO.NET to access a database: connected and disconnected.

Those of you who have read my book *Real World ASP.NET: Building a Content Management System* (Apress, 2002) might find some of the material similar, as you're going to be using the database I developed in that book.

What Is ADO.NET?

Databases are made up of tables, views, relationships, constraints, and stored procedures. They're usually the domain of the database architects, designers, developers, and administrators. ADO.NET, on the other hand, is how application developers get their hands on these (meaning the tables, views, and so forth—not the architects and designers, though sometimes I'd like to get my hands on the designers . . .). With ADO.NET, it's possible to keep these two diverse software developing worlds separate, letting the specialists in both fields focus on what they do best.

ADO.NET is a set of classes that encompasses all aspects of accessing data sources within the .NET architecture. It's designed to provide full support for either connected or disconnected data access, while using an Extensible Markup Language (XML) format for transmitting data when data transfer is required. Chapter 13 contains more details about XML, so don't worry about it for now. Just think of ADO.NET as a programmer's window into a data source, in this case the DVC_DB database.

The classes that make up ADO.NET are located primarily in two assemblies: System.Data.dll and System.Xml.dll. To reference these two assemblies, you need to either add the following two lines to the top of your application source:

```
#using <System.Data.dll>
#using <System.Xml.dll>
```

or add a reference to these assemblies in the project's Properties page.

The addition of the System.Xml.dll assembly is due to the heavy reliance on XML in the internals of ADO.NET and in particular the class XmlDataDocument.

Seven namespaces house all of ADO.NET's functionality. These namespaces are described at a high level in Table 12-1.

Table 12-1. *ADO.NET Namespaces*

Namespace	Description
System::Data	Contains most of the classes that make up ADO.NET. The classes found within this namespace are designed to work independently of the type of data source used. The most important class in this namespace is the DataSet class, which is the cornerstone of disconnected data source access.
System::Data::Common	Contains the common interfaces used by each of the managed providers.
System::Data::Odbc	Contains the classes that make up the ODBC managed provider, which allows access to ODBC-connected databases such as MySQL. The classes contained within this namespace are all prefixed with Odbc.
System::Data::OleDb	Contains the classes that make up the OLE DB managed provider, which allows access to databases such as Sybase, Microsoft Access, and Microsoft SQL Server 6.5. The classes contained within this namespace are all prefixed with OleDb.
System::Data::Oracle	Contains the classes that make up the Oracle managed provider, which allows access to Oracle8i and later databases. The classes contained within this namespace are all prefixed with Oracle.
System::Data::SqlClient	Contains the classes that make up the SQL Server managed provider, which allows access to Microsoft SQL Server 7.0 and later databases. The classes contained within this namespace are all prefixed with Sql.
System::Data::SqlTypes	Contains classes for native data types associated with SQL Server.

Now that you have a basic understanding of what ADO.NET is, let's take a small sidetrack from C++/CLI and see how to build a database using Visual Studio 2005.

Building a Database with Visual Studio 2005

Visual Studio 2005 is well equipped when it comes to the design and development of Microsoft SQL Server databases. It provides the functionality to create databases, tables, views, stored procedures, and many other features.

The starting point of all database utilities is Server Explorer. Select Server Explorer from the View menu to open it (see Figure 12-1). You will find your database in the Data Connections folder just above the Servers folder.

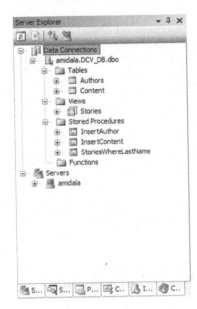

Figure 12-1. *Server Explorer*

Visual Studio 2005 provides Microsoft SQL Server databases with much of the functionality that comes with SQL Enterprise Manager. On the other hand, all the other database types are mostly restricted to viewing and editing records. This book focuses on Microsoft SQL Server and covers the functionality provided by Visual Studio 2005. If you are developing using any other database, much of the first part of this chapter will not help you because you will have to use the database maintenance tools provided by your database.

■**Tip** If you don't currently have a database installed on your system, I recommend that you install the MSDE 2000 database server or SQL Server 2005 Express. These databases are stripped-down versions of Microsoft SQL Server, and with either you'll get a good feel for the functionality provided by Visual Studio 2005. Plus, you can always uninstall it later and use the database of your choice.

There is nothing stopping you from building your Microsoft SQL Server databases outside of Visual Studio 2005, using the SQL Enterprise Manager, for example, and then adding the database to Server Explorer. Doing this is beyond the scope of this book, however.

Now you'll build your own simple content management database so that you can explore ADO.NET with intimate knowledge of its architecture, instead of as a black box as you would if you were using one of the preinstalled databases provided with Microsoft SQL Server.

Creating a New Database

The first step in database development isn't creating one. Obviously, creating the data model, designing the logical database, and designing the physical database should come first. But hey, I'm a programmer. I'll code first and then go ask questions. (I'm joking—really!)

Visual Studio 2005 makes creating databases so easy that it's almost not worth explaining how to do it.

The following steps create the database DCV_DB, which contains author information and their related stories. You will use this database throughout the chapter.

1. Select Server Explorer from the View menu.

2. Right-click the Data Connections folder.

3. Select the Create New SQL Server Database menu item, which displays the Create New SQL Server Database dialog box shown in Figure 12-2.

Figure 12-2. *The Create New SQL Server Database dialog box*

4. Enter the server name that the database will reside on (in my case, Amidala).

5. Enter DCV_DB in the New database name field.

6. Select the Use Windows Authentication radio button.

7. Click OK.

Microsoft SQL Server supports two types of security: Windows Authentication and SQL Server authentication. Covering these security systems is beyond the scope of this book. In the preceding database, I use the default security configuration. You should consult your DBA to see which security method you should use.

Now you should have a new database called DCV_DB in your database folder. You can expand it and see all the default folders built. If you click these folders, however, you will see that there is nothing in them. Okay, let's fix that and add some stuff.

Adding and Loading Tables and Views to a Database

An empty database is really quite useless, so now you'll add a couple of tables to the database to provide a place to store your content.

Note The tables and views you use in this chapter are purposely very simple (you might even call them minimal) and aren't the best schema around. I did this so that you don't get bogged down with the details of the database and so it doesn't take much effort or time for you to build these tables and views yourself.

The first table is for storing authors and information about them, and the second table is for storing headlines and stories. The two databases are linked together by a common AuthorID key. Figure 12-3 shows a data diagram of the database.

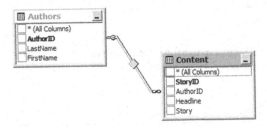

Figure 12-3. *The DCV_DB data diagram*

Having this separation means you have to store only one copy of the author information, even though the author may have written many stories. If you had created only one table to contain all the information, a lot of duplicated author information would have to be rekeyed each time a story is added to maintain the database. It also conveniently enables me to show you how to create a relationship between tables.

The process of building a new table is only slightly more difficult than creating a database. The hard part is figuring out what columns are needed and the format for each table in the database. It's nice to know you can spend most of your time designing the ultimate database schema instead of figuring out how to implement it.

Creating Tables

To create the first table, follow these steps:

1. Expand the Date Connections folder.

2. Expand the DCV_DB folder. Usually the server name will precede the database name and be followed by dbo. For my system, I expand the Amidala.DCV_DB.dbo folder.

3. Right-click the Tables folder.

4. Select the Add New Table menu item. You should now have an entry form in which to enter the database columns shown in Table 12-2. (Note that Description and Identity Specification are entered in the Column Properties view, which comes available when you select the column definition row.)

Table 12-2. *Authors Database Table Column Descriptions*

Column Name	Data Type	Length	Description	Identity Specification	Allow Nulls
AuthorID	int	4	Auto-generated ID number for the author	Yes	No
LastName	varchar	50	Last name of the author	No	No
FirstName	varchar	50	First name of the author	No	No

5. Right-click the AuthorID row and select Set Primary Key from the drop-down menu.

6. Select Save Table1 from the File menu.

7. Enter **Authors** into the text field in the dialog box.

8. Click OK.

Go ahead and repeat these steps for the second table, but use the information in Table 12-3 and use StoryID as the primary key. Save the table as Content.

Table 12-3. *Content Database Table Column Descriptions*

Column Name	Data Type	Length	Description	Identity Specification	Allow Nulls
StoryID	int	4	Auto-generated ID number for the story	Yes	No
AuthorID	int	4	Foreign key to the Authors database	No	No
Headline	varchar	80	Headline for the content	No	No
Story	text	16	Story portion of the content	No	No

In this book I don't go into what all the data types mean, but if you're interested, many good books on Microsoft SQL Server and SQL cover this topic in great detail.

The Identity Specification, when set to Yes, will turn on autonumber generation for the column. Why the field is called "Identity Specification" (instead of "Autonumber") is a mystery to me. I'm an application programmer, though, and not a database person. It's probably some special database term.

Okay, you now have your tables. The next step is to build a relationship between them. In this database, it is fairly obvious: AuthorID is the column that should link these two tables.

Creating a Relationship

To create a relationship between your tables, follow these steps:

1. Right-click the Content table in Server Explorer.
2. Select Open Table Definition from the menu.
3. Right-click anywhere on the Table Designer.
4. Select Relationships from the menu. This will bring up a Relationships property page similar to the one shown in Figure 12-4.

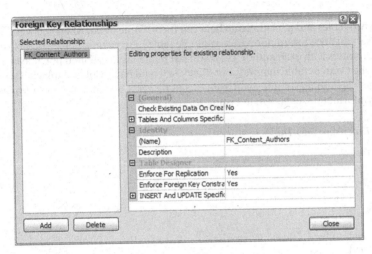

Figure 12-4. *The Foreign Key Relationships property page*

5. Click the Add button.
6. Click the Tables and Columns Specification property and click the ellipses. This will bring up a Tables and Columns dialog box similar to the one shown in Figure 12-5.

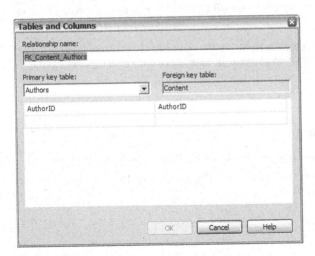

Figure 12-5. *The Tables and Columns property page*

7. Select Authors as the primary key side of the relationship from the Primary key table drop-down list.

8. Select AuthorID as the primary key in the grid beneath the Primary key table drop-down list.

9. Select AuthorID as the foreign key in the grid beneath the Foreign key.

10. Click OK.

11. Click Close.

Now you have two tables and a relationship between them. Quite often, when you want to get data from a database, you need information from multiple tables. For example, in this case, you might want to get all stories with each author's first and last name. As mentioned previously, you could have created the Content table that way, but then you would have a lot of duplicate data floating around. There is nothing stopping you from executing a SQL statement, also known as a *query*, that gets this information, as shown in Listing 12-1.

Listing 12-1. *Getting Data from Two Tables*

```
SELECT     FirstName,
           LastName,
           Headline,
           Story
FROM       Authors,
           Content
WHERE      Authors.AuthorID = Content.AuthorID
ORDER BY   StoryID ASC
```

Personally, I prefer to be able to write a query something like this instead:

```
SELECT FirstName, LastName, Headline, Story FROM Stories
```

This is exactly what you can do with database views. Basically, you might think of a view as a virtual table without any data of its own, based on a predefined query. If you know you are going to use the same set of data based on a query, you might consider using the view instead of coding.

Note Those of you who are knowledgeable about SQL and views might have noticed the ORDER BY clause. Microsoft SQL Server supports the ORDER BY clause in its views, unlike some older database systems.

Creating a View

Follow these steps to create a view:

1. Right-click the Views table from within the DCV_DB folder in Server Explorer.

2. Select Add New View from the menu. This will bring up an Add Table dialog box similar to the one shown in Figure 12-6.

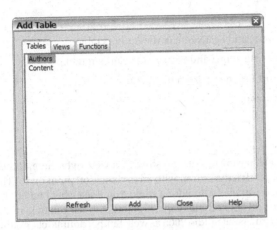

Figure 12-6. *The Add Table dialog box*

3. Select both Authors and Content.

4. Click the Add button. This generates a window similar to the one shown in Figure 12-7.

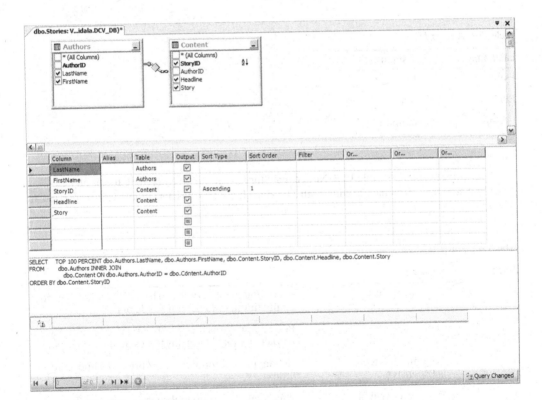

Figure 12-7. *The View Design window*

5. Click the Close button.

6. Click the check boxes for FirstName and LastName in the Authors table.

7. Click the check boxes for StoryID, Headline, and Story in the Content table.

8. Right-click StoryID and select Sort Ascending from the menu.

9. Select Save View1 from the File menu.

10. Enter Stories into text field.

11. Click OK.

Pretty painless, don't you think? You have the option of testing your view right there, too. Click the Run Query button on the main toolbar. (It's the button with an exclamation point on it.) The View Design window is pretty powerful. If you play with it for a while, you'll see what I mean.

Did you click the Run Query button and get nothing? Oops . . . I forgot to tell you to load some data into the database. You can do this with Visual Studio 2005 as well. Simply double-click either of the tables you created, and an editable table will appear.

First enter the data for the authors. If you don't, you won't have an author ID to enter into the AuthorID column in the Content view. Enter the data from Table 12-4. Notice that there are no author IDs to enter—this field is automatically created. In fact, Visual Studio 2005 will yell at you if you try to enter something in the AuthorID column.

Table 12-4. *Author Data*

LastName	FirstName
Doors	Bill
Ellidaughter	Larry
Fraser	Stephen

Now enter the data in Table 12-5. Notice that StoryID cannot be entered. It, too, is an auto-generated number. You do have to enter AuthorID, though, because it is not automatically generated in this table.

Table 12-5. *Content Data*

AuthorID	Headline	Story
1	.NET is the Best	According to my research. The .NET product has no competition, though I am a little biased.
2	Oracle is #1	Research suggests that it is the best database on the market, not that I have any biases in that conclusion.
3	Content Management is Expensive	Not anymore. It now costs the price of a book and a little work.
4	SQL Server Will Be #1	This database has no real competition. But then again, I am a little biased.

Building Stored Procedures

You don't have to use stored procedures, because anything you can run using stored procedures you can run using standard SQL. So, why cover this utility at all?

There are two main reasons. First, stored procedures let a software developer call database code using function calls with arguments. Second, and more important, the utility is compiled before it gets loaded. This makes the calls to the database faster and more efficient because it has already been optimized.

Because you haven't encountered ADO.NET code yet, you won't be able to do much with the stored procedure you'll create. Fortunately, Visual Studio 2005 provides an option so that it can be tested.

Unlike the previous utilities, you have to actually code stored procedures. If you don't know SQL, don't worry because the coding is short and, I think, pretty self-explanatory. As always, there are many good books you can read to get a better understanding of it.

You will create a stored procedure to insert data into the Authors table. You already did this process manually, so you should have a good idea of what the stored procedure needs to do.

To create a stored procedure, follow these steps:

1. Right-click the Stored Procedures table from within the DCV_DB folder in Server Explorer.

2. Select Add New Stored Procedure from the menu. This will bring up an editing session with the default code shown in Listing 12-2.

Listing 12-2. *Default Stored Procedure Code*

```
CREATE PROCEDURE dbo.StoredProcedure1
/*
    (
        @parameter1 datatype = default value,
        @parameter2 datatype OUTPUT
    )
*/
AS
    /* SET NOCOUNT ON */
    RETURN
```

First you have to set up the parameters that will be passed from the program. Obviously, you need to receive all the mandatory columns that make up the row. In the Authors table's case, that's the entire row except AuthorID, which is auto-generated. Listing 12-3 shows the changes that need to be made to the default code provided in order to add parameters. Note that the comments (/*...*/) are removed.

Listing 12-3. *Setting the Parameters*

```
CREATE PROCEDURE dbo.StoredProcedure1
    (
        @LastName NVARCHAR(32) = NULL,
        @FirstName NVARCHAR(32) = NULL
    )
AS
```

The SET NOCOUNT ON option prevents the number of rows affected by the stored procedure from being returned to the calling program every time it is called. If you need a count on the number of records affected, you can leave the SET NOCOUNT ON option commented out, or you can delete the option altogether. Because I will use the count in a later example, I left the option commented out.

Finally, you code the actual insert command. The key to this stored procedure is that instead of hard-coding the values to be inserted, you use the parameters you previously declared. Listing 12-4 is the final version of the stored procedure. Note that you rename the stored procedure to dbo.InsertAuthor.

Listing 12-4. *InsertAuthor Stored Procedure*

```
CREATE PROCEDURE dbo.InsertAuthor
    (
        @LastName NVARCHAR(32) = NULL,
        @FirstName NVARCHAR(32) = NULL
    )
AS
    /* SET NOCOUNT ON */

    INSERT INTO    Authors ( LastName,  FirstName)
    VALUES                 (@LastName, @FirstName)

    RETURN
```

All that's left is to save the stored procedure. Saving the file will create a stored procedure with the name on the CREATE PROCEDURE line. If you made a mistake while coding, the save will fail, and an error message will tell you where the error is.

To run or debug the stored procedure, just right-click the newly created stored procedure and select Run Stored Procedure or Step Into Stored Procedure.

You now have a database to work with for the rest of the chapter. Let's continue on and start looking at ADO.NET and how to code it using C++/CLI.

Managed Providers

Managed providers provide ADO.NET with the capability to connect to and access data sources. Their main purpose, as far as most developers are concerned, is to provide support for the DataAdapter class. This class is essentially for mapping between the data store and the DataSet.

Currently four (Microsoft supported) managed providers exist for ADO.NET:

- SQL Server managed provider: Connects to Microsoft SQL Server version 7.0 or higher databases

- OLE DB managed provider: Connects to several supported OLE DB data sources

- ODBC managed provider: Connects to ODBC-connected databases such as MySQL

- Oracle managed provider: Connects to the Oracle8i or higher databases

Determining which of these managed providers is actually used depends on the database that ADO.NET interfaces with. Currently, ADO.NET interfaces with four groups of database types: Microsoft SQL Server 7.0 and later, Oracle8*i* and later, databases that provide ODBC support, and databases that provide OLE DB support. Which database group you are using determines whether you implement the System::Data::SqlClient, System::Data::Oracle; System::Data::Odbc, or System::Data::OleDb namespace.

In addition, the group of databases interfaced with determines which classes you will use. You will find that if you are using the System::Data::SqlClient namespace, then all of your classes will be prefixed with Sql, as in SqlCommand() and SqlDataAdapter(). If you are using the System::Data::Oracle namespace, then the classes will be prefixed with Oracle, as in OracleCommand() and OracleDataAdapter(). If you are using the System::Data::Odbc namespace, then the classes will be prefixed with Odbc, as in OdbcCommand() and OdbcDataAdapter(). And, if you are using the System::Data::OleDb namespace, then the classes will be prefixed with OleDb, as in OleDbCommand() and OleDbDataAdapter().

Once you have learned one managed provider, you have pretty much learned all four because they are nearly the same, except for the Sql, OleDb, Odbc, and Oracle prefixes and a few other small differences.

Because this book uses Microsoft SQL Server 2000, I use the SQL Server managed provider and thus the namespace associated with it.

Connected ADO.NET

As I stated previously, you have two distinct ways of accessing a database using ADO.NET. I cover the one that's easier to visualize and code (at least for me) first: connected access.

With *connected access*, you are continually connected to the database during the entire time you work with it. Like file access, you open the database, work with it for a while, and then you close it. Also like file I/O, you have the option of buffering data written to the database. This buffered access to the database is better known as *transactional database access*. I discuss this access method after I cover nontransactional database access.

Using Simple Connected ADO.NET

You'll start with the easiest way of working with the database, where the commands you execute happen immediately to the database.

Figure 12-8 shows the basic flow of nontransactional database access.

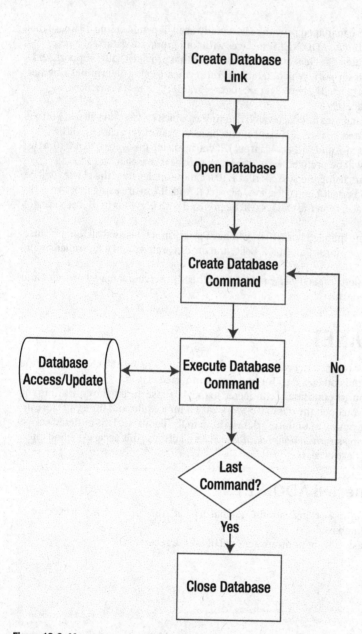

Figure 12-8. *Nontransactional database access*

1. Create a link to the database with a SqlConnection.
2. Open the database with the Open() method.
3. Create a database command with SqlCommand.

4. Execute the command by using one of the three methods within SqlCommand (see Table 12-6). The database is immediately updated.

Table 12-6. *The Main SqlCommand SQL Statement Execution Methods*

Method	Description
ExecuteNonQuery	Executes a statement that updates the database.
ExecuteReader	Executes a query to the database that could potentially return multiple rows from a database. This method returns a SqlDataReader object that provides forward-only read access to the retrieved data or result set.
ExecuteScalar	Executes a statement that returns a single value.

5. Repeat steps 3 and 4 until completed.

6. Close the database with the Close() method.

Note If you are using the SQL Server managed provider, use classes prefixed with Sql. On the other hand, when you are using the OLE DB managed provider, use classes starting with OleDb; when you are using the ODBC managed provider, use classes starting with Odbc; and when you are using the Oracle managed provider, use classes starting with Oracle.

Connecting to, Opening, and Closing a Database

With connected nontransactional access to a database, you will always be connecting to, opening, and closing your database. To handle this, you need to work with one of the Connection classes: SqlConnection, OleDbConnection, OdbcConnection, or OracleConnection. Which one of these you use depends on the managed provider you use.

This book uses Microsoft SQL Server, so you'll use the SQL Server managed provider. If you are using the OLE DB, ODBC, or Oracle managed provider, just remember to replace the prefix of every class starting with Sql with OleDb, Odbc, or Oracle and, of course, you will have to change the connection string, but I'll get to that shortly.

Listing 12-5 shows how to connect, open, and close a database in a nontransactional method.

Listing 12-5. *Connecting, Opening, and Closing a Database*

```
using namespace System;
using namespace System::Data;
using namespace System::Data::SqlClient;

void main()
{
    SqlConnection^ connection = gcnew SqlConnection();

#ifdef SQLAuth
    // SQL Server authentication
    connection->ConnectionString =
        "User ID=sa; Password=;"
        "Data Source=(local); Initial Catalog=DCV_DB;";
```

```
#else
    //  Windows Integrated Security
    connection->ConnectionString =
        "Persist Security Info=False; Integrated Security=SSPI;"
        "Data Source=(local); Initial Catalog=DCV_DB;";
#endif

    try
    {
        connection->Open();
        Console::WriteLine("We got a connection!");
    }
    catch (SqlException ^e)
    {
        Console::WriteLine("No connection the following error occurred: {0}",
            e->Message);
    }
    finally
    {
        connection->Close();
        Console::WriteLine("The connection to the database has been closed");
    }
}
```

The first thing you do (as with any other .NET application) is import the namespaces needed to access the ADO.NET basic functionality:

```
using namespace System;
using namespace System::Data;
using namespace System::Data::SqlClient;
```

For those of you using a database other than Microsoft SQL Server, use one of the following namespaces instead of System::Data::SqlClient: System::Data::OleDb, System::Data::Odbc, or System::Data::Oracle.

There is nothing special about creating a SqlConnection class. It is just a default constructor:

```
SqlConnection ^connection = gcnew SqlConnection();
```

The hardest part of this piece of coding is figuring out what the connection string is. For the SQL Server managed provider, this is fairly easy because it is usually made up of a combination of four out of six clauses:

- Data Source: The location of the database server. This field will normally be (local) for your local machine, or the server name or IP address when the server is remote. Since the database is local for me, I need to use (local).

- Initial Catalog: The name of the database. I am using the DCV_DB database.

- Persist Security Info: Use True when security-sensitive information is returned as part of the connection. Since this is not the case in this example, I use False.

- Integrated Security: When False (the default)True (or the equivalent and recommended SSPI). Since both are common, I show both types of security. Which gets implemented is determined by whether you define SQLAuth.

- User ID: The user ID (not recommended with Windows Integrated Security). I use the system-defined sa user ID, but I would recommend that you use one of your own creation.

- Password: The user password (not recommended with Windows Integrated Security). I use a blank password to simplify things, but this is severely frowned upon in a production environment.

Tip You can find the connection string in the connection string property when you select the database connection in the Server Explorer.

The connection string will look like this in the code:

```
connection->ConnectionString =
    "User ID=sa; Password=; Data Source=(local); Initial Catalog=DCV_DB;";
```

or

```
connection->ConnectionString =
    "Persist Security Info=False;Integrated Security=SSPI;"
    "Data Source=(local); Initial Catalog=DCV_DB;";
```

The connection string for the Oracle managed provider is very similar to the SQL Server managed provider, whereas the OLE DB and ODBC managed providers always add an additional clause: for OLE DB, the Provider clause, and for ODBC, the Driver clause. For example:

```
//OLE DB Connection string
connection->ConnectionString =
    "Provider=SQLOLEDB; Data Source=(local); Initial Catalog=DCV_DB; "
    "User ID=sa; Password=;";
```

and

```
// ODBC Connection string
connection->ConnectionString =
    "Driver={SQL Server}; Data Source=(local); Initial Catalog=DCV_DB; "
    "User ID=sa; Password=;";
```

Note In the preceding code example, I define two of the more common connection strings I use and use the compile-time directive #ifdef SQLAuth to allow me to choose the one I want. I do this to simplify things. In most cases, it would be better not to hard-code the connection string at all and instead retrieve it from a configuration file or registry.

You open and close the database in virtually the same way as you do a file, except the Open() method doesn't have any parameters:

```
connection->Open();
connection->Close();
```

You need to pay attention to the try statement. ADO.NET commands can abort almost anywhere, so it is always a good thing to enclose your ADO.NET logic within a try clause and capture any exceptions by catching SQLException (OleDbException, OdbcException, or OracleException).

It is also possible for ADO.NET to abort with the database still open. (Probably not in this example, but I felt having the correct code right from the beginning would make things clearer.) Therefore, it is a good idea to place your Close() method within a finally clause so that it will always be executed.

Figure 12-9 shows the results of the preceding example program. Impressive, no?

Figure 12-9. *The database is successfully opened and closed.*

Querying a Database

All queries made to a connected database are done using the `SqlCommand`, `OleDbCommand`, `OdbcCommand`, or `OracleCommand` class. As noted previously, the `SqlCommand` class provides three methods to send SQL commands to the database, with each depending on the type of command. To query the database, you need to use the `ExecuteReader()` method.

Before you run the `ExecuteReader()` method, you need to configure `SqlCommand` by placing the SQL command into it. There are two common ways of doing this. You can either place the SQL command, in text form, into the `CommandText` property or place the name of the stored procedure containing the SQL command into the same property. The default method is the command in text form. If you plan to use a stored procedure, you need to change the `CommandType` property to `CommandType::StoredProcedure`.

Listing 12-6 shows both methods. The first command uses a text-formatted command and retrieves the contents of the Authors database for authors with a specified LastName, in this case hard-coded to "Doors". The second command, using a stored procedure, retrieves all Stories view records where LastName equals the value passed to the stored procedure, in this case also "Doors".

Both calls to the `ExecuteReader()` method after being configured return an instance of `SqlDataReader`, which is then iterated through to display the retrieved content.

Listing 12-6. *The "Doors" Stories*

```
using namespace System;
using namespace System::Data;
using namespace System::Data::SqlClient;

void main()
{
    String ^Name = "Doors";

    SqlConnection ^connection = gcnew SqlConnection();

#ifdef SQLAuth
    //  SQL Server authentication
    connection->ConnectionString =
        "User ID=sa; Password=;"
        "Data Source=(local); Initial Catalog=DCV_DB;";
#else
    //  Windows Integrated Security
    connection->ConnectionString =
        "Persist Security Info=False; Integrated Security=SSPI;"
        "Data Source=(local); Initial Catalog=DCV_DB;";
#endif
```

```cpp
try
{
    SqlCommand ^cmd = gcnew SqlCommand();
    cmd->Connection = connection;

    cmd->CommandType = CommandType::Text;
    cmd->CommandText =
        String::Format("SELECT FirstName, LastName FROM Authors "
                       "WHERE LastName = '{0}'",
                       Name);

    connection->Open();

    SqlDataReader ^reader = cmd->ExecuteReader();

    while(reader->Read())
    {
        Console::WriteLine("{0} {1}",
            reader["FirstName"], reader["LastName"]);
    }
    reader->Close();

    // CREATE PROCEDURE dbo.StoriesWhereLastName
    //   (
    //       @LastName NVARCHAR(32) = NULL
    //   )
    // AS
    //   /* SET NOCOUNT ON */

    //   SELECT StoryID, Headline, Story FROM Stories
    //   WHERE  LastName = @LastName
    //
    //   RETURN

    cmd->CommandType = CommandType::StoredProcedure;
    cmd->CommandText = "StoriesWhereLastName";

    cmd->Parameters->Add(
        gcnew SqlParameter("@LastName",SqlDbType::VarChar));
    cmd->Parameters["@LastName"]->Value = Name;

    reader = cmd->ExecuteReader();

    Console::WriteLine("-------------------------------------------------");
    while(reader->Read())
    {
        Console::WriteLine(reader["StoryID"]);
        Console::WriteLine(reader["Headline"]);
        Console::WriteLine(reader["Story"]);
        Console::WriteLine();
    }
    reader->Close();
}
```

```
    catch (SqlException ^e)
    {
        Console::WriteLine("No connection the following error occurred: {0}",
            e->Message);
    }
    finally
    {
        connection->Close();
    }
}
```

The code to query a database with a CommandType of Text is pretty easy (if you know SQL, that is). First, you set the SqlCommand class's CommandType property to Text:

```
cmd->CommandType = CommandType::Text;
```

Next, you place the SQL command you want to execute in the CommandText property. What makes this process easy is that you can use standard String formatting to build the command, as you see here:

```
cmd->CommandText =
    String::Format("SELECT * FROM Authors WHERE LastName='{0}'", Name);
```

Finally, you run the SqlCommand class's ExecuteReader() method. This method returns a SqlDataReader class from which you process the result set produced from the query:

```
SqlDataReader ^reader = cmd->ExecuteReader();
```

The code to query a database with a CommandType of StoredProcedure is a little more difficult if passing parameters is required. (It is a little easier if no parameters are passed, as no SQL code has to be written by the application developer.) First, you set the SqlCommand class's CommandType property to StoredProcedure:

```
cmd->CommandType = CommandType::StoredProcedure;
```

Next, you place the name of the stored procedure you want to execute in the CommandText property:

```
cmd->CommandText = "StoriesWhereLastName";
```

Now comes the tricky part. You need to build a collection of SqlParameters, within which you will place all the parameters that you want sent to the stored procedure. The SqlCommand class provides a property called Parameters to place your collection of SqlParameters.

The first step is to use the Add() method off of the Parameters property collection to add all the SqlParameters making up all the parameters that will be passed to the stored procedure. The constructor for the SqlParameters class takes two or three parameters depending on the data type of the parameter that will be passed to the stored procedure. If the data type has a predefined length like int or a variable length like VarChar, then only two parameters are needed.

```
cmd->Parameters->Add(gcnew SqlParameter("@LastName", SqlDbType::VarChar));
```

On the other hand, if the data type needs its length specified like Char, then the third parameter is used to specify the length.

```
cmd->Parameters->Add(gcnew SqlParameter("@FixedSizeString",SqlDbType::Char,32));
```

When all the parameters are specified, you need to assign values to them so that the stored procedure can use them. You do this by assigning a value to the Value property of the indexed property, off of the Parameters property collection of the SqlCommand class. Clear as mud? The example should help:

```
cmd->Parameters["@LastName"]->Value = Name;
```

Finally, when all the parameters are assigned values, you call the SqlCommand class's ExecuteReader() method just like you did for a CommandType of Text:

```
reader = cmd->ExecuteReader();
```

The processing of the result set within the SqlDataReader object is handled in a forward-only manner. The basic process is to advance to the next record of the result set using the Read() method. If the return value is false, you have reached the end of the result set and you should call the Close() method to close the SqlDataReader. If the value is true, then you continue and process the next result set record.

```
while(reader->Read())
{
    Console::WriteLine(reader["StoryID"]);
    Console::WriteLine(reader["Headline"]);
    Console::WriteLine(reader["Story"]);
    Console::WriteLine("");
}
reader->Close();
```

There are two different methods of processing the record set. You can, as I did, use the indexed property to get the value based on the column header. You can also process the columns using an assortment of type-specific Getxxx() methods. The following code generates the same output as the preceding code:

```
while(reader->Read())
{
    Console::WriteLine(reader->GetInt32(0));
    Console::WriteLine(reader->GetString(1));
    Console::WriteLine(reader->GetString(2));
    Console::WriteLine("");
}
reader->Close();
```

Note the parameter passed in the position of the column starting at zero.

I personally find using column names easier, but the style you choose to use is up to you. Figure 12-10 shows the results of the preceding example program.

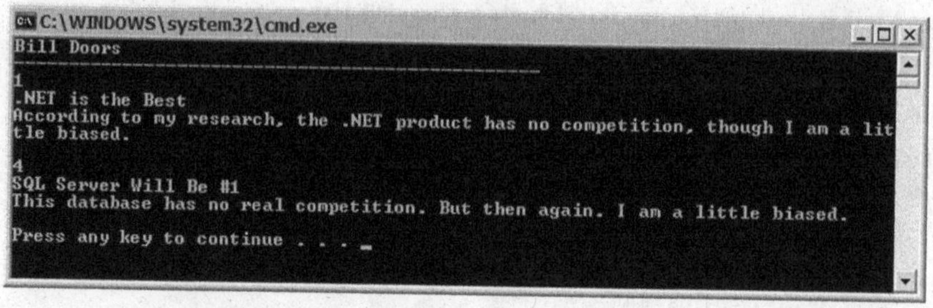

Figure 12-10. *Retrieving Bill Doors's stories*

Insert, Update, and Delete Commands

The code to modify the database (i.e., insert, update, and delete rows of the database) isn't much different from the code to query the database. Obviously, the SQL is different. The only other difference is that you call the SqlCommand class's ExecuteNonQuery() method instead of the ExecuteReader() method.

You can still use both CommandTypes and you still need to set up the SQLParameters the same way for stored procedures.

In Listing 12-7 you insert a new record into the database, you change the LastName on the record, and then you delete the record. (A lot of work for nothing, don't you think?)

Listing 12-7. *Modifying the Database*

```
using namespace System;
using namespace System::Data;
using namespace System::Data::SqlClient;

void main()
{
    String ^Name = "Doors";

    SqlConnection ^connection = gcnew SqlConnection();

#ifdef SQLAuth
    // SQL Server authentication
    connection->ConnectionString =
        "User ID=sa; Password=;"
        "Data Source=(local); Initial Catalog=DCV_DB;";
#else
    // Windows Integrated Security
    connection->ConnectionString =
        "Persist Security Info=False; Integrated Security=SSPI;"
        "Data Source=(local); Initial Catalog=DCV_DB;";
#endif

    try
    {
        SqlCommand ^cmd = gcnew SqlCommand();
        cmd->Connection = connection;
        connection->Open();
```

```
        cmd->CommandType = CommandType::StoredProcedure;
        cmd->CommandText = "InsertAuthor";

        cmd->Parameters->Add(gcnew SqlParameter("@LastName", SqlDbType::VarChar));
        cmd->Parameters->Add(gcnew SqlParameter("@FirstName",SqlDbType::VarChar));

        cmd->Parameters["@LastName"]->Value  = "Dope";
        cmd->Parameters["@FirstName"]->Value = "John";

        int affected = cmd->ExecuteNonQuery();
        Console::WriteLine("Insert - {0} rows are affected", affected);

        cmd->CommandType = CommandType::Text;
        cmd->CommandText = "UPDATE Authors SET LastName = 'Doe'"
                           "WHERE LastName = 'Dope'";

        affected = cmd->ExecuteNonQuery();
        Console::WriteLine("Update - {0} rows are affected", affected);

        cmd->CommandType = CommandType::Text;
        cmd->CommandText = "DELETE FROM Authors WHERE LastName = 'Doe'";

        affected = cmd->ExecuteNonQuery();
        Console::WriteLine("Delete - {0} rows are affected", affected);
    }
    catch (SqlException ^e)
    {
        Console::WriteLine("No connection the following error occurred: {0}",
            e->Message);
    }
    finally
    {
        connection->Close();
    }
}
```

As you can see, there is not much new going on here in the C++/CLI code, other than the call to
ExecuteNonQuery(). This method returns the number of rows affected by the SQL command.

```
int affected = cmd->ExecuteNonQuery();
```

Figure 12-11 shows the results of the preceding example program.

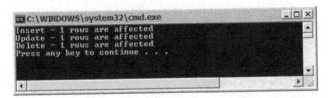

Figure 12-11. *A lot of modifications to the database for no gain*

Returning a Single Value from a Query

The final command-executing method of the SqlCommand class is ExecuteScalar(). This method is designed to return an Object handle as the result of the query. The returned Object points to a value like that produced by an aggregated SQL function such as COUNT or SUM. Again, like the database modifying command, there is not much changed between the source code needed to execute this type of method and that of a standard query.

Listing 12-8 shows how to count all the records in a database and also how to sum a column. (The database does not have a column that you would want to sum—I had to improvise.)

Listing 12-8. *Counting and Summing*

```
using namespace System;
using namespace System::Data;
using namespace System::Data::SqlClient;

void main()
{
    SqlConnection ^connection = gcnew SqlConnection();

#ifdef SQLAuth
    //  SQL Server authentication
    connection->ConnectionString =
        "User ID=sa; Password=;"
        "Data Source=(local); Initial Catalog=DCV_DB;";
#else
    //  Windows Integrated Security
    connection->ConnectionString =
        "Persist Security Info=False; Integrated Security=SSPI;"
        "Data Source=(local); Initial Catalog=DCV_DB;";
#endif

    try
    {
        SqlCommand ^cmd = gcnew SqlCommand();
        cmd->Connection = connection;
        connection->Open();

        cmd->CommandType = CommandType::Text;
        cmd->CommandText = "SELECT COUNT(*) FROM Authors";

        Object ^NumAuthors = cmd->ExecuteScalar();
        Console::WriteLine("The number of Authors are {0}", NumAuthors);

        cmd->CommandType = CommandType::Text;
        cmd->CommandText = "SELECT SUM(AuthorID) FROM Authors";
```

```
        Object ^UselessNum = cmd->ExecuteScalar();
        Console::WriteLine("The Sum of AuthorIDs for fun is {0}", UselessNum);
    }
    catch (SqlException ^e)
    {
        Console::WriteLine("No connection the following error occurred: {0}",
            e->Message);
    }
    finally
    {
        connection->Close();
    }
}
```

As you can see, other than the SQL code and the calling of the ExecuteScalar() method, there is not much new. The ExecuteScalar() method returns a handle to an Object, which you can type cast to the type of the return value. In both cases, you could have type cast the return Object handle to int, but the WriteLine() method can do it for you.

Figure 12-12 shows the results of the preceding example program.

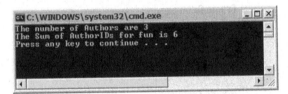

Figure 12-12. *Counting rows and summing a column*

Using Connected ADO.NET with Transactions

Think about this scenario. You buy a computer on your debit card, but while the purchase is being processed, the connection to the debit card company is lost. The response from the debit card reader is a failure message. You try again, and the debit card reader now responds that there is not enough money. You go home empty-handed, angry, and confused. Then a month later, your bank statement says you bought a computer with your debit card.

It can't happen, right? Wrong. If you use the preceding immediate updating method, it's very possible, as each update to the database is stand-alone. One command can complete, for example, the withdrawal, while a second command may fail, for example, the sale.

This is where transactions come in handy. They make sure all database commands needed to complete a process are completed successfully before allowing the database to commit (or write) these commands. If one or more of the commands fail, the database can reject all of the commands and return to its original state before any of the commands were completed. This is known as rolling back.

Figure 12-13 shows the basic flow of transactional database access.

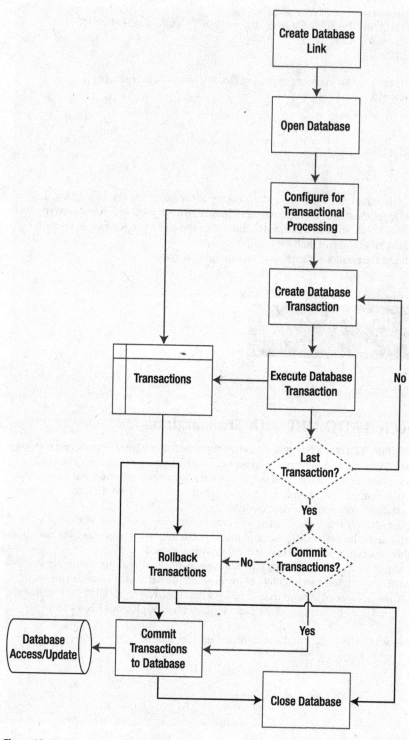

Figure 12-13. *Transactional database access*

1. Create a link to the database with a SqlConnection.

2. Open the database with the Open() method.

3. Configure for transactions.

4. Create a database transaction with the SqlCommand class.

5. Execute the transaction by using the ExecuteNonQuery() method of the SqlCommand class. The temporary copy of the database is updated.

6. Repeat steps 4 and 5 until completed.

7. When all transactions are complete, either commit the transactions to the database or roll them back.

8. Close the database with the Close() method.

Listing 12-9 shows how to convert the nontransactional example from Listing 12-7 into a transactional example.

Listing 12-9. *Transactional Database Updates*

```
using namespace System;
using namespace System::Data;
using namespace System::Data::SqlClient;

void main()
{
    String ^Name = "Doors";

    SqlConnection  ^connection = gcnew SqlConnection();
    SqlTransaction ^transaction;

#ifdef SQLAuth
    //  SQL Server authentication
    connection->ConnectionString =
        "User ID=sa; Password=;"
        "Data Source=(local); Initial Catalog=DCV_DB;";
#else
    //  Windows Integrated Security
    connection->ConnectionString =
        "Persist Security Info=False; Integrated Security=SSPI;"
        "Data Source=(local); Initial Catalog=DCV_DB;";
#endif

    try
    {
        connection->Open();

        SqlCommand ^cmd = gcnew SqlCommand();

        transaction = connection->BeginTransaction(
            IsolationLevel::Serializable, "AuthorTransaction");
```

```
        cmd->Connection  = connection;
        cmd->Transaction = transaction;

        cmd->CommandType = CommandType::StoredProcedure;
        cmd->CommandText = "InsertAuthor";

    cmd->Parameters->Add(gcnew SqlParameter("@LastName",  SqlDbType::Char,32));
    cmd->Parameters->Add(gcnew SqlParameter("@FirstName",SqlDbType::Char,32));

        cmd->Parameters["@LastName"]->Value  = "Dope";
        cmd->Parameters["@FirstName"]->Value = "John";

        int affected = cmd->ExecuteNonQuery();
        if (affected <= 0)
            throw gcnew Exception("Insert Failed");
        Console::WriteLine("Insert - {0} rows are affected", affected);

        cmd->CommandType = CommandType::Text;
        cmd->CommandText = "UPDATE Authors SET LastName = 'Doe'"
                            "WHERE LastName = 'Dope'";

        affected = cmd->ExecuteNonQuery();
        if (affected <= 0)
            throw gcnew Exception("Insert Failed");
        Console::WriteLine("Update - {0} rows are affected", affected);

        // This transaction will return 0 affected rows
        // because "Does" does not exist.
        // Thus, the if condition throws an execption which causes all
        // Transactions to be rolled back.
        cmd->CommandType = CommandType::Text;
        cmd->CommandText = "DELETE FROM Authors WHERE LastName = 'Does'";

        affected = cmd->ExecuteNonQuery();
        if (affected <= 0)
            throw gcnew Exception("Insert Failed");
        Console::WriteLine("Delete - {0} rows are affected", affected);

        transaction->Commit();
    }
    catch (Exception ^e)
    {
        transaction->Rollback("AuthorTransaction");
        Console::WriteLine("Transaction Not completed");
        Console::WriteLine("SQL error occurred: {0}", e->Message);
    }
    finally
    {
        connection->Close();
    }
}
```

As you can see, there have not been many changes. First, you need to declare a SqlTransaction (OleDbTransaction, OdbcTransaction, or OracleTransaction) class:

```
SqlTransaction ^transaction;
```

Next, you need to create a transaction set using the SqlConnection class's BeginTransaction() method. The BeginTransaction() method takes two parameters. The first parameter specifies the locking behavior of the transaction (see Table 12-7) and the second is the name of the transaction set:

```
transaction = connection->BeginTransaction(IsolationLevel::RepeatableRead,
                                     "AuthorTransaction");
```

Table 12-7. *Common Transaction IsolationLevels*

Level	Description
ReadCommitted	Specifies that locks are held while the data is read, but changes to the data can occur before the transaction is committed
ReadUncommitted	Specifies that changes can occur even while the data is being read
RepeatableRead	Specifies that locks are held on the data until the transaction is committed, but additional rows can be added or deleted
Serializable	Specifies that locks are held on the entire database until the transaction is committed

Now that you have a transaction set, you need to assign it to the SqlCommand class's property Transaction:

```
cmd->Transaction = transaction;
```

The last set of transactional database updates is to execute all the transactions. If everything completes successfully, then execute the SqlTransaction class's Commit() method:

```
transaction->Commit();
```

If, on the other hand, an error occurs, you would then execute the SqlTransaction class's Rollback() method:

```
transaction->Rollback("AuthorTransaction");
```

Figure 12-14 shows the results of the preceding example program failing because the name of the author was not found in the database.

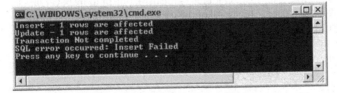

Figure 12-14. *Transactional database update rollback*

Disconnected ADO.NET

Let's switch gears and now look at disconnected ADO.NET. Disconnected data access is a key feature of ADO.NET. Basically, it means that most of the time when you're accessing a database, you aren't getting the data from the database at all. Instead, you're accessing a synchronized, in-memory copy of the data that was moved earlier to your client computer. Don't worry about all the technical issues surrounding this; just be glad that it works because it provides three major benefits:

- Less congestion on the database server because users are spending less time connected to it
- Faster access to the data because the data is already on the client
- Capability to work across disconnection networks such as the Internet

It also offers one benefit (associated with disconnected access) that is less obvious: Data doesn't have to be stored in a database-like format. Realizing this, Microsoft decided to implement ADO.NET using a strong typed XML format. The benefit is that having data in XML format enables data to be transmitted using standard HTTP. This causes a further benefit: Firewall problems disappear. An HTTP response with the body of XML flows freely through a firewall, unlike the pre-ADO.NET technology's system-level COM marshalling requests. If the previous bonus is Greek (or geek) to you, don't fret. In fact, be glad you have no idea what I was talking about.

The Core Classes

If you spend a lot of time working with ADO.NET, you may have an opportunity to work with almost all of ADO.NET's classes. For the purposes of this book, however, I've trimmed these classes down to the following:

- DataAdaptor
- DataSet
- DataTableCollection
- DataTable
- DataRow
- DataColumn
- DataRelationCollection
- DataRelation
- Constraint

All of these classes interact with each other in some way. Figure 12-15 shows the flow of the interaction. Essentially, the DataAdaptor connects the data store to the DataSet. The DataSet stores the data in a Tables property containing a DataTablesCollection made up of one or more DataTables. Each DataTable is made up of DataRows and DataColumns. All of the DataTables store their relationships in a Relations property containing a DataRelationCollection made up of DataRelations. Finally, each DataTable can be affected by Constraints. Simple, isn't it?

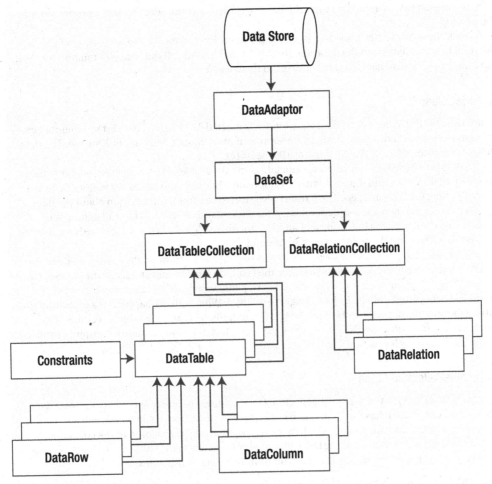

Figure 12-15. *The disconnected ADO.NET class interaction*

DataAdaptor

The DataAdaptor is the bridge between a data source (database) and the DataSet. Its purpose is to extract data out of the data source and place it in the DataSet. Then it updates, if required, the data source with the changes made in the DataSet.

It should be relatively easy to get comfortable with the SqlDataAdaptor, OleDbDataAdaptor, OdbcDataAdaptor, or OracleDataAdaptor, as they use (just like connected database access) a connection class to connect to the data source and a command class to add, update, and select data out of the data source.

The basic idea behind using the DataAdaptor is to provide SQL commands to the following four properties to handle sending and receiving data between the DataSet and the data store:

- SelectCommand
- InsertCommand
- UpdateCommand
- DeleteCommand

If you plan to only read data from the database, then only the SelectCommand property needs to be provided.

With these properties provided, it is a simple matter to call the DataAdaptor class's Fill() method to select data from the data store to the DataSet and to call the Update() method to insert, update, and/or delete data from the DataSet to the data store.

DataSet Class

The DataSet is the major controlling class for disconnected ADO.NET. A DataSet is a memory cache used to store all data retrieved from a data source, in most cases a database or XML file. The data source is connected to the DataSet using a DataAdaptor.

A DataSet consists of one or more data tables in a DataTableCollection class, which in turn is made up of data rows and data columns. Relationships between the tables are maintained via a DataRelationsCollection class. The DataSet also stores the format information about the data.

A DataSet is data source–independent. All it understands is XML. In fact, all data sent or received by the DataSet is in the form of an XML document. The DataSet has methods for reading and writing XML, and these are covered in Chapter 13.

A DataSet also provides transactional access to its data. To commit all changes made to the DataSet from the time it was created or since the last time it was committed, call the DataSet class's AcceptChanges() method. If you want to roll back changes since the DataSet was corrected or since it was last committed, call the RejectChanges() method. What actually happens is a cascading effect where the AcceptChanges() and RejectChanges() methods execute their table's versions of the method, which in turn calls the table's rows' version. Thus, it is also possible to commit or roll back at the table and row levels.

DataTableCollection Class

A DataTableCollection is a standard collection class made up of one or more DataTables. Like any other collection class, it has functions such as Add, Remove, and Clear. Usually, you will not use any of this functionality. Instead, you will use it to get access to a DataTable stored in the collection.

The method of choice for doing this will probably be to access the DataTableCollection indexed property, using the name of the table that you want to access as the index:

```
DataTable ^dt = dSet->Tables["Authors"];
```

It is also possible to access the same table using the overloaded array property version of Item:

```
DataTable ^dt = dSet->Tables[0];
```

With this method, you need to know which index is associated with which table. When you use the indexed property, it is a little more obvious.

Caution The first index in a DataTableCollection is 0.

DataTable Class

Put simply, a DataTable is one table of data stored in memory. A DataTable also contains constraints, which help ensure the integrity of the data it is storing.

It should be noted that a DataTable can be made up of zero or more DataRows, because it is possible to have an empty table. Even if the table is empty, the Columns property will still contain a collection of the headers that make up the table.

Many properties and methods are available in the DataTable, but in most cases you will simply use it to get access to the rows of the table. Two of the most common methods are enumerating through the Rows collection:

```
IEnumerator ^Enum = dt->Rows->GetEnumerator();
while(Enum->MoveNext())
{
    DataRow ^row = (DataRow^)(Enum->Current);
    //...Do stuff to row
}
```

and selecting an array of DataRows using the Select() method:

```
array<DataRow^>^ row =
    dt->Select(String::Format("AuthorID={0}", CurrentAuthorID));
```

Another method that you will probably come across is NewRow(), which creates a new DataRow, which will later be added to the DataTable Rows collection:

```
DataRow ^row = dt->NewRow();
//...Build row
dt->Rows->Add(row);
```

DataRow Class

The DataRow is where the data is actually stored. You will frequently access the data from the DataRow as indexed property, using the name of the column that you want to access as the index.

```
row["LastName"] = tbLastName->Text;
```

It is also possible to access the same column using the overloaded array property version:

```
row[0] = tbLastName->Text;
```

With this method, you need to know which index is associated with which column. When you use the indexed property, it is a little more obvious.

Caution The first index in a DataRow is 0.

DataColumn Class

You use the DataColumn class to define the columns in a DataTable. Each DataColumn has a data type that determines the kind of data it can hold. A DataColumn also has properties similar to a database, such as AllowNull and Unique. If the DataColumn auto-increments, then the AutoIncrement property is set. (Now, that makes more sense than Identity.)

DataRelationCollection Class

A DataRelationCollection is a standard collection class made up of one or more DataRelations. Like any other collection class, it has functions such as Add, Remove, and Clear. Usually, as with the DataTableCollection class, you will not use any of this functionality. Instead, you will simply use it to get access to the DataRelations it stores.

DataRelation Class

A DataRelation is used to relate two DataTables together. It does this by matching DataColumns between two tables. You can almost think of it as the ADO.NET equivalent of the foreign-key relationship in a relational database (like you previously set).

One important thing you have to keep in mind is that the DataColumns must be the same data type. Remember that ADO.NET has strong data types, and when comparing different data types, one data type must be converted to the other. This conversion is not done automatically.

Constraint Classes

The Constraint classes make it possible to add a set of constraints on a particular column in your DataTable. Two types of constraints are currently supported by ADO.NET:

- ForeignKeyConstraint disallows a row to be entered unless there is a matching row in another (parent) table.

- UniqueConstraint makes sure that a column is unique within a DataTable.

Creating a Table Manually in Code

Normally, database designers build the databases that you use, but the DataColumn, DataRelation, and Constraint classes allow you as a developer to build a DataTable dynamically. The following snippet of code shows how to create the Authors DataTable manually:

```
// Create an empty DataTable
DataTable ^Authors = gcnew DataTable("Authors2");

// Add all the columns
Authors->Columns->Add(gcnew DataColumn("AuthorID",
                                       Type::GetType("System.Int32")));
Authors->Columns->Add(gcnew DataColumn("LastName",
                                       Type::GetType("System.String")));
Authors->Columns->Add(gcnew DataColumn("FirstName",
                                       Type::GetType("System.String")));

// Add autoincrement to AuthorID
Authors->Columns["AuthorID"]->AutoIncrement = true;

// Make AuthorID unique
Authors->Constraints->Add(
    gcnew UniqueConstraint("PK_AuthorID", Authors->Columns["AuthorID"]));

// Make AuthorID the Primary key
array<DataColumn^>^ key = gcnew array<DataColumn^>(1);
key[0] = Authors->Columns["AuthorID"];
Authors->PrimaryKey = key;

// Create a relation between AuthorID in Authors and Content tables
dSet->Relations->Add("StoryLink",
     Authors2->Columns["AuthorID"],
     dSet->Tables["Content"]->Columns["AuthorID"]);

// add table to DataSet
dSet->Tables->Add(Authors);
```

Developing with Disconnected ADO.NET

In the final two examples of this chapter, you're going to build a couple of small Win Form applications to maintain the Authors DataTable that you've been working with throughout the chapter. These examples use disconnected data source access with full select, insert, update, and delete capabilities that can be either committed or rolled back. For the first example, you do all the work. For the second, you let Visual Studio 2005 do all the work. A good portion of the code (which you can find in the Downloads section of my Web site, www.ProCppCLI.net, or the Apress Web site, http://www.apress.com) is related to auto-generated Win Forms controls and isn't included here as it really has no relevance to this chapter's topic. What you'll see in the example is the code that wasn't auto-generated by Visual Studio 2005.

Figure 12-16 shows the final result of the first example, from which you can build your own Win Form.

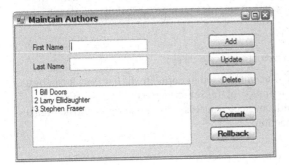

Figure 12-16. *The Author Maintenance tool*

Building the DataAdaptor

The first thing that you need to do is build the application's SqlDataAdaptor. Then you'll use the SqlDataAdaptor to place data in the DataSet. Eight major steps (three of which are optional) are involved in building a SqlDataAdaptor and populating and maintaining a DataSet:

1. Create a SqlConnection.

2. Create a SqlDataAdaptor.

3. Implement a SelectCommand property.

4. Implement an InsertCommand property (optional).

5. Implement an UpdateCommand property (optional).

6. Implement a DeleteCommand property (optional).

7. Create a DataSet.

8. Populate (fill) the DataSet.

You build a SqlConnection for a disconnected database in the same way as you build a connected database:

```
SqlConnection ^connect = gcnew SqlConnection();

#ifdef SQLAuth
    // SQL Server authentication
    connect->ConnectionString =
        "User ID=sa; Password=;"
        "Data Source=(local); Initial Catalog=DCV_DB;";
#else
    // Windows Integrated Security
    connect->ConnectionString =
        "Persist Security Info=False; Integrated Security=SSPI;"
        "Data Source=(local); Initial Catalog=DCV_DB;";
#endif
```

Creating the SqlDataAdapter is a simple constructor call. You probably want to also add the primary key information. This ensures that incoming records that match existing records are updated instead of appended:

```
dAdapt = gcnew SqlDataAdapter();
dAdapt->MissingSchemaAction = MissingSchemaAction::AddWithKey;
```

The SelectCommand is the SQL command that will be used to populate the DataSet. It can be as complex or as simple as you like. The implementation of the SelectCommand requires a standard SqlCommand like the one you created earlier with connected access. Notice that the constructor takes the SQL command and the data source connection:

```
dAdapt->SelectCommand =
    gcnew SqlCommand("SELECT AuthorID, LastName, FirstName"
                     "FROM Authors", connect);
```

The InsertCommand is the SQL command that will be executed to insert added DataSet rows back into the data source. The implementation of this property is a little tricky, as it requires parameters to be passed to the command. The Add() method to the Parameters property is similar to what you have seen previously, except it has one additional parameter and the size parameter is mandatory, even if it is obvious, as in the case of Int. The additional property is the name of the column that the data will be extracted from:

```
// Implement Insert command
dAdapt->InsertCommand =
    gcnew SqlCommand("INSERT INTO Authors (LastName, FirstName) "
                     "VALUES (@LastName, @FirstName)", connect);

// Add parameters
dAdapt->InsertCommand->Parameters->Add("@LastName", SqlDbType::VarChar, 50,
                                        "LastName");
dAdapt->InsertCommand->Parameters->Add("@FirstName", SqlDbType::VarChar, 50,
                                        "FirstName");
```

The UpdateCommand is the SQL command that will be executed to update rows in the data source that have been modified within the DataSet. The code does not contain anything new:

```
dAdapt->UpdateCommand =
    gcnew SqlCommand("UPDATE Authors SET "
                     "LastName = @LastName, FirstName = @FirstName, "
                     "WHERE AuthorID = @AuthorID", connect);
dAdapt->UpdateCommand->Parameters->Add("@LastName", SqlDbType::VarChar, 50,
                                        "LastName");
```

```
dAdapt->UpdateCommand->Parameters->Add("@FirstName", SqlDbType::VarChar, 50,
                                "FirstName");
dAdapt->UpdateCommand->Parameters->Add("@AuthorID", SqlDbType::Int, 4,
                                "AuthorID");
```

In the preceding WHERE clause, I use the key AuthorID, which is an auto-generated column that can't be changed, to find the row to update. This simplifies things because if the key used to find the row to update can be changed during the update process, then when it's changed the WHERE clause won't be able to find the right row due to the changed key not matching the original key in the database.

So, are you stuck with only being able to use unchangeable keys? Fortunately, the answer is no. When changed, DataRows store their original values so that they can be accessed for this exact reason (they can be used for rolling back changes as well). Let's pretend you can update AuthorID. Here is the code that needs to be changed:

```
dAdapt->UpdateCommand =
    gcnew SqlCommand("UPDATE Authors SET "
                    "LastName = @LastName, FirstName = @FirstName, "
                    "AuthorID = @AuthorID "
                    "WHERE AuthorID = @OldAuthorID", connect);
//...All the parameters plus
dAdapt->UpdateCommand->Parameters->Add("@OldAuthorID", SqlDbType::Int, 4,
    "AuthorID")->SourceVersion = DataRowVersion::Original;
```

The DeleteCommand is the SQL command that will be executed when a DataRow is removed from the DataSet, which needs to be deleted now from the data source. Nothing new to explore here in the code:

```
dAdapt->DeleteCommand =
    gcnew SqlCommand("DELETE FROM Authors "
                    "WHERE AuthorID = @AuthorID", connect);
dAdapt->DeleteCommand->Parameters->Add("@AuthorID", SqlDbType::Int, 4,
                                "AuthorID");
```

You create a DataSet with a simple constructor. To fill the DataSet, you call the SqlDataAdapter class's Fill() method. The Fill() method takes two parameters: a handle to the DataSet and the name of the data source table that you will be filling the DataSet with:

```
dSet = new DataSet();
dAdapt->Fill(dSet, "Authors");
```

Selecting Rows

You have many ways of selecting records from the DataSet. A common way of getting all the rows from a table is to use the DataRow collection found in the Rows property of the table and then enumerate through the collection. You populate the list box doing exactly that:

```
DataTable ^dt = dSet->Tables["Authors"];

if (dt == nullptr)
    throw gcnew Exception("No Authors Table");

IEnumerator ^Enum = dt->Rows->GetEnumerator();
while(Enum->MoveNext())
{
    DataRow ^row = (DataRow^)(Enum->Current);
    lbAuthors->Items->Add(ListBoxItem(row));
}
```

As you can see in the ListBoxItem() method, to grab the columns, you use the indexed property of the DataRow:

```
String ^ListBoxItem(DataRow ^row)
{
    return String::Format("{0} {1} {2}",
        row["AuthorID"],
        row["FirstName"],
        row["LastName"]);
}
```

A way of getting a specific set of DataRows from a DataTable is by using the DataTable's Select() method. The method takes as a parameter a filter of the primary key:

```
array<DataRow^>^ row =
    dt->Select(String::Format("AuthorID={0}", CurrentAuthorID));
```

You will see this code implemented later in updating and deleting rows.

Inserting Rows

Inserting a new row or, in this case, a new author is done by updating the text boxes with the information about the author and then clicking the Add button.

A good portion of the following code consists of validating, updating the list box, and cleaning up for text boxes. The actual ADO.NET-related code simply creates a new row, updates the columns with the information in the list boxes, and adds the row to the DataTable.

Notice that the actual insertion of the row into the data source with the Update() method is not found in this method. The reason for this is that I want to be able to commit or roll back all changes at one time using the Commit and Rollback buttons. Thus, the Update() method only occurs in the Commit button event. When the Update() method finally gets called, the UpdateCommand (which was coded previously) will get executed:

```
System::Void bnAdd_Click(System::Object^ sender, System::EventArgs^ e)
{
    // Make sure the text boxes are populated
    if (tbFirstName->Text->Trim()->Length == 0 ||
        tbLastName->Text->Trim()->Length == 0)
        return;

    // Create a new row in the DataTable
    DataTable ^dt = dSet->Tables["Authors"];
    DataRow ^row = dt->NewRow();

    // Update the columns with the new author information
    row["FirstName"] = tbFirstName->Text;
    row["LastName"]  = tbLastName->Text;

    // Add the row to the Rows collection
    dt->Rows->Add(row);

    // Add the new row to the list box
    lbAuthors->Items->Add(ListBoxItem(row));

    // Blank out the text boxes
    tbFirstName->Text = "";
    tbLastName->Text = "";
}
```

Updating Rows

Updating an author row is handled when you select a row out of the list box, update the text boxes, and finally click the Update button.

The ADO.NET-related code to update the author requires that you first select the row to be updated using the DataTable class's Select() method. Once you have the row, you update the author information in the row columns. Like when you inserted a row, the Update() method does not get called until the Commit button is clicked, but when the Update() method finally gets called, the UpdateCommand ends up being executed:

```
System::Void bnUpdate_Click(System::Object^ sender, System::EventArgs^ e)
{
    // Make sure we have a selected author from the listbox
    if (CurrentAuthorID < 0)
        return;

    // Select the author using its AuthorID
    DataTable ^dt = dSet->Tables["Authors"];
    array<DataRow^>^ row =
        dt->Select(String::Format("AuthorID={0}", CurrentAuthorID));

    // Since we know that AuthorID is unique only one row will be returned
    // Update the row with the text box information
    row[0]["FirstName"] = tbFirstName->Text;
    row[0]["LastName"]  = tbLastName->Text;

    // Update listbox
    lbAuthors->Items->Insert(lbAuthors->SelectedIndex, ListBoxItem(row[0]));
    lbAuthors->Items->RemoveAt(lbAuthors->SelectedIndex);
}
```

Deleting Rows

Deletion of an author DataRow happens when you click a row in the list box and then click the Delete button.

The code to handle deleting a row is a little tricky, as it requires the use of transactional access to the DataSet. First, you need to select the row. Then you call its Delete() method. Deleting a record in the DataSet does not actually occur until the change is accepted. At this point only, a flag is set in the DataRow.

Also, like inserting and updating, the actual updating of the database does not occur until the Update() method is called when the Commit button is clicked. Ultimately, when the Update() method is called, the DeleteCommand (built previously) will be executed:

```
System::Void bnDelete_Click(System::Object^ sender, System::EventArgs^ e)
{
    // Make sure we have a selected author from the listbox
    if (CurrentAuthorID < 0)
        return;

    // Select the author using its AuthorID
    DataTable ^dt = dSet->Tables["Authors"];
    array<DataRow^>^ row =
        dt->Select(String::Format("AuthorID={0}", CurrentAuthorID));
```

```
// Since we know that AuthorID is unique only one row will be returned
// Delete the row
row[0]->Delete();

// All went well, delete the row from list box
lbAuthors->Items->RemoveAt(lbAuthors->SelectedIndex);
}
```

Committing and Rolling Back Changed Rows

You commit all author DataRows changed when you click the Commit button.

Because a DataSet is disconnected from the database, anything that you do to it will not get reflected in the actual database until you force an update using the Update() method. Because this is the case, it is really a simple matter to either commit or roll back any changes that you have made to the DataSet.

To commit the changes to the database, simply call the Update() method, which will walk through the DataSet and update any changed records in its corresponding database record. Depending on the type of change, the appropriate SQL command (insert, update, or delete) will be executed. To commit the changes to the DataSet, you need to call the AcceptChanges() method, which will cause the DataSet to accept all changes that were made to it:

```
dAdapt->Update(dSet, "Authors");
dSet->AcceptChanges();
```

To roll back any changes, simply don't call the Update() method, and call the RejectChanges() method to delete all changes in the DataSet that you have made since you last committed:

```
dSet->RejectChanges();
```

No (Coding) Effort Development with Disconnected ADO.NET

Lots of hard work there don't you think? What if I were to tell you that you could provide the exact same functionality using Visual Studio 2005 with a few drag and drop operations and typing three lines of code? Hard to believe . . . but it's true. It's all due to the power of the Typed DataSet and the DataGridView.

Typed DataSet

A Typed DataSet is an extension of a DataSet class where all columns of the database table are implemented as strongly typed properties. What you add after that to the class is really up to you.

I bet you are wondering how many of the three lines of code you are going to have to type make up the Typed DataSet. Fortunately, the answer is none, as Visual Studio 2005 can create a Typed DataSet for you. Okay, I've heard from hardcore developers that the generated Typed DataSet is not perfect, but to me it works just fine.

The steps to creating a Typed DataSet are straightforward:

1. Right-click the project name in the Solution Explorer.

2. Select the menu items Add ➤ New Item. This displays the dialog box shown in Figure 12-17.

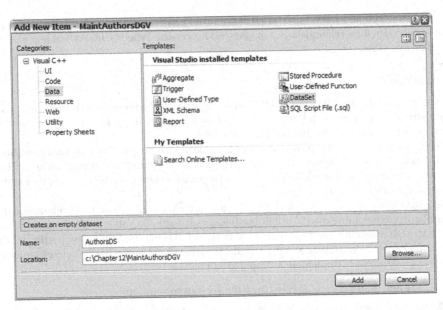

Figure 12-17. *Add New Item dialog box*

3. Select DataSet Template and then enter **AuthorsDS** as the name of the Typed DataSet. (This is my naming convention, i.e., table name followed by DS, but you can use any name you want.)

4. Click Add and then you get a (rather pretty) blue screen that gives you details on what to do next.

5. From within the Server Explorer, navigate to the Authors table.

6. Drag the Authors table to the blue screen and drop it.

7. You now have a screen that looks like Figure 12-18.

Figure 12-18. *AuthorsDS Typed DataSet*

You're finished. Okay, this was a rather simple example. You could also drag other tables, which incidentally retain their relationships, but I very seldom create Typed DataSets that are made up of more than one table.

DataGridView

Now comes that fun part. The DataGridView is probably one of the most powerful controls available in your screen design arsenal. It is also extremely easy to work with, but in this chapter I will barely even scratch the surface of the functionality it provides.

The DataGridView control provides a customizable table for displaying data with or without an underlying data source. In other words, you can either create your table manually or, as I will do in the example, generate it automatically by binding it to a data source. In this case, the data source is the Typed DataSet AuthorsDS.

The DataGridView class allows for a massive amount of customization. It provides more than 150 public properties, more than 80 public methods, and nearly 200 public events. Covering all these could take a fair-size book. Fortunately, at least as far as I'm concerned, all the properties, methods, and events I have to be concerned about are available via the Visual Studio 2005 Window form designer.

Here are the steps to implement a simple DataGridView:

1. Drag and drop the DataGridView from the Toolbox to your form.

2. Size it so that it nearly fills the form, but leave room for two buttons at the bottom.

3. Anchor the control to all four sides.

4. Click the triangle in the box in the top-right corner of the DataGridView.

5. Click the drop-down arrow next to the Choose Data Source text box. This displays a dialog box similar to the one in Figure 12-19.

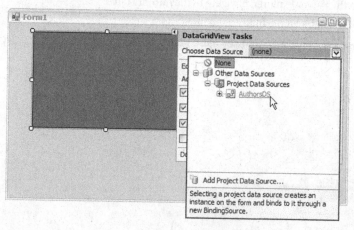

Figure 12-19. *DataGridView Tasks*

6. Select the AuthorsDS link. This adds two addition controls to the form, AuthorsDS and AuthorDSBindingSource.

7. Select the AuthorDSBindingSource control and select Authors from the DataMember property drop-down list. Presto, your DataGridView changes from a gray box into a table.

8. Right-click within the `DataGridView` and select Edit Columns. This presents you with a dialog box like the one in Figure 12-20.

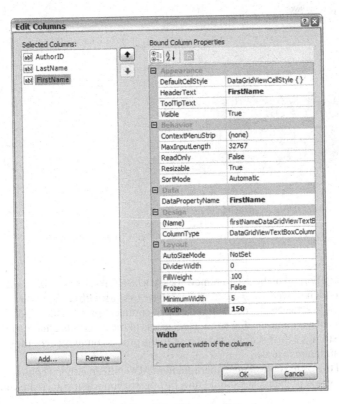

Figure 12-20. *DataGridView Edit Columns dialog box*

9. Go wild and change the look and feel of the `DataGridView` to your heart's content.

10. Click OK.

Go ahead and compile and run your form. You should get a table of all the records in your Authors table. You can even edit, add, and remove them. But oops . . . you can't save your changes to your database.

Here is where your three lines of code come in. Add two buttons, Commit and Rollback. Then in the Commit button's `click` event handler, add the following two lines:

```
this->AuthorsTableAdapter->Update(this->AuthorsDS->Authors);
this->AuthorsDS->AcceptChanges();
```

These lines provide the ability to commit the changes you made to the `DataGridView` to the database and then accept the changes to the `DataSet`. If you recall, you saw these same two lines in the Commit button in the prior example.

Finally, add your third and last line of code to the rollback button's `click` event handler:

```
this->AuthorsDS->RejectChanges();
```

This line rejects all changes you made and restores the `DataGridView` back to its original state or to its state when the `DataSet` was last committed.

Done! Figure 12-21 shows the final results of the second example.

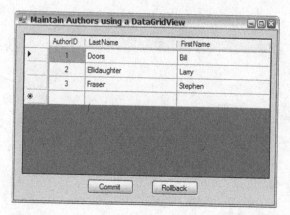

Figure 12-21. *Maintaining authors using a DataGridView*

Summary

In this chapter, you saw a large portion of the .NET Framework's ADO.NET. You started out by covering the basics of ADO.NET. You then moved on to creating a database to work with through the rest of the chapter using Visual Studio 2005. Next, you explored how to connect, query, insert, update, delete, count, and sum rows of a database using connected access to the database. Finally, you learned how to do the same things with disconnected access, in the process building a couple simple Windows Forms author maintenance tools.

You have now learned the code you will need to implement ADO.NET in either a connected or disconnected manner. The world of databases should now be open to you when you create your applications.

In the next chapter, you'll examine the mysterious world of XML, the last of the four common methods of getting input into and out of your .NET Windows applications.

CHAPTER 13

■■■

XML

Though you're covering XML last of the four most common .NET Framework class library input/output (I/O) mechanisms, it's hardly the least important. In fact, much of the underlying architecture of .NET relies on XML, so much so that the .NET Framework class library provides a plethora of ways of working with XML. This chapter covers some of the more common classes.

A major goal of the .NET Framework class library is to simplify XML development. It has done this. But if you come from a background of implementing XML in the worlds of Microsoft XML Parser (MSXML) or Java, what you've already learned isn't lost. In fact, you'll find many similarities between these implementations and the one provided by the .NET Framework class library.

This chapter isn't intended to provide details about XML, though to provide a level playing field I do include some high-level coverage. Instead, the goal is to show you how to implement the many facets of XML development provided by the .NET Framework class library. In particular, you'll learn how to read, write, update, and navigate an XML file. After you've covered the common areas of XML that you'll more than likely develop code for, you'll move on and look at using XML with ADO.NET.

What Is XML?

First off, XML is not a computer language. Rather, it is a meta-language for defining or specifying how to mark up a document in such a way as to identify its structure.

Say what?

How about this definition: XML is a method of arranging a document so that it's broken up into parts. For example, in this chapter you're going to create an XML document of role-playing monsters. The document will be broken up by monster name, hit dice, and weapon(s). (If you play Dungeons & Dragons [D&D], you know this is a very small subset of all the information available, but I didn't want or need to make the examples any more difficult.)

XML documents, in their simplest form, are made up of a hierarchy of two types of components: elements and attributes.

An *element* is made up of three parts:

- *Start element node*, often called the *start tag*. It is made up of an element text name enclosed in angle brackets: `<Element_Tag>`.

- *Content node(s)* made up of a combination of zero or more *text nodes* (text enclosed between start and end element nodes) and child or nested elements (hence the hierarchical nature of XML).

- *End element node*, often called the *end tag*. It is made up of a backslash and text, which must exactly match the text name of the start element node, enclosed in angle brackets: `</Element_Tag>`.

An *attribute* is an extension to the start element node. It provides more information about the element. Attributes are one or more name= "value" pairs added after the element text name but before the closing angle bracket: <Element_Tag name="value" >.

Two additional components that you will encounter are the XML header declaration and the comment. The *header declaration* indicates that the file should be parsed as XML and in most cases will simply read

```
<?xml version="1.0" encoding="utf-8"?>
```

Comments provide the reader of the XML file additional information that will be ignored by the XML parser. The syntax of a comment is <!-- comment_text -->.

Listing 13-1 shows the XML document that you'll be using throughout the chapter.

Listing 13-1. *An XML Monster File*

```xml
<?xml version="1.0" encoding="utf-8"?>
<!-- Monster List -->
<MonsterList>
  <!-- Easy Monster -->
  <Monster>
    <Name>Goblin</Name>
    <HitDice Dice="1d8" Default="4"/>
    <Weapon Number="1" Damage="1d4">Dagger</Weapon>
  </Monster>
  <!-- Medium Monster -->
  <Monster>
    <Name>Succubus</Name>
    <HitDice Dice="6d8+6" Default="33"/>
    <Weapon Number="2" Damage="1d3+1">Claw</Weapon>
    <Weapon Number="1" Damage="1d4">Dagger</Weapon>
  </Monster>
  <!-- Tough Monster -->
  <Monster>
    <Name>Red Dragon</Name>
    <HitDice Dice="22d12+110" Default="253"/>
    <Weapon Number="1" Damage="2d8">Bite</Weapon>
    <Weapon Number="2" Damage="2d6">Claw</Weapon>
    <Weapon Number="2" Damage="1d8">Wing</Weapon>
  </Monster>
</MonsterList>
```

The .NET Framework XML Implementations

The .NET Framework class library provides two ways of processing XML data:

- Fast, noncached, forward-only stream
- Random access via an in-memory Document Object Model (DOM) tree

Both methods of processing XML data are equally valid. However, each has a definite time when it is better suited. At other times, both will work equally well, and the decision of which to use is up to the developer's taste.

The major deciding factors for choosing one method over the other are whether all data needs to be in memory at one time (large files take up large amounts of memory, which in many cases isn't a good thing, but with the large amount of physical memory a computer can have nowadays the size of the XML file is almost irrelevant) and whether random access to the data is needed. When either of these factors occurs, the DOM tree should probably be used because the process of repeatedly starting from the beginning of the document and reading forward sequentially through it to find the right place in the stream of XML to read, update, or write random data is time consuming.

On the other hand, if the data can be processed sequentially, a forward-only stream is probably the better choice because it is easier to develop and uses fewer resources more efficiently than a DOM tree. However, there is nothing stopping you from using a DOM tree in this scenario as well.

Implementing code to process XML with the .NET Framework class library requires referencing the System.Xml.dll assembly. You would think that due to the heavy reliance on XML in the .NET Framework, it would be part of the mscorlib.dll assembly. Because it is not, your source code implementing XML requires the following code be placed at the top of your source code (this is done automatically for you by Visual Studio 2005 for Windows Forms applications but not for console applications):

```
#using <system.xml.dll>
```

Six namespaces house all of the XML functionality within the .NET Framework class library. Table 13-1 describes these namespaces at a high level.

Table 13-1. *XML Namespaces*

Namespace	Description
System::Xml	Provides the core of all XML functionality
System::Xml::Schema	Provides support for XML Schema definition language (XSD) schemas
System::Xml::Serialization	Provides support for serializing objects into XML formatted documents or streams
System::Xml::XPath	Provides support for the XPath parser and evaluation engine
System::Xml::Xsl	Provides support for Extensible Stylesheet Language Transformations (XSLT) transforms

Forward-Only Access

Forward-only access to XML is amazingly fast. If you can live with the restriction that you can process the XML data only in a forward-only method, then this is the way to go. The base abstract classes for implementing this method of access are named, intuitively enough, XmlReader and XmlWriter.

The .NET Framework class library's implementation of forward-only access, when you first look at it, seems a lot like the Simple API for XML (SAX), but actually they are fundamentally different. Whereas SAX uses a more complex push model, the class library uses a simple pull model. This means that a developer requests or pulls data one record at a time instead of having to capture the data using event handlers.

Coding using the .NET Framework class library's implementation of forward-only access seems, to me, more intuitive because you can handle the processing of an XML document as you would a simple file, using a good old-fashioned while loop. There is no need to learn about event handlers or SAX's complex state machine.

Reading from an XML File

To implement forward-only reading of an XML file you use the XmlReader class. This is a little tricky as the XmlReader is an abstract class. This means, instead of the normal creation of the class using a constructor, you use the static method Create(), in conjunction with the optional XmlReaderSettings class.

For those of you who developed XML code with a previous version of the .NET Framework, it is also possible to still use the XmlTextReader and XmlNodeReader classes, which inherit from XmlReader. With .NET Framework version 2.0, Microsoft has recommended the use of the XmlReader class, since using the Create() method with the XmlReaderSettings class you get the following benefits:

- The ability to specify the features you want supported by the created XmlReader instance.

- The ability to create an instance of XmlReaderSettings that can be reused to create multiple XmlReaders, each sharing the same features.

- The ability to create a unique instance or modify an existing instance of the XmlReaderSettings, allowing each XmlReader to have a different set of features.

- You can extend the features of the XmlReader. The Create() method can accept another XmlReader. The underlying XmlReader instance can be a reader such as an XmlTextReader, or another user-defined XmlReader instance that you add your own features to.

- Provides the ability to take advantage of all the new features added to the XmlReader class in .NET Framework version 2.0. Some features, such as better conformance checking and compliance to the XML 1.0 recommendation, are only available with XmlReader instances created using the Create() method.

I'll cover the XmlReaderSettings class when I discuss XML file validation later in the chapter, as much of this class pertains to validation.

The XmlReader class is made up of a number of properties and methods. Some of the more common properties you will probably encounter are as follows:

- AttributeCount is an Int32 that specifies the number of attributes in the current Element, DocumentType, or XmlDeclaration node. Other node types don't have attributes.

- Depth is an Int32 that specifies the depth of the current node in the tree.

- EOF is a Boolean that's true if the reader is at the end of the file; otherwise, it's false.

- HasAttributes is a Boolean that's true if the current node has attributes; otherwise, it's false.

- HasValue is a Boolean that's true if the current node has a value; otherwise, it's false.

- IsEmptyElement is a Boolean that's true if the current node is an empty element, or in other words, the element ends in />.

- Item is the String value of an attribute specified by index or name within the current node.
- LocalName is the String the local name of the current node. For example, Monster is the LocalName for the element <my:Monster>.
- Name is the String qualified name of the current node. For example, the fully qualified my:Monster is the Name for the element <my:Monster>.
- NodeType is an XmlNodeType enum class that represents the node type (see Table 13-2) of the current node.
- Prefix is the String namespace prefix of the current node. For example, my is the namespace for the element <my:Monster>.
- ReadState is a ReadState enum class of the current state of the XmlReader object. Possible states are: Closed, EndOfFile, Error, Initial, and Interactive.
- Value is the String value for the current node.

Here are a few of the more common XmlReader methods:

- Close() changes the ReadState of the reader to Closed.
- Create() is used to create an instance of an XmlReader.
- GetAttribute() gets the String value of the attribute.
- IsStartElement() returns the Boolean true if the current node is a start element tag.
- MoveToAttribute() moves to a specified attribute.
- MoveToContent() moves to the next node containing content.
- MoveToElement() moves to the element containing the current attribute.
- MoveToFirstAttribute() moves to the first attribute.
- MoveToNextAttribute() moves to the next attribute.
- Read() reads the next node.
- ReadAttributeValue() reads an attribute containing entities.
- ReadContentAs[data type]() reads the current content of the node as the [data type] specified. Examples are ReadContentAsInt() and ReadContentAsDouble().
- ReadElementContentAs[data type]() reads the value of element node as the [data type] specified. Examples are ReadElementContentAsInt() and ReadElementContentAsDouble().
- ReadElementString() is a helper method for reading simple text elements.
- ReadEndElement() verifies that the current node is an end element tag and then reads the next node.
- ReadStartElement() verifies that the current node is a start element tag and then reads the next node.
- ReadString() reads the contents of an element or text node as a String.
- Skip() skips the children of the current node.

The XmlReader class processes an XML document by tokenizing a text stream of XML data. Each token (or *node*, as it is known in XML) is then made available by the Read() method and can be handled as the application sees fit. A number of different nodes are available, as you can see in Table 13-2.

Table 13-2. *Common XML Node Types*

Node Type	Description
Attribute	An element attribute
Comment	A comment
Document	The root of a document tree providing access to the entire XML document
DocumentFragment	A subtree of a document
DocumentType	A document type declaration
Element	A start element tag
EndElement	An end element tag
EndEntity	The end of an entity declaration
Entity	The start of an entity declaration
EntityReference	A reference to an entity
None	The value placed in NodeType before any Read() method is called
SignificantWhitespace	White space between markups in a mixed content model or white space within the xml:space="preserve" scope
Text	The text content
Whitespace	White space between markups
XmlDeclaration	An XML declaration

The basic logic of implementing the XmlReader class is very similar to that of a file IO class:

1. Open the XML document.
2. Read the XML element.
3. Process the element.
4. Repeat steps 2 and 3 until the end of file (EOF) is reached.
5. Close the XML document.

The example in Listing 13-2 shows how to process the previous XML monster file. The output is to the console and contains a breakdown of the nodes that make up the XML file.

Listing 13-2. *Splitting the XML Monster File into Nodes*

```
#using <system.xml.dll>

using namespace System;
using namespace System::Xml;


String ^indent(Int32 depth)
{
    String ^ind = "";
    return ind->PadLeft(depth * 3, ' ');
}

void main()
{
    XmlReader ^reader;

    try
    {
        reader = XmlReader::Create("Monsters.xml");

        while (reader->Read())
        {
            switch (reader->NodeType)
            {
                case XmlNodeType::Comment:
                    Console::WriteLine(
                        "{0}Comment node: Value='{1}'",
                        indent(reader->Depth), reader->Value);
                    break;
                case XmlNodeType::Element:
                    Console::WriteLine(
                        "{0}Element node: Name='{1}'",
                        indent(reader->Depth), reader->Name);

                    if (reader->HasAttributes)
                    {
                        while (reader->MoveToNextAttribute())
                        {
                            Console::WriteLine(
                                "{0}Attribute node: Name='{1}' Value='{2}'",
                                indent(reader->Depth), reader->Name,
                                reader->Value);
                        }
                        reader->MoveToElement();
                    }
```

```
        if (reader->IsEmptyElement)
        {
            Console::WriteLine(
                "{0}End Element node: Name='{1}'",
                indent(reader->Depth), reader->Name);
        }
        break;
    case XmlNodeType::EndElement:
        Console::WriteLine(
            "{0}End Element node: Name='{1}'",
            indent(reader->Depth), reader->Name);
        break;
    case XmlNodeType::Text:
        Console::WriteLine(
            "{0}Text node: Value='{1}'",
            indent(reader->Depth), reader->Value);
        break;
    case XmlNodeType::XmlDeclaration:
        Console::WriteLine(
            "Xml Declaration node: Name='{1}'",
            indent(reader->Depth), reader->Name);

        if (reader->HasAttributes)
        {
            while (reader->MoveToNextAttribute())
            {
                Console::WriteLine(
                    "{0}Attribute node: Name='{1}' Value='{2}'",
                    indent(reader->Depth), reader->Name,
                    reader->Value);
            }
        }
        reader->MoveToElement();
        Console::WriteLine(
            "End Xml Declaration node: Name='{1}'",
            indent(reader->Depth), reader->Name);
        break;
    case XmlNodeType::Whitespace:
        // Ignore white space
        break;
    default:
        Console::WriteLine(
            "***UKNOWN*** node: Name='{1}' Value='{2}'",
            indent(reader->Depth), reader->Name, reader->Value);
    }
  }
}
```

```
catch (XmlException ^e)
{
    Console::WriteLine("\n\n\nSplitting XML Aborted with error: {0}",
        e->Message);
}
finally
{
    if (reader->ReadState != ReadState::Closed)
    {
        reader->Close();
    }
}
}
```

The preceding code, though longwinded, is repetitively straightforward and, as pointed out, resembles the processing of a file in many ways.

One neat little trick this example shows is how you can use the XmlReader class's Depth property to indent your output based on the depth the current node is within the tree. All I do is simply indent an additional three spaces for each depth:

```
String ^indent(Int32 depth)
{
    String ^ind = "";
    return ind->PadLeft(depth * 3, ' ');
}
```

You process all XML within an XmlException try/catch block because every XML method in the .NET Framework class library can throw an XmlException.

You start by opening the XML file. Then you read the file, and finally you close the file. You place the Close() method in a finally clause to ensure that the file gets closed even on an exception. Before you close the file, you verify that the file had in fact been opened in the first place. It is possible for the Create() method of the XmlReader class to throw an XmlException and never open the XML file:

```
XmlReader ^reader;
try
{
    reader = XmlReader::Create("Monsters.xml");
    while (reader->Read())
    {
        //...Process each node.
    }
}
catch (XmlException ^e)
{
    Console::WriteLine("\n\n\nSplitting XML Aborted with error: {0}",
        e->Message);
}
finally
{
    if (reader->ReadState != ReadState::Closed)
    {
        reader->Close();
    }
}
```

The processing of each of the nodes is done using a simple case statement on the node type of the current node:

```
switch (reader->NodeType)
{
    case XmlNodeType::Comment:
        //...Process a comment
        break;
    case XmlNodeType::Element:
        //...Process an element
        break;
    //...etc.
}
```

The processing of most of the node types in the preceding example involves simply writing either the name or the value to the console. One exception is the Element tag. It starts off like the other node type by writing its name to the console, but then it continues on to check if it has attributes. If it does, it moves through each of the attributes and writes them to the console as well. When it has finished processing the attributes, it moves the element back as the current node using the MoveToElement() method. You might think you have just broken the forward-only property, but in reality, attributes are only part of an element, so therefore the element is still the current node.

It is possible for an element to be empty using the syntax <tag/>, so you have to then check to see if the element is empty. If it is, you write the element's end tag to the console:

```
case XmlNodeType::Element:
    Console::WriteLine("{0}Element node: Name='{1}'",
                    indent(reader->Depth), reader->Name);

    if (reader->HasAttributes)
    {
        while (reader->MoveToNextAttribute())
        {
            Console::WriteLine("{0}Attribute node: Name='{1}' Value='{2}'",
                            indent(reader->Depth), reader->Name,
                            reader->Value);
        }
        reader->MoveToElement();
    }

    if (reader->IsEmptyElement)
    {
        Console::WriteLine("{0}End Element node: Name='{1}'",
                        indent(reader->Depth), reader->Name);
    }
    break;
```

Figure 13-1 shows the results of ReadXML.exe. It's hard to believe so much information is contained within such a small XML file.

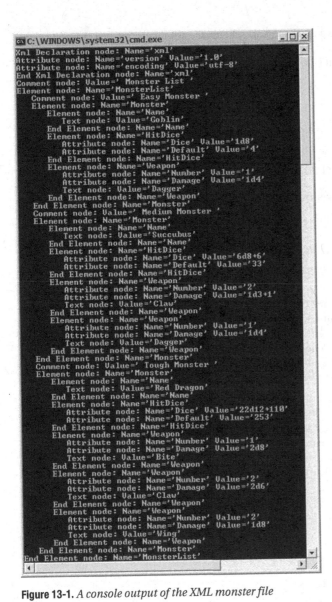

Figure 13-1. *A console output of the XML monster file*

Validating an XML File

The XmlReader class in conjunction with the XmlReaderSettings class can be used to verify that an XML file is *well formed*—in other words, that it follows all the syntax rules of an XML file. These classes don't verify, though, that the XML file is valid.

A valid XML file needs the nodes to be in a specific order, number, and type. You can use the following two standards for checking validity:

- Document type definition (DTD)
- XML schema definition (XSD)

Validating an XML file requires a DTD or a XSD schema file. Monsters.dtd (see Listing 13-3) is an example of a DTD for the Monsters.xml file. DTD is an older method of validating XML and is becoming more or less obsolete. But since it is still used, I thought I'd show an example.

Listing 13-3. *The Monsters.dtd File*

```
<!ELEMENT MonsterList (Monster)+ >
<!ELEMENT Monster (Name, HitDice, Weapon+) >
<!ELEMENT Name (#PCDATA) >
<!ELEMENT HitDice EMPTY >
<!ATTLIST HitDice Dice CDATA #IMPLIED Default CDATA #IMPLIED >
<!ELEMENT Weapon (#PCDATA) >
<!ATTLIST Weapon Number CDATA #IMPLIED Damage CDATA #IMPLIED >
```

You will also need to make this minor change to the XML file so that it knows where to find the DTD file:

```
<?xml version="1.0" encoding="utf-8"?>
<!DOCTYPE MonsterList SYSTEM "Monsters.dtd">
<!-- Monster List -->
```

The XSD is very different from the DTD. It is much more verbose, but since it is defined using XML it is a little easier to read. In addition, it is far more powerful. On the other hand, the application code is virtually the same for both standards, so we won't go into the details of the schema definitions. But just to give you an idea of what a schema definition looks like, Listing 13-4 is the XSD equivalent to Listing 13-3, which incidentally was auto-generated by clicking in the XML create schema toolbar button while the Monsters.xml file was being displayed in the Visual Studio 2005 code window.

Listing 13-4. *The Monsters.xsd File*

```
<?xml version="1.0" encoding="utf-8"?>
<xs:schema attributeFormDefault="unqualified"
           elementFormDefault="qualified"
           xmlns:xs="http://www.w3.org/2001/XMLSchema">
  <xs:element name="MonsterList">
    <xs:complexType>
      <xs:sequence>
        <xs:element maxOccurs="unbounded" name="Monster">
          <xs:complexType>
            <xs:sequence>
              <xs:element name="Name" type="xs:string" />
              <xs:element name="HitDice">
                <xs:complexType>
                  <xs:attribute name="Dice" type="xs:string"
                                use="required" />
                  <xs:attribute name="Default" type="xs:unsignedByte"
                                use="required" />
                </xs:complexType>
              </xs:element>
```

```
    <xs:element maxOccurs="unbounded" name="Weapon">
      <xs:complexType>
        <xs:simpleContent>
          <xs:extension base="xs:string">
            <xs:attribute name="Number" type="xs:unsignedByte"
                          use="required" />
            <xs:attribute name="Damage" type="xs:string"
                          use="required" />
          </xs:extension>
        </xs:simpleContent>
      </xs:complexType>
    </xs:element>
  </xs:sequence>
  </xs:complexType>
</xs:element>
</xs:sequence>
</xs:complexType>
</xs:element>
</xs:schema>
```

To verify an XML file, you need to add an instance of the XmlReaderSettings class within the Create() method of the XmlReader class. The XmlReaderSettings class basically extends the functionality of the XmlReader class by adding verification logic.

Note The XmlReaderSettings class extends features of the XmlReader besides those of validation, but these features are beyond the scope of this book.

The XmlReaderSettings class has a few properties and a method to extend the XmlReader class with validation support:

- IgnoreComments is a Boolean value to specify whether validation should ignore comments. The default is false.

- IgnoreWhiteSpace is a Boolean value to specify whether validation should ignore insignificant white space. The default is false.

- ProhibitDtd is a Boolean value to specify whether DTD validation is prohibited. The default is true.

- Reset() is a method that resets the instance of the XmlReaderSettings back to default values.

- Schemas is an XmlSchemaSet containing the collection of schemas used for validation.

- ValidationType is a ValidationType enumerator to which type of validation, DTD, Schema (XSD), or None, should be done. The default is None.

Caution If you want to validate using DTD, you must both set ProhibitDTD to false and set ValidationType to DTD.

Listing 13-5 shows in a minimal fashion how to validate an XML file with a DTD.

Listing 13-5. *Validating the Monsters.xml File*

```
using namespace System;
using namespace System::Xml;
using namespace System::Xml::Schema;

ref class ValidateXML
{
public:
    ValidateXML(String ^filename)
    {
        XmlReader ^vreader;
        try
        {
            XmlReaderSettings ^settings = gcnew XmlReaderSettings();
            settings->ProhibitDtd = false;
            settings->ValidationType = ValidationType::DTD;
            vreader = XmlReader::Create("Monsters.xml", settings);

            while(vreader->Read())
            {
                // ... Process nodes just like XmlTextReader()
            }
            Console::WriteLine("Finished Processing");
        }
        catch (Exception ^e)
        {
            Console::WriteLine(e->Message);
        }
        finally
        {
            if (vreader->ReadState != ReadState::Closed)
            {
                vreader->Close();
            }
        }
    }
};

void main()
{
    gcnew ValidateXML("Monsters.xml");
}
```

As you can see, there isn't much difference between implementing a simple XmlReader and a validated XmlReader. In fact, the only difference is that an instance of the XmlReaderSettings class is created and passed as a parameter to the XmlReader class's Create() method.

When you run this on the Monsters.xml file listed earlier, "Finished Processing" displays on the console. To test that validation is happening, change the Easy Monster to have its HitDice element placed after the Weapon element, as shown in Listing 13-6.

Listing 13-6. *Invalid Monsters.xml File*

```
<?xml version="1.0" encoding="utf-8"?>
<!DOCTYPE MonsterList SYSTEM "Monsters.dtd">
<!-- Monster List -->
<MonsterList>
    <!-- Easy Monster -->
    <Monster>
        <Name>Goblin</Name>
        <Weapon Number="1" Damage="1d4">Dagger</Weapon>
        <HitDice Dice="1d8" Default="4" />
    </Monster>
    <!-- The rest of the document -->
</MonsterList>
```

Now the program ValidateXML.exe will abort, as shown in Figure 13-2.

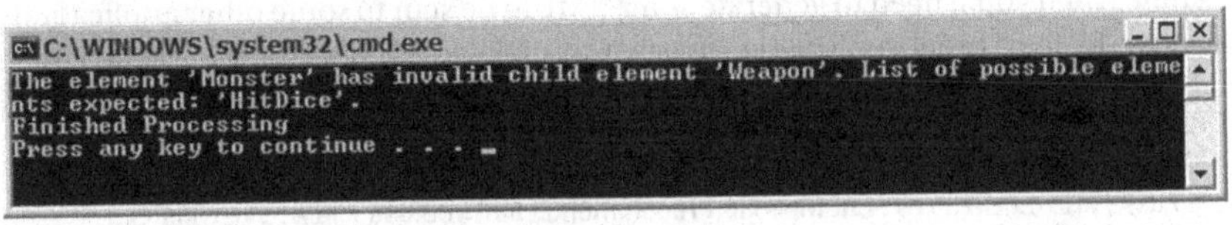

Figure 13-2. *Aborting the Monsters.xml file*

What happens if you want to handle the problems in the invalid XML file yourself, instead of just throwing the exception? You can override the exception being thrown by providing a handler to ValidationEventHandler of the XmlReaderSettings class. Within this handler, you can do whatever processing is necessary for the validation error.

ValidationEventHandler is triggered whenever a validation error occurs. The code for the handler is similar to all the other event handlers you've seen so far in this book. It takes two parameters: a pointer to an Object (which in this case you ignore), and a pointer to ValidationEventArgs. ValidationEventArgs provides in its properties information to tell you what caused the validation event to trigger.

Notice that you also need to import the System::Xml::Schema namespace:

```
using namespace System::Xml::Schema;
ref class ValidateXML
{
public:
    void ValidationHandler (Object ^sender, ValidationEventArgs ^vea)
    {
        Console::WriteLine(vea->Message);
    }
    //...the rest of class
};
```

Delegating the event handler follows the same process you've seen before:

```
XmlReaderSettings ^settings = gcnew XmlReaderSettings();
settings->ProhibitDtd = false;
settings->ValidationType = ValidationType::DTD;
settings->ValidationEventHandler +=
    gcnew ValidationEventHandler(this, &ValidateXML::ValidationHandler);
vreader = XmlReader::Create("Monsters.xml", settings);
```

or

```
XmlSchemaSet^ sc = gcnew XmlSchemaSet;
sc->Add( L"urn:monster-schema", L"Monsters.xsd" );

XmlReaderSettings ^settings = gcnew XmlReaderSettings();
settings->ValidationType = ValidationType::Schema;
settings->Schemas = sc;
settings->ValidationEventHandler +=
    gcnew ValidationEventHandler(this, &ValidateXML::ValidationHandler);
vreader = XmlReader::Create("Monsters.xml", settings);
```

Now when you execute the application, you get the same message displayed to the console, as that is the logic I placed in the handler, but the program continues on to the end of the file without an exception being thrown.

Writing a New XML Stream

There will come a time when you'll need to generate some XML to be sent to some other application or stored off for later use by the current application. An easy way of doing this is through the XmlWriter class and optional XmlWriterSettings class.

Note You can also use XmlTextWriter, but Microsoft recommends that you use XmlWriter instead. The benefits are more or less the same as those for XmlReader, which we discussed earlier.

Just like its counterpart XmlReader, XmlWriter is an abstract class and you create an instance using its Create() method. You can also pass as an argument a settings class. The XmlWriterSettings class is primarily used to tell XmlWriter how to format the output of its XML stream. Here are some of the more common properties you will set:

- Encoding is an Encoding enum class that represents the character encoding to use.
- Indent is a Boolean value that represents whether to indent elements. The default value is false.
- IndentChars is a String that represents what set of characters to use for indenting. This value is used when Indent is set to true.
- NewLineChars is a String that represents what set of characters to use for a line break. This value is used when NormalizeNewLines is set to true.
- NewLineHandling is a NewLineHandling enum class that represents whether the new lines are Entitize (preserve new line characters that would not be otherwise preserved by a normalizing XmlReader), None (unchanged), or Replaced.
- NewLineOnAttribute is a Boolean value that specifies whether to write attributes on a new line. The default value is false.
- OmitXmlDeclaration is a Boolean value that specifies whether to omit the XML declaration. The default value is false, which means the declaration is written.

The XmlWriter class is implemented as a forward-only XML stream writer. There aren't many commonly used properties when it comes to the XmlWriter class. Most likely you will only deal with a couple:

- Settings, which returns the XmlWriterSettings associated with the XmlWriter.

- WriteState, which is a WriteState enum class of the current state of the XmlWriter. Possible states are: Attribute value being written, Closed method was called, Content being written, Element start tag being written, Error, Prolog value being written, and Start (meaning a write method has yet to be called).

Instead of properties, the XmlWriter class depends on a number of methods. Some of the more common methods are as follows:

- Close() closes the streams associated with the XmlWriter.

- Create() creates an instance of XmlWriter.

- Flush() flushes the write buffers.

- WriteAttributes() writes all attributes at the current location.

- WriteAttributeString() writes an attribute.

- WriteBase64() encodes the specified binary bytes as Base64 and then writes them out.

- WriteBinHex() encodes the specified binary bytes as BinHex and then writes them out.

- WriteCharEntity() writes out a char entity for the specified Unicode character. For example, a © symbol would generate a char entity of ©.

- WriteChars() writes out a text buffer at a time.

- WriteComment() writes out a comment.

- WriteDocType() writes out a DOCTYPE declaration.

- WriteElementString() writes out an element.

- WriteEndAttribute() writes out an end attribute, closing the previous WriteStartAttribute.

- WriteEndDocument() writes out end attributes and elements for those that remain open and then closes the document.

- WriteEndElement() writes out an empty element (if empty) or a full end element.

- WriteEntityRef() writes out an entity reference.

- WriteFullEndElement() writes out a full end element.

- WriteName() writes out a valid XML name.

- WriteNode() writes out everything from the XmlReader to the XmlWriter and advances the XmlReader to the next sibling.

- WriteStartAttribute() writes out the start of an attribute.

- WriteStartDocument() writes out the start of a document.

- WriteStartElement() writes out the start tag of an element.

- WriteString() writes out the specified string.

- WriteValue() writes out a simple-typed value.

- WriteWhitespace() writes out specified white space.

As you can see from the preceding lists, there is a write method for every type of node that you want to add to your output file. Therefore, the basic idea of writing an XML file using the XmlWriter class is to open the file, write out all the nodes of the file, and then close the file.

The example in Listing 13-7 shows how to create an XML monster file containing only a Goblin.

Listing 13-7. *Programmatically Creating a Goblin*

```
using namespace System;
using namespace System::Xml;

void main()
{
    XmlWriter ^writer;
    try
    {
        XmlWriterSettings ^settings = gcnew XmlWriterSettings();
        settings->Indent = true;
        settings->IndentChars = ("    ");
        settings->NewLineOnAttributes = true;

        writer = XmlWriter::Create("Goblin.xml", settings);

        writer->WriteStartDocument();

        writer->WriteStartElement("MonsterList");

        writer->WriteComment("Program Generated Easy Monster");
        writer->WriteStartElement("Monster");

        writer->WriteStartElement("Name");
        writer->WriteString("Goblin");
        writer->WriteEndElement();

        writer->WriteStartElement("HitDice");
        writer->WriteAttributeString("Dice", "1d8");
        writer->WriteAttributeString("Default", "4");
        writer->WriteEndElement();

        writer->WriteStartElement("Weapon");
        writer->WriteAttributeString("Number", "1");
        writer->WriteAttributeString("Damage", "1d4");
        writer->WriteString("Dagger");
        writer->WriteEndElement();

        // The folling not needed with WriteEndDocument
        // writer->WriteEndElement();
        // writer->WriteEndElement();

        writer->WriteEndDocument();
```

```
        writer->Flush();
    }
    catch (Exception ^e)
    {
        Console::WriteLine("XML Writer Aborted -- {0}", e->Message);
    }
    finally
    {
        if (writer->WriteState != WriteState::Closed)
        {
            writer->Close();
        }
    }
}
```

This may seem like a lot of work to create just one monster in an XML file, but remember that all monsters have basically the same structure; therefore, you could create almost any number of Monster elements by removing the hard-coding and placing Weapon elements in a loop, as opposed to the expanded version shown in the preceding code. You, of course, also need some way of providing the monster information that you want placed in the XML file. (A random generator would be cool—tough to code, but cool.)

The Create() method of the XmlWriter class has several overloads. It can take as a parameter either a stream, filename, StringBuilder, TextWriter, or another XmlWriter. Along with each of these, Create() can also take an instance of an XmlWriterSettings class. I showed the constructor using a filename in the previous example. When using the filename, the constructor will automatically create the file or, if the filename exists, the constructor truncates it. In either case, you are writing to an empty file.

```
XmlWriter ^writer;
writer = XmlWriter::Create("Goblin.xml");
```

If you plan on allowing someone to read the generated XML, you might, as I stated earlier, want to consider passing to the Create() method an instance of the XmlWriterSettings class. In the previous example I used my favorite settings. First, I told XmlWriterSettings that I am going to indent the output with three spaces, instead of one long continuous stream of XML text:

```
XmlWriterSettings ^settings = gcnew XmlWriterSettings();
settings->Indent = true;
settings->IndentChars = ("   ");
```

Then I told it to put each attribute on a new line:

```
settings->NewLineOnAttributes = true;
writer = XmlWriter::Create("Goblin.xml", settings);
```

Okay, now to actually write the XML, the first thing you need to do is start the document using the WriteStartDocument() method. This method adds the following standard XML header to the XML document:

```
<?xml version="1.0" encoding="utf-8"?>
```

Next, you simply write the XML document. You use the WriteStartElement(), WriteString(), and WriteEndElement() methods to add elements, and for attributes you use the WriteAttributeString()

method. If you want to include comments, then you use the WriteComment() method. Once you've finished adding the XML document, you finish off with a WriteEndDocument() method. You might notice that the WriteEndDocument() method automatically ends any open elements.

```
writer->WriteComment("Add a weapon element");
writer->WriteStartElement("Weapon");
writer->WriteAttributeString("Number", "1");
writer->WriteAttributeString("Damage", "1d4");
writer->WriteString("Dagger");
writer->WriteEndElement();
```

Now that you have a new XML document, you must flush out any buffers and finally close the file so that some other process can access it. As you saw with the XmlReader class, you check the status of the file to make sure it even needs to be closed:

```
writer->Flush();
if (writer->WriteState != WriteState::Closed)
{
    writer->Close();
}
```

Figure 13-3 shows Goblin.xml, the output of WriteXML.exe, displayed in the Visual Studio 2005 editor.

Figure 13-3. *The generated Goblin.xml file*

Updating an Existing XML File

You have many ways to update an XML file. Using a standard editor comes to mind. Another option, especially if you are working with a repetitive operation, is to read in the XML file using the XmlReader class, make your changes, and then write out the edited XML with XmlWriter.

A catch to using this method is that there is no backtracking with either the reader or the writer. Therefore, you must make all changes as the element or attribute becomes available or store them temporarily.

There isn't anything new with this code. It simply isn't obvious how it's done. So here's an example of how to update an XML file in a forward-only manner. In Listing 13-8, you're adding the element <Encountered>False</Encountered> after the name of every monster.

Listing 13-8. *Updating the XML Monster File*

```cpp
using namespace System;
using namespace System::Xml;

void main()
{
    XmlReader ^reader;
    XmlWriter ^writer;
    try
    {
        reader = XmlReader::Create("Monsters.xml");

        XmlWriterSettings ^settings = gcnew XmlWriterSettings();
        settings->Indent = true;
        settings->IndentChars = ("    ");

        writer = XmlWriter::Create("New_Monsters.xml", settings);

        while (reader->Read())
        {
            switch (reader->NodeType)
            {
                case XmlNodeType::Comment:
                    writer->WriteComment(reader->Value);
                    break;
                case XmlNodeType::Element:
                    writer->WriteStartElement(reader->Name);
                    writer->WriteAttributes(reader, false);
                    if (reader->IsEmptyElement)
                        writer->WriteEndElement();
                    break;
                case XmlNodeType::EndElement:
                    writer->WriteEndElement();

                    // *** Add new Monster Element
                    if (reader->Name->Equals("Name"))
                    {
                        writer->WriteStartElement("Encountered");
                        writer->WriteString("False");
                        writer->WriteEndElement();
                    }
                    break;
                case XmlNodeType::Text:
                    writer->WriteString(reader->Value);
                    break;
                case XmlNodeType::XmlDeclaration:
                    writer->WriteStartDocument();
                    break;
            }
        }
```

```
        writer->Flush();

        Console::WriteLine("Done");
    }
    catch (Exception ^e)
    {
        Console::WriteLine("XML Update Aborted -- {0}", e->Message);
    }
    finally
    {
        if (writer->WriteState != WriteState::Closed)
        {
            writer->Close();
        }
        if (reader->ReadState != ReadState::Closed)
        {
            reader->Close();
        }
    }
}
```

Notice that there is no "open for update" mode for either the reader or the writer, so you need to open an input and an output file:

```
XmlReader ^reader = XmlReader::Create("Monsters.xml");
XmlTWriter ^writer = XmlWriter::Create("New_Monsters.xml", settings);
```

After that, the code is standard XmlReader and XmlWriter logic. Basically, you read in each element, attribute, comment, and so on and then write them out again. When the end element of Name shows up, write it out and then dump out the new element:

```
while (reader->Read())
{
    switch (reader->NodeType)
    {
        //...Other cases.
        case XmlNodeType::EndElement:
            writer->WriteEndElement();
            if (reader->Name->Equals("Name"))
            {
                writer->WriteStartElement("Encountered");
                writer->WriteString("False");
                writer->WriteEndElement();
            }
            break;
        //...The remaining cases.
```

Figure 13-4 shows New_Monsters.xml, the output of UpdateXML.exe, displayed in the Visual Studio 2005 editor.

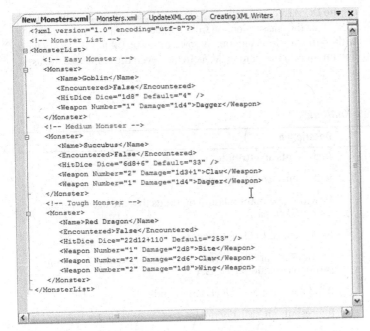

```
New_Monsters.xml  Monsters.xml  UpdateXML.cpp  Creating XML Writers            ▼ ✕
    <?xml version="1.0" encoding="utf-8"?>
    <!-- Monster List -->
 ⊟ <MonsterList>
      <!-- Easy Monster -->
 ⊟    <Monster>
         <Name>Goblin</Name>
         <Encountered>False</Encountered>
         <HitDice Dice="1d8" Default="4" />
         <Weapon Number="1" Damage="1d4">Dagger</Weapon>
      </Monster>
      <!-- Medium Monster -->
 ⊟    <Monster>
         <Name>Succubus</Name>
         <Encountered>False</Encountered>
         <HitDice Dice="6d8+6" Default="33" />
         <Weapon Number="2" Damage="1d3+1">Claw</Weapon>
         <Weapon Number="1" Damage="1d4">Dagger</Weapon>   I
      </Monster>
      <!-- Tough Monster -->
 ⊟    <Monster>
         <Name>Red Dragon</Name>
         <Encountered>False</Encountered>
         <HitDice Dice="22d12+110" Default="253" />
         <Weapon Number="1" Damage="2d8">Bite</Weapon>
         <Weapon Number="2" Damage="2d6">Claw</Weapon>
         <Weapon Number="2" Damage="1d8">Wing</Weapon>
      </Monster>
    </MonsterList>
```

Figure 13-4. *The generated New_Monsters.xml file*

Working with DOM Trees

The Document Object Model (DOM) is a specification for how to store and manipulate XML documents in memory. This differs significantly from the forward-only access just discussed, because for that method only a single node of the XML document is in memory at any one time. Having the entire document in memory has some major advantages and a couple of significant disadvantages compared to forward-only access.

The most important advantage is that because the entire XML document is in memory, you have the ability to access any portion of the XML document at any time. This means you can read, search, write, change, and delete anywhere at any time in the document. Best of all, once you are through, you can dump the XML document back to disk with a single command.

The major disadvantages are that the DOM tree can use up a lot more memory than forward-only access. especially if the XML document is large, and that there is often a delay as the DOM tree is loaded. Are these disadvantages significant? In most cases the answer is not really. Most computers have more than enough memory to handle all but the very largest XML documents (and when a document gets that large, the data should probably be in a database anyway). The slight delay is usually masked in the start-up of the application, and for the delay to be noticeable at all, the XML document needs to be quite sizable. (Again, when an XML document gets that large, it should probably be placed in a database.)

The core underlying class of the DOM tree is the abstract class XmlNode. You should be able to get comfortable quickly with XmlNode, as the classes derived from XmlNode have a close resemblance to the node types you worked with in the previous section. As you can see in Table 13-3, every type of node that is part of an XML document inherits from XmlNode. In fact, even the XmlDocument class is inherited from XmlNode.

Table 13-3. *Classes Derived from XmlNode*

Class	Description
XmlAttribute	Represents an attribute
XmlCDataSection	Represents a CDATA section
XmlCharacterData	Provides text manipulation methods that are used by several inherited classes
XmlComment	Represents an XML comment
XmlDataDocument	Provides the ability to store, retrieve, and manipulate data through a relational DataSet
XmlDeclaration	Represents the XML declaration node
XmlDocument	Represents an XML document
XmlDocumentFragment	Represents a fragment or hierarchical branch of the XML document tree
XmlDocumentType	Represents the DTD
XmlElement	Represents an element
XmlEntity	Represents an entity declaration
XmlEntityReference	Represents an entity reference node
XmlLinkedNode	Provides the ability to get the node before and after the current node
XmlNotation	Represents a notation declaration
XmlProcessingInstruction	Represents a processing instruction
XmlSignificantWhitespace	Represents white space between markup in a mixed content mode or white space within an xml:space= 'preserve' scope
XmlText	Represents the text content of an element or attribute
XmlWhitespace	Represents white space in element content

Because it's easier to visualize the XmlNode hierarchy than describe it in text, I've included the following illustration:

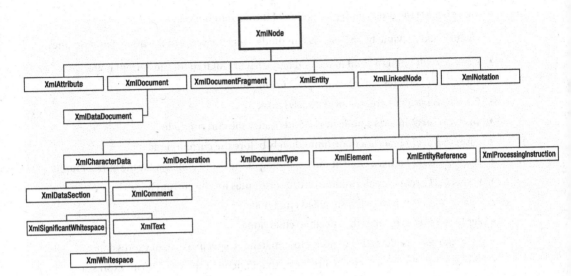

You use the properties and the methods defined in the XmlNode class to navigate, manipulate, and remove the nodes of the DOM tree. Here are some of the more common XmlNode properties:

- Attributes is an XmlAttributeCollection containing the attributes of the current node.

- ChildNodes is an XmlNodeList containing all the child nodes of the current node.

- FirstChild is an XmlNode of the first child of the current node, probably the XML declaration. If there is no first child node, then the value is null.

- HasChildNodes is a Boolean that is true if the node has any children; otherwise, it is false.

- InnerText is a String concatenation of the value of the current node and all of its children.

- InnerXml is a String representing the markup of the children of the current node. Setting this property replaces all the children of the current node.

- IsReadOnly is a Boolean that is true if the node is read-only; otherwise, it is false.

- Item is an XmlElement child of the current node specified by name.

- LastChild is an XmlNode of the last child of the current node.

- LocalName is a String representing the name of the current node without the namespace prefix.

- Name is a String representing the qualified name of the current node.

- NextSibling is the XmlNode with the same parent immediately following the current node. It has a value of null if no subsequent sibling exists.

- NodeType is an XmlNodeType enum class that represents the node type (see Table 13-2) of the current node.

- OuterXml is a String representing the markup of the current node and of the children of the current node.

- OwnerDocument is the XmlDocument of which the current node belongs.

- ParentNode is the XmlNode of the parent of the current node.

- PreviousSibling is the XmlNode with the same parent immediately before the current node. It has a value of null if no prior sibling exists.

- Value is a String representing the value of the current node.

As mentioned previously, XmlNode has methods. Here are some of the more common ones:

- AppendChild() adds a child to the end of the list of children for the current node.
- CloneNode() creates a duplicate of the current node.
- CreateNavigator() creates an XPathNavigator.
- InsertAfter() inserts a node immediately after the current node.
- InsertBefore() inserts a node immediately before the current node.
- PrependChild() adds a child at the beginning of the list of children for the current node.
- RemoveAll() removes all children and/or attributes for the current node.
- RemoveChild() removes the specified child node.
- ReplaceChild() replaces the specified child node.
- SelectNodes() selects a list of nodes that matches a specified XPath expression.
- SelectSingleNode() selects the first node that matches a specified XPath expression.
- WriteContentTo() saves all the children of the XmlDocument to an XmlWriter.
- WriteTo() saves the XmlDocument to an XmlWriter.

XmlNodes are placed in an XmlNodeList. This list is ordered and supports indexed as well as enumerated access. Any changes that you make to the XmlNodes in the DOM tree are immediately reflected in the XmlNodeList in which the XmlNodes reside. You can find the root of all XmlNodeLists in the DocumentElement property of the XmlDocument class.

The starting point of working with DOM trees is the XmlDocument class. Not only do you use this class to load and save the XML document to and from disk, but you also use it to query the DOM tree and create nodes to be added to the tree. As you might have noticed in Table 13-3, XmlDocument inherits from XmlNode, so the XmlDocument class has all the XmlNode class's properties and methods. Here are some of the more common properties unique to XmlDocument:

- DocumentElement is an XmlElement representing the root element of the document.
- DocumentType is an XmlDocumentType containing the DocumentType or DOCTYPE declaration if the document has one.
- PreserveWhitespace is a Boolean that is true if white space is to be preserved; otherwise, it is false.

As you can see, the XmlDocument class provides quite a bit of additional functionality over the XmlNode class. The following are some of the XmlDocument class's unique methods:

- CreateAttribute() creates an XmlAttribute.
- CreateCDataSection() creates an XmlCDataSection.
- CreateComment() creates an XmlComment.
- CreateDocumentFragment() creates an XmlDocumentFragment.
- CreateDocumentType() creates an XmlDocumentType.
- CreateElement() creates an XmlElement.
- CreateEntityReference() creates an XmlEntityReference.
- CreateNode() creates an XmlNode.
- CreateTextNode() creates an XmlText.

- CreateXmlDeclaration() creates an XmlDeclaration.
- GetElementById() gets an element based on a specified ID.
- GetElementsByTagName() gets an XmlNodeList of all elements that match the specified tag.
- ImportNode() imports a node for another XmlDocument.
- Load() loads into the XmlDocument a File, Stream, TextReader, or XmlReader.
- LoadXml() loads into the XmlDocument a String.
- ReadNode() creates an XmlNode based on the current position of an XmlReader.
- Save() saves the XmlDocument to a specified filename, Stream, TextWriter, or XmlWriter.

Reading a DOM Tree

You have many different ways of navigating through a DOM tree. You'll start out by using only the basic methods found in XmlDocument, XmlNode, and XmlNodeList. Later you'll look at an easier way of navigating using XPaths.

Because the DOM is stored in a tree in memory, it's a good candidate for navigating via recursion. The example in Listing 13-9 demonstrates an implementation of recursively following the tree branch and dumping the node information it passed along the way. You dump the tree to the system console.

Listing 13-9. *Reading a DOM Tree Recursively*

```
using namespace System;
using namespace System::Xml;

String ^indent(int depth)
{
    String ^ind = "";
    return ind->PadLeft(depth*4, ' ');
}

void Navigate(XmlNode ^node, int depth)
{
    if (node == nullptr)
        return;

    Console::WriteLine("{0}: Name='{1}' Value='{2}'",
        String::Concat(indent(depth),node->NodeType.ToString()),
        node->Name, node->Value);

    if (node->Attributes != nullptr)
    {
        for (int i = 0; i < node->Attributes->Count; i++)
        {
            Console::WriteLine("{0}Attribute: Name='{1}' Value='{2}'",
                indent(depth+1),node->Attributes[i]->Name,
                node->Attributes[i]->Value);
        }
    }
    Navigate(node->FirstChild, depth+1);
    Navigate(node->NextSibling, depth);
}
```

```
void main()
{
    XmlDocument ^doc = gcnew XmlDocument();

    try
    {
        XmlReader ^reader = XmlReader::Create("Monsters.xml");
        doc->Load(reader);
        reader->Close();

        XmlNode ^node = doc->FirstChild;  // I want the Xml Declaration

        // Recursive navigation of the DOM tree
        Navigate(node, 0);
    }
    catch (Exception ^e)
    {
        Console::WriteLine("Error Occurred: {0}", e->Message);
    }
}
```

As I stated before, you process all XML documents within an exception try block because every XML method in the .NET Framework class library can throw an exception.

Before you start reading the DOM tree, you need to load it. First, you create an XmlDocument to hold the tree. You do this using a standard constructor:

```
XmlDocument ^doc = gcnew XmlDocument();
```

Then you load the XML document into the XmlDocument. It is possible to pass the name of the XML file directly into the Load() method, which I think is a little easier. But, if you do it the following way, make sure you close the file after the load is complete, because the file resource remains open longer than it needs to be. Plus, if you try to write to the file, it will throw an exception because the file is already open.

```
XmlReader ^reader = XmlReader::Create("Monsters.xml");
doc->Load(reader);
reader->Close();
```

In the previous example, I call the XmlDocument class's FirstChild() method instead of the DocumentElement() method because I want to start reading the XML document at the XML declaration and not the first element of the document.

```
XmlNode ^node = doc->FirstChild;  // I want the Xml Declaration
```

Finally, you call a simple recursive method to navigate the tree. The first thing this method does is check to make sure that you have not already reached the end of the current branch of the tree:

```
if (node == nullptr)
    return;
```

Then it dumps to the console the current node's type, name, and value. Notice that I use the little trick I mentioned in Chapter 3 to display the enum class's (in this case, the NodeType's) String name:

```
Console::WriteLine("{0}: Name='{1}' Value='{2}'",
    String::Concat(indent(depth), node->NodeType.ToString()),
    node->Name, node->Value);
```

The method then checks to see if the element has any attributes. If it does, it then iterates through them, dumping each to the console as it goes:

```
if (node->Attributes != nullptr)
{
    for (int i = 0; i < node->Attributes->Count; i++)
    {
        Console::WriteLine("{0}Attribute: Name='{1}' Value='{2}'",
            indent(depth+1),
            node->Attributes[i]->Name,
            node->Attributes[i]->Value));
    }
}
```

The last thing the method does is call itself to navigate down through its children, and then it calls itself to navigate through its siblings:

```
Navigate(node->FirstChild, depth+1);
Navigate(node->NextSibling, depth);
```

Figure 13-5 shows the resulting console dump for ReadXMLDOM.exe of all the nodes and attributes that make up the monster DOM tree.

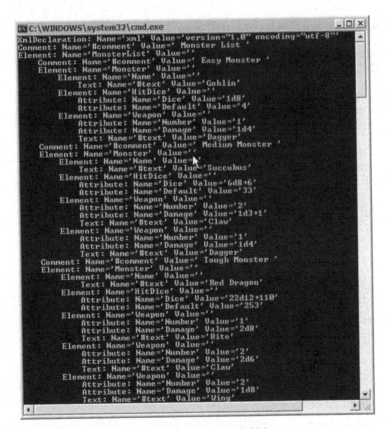

Figure 13-5. *The console dump of the monster DOM tree*

Updating a DOM Tree

The process of updating a DOM tree is as simple as finding the correct node and changing the appropriate values. Finally, after all of the changes are made, save the changes.

In Listing 13-10, you continue to recursively navigate the DOM tree of Listing 13-1, but this time you're looking for a Goblin node that was mistakenly given a Dagger. The Goblin was supposed to have a Saber. The trick is that you can just globally change all Daggers to Sabers because the Succubus node also has a Dagger, so you have to verify that it is the Goblin node's Dagger. There are many ways of doing this, and I can think of a couple (better ones) using flags, but the method in Listing 13-10 shows the implementation of the largest number of different methods to find a node (without being redundant).

Listing 13-10. *Updating the Monster DOM Tree*

```
using namespace System;
using namespace System::Xml;

void Navigate(XmlNode ^node)
{
    if (node == nullptr)
        return;

    if (node->Value != nullptr && node->Value->Equals("Dagger"))
    {
        if (node->ParentNode->ParentNode["Name"]->FirstChild->Value->
            Equals("Goblin"))
        {
            node->Value = "Saber";
            node->ParentNode->Attributes["Damage"]->Value = "1d8";
        }
    }

    Navigate(node->FirstChild);
    Navigate(node->NextSibling);
}


void main()
{
    XmlDocument ^doc = gcnew XmlDocument();

    try
    {
        doc->Load("Monsters.xml");
        XmlNode ^root = doc->DocumentElement;
```

```
        // Recursive navigation of the DOM tree
        Navigate(root);

        doc->Save("New_Monsters.xml");
    }
    catch (Exception ^e)
    {
        Console::WriteLine("Error Occurred: {0}", e->Message );
    }
}
```

The main method looks familiar enough. The primary difference is that you will write out the DOM tree when you are done to make sure the change actually occurred:

```
doc->Save("New_Monsters.xml");
```

The recursive function is pretty similar. Let's look closely at the if statement that does the update. First, you make sure the node has a value, as not all nodes have one. Calling the Equals() method on a node that doesn't have a value will cause an exception to be thrown:

```
if (node->Value != nullptr && node->Value->Equals("Dagger"))
```

So you now know that you have a node with a value of Dagger. How do you check to make sure it belongs to a Goblin node? You do this by checking the current node's grandparent's Name element for the value of Goblin:

```
if (node->ParentNode->ParentNode["Name"]->FirstChild->Value->Equals("Goblin"))
```

What I really want you to focus on in the preceding statement is ParentNode["Name"]. The default indexed property of a ParentNode contains a collection of its child elements. This collection can be either an indexed property (as previously) or an array property where it is passed the numeric index of the child: ParentNode[0].

To change the value of a node, you simply assign it a new value:

```
node->Value = "Saber";
```

The damage done by a Saber differs from a Dagger, so you need to change the Damage attribute of the Weapon node. Notice that it is the Weapon node, not the Saber node. The Saber node is an XmlText node. You need to navigate to the Saber node's parent first and then to its attributes. Notice that Attributes also has a default indexed property.

```
node->ParentNode->Attributes["Damage"]->Value = "1d8";
```

Figure 13-6 shows the new copy of the XML monster file created by UpdateXMLDOM.exe in the Visual Studio 2005 editor.

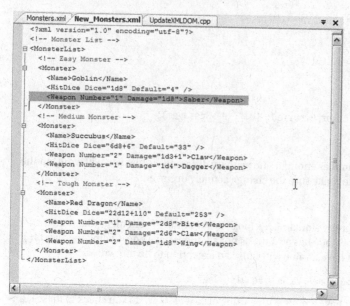

Figure 13-6. *The updated XML monster file*

Writing XmlNodes in a DOM Tree

You can truly get a good understanding of how a DOM tree is stored in memory by building a few XmlNodes manually. The basic process is to create a node and then append all its children on it. Then for each of the children, append all their children, and so on.

The last example (see Listing 13-11) before you get to XPaths shows how to add a new monster (a Skeleton node) after the Goblin node.

Listing 13-11. *Adding a New Monster to the DOM Tree*

```
using namespace System;
using namespace System::Xml;

XmlElement ^CreateMonster(XmlDocument ^doc)
{
    XmlElement ^skeleton = doc->CreateElement("Monster");

    // <Name>Skeleton</Name>
    XmlElement ^name = doc->CreateElement("Name");
    name->AppendChild(doc->CreateTextNode("Skeleton"));
    skeleton->AppendChild(name);

    // <HitDice Dice="1/2 d12" Default="3" />
    XmlElement ^hitdice = doc->CreateElement("HitDice");
    XmlAttribute ^att = doc->CreateAttribute("Dice");
    att->Value = "1/2 d12";
    hitdice->Attributes->Append(att);
    att = doc->CreateAttribute("Default");
    att->Value = "3";
    hitdice->Attributes->Append(att);
    skeleton->AppendChild(hitdice);
```

```
        // <Weapon Number="2" Damage="1d3-1">Claw</Weapon>
        XmlElement ^weapon = doc->CreateElement("Weapon");
        att = doc->CreateAttribute("Number");
        att->Value = "2";
        weapon->Attributes->Append(att);
        att = doc->CreateAttribute("Damage");
        att->Value = "1d3-1";
        weapon->Attributes->Append(att);
        weapon->AppendChild(doc->CreateTextNode("Claw"));
        skeleton->AppendChild(weapon);

        return skeleton;
}

void main()
{
        XmlDocument ^doc = gcnew XmlDocument();

        try
        {
                doc->Load("Monsters.xml");
                XmlNode ^root = doc->DocumentElement;

                // Skip comment and goblin
                XmlNode ^child = root->FirstChild->NextSibling;

                // Insert new monster
                root->InsertAfter(CreateMonster(doc), child);

                doc->Save("New_Monsters.xml");
        }
        catch (Exception ^e)
        {
                Console::WriteLine("Error Occurred: {0}", e->Message );
        }
}
```

The method of inserting XmlNodes, though not difficult, needs a quick explanation. I first wondered why you needed to pass a pointer to the XmlNode that you are going to place on the new XmlNode before or after. Why not just call the Insert method for this node instead, like this:

```
childNode->InsertBefore(newNode);   // wrong
childNode->InsertAfter(newNode);    // wrong
```

Then I realized that I am not actually inserting after the child node. Instead I am inserting into the parent node after or before the child node. Thus the correct syntax:

```
parentNode->InsertBefore(newNode, childNode);
parentNode->InsertAfter(newNode, childNode);
```

or as in the previous code:

```
root->InsertAfter(CreateMonster(doc), child);
```

Like the writing methods of forward-only access, it seems a lot of effort is required to create such a simple XmlElement. You need to remember that the correct way to do this is without hard-coding, thus making it reusable.

The first issue with creating nodes dynamically is that you need access to the XmlDocument, as all the XmlNode creation methods are found in it. You have two choices: pass XmlDocument as a parameter as was done in this example, or make XmlDocument a private member variable that all classes can access.

Now that you have access to the creation methods, it is a simple matter to create the element:

```
XmlElement ^skeleton = doc->CreateElement("Monster");
```

Then you create and append any of its child elements:

```
XmlElement ^weapon = doc->CreateElement("Weapon");
skeleton->AppendChild(weapon);
```

Of course, to create these child elements, you need to create and append the child elements attribute(s) and body text (which might have to create grandchildren nodes, and so on):

```
XmlAttribute ^att = doc->CreateAttribute("Number");
att->Value = "2";
weapon->Attributes->Append(att);

att = doc->CreateAttribute("Damage");
att->Value = "1d3-1";
weapon->Attributes->Append(att);

weapon->AppendChild(doc->CreateTextNode("Claw"));
```

Figure 13-7 shows the resulting new copy of the XML monster file from WriteXMLDOM.exe with the new inserted monster in the Visual Studio 2005 editor.

Figure 13-7. *The XML monster file with a new monster*

Navigating with XPathNavigator

Wouldn't it be nice to have easy sequential access through an XML file and the concept of a current location like you have with XmlReader discussed previously, but without the restriction of forward-only access? You do. It's called the XPathNavigator class.

If you were comfortable with the XmlReader class, then you should have no trouble adapting to the XPathNavigator class, as many of its properties and methods are very similar. Also, if you were comfortable with XmlDocument, you should have few problems with XPathNavigator because you will find a lot of overlap between them. The following are some of the more common XPathNavigator properties:

- HasAttributes is a Boolean that is true if the current node has attributes; otherwise, it is false.

- HasChildren is a Boolean that is true if the current node has children; otherwise, it is false.

- IsEmptyElement is a Boolean that is true if the current node is an empty element or, in other words, the element ends in />.

- LocalName is a String representing the name of the current node without the namespace prefix.

- Name is a String representing the qualified name of the current node.

- NodeType is an XmlNodeType enum class that represents the node type (see Table 13-2) of the current node.

- Value is a String representing the value of the current node.

- ValueAs<data type> is a <data type> representing the value of the current node. Some examples are ValueAsBoolean and ValueAsInt32.

Here are some of the more commonly used XPathNavigator class methods:

- ComparePosition() compares the position of the current navigator with another specified navigator.

- Compile() compiles an XPath String into an XPathExpression.

- Evaluate() evaluates an XPath expression.

- GetAttribute() gets the attribute with the specified LocalName.

- IsDescendant() determines whether the specified XPathNavigator is a descendant of the current XPathNavigator.

- IsSamePosition() determines whether the current and a specified XPathNavigator share the same position.

- Matches() determines whether the current node matches a specified expression.

- MoveTo() moves to the position of a specified XPathNavigator.

- MoveToAttribute() moves to the attribute that matches a specified LocalName.

- MoveToChild() moves to the child node specified.

- MoveToDescendant() moves to the descendant node specified.

- MoveToFirst() moves to the first sibling of the current node.

- MoveToFirstAttribute() moves to the first attribute of the current node.

- MoveToFirstChild() moves to the first child of the current node.

- MoveToId() moves to the node that has a specified String ID attribute.

- MoveToNext() moves to the next sibling of the current node.

- MoveToNextAttribute() moves to the next attribute of the current node.
- MoveToParent() moves to the parent of the current node.
- MoveToPrevious() moves to the previous sibling of the current node.
- MoveToRoot() moves to the root node of the current node.
- Select() selects a collection of nodes that match an XPath expression.
- SelectAncestor() selects a collection of ancestor nodes that match an XPath expression.
- SelectChildren() selects a collection of children nodes that match an XPath expression.
- SelectDescendants() selects a collection of descendant nodes that match an XPath expression.
- ValueAs() returns the current node value as the type specified.

As you can see by the list of methods made available by XPathNavigator, it does what its name suggests: navigates. The majority of the methods are for navigating forward, backward, and, as you will see when you add XPath expressions, randomly through the DOM tree.

Basic XPathNavigator

Let's first look at the XPathNavigator class without the XPath functionality or simply its capability to move around a DOM tree. The example in Listing 13-12 is your third and final read through the monster XML file. This time you are going to use XPathNavigator.

Listing 13-12. *Navigating a DOM Tree Using XPathNavigator*

```
using namespace System;
using namespace System::Xml;
using namespace System::Xml::XPath;

String ^indent(int depth)
{
    String ^ind = "";
    return ind->PadLeft(depth*4, ' ');
}

void Navigate(XPathNavigator ^nav, int depth)
{
    Console::WriteLine("{0}: Name='{1}' Value='{2}'",
        String::Concat(indent(depth), nav->NodeType.ToString()),
        nav->Name, nav->Value);

    if (nav->HasAttributes)
    {
        nav->MoveToFirstAttribute();
        do {
            Console::WriteLine("{0} Attribute: Name='{1}' Value='{2}'",
                indent(depth+1),nav->Name, nav->Value);
        }
        while(nav->MoveToNextAttribute());
        nav->MoveToParent();
    }
```

```
    if (nav->MoveToFirstChild())
    {
        Navigate(nav, depth+1);
        nav->MoveToParent();
    }
    if (nav->MoveToNext())
        Navigate(nav, depth);
}

void main()
{
    XmlDocument ^doc = gcnew XmlDocument();
    try
    {
        doc->Load("Monsters.xml");
        XPathNavigator ^nav = doc->CreateNavigator();
        nav->MoveToRoot();
        Navigate(nav, 0);
    }
    catch (Exception ^e)
    {
        Console::WriteLine("Error Occurred: {0}", e->Message);
    }
}
```

The first thing you have to remember when working with the XPathNavigator class is that you need to import the namespace System::Xml::XPath using the following command:

```
using namespace System::Xml::XPath;
```

I personally think of the XPathNavigator as a token that I move around that shows where I currently am in the DOM tree. In the preceding program I use only one XPathNavigator object pointer that gets passed around. This pointer eventually passes by every node of the DOM tree.

You create an XPathNavigator from any class that inherits from the XmlNode class using the CreateNavigator() method:

```
XPathNavigator ^nav = doc->CreateNavigator();
```

At this point, your navigator is pointing to the location of the node that you created it from. To set it at the first element of the DOM tree, you need to call the navigator's MoveToRoot() method:

```
nav->MoveToRoot();
```

Using recursion still holds true for XPathNavigator navigation as it does for standard XmlDocument navigation. You will probably notice that it has many similarities to the XmlDocument reader example. The biggest difference, though, is that with an XPathNavigator you need to navigate back out of a child branch before you can enter a new branch. Therefore, you see the use of the MoveToParent() method much more frequently.

Something that you have to get used to if you have been using XmlDocument and XmlNode navigation is that the move methods return Boolean success values. In other words, to find out if you successfully moved to the next node, you need to check whether the move method returned true. If the move method can't successfully move to the next node, then it returns false. The move ends up changing an internal pointer in the XPathNavigator. This is considerably different than navigating with XmlNodes, where the nodes return the value of the next node or null if they can't navigate as requested.

One other thing you'll probably notice is that the Value property returns a concatenation of all its child node Value properties, and not just its own Value. You might not think it helpful, but I'll show how you can use this feature as a shortcut in the next example.

Figure 13-8 shows the console dump, created by ReadXPathNav.exe, of all the nodes and attributes that make up the monster DOM tree.

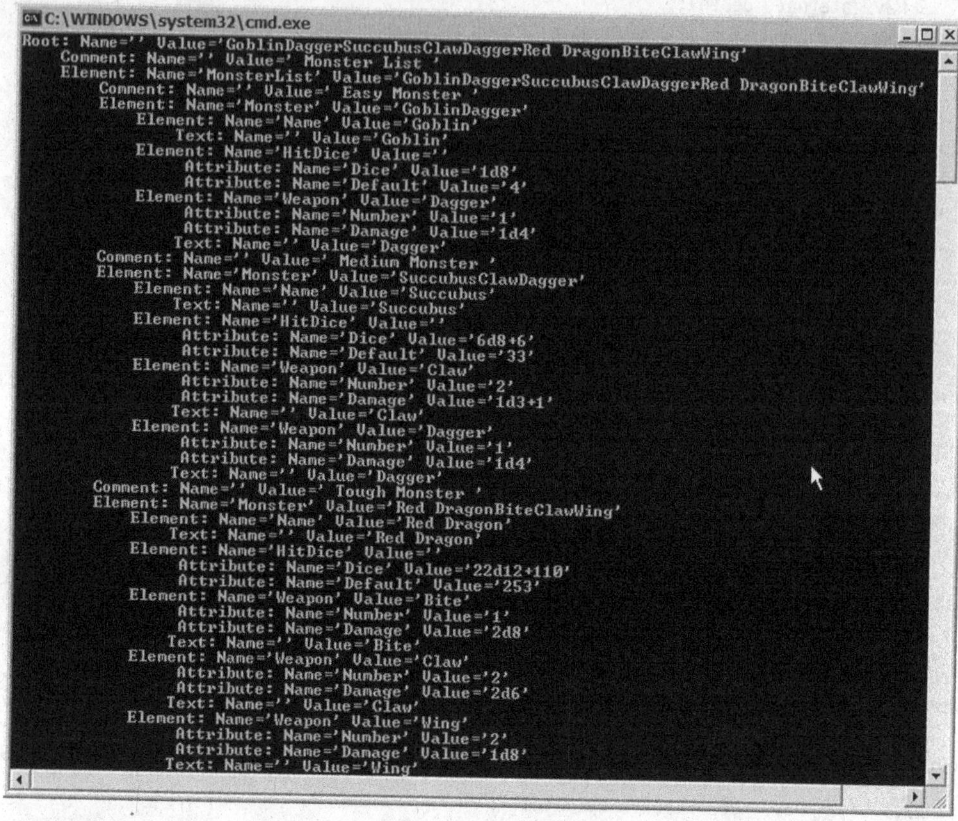

Figure 13-8. *A console list of all nodes of the XML monster file*

XPathNavigator Using XPath Expressions

Using any of the methods in the previous section to navigate an XML file or DOM tree is hardly trivial. If you're trying to get specific pieces of information out of your XML files, going through the trouble of writing all that code hardly seems worth the effort. If there wasn't a better way, I'm sure XML would lose its popularity. The better way is the XPath expression.

With XPath expressions, you can quickly grab one particular piece of information out of the DOM tree or a list of information. The two most common ways of implementing XPath expressions are via the XPathNavigator class's Select() method and the XmlNode class's SelectNodes() method.

The XPath expression syntax is quite large and beyond the scope of this book. If you want to look into the details of the XPath language, then I recommend you start with the documentation on XPath provided by the .NET Framework.

For now, let's make do with some simple examples that show the power of the XPath (almost wrote "Force" there—hmmm . . . I must have just seen *Star Wars*).

The first example is the most basic form of XPath. It looks very similar to how you would specify a path or a file. It is simply a list of nodes separated by the forward slash (/), which you want to match within the document. For example,

```
/MonsterList/Monster/Name
```

specifies that you want to get a list of all Name nodes that have a parent node of Monster and MonsterList. The starting forward slash specifies that MonsterList be at the root. Here is a method that will execute the preceding XPath expression:

```
void GetMonsters(XPathNavigator ^nav)
{
    XPathNodeIterator ^list =
        nav->Select("/MonsterList/Monster/Name");

    Console::WriteLine("Monsters\n--------");
    while (list->MoveNext())
    {
        XPathNavigator ^n = list->Current;
        Console::WriteLine(n->Value);
    }

// The required code to do the same as above if no
// XPathNavigator concatenation occurred.
/*
    list = nav->Select("/MonsterList/Monster/Name");

    Console::WriteLine("Monsters\n--------");
    while (list->MoveNext())
    {
        XPathNavigator ^n = list->Current;
        n->MoveToFirstChild();
        Console::WriteLine(n->Value);
    }
*/
}
```

Figure 13-9 presents the output of the snippet.

Figure 13-9. *Output for the XPath expression MonsterList/Monster/Name*

As promised earlier, this example shows how the concatenation of child values by the XPathNavigator can come in handy. Remember that the XmlText node is a child of the XmlElement node, so without the concatenation of the XPathNavigator class, the dumping of the values of the Name nodes will produce empty strings, because XmlElement nodes have no values.

That was simple enough. Let's look at something a little more complex. It is possible to specify that you don't care what the parents are by prefixing with a double forward slash (//). For example,

```
//Name
```

would get you all Name nodes in the document. Be careful, though: If you use the Name element start tag in different places, you will get them all.

Along the same lines, if you don't actually care what the parent is but you want only a node at a specific depth, you would use the asterisk (*) to match any element. For example,

```
/MonsterList/*/Name
```

would get all the names with a grandparent of MonsterList, but it would matter who the parent was.

Conditional expressions are possible. You enclose conditionals in square brackets ([ ]). For example,

```
//Monster[Name]
```

would result in all monsters that have the Name node (which would be all of them, as Name is a mandatory element—but that is another story). It is possible to specify an exact value for the conditional node or specify what values it cannot be. For example,

```
//Monster[Name = ''Goblin'']
//Monster[Name != ''Succubus'']
```

would result in the first expression grabbing the Monster node Goblin and the second expression grabbing every monster but the Succubus.

Here is a method that will execute a combination of a few of the expressions you covered previously. Also notice that just to be different, the example uses the XmlNode class's SelectNodes() method. Because XmlNodes don't concatenate child values, you need to navigate to the child to get the desired value:

```
void GetDragonsWeapons(XmlNode ^node)
{
    XmlNodeList ^list =
        node->SelectNodes("//Monster[Name='Red Dragon']/Weapon");

    Console::WriteLine("\nDragon's Weapons\n-------");

    IEnumerator ^en = list->GetEnumerator();
    while (en->MoveNext())
    {
        XmlNode ^n = (XmlNode^)en->Current;
        Console::WriteLine(n->FirstChild->Value);
    }
}
```

Figure 13-10 shows the output of the snippet.

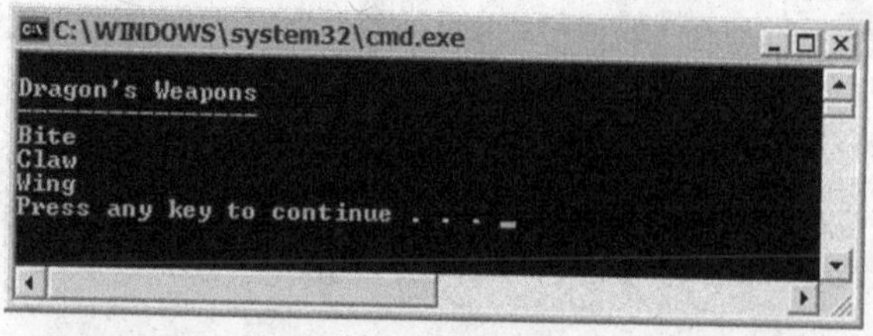

Figure 13-10. *Output for the XPath expression //Monster[Name='Red Dragon']/Weapon*

Let's expand on this expression just a little more. It is also possible to have conditionals with logical operators such as and, or, and not().

The following method shows the logical operator in practice. It also shows how to grab an attribute value out of the navigator:

```
void GetGoblinSuccubusHitDice(XPathNavigator ^nav)
{
    XPathNodeIterator ^list =
        nav->Select("//Monster[Name='Goblin' or Name='Succubus']/HitDice");

    Console::WriteLine("\nGoblin & Succubus HD\n-----------");
    while (list->MoveNext())
    {
        XPathNavigator ^n = list->Current;
        n->MoveToFirstAttribute();
        Console::WriteLine(n->Value);
    }
}
```

Figure 13-11 shows the output of the snippet.

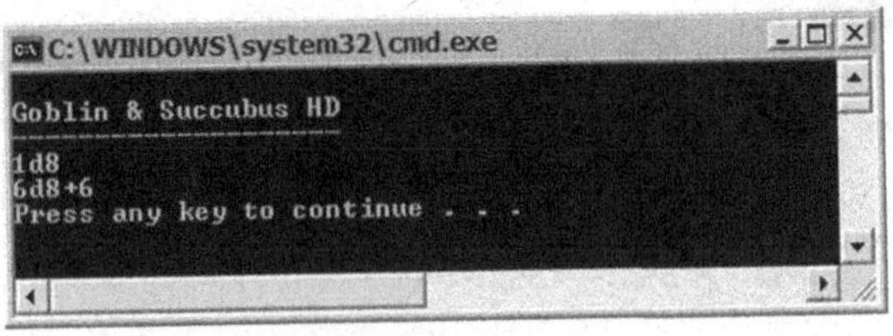

Figure 13-11. *Output for the XPath expression //Monster[Name='Goblin' or Name='Succubus']/HitDice*

To match attributes in an XPath expression, use the "at" sign (@) in front of the attribute's name. For example,

```
void GetGoblinSuccubusHitDice(XPathNavigator ^nav)
{
    XPathNodeIterator ^list =
        nav->Select("//Monster[Name='Goblin' or Name='Succubus']/HitDice/@Dice");

    Console::WriteLine("\nGoblin & Succubus HD\n----------");
    while (list->MoveNext())
    {
        XPathNavigator ^n = list->Current;
        Console::WriteLine(n->Value);
    }
}
```

results in the same output as the previous example. Notice that you no longer have to move to the attribute before displaying it.

As a final example, the following snippet shows that you can make numeric comparisons. In this example, I grab all Weapon elements with a Number attribute of less than or equal to 1:

```
void GetSingleAttackWeapons(XPathNavigator ^nav)
{
    XPathNodeIterator ^list =
        nav->Select("//Weapon[@Number <= 1]");

    Console::WriteLine("\nSingle Attack Weapons\n----------");
    while (list->MoveNext())
    {
        XPathNavigator ^n = list->Current;
        Console::WriteLine(n->Value);
    }
}
```

Figure 13-12 shows the output of the snippet.

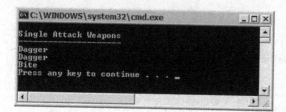

Figure 13-12. *Output for the XPath expression //Weapon[@Number <= 1]*

Table 13-4 is a list of the available operators that you have at your disposal when developing your XPath expressions.

Table 13-4. *XPath Operators*

Operator	Description
		Compute the union of node sets; for example: //monsters	//players would return a node set containing all monster and players (if players were part of the DOM)
+	Addition
-	Subtraction
*	Multiplication
div	Division
=	Equals
!=	Not equals
<	Less than
<=	Less than or equal to
>	Greater than
>=	Greater than or equal to
or	Or

Table 13-4. *XPath Operators*

Operator	Description
and	And
mod	Modulus (remainder)
not	Negation

XML and ADO.NET

This topic almost doesn't merit a section of its own, as only one class, XmlDataDocument, needs to be examined, and XmlDataDocument inherits from XmlDocument. What am I trying to get at? To use ADO.NET and XML together, you need to create a DataSet (see Chapter 12) and create an XmlDataDocument with it. Then you can manipulate the database data just as you did with XmlDocument.

The XmlDataDocument class adds properties and members to streamline some activities and to make them more "relational database"–like, but other than that you have already learned what you need to work with XML originating from an ADO.NET database:

- DataSet is the DataSet used to create the XmlDataDocument.
- CreateEntityReference() is a method that is not supported and throws an exception.
- GetElementById() is a method that is not supported and throws an exception.
- GetElementFromRow() gets an XmlElement associated with a specified DataRow.
- GetRowFromElement() gets a DataRow associated with a specified XmlElement.
- Load() loads into the XmlDocument using a filename, Stream, TextReader, or XmlReader, and then synchronizes with the DataSet.

The example in Listing 13-13 is an exact duplicate of Listing 13-9, except that the source of the XML data is the DCV_DB database created in Chapter 12.

Listing 13-13. *Dumping the DCV_DB Database to a Console Using XML*

```
using namespace System;
using namespace System::Data;
using namespace System::Data::SqlClient;
using namespace System::Xml;

String ^indent(int depth)
{
    String ^ind = "";
    return ind->PadLeft(depth*4, ' ');
}

void Navigate(XmlNode ^node, int depth)
{
    if (node == nullptr)
        return;
```

```cpp
        Console::WriteLine("{0}: Name='{1}' Value='{2}'",
            String::Concat(indent(depth),node->NodeType.ToString()),
            node->Name, node->Value);

        if (node->Attributes != nullptr)
        {
            for (int i = 0; i < node->Attributes->Count; i++)
            {
                Console::WriteLine("{0}Attribute: Name='{1}' Value='{2}'",
                    indent(depth+1),node->Attributes[i]->Name,
                    node->Attributes[i]->Value);
            }
        }

        Navigate(node->FirstChild, depth+1);
        Navigate(node->NextSibling, depth);
}

void main()
{
    XmlDocument ^doc = gcnew XmlDocument();

    try
    {
        SqlConnection ^connect = gcnew SqlConnection();

#ifdef SQLAuth
        //  SQL Server authentication
        connect->ConnectionString =
            "User ID=sa; Password=;"
            "Data Source=(local); Initial Catalog=DCV_DB;";
#else
        //  Windows Integrated Security
        connect->ConnectionString =
            "Persist Security Info=False; Integrated Security=SSPI;"
            "Data Source=(local); Initial Catalog=DCV_DB;";
#endif

        SqlDataAdapter ^dAdapt = gcnew SqlDataAdapter();
        DataSet ^dSet          = gcnew DataSet();
        dAdapt->SelectCommand  =
            gcnew SqlCommand("SELECT * FROM Authors", connect);

        dAdapt->Fill(dSet, "Authors");
        XmlDataDocument ^doc = gcnew XmlDataDocument(dSet);

        // Recursive navigation of the DOM tree
        Navigate(doc->DocumentElement, 0);
    }
    catch (Exception ^e)
    {
        Console::WriteLine("Error Occurred: {0}", e->Message);
    }
}
```

As you can see, the only code that is different from the original (Listing 13-9) is the standard code to create a DataSet and then the placing of the DataSet within an XmlDataDocument. If you need a refresher on creating a DataSet, please review Chapter 12.

```
SqlConnection ^connect = gcnew SqlConnection();

#ifdef SQLAuth
    //  SQL Server authentication
    connect->ConnectionString =
        "User ID=sa; Password=;"
        "Data Source=(local); Initial Catalog=DCV_DB;";
#else
    //  Windows Integrated Security
    connect->ConnectionString =
        "Persist Security Info=False; Integrated Security=SSPI;"
        "Data Source=(local); Initial Catalog=DCV_DB;";
#endif

    SqlDataAdapter ^dAdapt = gcnew SqlDataAdapter();
    DataSet ^dSet         = gcnew DataSet();
    dAdapt->SelectCommand = gcnew SqlCommand("SELECT * FROM Authors", connect);

    dAdapt->Fill(dSet, "Authors");
    XmlDataDocument ^doc = gcnew XmlDataDocument(dSet);
```

Figure 13-13 shows the resulting console dump by ADONET.exe of all the nodes and attributes that make up the DCV_DB database DOM tree.

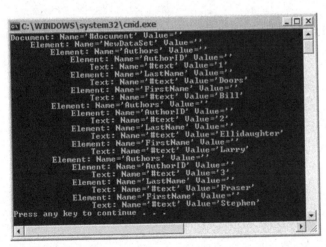

Figure 13-13. *The console dump of the DCV_DB database DOM tree*

Summary

In this chapter you covered the last of the .NET Framework class library's standard I/O mechanisms. You started with a quick refresher on XML. You then learned how to read, validate, write, and update XML documents using forward-only access. Then you looked at DOM trees and how to go about reading from, updating, and writing to them. Next, you took a brief look at the powerful XPath. You finished off by learning how simple it is to manipulate ADO.NET databases using XML.

Now with all four I/O systems covered, you should have no problems getting the necessary information into your system.

In the next chapter, you will explore the first of two service types covered in this book, the Windows service.

■ ■ ■

CHAPTER 14

Windows Services

The .NET Framework provides two considerably different types of services applications to the developer: the Windows service, which I cover in this chapter, and the Web service, which I cover in the next chapter. Although both are called services, they are very different. Windows services are standalone installed applications, while, as you shall see, Web services provide a service via a network to another application.

Windows services, I'd like to point out, is a bit of a misnomer, as this same functionality is also available on the Mono/Linux platform using what is called a monod, which (I believe) is an implementation of a forked daemon and has nothing to do with Windows at all. I am also pretty sure the other .NET-implemented platforms don't use Windows in any way to implement the functionality. Admittedly, I have not looked into it. Personally, I think Windows services should be called service processes, as the implementing .NET Framework namespace suggests.

That being said, so as to not confuse the Windows developer, this chapter will focus on the Windows implementation of the service process and use the term *Windows service*. This kind of makes sense, as C++/CLI currently only has (as far as I know) a Windows implementation. Hopefully, since Microsoft has released the standard to the ECMA, there will be other implementations on other platforms.

Note Windows Services do not run on Windows 98 or Windows ME. They require the NT kernel and thus run on Windows NT4, Windows 2000, Windows XP, and Windows 2003.

This chapter starts out by providing you with a general understanding of Windows services and its three parts: the service application, the service control application, and the service configuration application. Next, you will see how to create, install, and uninstall a Windows service. Then you will take a look at how to manage a Windows service. Finally, you will take a look at how to debug the Windows service, as it is done a little differently from the normal debugging process.

What Are Windows Services?

A Windows service, or what used to be known as an NT service, is an installed long-running executable application that runs in its own process space. Windows services can run without a user context (albeit only under Windows NT, Windows 2000, or Windows XP and Windows Vista at this point). They don't require a user to be logged in to function, and they generally run in a higher-powered security mode than do most users. A Windows service is normally automatically started when the computer boots, but it can be also started, paused, restarted, and stopped manually by a user.

Another telling aspect of Windows services is that it has no user interface, thus making it good for the scenario where the user needs some long-running functionality that does not interfere with users working on the computer. Also, due to the fact that the Windows service has no interface, it is ideal for running in the background thread on a server. Since I do not cover multithreading until later in the book (Chapter 16), I will not the cover placing of a Windows service in a background thread, but after you have read Chapter 16, you should have little difficulty doing so.

Note Not having an interface, though, does not make an application a service. Console applications can be written without an interface as well. Typically, services provide system-level support, including a system event log, performance counters, and a task scheduler, but again that does not make an application a service either.

As mentioned previously, a Windows service is installed into the registry as an executable object. As you will see, the `main()` method does not actually run the service; instead, it is used to install the service into the registry. To actually start a Windows service, you will need to use either the Services application, which is part of the Administrative Tools on the Control Panel (see Figure 14-1), or create your own service control application. (You can also configure your Windows service to automatically start at startup as well.)

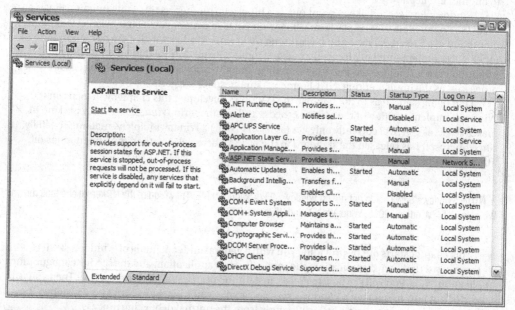

Figure 14-1. *The Administrative Tools' Services application*

In case you are interested, all Windows services installed on a computer can be found in the registry at

`HKEY_LOCAL_MACHINE\SYSTEM\CurrentControlSet\Services`

There are several different types of Windows services that can be created, but only two managed code types can be created with the .NET Framework. A Windows service made up of only a single service in a process is of type `Win32OwnProcess`, while a Windows service made up of multiple services in a single shared process is of type `Win32ShareProcess`.

You can find out the type of Windows service you are accessing by querying the property `ServiceController.ServiceType`. If the service was not created by .NET, then it is possible for this property to have other values as listed in Table 14-1.

Table 14-1. *Windows Service Types*

ServiceType	Description
Adapter	A service for a piece of hardware that needs its own driver.
FileSystemDriver	A file system driver. This is a specific type of kernel driver.
InteractiveProcess	A service that can communicate with the desktop.
KernelDriver	A low-level hardware device driver.
RecognizerDriver	A file system driver used during the system startup to determine file system types.
Win32OwnProcess	A service made up of only a single service in a process.
Win32ShareProcess	A service made up of multiple services in a single shared process.

Architecture of Windows Services

Unlike other application types, Windows services actually require three different programs to function properly. The first program is the service application itself. This program implements the functionality required by the Windows service. The second program is the service control application. This program provides the ability to start, pause, restart, stop, and send unique commands to the service application. The final program is the service configuration application. This program installs and configures the service application.

Service Application

The service application provides the functionality of the Windows service. But since it is a registry executable object, it is internally set up a little differently from other applications. The service application is also made up of three parts: the main, the service-main, and the handlers.

The main part provides the ability to register the true entry point or points of the service application, the service-main or service-mains. This dual functionality is required because a Windows service can be either of type `Win32OwnProcess` or `Win32ShareProcess`. Thus, when the Windows service is of type `Win32OwnProcess`, the main part must register the single service-main that makes up the Windows service. On the other hand, when the Windows service type is `Win32ShareProcess`, then the main part must register the multiple services that comprise the Windows service.

The service-main is the Windows service's interface to the outside world and is called when the service needs to be started. Once called, the service-main then needs to register a handler to the Service Control Manager (SCM).

The SCM is part of the operating system that communicates with the Windows service. It is the SCM that sends events to the third part of the service application, the handler. It is up to the handler to handle the start, pause, continue, stop, and custom events sent to it from the SCM.

Service Control Application

You don't have to write your own service control application, since the Windows operating system provides one for you, as you saw previously with the Administrative Tools' Services application. This tool provides limited functionality. It can only start, stop, pause, resume, and restart a Windows service.

When you write your own service control application, you can query and retrieve the properties of the Windows service. Plus, another cool feature of writing your own implementation of the service control application is you can write custom controls that allow you to perform more specialized tasks within the Windows service.

Whenever you use the Services application or your own service control application, you are still using the SCM to communicate with your Windows service. Your service application and service control application only have built-in functionality to communicate via the SCM. You can also use TCP/IP to directly communicate with the service application when the functionality provided by the SCM just doesn't cut it. Again, since I don't cover network programming until Chapter 17, I will not show how to write this code, but after you finish Chapter 17, you should have no trouble writing it yourself.

Service Configuration Application

The service configuration application does as its name suggests: it configures the Windows service. Through this application, you specify things like whether the Windows service is started automatically at startup, manually, or is disabled; the user to run the session under; and any dependencies that the services may have.

Windows services normally start when the computer is booted, but you have the option to determine manually when the service will be started. You use the service configuration application to set up the registry and then the service control application to perform the actual startup process. The Windows operating system provides you with a very limited service configuration application, as the Administrative Tools' Services application handles the setting up of automatic startup, manual startup, and disabling of the Windows service.

The Windows service can be run under four different security context groups as shown in Table 14-2.

Table 14-2. *Windows Service Security Contexts*

Context	Description
LocalService	Acts as a nonprivileged user on the local computer and uses anonymous credentials on any remote server
LocalSystem	Acts as a high-privileged user
NetworkService	Acts as a privileged user on the local computer and presents the computer's credentials to any remote server
User	Uses the privileges available to the specified user (the user may get challenged for a username and password unless both are set within the application)

The LocalSystem runs the Windows service in a high-privileged security context. Most services do not need this high level of privileges. I recommend the use of LocalService and NetworkService security context instead unless you truly need the high security.

Note LocalService and NetworkService are available only for Windows XP and Windows 2003.

During the startup process, there may be the requirement that certain services be available or loaded first. The service configuration application can be coded to let you know of missing dependencies and preload those dependencies that it has control over.

The ServiceProcess Namespace

Only one namespace is directly related to Windows services: the ServiceProcess namespace. In fact, you normally only have to deal with four of the classes within these namespaces. Table 14-3 shows a brief description of these classes. The rest of the chapter further expands on them.

Table 14-3. *ServiceProcess Namespace Classes*

Class	Description
ServiceBase	This class is used to create a service application and contains the handlers that your code will interact with.
ServiceController	This class is used to create a service controller application and allows you to connect, stop, start, etc., a Windows service.
ServiceInstaller	This class, along with the ServiceProcessInstaller, is used to create a service configuration application. This class provides properties unique to each service within a Windows service, in particular StartType (Automatic, Manual, Disabled), DisplayName, ServiceName, and ServicesDependentOn.
ServiceProcessInstaller	This class, along with the ServiceInstaller, is used to create a service configuration application. This class provides properties that pertain to all services that are contained within the Windows Service, in particular Username, Password, Context and Account.

One cool feature of using the preceding classes is that if you are using Visual Studio 2005, many of the properties can be manipulated using the Properties window, so you don't even have to look at the code. Don't worry. Not all of the class members can be handled this way. You will still need to write some code.

Creating Windows Services

Okay, I've shown you all the pieces, but how do you actually go about creating a Windows service? The example in this section shows you. Here I'll also explore a new feature to make things interesting: system event logs. The example will use system event logs to log all Windows service handlers that are triggered. The easy route would be to just use file I/O like what I covered in Chapter 8, but since the normal route for logging events in a Windows service is the system event log, I thought I'd do it that way (albeit stripped down and simplified).

But before we get into this new feature, let's start things off by creating the basic skeleton program from which almost all Windows services emerge.

Like any other application, the first step is to create the base application from a template using Visual Studio 2005. (For those of you doing this from a text editor, you will need to do a bit more typing.) This time the template to select is Windows Service, as shown in Figure 14-2. I gave the new project, created from the template, the name Simple. You will find that the template adds "WinService" to your service names automatically, so I felt it a bit redundant to add some derivative of "Windows service" to the project name. But obviously, you can call your projects anything you want to or change the names created by the template.

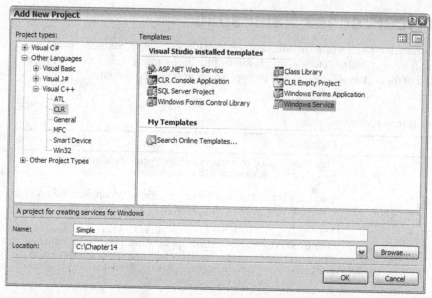

Figure 14-2. *Selecting the Windows Service template*

Unlike most of the other projects created from a Visual Studio 2005 template, this one is not a fully functional application when compiled. You still need to add installers to the project for the Windows service to run. I'll cover installers later in the chapter. What you do get is the service application part of the Windows service.

The template adds a number of files to the project, but really at this point only two are of interest. If you used "Simple" as your project name, then the two files will be called SimpleWinService.cpp and SimpleWinService.h.

Auto-generated Windows Service

SimpleWinService.cpp, shown in Listing 14-1, is the code automatically generated by the template. This code is basically used to start the registration process of the Windows service.

Listing 14-1. *Template-generated SimpleWinService.cpp*

```cpp
#include "stdafx.h"
#include <string.h>
#include "SimpleWinService.h"

using namespace Simple;
using namespace System::Text;
using namespace System::Security::Policy;
using namespace System::Reflection;

//To install/uninstall the service, type: "Simple.exe -Install [-u]"
int _tmain(int argc, _TCHAR* argv[])
{
  if (argc >= 2)
  {
    if (argv[1][0] == _T('/'))
    {
        argv[1][0] = _T('-');
    }

    if (_tcsicmp(argv[1], _T("-Install")) == 0)
    {
        array<String^>^ myargs = System::Environment::GetCommandLineArgs();
        array<String^>^ args = gcnew array<String^>(myargs->Length - 1);

        // Set args[0] with the full path to the assembly,
        Assembly^ assem = Assembly::GetExecutingAssembly();
        args[0] = assem->Location;

        Array::Copy(myargs, 2, args, 1, args->Length - 1);
        AppDomain^ dom = AppDomain::CreateDomain(L"execDom");
        Type^ type = System::Object::typeid;
        String^ path = type->Assembly->Location;
        StringBuilder^ sb =
            gcnew StringBuilder(path->Substring(0, path->LastIndexOf(L"\\")));
        sb->Append(L"\\InstallUtil.exe");
        Evidence^ evidence = gcnew Evidence();
        dom->ExecuteAssembly(sb->ToString(), evidence, args);
    }
  }
  else
  {
      ServiceBase::Run(gcnew SimpleWinService());
  }
}
```

Ugly, don't you think?

This code is really mostly legacy code from the Managed Extensions for C++ days due to Managed C++'s not being able to generate safe code. You used to need all this code to magically build a command to fool Windows into believing the code is safe. Now with C++/CLI, since safe code can be generated, most of this code can be thrown away. However, it's probably a good thing to keep this code in your arsenal if you plan on writing a Windows service that isn't safe. (You'll learn about unsafe code in Chapters 20 and 21.) On the other hand, if you plan on using safe code, then Listing 14-2 shows how I would change the preceding code.

Listing 14-2. *Conversion of SimpleWinService.cpp for Safe Code*

```
#include "stdafx.h"
#include "SimpleWinService.h"

using namespace Simple;
using namespace System::Collections;
using namespace System::ServiceProcess;

void main()
{
    array<ServiceBase^>^ ServicesToRun;

    // More than one user service may run within the same process. To add
    // another service to this process, change the following line to
    // create a second service object. For example,
    //
    //    ServicesToRun = gcnew array<ServiceBase^>
    //    {
    //        gcnew Service1(),
    //        gcnew Service2()
    //    };
    //
    ServicesToRun = gcnew array<ServiceBase^> { gcnew SimpleWinService() };

    ServiceBase::Run(ServicesToRun);
}
```

Notice most of the preceding code is comments. By the way, I can't lay claim to this code, as it is the code generated by the C# template converted into C++/CLI.

Note To use Listing 14-2, you must compile using the /clr:safe option. If the code compiles cleanly with this option, then you know your code is safe. By the way, you also need to remove the include files from stdafx.h as they contain unsafe code. (You don't need these include files anyway.)

What's the big difference between these two listings? Two things are different. The first is that to install Listing 14-1, you use the command Sample.exe -Install, and to uninstall, you use the command Simple -Install -u. For Listing 14-2, you use the command InstallUtil Simple.exe to install and InstallUtil -u Simple.exe to uninstall.

■ **Note** Actually, you are using the InstallUtil command for both listings, but the code in Listing 14-1 builds this code behind the scenes.

The second difference in the code generated by Listing 14-1 contains native code and may not be safe, while Listing 14-2 compiles to strictly safe code (if you use the /clr:safe option, that is).

Once you strip away all the magic code, all you are left with is

```
ServiceBase::Run(ServicesToRun);
```

All the ServiceBase::Run() method does (at least as far as you need to be concerned about) is load the service application into memory and provide the service-main entry point so that the service control application can start the application.

SimpleWinService.h, shown in Listing 14-3, is a little more exciting, as it is where you will spend most of your time coding the Windows service—in particular, the following two auto-generated handlers:

- OnStart(): Used to initialize the Windows service during the startup process
- OnStop(): Used to shut down everything opened up while the Windows service was executing

And the four handlers that you most likely will add yourself:

- OnContinue(): Runs when the continue event is sent by the Service Control Manager. The handler is used to start up any resources that you might have stopped when you paused the Windows service. This handler is only valid when the Windows service is in a paused state.
- OnCustomCommand(): Runs when the SCM sends a custom event to the Windows service.
- OnPause(): Runs when the SCM sends a pause event to the Windows service. You use this handler to shut down any resources that don't need to be active while the Windows service is paused.
- OnShutdown(): Runs just before the system shuts down. This is the last chance the Windows service has to shut down any resources that might be left running. Note that this is called when the computer shuts down, not the Windows service.

Listing 14-3. *Auto-generated SimpleWinService.h Code*

```cpp
#pragma once

using namespace System;
using namespace System::Collections;
using namespace System::ServiceProcess;
using namespace System::ComponentModel;

namespace Simple
{
    public ref class SimpleWinService : public ServiceProcess::ServiceBase
    {
    public:
        SimpleWinService()
        {
            InitializeComponent();
        }
```

```
    protected:
        ~SimpleWinService()
        {
            if (components)
            {
                delete components;
            }
        }

        virtual void OnStart(array<String^>^ args) override
        {
        }

        virtual void OnStop() override
        {
        }

    private:
        System::ComponentModel::Container ^components;

#pragma region Windows Form Designer generated code

        void InitializeComponent(void)
        {
            this->components = gcnew System::ComponentModel::Container();
            this->CanStop = true;
            this->CanPauseAndContinue = true;
            this->AutoLog = true;
            this->ServiceName = L"SimpleWinService";
        }
#pragma endregion
    };
}
```

Listing 14-3 has some interesting Boolean properties that you might want to be aware of (you can change them directly in the code or via the Properties window as shown in Figure 14-3):

- AutoLog: You set this to true when you want the Windows service to automatically log entries in the Windows system event log.

- CanHandlePowerEvent: You set this to true when you want the Windows service to receive power events like switch for AC power to battery.

- CanHandleSessionChangeEvent: You set this to true when you want the Windows service to receive the change event from a Terminal Services session.

- CanPauseAndContinue: You set this to true when you want to give the user the ability to pause the Windows service.

- CanShutdown: You set this to true when you want the Windows service to receive the Windows Shutdown message.

- CanStop: You set this to true if you want the user to be able to shut the Windows service down.

- ServiceName: This is the name of the service as it will appear in the Administrative Tools' Services application.

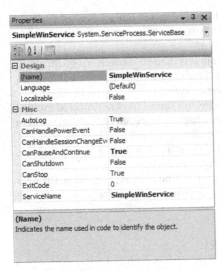

Figure 14-3. *The Windows ServiceProcess Properties View*

These properties (except for AutoLog and ServiceName) provide you with a way to restrict which events the Windows Service will receive.

Customizing the Windows Service

Procedurally, there really isn't much to customizing Windows services. You simply override the handlers provided by ServiceProcess::ServiceBase, which you inherited from automatically when creating a Windows service from the Visual Studio 2005 template. (Of course, the features you want to implement within the Windows service can be any level of complexity.)

Since creating Windows services is basically the same process, I can get away with a very simple example—the logging of all events sent to the Windows service from the SCM.

But before we do this, let's drag and drop an EventLog control from the components section of the toolbox to the SimpleWinService.h Design view. Once the EventLog icon is on the Design view, click it to enable the Properties window. Right-click the Log property drop-down and then select Application (since you are not logging errors or security info). Finally, in the Source property, enter SimpleWinService. Now, a few additional lines of code are added to your template, and you are ready to create system event logs using the following command:

```
eventLog1->WriteEntry("An system event log message go here");
```

Note There are many more options available to you when it comes to configuring system event logs, but they are beyond the scope of this chapter. For more information, consult the .NET Framework documentation.

OnStart()

The first event that your Windows service will probably handle is OnStart(). Frequently, this handler will be used to create a new background thread of execution for the Windows service to run under. Why a separate thread, you are probably asking?

My first thought (and probably yours as well) when I encountered Windows services was that I'd simply start the service in the main thread and then let it run. Then when it needs to pause, continue, or stop, just handle the event from the main thread. The problem is that a Windows service handler times out after 30 seconds. Thus, if the OnStart() does not return in 30 seconds, the Windows service aborts.

To get around this, you need to have OnStart() return in less than 30 seconds. To do this, you usually create either a System::Timers::Timer or another thread of execution to run your Windows service's activities and then let the main thread continue and return.

I'll show the System::Timers::Timer logic in the example, but since I have not covered multi-threading yet, I'll not show any of this code, but once you read Chapter 16, you should have no problem plugging a new thread of execution within the OnStart() handler in place of the Timer event.

Nearly any code you want to can be placed in the OnStart() handler so long as it takes less than 30 seconds to execute (and your security context has the privileges to run it).

Here's a simple and possibly somewhat redundant example of the OnStart() in action. I also for grins and giggles added timer event code and code to dump out the args that were passed:

```
virtual void OnStart(array<String^>^ args) override
{
    eventLog1->WriteEntry("SimpleWinService Started");

    if (args->Length == 0)
        eventLog1->WriteEntry("Empty args");
    else
    {
        for each (String ^s in args)
        {
            eventLog1->WriteEntry(s);
        }
    }
    double interval = 10000;  // 10 seconds - hard coded for simplicity
                              // but could be passed as an argument
    this->timer = gcnew System::Timers::Timer(interval);
    this->timer->Elapsed += gcnew System::Timers::ElapsedEventHandler(this,
                                        &SimpleWinService::timer_Tick);
    this->timer->Start();
}
```

As you can see, the example overrides the virtual handler provided by the Windows Service template, with a log to the system event log stating that the Windows service was started and a dump of the args using the system event log as well.

The code to create the timer is pretty easy. Create a Timer with an interval of 10 seconds. Notice that the timer itself is a member variable code:

```
private:
    System::Timers::Timer^  timer;
```

The reason the timer is a member variable is that other Windows service handlers are going to need access to it. Next, you add an event handler to the timer's Elapse handler. Here's the code for the handler:

```
private:
void timer_Tick(System::Object^ sender, System::Timers::ElapsedEventArgs^ e)
{
    this->timer->Stop();
    eventLog1->WriteEntry("SimpleWinService Elapsed Event Occurred");
    this->timer->Start();
}
```

This is pretty much the minimum code you can have for the elapse handler. Notice that you first Stop() the timer, perform whatever actions you want within the elapsed event, and then Start() the timer again. Doing this prevents any problems that might happen if the code takes longer than the timer elapse interval. If you are 100 percent certain that the process time of the handler will be less than the timer's elapsed time, then you can skip the Stop() and Start() steps.

Now, why is this code of the OnStart() handler redundant? If you have the AutoLog feature set to true, the Windows service will also automatically log this event. Because of this, when you finally get to run this example, you will have two system log events created, one automatically and this one that you created earlier.

This handler is the only one to take an argument, in this case, a string array of values that is sent to it from the Start command. If you use the Services application found in the Administrative Tools, you can add the arguments using the General tab on the Windows service's Properties window. To do this, select Windows service in the Services application, and then right-click and select the Properties menu item. This should present the Properties dialog window as shown in Figure 14-4. From here, just add the arguments to the Start Parameters text box.

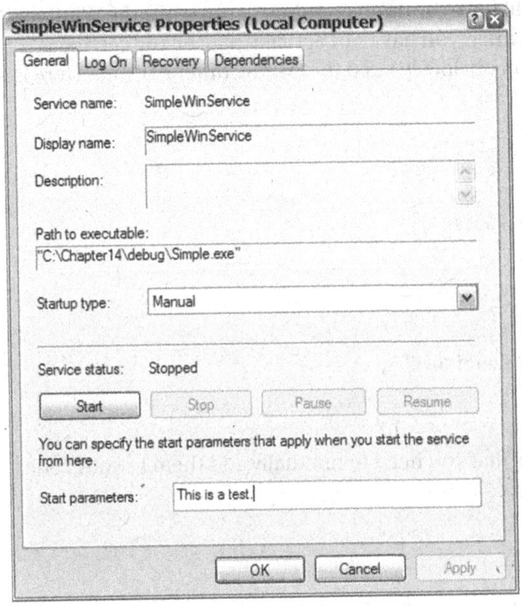

Figure 14-4. *Setting starting arguments using Services application*

I have yet to use this parameter, but I'm sure it is put to good use by somebody.

OnStop()

The second event that you will most probably have your Windows service handle is OnStop(). Here you place all the code you need to shut down your Windows service.

One thing that bit me once with the OnStop() handler is that it is never called when the CanStop property is set to false, even when the computer is shutting down. Instead, the SCM handles everything itself. (Also, you have no way to stop the Windows service, except killing the process or shutting down the machine.)

One nice thing is that you don't have to do anything special within the OnStop() handler to trigger the stop event for all the dependent services, as they are automatically triggered by the SCM.

Let's continue the example. Since I started a `Timer` in the `OnStart()`, I better stop it on the `OnStop()`. Plus, I will write a system event log entry stating that the Windows service was stopped. (Just like `OnStart()` if the `AutoLog` is true, the writing of this event log is sort of redundant.)

Here's all I need to do to shut down this simple example:

```
virtual void OnStop() override
{
    this->timer->Stop();
    eventLog1->WriteEntry("SimpleWinService Stopped");
}
```

OnPause() and OnContinue()

Two common event handlers you may implement are `OnPause()` and `OnContinue()`. Obviously these handles are triggered when the Windows services is paused and continued. You use these events to temporarily stop and then later restart any resources that don't need to be active while the Windows service is paused.

To continue our example, there is no need to have the timer continue to run while the Windows service is paused. (In fact, if you don't stop the timer, you have not actually paused the service.) When the Windows service finally continues, you obviously need to start the timer back up. Here is the code to handle the pause and continue process:

```
virtual void OnPause() override
{
    this->timer->Stop();
    eventLog1->WriteEntry("SimpleWinService Paused");
}

virtual void OnContinue() override
{
    eventLog1->WriteEntry("SimpleWinService Continued");
    this->timer->Start();
}
```

The only trick to using these two handlers is that you need to manually add them to your code, but as you can see, it's hardly rocket science.

Other ServiceBase Class Handlers

There are a few more ServiceBase class handlers that you might use, but I thought it a bit redundant showing examples of using them, as you code them the exact same way as the other handlers. There is one exception, the `OnCustomCommand()`, but I will hold off covering this handler until I cover managing Windows services later in the chapter.

Customized Example

Okay, SimpleWinService.cpp has remained unchanged from what was generated by the template (or the safe version, if you used that), but we've made quite a few changes to SimpleWinService.h. Since some of the code was auto-generated by Visual Studio 2005, I thought it would be helpful for those of you writing a Windows service without VS 2005 to see the customized SimpleWinService.h, shown in Listing 14-4, in its entirety.

Listing 14-4. *Customized SimpleWinService.h Code*

```cpp
#pragma once

using namespace System;
using namespace System::Collections;
using namespace System::ServiceProcess;
using namespace System::ComponentModel;

namespace Simple
{
    private:
    double interval;

    public ref class SimpleWinService : public ServiceProcess::ServiceBase
    {
    public:
        SimpleWinService()
        {
            InitializeComponent();
            interval = 15000; // 15 seconds - default
        }

    protected:
        ~SimpleWinService()
        {
            if (components)
            {
                delete components;
            }
        }

        virtual void OnStart(array<String^>^ args) override
        {
            eventLog1->WriteEntry("SimpleWinService Started");

            if (args->Length == 0)
                eventLog1->WriteEntry("Empty args");
            else
            {
                for each (String ^s in args)
                {
                    eventLog1->WriteEntry(s);
                }
            }

            this->timer = gcnew System::Timers::Timer(interval);
            this->timer->Elapsed +=
                gcnew System::Timers::ElapsedEventHandler(this,
                                          &SimpleWinService::timer_Tick);
            this->timer->Start();
        }
```

```cpp
        virtual void OnStop() override
        {
            this->timer->Stop();
            eventLog1->WriteEntry("SimpleWinService Stopped");
        }

        virtual void OnPause() override
        {
            this->timer->Stop();
            eventLog1->WriteEntry("SimpleWinService Paused");
        }

        virtual void OnContinue() override
        {
            eventLog1->WriteEntry("SimpleWinService Continued");
            this->timer->Start();
        }

    private:
        System::Diagnostics::EventLog^  eventLog1;
        System::Timers::Timer^  timer;

        System::ComponentModel::IContainer^  components;

#pragma region Windows Form Designer generated code

        void InitializeComponent(void)
        {
            this->components = (gcnew System::ComponentModel::Container());
            this->eventLog1 = (gcnew System::Diagnostics::EventLog());
            (cli::safe_cast<System::ComponentModel::ISupportInitialize^>
                (this->eventLog1))->BeginInit();
            //
            // eventLog1
            //
            this->eventLog1->Log = L"Application";
            this->eventLog1->Source = L"SimpleWinService";
            //
            // SimpleWinService
            //
            this->CanPauseAndContinue = true;
            this->ServiceName = L"SimpleWinService";
            (cli::safe_cast<System::ComponentModel::ISupportInitialize^>
                (this->eventLog1))->EndInit();
        }
```

```
#pragma endregion

    private:
        void timer_Tick(System::Object^ sender,
                        System::Timers::ElapsedEventArgs^ e)
        {
            this->timer->Stop();
            eventLog1->WriteEntry("SimpleWinService Elapsed Event Occurred");
            this->timer->Start();
        }
    };
}
```

Installing and Uninstalling Windows Services

With other application types, you would now be ready to compile and run. Not so with Windows services.

You now need to add one `ServiceProcessInstaller` class and a `ServiceInstaller` class for each service that makes up the Windows service. These classes then are used by the service configuration application to register the Windows service correctly within the registry. To perform the actual registering process, you normally use the service configuration application provided by .NET called InstallUtil.exe. (You can use other installation programs or even write your own, but doing this is beyond the scope of this book.)

Fortunately, the process for creating the `ServiceProcessInstaller` and `ServiceInstaller` class is mostly automated. Here are the steps you will follow:

1. Switch to the Design view of the service. You can double-click SimpleWinService.h to do this.

2. Right-click anywhere on the Design view window to bring up the menu as shown in Figure 14-5.

Figure 14-5. *Adding installer*

3. Select the Add Installer menu item. This will generate ProjectInstaller.cpp and ProjectInstaller.h.

4. Double-click ProjectInstaller.h in the Solution Explorer to switch to the Design view of the `ProjectInstaller`.

5. Select the `serviceInstaller1` component.

6. Set the `ServiceName` property to SimpleWinService if it isn't that already.

7. Set the StartType property to Automatic if you want the service to start automatically on startup or leave it as manual if you want the user to start the Windows service. (You might want to leave it as manual for now, as you will most probably be continually starting and stopping the service manually. Once everything is working properly, switch the property to Automatic.)

8. Select the serviceProcessInstaller1 component.

9. Set the Account property to the security context that most suits the need of the Windows service. (Being lazy, I usually just set this to LocalSystem or NetworkService during development and then change it to something more appropriate during final testing and release.)

10. Build your Windows service.

For those of you who are interested, the auto-generated code for ProjectInstall.cpp is shown in Listing 14-5, and ProjectInstaller.h is shown cleaned up in Listing 14-6.

Listing 14-5. *Auto-generated ProjectInstall.cpp*

```
#include "StdAfx.h"
#include "ProjectInstaller.h"
```

Listing 14-6. *Auto-generated ProjectInstall.h*

```
#pragma once

using namespace System;
using namespace System::ComponentModel;
using namespace System::Collections;
using namespace System::Configuration::Install;

namespace Simple
{
    [RunInstaller(true)]
    public ref class ProjectInstaller :
        public System::Configuration::Install::Installer
    {
    public:
        ProjectInstaller(void)
        {
            InitializeComponent();
        }

    protected:
        ~ProjectInstaller()
        {
            if (components)
            {
                delete components;
            }
        }
```

```cpp
private:
  System::ServiceProcess::ServiceProcessInstaller^ serviceProcessInstaller1;
    System::ServiceProcess::ServiceInstaller^  serviceInstaller1;
    System::Diagnostics::EventLogInstaller^ eventLogInstaller1;

    System::ComponentModel::Container ^components;

#pragma region Windows Form Designer generated code
    void InitializeComponent(void)
    {
        this->serviceProcessInstaller1 =
            (gcnew System::ServiceProcess::ServiceProcessInstaller());
        this->serviceInstaller1 =
            (gcnew System::ServiceProcess::ServiceInstaller());
        this->eventLogInstaller1 =
            (gcnew System::Diagnostics::EventLogInstaller());
        //
        // serviceProcessInstaller1
        //
        this->serviceProcessInstaller1->Account =
            System::ServiceProcess::ServiceAccount::LocalSystem;
        this->serviceProcessInstaller1->Password = nullptr;
        this->serviceProcessInstaller1->Username = nullptr;
        //
        // serviceInstaller1
        //
        this->serviceInstaller1->ServiceName = L"SimpleWinService";
        //
        // ProjectInstaller
        //
        this->Installers->AddRange(
            gcnew cli::array<System::Configuration::Install::Installer^>(2)
            {
                this->serviceProcessInstaller1,
                this->serviceInstaller1
            });
    }
#pragma endregion
    };
}
```

Now you should have a Windows service that you can finally install and run unless you have added resources to your Windows service that also need to be installed like the system event log. To install the system event log, switch to the Design view of SimpleWinService.h again, right-click the eventLog1 component, and select the Add Installer menu item. Now rebuild the project, and you will have a Windows service ready to be installed.

The first thing you do is navigate in the Visual Studio 2005 Command console window to the directory where your Windows service assembly is located. How you actually install your Windows services depends on which version of SimpleWinService.cpp you used, though behind the scenes, you are really doing the same thing.

To install your Windows service using the default template version, you use the command Sample.exe -Install at the command line. (To uninstall, you use the command Simple -Install -u.)

For the safe code version, you use the command InstallUtil Simple.exe at the command line to install the Windows service. (To uninstall, you use the command InstallUtil -u Simple.exe.)

Since both end up doing the same thing behind the scenes, both of the preceding installation methods will cause the output shown in Figure 14-6 to be generated in the command window.

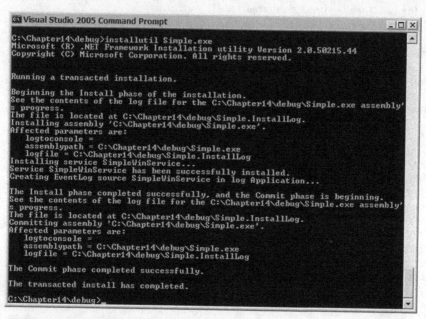

Figure 14-6. *Running the installer program*

Note that if you selected a security context of User, you will be asked to enter, as shown in Figure 14-7, the user and password you want to run the Windows service under. Make sure you use the full username by including your domain or workgroup as well as the username. For me this is Amidala\Stephen Fraser.

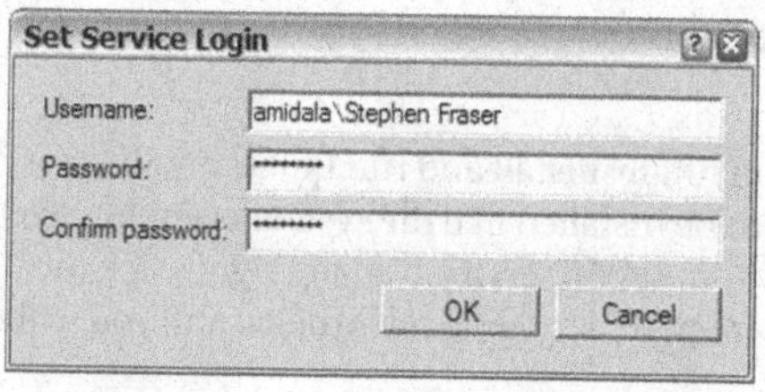

Figure 14-7. *Username and password to run Windows service.*

Managing Windows Services

The most basic method of managing Windows services is using the Administrative Tools' Services application provided by the Windows operating system. For most Windows services, this application will be all that you need. On the other hand, on those rare occasions .NET provides you with the

`System::ServiceProcess::ServiceController` class, which enables you to connect and control Windows services within your own custom application.

Services Application

The Administrative Tools' Services application (see Figure 14-8) is actually a snap-in to the Microsoft Management Console (MMC). Not only does this tool allow you to see, start, pause, continue, stop, and restart all services currently on your system, but it also allows you to perform some configurations on them as well.

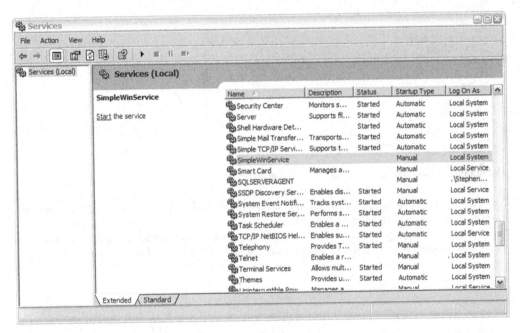

Figure 14-8. *The Administrative Tools' Services application*

As you can see in Figure 14-8, SimpleWinService is now available on your system, but the status is blank or currently not run. In addition, the startup type is manual and the Windows service uses the LocalSystem security context. Your implementation could be different if you selected different property values for `ServiceProcessInstaller` and `ServicesInstaller`.

Double-clicking the SimpleWinService line causes the Services application to present the Windows services properties dialog box as shown in Figure 14-9. The tabs across the top of the control point out the different properties that can be customize for the Windows service:

- Change state and startup method of Windows service.
- Specify user login security context for the Windows service.
- Specify action to perform on Windows service failure.
- View Windows service dependencies.

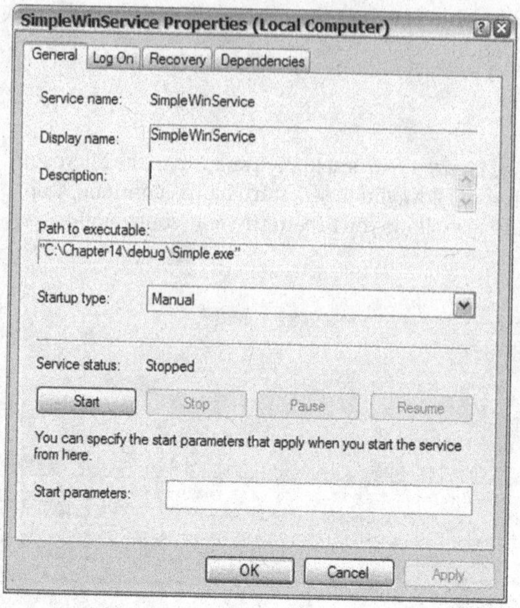

Figure 14-9. *Services application properties dialog box*

I usually only deal with the General tab, where I change the Windows service startup method from Manual (user controlled) to Automatic (system controlled started during startup process). You can also specify stop, start, etc. on the General tab, but I usually use the middle panel on the Services application or use the right-click context menu (see Figure 14-10) associated with the Windows service.

Figure 14-10. *Services application Windows services context menu*

Custom Service Control Application

There will come a time when the Services application just doesn't provide enough functionality. When that time comes, the ability to create your own custom service control application really comes in handy.

Usually, you will create a GUI service control application, but nothing is stopping you from making it a console application. In the following examples, I'll show you a couple of GUI tools, but you should have no trouble making equivalent console applications using the same basic logic.

It is remarkably easy to write your own custom service control application. All that really is required is to add an instance of a System::ServerProcess::ServiceController to your application. Link the controller instance to the Windows service you want to interface with, and then call the controller's methods. The actual communication between the controller and the Windows service is handled for you behind the scenes. Well, to be more accurate, the communication between your controller and the SCM is hidden from you. As mentioned previously, the Windows service gets its handles triggered from the SCM.

Visual Studio 2005 provides a drag and drop interface to simplify the creation of the controller instance for Windows applications. I'll show the steps here, though the code that gets generated is so simple, it is almost easier just to code it by hand.

1. Create a Windows application. (If you need a reminder on how to do this, I covered how in Chapters 9 and 10.)

2. Open up the Server Explorer.

3. Navigate to the Services branch of the tree as shown in Figure 14-11.

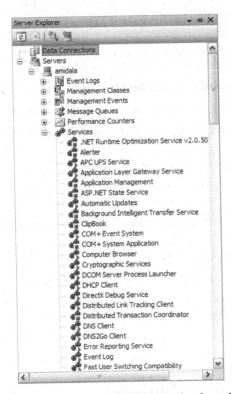

Figure 14-11. *Server Explorer, Services branch*

4. Select the service you want to interface with.

5. Right-click and select Add to Designer or simply drag the service directly onto the form.

Doing all that adds the following code to your Windows Form, assuming your server is called Amidala and the Windows service is called SimpleWinService:

```
private: System::ServiceProcess::ServiceController^ serviceController1;
this->serviceController1 = (gcnew System::ServiceProcess::ServiceController());
this->serviceController1->MachineName = L"amidala";
this->serviceController1->ServiceName = L"SimpleWinService";
```

Basically, now your application is connected to the Windows service. You have read access (and a few with write access) to a number of the Windows services properties and the ability to trigger the Windows service's handles by making `ServiceController` method calls. Table 14-4 shows some of the more common properties and methods available to you.

Table 14-4. *Commonly Used ServiceController Properties and Methods*

Property/Method	Description
CanPauseAndContinue	A property indicating whether the Windows service can be paused and continued
CanShutDown	A property indicating whether the Windows service receives shutdown events
CanStop	A property indicating whether the Windows service can stop after starting
Close()	A method that closes down this instance of `ServicesController` and releases all resources associated with the instance
Continue()	A method that triggers the `OnContinue()` handler
DependentServices	A property containing a list of all dependent Windows services
DisplayName	A property that allows you to get or set the friendly name of the Windows service
ExecuteCommand()	A method that triggers the `OnCustomCommand()` handler
GetServices()	A static method that retrieves an array of all Windows services on the system
MachineName	A property that allows you to get or set the name of the computer of where the Windows service resides
Pause()	A method that triggers the `OnPause()` handler
Refresh()	A method that refreshes all the Windows Services properties
ServiceName	A property that allows you to get or set the name of the service this instance of `ServicesController` is referencing
Start()	A method that triggers the `OnStart()` handler
Status	A property indicating the current status (state would be more accurate) of the Windows service
Stop()	A method that triggers the `OnStop()` handler
WaitForStatus()	A method that waits until the Windows services becomes a specified status (state)

The actual code to implement a custom service control application is nearly trivial. And as far as I can see, there is really only one gotcha. The properties in the `ServiceController` are a snapshot, and to get the most recent version of them, you need to call the `Refresh()` method.

To show you what I mean, add four buttons to the Windows Form that you created previously. The form should look something like Figure 14-12.

Figure 14-12. *SimpleWinServive controller*

Now let's add the ability for the service control application to start the Windows service. Once you have your Windows Form laid out, double-click the Start button so that you can edit the code for the start Windows service event handler. Here is the code:

```
System::Void bnStart_Click(System::Object^ sender, System::EventArgs^ e)
{
    serviceController1->Refresh();

    if (serviceController1->Status == ServiceControllerStatus::Stopped)
    {
        serviceController1->Start();
        MessageBox::Show("SimpleWinService Started");
    }
    else
    {
        MessageBox::Show("SimpleWinService Running");
    }
}
```

Yes, that's all it takes! Now let's take a closer look. The first thing you need to do is Refresh() the properties. If you don't, then the Status property will probably be out of sync with the actual Windows service. Then, before you call the Start() method, you need to make sure that the Windows services status is Stopped. Another option would be to enclose the Start() method in a try/catch block, as the Start() method throws an exception if the current start is not Stopped. I added the MessageBoxes so that you can verify all is well, but they are obviously not needed.

Now let's stop the service:

```
System::Void bnStart_Click(System::Object^ sender, System::EventArgs^ e)
{
    serviceController1->Refresh();

    if (serviceController1->Status == ServiceControllerStatus::Stopped)
    {
        serviceController1->Start();
        MessageBox::Show("SimpleWinService Started");
    }
    else
    {
        MessageBox::Show("SimpleWinService Running");
    }
}
```

The code is nearly identical. In fact most of the handler trigger methods are handled this exact same way. There is one major exception: ExecuteCommand().

The ExecuteCommand() method allows you to trigger an event on the Windows service based on a numeric value between 128 and 255. Windows reserves the values 0 through 127. The implementation of the custom command is made up of two parts.

First you need to add a call to your Windows Form to ExecuteCommand(), passing it a number representing the command that you want the Windows service to execute. Here is the code for the button Interval 15. (The code for button Interval 20 is virtually the same except the numeric value passed in the ExecuteCommand() method.)

```
System::Void bnIntv15_Click(System::Object^ sender, System::EventArgs^ e)
{
    serviceController1->Refresh();

    if (serviceController1->Status == ServiceControllerStatus::Running)
    {
        serviceController1->ExecuteCommand(150);
        MessageBox::Show("SimpleWinService Interval in 15 seconds");
    }
    else
    {
        MessageBox::Show("SimpleWinService Not Running");
    }
}
```

I'm pretty sure you are starting to see a pattern forming on these event handlers.

The second half the of the custom command is to add an OnCustomCommand() handler to your Windows service, which will process the numeric command sent by the ExecuteCommand() method. Here is an example that changes the interval time of the timer of the Windows service:

```
virtual void OnCustomCommand(int cmd) override
{
    if (cmd == 150)
        this->timer->Interval = 15000;
    else
        this->timer->Interval = 20000;
}
```

I used an if statement due to the fact that only two numeric values are being sent to the OnCustomCommand() handler. Normally, you would probably use a case statement on the cmd parameter.

Normally, I include a full example of the source code, but I see no real added value in doing so for this example, as all the code is so trivial. But if you need the code example, it is available on the Apress and ProCppCLI.net Web sites.

Debugging Windows Services

The process of debugging a Windows service is a little different from the generic Windows Forms application or console application, since you do not start or execute the service via the main() method. Fortunately, all is not lost, as you have two techniques for debugging your Windows service. Which debugging process you use depends on what functionality you are trying to test.

Attaching the Debugger to the Windows Service

The first process is outlined in the many C# books out there that cover Windows services: attach the debugger to the service after it is running. This allows you to use all the standard debugging features available on Visual Studio 2005. The process, while straightforward, is, as far as I'm concerned, far from intuitive. But once you know the steps, you can replicate it for any Windows service.

To attach the debugger to a Windows service requires the following steps:

1. Start your Windows service using the Services application or your own custom service control application.

2. Select from the main Visual Studio 2005 menu Debug and then the menu item Attach to Process. This will display a dialog box similar to the one in Figure 14-13.

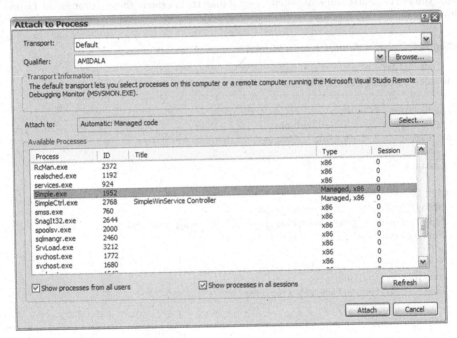

Figure 14-13. *Attach to Process dialog box*

3. Click Show processes from all users. You may not need this if you started the process using your own user security context.

4. Select your Windows service from the Available Processes list.

5. Click the Attach button.

When you complete these steps, the dialog box will disappear, the debugger will be attached to your Windows service, and you will be in debug mode of Visual Studio 2005. At this point, you can set break point, watches, etc., just like you would for any other Windows or console application.

The problem with this method is that you cannot test the OnStart() handler, as it has already run. And executing the OnStop() handler ends the debug session, so you can't restart the Windows service to test the OnStart() either.

This is where the other testing process comes in.

A Special Main() Function

A Windows service is really just a specialized application. Due to this fact, you can write a slightly modified main() function to test your Windows service's startup process. I think it's easier just to show you the code first and walk you through it than try to explain things beforehand. Listing 14-7 shows the new main() method.

Listing 14-7. *Debug-enhanced main() Method*

```
#include "stdafx.h"
#include "SimpleWinService.h"

using namespace Simple;
using namespace System::Collections;
using namespace System::ServiceProcess;

void main()
{
#ifndef COMMANDLINE_DEBUG
    array<ServiceBase^>^ ServicesToRun;
    ServicesToRun = gcnew array<ServiceBase^> { gcnew SimpleWinService() };
    ServiceBase::Run(ServicesToRun);
#else
    SimpleWinService ^svc = gcnew SimpleWinService();
    svc->OnStart(nullptr);
    Console::WriteLine("Any key stop stop");
    Console::ReadLine();
    svc->OnStop();
#endif
}
```

The code uses the #ifndef directive (covered in Chapter 4) to split the main() method into two parts. If you recall, the #ifndef directive causes the compiler only to compile code in the enclosed region (between #else, #elseif, or #endif) when the symbol specified does not exist. Thus, the first block compiles the code just like normal, if the symbol COMMANDLINE_DEBUG does not exist, whereas the second block compiles the special code allowing you to debug the OnStart() handler, if the symbol does exist.

You can place the symbol COMMANDLINE_DEBUG either as a #define directive in stdafx.h or in SimpleWinService.h anywhere before the line

```
#include "SimpleWinService.h"
```

or in the application's Processor Definitions property as shown in Figure 14-14. You need to place it before the preceding #include statement because SimpleWinService.h also uses the symbol, as I'll point out next.

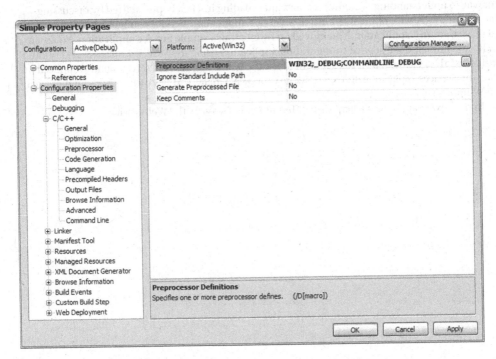

Figure 14-14. *Processor Definitions property*

One more issue remains. When you compile the preceding code, you get two errors telling you that the OnStart() and OnStop() methods are not accessible. The reason is the auto-generated template code for Windows services defines these two methods as protected and thus not accessible.

To fix this, add

```
#ifdef COMMANDLINE_DEBUG
    public:
#endif
```

right before the call to OnStart(). This will cause the methods to now be public when the symbol is defined.

Now you can compile and debug the Windows service exactly like any other Windows or console application. This, unfortunately, also means you cannot access the Windows service using the Services application or your custom service control application, as it has not actually been started as a service. So long as you don't try to interface it with either of these, it will behave just like the Windows service does when compiled as a service, with the added bonus that you can now debug the OnStart() method.

By the way, you can debug the other handlers as well by calling them in the main() function.

Summary

Admittedly, this chapter has simplified the coding of Windows services, but you should be well on your way to understanding Windows services after reading it. The chapter started by discussing what a Windows service is and its three parts: service application, service configuration application, and service control application. You moved on by creating a simple Service application. You then saw how to implement a service configuration application using the `ServiceProcessInstaller` and `ServiceInstaller` classes. Next, you saw how to use the Windows-provided service control application called the Services application and how to write your own. Finally, you saw two methods for debugging your Windows services.

In the next chapter, you'll explore a different kind of service, the Web service.

CHAPTER 15

Web Services

Web services are the central hub of everything that is .NET. The basic goal of Web services is to make distributed applications much easier to design and develop than ever before. They change the way Internet, intranet, extranet, or whichevernet-based applications are written. Basically, Web services put the "net" in .NET.

Web services aren't unique to Microsoft or .NET. In fact, all of the major industry players have a Web services offering. This chapter, however, focuses only on the Microsoft .NET Framework implementation of Web services.

The chapter starts by providing you with a general understanding of Web services. You'll discover how to implement and consume a simple Web service using C++/CLI. With the basics under your belt, you'll then be ready for a more elaborate implementation of a Web service, this time working with the ADO.NET skills you acquired back in Chapter 12.

What Are Web Services?

In simple terms, *Web services* are software components that can be accessed and executed remotely via a network by a client application using standard protocols such as Hypertext Transfer Protocol (HTTP) and Simple Object Access Protocol (SOAP), as shown in the following illustration.

Note Web services are not restricted to SOAP or HTTP, but this chapter will focus on these two as they are all I use and are the most common.

What does this mean in English? You can create a class, make it available on the Internet, and have someone on the other side of the world execute the methods on that class as if the methods were on their local machine. Likewise, Web services enable you to execute other developers' classes from anywhere around the world as long as they're hosted on the Internet. You can also place the class on a server within your LAN or WAN and execute it exactly the same way using your intranet, extranet, or whatevernet, but that simply isn't as exciting, so I'll stick to Web services' Internet capabilities in this chapter.

Another cool feature of Web services is that they aren't just a .NET thing. You can access Web services written in any computer language on any platform as long as they conform to an agreed-upon set of standards to communicate, nearly always HTTP and SOAP. This feature allows for simple integration of diverse legacy systems and new .NET applications.

For those of you who have been coding for a few years, Web services are a much improved alternative to DCOM, COBRA, and the like.

Components of a Web Service

Web services are based on well-established networking protocols and a few newer technologies. In truth, you really don't have to know much about any of these technologies because .NET handles them, for the most part, in the background for you. In fact, the first few Web services I wrote were in complete blissful ignorance of these technologies. But, of course, true to my developer nature, I wanted to see what happens behind the curtain.

Basically, for a Web service to function, you need

- A communication protocol so that the service and its consuming client can communicate
- A description service so that the consuming client will be able to understand how to use the Web service
- A discovery service so that the consuming client can find the Web service

In the following sections you'll take a look at each requirement in a little more detail.

Communication Protocols

Communication between .NET Web services and client consumers is handled via generic HTTP using, normally, port 80. (For those of you who are HTTP knowledgeable, you are aware that HTTP is not restricted to port 80.) If you know something about Internet technology, you will recognize this as the same communication method used by standard Web browsers. Thus, if your system supports a Web browser, it can also support Web services. This is a key aspect of Web services, as other distributed application methods use their own specific communication protocols.

Communication between a Web service and a consumer client is always initiated by the client. Clients communicate with the Web service over HTTP in two different ways:

- HTTP POST commands
- SOAP

If you have done any Web programming, you should be quite comfortable with using HTTP POST commands. Normally, you will not use this method when implementing Web services because it is limited to simple data types for passing between the client and the service.

Caution Make sure you are using HTTP POST and not HTTP GET. HTTP GET is supported by Web services, but you need to change your default machine.config file. (You must uncomment the line `<add name="HttpGet"/>`.) My guess is that Microsoft plans to phase this out, so I recommend that you don't use HTTP GET, and except for basic Web service testing, I don't really see any reason to use HTTP GET anyway.

SOAP is a powerful XML-based protocol that packages up a method call to be executed, along with any parameters it requires for implementing. This package is then sent using a standard HTTP request to the Web service. Upon the completion of the execution of a method, SOAP packages up any return values and sends them back to the client using a standard HTTP response.

The best part of SOAP, at least when it comes to .NET, is you get it for free in almost all cases, and you don't have to know anything about it so long as you code within the Common Language Specification (CLS) specified by .NET. As you will see later in this chapter when I show how to send a DataSet from a Web service to a client, it is possible to transmit fairly complex data objects using SOAP.

Description Service

It's all well and good that you send stuff back and forth between the client and the Web service. But before this communication can take place, the client needs some way to find out what it can request the Web service to do and what format the request needs to be in. (The format is also known as the *method signature*.) You might think that you could use SOAP to handle the descriptive service, but SOAP was not designed to describe method signatures, only to package them for transport.

The Web service provides this description of its interfaces using the standard called the *Web Services Description Language* (WSDL). Like SOAP, WSDL is XML based. But instead of packaging like SOAP, WSDL actually describes the method signatures. In fact, WSDL describes method signatures in such detail that Visual Studio 2005 imports the WSDL's XML definitions and uses them to provide IntelliSense help.

Like all the previous technologies for Web services, WSDL is completely handled by Visual Studio 2005.

Discovery Service

Even if you can communicate between a client and a Web service and describe how this communication needs to take place, it's all still moot if the client doesn't know where to find the required Web service it needs to execute. This is the job of the *discovery service*. .NET provides two discovery services:

- Web Services Discovery tool (DISCO)
- Universal Description, Discovery, and Integration (UDDI)

DISCO is used to describe each Web service in any given virtual directory and any related subdirectories. Originally, .NET was going to use DISCO as its primary method of discovery, but with the advent of the superior UDDI, DISCO has become optional. It is still created automatically by Visual Studio 2005 for those who want to stick with DISCO, but I think it will most probably disappear in the future.

UDDI's scope is more far-reaching than DISCO's. With UDDI, you register your Web service with a central agency. Once your Web service is registered, third parties can search the agency to locate your registered Web service.

Personally, I find discovery services only useful if I don't know the exact URL of the Web service (which for me is rarely as I am usually the author of the Web service). As you will see later in the chapter, if you know the URL of the Web service you can access it directly without worrying about directory services.

The Web Services Namespaces

Five namespaces within the .NET Framework are directly related to Web services development:

- System::Web::Services is the primary namespace for Web services development. It consists of classes required for Web services creation.

- System::Web::Services::Configuration consists of classes that configure how Web services are created using ASP.NET.

- System::Web::Services::Description provides classes to programmatically interface with the WSDL.

- System::Web::Services::Discovery provides classes to programmatically discover Web services on a Web server.

- System::Web::Services::Protocols defines the protocols for transmitting data to and from the client and Web service over the network.

Most of the time when you develop Web services, you can be almost completely ignorant of the preceding namespaces. Normally, all you will need when implementing a Web service is two attributes, WebServiceAttribute and WebMethodAttribute, and an optional class, WebService. You use this class as a base class from which to inherit your Web service. You can find all three in the System::Web::Services namespace.

You use the System::Web::Services::Protocols namespace as well, but only indirectly within auto-generated code created when you add a Web reference.

A Simple Web Service

Enough theory—let's look at some code. In this example, you'll create an overly simplified Web service that finds a zip code based on city and state. It's so oversimplified that it finds the zip code only for two city and state combinations. In truth, it really doesn't matter what the internal workings of a Web service are, as they're just (in the case of this book) standard C++/CLI classes. What is special is the ability to access these classes over a network.

The process of creating a Web service is very easy. The first step is the same as that of any other project: Select the appropriate template (in this case, the ASP.NET Web Service template) to start building your Web service and give it a name. As you can see in Figure 15-1, I gave the project the name FindZipCode.

Once the New Project Wizard finishes, you're left with (believe it or not) a fully functioning "Hello World" Web service. Okay, let's modify the "Hello World" service so that it provides zip code–finding functionality.

The first thing I usually do with the template is delete the generated Web service *.asmx, *.cpp, and *.h files. Then I add a new ASP.NET Web service with a more appropriate name. If you like the default name generated, then you can go ahead and use that one. In the case of this example, I actually like the default, FindZipCodeClass, so I won't go through the delete process.

The code generated by the Web service wizard uses the standard two-file format of C++/CLI (finally, a C++/CLI template that is done correctly!). Well, actually, to be more accurate, the code generated is a three-file format, since the template provides an .asmx file as well as the .cpp and .h files. An .asmx file is a Web service file that defines the class where the methods of the service reside.

Web services are not fully supported by C++/CLI and the only way to implement them is to precompile the source. In other languages, such as C# and Visual Basic .NET, there would be two additional attributes: the Language attribute, which specifies the language of the associated code, and the Codebehind attribute, which specifies the source file for the Web service. These other attributes allow the Web service to be compiled at runtime.

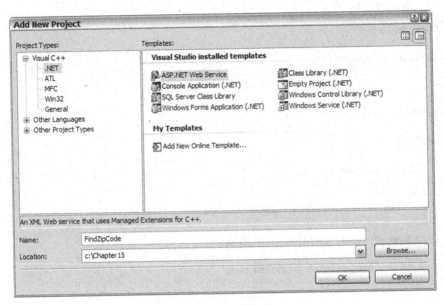

Figure 15-1. *Selecting the ASP.NET Web Service template*

The first file you should look at is FindZipCodeClass.asmx. In almost all cases, you will not change the contents of this file. As you can see in Listing 15-1, the file contains a single WebService directive containing a Class attribute that specifies the name of the associated class with this .asmx file.

Listing 15-1. *FindZipCodeClass.asmx*

```
<%@ WebService Class=FindZipCode.FindZipCodeClass %>
```

The next file of interest in this simple example is the FindZipCodeClass.h file, which contain the definitions of the methods that make up the Web service. Listing 15-2 shows the final version of FindZipCodeClass.h.

Listing 15-2. *FindZipCodeClass.h*

```
#pragma once

using namespace System;
using namespace System::Web;
using namespace System::Web::Services;

namespace FindZipCode {

    [WebServiceBinding(ConformsTo=WsiProfiles::BasicProfile1_1,
                    EmitConformanceClaims = true)]
    [WebService(Namespace="http://procppcli.net",
                Description = "Zip code retrieval service")]
    public ref class FindZipCodeClass : public WebService
    {
```

```
    public:
        FindZipCodeClass()
        {
            InitializeComponent();
        }

    protected:
        ~FindZipCodeClass()
        {
            if (components)
            {
                delete components;
            }
        }

    private:
        System::ComponentModel::Container ^components;

#pragma region Windows Form Designer generated code
        void InitializeComponent()
        {
        }
#pragma endregion

    public:
        [WebMethod(Description = "Get the zip code from city and state")]
        int GetZip(String ^city, String ^state);
    };
}
```

I removed the comments to save space. I also removed the redundant namespace qualifying because using namespace System::Web::Services does this for you. But you should probably leave the comments in and update them to reflect your Web service's functionality. Whether you use the redundant namespace qualifying is up to you.

You might also notice that the template auto-generated some designer code. This code will enable the designer to accept components that you drag onto it. I find this facility most helpful when I drag a database connection to the designer, as it auto-generates the connection string needed to connect to the dragged database.

The first noteworthy bit of generated code is the auto-generated but optional WebServiceBinding attribute. This attribute uses the ConformsTo property to specify which Web Services Interoperability (WSI) specification this Web service claims to conform to and the EmitConformanceClaims property to specify whether this claim is provided when a WSDL of the Web service is published. Personally, I have not done anything with this attribute and since it doesn't impact what I'm doing with the Web service I just leave it there.

As you might have noticed when you were entering the previous example, the second attribute WebService is not auto-generated. It is optional, though in this case I recommend always adding it. The WebService attribute provides the Web service with two important features:

- A guaranteed unique namespace (if used properly). Just like C++/CLI namespaces, this namespace resolves name clashes between multiple Web services.

- A description of the Web service for potential consumer clients to read and determine if it is the correct Web service to use.

How do you guarantee a unique namespace? It is possible for some third-party developer to create a Web service with the exact same name and members as your Web service. So to stop this from happening, a Web service uses your Web address as a root namespace, because a Web address is guaranteed to be unique for the Web server that hosts the Web service. Of course, it is still required that all Web services be unique on a single Web server.

Here is the code for the WebService attribute from the previous example:

```
[WebService(Namespace="http://procppcli.net",
            Description = "Zip code retrieval service")]
```

Notice that it uses standard attribute syntax.

The declaration of the ref class FindZipCodeClass and its public method GetZip() have nothing particularly special about them, except the attributes WebServiceBinding, WebService, and WebMethod.

Most of Web service magic resides in the last WebMethod attribute. The WebMethod attribute is the only required element (other than the .asmx file) for a Web service. You must add it to any public methods that you want to be accessible within the Web service.

Note Only public members with the [WebMethod] attribute are accessible within the Web service.

Even if the member is public, it will not be accessible unless it has a WebMethod attribute. Just like the WebService attribute, you can include an optional Description of the Method.

```
[WebMethod(Description = "Get the zip code from city and state")]
```

The last file generated by the template of current interest is FindZipCodeClass.cpp, shown in Listing 15-3.

Listing 15-3. *FindZipCodeClass.cpp*

```cpp
#include "stdafx.h"
#include "FindZipCodeClass.h"
#include "Global.asax.h"

namespace FindZipCode
{
    int FindZipCodeClass::GetZip(String ^city, String ^state)
    {
        // Obviously very simplified
        if (city->Equals("Louisville") && state->Equals("KY"))
            return 40241;
        else if (city->Equals("San Jose") && state->Equals("CA"))
            return 95138;
        else
            throw gcnew Exception("Zip Code not found");
    }
};
```

The public method GetZip() is nothing particularly special, except that it throws an exception on an error. I could have just as easily returned a predetermined value to handle the not found condition, but I want to show you that, when you build consuming clients later in the chapter, exception handling works even over the Internet.

Okay, let's compile and run the Web service. You can do this the same way as any other application. I use Ctrl-F5, but you can use any method you are comfortable with. What you should get is a Web page that looks something like the one shown in Figure 15-2.

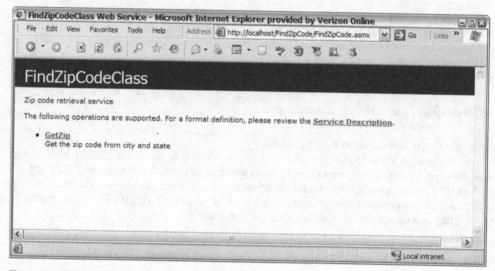

Figure 15-2. *The FindZipCode Web service Web page*

Tip You might get the error "Resource can't be found." If you do, check the URL that Visual Studio 2005 is trying to execute. Most likely it is using the solution's URL instead of the project's. To fix this, go to Debugging properties of the project and change the HTTP URL to point to the correct place. In my case the URL contains `http://localhost/Chapter15/findzipcode.asmx` and this needed to be changed to `http://localhost/FindZipCode/findzipcode.asmx`.

Tip You might get the error "Unable to load DLL 'msvcm80d.dll'." If you do, it means you compiled your Web service using the `/clr:pure` option, which has a dependency on this DLL. To get around this error, recompile the project using the `/clr:safe` option, which doesn't have this dependency.

I don't remember coding this Web page, do you? This Web page was automatically created when you compiled your Web service. This page is how a third-party developer will get information about your Web service. Note that I used the term "developer." The client application will get its information using WSDL. Because I wasn't very detailed in my descriptions on the `WebService` and `WebMethod` attributes, this page isn't very helpful. I personally recommend that you be as detailed as possible in those attribute descriptions. This will make it easier for a developer to use your Web service.

Go ahead and click the "Service Description" hyperlink to generate and display the WSDL for your Web service. As you can see in Listing 15-4, it's interesting, but I personally don't need to know anything about it. I'll let the computer figure all this out for me.

Listing 15-4. *FindZipCode's WSDL*

```
<?xml version="1.0" encoding="utf-8" ?>
  <wsdl:definitions xmlns:soap="http://schemas.xmlsoap.org/wsdl/soap/"
               xmlns:tm="http://microsoft.com/wsdl/mime/textMatching/"
               xmlns:soapenc="http://schemas.xmlsoap.org/soap/encoding/"
               xmlns:mime="http://schemas.xmlsoap.org/wsdl/mime/"
               xmlns:tns="http://procppcli.net"
```

```
                  xmlns:s="http://www.w3.org/2001/XMLSchema"
                  xmlns:soap12="http://schemas.xmlsoap.org/wsdl/soap12/"
                  xmlns:http="http://schemas.xmlsoap.org/wsdl/http/"
                  targetNamespace="http://procppcli.net"
                  xmlns:wsdl="http://schemas.xmlsoap.org/wsdl/">
<wsdl:documentation xmlns:wsdl="http://schemas.xmlsoap.org/wsdl/">
  Zip code retrieval service
</wsdl:documentation>
<wsdl:types>
  <s:schema elementFormDefault="qualified"
            targetNamespace="http://procppcli.net">
    <s:element name="GetZip">
      <s:complexType>
        <s:sequence>
          <s:element minOccurs="0" maxOccurs="1"
                     name="city" type="s:string" />
          <s:element minOccurs="0" maxOccurs="1"
                     name="state" type="s:string" />
        </s:sequence>
      </s:complexType>
    </s:element>
    <s:element name="GetZipResponse">
      <s:complexType>
        <s:sequence>
          <s:element minOccurs="1" maxOccurs="1"
                     name="GetZipResult" type="s:int" />
        </s:sequence>
      </s:complexType>
    </s:element>
  </s:schema>
</wsdl:types>
<wsdl:message name="GetZipSoapIn">
    <wsdl:part name="parameters" element="tns:GetZip" />
</wsdl:message>
  <wsdl:message name="GetZipSoapOut">
    <wsdl:part name="parameters" element="tns:GetZipResponse" />
</wsdl:message>
<wsdl:portType name="FindZipCodeClassSoap">
  <wsdl:operation name="GetZip">
    <wsdl:documentation xmlns:wsdl="http://schemas.xmlsoap.org/wsdl/">
      Get the zip code from city and state
    </wsdl:documentation>
    <wsdl:input message="tns:GetZipSoapIn" />
    <wsdl:output message="tns:GetZipSoapOut" />
  </wsdl:operation>
</wsdl:portType>
<wsdl:binding name="FindZipCodeClassSoap" type="tns:FindZipCodeClassSoap">
  <soap:binding transport="http://schemas.xmlsoap.org/soap/http" />
    <wsdl:operation name="GetZip">
      <soap:operation soapAction="http://procppcli.net/GetZip"
                      style="document" />
        <wsdl:input>
          <soap:body use="literal" />
        </wsdl:input>
```

```
            <wsdl:output>
              <soap:body use="literal" />
            </wsdl:output>
        </wsdl:operation>
    </wsdl:binding>
    <wsdl:binding name="FindZipCodeClassSoap12"
                  type="tns:FindZipCodeClassSoap">
      <soap12:binding transport="http://schemas.xmlsoap.org/soap/http" />
        <wsdl:operation name="GetZip">
          <soap12:operation soapAction="http://procppcli.net/GetZip"
                            style="document" />
          <wsdl:input>
            <soap12:body use="literal" />
          </wsdl:input>
          <wsdl:output>
            <soap12:body use="literal" />
          </wsdl:output>
        </wsdl:operation>
    </wsdl:binding>
    <wsdl:service name="FindZipCodeClass">
      <wsdl:documentation xmlns:wsdl="http://schemas.xmlsoap.org/wsdl/">
        Zip code retrieval service
      </wsdl:documentation>
      <wsdl:port name="FindZipCodeClassSoap"
                 binding="tns:FindZipCodeClassSoap">
        <soap:address
          location="http://localhost/FindZipCode/FindZipCode.asmx" />
      </wsdl:port>
        <wsdl:port name="FindZipCodeClassSoap12"
                   binding="tns:FindZipCodeClassSoap12">
          <soap12:address
            location="http://localhost/FindZipCode/FindZipCode.asmx" />
      </wsdl:port>
    </wsdl:service>
  </wsdl:definitions>
```

Now go back to the previous page and click the GetZip hyperlink. On this page, you get a simple dialog box to test your Web service. I'll show you the code to do this yourself a little later in this chapter.

Another interesting, but unnecessary, bit of information provided on this page are the HTTP request (see Listing 15-5) and response (see Listing 15-6) SOAP wrappers for your Web service. The reason that I think that they are provided (other than they look cool) is that other platforms are not as lucky as .NET and have to build and parse these SOAP wrappers themselves.

Listing 15-5. *FindZipCode's Request SOAP Wrapper*

```
POST /FindZipCode/FindZipCode.asmx HTTP/1.1
Host: localhost
Content-Type: text/xml; charset=utf-8
Content-Length: length
SOAPAction: "http://procppcli.net/GetZip"
```

```
<?xml version="1.0" encoding="utf-8"?>
<soap:Envelope xmlns:xsi="http://www.w3.org/2001/XMLSchema-instance"
xmlns:xsd="http://www.w3.org/2001/XMLSchema"
xmlns:soap="http://schemas.xmlsoap.org/soap/envelope/">
  <soap:Body>
    <GetZip xmlns="http://procppcli.net">
      <city>string</city>
      <state>string</state>
    </GetZip>
  </soap:Body>
</soap:Envelope>
```

Listing 15-6. *FindZipCode's Response SOAP Wrapper*

```
HTTP/1.1 200 OK
Content-Type: text/xml; charset=utf-8
Content-Length: length
<?xml version="1.0" encoding="utf-8"?>
<soap:Envelope xmlns:xsi="http://www.w3.org/2001/XMLSchema-instance"
xmlns:xsd="http://www.w3.org/2001/XMLSchema"
xmlns:soap="http://schemas.xmlsoap.org/soap/envelope/">
  <soap:Body>
    <GetZipResponse xmlns="http://procppcli.net">
      <GetZipResult>int</GetZipResult>
    </GetZipResponse>
  </soap:Body>
</soap:Envelope>
```

The last things shown on this page are the request (see Listing 15-7) and response (see Listing 15-8) for an HTTP POST. You'll probably use this information only in the simplest of Web services and, even then, probably only during the debug phase of that Web service's development. Other platforms, on the other hand, may need to use this information because they don't have SOAP support.

Listing 15-7. *FindZipCode's HTTP POST Request*

```
POST /FindZipCode/FindZipCode.asmx/GetZip HTTP/1.1
Host: localhost
Content-Type: application/x-www-form-urlencoded
Content-Length: length

city=string&state=string
```

Listing 15-8. *FindZipCode's HTTP POST Response*

```
HTTP/1.1 200 OK
Content-Type: text/xml; charset=utf-8
Content-Length: length

<?xml version="1.0" encoding="utf-8"?>
<int xmlns="http://procppcli.net">int</int>
```

Congratulations, you've made your first C++/CLI Web service! Now let's look at an assortment of ways to access your Web service.

Accessing a Web Service Using HTTP POST

Using HTTP POST commands is the easier of the two methods of consuming your Web service. All it requires is some simple HTML code and a Web browser. The problem with using HTTP POST is that the response back from the Web service is an XML document that you will need to parse yourself.

Listing 15-9 shows a sample of some HTML code you might use to consume the Web service. It is basically a stripped-down version of the code generated when you access FindZipCode.asmx.

Listing 15-9. *HTML to Consume the FindZipCode Web Service*

```html
<HTML>
    <BODY>
        To execute click the 'Invoke' button.
        <form action='http://localhost/FindZipCode/FindZipCode.asmx/GetZip'
            method="POST">
            <table>
                <tr>
                    <td>Parameter</td>
                    <td>Value</td>
                </tr>
                <tr>
                    <td>city:</td>
                    <td><input type="text" name="city"></td>
                </tr>
                <tr>
                    <td>state:</td>
                    <td><input type="text" name="state"></td>
                </tr>
                <tr>
                    <td colspan="2" align="center">
                        <input type="submit" value="Invoke">
                    </td>
                </tr>
            </table>
        </form>
    </BODY>
</HTML>
```

As you can see, there is not much to this HTML. The only tricky parts are as follows:

- Use a form action attribute that is made up of the Web service's name, including the .asmx suffix, followed by the name of the method you want to consume.

- Remember to use within your <form> tag a method attribute of POST and not the more common GET.

- Make sure the names of the input types match the Web service method parameters' names.

Figure 15-3 shows the data entry code getzip.html in action. Figure 15-4 shows what the response is after you click the Invoke button.

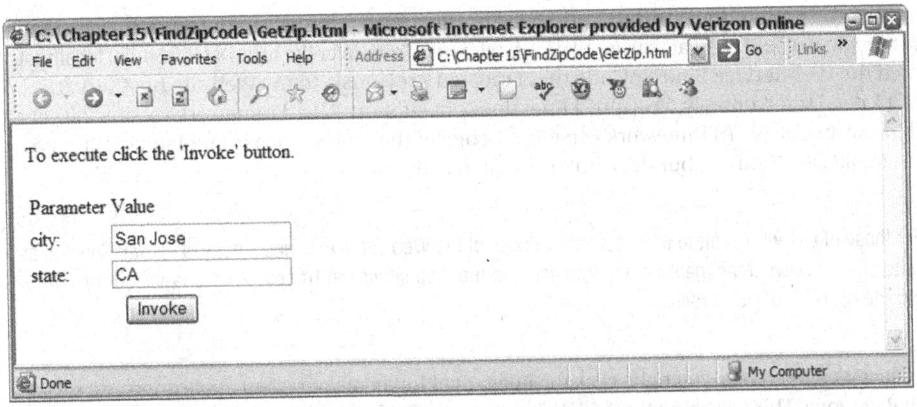

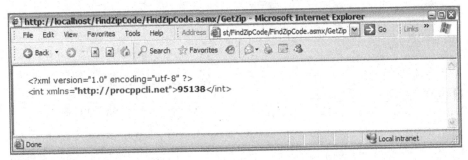

Figure 15-3. *Consuming the FindZipCode Web service using getzip.html*

```
<?xml version="1.0" encoding="utf-8" ?>
<int xmlns="http://procppcli.net">95138</int>
```

Figure 15-4. *Response to getzip.html from the FindZipCode Web service*

Accessing a Web Service Using SOAP

With .NET, the only real way to consume Web services is to use SOAP. As you saw previously, the SOAP wrapper is quite complex. Fortunately, if you're using Visual Studio 2005 and C++/CLI (or any other .NET language, for that matter) you don't have to know squat about SOAP, because pretty well everything about SOAP is taken care of for you. (If you use complex objects you might have to mark up the objects with attributes in order describe how to serialize the object, but that is beyond the scope of this book.)

Normally, when you're working with distributed programs, the client would be either a Windows Form or a Web Form. In the following example, on the other hand, I use a console to be different and to prove that it can be done. In a later example, I show how to use the more normal Windows Form.

The following example shows how to implement a client using the console. In this example, the client simply requests three zip codes. The first two are valid city/state combinations and the third is an invalid combination. The response to all three requests is written to the console. The third response ends up being a caught exception.

Start by creating a new Console Application (.NET) project. (In the example, I added this project to the chapter solution just to keep all the same code for a chapter together.)

Once the wizard has done its thing, you need to add a Web reference to the FindZipCode Web service. I thought it would be neat to use a real Web reference from over the Internet instead of localhost, so I copied the Web service FindZipCode that I created previously to my Web site host server, ProCppCLI.net. Unfortunately, ProCppCLI.net does not support .NET Framework version 2.0 yet, so I had to use an old .NET Framework version 1.1 copy of the Web service from ManagedCpp.net (which is an old site of mine), but the result is ultimately the same.

Tip For those of you who want to try out a remote copy of the Web service, I keep a copy of FindZipCode on an old Web site of mine: www.ManagedCpp.net. You can find the Web service at `http://www.managedcpp.net/FindZipCode/FindZipCode.asmx`.

To add a Web reference, you right-click the References folder of your client application and select Add Web Reference. This will cause the Add Web Reference dialog box to appear (see Figure 15-5).

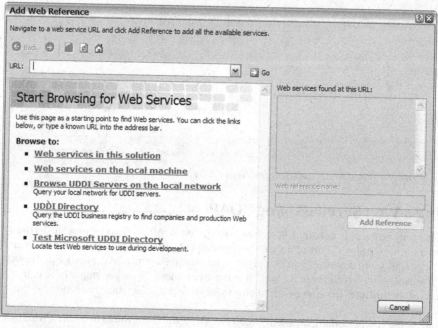

Figure 15-5. *The Add Web Reference dialog box that appears before you select a Web service*

From here, you can either click one of the links within the dialog box to search for the Web service or type the URL of the Web service in the supplied text box. In Figure 15-5, I typed in the URL of the Web service, but if you don't have access to a Web server or don't want to use my copy of the Web service, then select the "Web services on the local machine" link, which will find and make available the Web service you built previously. Once you select the Web service, you want the Add Web Reference dialog box changes to look like Figure 15-6.

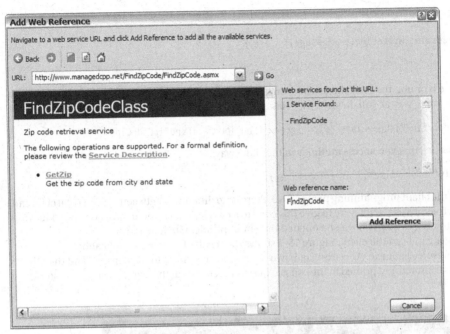

Figure 15-6. *The Add Web Reference dialog box after you have selected a Web service*

Now all you have to do is change the Web reference name to something more appropriate than the Web server's name, and then click the Add Reference button.

The addition of a Web reference adds a number of files to your project. Among them are a WSDL file and a DISCO file. Both are nice to look at but, in most cases, you will do nothing with them directly. The only file of real importance is the include file with the same name as the Web reference name you changed previously. All you need to do with this file is include it at the top of your client application. If you are curious, you can open this file to see some of the details of how the connection to the Web service is made.

Now you need to make the changes to your main .cpp file, as shown in Listing 15-10.

Listing 15-10. *A Console Web Services Client Application*

```cpp
#include "FindZipCode.h"

using namespace System;

void main()
{
    FindZipCode::FindZipCodeClass ^fzc = gcnew FindZipCode::FindZipCodeClass();

    try
    {
        Console::WriteLine(fzc->GetZip("Louisville", "KY").ToString());
        Console::WriteLine(fzc->GetZip("San Jose", "CA").ToString());
        Console::WriteLine(fzc->GetZip("xx", "cc").ToString());
    }
```

```
        catch (Exception ^e)
        {
            Console::WriteLine(e->Message);
        }
}
```

Believe it or not, that's all the coding you have to do. Notice that you instantiate a Web service class in the same way as you do any other class:

```
FindZipCode::FindZipCodeClass ^fzc = gcnew FindZipCode::FindZipCodeClass();
```

Also notice that you access methods in the same way:

```
fzc->GetZip("Louisville", "KY").ToString();
```

From the client programming perspective, there is no difference between using a local class and using a Web service class. If I were to give this code to a developer, he would have no way of knowing it uses Web services unless he or she opened the FindZipCode.h include file.

Go ahead and run the client. Figure 15-7 shows the result of the client application ZipCodeConsoleClient.exe. As is expected, two zip codes are printed to the console, and then the exception is captured and printed to the console (just as I predicted at the beginning of this example).

Figure 15-7. *The client consumer of Web service FindZipCode in action*

Debugging a Web Service

Debugging a Web service on its own is really no different than debugging any other .NET application. Simply compile within the debug solution configuration and then set breakpoints where you want the execution to stop.

There is only one scenario that requires you to do anything special, and that is if you create your Web service within a solution that has a different name than the Web service. When you do this, starting the debugger causes the error shown in Figure 15-8.

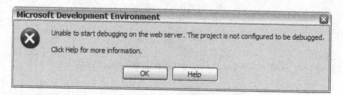

Figure 15-8. *The debugging Web service error*

The wording of the error doesn't really explain what caused the error. But it's very easy to solve the problem. What has happened is that the URL to your Web service is incorrect. When you build a Web service from an existing solution, Visual Studio 2005 creates a URL to your Web service using the solution's path instead of the Web service's. Thus, if you look in the Web service project properties under the Configuration Properties ➤ Debugging folder, you'll find that the HTTP URL has a value of http://localhost/solutiondir/webservicename.asmx when it should have the value http://localhost/webservicedir/webservicename.asmx. To fix the problem, simply type the correct HTTP URL in the text box.

Debugging a Web service when it is being consumed by a client is, on the other hand, not as simple and could require a little more effort to set up, depending on how your environment is set up.

The first scenario is when the client and Web service are in two different solutions. If this is the case, simply start up the Web service solution in debug mode and when the client calls the Web service the breakpoint will be triggered.

The second scenario is when the client and Web service are in the same solution but in different projects. In this case, I use the following two procedures (there are probably others that I don't know).

Procedure 1

The first step is to set a breakpoint in the client calling the Web service just before the first time you want to call the Web service with the debugger.

Then, the only way you can get the debugger to work within the Web service is to *step into* the Web service. Once you have stepped into Web service, from then on you can debug the Web service just like any other part of the application. In other words, breakpoints within the Web service don't work unless you step into the Web service at least once first.

Procedure 2

Open up two instances of Visual Studio 2005 for the solution. One will open a dialog box (see Figure 15-9) stating that the .ncb file could not be opened for writing.

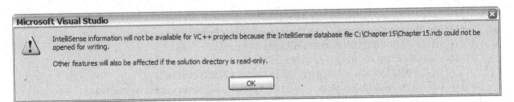

Figure 15-9. *The .ncb file cannot be edited by multiple concurrent instances of Visual Studio.*

Remember which instance generated this error, as you don't want to make any modification to the code with this instance of Visual Studio 2005.

Now, in either instance start up the Web service in debug mode. Once it has started, open up the client in the other instance. Now when a call to the Web service is made the first instance of Visual Studio 2005 will stop at any breakpoints you may have set up (without needing to step into it like you did in the first procedure).

Passing Data Using a Web Service

I'm going to finish this chapter with a more elaborate example of a Web service. It will take the MaintAuthors detached database project example you created back in Chapter 12 and convert it to a Web service.

With this example, you will truly see a detached (figuratively speaking) database, where the client is on one system and the Web service (database) is located somewhere else on the Internet.

The Web service consists of two methods. The first returns a DataSet of authors, and the second takes in a DataSet of authors and updates the database based on the batched processes made by the client to the authors DataSet. You should note that this example considers no concurrency issues (i.e., what happens if multiple clients update the database via the multiple Web service instances at the same time?).

The Windows Form client application receives a DataSet of authors and then allows additions, updates, and deletions to the DataSet.

Using Web Service GUI Designer Tool

One neat feature of Visual Studio 2005 is the ability to drag and drop a SqlConnection to a Web service. Not only does this spare you the time and effort of writing the code for the SqlConnection, but it also saves you from having to figure out the connection string to connect to a database.

The steps are… actually, the *step* is quite simple. Directly out of the Server Explorer, drag the data connection to the database you want to add a connection to, and drop it on the designer screen of the web service's .h file. Once you do that, the code needed to create a SqlConnection is automatically added to the actual .h file. Listing 15-11 shows the auto-generated code (both by the project template and by dropping and dragging a connection) along with the definition of the two Web service methods needed to implement the detached database.

Listing 15-11. *AuthorWSClass.h*

```
using namespace System;
using namespace System::Data;
using namespace System::Data::SqlClient;
using namespace System::Web;
using namespace System::Web::Services;

namespace AuthorWS
{
    [WebServiceBinding(ConformsTo=WsiProfiles::BasicProfile1_1,
                       EmitConformanceClaims = true)]
    [WebService(Namespace="http://procppcli.net",
                Description = "Author table access Web service")]
    public ref class AuthorWSClass : public System::Web::Services::WebService
    {

    public:
        AuthorWSClass()
        {
            InitializeComponent();
        }

    protected:
        ~AuthorWSClass()
        {
            if (components)
            {
                delete components;
            }
        }

    private: System::Data::SqlClient::SqlConnection^  sqlConnection;
    private: System::ComponentModel::IContainer^  components;
```

```
private:
    void InitializeComponent()
    {
        this->sqlConnection =
            gcnew System::Data::SqlClient::SqlConnection();
        //
        // sqlConnection
        //
        this->sqlConnection->ConnectionString =
            L"Server=Amidala;Integrated Security=True;Database=DCV_DB";
        this->sqlConnection->FireInfoMessageEventOnUserErrors = false;
    }

public:
    [WebMethod(Description =
        "Method to retrieve All Authors from the database")]
    DataSet ^GetAuthors();

    [WebMethod(Description =
        "Method to Commit changed made on client with Server database")]
    void UpdateAuthors(DataSet ^dSet);
};
}
```

Returning a DataSet

The easier of the two Web service methods to implement relates to filling a DataSet of all authors and then sending the DataSet from the Web service to the consuming client (see Listing 15-12).

Listing 15-12. *Building the Authors DataSet Web Service*

```
DataSet^ AuthorWSClass::GetAuthors()
{
    SqlDataAdapter ^dAdapt;
    DataSet ^dSet;

    dAdapt = gcnew SqlDataAdapter();
    dAdapt->MissingSchemaAction = MissingSchemaAction::AddWithKey;

    dAdapt->SelectCommand =
        gcnew SqlCommand("SELECT AuthorID, LastName, FirstName FROM Authors",
                        sqlConnection);
    dSet = gcnew DataSet();
    dAdapt->Fill(dSet, "Authors");

    return dSet;
}
```

As you can see, a Web service has no problems sending the complex DataSet object using SOAP. In fact, if it wasn't for the WebMethod attribute found in the method's declaration, this method would look like any other ADO.NET DataSet fill method.

One big difference, though, is that this method uses its own method scope version of the SqlConnection (auto-generated), DataAdapter, and DataSet. The reason is that a Web service (unless otherwise specified using the EnableSession property of the WebMethod attribute) is stateless. Basically, each time the Web service is called, it is from scratch. Thus, there is no need to have the SqlConnection, DataAdapter, or DataSet stick around after the Web service method has finished. For this same reason, there is no reason to assign the InsertCommand, UpdateCommand, and DeleteCommand properties to the DataAdapter as they are not used in the method.

Inserting, Updating, and Deleting Rows in a DataSet

Inserting, updating, and deleting rows in a DataSet via a Web service is handled in virtually the same way as standard, nondistributed ADO.NET. The UpdateAuthors() method (see Listing 15-13) is made up of code that is almost exactly the same as what you saw in Chapter 12.

Listing 15-13. *Updating the Authors Database Web Service*

```
void AuthorWSClass::UpdateAuthors(DataSet ^dSet)
{
    SqlDataAdapter ^dAdapt;

    dAdapt = gcnew SqlDataAdapter();
    dAdapt->MissingSchemaAction = MissingSchemaAction::AddWithKey;

    dAdapt->InsertCommand =
        gcnew SqlCommand("INSERT INTO Authors (LastName, FirstName) "
                         "VALUES (@LastName, @FirstName)",
                         sqlConnection);
    dAdapt->InsertCommand->Parameters->Add("@LastName", SqlDbType::VarChar,
                                           50, "LastName");
    dAdapt->InsertCommand->Parameters->Add("@FirstName", SqlDbType::VarChar,
                                           50, "FirstName");

    dAdapt->UpdateCommand =
        gcnew SqlCommand("UPDATE Authors SET LastName = @LastName,"
                                           "FirstName = @FirstName "
                         "WHERE AuthorID = @AuthorID",
                         sqlConnection);
    dAdapt->UpdateCommand->Parameters->Add("@LastName", SqlDbType::VarChar,
                                           50, "LastName");
    dAdapt->UpdateCommand->Parameters->Add("@FirstName", SqlDbType::VarChar,
                                           50, "FirstName");
    dAdapt->UpdateCommand->Parameters->Add("@AuthorID", SqlDbType::Int,
                                           4, "AuthorID");

    dAdapt->DeleteCommand =
        gcnew SqlCommand("DELETE FROM Authors WHERE AuthorID = @AuthorID",
                         sqlConnection);
    dAdapt->DeleteCommand->Parameters->Add("@AuthorID", SqlDbType::Int,
                                           4, "AuthorID");

    dAdapt->Update(dSet, "Authors");
}
```

I'm sure you are seeing the pattern here. Distributed code using Web services is usually very close to, if not the same as, its nondistributed equivalent. The only real difference is that the class state is not maintained. Therefore, you have to be careful about global and class variables.

Unlike the plain ADO.NET version in Chapter 12, the Web service creates a new version of the DataAdapter each time a DataSet update is required. The reason, as I stated previously, is that the Web service is stateless, so on the call to the AuthorUpdate() method, no DataAdapter object exists. Having a new or different DataAdapter from the one when the DataSet was created is not an issue, because a DataAdapter is not strongly linked to the DataSet it is supporting. In fact, as long as the database schema is the same, DataSets are interchangeable as far as DataAdapters are concerned. As you will see later, the DataSet of the Update process can be a subset of the one sent by the GetAuthors() method, because only changed rows are contained within this DataSet.

What is neat about this method is that it can handle inserted, updated, and deleted records, all in a batch-like manner, instead of requiring a separate method for each of these process types.

Caution To simplify this example, I didn't add any code to handle database concurrency.

One major issue that you may encounter when you try to access a database from within a Web service is that the Web service does not have the rights to access it. Instead you get the following error:

```
Exception Details: System.Data.SqlClient.SqlException: Login failed for user
'COMPUTERNAME\ASPNET'.
```

What this means in layman terms is that the Web service logs in to the database using the login ID of COMPUTERNAME\ASPNET and not your login ID. Thus, if the database is not set up to accept this login ID, then things don't go very well for your Web service.

The solution is simple (once you know it). Add COMPUTERNAME\ASPNET as a user who can log in to the database in question. To do this, you need to run the following commands (I use SQL Query Analyzer but you can use the command osql in a command window as well):

```
USE DATABASENAME
EXEC sp_grantlogin 'COMPUTERNAME\ASPNET'
EXEC sp_grantdbaccess 'COMPUTERNAME\ASPNET'
EXEC sp_addrolemember 'db_owner', 'COMPUTERNAME\ASPNET'
go
```

where COMPUTERNAME is the name of the computer the Web service is running on.

Authors DataSet Processing Web Service Client

In truth, there is little reason to include this section in the chapter other than to show that very little has changed in the Web service client application when you compare it to the ADO.NET example in Chapter 12. Listing 15-14 has been included so that you can compare it to the source code of the MaintAuthors example in Chapter 12.

Listing 15-14. *Web Server Version of the MaintAuthors Application*

```cpp
namespace MaintAuthors
{
    using namespace System;
    using namespace System::ComponentModel;
    using namespace System::Collections;
    using namespace System::Windows::Forms;
    using namespace System::Data;
    using namespace System::Drawing;

    public ref class Form1 : public System::Windows::Forms::Form
    {
    public:
        Form1(void)
        {
            InitializeComponent();

            authors = gcnew AuthorWS::AuthorWSClass();
            dSet = authors->GetAuthors();

            DataTable ^dt = dSet->Tables["Authors"];

            if (dt == nullptr)
                throw gcnew Exception("No Authors Table");

            for each (DataRow ^row in dt->Rows::get())
            {
                lbAuthors->Items->Add(ListBoxItem(row));
            }

            CurrentAuthorID = -1;
        }

    protected:
        ~Form1()
        {
            if (components)
            {
                delete components;
            }
        }

        DataSet ^dSet;
        int CurrentAuthorID;
        AuthorWS::AuthorWSClass ^authors;

        void InitializeComponent(void)
        //... Not shown to save space
```

```cpp
private:
    String ^ListBoxItem(DataRow ^row)
    {
        return String::Format("{0} {1} {2}",
            row["AuthorID"],
            row["FirstName"],
            row["LastName"]);
    }

    System::Void bnRollback_Click(System::Object^ sender,
                                  System::EventArgs^ e)
    {
        dSet->RejectChanges();

        lbAuthors->Items->Clear();

        DataTable ^dt = dSet->Tables["Authors"];

        for each (DataRow^ row in dt->Rows)
        {
            lbAuthors->Items->Add(ListBoxItem(row));
        }
        CurrentAuthorID = -1;
    }

    System::Void bnCommit_Click(System::Object^ sender,
                                System::EventArgs^ e)
    {
        authors->UpdateAuthors(dSet->GetChanges());
        dSet->AcceptChanges();

        lbAuthors->Items->Clear();

        DataTable ^dt = dSet->Tables["Authors"];

        for each (DataRow^ row in dt->Rows)
        {
            lbAuthors->Items->Add(ListBoxItem(row));
        }
        CurrentAuthorID = -1;
    }

    System::Void bnDelete_Click(System::Object^ sender,
                                System::EventArgs^  e)
    {
        if (CurrentAuthorID < 0)
            return;

        DataTable ^dt = dSet->Tables["Authors"];
        array<DataRow^>^ row =
            dt->Select(String::Format("AuthorID={0}", CurrentAuthorID));

        row[0]->Delete();
```

```cpp
        lbAuthors->Items->RemoveAt(lbAuthors->SelectedIndex);
    }

    System::Void bnUpdate_Click(System::Object^ sender,
                                System::EventArgs^ e)
    {
        if (CurrentAuthorID < 0)
            return;

        DataTable ^dt = dSet->Tables["Authors"];
        array<DataRow^>^ row =
            dt->Select(String::Format("AuthorID={0}", CurrentAuthorID));

        row[0]["FirstName"] = tbFirstName->Text;
        row[0]["LastName"]  = tbLastName->Text;

        lbAuthors->Items->Insert(lbAuthors->SelectedIndex,
                                 ListBoxItem(row[0]));
        lbAuthors->Items->RemoveAt(lbAuthors->SelectedIndex);
    }

    System::Void bnAdd_Click(System::Object^ sender, System::EventArgs^ e)
    {
        if (tbFirstName->Text->Trim()->Length == 0 ||
            tbLastName->Text->Trim()->Length == 0)
            return;

        DataTable ^dt = dSet->Tables["Authors"];

        DataRow ^row = dt->NewRow();

        row["FirstName"] = tbFirstName->Text;
        row["LastName"]  = tbLastName->Text;

        dt->Rows->Add(row);

        lbAuthors->Items->Add(ListBoxItem(row));

        tbFirstName->Text = "";
        tbLastName->Text = "";
    }

    System::Void lbAuthors_SelectedIndexChanged(System::Object^ sender,
                                                System::EventArgs^ e)
    {
        array<System::Char>^ ASpace = gcnew array<System::Char>{' '};

        if (lbAuthors->SelectedItem == nullptr)
        {
            CurrentAuthorID = -1;
            tbFirstName->Text = "";
            tbLastName->Text = "";
            return;
        }
```

```
        array<String^>^ split =
            lbAuthors->SelectedItem->ToString()->Split(ASpace);

        CurrentAuthorID = Convert::ToInt32(split[0]);
        tbFirstName->Text = split[1];
        tbLastName->Text = split[2];
    }
};
}
```

As you can see, the code is the same except that the ADO.NET `DataAdapter` and `DataSet` logic has been removed. In actuality, this logic should probably have been moved to its own class in the example in Chapter 12, but this was not done because it simplifies the code listing.

Figure 15-10 shows the Web service version of MaintAuthors.exe in action. Those of you looking for differences between this and the original version in Chapter 12 won't find any.

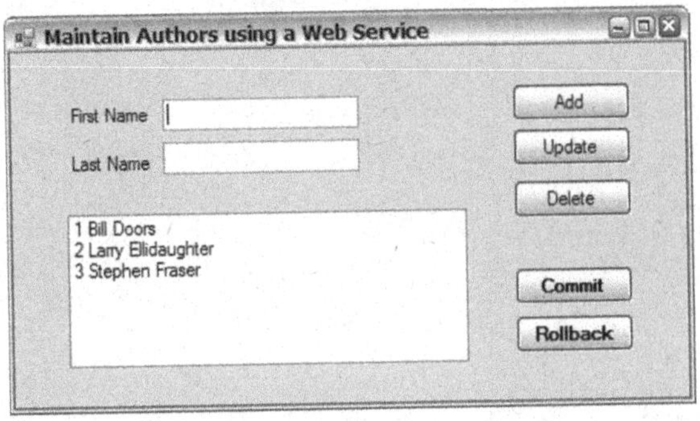

Figure 15-10. *Web service version of MaintAuthors*

Summary

In this chapter you examined the "net" in .NET: Web services. What you found out is that Web services are extremely easy to develop and code because you aren't doing anything different when coding Web services as compared to developing any other class. In general, any complexities associated with the distributed application nature of Web services are hidden from you. The only real difference of note is that Web services are generally coded in a stateless manner.

You started the chapter by covering the basics of Web services. Then you moved on to examine two different examples of Web services and multiple ways to write consumer clients. The second example was relatively complex, but the complex logic actually had very little to do with Web services and more to do with coding ADO.NET in a stateless manner.

In the next chapter, you'll take a look at a third way of working over a network. This time, you will take complete control and code at the socket level.

CHAPTER 16

■ ■ ■

Multithreaded Programming

Normally, multithreaded programming would be one of the more advanced topics, if not the most advanced topic, in a book, but due to the .NET Framework, it is no more advanced than any other topic in this book. Why, you might ask? Well, the answer is that the .NET Framework (as usual) has hidden most of the complexities of this habitually complex area of software development within its classes.

Having the complexities hidden doesn't mean it's any less powerful or flexible than your doing the entire complex coding yourself. In fact, true to the nature of the .NET Framework, if you want to get lost in the details, you can still do so. On the other hand, because this chapter is about developing multithreaded programs using C++/CLI and not about multithreaded programming in general, I try to stay away from these details and let the .NET Framework deal with them. However, for those of you who like to delve into the details, I try to point you in the right direction for future exploration.

This chapter starts off by covering multithreaded programming at a high level, so those of you who are new to multithreaded programming can get comfortable with the concept. Next, you'll explore the more commonly used and, fortunately, easy-to-understand multithreaded programming features provided by the .NET Framework. With the basics covered, you'll explore some of the more complex areas of multithreaded programming, including thread states, priorities, and the weighty topic of synchronization. Finally, you'll learn about a second way of handling multithreaded programming: thread pools.

What Is Multithreaded Programming?

Most developers are comfortable with the concept of *multitasking*, or the capability of computers to execute more than one application or process at the same time. However, *multithreading* may be a more alien term. Many programmers have not had any reason to program in a multithreaded fashion. In fact, for some programming languages, there is no way to do multithreaded programming without jumping through some very convoluted programming hoops.

So, what is multithreaded programming? You might want to think of it as multitasking at the program level. A program has two options for executing itself. The first option is to run itself in one thread of execution. In this method of execution, the program follows the logic of the program from start to end in a sequential fashion. You might want to think of this method of execution as *single threaded*. The second option is that the program can break itself into multiple threads of execution or, in other words, split the program into multiple segments (with beginning and end points) and run some of them concurrently (at the same time). This is what is better known as *multithreading*. It should be noted, though, that the end result of either a single-threaded or a multithreaded program will be the same.

Of course, if you have a single processor machine, true concurrency is not possible, as only one command can be run at a time through the CPU. (With Intel Corporation's new Hyper-Threading Technology, you can execute more than one command at the same time on a single CPU, but that is a topic for another book altogether.) This is an important concept to grasp because many programmers mistakenly think that if they break a computationally bound section of a program into two parts and run them in two threads of execution, then the program will take less time to run. The opposite is actually the case—it will take longer. The reason is that the same amount of code is being run for the program, plus additional time must be added to handle the swapping of the thread's context (the CPU's registers, stack, and so on).

So for what reason would you use multithreading for a single process computer if it takes longer than single threading? The reason is that, when used properly, multithreading can provide better I/O-related response time, as well as better use of the CPU.

Wait a second, didn't I just contradict myself? Well, actually, I didn't.

The key point about proper use of multithreading is the types of commands the threads are executing. Computational bound threads (i.e., threads that do a lot of calculations) gain very little when it comes to multithreading, as they are already working overtime trying to get themselves executed. Multithreading actually slows this type of thread down. I/O threads, on the other hand, gain a lot. This gain is most apparent in two areas: better response and CPU utilization.

I'm sure you've all come across a program that seemed to stop or lock up and then suddenly came back to life. The usual reason for this is that the program is executing a computationally bound area of the code. And, because multithreading wasn't being done, there were no CPU cycles provided for user interaction with the computer. By adding multithreading, it's possible to have one thread running the computational bound area and another handling user interaction. Having an I/O thread allows the user to continue to work while the CPU blasts its way through the computational bound thread. True, the actual computational bound thread will take longer to run, but because the user can continue to work, this minute amount of time usually doesn't matter.

I/O threads are notorious for wasting CPU cycles. Humans, printers, hard drives, monitors, and so forth are very slow when compared to a CPU. I/O threads spend a large portion of their time simply waiting, doing nothing. Thus, multithreading allows the CPU to use this wasted time.

Basic .NET Framework Class Library Threading

There is only one namespace that you need to handle threading: System::Threading. What you plan to do while using the threads will determine which of the classes you will use. Many of the classes provide different ways to do the same thing, usually differing in the degree of control. Here is a list of some of the more common classes within the System::Threading namespace:

- AutoResetEvent notifies a waiting thread that an event has occurred. You use this class to allow communication between threads using signaling. Typically, you use this class for threads that need exclusive access.

- Interlocked allows for atomic operation on a variable that is shared between threads.

- `ManualResetEvent` notifies one or more threads that an event has occurred. You use this class to allow communication between threads using signaling. Typically, you use this class for scenarios where one thread must complete before other threads can proceed.

- `Monitor` provides a mechanism to synchronize access to objects by locking access to a block of code, commonly called a *critical section*. While a thread owns the lock for an object, no other thread can acquire that lock.

- `Mutex` provides a synchronization primitive that solves the problem of two or more threads needing access to a shared resource at the same time. It ensures that only one thread at a time uses the resource. This class is similar in functionality to `Monitor`, except `Mutex` allows for interprocess synchronization.

- `ReaderWriterLock` allows a single writer and multiple readers access to a resource. At any given time, it allows either concurrent read access for multiple threads or write access to a single thread.

- `Semaphore` limits the number of threads that can access a particular system resource.

- `Thread` is the core class to create a thread to execute a portion of the program code.

- `ThreadPool` provides access to a pool of system-maintained threads.

- `WaitHandle` allows for the taking or releasing of exclusive access to a shared system-specific resource.

From the preceding list of classes, you can see that the .NET Framework class library provides two ways to create threads:

- `Thread`

- `ThreadPool`

The difference between the two primarily depends on whether you want to maintain the `Thread` object or you want the system to handle it for you. In effect, nearly the same results can be achieved with either method. I cover `Thread` first, as it provides you with complete control of your threads. Later in this chapter, I cover `ThreadPool`, where the system maintains the process threads—though, even with this reduction in control, you will see later in the chapter that `ThreadPool`s can be used just as effectively as `Thread`s. But, before you explore either method, you'll take a look at thread state and priority.

Thread State

The .NET Framework thread model is designed to model an execution thread. Many of the `Threading` namespace classes and members map directly to an execution state of a thread. Personally, I found knowing the execution states of a thread ultimately made it easier for me to understand threading, so using Figure 16-1 and Table 16-1, I'll walk you through the state and the action required to change states within the .NET Framework thread model.

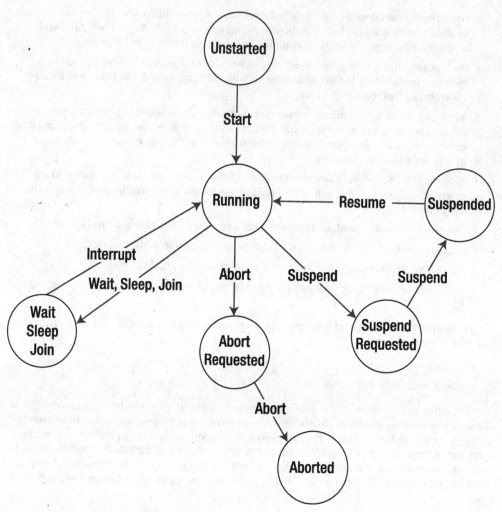

Figure 16-1. *The execution states of a thread*

You might want to note that the states in Table 16-1 map directly to the System::Threading::ThreadState enumeration. And, if you need to determine the current state, you would look in the ThreadState property in the Thread class.

Table 16-1. *The Execution States of a Thread*

Action	State
The thread is created with the CLR and has not been invoked.	Unstarted
The thread executes its start process.	Running
The thread continues to run until another action occurs.	Running
The running thread calls sleep for a specified length of time.	WaitSleepJoin
The running thread calls wait on a locked resource.	WaitSleepJoin

Table 16-1. *The Execution States of a Thread*

Action	State
The running thread calls join on another thread.	WaitSleepJoin
Another thread calls interrupt on the WaitSleepJoin thread.	Running
Another thread calls suspend on the thread.	SuspendRequest
The SuspendRequested thread processes the suspend call.	Suspended
Another thread calls resume on a Suspended thread.	Running
Another thread calls abort on the thread.	AbortRequest
The AbortRequested thread processes the abort call.	Aborted

In addition to these states is a Background state, which means the thread is executing in the background (as opposed to in the foreground). The biggest difference between a background thread and a foreground thread is that a background thread ends when the main application thread ends. A foreground thread continues executing until it is aborted or finishes executing. You set a thread to be in the background by setting the IsBackground property of the Thread class.

Thread Priorities

Not all threads are created equal. Well, that's not really true, all threads are created equal. You just make them unequal later by updating the Priority property of the Thread class. With the .NET Framework, you have five levels of priorities available to place on a thread:

- Highest
- AboveNormal
- Normal
- BelowNormal
- Lowest

You can find each of the preceding priorities in the System::Threading:ThreadPriority enumeration.

The basic idea behind priorities is that all threads are created at a Normal priority. When unaltered, each "running" thread gets an equal share of processor time. If, on the other hand, you change the priority of the thread to a higher level—AboveNormal, for example—then the documentation says it will be scheduled to execute prior to threads at a lower level. Well, this is sort of the case. If that were truly how the Framework did it, then lower-level threads would never run (in other words, they would *starve*) until the higher-level thread finished. This doesn't happen, so it appears that the .NET Framework has additional logic in it to allow lower-level priority threads to have at least a little processor time.

Normally you don't want to mess with priorities, but for those rare occasions, the functionality, as you have come to expect with the .NET Framework, is provided.

Using Threads

Of the two methods available in the .NET Framework for creating threads, Thread and ThreadPool, the System::Threading::Thread class provides you with the most control and versatility. The cost is a minor amount of additional coding complexity.

Like all classes in the .NET Framework, the Thread class is made up of properties and methods. The ones you will most likely use are as follows:

- Abort() is a method that raises a ThreadAbortException in the thread on which it is invoked, which starts the process of terminating the thread. Calling this method normally results in the termination of the thread.

- CurrentThread is a static Thread property that represents the currently running thread.

- Interrupt() is a method that interrupts a thread that is currently in the WaitSleepJoin thread state, thus resulting in the thread returning to the Running thread state.

- IsBackground is a Boolean property that represents whether a thread is a background or a foreground thread. The default is false.

- Join() is a method that causes the calling thread to block until the called thread terminates.

- Name is a String property that represents the name of the thread. You can write the name only once to this property.

- Priority is a ThreadPriority enumerator property that represents the current priority of the thread. The default is Normal.

- Resume() is a method that resumes a suspended thread and makes its thread state Running.

- Sleep() is a method that blocks the current thread for a specified length of time and makes its thread state WaitSleepJoin.

- Start() is a method that causes the thread to start executing and changes its thread state to Running.

- Suspend() is a method that causes the thread to suspend. The thread state becomes Suspended.

- ThreadState is a ThreadState enumerator property that represents the current thread state of the thread.

The idea of running and keeping track of two or more things at the same time can get confusing. Fortunately, in many cases with multithreaded programming, you simply have to start a thread and let it run to completion without interference.

I start off by showing you that exact scenario first. Then I show you some of the other options available to you when it comes to thread control.

Starting Threads

The first thing that you need to do to get the multithreaded programming running is to create an instance of a Thread. In prior versions of the .NET Framework 2.0, you didn't have much in the way of options, as there was only one constructor:

```
System::Threading::Thread(System::Threading::ThreadStart ^start);
```

The parameter ThreadStart is a delegate to the method that is the starting point of the thread. The signature of the delegate is a method with no parameters that returns void:

```
public delegate void ThreadStart();
```

Version 2.0 of the .NET Framework has expanded the constructors by an additional three. All these additions help to overcome a shortcoming of thread creation. The first addition is to allow the specification of a ParameterizedThreadStart, instead of a simple ThreadStart, thus allowing an Object parameter to be passed to the thread.

```
System::Threading::Thread(System::Threading::ParameterizedThreadStart ^start);
```

The third and fourth additional constructors expand the other two constructors by allowing the maximum stack size to be specified. Such fine-tuning of threads is beyond the scope of this book, but I thought I'd let you know it was available, just in case you need it.

```
Thread(ThreadStart ^start, Int32 mazStackSize);
Thread(ParameterizedThreadStart ^start, Int32 mazStackSize);
```

Caution The maxStackSize passed to the Thread constructor must be greater than 128K (131072) bytes or an ArgumentOutOfRangeException will be thrown.

One thing that may not be obvious when you first start working with threads is that creating an instance of the Thread object doesn't cause the thread to start. The thread state after creating an instance of the thread is, instead, Unstarted. To get the thread to start, you need to call the Thread class's Start() method. It kind of makes sense, don't you think?

I think it's about time to look at some code. Take a look at the example of a program that creates two threads in Listing 16-1. The first thread executes a static method of a class, and the second thread executes a member class that passes a parameter.

Listing 16-1. *Starting Two Simple Threads*

```
using namespace System;
using namespace System::Threading;

ref class MyThread
{
public:
    static void StaticThread();
    void NonStaticThread(Object ^name);
};

void MyThread::StaticThread()
{
    for (int i = 0; i < 50000001; i++)
    {
        if (i % 10000000 == 0)
            Console::WriteLine("Static Thread {0}", i.ToString());
    }
}

void MyThread::NonStaticThread(Object ^name)
{
    for (int i = 0; i < 50000001; i++)
    {
```

```
            if (i % 10000000 == 0)
                Console::WriteLine("Member {0} Thread {1}",
                name, // Parameter passed
                i.ToString());
        }
    }

    void main()
    {
        Console::WriteLine("Main Program Starts");

        // Creating a thread start delegate for a static method
        ThreadStart ^thrStart = gcnew ThreadStart(&MyThread::StaticThread);
        // Use the ThreadStart to create a Thread handle Object
        Thread ^thr1 = gcnew Thread(thrStart);

        MyThread ^myThr = gcnew MyThread();
        // Creating a Thread reference object in one line from a member method
        Thread ^thr2 = gcnew Thread(
            gcnew ParameterizedThreadStart(myThr, &MyThread::NonStaticThread));

    //  Uncomment for background vs foreground exploration
    //  thr1->IsBackground = true;
    //  thr2->IsBackground = true;

        // Actually starting the threads
        thr1->Start();
        thr2->Start("Parameterized");

        Console::WriteLine("Main Program Ends");
    }
```

The first thing of note is the difference between creating an instance of a delegate from a static method and creating an instance of a delegate from a member method:

```
gcnew ThreadStart(MyThread::StaticThread)
gcnew ThreadStart(myThr, &MyThread::MemberThread)

gcnew ParameterizedThreadStart(MyThread::StaticThread)
gcnew ParameterizedThreadStart(myThr, &MyThread::MemberThread)
```

The first parameter is a handle to the class that contains the delegate method. For a static method, there is no class handle, so the first parameter is not passed. The second parameter is a fully qualified method.

The second thing of note is that I had to use really big loops for this example to show the threading in process. For smaller loops, the first thread finished before the second thread even started. (Wow, computers are fast!)

Okay, execute StartingThreads.exe by pressing Ctrl-F5. This will compile the program and start it without the debugger. If no error results, you should get something like Figure 16-2.

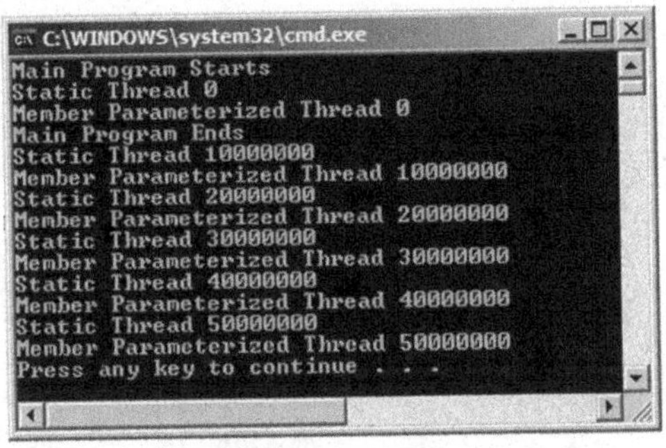

Figure 16-2. *The StartingThreads program in action*

Take a look at the top of your output. Your main program started and ended before the threads even executed their first loop. As you can see, foreground threads (which these are) continue to run even after the main thread ends.

If you were to uncomment these two lines, before the start method calls, with the lines

```
thr1->IsBackground = true;
thr2->IsBackground = true;
```

then you would find that the threads stop abruptly without completing when the main thread ends, just as you would expect. Something you might not expect, though, is that if you set only one of the threads to the background, it doesn't end when the main thread ends but instead continues until the second "foreground" thread completes.

Getting a Thread to Sleep

When you develop your thread, you may find that you don't need it to continually run or you might want to delay the thread while some other thread runs. To handle this, you could place a delay loop like a "do nothing" for loop. However, doing this wastes CPU cycles. What you should do instead is temporarily stop the thread or put it to sleep.

Doing this couldn't be easier. Simply add the following static Thread method:

```
Thread::Sleep(timeToSleepInMilliseconds);
```

This line causes the current thread to go to sleep for the interval specified either in milliseconds or using the TimeSpan structure. The TimeSpan structure specifies a time interval and is created using multiple overloaded constructors:

```
TimeSpan(Int64 ticks);
TimeSpan(Int32 hours,Int32 minutes,Int32 seconds);
TimeSpan(Int32 days,Int32 hours,Int32 minutes,Int32 seconds);
TimeSpan(Int32 days,Int32 hours,Int32 minutes,Int32 seconds,Int32 milliseconds);
```

The Sleep() method also takes two special values: Infinite, which means sleep forever, and 0, which means give up the rest of the thread's current CPU time slice.

A neat thing to notice is that main() and WinMain() are also threads. This means you can use Thread::Sleep() to make any application sleep. In Listing 16-2, both worker threads and the main thread are all put to sleep temporarily.

Listing 16-2. *Making a Thread Sleep*

```
using namespace System;
using namespace System::Threading;

ref class MyThread
{
public:
    static void ThreadFunc(Object ^Name);
};

void MyThread::ThreadFunc(Object ^Name)
{
    for (int i = 0; i < 101; i++)
    {
        if (i % 10 == 0)
            Console::WriteLine("{0} {1}", Name, i.ToString());
        Thread::Sleep(10);
    }
}

void main()
{
    Console::WriteLine("Main Program Starts");

    Thread ^thr1 =
        gcnew Thread(gcnew ParameterizedThreadStart(&MyThread::ThreadFunc));
    Thread ^thr2 =
        gcnew Thread(gcnew ParameterizedThreadStart(&MyThread::ThreadFunc));

    thr1->Start("Thread1");
    thr2->Start("Thread2");

    int iHour = 0;
    int iMin = 0;
    int iSec = 1;
    Thread::Sleep(TimeSpan(iHour, iMin, iSec));

    Console::WriteLine("Main Program Ends");
}
```

Listing 16-2 has a couple of additional bits of bonus logic. First, it shows how to get a handle to the current thread using the Thread class's CurrentThread property:

```
Thread ^thr = Thread::CurrentThread;
```

Second, it shows how to assign a name to a thread using the Thread class's Name property, which you can retrieve later within the thread:

```
// When creating thread add
thr1->Name = "Thread1";
// Then later in thread itself
String ^threadName = Thread::CurrentThread->Name;
```

The results of SleepingThreads.exe are shown in Figure 16-3.

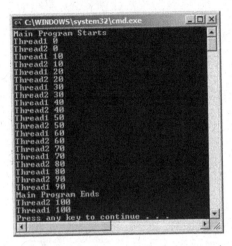

Figure 16-3. *The SleepingThreads program in action*

Notice that the main thread ends in the middle of the thread execution, instead of before it starts, like in the previous example. The reason is the main thread is put to sleep while the worker threads run, and then it wakes up just before the other threads end.

Aborting Threads

You might, on occasion, require that a thread be terminated within another thread before it runs through to its normal end. In such a case, you would call the `Abort()` method. This method will, normally, permanently stop the execution of a specified thread.

Notice that I used the term "normally." What actually happens when a thread is requested to stop with the `Abort()` method is that a `ThreadAbortException` exception is thrown within the thread. This exception, like any other, can be caught but, unlike most other exceptions, `ThreadAbortException` is special as it gets rethrown at the end of the `catch` block unless the aborting thread's `ResetAbort()` method is called. Calling the `ResetAbort()` method cancels the abort, which in turn prevents `ThreadAbortException` from stopping the thread.

■**Caution** Something that you must be aware of is that an aborted thread can't be restarted. If you attempt to do so, a `ThreadStateException` exception is thrown instead.

Listing 16-3 shows the `Abort()` method in action. First it creates two threads, and then it aborts them. Just for grins and giggles, I then try to restart an aborted thread, which promptly throws an exception.

Listing 16-3. *Aborting a Thread*

```
using namespace System;
using namespace System::Threading;

ref class MyThread
{
public:
    static void ThreadFunc(Object ^Name);
};

void MyThread::ThreadFunc(Object ^Name)
{
    Thread ^thr = Thread::CurrentThread;
    try
    {
        for (int i = 0; i < 100; i++)
        {
            Console::WriteLine("{0} {1}", Name, i.ToString());
            Thread::Sleep(1);
        }
        return;
    }
    catch (ThreadAbortException^)
    {
        Console::WriteLine("{0} Aborted", Name);
        // Reset the abort so that the method will continue processing
        // thr->ResetAbort();
    }
}

void main()
{
    Console::WriteLine("Main Program Starts");

    Thread ^thr1 =
        gcnew Thread(gcnew ParameterizedThreadStart(&MyThread::ThreadFunc));
    Thread ^thr2 =
        gcnew Thread(gcnew ParameterizedThreadStart(&MyThread::ThreadFunc));

    thr1->Start("Thread1");
    thr2->Start("Thread2");

    Thread::Sleep(20);
    thr1->Abort();
    Thread::Sleep(40);
    thr2->Abort();
```

```
try
{
    thr1->Start();
}
catch (ThreadStateException ^tse)
{
    Console::WriteLine(tse->ToString());
}
Console::WriteLine("Main Program Ends");
}
```

In the exception of the Thread method, I've added (but commented out) the code required to reset the abort so that the thread continues instead of ending.

Figure 16-4 shows AbortingThreads.exe in action. As you can see, even though I catch the ThreadAbortException exception in the thread, the thread still aborts after leaving the catch block. As expected, when I try to restart a thread, a ThreadStateException exception is thrown.

Figure 16-4. *The AbortingThreads program in action*

Joining Threads

Back in the first example in this chapter, you saw that after you created your threads and started them, the main program then proceeded to terminate. In the case of the first example this is fine, but what if you want to execute something after the threads finish? Or, more generally, how do you handle the scenario where one thread needs to wait for another thread to complete before continuing?

What you need to do is join the threads using the Thread class's Join() method. You can join threads in three different ways by using one of the three overloaded Join() methods. The first overloaded method takes no parameters and waits until the thread completes, and the second takes an int parameter and then waits the parameter's specified number of milliseconds or for the thread to terminate, whichever is shorter. The third overload takes a TimeSpan struct and functions the same as the previous overload.

The simple example in Listing 16-4 joins the main thread to the first worker thread and then waits for the worker thread to complete before starting the second worker thread.

Listing 16-4. *Joining Threads*

```
using namespace System;
using namespace System::Threading;

ref class MyThread
{
public:
    static void ThreadFunc(Object ^Name);
};

void MyThread::ThreadFunc(Object ^Name)
{
    for (int i = 0; i < 5; i++)
    {
        Console::WriteLine("{0} {1}", Name, i.ToString());
        Thread::Sleep(1);
    }
}

void main()
{
    Console::WriteLine("Before starting thread");

    Thread ^thr1 =
        gcnew Thread(gcnew ParameterizedThreadStart(&MyThread::ThreadFunc));
    Thread ^thr2 =
        gcnew Thread(gcnew ParameterizedThreadStart(&MyThread::ThreadFunc));

    thr1->Start("Thread1");
    thr1->Join();

    thr2->Start("Thread2");

    Console::WriteLine("End of Main");
}
```

Figure 16-5 shows JoiningThreads.exe in action. Notice that the main thread terminates again after both threads are started, but this time the main thread waited for the first worker thread to end before starting the second thread.

Figure 16-5. *The JoiningThreads program in action*

Interrupting, Suspending, and Resuming Threads

It is completely possible to take a worker thread and place it in a tight loop, waiting for some event to occur. Doing this would be a big waste of CPU cycles. It would be better to let the worker thread sleep and then be woken up when the event occurs. You can do exactly that using a combination of Sleep() and Interrupt() methods, in conjunction with the System::Threaded::ThreadInterruptedException exception.

The basic idea is to put the worker thread to sleep using the static Sleep() method, and then interrupt (the sleep of) the worker thread when the required event occurs using the Interrupt() member method. Simple enough, I think, except that the Interrupt() method throws a ThreadInterruptedException exception instead of just terminating the Sleep() method. Thus, you need to place the Sleep() method in the try of a try/catch block, and then have the worker thread continue execution in the catch.

Here's the worker thread:

```
try
{
    // Wait for event to occur
    Thread::Sleep(Timeout::Infinite);
}
catch(ThreadInterruptedException^)
{
    /*continue processing*/
}
```

Here's some other thread:

```
WorkerThread->Interrupt();
```

The preceding scenario will work if the worker thread knows when to go to sleep. It may also be necessary to allow another thread to temporarily stop a different thread and then restart it again later.

For example, a worker thread could be doing some intense number crunching when along comes another thread that needs to put a large graphic up on the monitor as soon as possible (the user interface should almost always get priority).

You can resolve this scenario in at least three ways. First, you could do nothing special and let the multithreading engine slowly display the graphic. Second, you could raise the priority of the graphic display thread (or lower the priority of the worker thread), thus giving the graphic display more cycles. Or third, you could suspend the worker thread, then draw the graphic and, finally, resume the worker thread. Doing it this way requires two methods and would be done like this:

```
WorkerThread->Suspend();
// Do stuff
WorkerThread->Resume();
```

■ **Caution** Choosing either the second or third methods mentioned previously can have some negative side effects. Changing priorities could lead to sluggish interface response time because the interface thread is now a lower priority. Suspending a thread could lead to thread deadlocking or starvation as the suspended thread might hold resources needed by other threads.

For example, the worker thread from the preceding example may hold a lock on a database that the drawing thread uses to draw the display. Since the worker thread is suspended, it will never relinquish its hold on the database, and the drawing thread will wait forever for the hold on the database to be released.

> **Note** The Suspend() and Resume() methods have been marked as obsolete in version 2.0 of the .NET Framework and will probably disappear in future releases. The reason is they are so deadlock-prone that using them in all but the simplest cases is problematic. Microsoft suggests using the Monitor, Mutex, Event, or Semaphore instead, which I cover later in the chapter (except for Event, as I covered that way back in Chapter 4). I am leaving this section (from the previous version of the book) in the book for those of you who have used these methods in the past, but I suggest that you refrain from implementing anything new using them.

Listing 16-5 shows how to implement both of the Thread class's sleep/interrupt and suspend/resume functionalities.

Listing 16-5. *Sleeping/Interrupting and Suspending/Resuming a Thread*

```
using namespace System;
using namespace System::Threading;

ref class MyThread
{
public:
    static void ThreadFunc1();
    static void ThreadFunc2();
};

void MyThread::ThreadFunc1()
{
    Console::WriteLine("Before long sleep");
    try
    {
        Thread::Sleep(Timeout::Infinite);
    }
    catch(ThreadInterruptedException^){/*continue processing*/}
    Console::WriteLine("After long sleep");
}

void MyThread::ThreadFunc2()
{
    for (int i = 0; i < 5; i++)
    {
        Console::WriteLine("Thread {0}",i.ToString());
        Thread::Sleep(2);
    }
}

void main()
{
    Thread ^thr1 = gcnew Thread(gcnew ThreadStart(&MyThread::ThreadFunc1));
    Thread ^thr2 = gcnew Thread(gcnew ThreadStart(&MyThread::ThreadFunc2));

    Console::WriteLine("Sleep/interrupt thread");
    thr1->Start();
```

```
    Thread::Sleep(4);
    for (int i = 0; i < 4; i++)
    {
        Console::WriteLine("**Main2 {0}", i.ToString());
        Thread::Sleep(2);
    }
    thr1->Interrupt();
    thr1->Join();

    Console::WriteLine("\nSuspend/resume thread");
    thr2->Start();

    Thread::Sleep(8);
    thr2->Suspend();

    for (int i = 0; i < 4; i++)
    {
        Console::WriteLine("**Main1 {0}", i.ToString());
        Thread::Sleep(2);
    }
    thr2->Resume();
}
```

You can see the results of ISRingThreads.exe in Figure 16-6.

Figure 16-6. *The ISRingThreads program in action*

Notice how both provide a similar flow through their threads. The major difference between sleep/interrupt and suspend/resume is which thread initiates the temporary stopping of the worker thread.

Using ThreadPools

As the name of the class suggests, System::Threading::ThreadPool provides a system-managed pool of threads on which to run your application's threads. Being managed by the system, your multi-threaded application loses control of how threads are created, managed, and cleaned up. But, in many cases, your application has no real need to manage threads, as aborting, joining, interrupting, suspending, and resuming a thread in an application is not always needed.

What you lose in control you get back in ease of use. Plus, it simplifies multithreaded programming, especially if your application is made up of numerous threads. With thread pooling, you're able to focus on developing your business logic without getting bogged down with thread management.

For those of you who are interested, this is, at a high level, how a thread pool works. Basically, a thread pool is created the first time ThreadPool is called. Thread pools use a queuing system that places a work item (a thread request) on an available thread pool thread. If no thread pool thread is available, then a new one is created up to a default maximum of 25 threads per available processor. (You can change this maximum using CorSetMaxThreads, defined in the mscoree.h file.) If the maximum number of threads is reached, then the work item remains on a queue until a thread pool thread becomes available. There is no limit to the number of work items that can be queued. (Well, that's not quite true. You are restricted to available memory.)

Each thread pool thread runs at the default priority and can't be cancelled.

Note Thread pool threads are background threads. As such, you need the main program thread or some other foreground thread to remain alive the entire life of the application.

You add a work item to the thread pool queue by calling the ThreadPool class's static QueueUserWorkItem() method. The QueueUserWorkItem() method takes a WaitCallback delegate as a parameter and an Object handle parameter to allow you to pass information to the generated thread. (The method is overloaded so that you don't have to pass an Object parameter if none is required.) The WaitCallback delegate has the following signature:

```
public delegate void WaitCallback(Object^ state);
```

The Object^ state parameter will contain the Object handle that was passed as the second parameter to the QueueUserWorkItem() method. The QueueUserWorkItem() method returns true if the method successfully queues the work item; otherwise, it returns false.

The example in Listing 16-6 shows how simple it is to create two ThreadPool threads.

Listing 16-6. *Using Thread Pools*

```
using namespace System;
using namespace System::Threading;

ref class MyThread
{
public:
    void ThreadFunc(Object^ stateInfo);
};

void MyThread::ThreadFunc(Object^ stateInfo)
{
    for (int i = 0; i < 10; i++)
    {
        Console::WriteLine("{0} {1}", stateInfo, i.ToString());
        Thread::Sleep(100);
    }
}
```

```
void main()
{
    Console::WriteLine("Main Program Starts");

    MyThread ^myThr1 = gcnew MyThread();

    ThreadPool::QueueUserWorkItem(
        gcnew WaitCallback(myThr1, &MyThread::ThreadFunc), "Thread1");
    ThreadPool::QueueUserWorkItem(
        gcnew WaitCallback(myThr1, &MyThread::ThreadFunc), "Thread2");

    Thread::Sleep(2000);
    Console::WriteLine("Main Program Ends");
}
```

There are only a couple of things of note in the preceding example. The first is the second parameter in the call to the QueueUserWorkItem() method. This parameter is actually extremely flexible, as you can pass it any managed data type supported by the .NET Framework. In the preceding example, I passed a String, but you could pass it an instance to an extremely large and complex class if you want.

The second thing of note is the Sleep() method used to keep the main thread alive. Once the main thread dies, so do all the threads in the ThreadPool, no matter what they are doing.

You can see the results of ThreadPooling.exe in Figure 16-7.

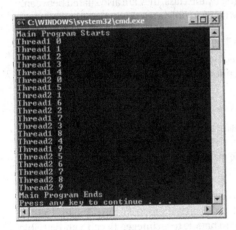

Figure 16-7. *The ThreadPooling program in action*

Synchronization

As threads become more complex, you will find that they more than likely start to share resources between themselves. The problem with shared resources is that only one thread can safely update them at any one time. Multiple threads that attempt to change a shared resource at the same time will eventually have subtle errors start to occur in themselves.

These errors revolve around the fact that Windows uses preemptive mode multithreading and that C++/CLI commands are not atomic or, in other words, require multiple commands to complete. This combination means that it is possible for a single C++/CLI operation to be interrupted partway through its execution. This, in turn, can lead to a problem if this interruption happens to occur when updating a shared resource.

For example, say two threads are sharing the responsibility of updating a collection of objects based on some shared integer index. As both threads update the collection using the shared index, most of the time everything will be fine, but every once in a while something strange will happen due to the bad timing of the preemptive switch between threads. What happens is that when thread 1 is in the process of incrementing the shared integer index and just as it is about to store the newly incremented index into the shared integer, thread 2 takes control. This thread then proceeds to increment the shared value itself and updates the collection object associated with the index. When thread 1 gets control back, it completes its increment command by storing its increment value in the stored index, overwriting the already incremented value (from thread 2) with the same value. This will cause thread 1 to update the same collection object that thread 2 has already completed. Depending on what updates are being done to the collection, this repeated update could be nasty. For example, maybe the collection was dispersing $1 million to each object in the collection and now that account in question has been dispersed $2 million.

The ThreadStatic Attribute

Sometimes your synchronizing problem is the result of the threads trying to synchronize in the first place. What I mean is you have static class scope variables that store values within a single threaded environment correctly but, when the static variables are migrated to a multithreaded environment, they go haywire.

The problem is that static variables are not only shared by the class, they are also shared between threads. This may be what you want, but there are times when you only want the static variables to be unique between threads.

To solve this, you need to use the System::Threading::ThreadStaticAttribute class. A static variable with an attribute of [ThreadStatic] is not shared between threads. Each thread has its own separate instance of the static variable, which is independently updated. This means that each thread will have a different value in the static variable.

Caution You can't use the class's static constructor to initialize a [ThreadStatic] variable because the call to the constructor only initializes the main thread's instance of the variable. Remember, each thread has its own instance of the [ThreadStatic] variable and that includes the main thread.

Listing 16-7 shows how to create a thread static class variable. It involves nothing more than placing the attribute [ThreadStatic] in front of the variable that you want to make thread static. I added a little wrinkle to this example by making the static variable a handle to an integer. Because the variable is a handle, you need to create an instance of it. Normally, you would do that in the static constructor, but for a thread static variable this doesn't work, as then only the main thread's version of the variable has been allocated. To fix this, you need to allocate the static variable within the thread's execution.

Listing 16-7. *Synchronizing Using the ThreadStatic Attribute*

```
using namespace System;
using namespace System::Threading;

ref class MyThread
{
public:

    [ThreadStatic]
```

```
    static int ^iVal;

public:
    static MyThread()
    {
        iVal = gcnew int;
    }

    void ThreadFunc();
    void SubThreadFunc();
};

void MyThread::ThreadFunc()
{
    iVal = gcnew int;
    iVal = 7;

    SubThreadFunc();
}

void MyThread::SubThreadFunc()
{
    int max = *iVal + 5;

    while (*iVal < max)
    {
        Thread ^thr = Thread::CurrentThread;
        Console::WriteLine("{0} {1}", thr->Name, iVal->ToString());
        Thread::Sleep(1);
        (*iVal)++;
    }
}

void main()
{
    Console::WriteLine("Before starting thread");

    MyThread ^myThr1 = gcnew MyThread();

    Thread ^thr1 =
        gcnew Thread(gcnew ThreadStart(myThr1, &MyThread::ThreadFunc));
    Thread ^thr2 =
        gcnew Thread(gcnew ThreadStart(myThr1, &MyThread::ThreadFunc));

    Thread::CurrentThread->Name = "Main";
    thr1->Name = "Thread1";
    thr2->Name = "Thread2";

    thr1->Start();
    thr2->Start();

    myThr1->iVal = 5;
    myThr1->SubThreadFunc();
}
```

Unsafe Code Referencing a member variable by address is classified as unsafe, so to get this example to compile, you need to use the `/clr:pure` or just plain `/clr` option.

First off, when you comment out the `[ThreadStatic]` attribute and run the ThreadStaticVars.exe program, you get the output shown in Figure 16-8. Notice how the value is initialized three times and then gets incremented without regard to the thread that is running. Maybe this is what you want, but normally it isn't.

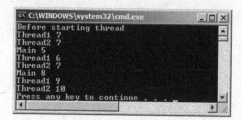

Figure 16-8. *The attribute commented-out ThreadStaticVars program in action*

Okay, uncomment the `[ThreadStatic]` attribute and run ThreadStaticVars.exe again. This time you'll get the output shown in Figure 16-9. Notice now that each thread (including the main thread) has its own unique instance of the static variable.

Figure 16-9. *The ThreadStaticVars program in action*

Notice that the static constructor works as expected for the main thread, whereas for worker threads you need to create an instance of the variable before you use it. To avoid having the main thread create a new instance of the static variable, the class separates the logic of initializing the variable from the main logic that the thread is to perform, thus allowing the main thread to call the application's logic without executing the static variable's gcnew command.

The Interlocked Class

The opposite of the thread static variable is the interlocked variable. In this case, you want the static variable to be shared across the class and between threads. The `Interlocked` class provides you with a thread-safe way of sharing an integer type variable (probably used for an index of some sort) between threads.

For the sharing of an integer to be thread-safe, the operations to the integer must be atomic. In other words, operations such as incrementing, decrementing, and exchanging variables can't be preempted partway through the operation. Thus, the $2 million problem from earlier won't occur.

Using an interlocked variable is fairly straightforward. Instead of using the increment (++) or decrement (--) operator, all you need to do is use the corresponding static System::Threading::Interlocked class method. Notice in the following declarations that you pass a handle to the variable you want interlocked and not the value:

```
static Int32 Interlocked::Increment(Int32 ^ival);
static Int64 Interlocked::Decrement(Int64 ^lval);
static Object^ Exchange(&Object^ oval, Object ^oval);
```

Listing 16-8 shows a thread-safe way of looping using an interlocked variable.

Listing 16-8. *Using the Interlocked Class*

```
using namespace System;
using namespace System::Threading;

ref class MyThread
{
    static int iVal;

public:

    static MyThread()
    {
        iVal = 5;
    }

    void ThreadFunc();
};

void MyThread::ThreadFunc()
{
    while (Interlocked::Increment(iVal) < 15)
    {
        Thread ^thr = Thread::CurrentThread;
        Console::WriteLine("{0} {1}", thr->Name, iVal);
        Thread::Sleep(1);
    }
}


void main()
{
    MyThread ^myThr1 = gcnew MyThread();

    Thread ^thr1 =
        gcnew Thread(gcnew ThreadStart(myThr1, &MyThread::ThreadFunc));
    Thread ^thr2 =
        gcnew Thread(gcnew ThreadStart(myThr1, &MyThread::ThreadFunc));
```

```
    thr1->Name = "Thread1";
    thr2->Name = "Thread2";

    thr1->Start();
    thr2->Start();
}
```

Notice that unlike the thread static variable, the static constructor works exactly as it should as there is only one instance of the static variable being shared by all threads.

Figure 16-10 shows InterlockedVars.exe in action, a simple count from 6 to 14, though the count is incremented by different threads.

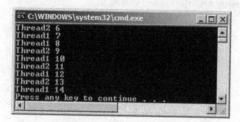

Figure 16-10. *The InterlockedVars program in action*

The Monitor Class

The Monitor class is useful if you want a block of code to be executed as single threaded, even if the code block is found in a thread that can be multithreaded. The basic idea is that you use the static methods found in the System::Threading::Monitor class to specify the start and end points of the code to be executed as a single task.

It is possible to have more than one monitor in an application. Therefore, a unique Object is needed for each monitor that you want the application to have. To create the Object to set the Monitor lock on, simply create a standard static Object:

```
static Object^ MonitorObject = gcnew Object();
```

You then use this Object along with one of the following two methods to specify the starting point that the Monitor will lock for single thread execution:

- Enter() method
- TryEnter() method

The Enter() method is the easier and safer of the two methods to use. It has the following syntax:

```
static void Enter(Object^ MonitorObject);
```

Basically, the Enter() method allows a thread to continue executing if no other thread is within the code area specified by the Monitor. If another thread occupies the Monitor area, then this thread will sit and wait until the other thread leaves the Monitor area (known as *blocking*).

The TryEnter() method is a little more complex in that it has three overloads:

```
static bool TryEnter(Object^ MonitorObject);
static bool TryEnter(Object^ MonitorObject, int wait);
static bool TryEnter(Object^ MonitorObject, TimeSpan wait);
```

The first parameter is the MonitorObject, just like the Enter() method. The second parameter that can be added is the amount of time to wait until you can bypass the block and continue. Yes, you read that right. The TryEnter() method will pass through even if some other thread is currently in the Monitor area. The TryEnter() method will set the start of the Monitor area only if it entered the Monitor when no other thread was in the Monitor area. When the TryEnter() method enters an unoccupied Monitor area, then it returns true; otherwise, it returns false.

This doesn't sound very safe, does it? If this method isn't used properly, it isn't safe. Why would you use this method if it's so unsafe? It's designed to allow the programmer the ability to do something other than sit at a blocked monitor and wait, possibly until the application is stopped or the machine reboots. The proper way to use the TryEnter() method is to check the Monitor area. If it's occupied, wait a specified time for the area to be vacated. If, after that time, it's still blocked, go do something other than enter the blocked area:

```
if (!Monitor::TryEnter(MonitorObject))
{
    Console::WriteLine("Not able to lock");
    return;
}
//...Got lock go ahead
```

Of course, as you continue into the blocked Monitor area, your code is no longer multithread-safe. Not a thing to do without a very good reason. If you code the TryEnter() method to continue into the Monitor area, even if the area is blocked, be prepared for the program to not work properly.

To set the end of the Monitor area, you use the static Exit() method, which has the following syntax:

```
static void Exit(Object^ MonitorObject);
```

Not much to say about this method other than once it's executed, the Monitor area blocked by either the Entry() method or the TryEnter() method is opened up again for another thread to enter.

In most cases, using these three methods should be all you need. For those rare occasions, the Monitor provides three additional methods that allow another thread to enter a Monitor area even if it's currently occupied. The first method is the Wait() method, which releases the lock on a Monitor area and blocks the current thread until it reacquires the lock. To reacquire a lock, the block thread must wait for another thread to call a Pulse() or PulseAll() method from within the Monitor area. The main difference between the Pulse() and PulseAll() methods is that Pulse() notifies the next thread waiting that it's ready to release the Monitor area, whereas PulseAll() notifies all waiting threads.

Listing 16-9 shows how to code threads for a Monitor. The example is composed of three threads. The first two call synchronized Wait() and Pulse() methods, and the last thread calls a TryEnter() method, which it purposely blocks to show how to use the method correctly.

Listing 16-9. *Synchronizing Using the Monitor Class*

```
using namespace System;
using namespace System::Threading;

ref class MyThread
{
    static Object^ MonitorObject = gcnew Object();

public:
    void TFuncOne();
    void TFuncTwo();
    void TFuncThree();
};
```

```cpp
void MyThread::TFuncOne()
{
    Console::WriteLine("TFuncOne    enters monitor");
    Monitor::Enter(MonitorObject);
    for (Int32 i = 0; i < 3; i++)
    {
        Console::WriteLine("TFuncOne    Waits {0}", i.ToString());
        Monitor::Wait(MonitorObject);
        Console::WriteLine("TFuncOne    Pulses {0}", i.ToString());
        Monitor::Pulse(MonitorObject);
        Thread::Sleep(1);
    }
    Monitor::Exit(MonitorObject);
    Console::WriteLine("TFuncOne    exits monitor");
}

void MyThread::TFuncTwo()
{
    Console::WriteLine("TFuncTwo    enters monitor");
    Monitor::Enter(MonitorObject);
    for (Int32 i = 0; i < 3; i++)
    {
        Console::WriteLine("TFuncTwo    Pulses {0}", i.ToString());
        Monitor::Pulse(MonitorObject);
        Thread::Sleep(1);
        Console::WriteLine("TFuncTwo    Waits {0}", i.ToString());
        Monitor::Wait(MonitorObject);
    }
    Monitor::Exit(MonitorObject);
    Console::WriteLine("TFuncTwo    exits monitor");
}

void MyThread::TFuncThree()
{
    if (!Monitor::TryEnter(MonitorObject))
    {
        Console::WriteLine("TFuncThree was not able to lock");
        return;
    }
    Console::WriteLine("TFuncThree got a lock");

    Monitor::Exit(MonitorObject);
    Console::WriteLine("TFuncThree exits monitor");
}


void main()
{
    MyThread ^myThr1 = gcnew MyThread();

    (gcnew Thread(gcnew ThreadStart(myThr1, &MyThread::TFuncOne)))->Start();
    Thread::Sleep(2);
```

```
(gcnew Thread(gcnew ThreadStart(myThr1, &MyThread::TFuncTwo)))->Start();
Thread::Sleep(2);

for (int i = 0; i < 2; i++)
{
    (gcnew Thread(
        gcnew ThreadStart(myThr1, &MyThread::TFuncThree)))->Start();
    Thread::Sleep(50);
}
}
```

Notice that a Monitor area need not be a single block of code but, instead, can be multiple blocks spread out all over the process. In fact, it's not apparent due to the simplicity of the example, but the Monitor object can be in another class, and the Monitor areas can spread across multiple classes so long as the Monitor object is accessible to all Monitor area classes and the Monitor areas fall within the same process.

The Wait() and Pulse() methods can be tricky to synchronize and, if you fail to call a Pulse() method for a Wait() method, the Wait() method will block until the process is killed or the machine is rebooted. You can add timers to the Wait() method in the same fashion as you do the TryEnter() method, to avoid an infinite wait state. Personally, I think you should avoid using the Wait() and Pulse() methods unless you have no other choice.

Figure 16-11 shows SyncByMonitor.exe in action.

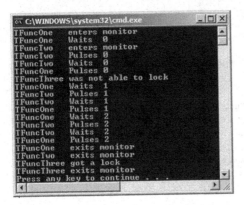

Figure 16-11. *The SyncByMonitor program in action*

The Mutex Class

The Mutex class is very similar to the Monitor class in the way it synchronizes between threads. You define regions of code that must be single threaded or MUTually EXclusive, and then, when a thread runs, it can only enter the region if no other thread is in the region. What makes the Mutex class special is that it can define regions across processes. In other words, a thread will be blocked in process 1 if some thread in process 2 is in the same name Mutex region.

Before I go into detail about Mutex, let's sidetrack a little and see how you can have the .NET Framework start one process within another. Creating a process inside another process is fairly easy to do, but within the .NET Framework it's far from intuitive because the methods to create a process are found within the System::Diagnostic namespace.

The procedure for creating a process is similar to that of a thread in that you create a process and then start it. The actual steps involved in creating a process, though, are a little more involved. To create a process, you simply create an instance using the default constructor:

```
Process^ proc = gcnew Process();
```

Next, you need to populate several properties found in the StartInfo property. These properties will tell the CLR where the process is, what parameters to pass, whether to start the process in its own shell, and whether to redirect standard input. There are several other properties as well, but these are the most important:

```
proc->StartInfo->FileName = "../debug/SyncByMutex.exe";
proc->StartInfo->Arguments = "1";
proc->StartInfo->UseShellExecute = false;
proc->StartInfo->RedirectStandardInput = true;
```

Finally, once the process is defined, you start it:

```
proc->Start();
```

Listing 16-10 shows how to start two copies of the Mutex process that you will build next in this chapter.

Listing 16-10. *Creating Subprocesses*

```
using namespace System;
using namespace System::Diagnostics;
using namespace System::Threading;


void main()
{
    Process^ proc1 = gcnew Process();
    proc1->StartInfo->FileName = "../debug/SyncByMutex.exe";
    proc1->StartInfo->Arguments = "1";
    proc1->StartInfo->UseShellExecute = false;
    proc1->StartInfo->RedirectStandardInput = true;
    proc1->Start();

    Process^ proc2 = gcnew Process();
    proc2->StartInfo->FileName = "../debug/SyncByMutex.exe";
    proc2->StartInfo->Arguments = "2";
    proc2->StartInfo->UseShellExecute = false;
    proc2->StartInfo->RedirectStandardInput = true;
    proc2->Start();

    Thread::Sleep(5000);  // Added just to clean up console display
}
```

You don't need to use MutexSpawn.exe to run the following Mutex example, but it makes things easier when you're trying to test multiple processes running at the same time.

Okay, let's move on to actually looking at the Mutex class. In general, you'll use only three methods on a regular basis within the Mutex class:

- The constructor
- WaitOne()
- ReleaseMutex()

Unlike the Monitor class, in which you use a static member, the Mutex class requires you to create an instance and then access its member methods. Like any other class, to create an instance of Mutex requires you call its constructor. The Mutex constructor provides five overloads:

```
Mutex();
Mutex(Boolean owner);
Mutex(Boolean owner, String^ name);
Mutex(Boolean owner, String^ name, &Boolean createdNew);
Mutex(Boolean owner, String^ name, &Boolean createdNew,
                          MutexSecurity^ mutexSecurity);
```

When you create the Mutex object, you specify whether you want it to have ownership of the Mutex or, in other words, block the other threads trying to enter the region. Be careful, though, that the constructor doesn't cause a thread to block. This requires the use of the WaitOne() method, which you'll see later in the chapter.

You can create either a named or unnamed instance of a Mutex object but, to share a Mutex across processes, you need to give it a name. When you provide a Mutex with a name, the Mutex constructor will look for another Mutex with the same name. If it does find one, then they will synchronize blocks of code together.

The third constructor adds an output parameter that will have a value of true if this call was the first constructor to build a Mutex of the specified name; otherwise, the name already exists and will have the value of false.

The last constructor adds access control security to be applied to the named Mutex. This form of the constructor is beyond the scope of this book, but basically it allows the addition of access right rules to the named Mutex.

Once a Mutex object exists, you then must tell it to wait for the region to be unoccupied before entering. You do this using the Mutex class's WaitOne() member method:

```
bool WaitOne();
bool WaitOne(int milliseconds, bool exitContext);
bool WaitOne(TimeSpan span, bool exitContext);
```

The WaitOne() method is similar to a combination of the Monitor class's Enter() and TryEnter() methods, in that the WaitOne() method will wait indefinitely like the Monitor::Enter() method if you pass it no parameters. If you pass it parameters, though, it blocks for the specified time and then passes through like the Monitor::TryEnter() method. Just like the TryEnter() method, you should not, normally, let the thread execute the code within the Mutex region, as that will make the region not thread-safe.

Note The exitContext parameter you will probably ignore and set to false, as it is an advanced feature of Mutex where the WaitOne() method is called from inside a nondefault managed context. This can happen if your thread is inside a call to an instance of a class derived from ContextBoundObject. (Probably something that you won't do unless you are performing some rather advanced C++/CLI coding.)

To specify the end of the Mutex region, you use the Mutex class's ReleaseMutex() member method. Just like Monitor's Enter() and Exit() method combination, you need to match WaitOne() calls with ReleaseMutex() calls.

Listing 16-11 shows how to code a multithreaded single process. There is nothing special about it. In fact, I would normally just use a Monitor. Where this example really shines is when it is used in conjunction with MutexSpawn.exe, as it shows the Mutex class's real power of handling mutually exclusive regions of code across processes.

Listing 16-11. *Synchronizing Using the Mutex Class*

```
using namespace System;
using namespace System::Threading;

ref class MyThread
{
    static Mutex ^m = gcnew Mutex(false, "SyncByMutex");
public:
    static void ThreadFunc();
};

void MyThread::ThreadFunc()
{
    Random^ Rand = gcnew Random;

    Thread ^thr = Thread::CurrentThread;

    for (int i = 0; i < 4; i++)
    {
        m->WaitOne();

        Console::WriteLine("{0} Enter - {1}", thr->Name, i);
        Thread::Sleep(Rand->Next(20, 100)); // Simulate Work
        Console::WriteLine("{0} Exit  - {1}", thr->Name, i);
        m->ReleaseMutex();

        Thread::Sleep(Rand->Next(20, 100));
    }
}

int main(int argc, char *argv[])
{
    MyThread ^myThr = gcnew MyThread();

    Thread ^thr1 = gcnew Thread(gcnew ThreadStart(&MyThread::ThreadFunc));
    Thread ^thr2 = gcnew Thread(gcnew ThreadStart(&MyThread::ThreadFunc));

    thr1->Name =
        String::Format("Process {0} - Thread 1", gcnew String(argv[1]));
    thr2->Name =
        String::Format("Process {0} - Thread 2", gcnew String(argv[1]));

    thr1->Start();
    Thread::Sleep(50);
    thr2->Start();
}
```

Because you've already seen how to use the Monitor, the preceding example should be quite straightforward. The only real difference (other than the names of the methods being different, of course) is that the Mutex uses an instance object and member method calls, and the Monitor uses static method calls.

Figure 16-12 shows SyncByMutex.exe in action. Notice that threads in both processes are blocked and get access to the named Mutex region. Also notice that every enter line has a corresponding exit line printed before a new thread takes over the Mutex region.

Unsafe Code Passing arguments to the main() function is unsafe code as it uses pointers to pass the values. You need to use the /clr compiler option.

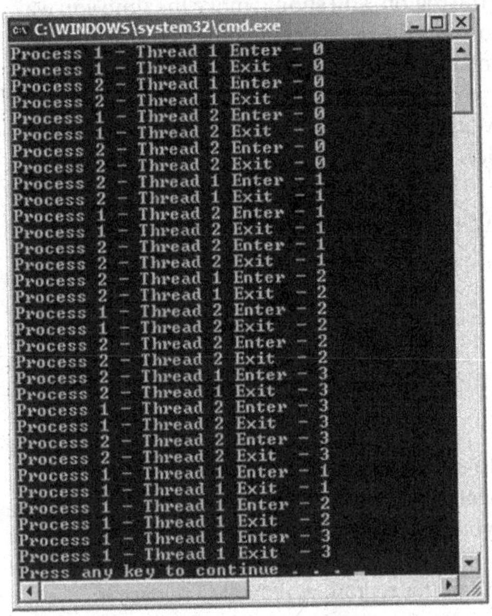

Figure 16-12. *A pair of SyncByMutex programs in action*

The ReaderWriterLock Class

The System::Threading::ReaderWriterLock class is a little different from the previous two types of synchronization in that it uses a multiple-reader/single-writer mechanism instead of the all-or-nothing approach. What this means is that the ReaderWriterLock class allows any number of threads to be in a block of synchronized code so long as they are only reading the shared resource within it. On the other hand, if a thread needs to change the shared resource, then all threads must vacate the region and give the updating thread exclusive access to it.

This type of synchronization makes sense because if a thread isn't changing anything, then it can't affect other threads. So, why not give the thread access to the shared resource?

The ReaderWriterLock class is very similar to both the Monitor class and the Mutex class. You specify a region to be synchronized and then have the threads block or pass into this area based on whether an update is happening in the region.

Like the Mutex class, you create an instance of the ReaderWriterLock class and work with its member method. To create an instance of the ReaderWriterLock object, you call its default constructor:

```
ReaderWriterLock();
```

Once you have a ReaderWriterLock object, you need to determine whether the region of code you want to block will do only reading of the shared resource or if it will change the shared resource.

If the region will only read the shared resource, then use the following code to set the region as read-only:

```
void AcquireReaderLock(int milliseconds);
void AcquireReaderLock(TimeSpan span);
```

You pass both of these overloaded methods a parameter, so specify the length of time you're willing to wait before entering the region. Due to the nature of this synchronization method, you can be sure of one thing: If you're blocked by this method call, then some other thread is currently updating the shared resource within. The reason you know some other thread is writing to the region is because the thread doesn't block if other threads in the region are only reading the shared resource.

Because you know that some thread is writing in the region, you should make the time you wait longer than the time needed to complete the write process. Unlike any of the other synchronization methods you've seen in this chapter, when this method times out, it throws an ApplicationException exception. So if you specify anything other than an infinite wait, you should catch the exception. The reason these methods throw an exception is that the only reason the wait time should expire is due to a thread deadlock condition. *Deadlock* is when two threads wait forever for each other to complete.

To specify the end of a synchronized read-only region, you need to release the region:

```
void ReleaseReaderLock();
```

If the region will require updating of the shared resource within the region, then you need to acquire a different lock:

```
void AcquireWriterLock(int milliseconds);
void AcquireWriterLock(TimeSpan span);
```

Like the reader, these methods pass parameters to avoid the deadlock situation. Unlike the reader lock, though, these methods block no matter what type of thread falls within the region, because they allow only one thread to have access. If you were to use only writer locks, then you would, in effect, be coding a Monitor or a Mutex.

As you would expect, once you're finished with the writer region, you need to release it:

```
void ReleaseWriterLock();
```

Listing 16-12 shows how to implement a multithread application using ReaderWriterLock. Also, just for grins and giggles, I added an Interlocked::Decrement() method to show you how that works as well.

Listing 16-12. *Synchronizing Using the ReaderWriterLock Class*

```
using namespace System;
using namespace System::Threading;

ref class MyThread
{
    static ReaderWriterLock ^RWLock = gcnew ReaderWriterLock();
    static int iVal = 4;

public:
    static void ReaderThread();
    static void WriterThread();
};

void MyThread::ReaderThread()
{
    String ^thrName = Thread::CurrentThread->Name;
    while (true)
    {
        try
        {
```

```
        RWLock->AcquireReaderLock(2);

        Console::WriteLine("Reading in {0}. iVal is {1}",
            thrName, iVal);

        RWLock->ReleaseReaderLock();
        Thread::Sleep(4);
    }
    catch (ApplicationException^)
    {
        Console::WriteLine("Reading in {0}. Timed out", thrName);
    }
    }
}

void MyThread::WriterThread()
{
    while (iVal > 0)
    {
        RWLock->AcquireWriterLock(-1);

        Interlocked::Decrement(iVal);
        Console::WriteLine("Writing iVal to {0}", iVal);
        Thread::Sleep(20);

        RWLock->ReleaseWriterLock();
    }
}

void main()
{
    Thread ^thr1 = gcnew Thread(gcnew ThreadStart(&MyThread::ReaderThread));
    Thread ^thr2 = gcnew Thread(gcnew ThreadStart(&MyThread::ReaderThread));
    Thread ^thr3 = gcnew Thread(gcnew ThreadStart(&MyThread::WriterThread));

    thr1->Name = "Thread1";
    thr2->Name = "Thread2";

    thr1->IsBackground = true;
    thr2->IsBackground = true;

    thr1->Start();
    thr2->Start();
    thr3->Start();

    thr3->Join();
    Thread::Sleep(2);
}
```

In actuality, the preceding code shouldn't need to use Interlock because the region is already locked for synchronization. Notice that I created infinite loops for my reader threads. To get these threads to exit at the completion of the program, I made the background threads.

Figure 16-13 shows SyncByRWLock.exe in action. Notice that I purposely don't specify a long-enough wait for the writing process to complete so that the exception is thrown.

Figure 16-13. *The SyncByRWLock program in action*

Summary

In this chapter, you examined multithreaded programming within the .NET Framework. You started by learning the basics of multithreaded programming. Next, you moved on and explored the two ways of creating threads: Thread and ThreadPool. You finished off the chapter by covering the weighty topic of thread synchronization.

This is a rather complex topic, and I have barely scratched the surface of it. In fact, most of the text in this chapter relates to how to implement multithreaded programming using the .NET Framework and not the theory behind it. If you find this topic interesting, there are many books and articles available on the proper implementation of multithreaded programming.

Now that you know how to write multithreaded code (which you'll need for the next chapter) you can move on to the next chapter and take a look at a third way of working over a network. This time, you will take complete control and code at the socket level.

CHAPTER 17

■ ■ ■

Network Programming

You have looked at using C++/CLI to create Web services, but what if you want to go a level deeper and create your own network-enabled applications? Maybe you are one of the thousands dreaming of making the next greatest multiplayer game (or possibly massively multiplayer game). Well, the .NET Framework will not disappoint you in that regard as it has taken good old socket programming and made it into a much easier and (I think) more powerful interface to work with.

Network programming is an extremely meaty topic, and many books have been written about it. Apress has a great book on the topic by Andrew Krowczyk, Vinod Kumar, Nauman Laghari, Ajit Mungale, Christian Nagel, Tim Parker, Alexandru Serban, and Srinivasa Sivakumar called *Pro .NET 1.1 Network Programming, Second Edition.* (A .NET 2.0 version is planned for summer 2006.) Like other books I've mentioned, this one is for C# developers, but you should be able to get the basics from it without any problems. If you are new to network development I recommend that you learn the basics first from a book like this before you read this chapter. I am going to assume you know about sockets, ports, packets, TCP, UDP, and the plethora of other concepts, features, and technologies associated with network programming. Because the topic is so large, what I will be covering instead is how to use C++/CLI and .NET Framework 2.0 to develop network-enabled applications.

More specifically, this chapter will examine .NET Framework socket coding in C++/CLI for both connected (TCP) and connectionless (UDP) sockets in both synchronous and asynchronous approaches. Along the way I will also cover some of the more commonly used helper classes provided by the .NET Framework.

I had originally thought I'd put this chapter after the one on Web services, but as this chapter developed I found that a chapter on threads was needed before I could cover the network programming concepts found in this chapter. So if you skipped the previous chapter on multithreaded programming, you might want to go back and give it a read.

The Network Namespaces

Both connected-oriented and connectionless networks use the same namespaces, System::Net and System::Net::Socket, to provide their functionality. Most protocol-related classes are found in System::Net, while System::Net::Socket contains a managed implementation of the Windows Sockets (Winsock) interface.

Therefore, you will probably find that all of your network-related code will include

```
using namespace System::Net;
using namespace System::Net::Sockets;
```

at the top of the class implementation files. Fortunately, because of their frequent use in the .NET Framework, the actual assembly containing the network functionality is system.dll, which is always included for you so you don't have to manually reference anything.

Connection-Oriented Sockets

I'm not sure I understand why some programmers try to present an aura of mystery around connection-oriented sockets, better known by its implementation method: TCP (Transmission Control Protocol). In its simplest form, you have two parties, a client and a server, that want to communicate with each other. To accomplish this, the server opens up a socket and then the client connects to it. Once the connection is made, messages, or more accurately data packets, are sent back and forth between them, and finally the connection between the two is closed.

Okay, you can complicate things by making elaborate message protocols between the client and server, but that is not always necessary. In fact, I would argue that if it is extremely complex, then maybe you might want to sit down and think your protocol through again.

The TCP Server

There are (at least) two parties involved in setting up a TCP connection: the client (or clients) and the server. Let's start with the server as it is in charge of providing a location to which the client(s) connect.

Four tasks must be performed by the server to create a location and establish a connection to a client:

1. Create a socket.

2. Bind the socket to an IPEndPoint. (An IPEndPoint is a combination of an IP address and a port.)

3. Set the socket to listening mode.

4. Accept the connection from the client in the socket.

Once the connection is established, then nearly any type of data can be sent from the server or received from the client. Usually communication between the client and server is transactional: One side sends a message and the other responds. But that is not always the case. It is perfectly all right for only one side to do all the sending, or to send multiple messages and then periodically receive a message. Basically, the sky's the limit. By the way, this sending and receiving of messages describes what is called a protocol, and as you can see, the complexity of the protocol can range from very simple to extremely complex.

In network programming, setting up the connection, sending and receiving messages, and closing the connection is the easy part. (Okay, under the covers, magic is happening but most programmers don't have to worry about that.) I think it's so easy that I'm going to jump ahead and show you one way to make a connection that can receive multiple clients. There are many methods of doing this, but I think the one I'm presenting here is the most straightforward (if you read the last chapter on multithreading, that is). Another reason for jumping ahead is because you are seldom going to write a server that connects to only a single client.

The process of creating a multiconnection server involves the same four steps mentioned earlier plus a fifth, which puts the accepted connection on its own thread to run stand-alone.

Create a Socket

Before you can do any TCP communication, you need to create a socket through which the messages will flow. For a TCP connection there is only one constructor that you have to worry about:

```
Socket^ socket = gcnew Socket(AddressFamily::InterNetwork,
                    SocketType::Stream,
                    ProtocolType::Tcp);
```

You may have to change the socket's name, but the rest of this code will pretty much stay the same until the new and improved version 6 IP addresses become more prevalent. At that time, the standard address family will most likely become InterNetworkV6 with a fallback to InterNetwork, if InterNetworkV6 isn't available.

The constructor shown here creates a socket to a version 4 IP address, which supports reliable, two-way, connection-based byte streams without duplication of data and without preservation of boundaries using the TCP protocol. (Now that is a mouthful!) We'll come back to this later as it has one potential gotcha for the unwary.

Bind the Socket to an IPEndPoint

Now that you have a socket sitting out there in the ether, it's time to bind it to a physical (sort of) address on your server machine. There are several ways of creating an IP endpoint address, but for the server you will probably use one of two ways, depending on the number of network interface cards (NICs) you have on your machine and how restrictive you want to make the connection to your server machine.

If you have only one NIC on your machine or you don't care which IP address the client connects on, then you use the following:

```
IPEndPoint^ iped = gcnew IPEndPoint(IPAddress::Any, portnumber);
```

This method says: listen on any IP address available on the machine or allow the client to connect on any IP address available on the machine. If on the other hand you want to restrict the client to a single IP address (most useful when you have more than one NIC), then you use something more like this:

```
IPEndPoint^ iped = gcnew IPEndPoint(IPAddress::Parse("127.0.0.1"), portnumber);
```

or any of the other available methods that resolve the IPAddress parameter to a single IP address. (There is a multitude of ways to get an IP address, but these two are the only ways I have needed for configuring a server.)

The port number can be any number from 0 to 65535, but to avoid conflicting with the *well-known* ports you should start at 1024 instead of 0. Also, you might find that another application is using your chosen port and then the system will not let you use it. To avoid this possibility, you should not hard-code the port within your code but instead make it an app.config, web.config, or Registry entry. (Of course, I'm not going to listen to my own advice and hard-code them but this is just to simplify the examples.)

By the way, to bind to a socket you simply call the following code:

```
socket->Bind(iped);
```

Set the Socket to Listening Mode

There isn't much to setting a socket to listening mode. You just call the Listen() method of the Socket class:

```
socket->Listen(10);
```

As you can see, it's hardly what I would call rocket science.

The Listen() method shown here takes a parameter of the number of pending connections allowed to be queued. Normally, you will just leave it at 10 and forget about it. But what happens if you are getting periodic connection request spikes that cause the pending connections queue to be exceeded? At this point the clients are told, "Sorry we're full, call back later..." (or something to that effect). To alleviate this, it is possible to tell the Listen() method to increase the size of the pending connection queue by setting the Listen() method's parameter to a higher value.

One possible problem is that you exceed the maximum pending connection queue size that the machine supports. To stop this from happening, you must make sure that the value you pass is less than or equal to SocketOptionName::MaxConnections. Here is the code to set the maximum pending connection queue size:

```
socket->Listen((int)SocketOptionName::MaxConnections);
```

Caution Even though SocketOptionName::MaxConnections appears to be a value that you would get or set using the GetSocketOption() or SetSocketOption() method, you actually just use it like a constant. I cover socket options later in the chapter.

Accept the Connection

The accepting of a connection is not any more difficult than any of the preceding steps; it's just one line of code:

```
Socket^ client = socket->Accept();
```

As you can see, you don't have much in the way of options. But believe it or not, how this command is processed is crucial in determining whether the server processes one or multiple clients. The reason is that the Accept() method blocks. That is to say, it waits until it gets a connection from a client. What this means to the program is that, without more than one thread of execution, the program will stop cold on this method, waiting for a connection.

So how do you get around this? There are multiple ways people have implemented their code to address this. I will show you the easiest method here (at least I think it's the easiest).

Place the Accepted Connection on Its Own Thread

Here is the simplest approach: Put the Accept() method in an infinite where loop and then create threads for each accepted client:

```
while(true)
{
    Console::WriteLine("Waiting for client connection.");
    Socket^ client = tcpListener->Accept();

    Thread ^thr = gcnew Thread(
        gcnew ParameterizedThreadStart(server, &TcpServer::ProcessThread));
    thr->Start(client);
}
```

With the addition of the ParameterizedThreadStart delegate in version 2.0 of the .NET Framework, things have gotten so easy. Just create a thread and pass on the newly accepted client socket. (Prior to version 2.0 you had to figure out some method of passing the client socket to the thread.)

You might want to review Chapter 16 if the above code looks strange to you, as I covered threads and ParameterizedThreadStart in quite a bit of detail in that chapter.

Now that there is an accepted client-server socket all set and ready, this is where things can get more complicated because now developers actually get a chance to do their own thing.

Send a Message

There are two ways of sending a message: either synchronously or asynchronously. I'll cover asynchronous in detail later in the chapter, but here is the basic difference: Synchronous sending blocks until the message is sent, whereas asynchronous sending does not block and continues execution of the code without stopping for the send to complete.

To send a message synchronously, you use one of the following overloaded Send() methods:

- Socket.Send (array<unsigned char>^)
- Socket.Send (array<unsigned char>^, SocketFlags)
- Socket.Send (array<unsigned char>^, int length, SocketFlags)
- Socket.Send (array<unsigned char>^, int start, int length, SocketFlags)

As you can see, each just expands upon the parameters from the other. The first parameter is the unsigned byte array of the message being sent. The first added parameter is SocketFlags (for a server it will most likely be None). Next is the length of the message being sent, and finally comes the start point within the unsigned char array (use this if you want to start sending from someplace other than the actual start of the message array).

With version 2.0 of the .NET Framework, two additional Send() methods were added, both allowing for the sending of unsigned char data within Generic ILists:

- Socket.Send (Generic IList)
- Socket.Send (Generic IList, SocketFlags)

When sending a message from a server, I usually use

```
array<unsigned char>^ message =
    Encoding::ASCII->GetBytes("Successful connection");
client->Send(message);
```

when the message buffer length matches the length of the data being sent (as shown here), or I use

```
client->Send(message, messagelength, SocketFlags::None);
```

when the message buffer length does not match the length of the data being sent—for example, when a generic length buffer is populated by a variable-length message.

Receive a Message

Just as when you're sending a message, you have two ways of receiving a message: synchronous or asynchronous. I'll cover asynchronous receive in detail later in the chapter, but the basic difference is as follows: Synchronous receiving blocks until the message is received, whereas asynchronous receiving sets up an event that waits for the message to be received and then continues on without stopping. Then when the message is finally received, the previously set up event is triggered.

The Receive() method overloads are exactly the same as the sends:

- int Socket.Receive (array<unsigned char>^)
- int Socket.Receive (array<unsigned char>^, SocketFlags)
- int Socket.Receive (array<unsigned char>^, int length, SocketFlags)
- int Socket.Receive (array<unsigned char>^, int start, int length, SocketFlags)

The first parameter is the received unsigned byte array of the message. The next parameter is SocketFlags—for a server most likely None or Peek (Peek allows you to look into the buffer without actually taking it out). Next is the length of the message to extract from the receive stream, and finally comes the start point within the receiving unsigned char array (use this if you want to place the incoming message someplace other than the actual start of the message array).

With version 2.0 of the .NET Framework, two additional Receive() methods were added, both allowing for the receiving of unsigned char data within Generic ILists:

- Socket.Receive (Generic IList)
- Socket.Receive (Generic IList, SocketFlags)

All receive methods return the number of unsigned char received or zero [0] if the connection was closed by the client. I use the zero [0] return value to my advantage as I use it to break out of my data input loops for each instance of a socket connection.

In the following simple example, since the number of unsigned chars being received is unknown (and also irrelevant), I use the following code to receive data:

```
if ((rcv = client->Receive(message)) == 0)
    break;
```

Normally, with more advanced servers you place the length of the following received message, formatted as an int, in the unsigned char array buf:

```
if (client->Receive(buf, 4, SocketFlags::Peek) > 0)
{
    int length = BitConverter::ToInt32(buf, 0);
    buf = gcnew array<Byte>(length);
}
```

Then to actually receive the message you use a while loop:

```
int total = 0;
int recv;
int dataLeft = length;
while (total < length)  // TCP has an unprotected Message boundary
{
    if ((recv = client->Receive(buf, total, dataLeft, SocketFlags::None)) == 0)
    {
        client->Close();
        break;
    }
    total += recv;
    dataLeft -= recv;
}
```

Why is all of this code needed? Remember earlier I mentioned a gotcha? TCP simply sends a stream of data. There is a guarantee that the data will get to its destination and in order, but there is no guarantee that it will all get there at the same time. It is perfectly possible that half the sent message will get to the receiver process at the time the Receive() method is called. With the previous code, the Receive() method will read the rest of the message when it finally arrives. Likewise, it is possible that two messages will be received at one time. Thus, this process will allow the two messages to be split and processed separately (assuming that in your sent message you prefix the sent data with the number of bytes of data sent).

Example TCP Server

Okay, now that we have reviewed all the pieces, let's see a complete TCP server example. Listing 17-1 is the de facto "Hello World" of network software development: the echo server. It takes in a stream of data from a client (which we will cover next), dumps it to the server console, and then sends the same message back to the client. Unlike most introductory versions of the echo, which show a server that can handle only one client at a time, I skipped ahead and have shown how to write the server so that it can process any number of concurrent (at the same time) clients.

Listing 17-1. *A TCP Server That Accepts Multiple Concurrent Clients*

```
using namespace System;
using namespace System::Net;
using namespace System::Net::Sockets;
using namespace System::Threading;
using namespace System::Text;

ref class TcpServer
{
public:
    void ProcessThread(Object ^clientObj);
};

void TcpServer::ProcessThread(Object ^clientObj)
{
    Socket^ client = (Socket^)clientObj;
    IPEndPoint^ clientEP = (IPEndPoint^)client->RemoteEndPoint;

    Console::WriteLine("Connected on IP: {0} Port: {1}",
                    clientEP->Address, clientEP->Port);

    array<unsigned char>^ msg = Encoding::ASCII->GetBytes(
        String::Format("Successful connection to the server on port {0}",
                    clientEP->Port));
    client->Send(msg);

    int rcv;
    while (true)
    {
        msg = gcnew array<unsigned char>(1024);

        if ((rcv = client->Receive(msg)) == 0)
            break;

        Console::WriteLine("Port[{0}] {1}",
            clientEP->Port, Encoding::ASCII->GetString(msg, 0, rcv));

        client->Send(msg, rcv, SocketFlags::None);
    }
    client->Close();
    Console::WriteLine("Connection to IP: {0} Port {1} closed.",
        clientEP->Address, clientEP->Port);
}

void main()
{
    TcpServer^ server = gcnew TcpServer();

    Socket^ tcpListener = gcnew Socket(AddressFamily::InterNetwork,
                                SocketType::Stream, ProtocolType::Tcp);
```

```
IPEndPoint^ iped = gcnew IPEndPoint(IPAddress::Any, 12345);
tcpListener->Bind(iped);

tcpListener->Listen((int)SocketOptionName::MaxConnections);


while(true)
{
    Console::WriteLine("Waiting for client connection.");
    Socket^ client = tcpListener->Accept();

    Thread ^thr = gcnew Thread(
        gcnew ParameterizedThreadStart(server, &TcpServer::ProcessThread));
    thr->Start(client);
}
}
```

I've already covered every bit of this code, but I would like to point out that this code has no way of exiting unless you kill the console (or press Ctrl-C). I did this so as so as not to add add any additional complexity to the network code in the example. There are many solutions to this problem, most involving event handling of keystrokes received on the server machine, but for this example, killing the window just suited it fine. When you run TcpServer.exe, you should get something like Figure 17-1.

Figure 17-1. *The TCP server in action*

The TCP Client

A TCP client is simpler than a TCP server, at least when it comes to establishing a connection. The code for processing a message, on the other hand, is just as simple or complex as that of the server, since they are mirror images of each other. In other words, when the server sends a message, the client receives it, and vice versa.

Only two tasks need to be performed by the client to establish a connection to a client:

1. Create a socket.

2. Connect to a server IPEndPoint.

The process of creating a TCP client socket is the same as that for a TCP server socket:

```
Socket^ socket = gcnew Socket(AddressFamily::InterNetwork,
                              SocketType::Stream,
                              ProtocolType::Tcp);
```

Also just like a TCP server, this constructor creates a socket to a version 4 IP address that supports reliable, two-way, connection-based byte streams without duplication of data and without preservation of boundaries using the TCP protocol.

Since there is nothing new here, let's move on.

Connect to a Server IPEndPoint

Connecting to a TCP server's IPEndPoint starts with the creation of an IPEndPoint that points to the server. Just as you do with the server, you will probably create the IPEndPoint using

```
IPEndPoint^ iped = gcnew IPEndPoint(IPAddress::Parse("127.0.0.1"), port);
```

But there is nothing stopping you from using any of the myriad of other ways available to you.

Look carefully at the code. It looks the same as that for the server, but there is a difference. Instead of the IP address pointing to the local machine where the socket resides, it points to the IP address of the remote machine where you want the connection to be made.

Once you have an IPEndPoint that points to the server, all it takes to make a connection to the server is this:

```
try
{
    server->Connect(iped);
}
catch (SocketException^ se)
{
    Console::WriteLine("Connection to server failed with error: {0}",
                        se->Message);

    return;
}
```

Notice that I made the call to the Connect() method within a try/catch block. The reason is that if the connection attempt fails, then a SocketException is thrown. In the previous example I immediately give up, but in your code more than likely you will capture the exception, note it somehow, and then try again.

Example TCP Client

I'm going to move on to the TCP client example as there is no new code to explore when it comes to sending and receiving messages.

Listing 17-2 is just a simple program that connects to a TCP server, receives a connection message from the server, and then proceeds to send messages (which you type in from the console) to the server. After the message is sent, the program waits for the server to send (echo) it back.

Listing 17-2. *A TCP Client*

```
using namespace System;
using namespace System::Net;
using namespace System::Net::Sockets;
using namespace System::Threading;
using namespace System::Text;

void main()
{
    Socket^ server = gcnew Socket(AddressFamily::InterNetwork,
                            SocketType::Stream, ProtocolType::Tcp);

    try
    {
        IPEndPoint^ iped =
            gcnew IPEndPoint(IPAddress::Parse("127.0.0.1"), 12345);
        server->Connect(iped);
    }
```

```
        catch (SocketException^ se)
        {
            Console::WriteLine("Connection Failed with error: {0}", se->Message);
            return;
        }


        array<unsigned char>^ msg = gcnew array<unsigned char>(1024);
        int rcv = server->Receive(msg);

        Console::WriteLine(Encoding::ASCII->GetString(msg, 0, rcv));

        while (true)
        {
            Console::Write("Message ('q' to quit): ");
            String^ input = Console::ReadLine();

            if (input->ToLower()->Equals("q"))
                break;

            msg = Encoding::ASCII->GetBytes(input);
            server->Send(msg, msg->Length, SocketFlags::None);

            msg = gcnew array<unsigned char>(1024);
            rcv = server->Receive(msg);
            Console::WriteLine(Encoding::ASCII->GetString(msg, 0, rcv));
        }
        Console::WriteLine("Ended connection with server.");
        server->Shutdown(SocketShutdown::Both);
        server->Close();
}
```

Notice this time that unlike the server, the client does have a way of exiting cleanly.

Closing the Connection

Without a close process, a clean break between the server and the client is not possible, as once a connection is made the only clean way of closing the connection is by the client (as in this case) or the server executing a Close() method on the Socket.

What happens if you don't call the Close() method and just exit the client? The answer is that the next time the server tries to do a read it throws a SocketException. Okay, you could just capture the exception, but that is not the cleanest way of shutting down the connection.

It is the Close() method that causes the Receive() method to receive a zero byte stream (along with some complicated hidden connection cleanup stuff that we don't have to worry about).

This leaves the unexplained Shutdown() method. This method is designed to make the shutdown process cleaner as it disables the sender, receiver, or both sockets. Thus, it stops extraneous messages from being sent during the disconnection process.

Disconnecting from a Socket

What happens if you want to change the server being connected to partway through the process? You could close the connection and create a new one from scratch, or you can disconnect from the current socket using the Disconnect() method and then reconnect it to a new server.

The Disconnect() method takes one parameter, a Boolean value that when set to true allows the socket to be reused. When the parameter is set to false the Disconnect() method acts like a Close() method. Here is a snippet of code showing the Disconnect() method in action:

```
client->Shutdown(SocketShutdown::Both);
client->Disconnect(true);

if (client->Connected)
{
    Console::WriteLine("Not good I'm still connnected!");
}
else
{
    try
    {
        IPEndPoint^ iped =
            gcnew IPEndPoint(IPAddress::Parse("127.0.0.1"), 12345);
        server->Connect(iped);
    }
    catch (SocketException^ se)
    {
        Console::WriteLine("Connection Failed with error: {0}", se->Message);
        return;
    }
}
```

In this code I also show the Connected property that, as you can see, indicates whether a socket is currently connected.

Okay, now that you are dangerous when it comes to TCP, let's move on and take a look at connectionless sockets and UDP (User Datagram Protocol), its most common method of being implemented.

When you run TcpClient.exe, you should get something like Figure 17-2.

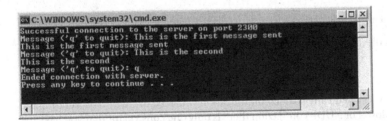

Figure 17-2. *The TCP client in action*

Connectionless Sockets

Developing connectionless sockets code is still primarily based on the client-server architecture. However, a client-server architecture need not be as strictly enforced as it is with TCP, as once a socket is open it can send to and receive from many different sockets during the course of the socket's lifetime.

Developing connectionless sockets code using UDP takes a different mind-set than developing connected socket code with TCP. There are primarily four reasons why this is so:

- Data is sent in self-contained packages instead of a stream of data.
- Network messages are not guaranteed to arrive in the same order as they were sent.
- There is no guarantee that duplicated messages won't arrive.
- Network messages are not guaranteed to arrive at the destination.

So how does this change your mind-set? First off, since data comes in packages you don't have to worry about the boundaries of the message being sent. In other words, when you read a UDP package, you know you have all the data that was sent for that particular package. That is a major plus in my book, as much of the code to implement TCP involves extracting data out of a stream.

But I guess there has to be a little bad with the good, because you are not guaranteed that messages will arrive in the order sent or, even worse, that messages will arrive at all. Many approaches have been developed to address these issues. Most of them involve a sequence number and either a positive or negative acknowledgment.

Personally, I have a simple approach to UDP coding. I read packages, and if the sequence number is greater than the last, I keep it and throw away the rest. How can I do this? I use UDP in only one scenario: computer games where messages come in fast and furious and if you miss one it doesn't really matter since the next will fill you in on what you missed. For every other scenario, I use TCP. I have developed a simple implementation based on positive acknowledgments that allows a client to re-send specific messages if they did not arrive at the destination (but this is well out of the scope of this book).

What does this all mean to you? Use TCP unless order and missed packages are not significant (or you are really good at coding in UDP, in which case you are probably not reading this book).

UDP Server

There really isn't much difference between the server and the client except that the server is waiting for packages from someplace, and a client is initiating the conversation and expecting some type of action from the server (though not necessarily a response package).

Only two tasks need to be performed by the server to create a location for a client to connect to:

1. Create a socket.

2. Bind the socket to an IPEndPoint.

The code for both of these is very similar to that for TCP.

Create a Socket

Just like with TCP, before you can do any UDP communication you need to create a socket through which the messages will flow. For a UDP connection there is only one constructor that you have to worry about:

```
Socket^ socket = gcnew Socket(AddressFamily::InterNetwork,
                              SocketType::Dgram,
                              ProtocolType::Udp);
```

This constructor creates a socket to a version 4 IP address that supports connectionless, unreliable messages (messages might be lost or duplicated, or arrive out of order) of a fixed (usually small) maximum length using the UDP protocol.

Bind the Socket to an IPEndPoint

There is no difference in creating an IPEndPoint for either TCP or UDP. Because of the nature of UDP, you will probably use the IPEndPoint frequently. The reason is that you need an EndPoint class to send and receive data, and one of the easiest ways to create an EndPoint is to create an IPEndPoint and then typecast it to the EndPoint.

As you'll recall from our earlier discussion, you will most likely use one of the following methods to create an IPEndPoint:

- `IPEndPoint^ iped = gcnew IPEndPoint(IPAddress::Any, portnumber);`

- `IPEndPoint^ iped = gcnew IPEndPoint(IPAddress::Parse("127.0.0.1"), portnumber);`

TCP and UDP have different purposes for binding to a socket. For TCP, you are creating one endpoint of a corridor between two specific endpoints. For UDP, on the other hand, you are creating a two-way door into your system from which you can communicate with any other system and any other system can communicate with your system.

All you need to know to send a package with another system is that system's IPEndPoint and the communication protocol used by that system. The reverse is also true; for another system to communicate with your system, all it needs to know is your system's IPEndPoint and your system's communication protocol.

The communication protocol can be simple as the echo system (what I get, I will send back), as extremely complex as a multiplayer gaming system (passwords, multiple packet formats, system states, etc.), or anything in between.

By the way, to bind to a socket in UDP you simply call the following code:

```
socket->Bind(iped);
```

Receive a Message

One of the best aspects of UDP is that when you receive a message packet, it is the complete package. (You just have to remember that the order, the number, and even whether you get all the sent messages are always in question.)

Another good feature of the UDP receive method is that you are not restricted to only one source of messages but instead can receive a message from any UDP sender, as long as the sender knows the receiver's IPEndPoint. Because of this, there is no need to spawn threads to handle all connections to the server. An IPEndPoint, and therefore a single thread, can handle all incoming messages from all clients.

The actual code for the ReceiveFrom() method that is used to receive messages using UDP is a bit more involved than that of the connected Receive() method, for two reasons.

First, you need to allocate a buffer to be populated by the ReceiveFrom() method. Be aware that if you specify a buffer that is too small, then the ReceiveFrom() method will fill as much data as it can in the buffer, discard all the extra unread data of the packet, and then throw a SocketException.

Second, due to the fact that the ReceiveFrom() method can get messages from any client, the method needs some way of providing the origin of the message. To accomplish this, an EndPoint is created and passed as a parameter to the ReceiveFrom() method. Then, when the ReceiveFrom() method is executed, the passed EndPoint receives the IPEndPoint of the sending client.

This may sound complex, but as you can see from the following code, it is anything but:

```
array<unsigned char>^ message = gcnew array<unsigned char>(1024);
EndPoint^ Remote = (EndPoint^) gcnew IPEndPoint(IPAddress::Any, 0);
int recv = socket->ReceiveFrom(message, Remote);
```

Notice that I use the IPEndPoint constructor to create an EndPoint. You must do this as the EndPoint class is abstract and you cannot directly create an instance of it.

To receive a message, you use one of the following overloaded ReceiveFrom() methods:

- `Socket.ReceiveFrom(array<unsigned char>^, EndPoint)`
- `Socket.ReceiveFrom(array<unsigned char>^, SocketFlags, EndPoint)`
- `Socket.ReceiveFrom(array<unsigned char>^, int, SocketFlags, EndPoint)`
- `Socket.ReceiveFrom(array<unsigned char>^, int, int, SocketFlags, EndPoint)`

Again, each just expands upon the other. The first parameter is the unsigned char array of the message being received, and the last parameter is the EndPoint of the sender. The first added parameter is SocketFlags (most likely None); next is the size of the message to be received; and finally we have the start point within the unsigned char array (use this if you want to place the received message someplace other than the actual start of the message array).

Just like the connected Receive() method, the ReceiveFrom() method returns the number of bytes received. But unlike the connected Receive() method, the unconnected ReceiveFrom() method does not receive any message when a client closes its IPEndPoint. Since this is the case, if you need your server (or client) to be aware of the demise of its opposite IPEndPoint, you must send some type of message to notify the server or client of this fact.

Send a Message

Just as when receiving a message, to send a message you need an EndPoint. To acquire an EndPoint, you will most likely use one created from scratch using an IPEndPoint constructor:

```
EndPoint^ Remote = gcnew IPEndPoint(IPAddress::Parse("127.0.0.1"), 54321);
array<unsigned char>^ message = Encoding::ASCII->GetBytes("Message");
socket->SendTo(message, Remote);
```

or use an EndPoint received from a ReceiveFrom() method:

```
socket->ReceiveFrom(inMessage, Remote);
array<unsigned char>^ outMessage = Encoding::ASCII->GetBytes("Message");
socket->SendTo(outMessage, Remote);
```

Kind of convenient, don't you think?

One cool thing about the UDP SendTo() method is that you can send it to many different EndPoints. Thus, you can use the same block of code to send the same message to multiple clients (or servers).

The SendTo() method overloads are exactly the same as with the ReceiveFrom() method:

- `Socket.SendTo(array<unsigned char>^, EndPoint)`
- `Socket.SendTo(array<unsigned char>^, SocketFlags, EndPoint)`
- `Socket.SendTo(array<unsigned char>^, int, SocketFlags, EndPoint)`
- `Socket.SendTo(array<unsigned char>^, int, int, SocketFlags, EndPoint)`

Once again, each just extends from the other. The first parameter is the unsigned char array of the message being received; the last parameter is the EndPoint of the destination of the message. The first added parameter is SocketFlags (most likely None); next is the size of the message to be sent; and next is the start point within the unsigned char array (use this if you want to start sending from someplace other than the actual start of the message array).

Example UDP Server

Now that we have all the pieces, let's take a look at Listing 17-3, another example of an echo server but this time using connectionless UDP.

Listing 17-3. *A UDP Server That Accepts Multiple Concurrent Clients*

```
using namespace System;
using namespace System::Net;
using namespace System::Net::Sockets;
using namespace System::Text;

void main()
{
    Socket^ socket = gcnew Socket(AddressFamily::InterNetwork,
                            SocketType::Dgram, ProtocolType::Udp);
    IPEndPoint^ ipep = gcnew IPEndPoint(IPAddress::Any, 54321);

    socket->Bind(ipep);

    Console::WriteLine("Waiting for client connection.");

    while(true)
    {
        array<unsigned char>^ message = gcnew array<unsigned char>(1024);
        EndPoint^ Remote = (EndPoint^) gcnew IPEndPoint(IPAddress::Any, 0);

        int recv = socket->ReceiveFrom(message, Remote);

        Console::WriteLine("[{0}] {1}",
            Remote->ToString(), Encoding::ASCII->GetString(message, 0, recv));

        socket->SendTo(message, recv, SocketFlags::None, Remote);
    }
}
```

The first thing you'll probably notice is that the code contains no special logic to handle multiple concurrent clients. The second thing you'll notice is that there is no logic to handle missing, duplicate, or wrong-order messages. As I mentioned earlier, I usually ignore the problems since I don't use UDP when message reliability is needed. If it is, I use TCP.

Also note that there is no way to exit the main loop other than killing the application or pressing Ctrl-C on the console. This is also by design (and to make the example simple) as killing the app works fine for me as a way to kill the server.

When you run UdpServer.exe, you should get something like Figure 17-3.

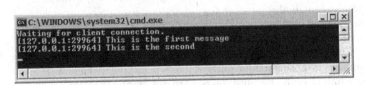

Figure 17-3. *The UDP server in action*

UDP Client Example

No new code is required to create a UDP client, so I'll just dive directly into the Echo client console application shown in Listing 17-4.

Listing 17-4. *A UDP Client*

```
using namespace System;
using namespace System::Net;
using namespace System::Net::Sockets;
using namespace System::Text;

void main()
{
    Socket^ socket = gcnew Socket(AddressFamily::InterNetwork,
                            SocketType::Dgram, ProtocolType::Udp);

// IPEndPoint^ ipep = gcnew IPEndPoint(IPAddress::Any, 54322);
// socket->Bind(ipep);

    EndPoint^ Remote = gcnew IPEndPoint(IPAddress::Parse("127.0.0.1"),
                            54321);

    while (true)
    {
        Console::Write("Message ('q' to quit): ");
        String^ input = Console::ReadLine();

        if (input->ToLower()->Equals("q"))
            break;

        array<unsigned char>^ message = Encoding::ASCII->GetBytes(input);
        socket->SendTo(message, Remote);

        message = gcnew array<unsigned char>(1024);
        int recv = socket->ReceiveFrom(message, Remote);
        Console::WriteLine("[{0}] {1}",
        Remote->ToString(), Encoding::ASCII->GetString(message, 0, recv));
    }
}
```

The first thing that should jump out at you from this code is that there is no bind to an IPEndPoint. In the example, there is no need since the first method call used by the socket class is the SendTo() method. This method has a handy built-in feature: It does the bind for you. Once you call the SendTo() method, all subsequent sends and receives will come through the randomly generated IPEndPoint assigned by that SendTo() method.

There is nothing stopping you from binding the socket yourself. Well, actually, I take that back. There is. You cannot bind twice to the same IPEndPoint. So you must use a unique IP address (or port) for each client and server. Either method is easy if clients and servers are on different machines. On the same machine, I recommend just using unique ports as things get a little trickier for IP addresses, especially if you have only one NIC, because you need to use specific IP addresses like 192.168.1.102 for the one IP and 127.0.0.1 for the other.

Another thing that should stand out in the previous program is that the client must know the specific IPEndPoint, bound by the server, that it is connecting with. Without this, the client cannot connect to the server.

Using Connect() with UDP

What if you are always sending and receiving from the same EndPoint? It seems a little redundant to continually send and receive the same address over and over. Well, you are in luck; UDP provides the ability to "sort of" connect to an EndPoint using a socket class Connect() method:

```
EndPoint^ Remote = gcnew IPEndPoint(IPAddress::Parse("127.0.0.1"), 54321);
socket->Connect(Remote);
```

The Connect() method does not cause a true connection but instead allows you to use the Send() and Receive() methods, which don't require the repeated use of an EndPoint. The syntax of the Send() and Receive() methods is the same as what is shown here in connection-oriented sockets.

Listing 17-5 shows a connected UDP client echo application.

Listing 17-5. *A UDP Client Using Connect()*

```cpp
using namespace System;
using namespace System::Net;
using namespace System::Net::Sockets;
using namespace System::Text;

void main()
{
    Socket^ socket = gcnew Socket(AddressFamily::InterNetwork,
                        SocketType::Dgram, ProtocolType::Udp);

    EndPoint^ Remote = gcnew IPEndPoint(IPAddress::Parse("127.0.0.1"),
                        54321);
    socket->Connect(Remote);

    while (true)
    {
        Console::Write("Message ('q' to quit): ");
        String^ input = Console::ReadLine();

        if (input->ToLower()->Equals("q"))
            break;

        array<unsigned char>^ message = Encoding::ASCII->GetBytes(input);
        socket->Send(message);

        message = gcnew array<unsigned char>(1024);
        int recv = socket->Receive(message);

        Console::WriteLine("[{0}] {1}",
            Remote->ToString(), Encoding::ASCII->GetString(message, 0, recv));
    }
}
```

As you can see, the code in Listing 17-4 is functionally equivalent to that in Listing 17-5; both can send to and receive messages from the same server. The only difference is that using the `Connect()` method in Listing 17-5 has allowed us to use the simplified `Send()`/`Receive()` method syntax instead of the (slightly more complex) `SendTo()`/`ReceiveFrom()` method syntax, at the expense of the socket being able to talk to only a single preset `EndPoint`.

When you run UdpClient.exe, you should get something like Figure 17-4.

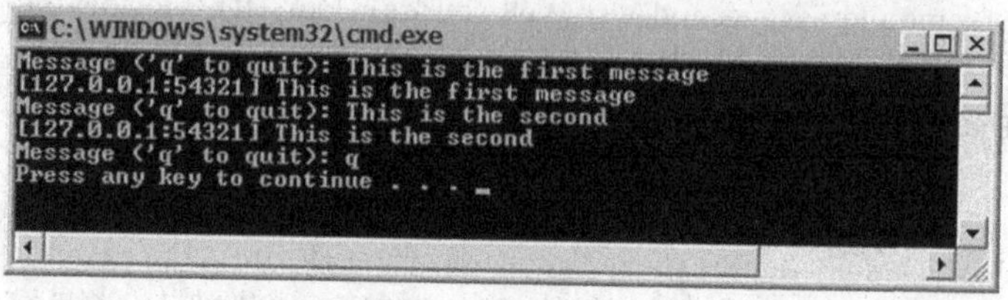

Figure 17-4. *The UDP client in action*

Socket Helper Classes and Methods

Okay, I've shown you the hard way to create connection-oriented and connectionless network code. Let's see if there is an easier way of doing the same thing—maybe at the expense of a little (usually unneeded) control.

TcpListener

Since the code to establish a TCP server connection is almost always the same no matter the implementation, the .NET Framework has provided `TcpListener`, a class that simplifies the whole process.

The `TcpListener` constructor has two overloads (there is a third but it is marked as obsolete), each providing a different way of determining the `IPEndPoint` that the TCP connection will be established on:

- `TcpListener(IPAddress^ address, int port)`
- `TcpListener(IPEndPoint^ ipep)`

The first overload allows you to pass the IP address and the port on which you want to make the connection. The second constructor allows you to build the `IPEndPoint` yourself and pass it into the `TcpListener` class.

Once you have an instance to a `TcpListener` object, you must start the listener up with the aptly named `Start()` method.

Now you are ready to accept socket connections on the `IPEndPoint` using the `AcceptSocket()` method. Listing 17-6 is the main method of a simplified version of Listing 17-1 using the `TcpListener` helper class. I did not include the `TcpServer` class's code as it is identical to that of Listing 17-1.

Listing 17-6. *A TCP Server's Main Method Using TcpListener*

```
using namespace System;
using namespace System::Net;
using namespace System::Net::Sockets;
using namespace System::Threading;
using namespace System::Text;
```

```
//... TcpServer class

void main()
{
    TcpServer^ server = gcnew TcpServer();

    TcpListener^ socket = gcnew TcpListener(IPAddress::Any, 12345);
    socket->Start();

    while(true)
    {
        Console::WriteLine("Waiting for client connection.");
        Socket^ client = socket->AcceptSocket();

        Thread ^thr = gcnew Thread(
            gcnew ParameterizedThreadStart(server, &TcpServer::ProcessThread));
        thr->Start(client);
    }
}
```

Cleans up the code nicely, doesn't it? But we're not done with the simplifications.

TcpClient

TCP communication is via a stream, right? So why not allow sending and receiving of messages to be handled as a stream instead of using the TCP Send() and Receive() methods? The TcpClient provides this functionality by providing a stream interface to TCP messages.

Just to confuse things, you can (and probably will) use the TcpClient on both the client and the server, as the code to set up the connection as a stream works equally well in both instances. The only real difference is that on a server you will accept a TcpClient using the AcceptTcpClient() method instead of the AcceptSocket() method like this:

```
TcpClient^ client = socket->AcceptTcpClient();
```

While on the client, you will create your own instance of it.

While creating an instance of TcpClient, you have the option of just using the constructor to connect to the server or using the Connect() method later on. The overloads to both are nearly the same; the main difference I see is that the Connect() method allows you to make the connection at a different time than when creating the instance of TcpClient.

- TcpClient()
- TcpClient(AddressFamily^)
- TcpClient(IPEndPoint^)
- TcpClient(String^ hostname, Int32 port)

The first two constructors don't provide the ability to immediately connect to a server for the obvious reason that the server's address has not been specified. The difference between these two constructors is that the second constructor allows TcpClient to use version 6 IP addresses by passing an address family of InterNetworkV6.

The second and third constructors will automatically attempt to connect to the server specified by the passed parameter. You have already seen the IPEndPoint, so let's move on to the last constructor. This neat little constructor allows you to pass either the IP address or the DNS host name (sweet! if you ask me), and the port to connect on. A DNS host name is the more human-friendly name you type in when you are using Internet Explorer, Firefox, or whatever browser you prefer—for example, www.managedcpp.net or www.procppcli.net (just a little plug for my C++/CLI Web site).

As I said earlier, the Connect() method takes very similar parameters:

- Connect(IPEndPoint^)
- Connect(IPAddress^ addr, Int32 port)
- Connect(array<IPAddress^>^ addrs, Int32 port)
- Connect(String^ hostname, Int32 port)

All the parameters passed to the Connect() method should be familiar to you except the third overload. With this overload, Connect() is expecting an array of IPAddresses. Why is this overload needed, you might ask? The reason is it works perfectly with the static Dns::ResolveToAddresses(String^ hostname) method, which returns an array of IPAddresses. This static method is helpful in that it allows you to give it a DNS host name and it spits out all IP addresses associated with it.

Okay, now that you are connected, you can use the TcpClient class's GetStream() method (why not a property?) to provide a Stream object from which you can access the TCP port as a stream of data:

```
TcpClient^ client = gcnew TcpClient();
client->Connect("www.procppcli.net", 12345);
NetworkStream^ ns = client->GetStream();
```

TCP Helper Class Example

Listing 17-7 and Listing 17-8 show how you can use TCPListener and TcpClient to communicate in a client-server fashion using strictly streams of String objects.

Listing 17-7. *A TCP Server Implementing Helper Classes*

```
using namespace System;
using namespace System::IO;
using namespace System::Net;
using namespace System::Net::Sockets;
using namespace System::Threading;

ref class TcpServer
{
public:
    void ProcessThread(Object ^clientObj);
};

void TcpServer::ProcessThread(Object ^clientObj)
{
    TcpClient^ client = (TcpClient^)clientObj;

    IPEndPoint^ clientEP = (IPEndPoint^)client->Client->RemoteEndPoint;

    Console::WriteLine("Connected on IP: {0} Port: {1}",
                        clientEP->Address, clientEP->Port);

    StreamWriter^ writer = gcnew StreamWriter(client->GetStream());
    StreamReader^ reader = gcnew StreamReader(client->GetStream());
```

```
writer->WriteLine("Successful connection to the server on port {0}",
                  clientEP->Port);
writer->Flush();

String^ msg;
while (true)
{
    try
    {
        msg = reader->ReadLine();
        Console::WriteLine("Port[{0}] {1}", clientEP->Port, msg);

        writer->WriteLine(msg);
        writer->Flush();
    }
    catch (IOException^)
    {
        break;  // connection lost
    }
}
client->Close();

Console::WriteLine("Connection to IP: {0} Port {1} closed.",
    clientEP->Address, clientEP->Port);
}

void main()
{
    TcpServer^ server = gcnew TcpServer();

    TcpListener^ socket = gcnew TcpListener(IPAddress::Any, 12345);
    socket->Start();

    while(true)
    {
        Console::WriteLine("Waiting for client connection.");
        TcpClient^ client = socket->AcceptTcpClient();

        Thread ^thr = gcnew Thread(
            gcnew ParameterizedThreadStart(server, &TcpServer::ProcessThread));
        thr->Start(client);
    }
}
```

As you can see from the code, all sending and receiving of data is of type String. What's more interesting is that I am able to use standard WriteLine() and ReadLine() methods to handle communication over the Internet! The following two lines make this possible:

- `StreamWriter^ writer = gcnew StreamWriter(client->GetStream());`
- `StreamReader^ reader = gcnew StreamReader(client->GetStream());`

These lines create a StreamWriter and StreamReader object (which I covered in Chapter 8) from the NetworkStream object returned by the TcpClient class's GetStream() method.

All that socket stuff is now (almost) completely hidden. There are only two catches: First, you need to flush the messages manually using the Flush() method, or the messages stay in the stream's buffer until the buffer is full. Second, you need to catch an IOException from the ReadLine() and WriteLine() methods. When this exception happens, you can assume that the network connection has been closed and you can go ahead and close things up.

Listing 17-8. *A TCP Client Implementing Helper Classes*

```
using namespace System;
using namespace System::IO;
using namespace System::Net;
using namespace System::Net::Sockets;

void main()
{
    TcpClient^ server;
    StreamWriter^ writer;
    StreamReader^ reader;
    String^ msg;

    try
    {
        server = gcnew TcpClient("127.0.0.1", 12345);

        writer = gcnew StreamWriter(server->GetStream());
        reader = gcnew StreamReader(server->GetStream());
    }
    catch (SocketException^ se)
    {
        Console::WriteLine("Connection to server failed with error: {0}",
                            se->Message);
        return;
    }

    msg = reader->ReadLine();
    Console::WriteLine(msg);

    while (true)
    {
        Console::Write("Message ('q' to quit): ");
        msg = Console::ReadLine();

        if (msg->ToLower()->Equals("q"))
            break;

        try
        {
            writer->WriteLine(msg);
            writer->Flush();

            msg = reader->ReadLine();
            Console::WriteLine(msg);
        }
```

```
    catch (IOException^)
    {
        break;  // connection lost
    }
}
Console::WriteLine("Ended connection with server.");
server->Close();
}
```

Okay, I sort of fibbed. There is a third catch. To simplify the client, you should also use a StreamWriter and StreamReader, as shown in Listing 17-8.

Notice that the client also places the WriteLine() and ReadLine() methods within a try/catch block. In most cases, a server should not come down with clients attached, but there are no rules saying it can't. Thus, if the WriteLine() or ReadLine() method throws an IOException, you can assume that the server has severed its connection and that you need to close the client connection. One bonus of TcpClient is that it shuts down gracefully on its own and therefore doesn't even provide a Shutdown() method like the Socket class does.

UdpClient

Since there is a TcpClient, you must be thinking that there has to be a UdpClient (and you'd be right). The UdpClient simplifies the already simple UDP socket in two ways, though there already isn't much left to simplify.

One area that is made easier is that you don't need to worry about binding; the myriad of UdpClient constructors handles it for you. Here is a list of the constructors available to you:

- UdpClient()
- UdpClient(AddressFamily^)
- UdpClient(Int32 port)
- UdpClient(IPEndPoint^)
- UdpClient(Int32 port, AddressFamily^)
- UdpClient(String^ hostname, Int32 port)

We have examined all these parameters already in some form in the constructor already covered, but I'll recap them so you don't have to go searching for them. The AddressFamily can be either InterNetwork (version 4 IP address) or InterNetworkV6 (version 6 IP address). The port parameter is an integer from 0 to 65535, but you should not use 0–1024 as these numbers are reserved as *well-known* ports. IPEndPoint is a combination of the IP address and the port. Finally, hostname is the human-friendly(ish) name you give to an IP address, like the one you type into Internet Explorer.

The other benefit of using UdpClient is that you no longer have to worry about not receiving the whole message package by allocating too small a buffer. With UdpClient the Receive() method returns the buffer; all you have to do is provide a handle to return it to.

Listings 17-9 and 17-10 contain all the basic code needed for a UDP client-server application using UdpClient.

Listing 17-9. *A UDP Server That Accepts Multiple Concurrent Clients Using UdpClient*

```
using namespace System;
using namespace System::Net;
using namespace System::Net::Sockets;
using namespace System::Text;
```

```cpp
void main()
{
    IPEndPoint^ ipep = gcnew IPEndPoint(IPAddress::Any, 54321);
    UdpClient^ server = gcnew UdpClient(ipep);

    Console::WriteLine("Waiting for client connection.");

    array<unsigned char>^ message;

    while(true)
    {
        IPEndPoint^ Remote = gcnew IPEndPoint(IPAddress::Any, 0);
        message = server->Receive(Remote);

        Console::WriteLine("[{0}] [{1}]",
            Remote->ToString(), Encoding::ASCII->GetString(message, 0,
            message->Length));

        server->Send(message, message->Length, Remote);
    }
}
```

Listing 17-10. *A UDP Client Using UdpClient*

```cpp
using namespace System;
using namespace System::Net;
using namespace System::Net::Sockets;
using namespace System::Text;

void main()
{
    UdpClient^ client = gcnew UdpClient();

    IPEndPoint^ Remote =
        gcnew IPEndPoint(IPAddress::Parse("127.0.0.1"), 54321);

    while (true)
    {
        Console::Write("Message ('q' to quit): ");
        String^ input = Console::ReadLine();

        if (input->ToLower()->Equals("q"))
            break;

        array<unsigned char>^ message = Encoding::ASCII->GetBytes(input);
        client->Send(message, message->Length, Remote);

        message = client->Receive(Remote);
        Console::WriteLine("[{0}] {1}",
            Remote->ToString(),
            Encoding::ASCII->GetString(message, 0, message->Length));
    }
}
```

There is not much difference between client and server, is there? In Listing 17-10, I threw in the UdpClient class's Send() method's ability to auto-bind to a port, but you could have just as easily used a UdpClient constructor with more information so that the constructor itself would bind to the port. Just remember that if you do this, the client and IP address and the port pairs must be different.

Changing Socket Options

I guess I'm kind of obligated to cover socket options here, as I did mention them in the caution way up near the start of the chapter. In most programs you write, you will not normally have to worry about the options on a socket. In fact, nearly all of the options are beyond the scope of this book. But, on those occasions that the defaults need to be tweaked or retrieved, the Socket class provides you with the aptly named methods SetSocketOption() and GetSocketOption().

The SetSocketOption() method has four different overloads. The reason is that different options require different data types to be set. Thus, each overload provides one of these data types:

- void SetSocketOption(SocketOptionLevel, SocketOptionName, Boolean)
- void SetSocketOption(SocketOptionLevel, SocketOptionName, array<Byte>^)
- void SetSocketOption(SocketOptionLevel, SocketOptionName, Int32)
- void SetSocketOption(SocketOptionLevel, SocketOptionName, Object^)

As you can see, each of these methods has two parameters in common: SocketOptionLevel, which specifies what level of socket to apply the set to (IP, IPv6, Socket, Tcp, or Udp), and SocketOptionName, which specifies which option to set. There are quite a few options that you can tweak, if you feel adventurous. Personally, I only recall using Linger, which keeps the socket open if unsent data exists, and ReceiveTimeout, which specifies how long to wait on a receive command before giving up and throwing an exception.

The GetSocketOption() method is also overloaded but only three times:

- object GetSocketOption(SocketOptionLevel, SocketOptionName)
- void GetSocketOption(SocketOptionLevel, SocketOptionName, array<Byte>^ value)
- array<Byte>^ Socket::GetSocketOption(SocketOptionLevel, SocketOptionName, Int32)

Just like the SetSocketOption() method, the first two parameters are SocketOptionLevel and SocketOptionName. In most cases, you use the first version of the GetSocketOption() method, but for those options that deal in byte arrays the other two versions are also available.

Listing 17-11 is an example of using the ReceiveTimeout option with UDP. You might find this option helpful if you want a simple way to help check that a package was sent successfully, by way of having the receiver of the package immediately send back an acknowledgment package. Since you have a timeout set on the ReceiveFrom() method, if the acknowledgment package doesn't come back in a timely fashion you know one of two things: The package was never received or the acknowledgment package was lost. (I never said it would check that the package was sent successfully, but only that it would help in checking.)

Listing 17-11. *A UDP Client with a Timeout*

```
using namespace System;
using namespace System::Net;
using namespace System::Net::Sockets;
using namespace System::Text;


void main()
{
    Socket^ socket = gcnew Socket(AddressFamily::InterNetwork,
                        SocketType::Dgram, ProtocolType::Udp);
```

```
EndPoint^ Remote = gcnew IPEndPoint(IPAddress::Parse("127.0.0.1"),
                                    54321);

if ((int)socket->GetSocketOption(SocketOptionLevel::Socket,
                    SocketOptionName::ReceiveTimeout) < 5000)
{
    socket->SetSocketOption(SocketOptionLevel::Socket,
                    SocketOptionName::ReceiveTimeout, 5000 );
}

while (true)
{
    Console::Write("Message ('q' to quit): ");
    String^ input = Console::ReadLine();

    if (input->ToLower()->Equals("q"))
        break;

    array<unsigned char>^ message = Encoding::ASCII->GetBytes(input);
    socket->SendTo(message, Remote);

    message = gcnew array<unsigned char>(1024);
    try
    {
        int recv = socket->ReceiveFrom(message, Remote);
        Console::WriteLine("[{0}] {1}",
          Remote->ToString(), Encoding::ASCII->GetString(message, 0, recv));
    }
    catch (SocketException^)
    {
        Console::WriteLine("Receive failed with a time out.");
        Console::WriteLine("Make sure server is running.");
    }
}
}
```

In the code, the use of GetSocketOption() is redundant as the default value is 0, but I wanted to show an example of it being used.

One thing that threw me is that the ReceiveFrom() method throws a SocketException if no socket is bound to the IPEndPoint it is expecting to receive data from. I first thought that the timeout was working, but when I extended the timeout value, the SocketException still happened immediately. It wasn't until I had the server bind to the socket that the timeout started working properly.

Asynchronous Sockets

It is time to change gears and look at another way of coding network programs. In all of the previous examples when the program called a network function, the program blocked (stopped/suspended) until the network function returned or timed out. In many programs this is just fine, and with multi-threading that's usually all you need.

But there will come a time when you will need the program to not stop/suspend when it encounters a network function, and in those cases you will use asynchronous network functions. (In previous versions of .NET, you would refer to this as *asynchronous socket functions*, but with version 2 of the .NET Framework TcpListener, TcpClient, and UdpClient were expanded to support asynchronous functionality. Yeah, I know down in their depths these three are socket code as well, so if you want to be picky I guess you can use the term *asynchronous socket function* and be completely correct.)

Asynchronous functions cause the execution of the code to be broken into two threads. When an asynchronous function is called, the processing of the network functionality breaks off and runs in another thread, while the application continues to run on the original thread. Then when the network functionality thread completes, you process any results in a callback function.

There really isn't anything that special about writing asynchronous network code; once you figure out how to do it for one asynchronous method, then you know how to do it for them all. The reason is that you code all asynchronous methods in almost exactly the same way.

Asynchronous methods are basically synchronous methods divided into two parts: the BeginXxx() method, which specifies the callback method and causes the thread to split, and the EndXxx() method, which processes the callback method when the network functionality completes.

Accepting Connections

As with synchronous connection-oriented code, you need to set up a Socket or TcpListener so that it can accept connections. There is no asynchronous method for the process of creating a socket or TcpListener; therefore, you use the same code as you did for your synchronous code. This makes sense because this code is not dependent on a remote client.

The first step, in which a server starts to communicate with a client (an extensive wait may occur while this communication process occurs), is the accept stage. You have three options when accepting connections:

- The Socket class's BeginAccept() method
- The TcpListener class's BeginAcceptSocket() method
- The TcpListener class's BeginAcceptTcpClient() method

All three of these methods have overloaded parameter sets similar to their synchronous equivalent, with the addition of two more parameters: a handle to the AsyncCallback method, which gets executed when the accept completes, and a handle to an Object class to hold information to pass from the Begin method to the End method. In addition, all three methods also return a handle to an IAsyncResult class. (You probably will not need to use this return value.)

To invoke the BeginAccept() method, you must first create a socket and the AsyncCallback method to handle the results of the accept operation. You have seen the steps to create a socket earlier (in our discussion of connection-oriented sockets), so I won't repeat myself here. Creating an AsyncCallback, on the other hand, is new. The AsyncCallback has two constructors. Which you use depends on whether the actual callback method is a static method:

```
AsyncCallback^ method = gcnew AsyncCallback(&TcpServer::AcceptCB);
```

or a member method:

```
AsyncCallback^ method = gcnew AsyncCallback(server, &TcpServer::AcceptCB);
```

Normally, you will just embed this code directly in the BeginAccept() method call like this:

```
socket->BeginAcceptSocket(gcnew AsyncCallback(&TcpServer::AcceptCB), socket);
```

The actual callback method (AcceptCB in this case) looks like this:

```
void TcpServer::AcceptCB(IAsyncResult^ iar)
{
    //...
}
```

where AcceptCB is declared as one of the following:

```
public:
    void AcceptCB(IAsyncResult^ iar);
```

or

```
public:
    static void AcceptCB(IAsyncResult^ iar);
```

When the BeginAccept() method is called, it creates a new thread to wait on the completion of a socket accept and then lets the original thread continue on its merry way. When the socket accept finally completes, the program now has two threads running concurrently: the original thread, plus the socket's accept thread, which starts to execute (as far as you are concerned anyway) from the beginning of the callback method.

The first thing you would normally do in the callback method is get back the socket that the original BeginAccept() method was run on. You get this from the AsyncState property on the IAsyncResult parameter of the callback method. This value is there because you passed it as a parameter of the BeginAccept() method.

```
TcpListener^ tcpListener = (TcpListener^)iar->AsyncState;
```

Now that you have the original socket you can call the EndAccept() method to get the accepted socket and finish off the accept operation:

```
Socket^ client = tcpListener->EndAccept(iar);
```

Now comes the tricky part. Remember you have two threads running, but unlike synchronous sockets the main thread has no knowledge of the newly accepted client; therefore, the main thread cannot handle the socket sends or receives without jumping through some hoops (I've never explored how to do this but you are free to explore on your own).

What I do instead is use the new thread to handle the sends and receives and basically let the original thread do whatever it was doing. What ultimately happens is that a callback method throws off a chain of calls to other callbacks and then exits gracefully. However, the number of threads spawned can get large, and in the case of an error, you have to figure out what thread went wrong.

Connecting to a Connection

A client using asynchronous code must connect to a server just like its synchronous counterpart. The difference as I'm sure you suspect is that you will use the BeginConnect()/EndConnect() method pair instead of the Connect() method. Also, just like the server, there is no asynchronous method for the process of creating a socket or TcpClient; therefore, you use the same code as you did for your synchronous code.

The first step, in which a client starts to communicate with a server (again, an extensive wait may occur while this communication process occurs), is the connection stage. You have two options when connecting:

- The Socket class's BeginConnect() method
- The TcpClient class's BeginConnect() method

As I said in the beginning of this section, once you know how to use one asynchronous method you know how to use them all. Just like the BeginAccept() method, the BeginConnect() method has overloaded parameter sets similar to their synchronous equivalent with the addition of two more parameters: a handle to the AsyncCallback method and a handle to an Object class (in which you should place the socket handle). Both methods also return a handle to a c. For example:

```
IAsyncResult^ ret =
  socket->BeginConnect(iep, gcnew AsyncCallback(&TcpClient::ConnectCB), socket);
```

When the connection operation completes, the callback method is executed (on its own thread):

```
void TcpClient::ConnectCB(IAsyncResult^ iar)
{
    //...
}
```

The first thing you do is get the Socket that was used to call the BeginConnect() method. You get this from the AsyncState property on the IAsyncResult parameter of the callback method:

```
Socket^ socket = (Socket^)iar->AsyncState;
```

Next, you execute the EndConnect() method, usually in a try/catch block, to complete the connection process:

```
try
{
    socket->EndConnect(iar);
}
catch (SocketException^ se)
{
    Console::WriteLine("Connection failed with error {0}", se->Message);
}
```

Disconnecting from a Connection

Your client applications have available to them only one asynchronous disconnect method pair from which you can reconnect to other servers. As with all asynchronous methods, you initiate the disconnect with the Begin method, in this case BeginDisconnect(). The BeginDisconnect() takes three parameters—the Boolean value that you specify if the socket will be reused, a handle to the AsyncCallback method, and a handle to an Object class—and returns an IAsyncResult. (The last two methods and the return value should, by now, look fairly familiar.)

```
IAsyncResult^ ret =
    socket->BeginDisconnect(true, gcnew AsyncCallback(&TcpClient::DisconnectCB),
                            socket);
```

When the disconnect operation completes, the callback method is executed (on its own thread):

```
void TcpClient::DisconnectCB(IAsyncResult^ iar)
{
    //...
}
```

The first thing you do (like with any other asynchronous callback) is get the Socket that was used to call the BeginDisconnect() method. You get this from the AsyncState property on the IAsyncResult parameter of the callback method:

```
Socket^ socket = (Socket^)iar->AsyncState;
```

Next, you execute the EndDisconnect() method, thus completing the disconnect process:

```
socket->EndDisconnect(iar);
```

Sending a Message

You have three options when it comes to sending messages asynchronously:

- The Socket class's BeginSend() method
- The Socket class's BeginSendTo() method
- The UDPClient class's BeginSend() method

All three of these methods have overloaded parameter sets similar to their synchronous equivalent, with the addition of two more parameters: a handle to the AsyncCallback method and a handle to an Object class. All three methods also return a handle to an IAsyncResult class. Here's an example:

```
IAsyncResult^ ret =
    client->BeginSend(msg, 0, msg->Length, SocketFlags::None,
                    gcnew AsyncCallback(&TcpServer::SendCB), client);
```

When the send operation completes, the callback is executed. Within the callback you will get the socket and then execute the EndSend() method:

```
void TcpServer::SendCB(IAsyncResult^ iar)
{
    Socket^ client = (Socket^)iar->AsyncState;
    client->EndSend(iar);
}
```

Receiving a Message

Like the asynchronous send, the receive has three options:

- The Socket class's BeginReceive() method
- The Socket class's BeginReceiveFrom() method
- The UDPClient class's BeginReceive() method

All three of these methods have overloaded parameter sets similar to their synchronous equivalent, along with two more parameters: a handle to the AsyncCallback method and a handle to an Object class. All three methods also return a handle to an IAsyncResult class.

One thing that is different about asynchronous receive is that you should not pass the socket in the final parameter of the Socket class asynchronous methods. (Send the socket in the UdpClient version as you would normally.) Instead, you send a custom class that is made up of a handle to the socket and a handle to the message buffer to receive the message. Here is an example:

```
ref class StateObject
{
public:
    property int bufSize;
    property Socket ^workSocket;
    property array<unsigned char>^ message;

    StateObject(Socket^ sock, int bufsize)
    {
        workSocket = sock;
        bufSize = bufsize;
        message = gcnew array<unsigned char>(bufsize);
    }
};
```

The reason for this is that the receive callback method needs both of these handles to run correctly. Here's how you would call the BeginReceive() method:

```
StateObject^ so = gcnew StateObject(client, 1024);
client->BeginReceive(so->message, 0, so->bufSize, SocketFlags::None,
    gcnew AsyncCallback(&TcpServer::ReceiveCB), so);
```

Now, when the receive operation completes, the callback is executed just like any other asynchronous callback, but this time, instead of just grabbing the socket from the AsyncState property on the IAsyncResult parameter, you grab the StateObject and then get the socket and the message buffer from it:

```
void TcpServer::ReceiveCB(IAsyncResult^ iar)
{
    StateObject^ so = (StateObject^)iar->AsyncState;
    Socket^ client = so->workSocket;

    int rcv;
    if ((rcv = client->EndReceive(iar)) > 0) // get message
    {
    //... the received data is in: so->message
    }
    else // connection closed
    {
        client->Close();
    }
}
```

Asynchronous TCP Server

Okay, let's take one last look at the TCP server in Listing 17-12. This time I've rewritten it so that it uses asynchronous methods. The functionality is exactly the same as the synchronous version. In fact, you can use the TCP clients that you wrote earlier to connect to it.

Personally, I find following the logic of asynchronous code a little more complex than that of synchronous and prefer not to use it. The only benefit I see of this version over my original is that you don't have to maintain the threads of the program yourself.

The example program relies heavily on asynchronous callback chaining. Here is the basic outline of how the program runs:

1. The main program calls accept, then waits for a return key to end the program.
2. Accept calls send, receive, and then recalls accept. Finally the program exits and ends the thread.
3. Send ends without calling anything, thus ending the thread.
4. Receive either calls send and then recalls receive, or it closes the connection. Finally, the method ends, ending the thread.

What ultimately results is a threaded loop that accepts new clients and multiple threaded loops that receive messages for each client.

Listing 17-12. *A TCP Server Asynchronous Style*

```
using namespace System;
using namespace System::Net;
using namespace System::Net::Sockets;
using namespace System::Threading;
```

```cpp
using namespace System::Text;

ref class StateObject
{
public:
    property int bufSize;
    property Socket ^workSocket;
    property array<unsigned char>^ message;

    StateObject(Socket^ sock, int bufsize)
    {
        workSocket = sock;
        bufSize = bufsize;
        message = gcnew array<unsigned char>(bufsize);
    }
};

ref class TcpServer
{
public:
    static void AcceptCB(IAsyncResult^ iar);
    static void SendCB(IAsyncResult^ iar);
    static void ReceiveCB(IAsyncResult^ iar);
};

void TcpServer::AcceptCB(IAsyncResult^ iar)
{
    TcpListener^ tcpListener = (TcpListener^)iar->AsyncState;
    Socket^ client = tcpListener->EndAcceptSocket(iar);

    IPEndPoint^ clientEP = (IPEndPoint^)client->RemoteEndPoint;

    Console::WriteLine("Connected on IP: {0} Port: {1}",
                    clientEP->Address, clientEP->Port);

    // Send socket successful connection message
    array<unsigned char>^ msg = Encoding::ASCII->GetBytes(
        String::Format("Successful connection to the server on port {0}",
                    clientEP->Port));
    client->BeginSend(msg, 0, msg->Length, SocketFlags::None,
        gcnew AsyncCallback(&TcpServer::SendCB), client);

    // Get message from client
    StateObject^ so = gcnew StateObject(client, 1024);
    client->BeginReceive(so->message, 0, so->bufSize,
        SocketFlags::None, gcnew AsyncCallback(&TcpServer::ReceiveCB), so);

    // Get the next socket connection
    Console::WriteLine("Waiting for client connections. [Return to Exit]");
    tcpListener->BeginAcceptSocket(gcnew AsyncCallback(&TcpServer::AcceptCB),
        tcpListener);
}
```

```
void TcpServer::SendCB(IAsyncResult^ iar)
{
    Socket^ client = (Socket^)iar->AsyncState;
    client->EndSend(iar);
}

void TcpServer::ReceiveCB(IAsyncResult^ iar)
{
    StateObject^ so = (StateObject^)iar->AsyncState;
    Socket^ client = so->workSocket;
    IPEndPoint^ clientEP = (IPEndPoint^)client->RemoteEndPoint;

    int rcv;
    if ((rcv = client->EndReceive(iar)) > 0) // get message
    {
        Console::WriteLine("Port[{0}] {1}",
            clientEP->Port, Encoding::ASCII->GetString(so->message, 0, rcv));

        // echo message
        client->BeginSend(so->message, 0, rcv, SocketFlags::None,
            gcnew AsyncCallback(&TcpServer::SendCB), client);

        // set up for next receive
        so = gcnew StateObject(client, 1024);
        client->BeginReceive(so->message, 0, so->bufSize,
            SocketFlags::None, gcnew AsyncCallback(&TcpServer::ReceiveCB), so);
    }
    else // connection closed
    {
        client->Close();
        Console::WriteLine("Connection to IP: {0} Port {1} closed.",
            clientEP->Address, clientEP->Port);
    }
}

void main()
{
    TcpListener^ socket = gcnew TcpListener(IPAddress::Any, 12345);
    socket->Start();

    Console::WriteLine("Waiting for client connections. [Return to Exit]");
    socket->BeginAcceptSocket(gcnew AsyncCallback(&TcpServer::AcceptCB),
        socket);

    // Exit on return key
    Console::ReadLine();
}
```

I added comments to the code to help you walk through. As you can see, asynchronous network programming can get complex fast.

When you run TcpServer_Async.exe, you should get something like Figure 17-5.

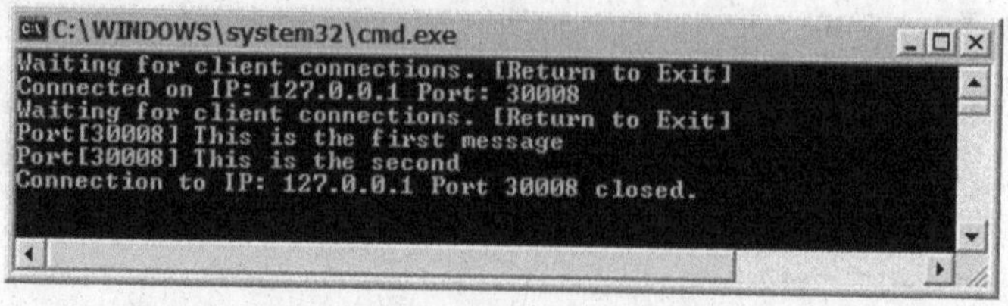

Figure 17-5. *The asynchronous TCP server in action*

Summary

In this chapter you got a fairly high level look at the weighty topic of network programming. I started out looking at connection-oriented client-server sockets, in particular a TCP server and client. I then looked at connectionless client-server sockets or, more specifically, a UDP server and client. Next, I looked at some of the helper functions provided by the .NET Framework to simplify network programming. Finally, I covered asynchronous network programming.

In the next chapter of this book, you'll cover assembly programming and how you can augment your assemblies with resources, localization, attributes, and type reflection.

CHAPTER 18

■ ■ ■

Assembly Programming

Before you roll your eyes and mumble under your breath, "Not another chapter on assemblies," read the chapter title again. This chapter is about programming an assembly, and not about the assembly. By now I'm assuming you know what an assembly is, its structure, how it eliminates DLL Hell, and so forth. Instead, this chapter focuses on programmatically playing with the assembly.

As I've pointed out a few times in this book, the assembly is the cornerstone of .NET Framework deployment. To paraphrase, all roads lead to the assembly. Because this is the case, it only makes sense that the .NET Framework provides the programmer many programmatic tools to interact directly with the assembly.

In this chapter, you'll look at some of these programming tools. Most of these tools are for the more advanced C++/CLI programmer. In most cases, you won't have to use them for most of your programs. On the other hand, knowing these tools will provide you with powerful weapons in your .NET software development arsenal and, inevitably, sometime in your coding career you'll need to use each of these tools.

The first tool, reflection, gives you the ability to look inside an assembly to see how it works. You've used system-defined attributes on several occasions in this book. In this chapter you'll have the opportunity to create some of your own attributes. Up until now, you've worked only with private assemblies, but it's also possible to share them. Most of the time, you'll take versioning (the second tool) for granted, but you can take a much more active role. Assemblies need not be just metadata and MSIL code. They can house almost any resource that your program needs to run. The last tool—but definitely not the least—is globalization and localization. Your culture may be central to your life, but there are many other cultures out there. Why not make your programs work with these cultures as well?

Reflection

Reflection is the ability to retrieve and examine at runtime the metadata that describes the contents of assemblies, i.e., classes, enums, methods, variables, etc. Then, for example, using the retrieved information, you can turn around and create dynamically an instance of one of these described classes, and invoke its methods or access its properties or member variables.

The System::Reflection namespace, which the .NET Framework uses to support reflection, is made up of more than 40 classes. Most of these classes you will probably not use directly, if at all. Several of the more common classes you will use are listed in Table 18-1.

Table 18-1. *Common System::Reflection Namespace Classes*

Class Name	Description
Assembly	Defines an assembly
AssemblyName	Provides access to all the parts of an assembly's name
ConstructorInfo	Provides access to the constructor's attributes and metadata
CustomAttributeData	Provides access to custom attribute data for assemblies, modules, types, members, and parameters
EventInfo	Provides access to the event's attributes and metadata
FieldInfo	Provides access to the field's attributes and metadata
MemberInfo	Provides access to the member's attributes and metadata
MethodInfo	Provides access to the method's attributes and metadata
Module	Defines a module
ParameterInfo	Provides access to the parameter's attributes and metadata
PropertyInfo	Provides access to the property's attributes and metadata
TypeDelegator	Provides a wrapper for an object and then delegates all methods to that object

Just to make things a little confusing, the key to .NET Framework reflection is the System::Type class which, as you can see, isn't even found within the Reflection namespace. My guess for its not being placed in the Reflection namespace is because it's used frequently, and the designers of the Framework didn't want to force the import of the Reflection namespace.

Examining Objects

A key feature of reflection is the ability to examine metadata using the System::Type class. The basic idea is to get a Type reference of the class you want to examine and then use the Type class's members to get access to the metadata information about the type, such as the constructors, methods, fields, and properties.

Getting the Type Reference

In most cases, you will get the Type reference to the class by one of four methods:

- Using the typeid keyword
- Calling the class's GetType() method
- Calling the Type class's static GetType() method, passing it the name of the class to be examined as a String
- Iterating through a collection of all types within an assembly retrieved by the Assembly class's GetTypes() method

The first method, typeid, is the easiest of the four ways to get a Type reference, but it must be able to be evaluated at compile time. The typeid keyword returns a Type of the specified type:

```
System::Type ^myClassType = MyClass::typeid;
```

To use the second method, you need to already have an instance of the managed object you want to examine, and with this instance you call its GetType() method. The key to the second method is the fact that all ref classes and value types inherit from the Object class and the Object class has a GetType() method. For example, here is how you would get the Type reference to the myClass class:

```
ref class myClass
{
    // members
};
MyClass ^myClass = gcnew MyClass();
Type ^myClassType = myClass->GetType();
```

The third method is kind of cool in that you pass the string equivalent of the type you want to reference to the Type class's static GetType() method. You might want to note that Type is an abstract class, so you can't create an instance of it but, as you can see here, you can still call its static methods:

```
Type ^myClassRef = Type::GetType("MyClass");
```

Tip Since Type::GetType() takes a string as a parameter, you can use this function to create nearly any type you want at runtime. In fact, in my current project, I use a database of class names (the actual classes all derived from a common interface) to populate this method. Then I use the polymorphic abilities of C++/CLI to provide the appropriate functionality of the class selected from the database.

One thing all the preceding methods have in common is that you need to have something of the type you want to reference at runtime—either the data type and instance of the type, or the name of the type. The fourth method allows you to get a Type reference without any knowledge of the object beforehand. Instead, you retrieve it out of a collection of Types with an assembly:

```
Assembly^ assembly = Assembly::LoadFrom("MyAssembly.dll");
array<Type^>^ types = assembly->GetTypes();
for each (Type ^type in types)
{
    Type ^myClassType = type;
}
```

Getting the Metadata

Getting the metadata out of a Type reference is the same no matter what method you use to attain the Type reference. The Type class contains numerous methods, many of which allow you to access metadata associated with the type. Table 18-2 lists of some of the more common methods available to you for retrieving metadata.

Table 18-2. *Common Type Metadata Retrieval Methods*

Method	Description
GetConstructor()	Gets a ConstructorInfo object for a specific constructor of the current Type
GetConstructors()	Gets a collection of ConstructorInfo objects for all the constructors for the current Type
GetEvent()	Gets an EventInfo object for a specific event declared or inherited from the current Type
GetEvents()	Gets a collection of EventInfo objects for all the events declared or inherited from the current Type
GetField()	Gets a FieldInfo object for a specific member variable from the current Type
GetFields()	Gets a collection of FieldInfo objects for all the member variables from the current Type
GetInterface()	Gets a Type object for a specific interface implemented or inherited from the current Type
GetInterfaces()	Gets a collection of Type objects for all the interfaces implemented or inherited from the current Type
GetMember()	Gets a MemberInfo object for a specific member from the current Type
GetMembers()	Gets a collection of MemberInfo objects for all the members from the current Type
GetMethod()	Gets a MethodInfo object for a specific member method from the current Type
GetMethods()	Gets a collection of MethodInfo objects for all the member methods from the current Type
GetProperty()	Gets a PropertyInfo object for a specific property from the current Type
GetProperties()	Gets a collection of PropertyInfo objects for all the properties from the current Type

Along with the "Get" methods, the Type class also has a number of "Is" properties (see Table 18-3), which you use to see if the current type "is" something.

Table 18-3. *Common "Is" Properties*

"Is" Property	Description
IsAbstract	Is a Boolean that represents whether the Type is abstract
IsArray	Is a Boolean that represents whether the Type is a managed array
IsClass	Is a Boolean that represents whether the Type is a ref class
IsEnum	Is a Boolean that represents whether the Type is an enumeration
IsImport	Is a Boolean that represents whether the Type is an interface

Table 18-3. *Common "Is" Properties*

"Is" Property	Description
IsNotPublic	Is a Boolean that represents whether the Type is not public
IsPrimitive	Is a Boolean that represents whether the Type is a .NET primitive (Int32, Single, Char, and so on)
IsPublic	Is a Boolean that represents whether the Type is public
IsSealed	Is a Boolean that represents whether the Type is sealed
IsSerializable	Is a Boolean that represents whether the Type is serializable
IsValueType	Is a Boolean that represents whether the Type is a value type

Listing 18-1 shows how to build a handy little tool that displays the member methods, properties, and variables of the classes found in the six most commonly referenced assemblies in the .NET Framework using reflection.

> **Note** To save space and because it isn't directly relevant, all the code examples in this chapter don't include the auto-generated Windows Form GUI code. (See Chapters 9 and 10 for more information on Windows Form development.)

Listing 18-1. *Referencing the Class Members of the .NET Framework*

```
namespace Reflecting
{
    //...Standard Usings
    using namespace System::Reflection;

    public ref class Form1 : public System::Windows::Forms::Form
    {
        //...Auto-generated GUI interface code

    private: array<Type^>^ types;
    private: static array<String^>^ assemblies =
            {
                "System",
                "System.Drawing",
                "System.Xml",
                "System.Windows.Forms",
                "System.Data",
                "mscorlib"
            };

    private:
        System::Void Form1_Load(System::Object^ sender, System::EventArgs^ e)
        {
```

```cpp
            for each (String ^assembly  in assemblies)
            {
                cbAssemblies->Items->Add(assembly);
            }
            cbAssemblies->SelectedIndex = 0;
        }

    private:
        System::Void cbAssemblies_SelectedIndexChanged(System::Object^ sender,
                                                       System::EventArgs^  e)
        {
            Assembly^ assembly = Assembly::LoadWithPartialName(
                            assemblies[cbAssemblies->SelectedIndex]);

            types = assembly->GetTypes();

            cbDataTypes->Items->Clear();

            for (int i = 0; i < types->Length; i++)
            {
                cbDataTypes->Items->Add(types[i]->ToString());
            }
            cbDataTypes->SelectedIndex = 0;
        }

    private:
        System::Void cbDataTypes_SelectedIndexChanged(System::Object^ sender,
                                                      System::EventArgs^  e)
        {
            Type ^type = types[cbDataTypes->SelectedIndex];

            array <MemberInfo^>^ methods = type->GetMethods();
            lbMethods->Items->Clear();
            for (int i = 0; i < methods->Length; i++)
            {
                lbMethods->Items->Add(methods[i]->ToString());
            }

            array <PropertyInfo^>^ properties = type->GetProperties();
            lbProperties->Items->Clear();
            for (int i = 0; i < properties->Length; i++)
            {
                lbProperties->Items->Add(properties[i]->ToString());
            }

            array <MemberInfo^>^ variables = type->GetFields();
            lbVariables->Items->Clear();
            for (int i = 0; i < variables->Length; i++)
            {
                lbVariables->Items->Add(variables[i]->ToString());
            }
        }
    };
}
```

As you can see from the code in the preceding example, reflection can be fairly easy to work with. Simply "Get" the metadata needed and then loop through the metadata. Admittedly, the example is not the most elaborate, but it still shows the potential power it has in making the metadata information within an assembly available.

Most of the preceding code is simply to load the appropriate GUI controls, but one thing new in the preceding example that hasn't been covered before is the use of the System::Reflection::Assembly class. The Assembly class is a core building block of all .NET Framework applications, though normally, even as a .NET developer, you seldom have to know of its existence.

When it comes to reflection, the Assembly class contains the starting point for retrieving any public metadata information you want about the current active assembly or one that you load using one of the many different loading methods. The only reason I see that there are multiple load methods (each has multiple overload) is due to the duplicated method signature required to support the myriad ways available to load an assembly. Essentially, all load methods do the same thing—load the assembly—with the only differences relating to the amount of information known about the assembly being loaded and the source of the assembly.

The LoadWithPartialName() method requires the least amount of information—simply the name of an assembly. It does not care about version, culture, and so on. It is also the method that the .NET Framework frowns upon using for that exact reason. In fact, Microsoft has gone and made it obsolete in version 2 of the .NET Framework. But in the case of this example, it works just fine.

Figure 18-1 shows Reflecting.exe in action. As you can see, it's made up of two ComboBoxes and three ListBoxes. The first ComboBox provides a way of selecting the assembly, and the second allows you to select the type. The results of these two selections are the methods, properties, and variables displayed in the ListBoxes.

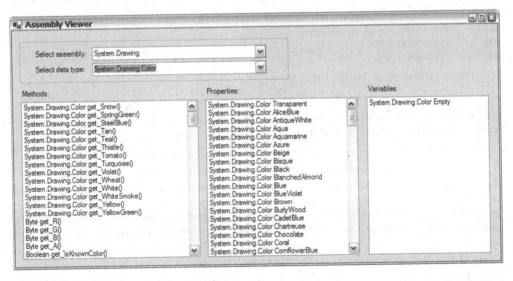

Figure 18-1. *The Reflecting program in action*

Dynamically Invoking or Late-Binding Objects

Reflection provides you with the rather powerful feature known as *late binding*. Late binding is the ability for different methods or objects to be invoked at runtime. These methods and objects are not statically known at compile time.

A cool thing about reflection is that once you have a reference to the method you want to invoke (which I showed how to do previously), it is not a large step to execute that method in a dynamic fashion. In fact, all you have to do is invoke the method using the (you guessed it) MethodInfo::Invoke() method.

The trickiest part of invoking methods using reflection is realizing that there are two types of methods: static and instance. *Static* methods are the easiest to handle, as you don't need to create an instance of the method's class to invoke it. Simply find the Method reference type and then use the Invoke() method:

```
MethodInfo ^method = type->GetMethod();
method->Invoke(nullptr, nullptr);
```

Notice that in the preceding example the Invoke() method has two parameters. The first is the instance of the class for which you are invoking the method. The second is an array of parameters that will be passed to the method. As you can now tell, the preceding example is not only a static method. It also takes no parameters.

If the method you want to invoke is an *instance* method, it is not quite as easy because you need to create an instance of the type for that method. The .NET Framework provides you help in the way of the System::Activator class, which contains the static CreateInstance() method to create objects:

```
Type ^type = assembly->GetType("MyType");
Object ^typeInstance = Activator::CreateInstance(type);
```

Now that you have an instance of the method class, all you have to do is pass it as the first parameter:

```
method->Invoke(typeInstance, nullptr);
```

To pass parameters to the Invoke() method, simply create an array of them and assign the array to the second parameter:

```
array<Object^>^ args = gcnew array<Object^>(2);
args[0] = parameterOne;
args[1] = parameterTwo;
```

That's really all there is to late binding.

Note This is a second Invoke() method, but I have yet to use it as it is much more involved. If you are interested, it can be found in the .NET Framework documentation.

Listing 18-2 shows how to execute both a static and an instance method using reflection. The first thing the example does is create an array using reflection of all the static color properties of the Color structure. It then displays the color as the background of a label by invoking the property's getter method. Next, the example dynamically invokes a method from one of two different classes to display the color name in the label. (There are much easier ways to do this without reflection, obviously.)

Listing 18-2. *Using Reflection to Change the Properties of a Label*

```
namespace Invoking
{
    //... Standard Usings
    using namespace System::Reflection;

    public ref class Form1 : public System::Windows::Forms::Form
    {
        // Auto-generated GUI Interface code
```

```cpp
private:
    array <PropertyInfo^>^ colors;

private:
    System::Void Form1_Load(System::Object^ sender, System::EventArgs^ e)
    {
        Type^ colorType = Color::typeid;
        colors = colorType->GetProperties();

        for (int i = 0; i < colors->Length; i++)
        {
            if (colors[i]->ToString()->IndexOf("System.Drawing.Color") >= 0)
                cbColor->Items->Add(colors[i]->ToString());
        }
        cbColor->SelectedIndex = 0;
    }

    System::Void comboBox1_SelectedIndexChanged(System::Object^ sender,
                                                System::EventArgs^ e)
    {
        static bool alternateWrite = true;
        PropertyInfo ^ColorProp = colors[cbColor->SelectedIndex];

        MethodInfo ^PropMethod = ColorProp->GetGetMethod();

        lbColor->BackColor = (Color)PropMethod->Invoke(nullptr,nullptr);

        Assembly ^assembly = Assembly::Load("Invoking");

        Type ^type;
        if (alternateWrite)
            type = assembly->GetType("Invoking.Writer1");
        else
            type = assembly->GetType("Invoking.Writer2");

        alternateWrite = !alternateWrite;

        MethodInfo ^ColorMethod = type->GetMethod("aColor");

        Object ^writerInst = Activator::CreateInstance(type);

        array <Object^>^ args = gcnew array <Object^>(1);
        args[0] = PropMethod->Invoke(nullptr,nullptr);

        lbColor->Text = (String^)ColorMethod->Invoke(writerInst, args);
    }
};
```

```
ref class Writer1
{
public:
    String ^aColor(Color ^col)
    {
        return String::Format("[Writer 1] {0}", col->ToString());
    }
};

ref class Writer2
{
public:
    String ^aColor(Color ^col)
    {
        return String::Format("[Writer 2] {0}", col->ToString());
    }
};
}
```

Note The GetType() method uses C# syntax when looking at the type within the assembly. Therefore, it uses a period (.) in place of a double colon (::).

As you can see from the preceding example, there is quite a bit of overhead involved in reflection and late binding, so you should use these techniques sparingly.

Figure 18-2 shows Invoking.exe in action. Pay attention to the text that prefixes the color displayed in the label as it alternates from "[Writer 1]" to "[Writer 2]".

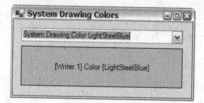

Figure 18-2. *The Invoking program in action*

Attributes

You have seen .NET Framework–defined attributes used a few times already in this book. For example:

- In Chapter 8, you used the Serializable attribute to enable serialization for a ref class.

- In Chapter 15, you used the WebService and WebMethod attributes to enable a class and a method to be Web services.

- In Chapter 16, you used the ThreadStatic attribute to make a static variable unique in each thread.

The overriding theme in every .NET Framework attribute is that it provides additional information to the class, enum, method, etc., for which it is associated. Basically, you can think of attributes as declarative tags that are written to an assembly at compile time to annotate or mark up a class and/or its members so that class and/or its members can be later extracted at runtime, possibly to change its normal behavior.

To add an attribute to a class or its members, you add code in front of the element you want to annotate with the following syntax:

```
[AttributeName(ConstructorArguments, optionalpropertyname=value)]
```

If you want to add more than one attribute, you simply add more than one attribute within the square brackets, delimited by commas:

```
[Attribute1(), Attribute2()]
```

An important feature to you (other than the changed behavior caused by the .NET Framework attributes) is that you can access attributes using reflection. A more important feature is that you can create your own custom attributes.

Creating a Custom Attribute

According to the Microsoft documentation, a *custom attribute* is just a class that is derived from the System::Attribute class with a few minor additional criteria.

The additional criteria are as follows:

- The custom attribute class needs to be public.
- By convention, the attribute name should end in "Attribute". A neat thing is that when you implement the attribute, you don't have to add the trailing "Attribute", as it's automatically added. In other words, as you saw in Chapter 15, WebMethod and WebMethodAttribute are the same.
- There's an additional AttributeUsageAttribute that you can apply to your custom attribute.
- All properties that will be written to the metadata need to be public.
- The properties available to be written to the metadata are restricted to Integer type (Byte, Int32, and so on), floating point (Single or Double), Char, String, Boolean, or Enum. Note that this means the very common DateTime data type isn't supported. (I show you how to get around this limitation later in this chapter.)

Of all the additional criteria, the only one you need to look at in more detail is the AttributeUsageAttribute attribute. This attribute controls the manner in which the custom attribute is used. To be more accurate, it defines three behaviors: which data types the custom attribute is valid on, if the custom attribute is inherited, and whether more than one of the custom attributes can be applied to a single data type.

You can specify that the custom attribute can be applied to any assembly entity (see Table 18-4) by giving the AttributeUsageAttribute attribute an AttributeTargets::All value. On the other hand, if you want to restrict the custom attribute to a specific type or a combination of types, then you would specify one or a combination (by ORing) of the AttributeTargets enumerations in Table 18-4.

Table 18-4. *AttributeTargets Enumeration*

All	Assembly	Class	Constructor	Delegate
Enum	Event	Field	Interface	Method
Module	Parameter	Property	ReturnValue	Struct

The second parameter of the AttributeUsageAttribute attribute specifies whether any class that inherits from a class that implements the custom attribute inherits that custom attribute. The default is that a class does inherit the custom attribute.

The final parameter allows a custom attribute to be applied more than one time to a single type. The default is that only a single custom attribute can be applied.

There are three ways that you can have data passed into the attribute when implementing. The first is by the custom attribute's construction. The second is by a public property. The third is by a public member variable.

Listing 18-3 and Listing 18-4 show the creation of two custom documentation attributes. The first is the description of the element within the class, and the second is a change history. By nature you should be able to apply both of these attributes to any type within a class and you should also have the attributes inherited. These attributes mostly differ in that a description can be applied only once to an element in a class, whereas the change history will be used repeatedly.

Listing 18-3. *Documentation Custom Attributes Definition*

```
using namespace System::Reflection;

namespace Documentation
{
    [AttributeUsage(AttributeTargets::All, Inherited=true, AllowMultiple=false)]
    public ref class DescriptionAttribute : public Attribute
    {
        String  ^mAuthor;
        DateTime mCompileDate;
        String  ^mDescription;

    public:
        DescriptionAttribute(String ^Author, String ^Description);

        property String^ Author { String^ get(); }
        property String^ Description { String^ get(); }
        property String^ CompileDate { String^ get(); }
    };

    [AttributeUsage(AttributeTargets::All, Inherited=true, AllowMultiple=true)]
    public ref class HistoryAttribute : public Attribute
    {
        String  ^mAuthor;
        DateTime mModifyDate;
        String  ^mDescription;

    public:
        HistoryAttribute(String ^Author, String ^Description);

        property String^ Author { String^ get(); }
        property String^ Description { String^ get(); }
        property String^ ModifyDate
        {
            String^ get();
            void set(String^ value);
        }
    };
}
```

Listing 18-4. *Documentation Custom Attributes Implemenation*

```cpp
#include "Documentation.h"

namespace Documentation
{
    // ------------- DescriptionAttribute -------------------

    DescriptionAttribute::DescriptionAttribute(String ^Author,
                                               String ^Description)
    {
        mAuthor = Author;
        mDescription = Description;
        mCompileDate = DateTime::Now;
    }

    String^ DescriptionAttribute::Author::get()
    {
        return mAuthor;
    }

    String^ DescriptionAttribute::Description::get()
    {
        return mDescription;
    }

    String^ DescriptionAttribute::CompileDate::get()
    {
        return mCompileDate.ToShortDateString();
    }

    // ------------- HistoryAttribute -------------------

    HistoryAttribute::HistoryAttribute(String ^Author, String ^Description)
    {
        mAuthor = Author;
        mDescription = Description;
        mModifyDate = DateTime::Now;
    }

    String^ HistoryAttribute::Author::get()
    {
        return mAuthor;
    }

    String^ HistoryAttribute::Description::get()
    {
        return mDescription;
    }

    String^ HistoryAttribute::ModifyDate::get()
    {
        return mModifyDate.ToShortDateString();
    }
```

```
void HistoryAttribute::ModifyDate::set(String ^value)
{
    mModifyDate = Convert::ToDateTime(value);
}
}
```

As you can see by the code, other than the [AttributeUsage] attribute (which is inherited from System::Attribute), there is nothing special about these classes. They are simply classes with a constructor and a few public properties and private member variables.

The only thing to note is the passing of dates in the form of a string, which are then converted to DateTime structure. Attributes are not allowed to pass the DateTime structure as pointed out previously, so this simple trick fixes this problem.

Implementing a Custom Attribute

As you can see in the example shown in Listing 18-5, you implement custom attributes in the same way as you do .NET Framework attributes. In this example, the DescriptionAttribute attribute you created earlier is applied to two classes, a constructor, a member method, and a property. Also, the HistoryAttribute attribute is applied twice to the first class and then later to the property.

Listing 18-5. *Implementing the Description and History Attributes*

```
using namespace System;
using namespace Documentation;

namespace DocTestLib
{
    [Description("Stephen Fraser",
                 "This is TestClass1 to test the documentation Attribute.")]
    [History("Stephen Fraser", "Original Version.", ModifyDate="11/27/02")]
    [History("Stephen Fraser", "Added DoesNothing Method to do nothing.")]
    public ref class TestClass1
    {
    public:
        [Description("Stephen Fraser",
                     "This is default constructor for TextClass1.")]
        TestClass1() {}

        [Description("Stephen Fraser",
                     "This is method does nothing for TestClass1.")]
        void DoesNothing() {}

        [Description("Stephen Fraser", "Added Variable property.")]
        [History("Stephen Fraser", "Removed extra CodeDoc Attribute")]
        property String^ Variable;
    };

    [Description("Stephen Fraser",
                 "This is TestClass2 to test the documentation Attribute.")]
    public ref class TestClass2
    {
    };
}
```

Notice in Listing 18-5 that "Attribute" is stripped off the end of the attributes. This is optional, and it is perfectly legal to keep "Attribute" on the attribute name.

Another thing that you might want to note is how to implement a named property to an attribute. This is done in the first use of the History attribute where I specify the date that the change was made:

```
[History("Stephen Fraser", "Original Version.", ModifyDate="11/27/02")]
```

The modified date is also a string and not a DateTime as you would expect. This is because (as I pointed out previously) it is not legal to pass a DateTime to an attribute.

Using a Custom Attribute

You looked at how to use custom attributes when you learned about reflection. Custom attributes are just placed as metadata onto the assembly and, as you learned in reflection, it is possible to examine an assembly's metadata.

The only new thing about assembly reflection and custom attributes is that you need to call the GetCustomAttribute() method to get a specific custom attribute or the GetCustomAttributes() method to get all custom attributes for a specific type.

The tricky part with either of these two methods is that you have to typecast them to their appropriate type, as both return an Object type. What makes this tricky is that you need to use the full name of the attribute or, in other words, unlike when you implemented it, you need the "Attribute" suffix added. If you created a custom attribute that doesn't end in "Attribute" (which is perfectly legal, I might add), then this won't be an issue.

Both of these methods have a few overloads, but they basically break down to one of three syntaxes. To get all custom attributes:

```
public: Object ^GetCustomAttributes(Boolean useInhertiance);
// For example:
array <Object^>^ CustAttr = info->GetCustomAttributes(true);
```

To get all of a specific type of custom attribute:

```
public: Object ^GetCustomAttributes(Type ^type, Boolean useInhertiance);
// For example:
array <Object^>^CustAttr = info->GetCustomAttributes(HistoryAttribute::typeid,
                                                      true);
```

Or to get a specific attribute for a specific type reference:

```
public: static Attribute^ GetCustomAttribute(ReflectionReference^, Type^);
// For Example
Attribute ^attribute =
    Attribute::GetCustomAttribute(methodInfo, DescriptionAttribute::typeid);
```

Caution If the type allows multiple custom attributes of a single type to be added to itself, then the GetCustomAttribute() method returns an Array and not an Attribute.

Listing 18-6 is really nothing more than another example of assembly reflection, except this time it uses an additional GetCustomAttribute() and GetCustomAttributes() method. The example simply walks through an assembly that you passed to it and displays information about any class, constructor, method, or property that is found within it. Plus, it shows any custom Description or History attributes that you may have added.

Listing 18-6. *Using Custom Attributes to Document Classes*

```cpp
using namespace System;
using namespace Reflection;
using namespace Documentation;

void DisplayDescription(Attribute ^attr)
{
    if (attr != nullptr)
    {
        DescriptionAttribute ^cd = (DescriptionAttribute^)attr;
        Console::WriteLine("  Author: {0} -- Compiled: {1}",
            cd->Author, cd->CompileDate);
        Console::WriteLine("  Description: {0}", cd->Description);
        Console::WriteLine("    ---- Change History ----");
    }
    else
        Console::WriteLine("    No Documentation");
}

void DisplayHistory(array<Object^>^ attr)
{
    if (attr->Length > 0)
    {
        for each (HistoryAttribute^ cd in attr)
        {
            Console::WriteLine("    Author: {0} -- Modified: {1}",
                cd->Author, cd->ModifyDate);
            Console::WriteLine("    Description: {0}", cd->Description);
        }
    }
    else
        Console::WriteLine("    No changes");
}

void DisplayAttributes(MemberInfo ^info)
{
    DisplayDescription(Attribute::GetCustomAttribute(info,
                        DescriptionAttribute::typeid));
    DisplayHistory(info->GetCustomAttributes(HistoryAttribute::typeid, true));
}

void PrintClassInfo(Type ^type)
{
    Console::WriteLine("Class: {0}", type->ToString());
    DisplayAttributes(type);

    array<ConstructorInfo^>^ constructors = type->GetConstructors();
    for (int i = 0; i < constructors->Length; i++)
    {
        Console::WriteLine("Constructor: {0}", constructors[i]->ToString());
        DisplayAttributes(constructors[i]);
    }
```

```
    array <MethodInfo^>^ methods = type->GetMethods((BindingFlags)
        (BindingFlags::Public|BindingFlags::Instance|BindingFlags::DeclaredOnly));
    for (int i = 0; i < methods->Length; i++)
    {
        Console::WriteLine("Method: {0}", methods[i]->ToString());
        DisplayAttributes(methods[i]);
    }

    array<PropertyInfo^>^ properties = type->GetProperties((BindingFlags)
        (BindingFlags::Public|BindingFlags::Instance|BindingFlags::DeclaredOnly));
    for (int i = 0; i < properties->Length; i++)
    {
        Console::WriteLine("Property: {0}", properties[i]->ToString());
        DisplayAttributes(properties[i]);
    }
}

void main(array<System::String ^> ^args)
{
    try
    {
        Assembly ^assembly = Assembly::LoadFrom(args[0]);

        array<Type^>^ types = assembly->GetTypes();

        for (int i = 0; i < types->Length; i++)
        {
            PrintClassInfo(types[i]);
            Console::WriteLine();
        }
    }
    catch(System::IO::FileNotFoundException^)
    {
        Console::WriteLine("Can't find assembly: {0}\n", args[0]);
    }
}
```

One thing that this example has that the previous reflection example doesn't is the use of the BindingFlags enumeration. The BindingFlags enum specifies the way in which the search for members and types within an assembly is managed by reflection. In the preceding example I used the following flags:

```
BindingFlags::Public | BindingFlags::Instance | BindingFlags::DeclaredOnly
```

This combination of flags specified that only public instance members that have only been declared at the current level (in other words, not inherited) will be considered in the search.

Also notice that even though the DisplayAttributes() method is called with a parameter of type Type, ConstructorInfo, MethodInfo, or PropertyInfo, it is declared using a parameter of type MemberInfo. The reason this is possible is because all the previously mentioned classes inherit from the MemberInfo class.

Figure 18-3 shows DocumentationWriter.exe in action. The dates in Figure 18-3 are based on when I compiled the assembly and most likely will differ from your results.

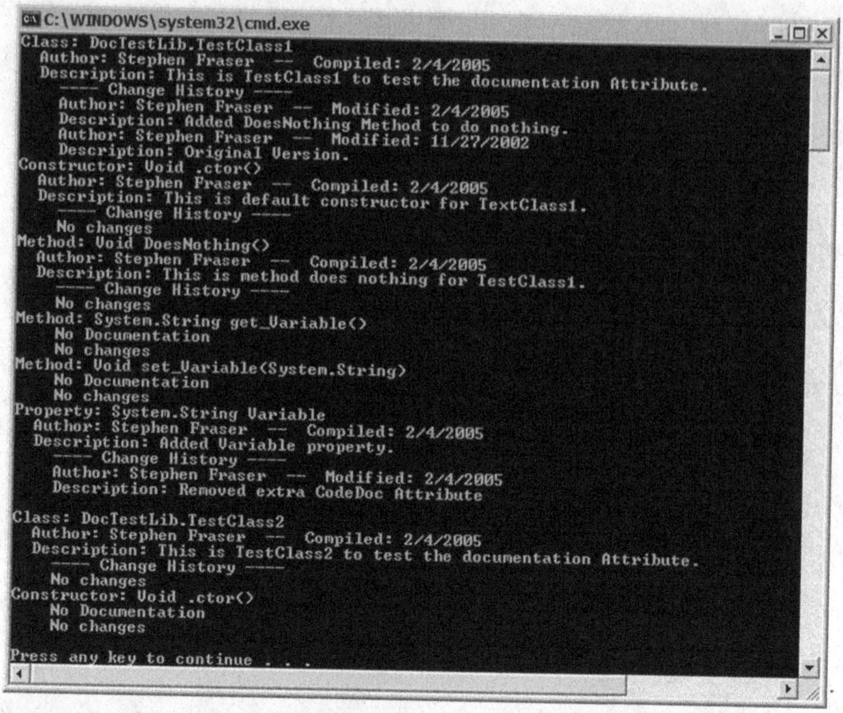

Figure 18-3. *The DocumentationWriter program in action*

Shared Assemblies

Up until now you have been developing only private assemblies. In other words, you have been developing assemblies that are local to the application and that can be accessed only by the application. In most cases, private assemblies will be all you really need to develop. But what happens if you have multiple applications that share a common assembly? You could make a copy of the assembly and copy it to each application's directory. Or you could use the second type of assembly, a *shared assembly*.

Shared assemblies are accessible to any program that is run on the same machine where the assembly resides. By the way, you work with shared assemblies whenever you use any of the classes or any other data type of the .NET Framework. This seems logical, as every .NET application shares these assemblies.

The Global Assembly Cache

Unlike private assemblies, shared assemblies are placed in a common directory structure known as the *global assembly cache* (GAC). If and when you go looking for the GAC, you will find it off of your <WINDIR> (Windows or Windows NT) directory, in a subdirectory aptly called assembly.

When you open the assembly directory in Windows Explorer, it has the appearance of being one big directory made up of many different assemblies (see Figure 18-4). In reality, the assembly directory has a complex directory structure that gets hidden (thankfully) by Windows Explorer.

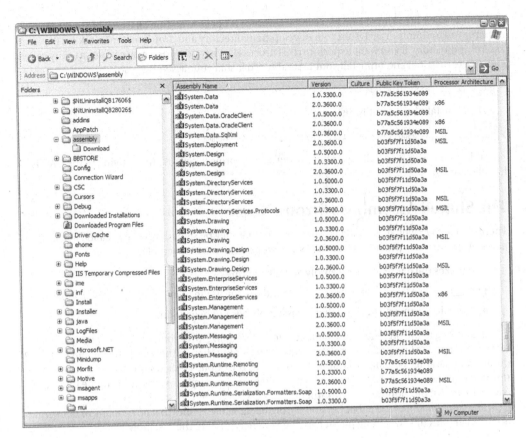

Figure 18-4. *The GAC*

In fact, the assembly directory itself only contains subdirectories. One subdirectory is called GAC, which in turn contains subdirectories for each assembly. Each of these subdirectories contains one or more subdirectories, one for each version of the assembly in the GAC. This directory finally contains the assembly's .dll file that your own assemblies reference.

Off of the <WINDIR>\assembly directory you will also find other subdirectories. You will find directories for each version of natively compiled code used by your system (i.e., any code that is precompiled in the machine language of the host machine). Normally, you work with MSIL code, but because this needs the additional step of compiling to machine code, the .NET Framework precompiles some of its more frequently used assemblies to save the time of performing this compile step. You will find that the native code directory structure is similar to that of the GAC.

There is also the possibility of finding another directory structure off of <WinDIR>\assembly. This one contains assemblies downloaded by ASP.NET, so that they can be used by Web Forms.

Note You can see the real structure of the GAC by accessing it via the command line. (Believe me... it isn't pretty.)

Adding Assemblies to the GAC

Fortunately, you can and probably should have remained ignorant of the complex nature of the GAC. (But I'm pretty sure most of you at one point or another will look into the GAC, so I decided to give you a heads-up.) The reason you can be ignorant is because adding an assembly to the GAC requires you to simply drag it from your development directory and drop it on the Windows Explorer assembly directory. If you want to perform this process in a batch routine, you can use a utility called gacutil.exe to install and uninstall your assembly. To install your assembly, use

```
> gacutil /i <assembly name>.dll
```

To uninstall the assembly, use

```
> gacutil /u <assembly name>.dll, Version=<version number>
```

It is even easier to install assemblies using a setup project because the copying to the GAC is handled for you.

The Shared Assembly's Strong Name

There is a catch to global assemblies. They require that they be signed by what is called a *strong name*. A strong name provides three necessary enhancements to assemblies:

- It makes the name of the assembly globally unique.
- It makes it so that no one else can steal and use the name (generally known as *spoofing*).
- It provides a means to verify that an assembly has not been tampered with.

The strong name provides these enhancements by adding three things to the assembly: a simple text name, a public key, and a digital signature. The combination of the simple text name and the public key guarantees the name is globally unique, as the public key is unique to the party creating the assembly, and it is assumed that the party will make the simple text assembly name unique within their own development environment.

The combination of the public key and the digital signature verifies that no spoofing or tampering occurred. It does this by adding public/private key encryption to the assembly.

Note Public/private key encryption uses two keys as its name suggests. The private key is used to encrypt something, and the public key is used to decrypt it. What makes this combination secure is that only a corresponding public key can be used to decrypt something encrypted by the private key.

So how does public/private key encryption apply to global assemblies? Before you get all excited, you should know that an assembly is not encrypted. Instead, at compile time the compiler creates a hash signature based on the contents of the assembly and then uses the private key (of public/private encryption) to encrypt the hash signature into a digital signature. Finally, the digital signature is added to the assembly. Later, when the assembly is loaded by the CLR, the digital signature is decrypted using the public key back into the hash signature, and the hash signature is verified to make sure that the assembly is unchanged.

The reason this all works is that only the owner of the private key can create a valid digital signature that can be decrypted by the public key.

Like most things in .NET application development, what actually happens is a lot more complex than what you need to do to get it the happen. In this case, to add a strong name to an assembly requires two very simple steps. First, you create a strong name key file by typing the following statement at the command prompt:

```
> sn -k StrongNameFileName.snk
```

Then you update [AssemblyKeyFileAttribute] in the AssemblyInfo.cpp file, which incidentally is created by all C++/CLI templates:

```
[assembly:AssemblyKeyFileAttribute("StrongNameFileName.snk")];
```

You can place the key in the project directory as the preceding example shows, or you can place it anywhere on your computer and provide a full path to the attribute.

Re-signing an Assembly

If you are security conscious, you may have seen a big problem in the preceding strong name system. If you are developing software in a team environment, everyone who needs to update the assembly must have access to the private key so that the assembly can be accessed using the same public key. This means there are a lot of potential areas for security leaks.

To remedy this, the strong name utility sn.exe has an additional option. It provides the capability for an assembly to be re-signed. This allows privileged developers a chance to sign the assembly with the company's private key before releasing it to the public. The command you need to type at the command line is

```
> sn -R <assembly name> <strong key file name>
```

Notice this time instead of the –k option you use the –R option, stating you want to replace the key instead of create one. You also provide the utility a completed assembly and a previously created strong key file.

Signcoded Digital Signature

Nowhere in the preceding strong name process is the user of the assembly guaranteed that the creator of the strong key is a trusted source, only that it is unchanged from the time it was created.

To remedy this, you need to execute the signcode.exe wizard on your assembly to add an authentic digital certificate created by a third party. Once you have done this, the user of the assembly can find out who created the assembly and decide whether he or she wants to trust it.

Caution You need to compile the assembly with the "final" strong name before you signcode it. The signcode.exe wizard only works with strong named assemblies. Also, re-signing a signcoded assembly invalidates its authentic digital certificate.

Versioning

Anyone who has worked with Windows for any length of time will probably be hit at least once with DLL Hell, the reason being that versioning was not very well supported in previous Windows developing environments. It was possible to swap different versions of .dlls in and out of the registry, which caused all sorts of compatibility issues. Well, with .NET this is no longer the case, as versioning is well supported.

That being said, a word of caution: The CLR ignores versioning in private assemblies. If you include a private assembly in your application's directory structure, the CLR assumes you know what you are doing and will use that version, even if the correct version, based on version number, is in the GAC.

The .NET Framework supports a four-part version: major, minor, build, and revision. You will most frequently see version numbers written out like this: 1.2.3.4. On occasion, however, you will see them like this: 1:2:3:4. By convention, a change in the major and minor numbers means that an incompatibility has been introduced, whereas a change in the build and revision numbers means compatibility has been retained. How you actually use version numbers, on the other hand, is up to you.

Here is how the .NET Framework handles versioning in a nutshell: Only the global assembly version that was referenced at compile time will work in the application. That is, all four version parts need to match. (Well, that is not quite true. You will see a way to overrule which version number to use later in this chapter.) This should not cause a problem even if there is more than one version of a shared assembly available, because multiple versions of a shared assembly can be placed without conflict into the GAC (see Figure 18-5). Okay, there might be a problem if the shared assembly with the corresponding version number is not in the GAC, as this throws a `System::IO::FileNotFoundException` exception.

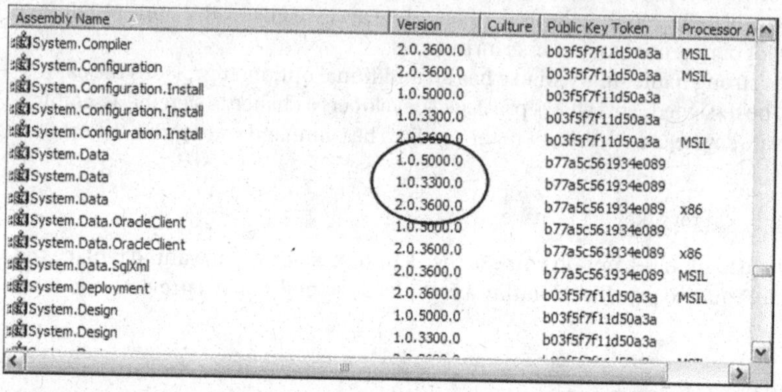

Assembly Name	Version	Culture	Public Key Token	Processor A
System.Compiler	2.0.3600.0		b03f5f7f11d50a3a	MSIL
System.Configuration	2.0.3600.0		b03f5f7f11d50a3a	MSIL
System.Configuration.Install	1.0.5000.0		b03f5f7f11d50a3a	
System.Configuration.Install	1.0.3300.0		b03f5f7f11d50a3a	
System.Configuration.Install	2.0.3600.0		b03f5f7f11d50a3a	MSIL
System.Data	1.0.5000.0		b77a5c561934e089	
System.Data	1.0.3300.0		b77a5c561934e089	
System.Data	2.0.3600.0		b77a5c561934e089	x86
System.Data.OracleClient	1.0.5000.0		b77a5c561934e089	
System.Data.OracleClient	2.0.3600.0		b77a5c561934e089	x86
System.Data.SqlXml	2.0.3600.0		b77a5c561934e089	MSIL
System.Deployment	2.0.3600.0		b03f5f7f11d50a3a	MSIL
System.Design	1.0.5000.0		b03f5f7f11d50a3a	
System.Design	1.0.3300.0		b03f5f7f11d50a3a	

Figure 18-5. *Multiple versions of an assembly in the GAC*

Setting the Version Number

Version numbers are stored as metadata within the assembly, and to set the version number requires that you update the `AssemblyVersionAttribute` attribute. To make things easier for you, the Visual Studio 2005 project template wizard automatically provides a default `AssemblyVersionAttribute` attribute within the AssemblyInfo.cpp file.

You set the version number by simply changing the dummy value

```
[assembly:AssemblyVersionAttribute("1.0.*")];
```

to a value that makes sense in your development environment, for example:

```
[assembly:AssemblyVersionAttribute("3.1.2.45")];
```

Notice the asterisk (*) in the default version number value provided by Visual Studio 2005. This asterisk signifies that the compiler will automatically create the build and revision numbers for you. When the compiler does this, it places the number of days since January 1, 2000, in the build and the number of seconds since midnight divided by two in the revision.

Personally, I think it's a mistake to use the auto-generated method, as the version numbers then provide no meaning. Plus, using auto-generated numbers forces you to recompile the application referencing the assembly every time you recompile the shared assembly. Auto-generated numbers aren't so bad if the application and the shared reference share into the same solution, but they aren't so good if the application and the shared reference share into different solutions, and even worse if different developers are developing the application and shared assembly.

Getting the Version Number

It took me a while to figure out how to get the version number out of the assembly (but that might just be me). As I found out, though, it's really easy to do, because it's just a property of the name of the assembly. I think the code is easier to understand than the explanation:

```
Assembly ^assembly = Assembly::GetExecutingAssembly();
Version ^version = assembly->GetName()->Version;
```

The only tricky part is getting the currently executing assembly, which isn't too tricky because the .NET Framework provides you with a static member to retrieve it for you.

No DLL Hell Example

Now that you've covered everything you need to create a shared assembly, you'll create one. Listing 18-7 shows the source code of a very simple class library assembly containing one class and one property. The property contains the version of the assembly.

Listing 18-7. *A Shared Assembly That Knows Its Version*

```
using namespace System;
using namespace System::Reflection;

namespace SharedAssembly
{
    public ref class SharedClass
    {
    public:
        property System::Version^ Version()
        {
            System::Version^ get()
            {
                Assembly ^assembly = Assembly::GetExecutingAssembly();
                return assembly->GetName()->Version;
            }
        }
    };
}
```

The code is short, sweet, and offers no surprises. Listing 18-8 contains a filled-in AssemblyInfo.cpp file. To save space, all the comments have been removed.

Listing 18-8. *A Standard AssemblyInfo.cpp File*

```
using namespace System::Reflection;
using namespace System::Runtime::CompilerServices;

[assembly:AssemblyTitleAttribute("A Shared Assembly")];
[assembly:AssemblyDescriptionAttribute("An assembly that knows its version")];
[assembly:AssemblyConfigurationAttribute("Release Version")];
[assembly:AssemblyCompanyAttribute("ProCppCLI")];
[assembly:AssemblyProductAttribute("Pro C++/CLI Series")];
[assembly:AssemblyCopyrightAttribute("Copyright (C) by Stephen Fraser 2005")];
[assembly:AssemblyTrademarkAttribute("ProCppCLI is a Trademark of blah")];
[assembly:AssemblyCultureAttribute("")];
```

```
[assembly:AssemblyVersionAttribute("1.0.0.0")];

[assembly:AssemblyDelaySignAttribute(false)];
[assembly:AssemblyKeyFileAttribute("SharedAssembly.snk")];
[assembly:AssemblyKeyNameAttribute("")];
```

You saw most of the important code earlier in this chapter, so I won't go over this in detail. I also think that most of the rest of the code is self-explanatory. Only the AssemblyCultureAttribute attribute needs to be explained, and I do that a little later in this chapter.

Of all the attributes in the preceding source file, only two attributes need to be filled in to enable an assembly to be a shared one. The first attribute is AssemblyVersionAttribute. It already has a default value but I changed it to give it more meaning to me.

The second attribute is AssemblyKeyFileAttribute, in which you place the strong key. Remember, you can either pass a full path to the attribute or use a key in the project source directory. Because I'm using a strong key file in the project source, I have to copy my key file SharedAssembly.snk into the project's source directory.

Before you compile the project, change the project's output directory to be local to the project and not the solution. In other words, change the project's configuration properties' output directory to read only $(ConfigurationName) and not the default $(SolutionDir)$(ConfigurationName). The reason you want to do this is that you don't want a copy of SharedAssembly.dll in the same directory as the application assembly referencing it, because otherwise it will be used instead of the copy in the GAC.

Now, when you compile the project, an assembly called SharedAssembly.dll is generated in the project's Debug or Release directory, depending on which environment you're doing the build in. This file needs to be copied to the GAC either by dragging and dropping it there or via gacutil.exe. Figure 18-6 shows what the entry in the Windows Explorer GAC display looks like.

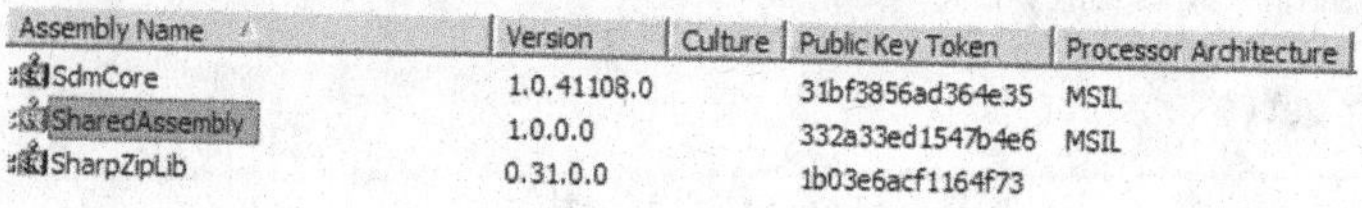

Assembly Name	Version	Culture	Public Key Token	Processor Architecture
SdmCore	1.0.41108.0		31bf3856ad364e35	MSIL
SharedAssembly	1.0.0.0		332a33ed1547b4e6	MSIL
SharpZipLib	0.31.0.0		1b03e6acf1164f73	

Figure 18-6. SharedAssembly in the GAC

Now you'll create an application assembly to reference the shared assembly (see Listing 18-9). All this application does is write out the version number of the shared assembly.

Listing 18-9. Referencing a Shared Assembly

```
using namespace System;
using namespace SharedAssembly;

void main()
{
    SharedClass ^sa = gcnew SharedClass();
    Console::WriteLine(sa->Version);
}
```

The code is not new, but to get this to work you need to reference the assembly SharedAssembly.dll. It is important to understand that the assembly you reference during the compile does not need to be the same as the one that you actually execute at runtime. They just have to have the same name, version, and public key token. Therefore, even though you are going to use the assembly within the GAC, you reference the assembly within the solution to get the definition of the SharedClass class and the Version property.

To reference SharedAssembly.dll, you need to perform the following steps:

1. Open the Properties window.

2. Select the References folder.

3. Click the Add New Reference button. This will bring up the Add Reference dialog box.

4. Select the Projects tab.

5. Select the shared assembly from the list.

    Or, if the shared assembly is in a different solution, click Browse, navigate to the location of the assembly, and then select the assembly.

6. Click OK.

7. In Build Properties, set Local copy to False (see Figure 18-7).

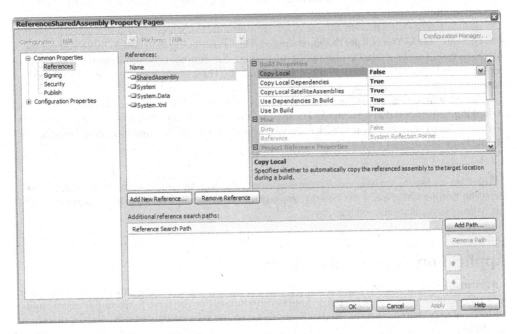

Figure 18-7. *The Add Reference dialog box*

The most important step of the preceding sequence is step 7. This step causes the build process not to make a local copy of the assembly and instead causes the GAC to be used as the source of the assembly.

Caution Don't miss step 7. If you do, then you are not using a shared assembly, just a local copy of the assembly that gets moved to the application's root directory during the compile process.

Run ReferenceSharedAssembly.exe. You should get something similar to what is shown in Figure 18-8.

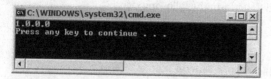

Figure 18-8. *The result of executing ReferenceSharedAssembly*

Now let's see what happens if you change your shared assembly and give it a new version number like this:

```
[assembly:AssemblyVersionAttribute("1.1.0.0")];
```

Recompile only the SharedAssembly project and then move the new assembly SharedAssembly.dll to the GAC. First off, notice that now there are two SharedAssembly entries in the GAC that differ by version number.

Run ReferenceSharedAssembly.exe again. (Important: *Do not* recompile when asked.) Nothing has changed, has it? You still get the same output. This is versioning in action. Why do you get the original version of the shared assembly? Because when you compiled the application program, you tightly bound it to version 1.0.0.0 of the shared assembly. Thus, when it executes, it can only load version 1.0.0.0.

Just for grins and giggle, delete version 1.0.0.0 from the GAC and run ReferenceSharedAssembly.exe a third time. Nice abort don't you think? The reason the program aborts is because even though there is a copy of SharedAssembly in the GAC, it is the wrong version (1.1.0.0). ReferenceSharedAssembly.exe is tightly bound to version 1.0.0.0.

Tip If you are like me and have your compile environment automatically compile all changed modules before executing, then the easiest way to test this is to compile only SharedAssembly and then go to the command line and run ReferenceSharedAssembly.exe from there.

Application Configuration Files

An alarm might be going off in your head right now. Does this mean that whenever you change a shared assembly, you have to keep the same version number or you have to recompile every application that uses shared assembly so that it can be accessed? How do you release a fix to a shared assembly?

The .NET Framework provides a solution to this problem by adding a configuration file to the application that specifies which assembly you want to load instead of the bound version. The application configuration file has the same name as the executable plus a suffix of .config. Therefore, for the preceding example, the application configuration file would be called ReferenceSharedAssembly.exe.config. Yes, the .exe is still in the name.

The application configuration file will look something like Listing 18-10.

Listing 18-10. *An Application Configuration File*

```
<configuration>
  <runtime>
    <assemblyBinding xmlns="urn:schemas-microsoft-com:asm.v1">
      <dependentAssembly>
        <assemblyIdentity name="SharedAssembly"
                          publicKeyToken="332a33ed1547b4e6" />
        <bindingRedirect  oldVersion="1.0.0.0"
                          newVersion="1.1.0.0" />
      </dependentAssembly>
    </assemblyBinding>
  </runtime>
</configuration>
```

The only two elements you have to worry about in the file are `<assemblyIdentity>` and `<bindingRedirect>`. `<assemblyIdentity>` contains the identity of the shared assembly that you want to use a different version with. Notice that all the information you need to identify the shared assembly can be found in the Windows Explorer GAC view.

Next is the key to assigning a different version to the `<bindingRedirect>` element. This element specifies the old version, or the version that the application assembly currently references, and then the new version that you want it to access instead. A cool feature is that the `oldVersion` tag can take a range:

```
<bindingRedirect oldVersion="1.0-1.1" newVersion="1.1.0.0" />
```

Now that you have the file created, place it in the same directory as the executable and run ReferenceSharedAssembly.exe again. (Important: *Do not* recompile when asked.) This time you will get the output shown in Figure 18-9.

Figure 18-9. *The result of executing ReferenceSharedAssembly with an application configuration file*

As a final note to application configuration files, you can also set the `newVersion` tag to a prior version of the assembly:

```
<bindingRedirect oldVersion="1.1.0.0" newVersion="1.0.0.0" />
```

This comes in handy when the new version is found to not be compatible and you need to fall back to a previous version.

Resources

When you finally get to the point of running your software, usually there are other things needed for it to run besides the executable. For example, you might find that you need images, icons, cursors, or, if you are going to globalize the application, a culture's set of strings. You could fill your application directory full of a bunch of files containing these "resources." But if you did, you would run the risk of forgetting something when you deployed your application. I think a better solution is to group common resources into .resources files. Then, optionally, embed the .resources files into the assembly that uses the contents of the .resources files. My thought is that with fewer files floating around, fewer things can get lost.

You have three ways to work with grouped resources in the .NET Framework:

- You can place the grouped resources in .resources files and then work with them as separate entities. This allows you to switch and swap the .resources files as needed. It also allows you to work with the resources within the .resources files in a dynamic fashion.

- You can embed the resources directly into the assembly that uses them. This method has the least flexibility, but you can be secure in the knowledge that everything you need to run the assembly is available.

- You can combine the two previous methods and create what the .NET Framework calls *satellite assemblies*. These are assemblies containing only resources, but at the same time, they directly link to the assembly that uses the resources within them. You will see this use of resources when you look at globalization and localization later in this chapter.

Creating Resources

The .NET Framework provides you with two text formats for creating .resources files: a text file made up of name/value pairs and an XML-formatted file called a .resx file. Of the two, the name/value-formatted file is much easier to use, but it has the drawback of supporting only string resources. On the other hand, .resx files support almost any kind of resource, but unfortunately they are extremely hard to hand code. Most likely, because .resx files are so complex, you will choose a third way, which is to write a simple program to add nontext-formatted resources to a .resources file. I show you how to write the program later in this section.

Because .resx files are so complex, why are they included? They are what Visual Studio 2005 uses to handle resources. In fact, you will use them quite extensively when you look at globalization and localization later in this chapter, but you will probably not even be aware that you are.

Building Text Name/Value Pair Resource Files

The simplest type of resource that you can create is the string table. You will probably want to create this type of resource using name/value pair files, as the format of the name/value pair file maps quite nicely to a string table. Basically, the name/value pair file is made up of many lines of name and value pairs separated by equal signs (=). Here is an example:

```
Name = Stephen Fraser
Email Address = stephen.fraser@apress.com
Phone Number = (502) 555-1234
Favorite Equation = E=mc2
```

As you can see, spaces are allowed for both the name and the value. Also, the equal sign can be used in the value (but not the name), as the first equal sign is used to delimit the name and the value.

▪ **Caution** Don't try to line up the equal signs, because the spaces will become part of the name. As you'll see later in the chapter, doing this will make it harder to code the resource accessing method.

ResGen

The text file you created previously is only an intermediate file. You might think of it as a source file just like a .cpp or .h file. You need to convert it to a .resources file so that your program will be able to process it as a resource. (By the way, you could process the file as a standard string file, but then you would lose many of the resource features provided by the .NET Framework.) To convert your text file, use the .NET Framework's ResGen.exe utility. There is not much to running the utility:

```
> ResGen filename.txt
```

When you run the preceding code, assuming that the text file consists of valid name/value pairs, you get an output file of filename.resources in the directory where you ran the utility. You can work with these files as separate entities, or you can embed them into your assembly. You will see how to do that later in this chapter.

One more thing, if you are a glutton for punishment and write resource files using .resx files, then you would use the ResGen utility to convert them into .resources files as well.

ResourceWriter

As I stated previously, adding nontext resources is not possible using name/value pair files, and the .resx file is a bear to work with. So what are you to do if you simply need to create nontext resources (e.g., an image table)?

You can use the System::Resources::ResourceWriter class, because this class has the capability to place almost any type of data within a .resources file, so long as the total combined size of the file does not exceed 2GB. In fact, this class is what ResGen.exe uses to generate its .resources file. Why they didn't make ResGen.exe more robust and allow other types of data types escapes me.

Using the ResourceWriter class requires you to perform only three steps:

1. Open up a .resources file using the ResourceWriter class's constructor.

2. Add resources to the .resources file using the AddResources() method.

3. Close the .resources file using the Close() method.

Listing 18-11 presents all the code you need to add an image to a .resources file from a .jpg file.

Listing 18-11. *Adding an Image to a .resources File*

```
#using <System.Drawing.dll>  // Add the reference as it's not a default

using namespace System;
using namespace System::Resources;
using namespace System::Drawing;

void main()
{
    ResourceWriter ^rwriter = gcnew ResourceWriter("filename.resources");
    rwriter->AddResource("ImageName", Images::FromFile("Imagefile.jpg"));
    rwriter->Close();
}
```

Embedding Resources

One way to make sure that everything that you need to execute an assembly is available is to put everything in the assembly itself. This way, executing an assembly is as easy as double-clicking the assembly's .exe file.

To embed resources from the command line, you use the assembly generation tool, al.exe, passing it the /embed option along with the name of the .resources file.

If you are using Visual Studio 2005, embedding resources is also fairly straightforward. In fact, if you are using .resx files as the source of your resources, you have to do nothing, because Visual Studio 2005 will automatically handle everything for you. To embed resources using name/value pair files and prebuilt .resources files is not much more difficult.

I think the easiest way to explain how to embed resources is to actually walk through the process. In the following example, you will embed Animal.resx, Color.txt (name/value pair file), and Fruit.resources into an assembly called EmbeddingResources.exe.

The first step, as with any other .NET application project, is to use the project template wizard to build the basic structure of your project. In this case, you will build a standard Console Application (.NET) project and name it EmbeddingResources. To complete this project, perform the following steps:

1. Add a new item of type Assembly Resource File (.resx) and name it **Animal**. Then add some name/value pairs, as shown in Figure 18-10.

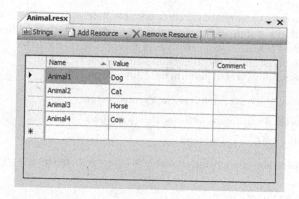

Figure 18-10. *The Animal resource file*

2. Add a new item of type Text File (.txt) and name it **Color**. Then add the following name/value pairs:

```
Color1 = Blue
Color2 = Red
Color3 = Yellow
Color4 = Green
```

3. Add an existing item called **Fruit.resources**. You will need to create this file at the command line using the ResGen tool on the name/value pair file containing the following entries:

```
Fruit1 = Apple
Fruit2 = Orange
Fruit3 = Grape
Fruit4 = Lemon
```

Now that you have all the resources ready, go ahead and embed them into the assembly. As I said previously, you don't have to do anything to embed a .resx file. Personally, though, I don't like the name that Visual Studio 2005 gives the resource when it's embedded, so let's change it:

1. Right-click Animal.resx in Solution Explorer and select the Properties menu item.

2. Select All Configurations from the Configuration drop-down list.

3. Change the Resource File Name entry in Managed Resources ➤ General to **$(IntDir)\$(RootNamespace).Animal.resources** (see Figure 18-11). This will give the resource the name EmbeddingResources.Animal. I think this is better than the default EmbeddingResources.ResourceFiles.

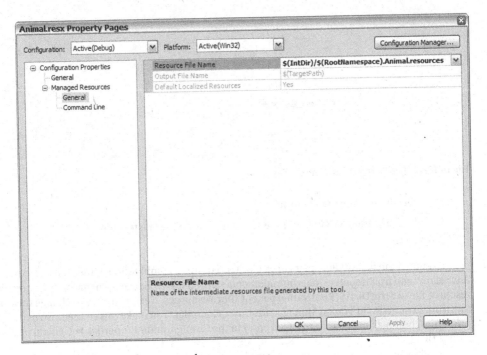

Figure 18-11. *Changing the generated resource name*

4. Click OK.

To embed an already-created .resources file requires that you add it as an input to the assembly linker. (By the way, you don't have to add the .resources file to Solution Explorer to get this to work—it just has to be in the project directory. I put the .resources file there so I remember that, in fact, I am embedding it.) The steps this time are a little different:

1. Right-click the EmbeddingResources project in Solution Explorer and select the Properties menu item. This will bring up a dialog box similar to the one in Figure 18-12.

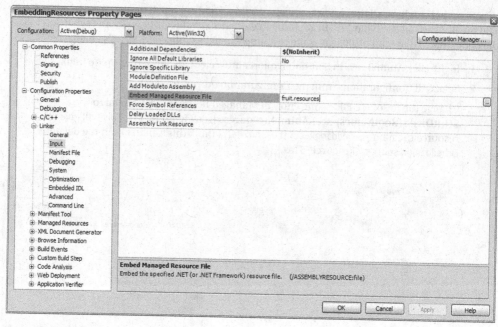

Figure 18-12. *Adding embedded resources*

2. In the Linker folder, select Input.

3. Enter **fruit.resources** in the Embed Managed Resource File text box.

4. Click OK.

To embed the name/value pairs file Color.txt requires a combination of the steps used to add Animal.resx and fruit.resources, plus one additional step: First you change the name of the generated resource file to **$(IntDir)\$(RootNamespace).Color.resources**. Next, you have to change the build tool from Custom Build Tool to Managed Resource Compiler. You make this change also in the file's properties, but this time change the Tool entry in the Configuration Properties ➤ General page (see Figure 18-13).

Finally, you add the resource to the Linker inputs using the exact same name you used previously, in this case: **$(IntDir)\$(RootNamespace).Color.resources** (see Figure 18-14).

When you compile the project, you will have three resources embedded into the application assembly. If you want proof, look in the assemblies manifest and you will find the following three entries:

```
.mresource public fruit.resources
{
}
.mresource public EmbeddingResources.Color.resources
{
}
.mresource public EmbeddingResources.Animal.resources
{
}
```

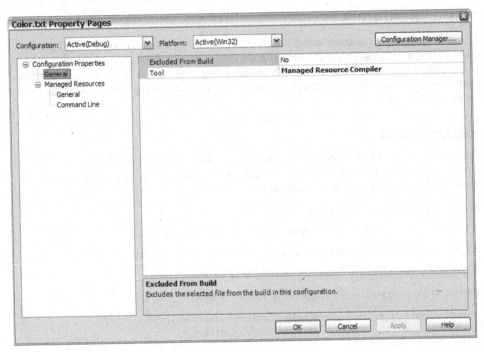

Figure 18-13. *Changing the tool to Managed Resource Compiler*

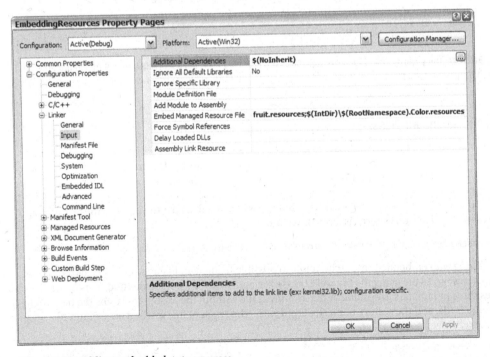

Figure 18-14. *Adding embedded .txt resources*

Accessing Resources

You've looked at creating resources and then embedding resources. Both are kind of neat, but by themselves are quite useless unless you have some way of accessing these resources within your application. Obviously, the .NET Framework provides a class to get access to the resources. In fact, depending on where the resource is stored, it may provide two ways: the ResourceReader class and the ResourceManager class.

ResourceReader Class

The ResourceReader class is the counterpart of the ResourceWriter class. It enables you to iterate through a .resources file, treating it as though it were a simple file. Just like the ResourceWriter class, the ResourceReader class is very easy to implement:

1. Open the .resources file using the ResourceReader constructor.

2. Get IDictionaryEnumerator from the ResourceReader class's GetEnumerator() method.

3. Use the MoveNext() method to process all the entries in the .resources file.

4. Close the ResourceReader class with the Close() method.

Here is all the code you need to implement ResourceReader:

```
ResourceReader ^rreader = gcnew ResourceReader("filename.resources");
IDictionaryEnumerator ^denum = rreader->GetEnumerator();
while (denum->MoveNext())
{
    Console::WriteLine("{0} = {1}", denum->Key, denum->Value );
}
rreader->Close();
```

■**Caution** The order in which the key/value pairs are retrieved from the assembly may not match the order in which they were written.

ResourceManager Class

Although the ResourceReader class is restricted to .resources files, the ResourceManager class gives you access to either .resources files or embedded resources. Another feature of the ResourceManager class that you will see later in this chapter is that it can access the resources in a culture-specific manner.

To create an instance of a ResourceManager class, you need to pass the name of the resource and the assembly that the resource is embedded into:

```
ResourceManager^ rmgr = gcnew ResourceManager("resourceName", assembly);
```

Along with embedded resources, it is also possible to open an instance of the ResourceManager from a .resources file using the CreateFileBasedResourceManager() static method. This method takes three parameters: the name of the .resources file without the .resources suffix, the path to the .resources file, and the culture to mask output with. The result of this method is a pointer to a ResourceManager:

```
ResourceManager^ rmgr =
    ResourceManager::CreateFileBasedResourceManager("resourceFilename", "",
                                                     nullptr);
```

Once you have the instance of the ResourceManager, all you have to do is pass the name of the resource item you want to either the GetString() or GetObject() method to return the value of the following:

```
String ^Value = rmgr->GetString("Name");
Object ^Value = rmgr->GetObject("Name");
```

Listing 18-12 expands on the previous section's project, EmbeddingResources. This example displays the Fruit.resources file using both the ResourceReader and ResourceManager and then continues on to display the embedded version of the Fruit resource using ResourceManager again.

Listing 18-12. *EmbeddedResources Display Function*

```
using namespace System;
using namespace System::Collections;
using namespace System::Reflection;
using namespace System::Resources;

void main()
{
    Console::WriteLine("*** ResourceReader ***");
    ResourceReader ^rreader = gcnew ResourceReader("Fruit.resources");
    IDictionaryEnumerator ^denum = rreader->GetEnumerator();
    while (denum->MoveNext())
    {
        Console::WriteLine("{0} = {1}", denum->Key, denum->Value);
    }
    rreader->Close();

    ResourceManager ^rmgr;

    Console::WriteLine("\n*** ResourceManager From File ***");
    rmgr = ResourceManager::CreateFileBasedResourceManager("Fruit", "",
                                                            nullptr);
    Console::WriteLine(rmgr->GetString("Fruit1"));
    Console::WriteLine(rmgr->GetString("Fruit2"));
    Console::WriteLine(rmgr->GetString("Fruit3"));
    Console::WriteLine(rmgr->GetString("Fruit4"));

    Console::WriteLine("\n*** ResourceManager From Assembly ***");
    Assembly ^assembly = Assembly::GetExecutingAssembly();
    rmgr = gcnew ResourceManager("Fruit", assembly);
    Console::WriteLine(rmgr->GetObject("Fruit1"));
    Console::WriteLine(rmgr->GetObject("Fruit2"));
    Console::WriteLine(rmgr->GetObject("Fruit3"));
    Console::WriteLine(rmgr->GetObject("Fruit4"));
}
```

Notice that you can use either GetString() or GetObject() to extract a String resource item. If, on the other hand, you were extracting an Image type resource item, you would need to use the GetObject() method and then typecast it back to an Image:

```
Image ^img = (Image^)rmgr->GetObject("ImageName");
```

Figure 18-15 shows EmbeddedResources.exe in action.

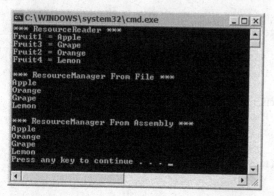

Figure 18-15. *The result of executing the EmbeddedResources program*

Globalization and Localization

The terms "globalization" and "localization" are frequently confused. Often people choose one of the terms to mean both when, in fact, each has a specific meaning:

- *Globalization* refers to designing and developing software that supports localized user interfaces and regional data for users of multiple cultures.

- *Localization* refers to the translation of the application's resources into localized versions for each culture supported by the application.

As you can see, you need both globalization and localization for an application to support multiple cultures. Basically, globalization is the underlying architecture, and localization is the actual translation. This is why the .NET Framework provides a System::Globalization namespace and not a localization one.

To globalize an application, you need to be able to specify cultural differences in things such as numbers, dates, and calendars. For example, Table 18-5 shows some number formats based on culture.

Table 18-5. *Number Formats Based on Culture*

Culture	Number Format
France (French)	123 456 789,01
Germany (German)	123.456.789,01
Switzerland (German)	123'456'789.01
U.S. (English)	123,456,789.01

Notice in Table 18-5 that there are two different ways of displaying numbers for a German culture. The Swiss have what is known as a *subculture* (but don't tell the Swiss that!). This points out that to support globalization, an application must also support subcultures. Seems to me things are starting to get complex. Okay, let's throw Chinese and Japanese character sets into the mix—now you're talking complex!

Fortunately, the .NET Framework has a few things up its sleeve to help support all these complexities. Don't get me wrong: Writing globalization code isn't for the faint of heart. It's tough! This section will only show you where to begin in globalizing your application. Please consult the many books that have been written on the subject for further information; for example, *Internationalization and Localization Using Microsoft .NET* by Nick Symmonds (Apress, 2002). (Like other books suggested earlier, this one is for C#, but you should have no problem working your way through it.)

The Globalization Tools

The first line of attack for handling globalization by the .NET Framework is that it uses Unicode to support the various culture-specific encoding types you may use in your applications. Unicode allows you to support complex character sets such as Chinese and Japanese, as well as the generic ASCII character set.

The next thing the .NET Framework does is provide intelligence in its classes and structures to support multiple cultures. For example, the DateTime and String objects generate appropriate culture-specific information. To add this intelligence, the .NET Framework relies on the System:: Globalization namespace (see Table 18-6) to provide support.

Table 18-6. *Common System::Globalization Namespace Classes*

Class Name	Description
Calendar	Specifies how to divide time into pieces (e.g., weeks, months, and years)
CultureInfo	Provides specific information about a culture
DateTimeFormatInfo	Specifies how dates and times are formatted
NumberFormatInfo	Specifies how numbers are formatted
RegionInfo	Provides information about the country and region
TextInfo	Specifies the properties and behaviors of the writing system

The final thing that the .NET Framework does to help support globalization was hinted at previously when I covered resources. The .NET Framework supports culture-specific resources using the ResourceManager class.

Culture

A *culture* in computer terms is a set of display preferences based on the language, beliefs, social norms, and so on (i.e., culture) of the user. How a computer processes the actual program internally does not differ based on culture. Culture only changes how the information is finally displayed. For example, adding two Int32s together using the German culture will not differ from how it is done using the French culture—the difference lies in how the final outcome is displayed.

The .NET Framework uses culture names based on RFC1766. If that means nothing to you, don't worry. It just means the .NET Framework uses a two-letter language and a two-letter country/ region code separated by a hyphen (-) to specify a culture. It's possible to only specify a two-letter language if the country/region isn't significant.

Table 18-7 lists a very small subset of the many cultures available to you.

Table 18-7. *Computer Cultures*

Name	Code
English	en
English (Canada)	en-ca
English (United Kingdom)	en-gb
English (United States)	en-us
French	fr
French (Canada)	fr-ca
French (France)	fr-fr
German	de
German (Germany)	de-de
German (Switzerland)	de-ch

You use the System::Globalization::CultureInfo class to convert one of the codes in Table 18-7 into something that the .NET Framework understands:

```
CultureInfo ^cinfo = gcnew CultureInfo("en-ca");
```

Setting the Culture

To get globalization to work within the CLR, you need to do one of two things:

- Use a special version of the ToString() method that takes the culture as a parameter.

- Set the culture you wish to use in the thread of execution.

The first method enables you to restrict globalization only to areas of your application that you specify. The second method of changing the CultureInfo in the CurrentThread changes the culture everywhere.

For example, if you want to display a date in multiple cultural styles, you could code it as shown in Listing 18-13.

Listing 18-13. *Multicultural Dates*

```
using namespace System;
using namespace System::Globalization;

void main()
{
    DateTime dt = DateTime::Now;

    Console::WriteLine("en-us {0}",dt.ToString("D",gcnew CultureInfo("en-us")));
    Console::WriteLine("en-gb {0}",dt.ToString("D",gcnew CultureInfo("en-gb")));
    Console::WriteLine("fr-fr {0}",dt.ToString("D",gcnew CultureInfo("fr-fr")));
    Console::WriteLine("de-de {0}",dt.ToString("D",gcnew CultureInfo("de-de")));
}
```

Figure 18-16 shows MulticulturalDates.exe run on December 4, 2002.

Figure 18-16. *The result of executing the MulticulturalDates program*

Now here comes a tricky part. There are two cultures you can set in the CurrentThread. The first is CurrentCulture, which is used by the Globalization namespace to handle culture-specific formatting. The second is CurrentUICulture, which is used by the ResourceManager to handle culture-specific resources. You may need to set one or both depending on what you are doing. Here is how you can set both to the French (France) culture:

```
Thread::CurrentThread->CurrentCulture = gcnew CultureInfo("fr-fr");
Thread::CurrentThread->CurrentUICulture = Thread::CurrentThread->CurrentCulture;
```

The Localization Tools

Once you have an application designed and coded for multiple cultures, you then have to go through the long process of localizing it for each culture you want to support. Fortunately, Visual Studio 2005 provides much of the functionality you need to localize your application if you happen to be building a Windows application. It also supplies much of the localization functionality for a console application, providing you use a minor trick.

The way in which localization works is actually very elegant. First, you create a default version of all of your display elements, placing each in a resource file. Then for every other culture, you create a satellite resource file. Within that satellite resource file are replacement elements for the default view. Thus, when the culture is changed, the ResourceManager looks into the satellite resource of that culture first for display elements. If it finds the element it wants there, then it uses it. If it doesn't find the element it wants there, then it takes the default value.

Building a Multicultural Windows Application

The addition of localization to a Windows application is quite impressive. You really don't see how impressive it is until you try it yourself. Let's start off by creating a very simple Windows Form containing a single label that looks like the one in Figure 18-17.

Figure 18-17. *A very simple Windows Form*

When you look at the auto-generated code in the InitializeComponent() method, as shown in Listing 18-14, you see pretty standard and unimpressive code.

Listing 18-14. *Very Simple Windows Form Code*

```
void InitializeComponent(void)
{
    this->lbHello = (gcnew System::Windows::Forms::Label());
    this->SuspendLayout();
    //
    // lbHello
    //
    this->lbHello->Font =
        (gcnew System::Drawing::Font(L"Microsoft Sans Serif", 12,
            System::Drawing::FontStyle::Bold,
            System::Drawing::GraphicsUnit::Point,
            static_cast<System::Byte>(0)));
    this->lbHello->Location = System::Drawing::Point(12, 9);
    this->lbHello->Name = L"lbHello";
    this->lbHello->Size = System::Drawing::Size(364, 23);
    this->lbHello->TabIndex = 0;
    this->lbHello->Text = L"Hello, my name is Stephen";
    //
    // Form1
    //
    this->AutoScaleDimensions = System::Drawing::SizeF(6, 13);
    this->AutoScaleMode = System::Windows::Forms::AutoScaleMode::Font;
    this->ClientSize = System::Drawing::Size(390, 48);
    this->Controls->Add(this->lbHello);
    this->Name = L"Form1";
    this->Text = L"English";
    this->ResumeLayout(false);
}
```

Okay, now let's take this same code and make it localizable. To do this, simply set the Form's Localizable property to true (see Figure 18-18).

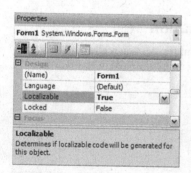

Figure 18-18. *Setting the Localizable flag to true*

Now take a look at the code in the InitializeComponent() method (see Listing 18-15).

Listing 18-15. *Localizable Simple Application*

```
void InitializeComponent(void)
{
    System::ComponentModel::ComponentResourceManager^ resources =
        (gcnew System::ComponentModel::ComponentResourceManager(Form1::typeid));
    this->lbHello = (gcnew System::Windows::Forms::Label());
    this->SuspendLayout();
    //
    // lbHello
    //
    resources->ApplyResources(this->lbHello, L"lbHello");
    this->lbHello->Name = L"lbHello";
    //
    // Form1
    //
    resources->ApplyResources(this, L"$this");
    this->AutoScaleMode = System::Windows::Forms::AutoScaleMode::Font;
    this->Controls->Add(this->lbHello);
    this->Name = L"Form1";
    this->ResumeLayout(false);
}
```

Where did all the code go? Don't panic, every aspect of the label has now become a resource. As such, it can take on any look and feel you want based on the values you place within the resource file that populates this label. At this point, all the information about the label and the form is stored in a resource file called Form1.resx. Now, instead of hard coding everything, the application at runtime dynamically applies the look and feel using the ApplyResources() method of the ComponentResourceManager class.

Currently, the resource file only contains all the default information about the Windows Form, as I pointed out as the first part of localization.

Now you'll add a new culture, French (France), to the form. To do this you set the form's Language property to French (France). Scrolling up and down in the Language property's selection displays quite a few cultures, don't you think?

Notice any difference in the Windows Form design? Nope, me neither. Here's the fun part: Go wild and change any property of the label, but just don't delete it. Now toggle between the default language and the French (France) language. Notice that they retain the information specific to each culture. (Well, apparently you can't go too wild there, as it seems a few of the properties aren't stored in the resource file automatically. Border and background color are two that surprised me by not working.)

Go ahead and do the same for the German (Germany) culture. Notice how everything reverts to the default culture look and feel again (if you were in the French language version anyway). Whenever you start a new culture, Visual Studio 2005 reverts back to the default so that you will always have a consistent starting point to make your culture-specific changes.

Anyway, now that you've created a French (France) culture and German (Germany) culture, notice there's now a Form1.fr-fr.resx and a Form1.de-DE.resx resource file added to your Solution Explorer.

Now let's see what happens when you compile the Windows Form application. After you compile the application, go ahead and open Windows Explorer and navigate to the directory structure where the application runs. There are now two directories, one for each culture using the culture's RFC1766 code as a name. Also, in each directory is a file called [ApplicationName].resources.dll, as shown in Figure 18-19. These two new .dll files are your satellite assemblies.

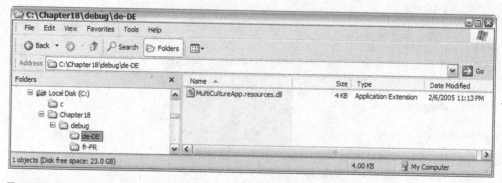

Figure 18-19. *The Windows Explorer view of satellite assemblies*

Run your new multicultured application. You see none of your French or German stuff, right? That is because your native culture is not French (France) or German (Germany), so the ResourceManager took the default resource values and not the French or German one. (Oh, of course, if you are reading this book in France or Germany and your machine is configured for French or German, then you would see the French or German. French or German readers might try some other culture for this example.)

As I stated previously, you need to change the CurrentThread class's CurrentUICulture to the satellite assembly's culture you want to access. Do this by adding the following lines before you call the InitializeComponent() method:

```
Thread::CurrentThread->CurrentCulture = gcnew CultureInfo("fr-fr");
Thread::CurrentThread->CurrentUICulture = Thread::CurrentThread->CurrentCulture;
```

Figure 18-20 shows MultiCulturalApp.exe French (France) culture in action.

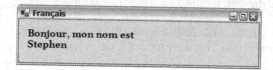

Figure 18-20. *The result of executing the MultiCulturalApp program*

Building a Multicultural Console Application

When you build an assembly that isn't a Windows application, things aren't quite as easy. But it doesn't take much to fool Visual Studio 2005 into believing it's building Windows-like satellite assemblies.

Let's create a simple little program called MulticultureConsole (see Listing 18-16) that writes four colors stored in a resource string table.

Listing 18-16. *Writing Out Four Colors from a Resource*

```
using namespace System;
using namespace System::Reflection;
using namespace System::Resources;
using namespace System::Threading;
using namespace System::Globalization;
```

```
void main()
{
    Assembly ^assembly = Assembly::GetExecutingAssembly();
    ResourceManager ^rmgr =
        gcnew ResourceManager("MulticultureConsole.Colors", assembly);

    Console::WriteLine(rmgr->GetObject("Color1"));
    Console::WriteLine(rmgr->GetObject("Color2"));
    Console::WriteLine(rmgr->GetObject("Color3"));
    Console::WriteLine(rmgr->GetObject("Color4"));
}
```

Add a new item of type Assembly Resource File (.resx) and name it **Colors**. Then add the string resources as shown in Figure 18-21. Finally, rename the generated resource file as **$(IntDir)/$(RootNamespace).Colors.resources**.

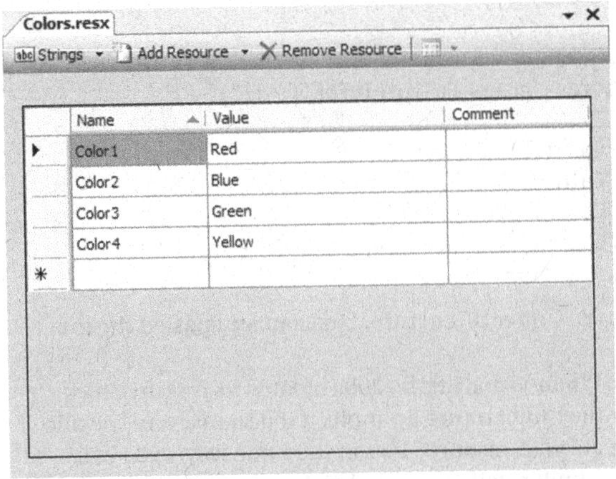

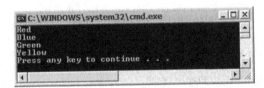

Figure 18-21. *The Colors assembly resource file*

When you run MulticultureConsole.exe, you should get something like Figure 18-22. There is nothing new so far.

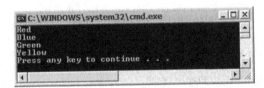

Figure 18-22. *The first result of MulticultureConsole*

Now let's make the program multicultural. The first step is to add the code to the application so that it will display based on another culture or, in other words, you globalize the application. You do this by setting the CurrentThread CurrentUICulture to something else. Let's change it to "fr-fr" or French (France), as shown in Listing 18-17.

Listing 18-17. *Writing Out Four Colors from a Resource Multiculturally*

```
using namespace System;
using namespace System::Reflection;
using namespace System::Resources;
using namespace System::Threading;
using namespace System::Globalization;

void main()
{
    Assembly ^assembly = Assembly::GetExecutingAssembly();
    ResourceManager ^rmgr =
        gcnew ResourceManager("MulticultureConsole.Colors", assembly);

    Console::WriteLine(rmgr->GetObject("Color1"));
    Console::WriteLine(rmgr->GetObject("Color2"));
    Console::WriteLine(rmgr->GetObject("Color3"));
    Console::WriteLine(rmgr->GetObject("Color4"));

    Thread::CurrentThread->CurrentUICulture = gcnew CultureInfo("fr-fr");

    Console::WriteLine(rmgr->GetObject("Color1"));
    Console::WriteLine(rmgr->GetObject("Color2"));
    Console::WriteLine(rmgr->GetObject("Color3"));
    Console::WriteLine(rmgr->GetObject("Color4"));
}
```

The only new thing you did was change the CurrentUICulture. I just cut and pasted the four lines that display the colors.

Now it's time to fool Visual Studio 2005. When Visual Studio 2005 created its resource files (which later became satellite assemblies) for the multiculture example, it did so in a very specific manner. The fortunate thing is that if you create your resource files in the same way, even in a console application, you will also get correctly built satellite assemblies.

Basically, here is how you do it. Create an assembly resource file (.resx) named **WhatYouWant.resx** that contains all the resource items for the default language. Also rename the auto-generated resource file as **$(IntDir)/$(RootNamespace).WhatYouWant.resources**. Notice that this is the same procedure you followed earlier when you embedded the standard resource file.

Now here's the trick to add, let's say, a French culture. Create a new assembly resource file (.resx) and name it **WhatYouWant.fr-fr.resx**. Add all the replacement values that you want for that culture. Then rename the auto-generated resource file as **$(IntDir)/$(RootNamespace). WhatYouWant.fr-fr.resources**. That's it! Placing the culture just before the .resx and .resources files is enough to trick Visual Studio 2005 into creating a culture-specific satellite assembly.

So for the previous MulticultureConsole example, create an assembly resource file (.resx) named **Colors.fr-fr.resx**. Then add the string resources as shown in Figure 18-23.

As you can see, once you change the culture to French, the ResourceManager looks first in the French satellite assembly for the value. Because there is no Color2, the English (default) value is written.

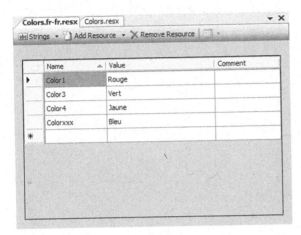

Figure 18-23. *French Colors assembly resource file*

Notice that it is important that the names of the name/value pairs match between the default and the French resource files. Finally, rename the generated resource file as **$(IntDir)/ $(RootNamespace).fr-fr.Colors.resources**.

When you run the revised MulticultureConsole.exe, you should get something like Figure 18-24. There is nothing new so far.

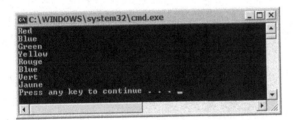

Figure 18-24. *Revised result of MulticultureConsole*

Summary

In this chapter, you looked at several ways to programmatically play with the .NET Framework assembly. You started by exploring reflection and then its counterpart, attributes. You moved on to look at shared assemblies. Next, you learned how to add more to assemblies than just code using resources. You finished off the chapter by looking at globalization and localization.

Programming with assemblies, like many of the other topics covered in this book, is a weighty topic. I feel the only way to really learn how to program the assembly is to do so yourself. This chapter should have opened up many doors on how to do this.

The programming world has gone security crazy—unfortunately, justifiably so. In the next chapter, we will look at what C++/CLI and the .NET Framework have to help secure your code.

CHAPTER 19

■ ■ ■

Security

Even though this is the last chapter specifically addressing managed code, it is hardly the least important. In fact, to many developers it is one of the more important ones. The only reason it is placed here, instead of earlier, is that it is easier to understand security if you already have a good knowledge of both managed code and the .NET Framework—which you should have by now.

Another reason I placed the chapter here is because this is the last chapter that deals solely with managed code. To put it simply, .NET Security works only with managed code (and, as you'll see in this chapter, managed data). So what you will be learning in the chapters following this one will not be bound by what is covered in this chapter. (Okay, that is not quite accurate. The code to access or call unsafe code still falls under the .NET security umbrella, but the unsafe code itself does not.)

In general, .NET security focuses on code that has an origin other than your local hard drive, or what is often called mobile code. Normally, code that originates on your local hard drive has authority to do anything on your computer that the operating system security allows. You can change this, but in most cases there is no need.

Security in .NET is a problematic topic when it comes to C++/CLI as you have the ability to very easily step outside the safe .NET sandbox if you are not paying attention. You may find that code that works just fine when run from your local hard drive continually throws exceptions when run as mobile code. The most probable reason for these exceptions is because of the code's or the user's lack of permission to execute a particular functionality or access a specific resource.

Understanding the reason for these exceptions and providing methods for solving them is the goal of this chapter.

Note If parts of your code are unsafe, it causes the common language runtime (CLR) to get upset and throw an exception tantrum. There is an easy way to combat accidentally introducing unsafe code: Always compile code that you want to be secure with the `/clr:safe` option. This option never compiles successfully if unsafe code is present. I discuss unsafe code in some detail in the last two chapters of this book.

This chapter will look at the two forms of security provided by .NET: role-based and code access security. I'll start off with role-based security as I feel it is the easier of the two security types. Then I'll move on to the more involved (though not much more complex) code access security.

The Security Namespaces

The .NET Framework breaks security functionality into two large namespaces: `System::Web::Security` for the ASP.NET and Web services worlds and `System::Security` for the Windows application, console, and Windows services worlds. Since the functionality of `System::Security` is so complex, the .NET Framework also breaks it up into the following:

- `System::Security` is the primary namespace that provides the underlying structure of the .NET security system.

- `System::Security::AccessControl` provides security access information on objects like Active Directory, files, the Registry, mutex, and Semaphores.

- `System::Security::Authentication` contains a set of enumerations that describe the security of a connection.

- `System::Security::Cryptography` provides cryptographic services, including secure encoding and decoding of data.

- `System::Security::Permissions` provides classes that control access to operations and resources based on policy.

- `System::Security::Policy` contains code groups, membership conditions, and evidence.

- `System::Security::Principal` defines a principal object that represents the security context under which code is running. In other words, it is a user, machine, or server that can be positively identified via authentication.

Which combination of namespaces you use depends mainly on the type of security your application is performing. For the most part, with role-based security you will use `System::Security`, `System::Security::Principal`, and `System::Security::Permissions`, and for code access security you will use `System::Security`, `System::Security::Policy`, and `System::Security::Permissions`.

Role-Based Security

When someone traditionally thinks of securing their computer system, role-based is usually what they are thinking about. It is the process of specifying and then allowing a user to access specific resources and functionalities of your system based on the role that the user performs. Common roles are administrator, user, and guest. Each of these roles has a set of resources that the user can access and functionalities that they may perform. Roles are not mutually exclusive; in fact, it is a common practice to combine roles into a hierarchy where the top of the hierarchy provides unlimited access and functionality and as you navigate down the hierarchy the role's rights become more restrictive. Of course, you can also build security in a haphazard way where roles have no interdependencies (though nearly always there is an administrative role that has the rights and privileges of all other roles).

.NET's role-based security works well in conjunction with Windows' user accounts and Active Directory (AD) users, but you are not restricted to either of these, since you can create roles dynamically at runtime that are neither a Windows user account nor an AD user.

To implement role-based security in .NET, you need two pieces: the user and the roles that the user belongs to. In .NET-speak, the user is represented by the identity object and the roles that the identity object belongs to are represented by the principal object. (I would have been quite happy with simply the user object and roles object, but hey, I didn't write the .NET Framework.)

Identities

The .NET Framework provides two identity objects: `WindowsIdentity` and `GenericIdentity`. The `WindowsIdentity` object consists of Windows users that you maintain using the Computer Management administrative tool, as shown in Figure 19-1.

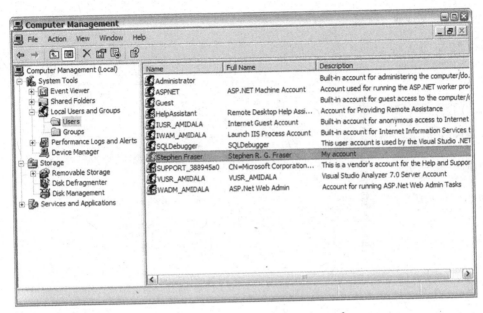

Figure 19-1. *Users in the Computer Management administrative tool*

The GenericIdentity, on the other hand, consists of users that you create dynamically at runtime. Both WindowsIdentity and GenericIdentity share the interface IIdentity, which makes things easier as methods need only use the interface to handle both types of identity.

Note You can create your own custom identities using the IIdentity interface, though personally I have found that GenericIdentity has provided all the functionality I've needed.

The IIdentity interface exposes three simple properties:

- AuthenticationType is a string that indicates the type of authentication used by the identity object. When you are working with Windows, this value will be either Basic, Forms, Kerberos, NTLM, or Passport. (You will most likely find this value is NTLM as it is used by Windows for logon authentication on stand-alone systems.)

- IsAuthenticated is a Boolean value that represents whether the identity object has been authenticated.

- Name is, well, you know… the name associated with the identity object.

Principal

Like the identity, the .NET Framework provides two principal objects: WindowsPrincipal and GenericPrincipal. The WindowsPrincipal object more or less maps to the Windows group and is also maintained by the Computer Management tool, as shown in Figure 19-2. (*Group, principal*, and *role* are all basically the same thing when it comes to role-based security… hmmm, let's just make things confusing, shall we?)

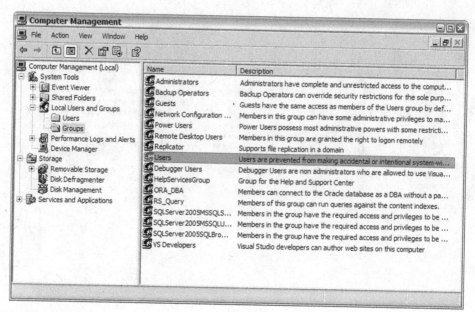

Figure 19-2. *Groups in the Computer Management tool*

The GenericPrincipal is an object that contains the roles of an identity that you create dynamically at runtime. Both WindowsPrincipal and GenericPrincipal share the interface IPrincipal, which again makes things easier since methods need only use the interface to handle both types of principal.

Note Just as with identities, you can create your own custom principals using the IPrincipal interface, though I have found that GenericPrincipal has provided all the functionality I've needed.

The IPrincipal interface exposes one property and one method:

- Identity is a property that contains a handle to the identity associated with the principal.
- IsInRole() takes as its parameter a role and returns a Boolean specifying if the principal has that role.

Working with Identities and Principals

Since the principal and identity objects contain very few properties and methods, they are rather easy to code. There are only a couple of things that you might find tricky.

The first thing you need to know about principals is how to get access to them. You find them using the static property CurrentPrincipal on the Thread object. Since this property returns an IPrincipal, you normally typecast it to either the WindowsPrincipal or the GenericPrincipal like this:

```
WindowsPrincipal ^wPrinc = (WindowsPrincipal^)Thread::CurrentPrincipal;
GenericPrincipal ^gPrinc = (GenericPrincipal^)Thread::CurrentPrincipal;
```

The other issue you need to be aware of is that you have to specify how principal and identity objects should be created for the application domain in which the thread is running. You do this by invoking the AppDomain::CurrentDomain->SetPrincipalPolicy() method using as its parameter the appropriate PrincipalPolicy enumeration. The default is PrincipalPolicy::UnauthenticatedPrincipal, which means that the principal has its Name property set to an empty string ("") and its IsAuthenticated property set to false. What you need to set it to is PrincipalPolicy::WindowsPrincipal, which will return the current user associated with the thread along with all the groups it is in as roles. There is also PrincipalPolicy::NoPrincipal, which will cause a nullptr to be returned (not that you will need this when doing role-based security). Here is how you would code it:

```
AppDomain::CurrentDomain->SetPrincipalPolicy(PrincipalPolicy::WindowsPrincipal);
```

Why is PrincipalPolicy::UnauthenticatedPrincipal the default? I'm not sure, as it is not normally what you are looking for. Oh, and one final gotcha. You need to set PrincipalPolicy before you call the Thread::CurrentPrincipal method because the SetPrincipalPolicy() method does not change the principal's type once it's been created.

Listing 19-1 is a simple example that first gets the Thread's current WindowsPrincipal and WindowsIdentity and displays their information, and then resets the CurrentThread so that it contains a dynamically created GenericPrincipal and GenericIdentity.

Listing 19-1. *Getting and Setting Principals and Identities*

```
using namespace System;
using namespace System::Security;
using namespace System::Security::Principal;
using namespace System::Threading;

void main()
{
    // set policy from UnauthenticatedPrincipal to WindowsPrincipal
    AppDomain::CurrentDomain->SetPrincipalPolicy(
                                    PrincipalPolicy::WindowsPrincipal);
    // ----------------------------------------------------------------
    // Get Windows Principal and Identity
    // ----------------------------------------------------------------
    Console::WriteLine("Windows Principal & Identity");
    Console::WriteLine("----------------------------");

    WindowsPrincipal ^wPrinc = (WindowsPrincipal^)Thread::CurrentPrincipal;

    Console::WriteLine("Is an Administrator?: {0}",
                    wPrinc->IsInRole(WindowsBuiltInRole::Administrator));
    Console::WriteLine("Is a Hacker?: {0}", wPrinc->IsInRole("Hacker"));

    WindowsIdentity ^wIdent = (WindowsIdentity^)wPrinc->Identity;

    Console::WriteLine("\nWindows Login Name: {0}", wIdent->Name);
    Console::WriteLine("Authentication Type: {0}", wIdent->AuthenticationType);
    Console::WriteLine("Is Authenticated: {0}", wIdent->IsAuthenticated);
    Console::WriteLine("Is System Account: {0}", wIdent->IsSystem);
    // ----------------------------------------------------------------
    // Create (Hacker) Principal and Identity
    // ----------------------------------------------------------------
    Console::WriteLine("\n\nGeneric Principal & Identity");
    Console::WriteLine("----------------------------");

    array<String^>^ rolesArray = {"Hacker"};
```

```
    // Set the principal to a new generic principal.
    Thread::CurrentPrincipal =
        gcnew GenericPrincipal(gcnew GenericIdentity("John Doe"), rolesArray);

    GenericPrincipal ^gPrinc = (GenericPrincipal^)Thread::CurrentPrincipal;

    Console::WriteLine("Is an Administrator?: {0}",
                        gPrinc->IsInRole("BUILTIN\\Administrator"));
    Console::WriteLine("Is a Hacker?: {0}", gPrinc->IsInRole("Hacker"));

    GenericIdentity ^gIdent = (GenericIdentity^)gPrinc->Identity;

    Console::WriteLine("\nUser Name: {0}", gIdent->Name);
    Console::WriteLine("Is Authenticated: {0}\n", gIdent->IsAuthenticated);
}
```

One thing you should note from Listing 19-1 is how you create a GenericPrincipal. First, you create a GenericIdentity using its constructor and then pass it along with an array of string-formatted roles to the GenericPrincipal constructor. Very simple and, I think, elegant.

Figure 19-3 shows the result of PrincipalIdentity.exe in action. Notice that my account has administrative rights. Yours, on the other hand, may not.

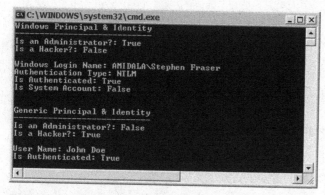

Figure 19-3. *The results of PrincipalIdentity.exe*

You may be wondering, when would I ever need to create a GenericPrincipal? Why not just use the WindowsPrincipal? Well, you'd want to use the GenericPrincipal when you want roles not bound to Windows groups. Basically, you use them when you want roles to be authorized based on a set defined by your application and not by Windows or Active Directory groups.

Securing Your Code Using Roles

Okay, having principals and identities is all very nice, but how does that secure your code? The simple answer is that it doesn't. You still have to add code to your program that provides this security. There are three techniques of doing this.

The first technique you have already seen (though you may not have been aware of it). You surround the code that you want restricted to specific roles with the IsInRole() method, like this:

```
if (wPrinc->IsInRole(WindowsBuiltInRole::Administrator))
{
    // do administrative stuff
}
```

Easy enough, but to use this technique you need to get the principal of the executing thread—though as you have already seen, getting `Thread::CurrentPrincipal` is not difficult.

The second technique of securing your code by role is by using what is known as declarative role-based security. With this technique you declare a method with the additional attribute `PrincipalPermissionAttribute` that specifies which roles areallowed to execute it. (I cover other `PermissionAttributes` later in the chapter, and I will go into greater detail at that time.) Basically, you demand that a principal have a specified role like this:

```
[PrincipalPermissionAttribute(SecurityAction::Demand,
                        Role="BUILTIN\\Administrator")]
void DeclarativeSecurity()
{
    // do administrative stuff
}
```

The third technique is a kind of a mix of the prior two techniques, called imperative role-based security. With this technique, you demand that a principal have a specific role but you make the demand (normally) just before the secured code. This technique requires that you create an instance of a `PrincipalPermission` and then execute its `Demand()` method. I usually do this in one line like this:

```
(gcnew PrincipalPermission(nullptr, "BUILTIN\\Administrator"))->Demand();
```

But you can break it up into its parts and it works just the same.

Notice the first parameter of the `PrincipalPermission` is a `nullptr`. This parameter allows you to specify a specific principal's name as well as a role. By passing `nullptr` you tell the `PrincipalPermission` to use any user principal with this role. If you were to specify a principal name, then only that specific principal/role pair would be used—which means you are no longer using role-based security and instead are using principal-based (user-based) security.

One major difference between technique 1 (the `IsInRole`) and technique 2 (declarative) and 3 (imperative) is that if the demand fails on techniques 2 and 3 a `SecurityException` is thrown. In the case of technique 1, only a `false` condition occurs.

Listing 19-2 shows how you can implement declarative and imperative role-based security. It also changes principal and identity midstream so that you can see that both methods react a different way depending on whether the role is found on the principal.

Listing 19-2. *Implementing Role-Based Security*

```
using namespace System;
using namespace System::Security;
using namespace System::Security::Principal;
using namespace System::Security::Permissions;
using namespace System::Threading;

[PrincipalPermissionAttribute(SecurityAction::Demand, Role = "NotAHacker")]
void DeclarativeSecurity()
{
    Console::WriteLine("I'm in the Declarative Security Function");
}

void DemandSecurity()
{
    (gcnew PrincipalPermission(nullptr, "NotAHacker"))->Demand();

    Console::WriteLine("I'm in the Demand Security Function\n");
}
```

```
void main()
{
    try
    {
        DeclarativeSecurity();
    }
    catch (SecurityException^)
    {
        Console::WriteLine("SECURITY ERROR in Declarative Security Function");
    }

    try
    {
        DemandSecurity();
    }
    catch (SecurityException^)
    {
        Console::WriteLine("SECURITY ERROR in Demand Security Function\n");
    }

    Console::WriteLine("Set CurrentPrincipal to John with role of NotAHacker");
    array<String^>^ rolesArray = {"NotAHacker"};
    Thread::CurrentPrincipal = gcnew GenericPrincipal(
                                    gcnew GenericIdentity( "John" ),
                                    rolesArray );
    try
    {
        DeclarativeSecurity();
    }
    catch (SecurityException^)
    {
        Console::WriteLine("SECURITY ERROR in Declarative Security Function");
    }

    try
    {
        DemandSecurity();
    }
    catch (SecurityException^)
    {
        Console::WriteLine("SECURITY ERROR in Demand Security Function");
    }
}
```

Notice the liberal use of try/catch blocks. These are needed so that the code can continue when a demand fails. If you don't use these try/catch blocks, then you will get an exception like what is shown in Figure 19-4. Normally when you code, you want a more gracious exit to your programs, but there is nothing stopping you from letting your programs die, then and there, when a principal doesn't have the roles needed to execute.

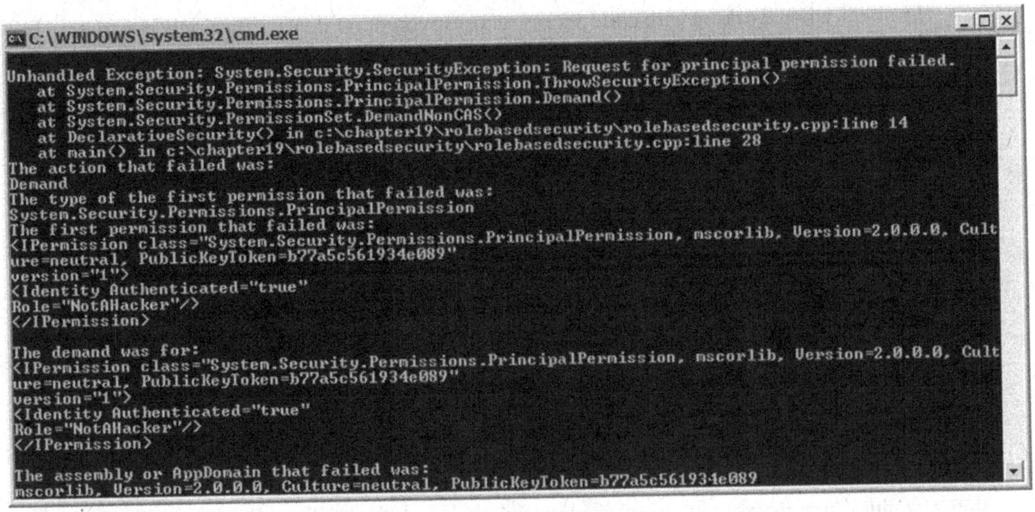

Figure 19-4. *An ugly SecurityException if try/catch is not used*

Figure 19-5 shows the result of RoleBasedSecurity.exe in action. Unless you actually have a Windows group of "NotAHacker" your results will be the same.

Figure 19-5. *The results of RoleBasedSecurity.exe*

Code Access Security

When I first started working with .NET security, I was totally baffled by code access security (sometimes known by its acronym, CAS), but as I started working with it, I realized that conceptually it doesn't differ much from role-based security. I find it easier to think of code access security as a form of evidence-based security. Basically, instead of using roles to determine what code can be run, you use evidence. Evidence means things like site or URL of origin and strong name.

Okay, it's a little more complicated than that, but thinking of it this way makes things easier, at least for me.

Code-based security is based on four concepts: permissions, policy, code groups, and evidence. Let's take a look at each.

Permissions

Permissions, as you can probably guess, represent the right to access or deny access to resources and functionalities. The .NET Framework provides many permission classes, such as FileIOPermission (permission to access files) and UIPermission (permission to access the user interface).

Normally, when working with code access security, you don't deal with a single permission but instead work with permission sets. Permission sets allow you to group permissions together that simplify your coding since you don't have to deal with each of the permissions individually.

The .NET Framework provides you with several preconfigured permission sets. The following five are the ones you will most likely come in contact with:

- FullTrust grants full access to all protected resources.
- LocalIntranet is the default permission set suitable for running code from within an enterprise.
- Internet is the default permission set suitable for running code from an unknown source.
- Execution gives permission to run but no rights to access protected resources.
- Nothing means no permissions (cannot run).

It is also fairly easy to create your own permission sets. You can do it using the Microsoft .NET Framework 2.0 Configuration tool or the command-line tool caspol.exe, but since this is a book about C++/CLI, I'll show you how to code the creation of the permission sets directly in C++/CLI. (There are many books and Web sites that cover creating permission sets, if you insist on doing it that way. But I'm pretty sure once you see how you do it in code you'll not have much trouble doing it with either of the aforementioned tools.)

The first step, quite logically, is to create a permission set:

```
PermissionSet^ permSet = gcnew PermissionSet(PermissionState::None);
```

Since this is a custom permission set, you start it off empty by assigning it a PermissionState::None. If you were to assign it a PermissionState::Unrestricted, then you would in effect be giving the permission set FullTrust. You can also pass an predefined permission set, to which you can add more permissions.

Now that you have an empty permission set, all you have to do is add the permission you want to it using its AddPermission() method:

```
permSet->AddPermission(gcnew SecurityPermission(PermissionState::Unrestricted));
permSet->AddPermission(gcnew UIPermission(PermissionState::Unrestricted));
permSet->AddPermission(gcnew FileIOPermission(FileIOPermissionAccess::Read,
                                              "C:\\"));
```

There is a minor gotcha that you have to address when starting a permission set from scratch. You need to give the permission set the rights to execute your code. You do this by adding an instance of the SecurityPermission object. You also have to allow the permission set the ability to show the user interface. This is done with the addition of an instance of the UIPermission object. You want to give both of these objects unrestricted permissions.

Now that you have the required permissions added, you will want to add the permission you specifically want to give to the permission set. In the previous code, I allow only file IO read access to the C:\ directory by adding an instance of the FileIOPermission object.

Numerous permissions are available to you. If you need to look them up, you can use the MSDN documentation. They are found in the System::Security::Permissions namespace.

Policy Statement

A policy statement is a set of rules that the CLR follows to determine what is granted permission to execute. There are four policies that you can apply policy statements to in code access security: Enterprise, Machine, User, and Application Domain. These policies are organized in a hierarchy as follows:

- Enterprise, or all managed code in the enterprise
- Machine, or all managed code on the machine
- User, or all managed code in processes owned by current user
- Application Domain, or all managed code within the application domain

Each level of the hierarchy is more restrictive, so for example an Enterprise's policy statement can overrule all other policy statements, while a Machine's policy statement can overrule a User's and an Application Domain's policy statement. What this boils down to is that what is granted permission to execute is determined by an intersection of all the policy statements within the four code access security policies, as depicted in Figure 19-6.

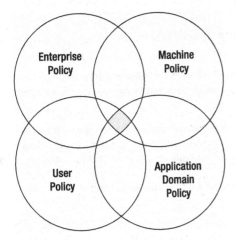

Figure 19-6. *Intersection of policies determining code to execute*

There are two constructors available for creating a policy statement. The simpler one just takes a permission set. Continuing with our example, the constructor would look like this:

```
PolicyStatement^ policy = gcnew PolicyStatement(permSet);
```

The second constructor provides you with a little more power as it allows you to override the default method of determining what is granted permission to be executed. This constructor takes an additional parameter of type `PolicyStatementAttribute`:

```
PolicyStatement^ policy =
    gcnew PolicyStatement(permSet, PolicyStatementAttribute.LevelFinal);
```

There are two attributes that you might want to set with this constructor:

- `Exclusive` means that only this policy statement (at this hierarchical level) will be used in determining what gets granted permission to execute.
- `LevelFinal` causes policy levels below this one to be ignored, effectively allowing a policy level to override its lower levels.

Code Groups

A code group is a logical grouping of code by means of one and only one common membership condition. That isn't to say that the same logical grouping of code can't be a member of more than one code group. In fact, code groups are organized in a hierarchy from "all code" to very (possibly) specific conditions. (Doesn't this sound familiar? Hint: a roles hierarchy.) Thus, if a logical group of code has evidence to support that it is a member of the lowest level of the hierarchy, then it is also a member by default of all parent code groups.

The .NET Framework provides several membership conditions for preconfigured code groups:

- *All code*: All code meets this condition.
- *Application directory*: Code in the directory or a child directory of the running application.
- *Custom*: Code matching a user-specified condition.
- *GAC*: Code that resides in the global assembly cache (GAC).
- *Hash*: Code with a hash that matches the given hash.
- *Publisher*: Code digitally signed with a specified certificate.
- *Site*: Code downloaded from a specified site.
- *Strong Name*: Code with a specified strong name and public key.
- *URL*: Code downloaded from a specified URL.
- *Zone*: Code that originates from one of five specified zones: My Computer, Internet, Local Intranet, Trusted Sites, and Untrusted Sites. (These zones are maintained within the security options of Internet Explorer.)

The process of coding membership condition is pretty easy; you just have to create an instance of it using the appropriate .NET Framework constructor. Conveniently there happens to be a class and simple constructor for each of the preconfigured code group membership conditions listed here in the System::Security::Policy namespace.

For example, if you want to create a URL membership condition you would create an instance of the UrlMembershipCondition class like this:

```
IMembershipCondition^ membership =
    gcnew UrlMembershipCondition("http://192.168.1.102/Chapter19/*");
```

Now that you have both a policy and a membership condition, you can create a code group, or more accurately add to the union the current code group's policy statement, with the policy statement of all its matching child code groups. This is done with the UnionCodeGroup class.

```
CodeGroup^ codeGroup = gcnew UnionCodeGroup(membership, policy);
```

Notice that I am creating an instance of a CodeGroup, not a UnionCodeGroup. The CodeGroup class is an abstract base class and you can't create it directly.

The CodeGroup has a few properties and members. The few I most commonly use are shown in Table 19-1.

Table 19-1. *Commonly Used CodeGroup Properties and Methods*

Member	Description
AddChild()	Method to add a child code group to the current code group.
Children	An ordered list of all child code groups.
Description	The description of the code group. This is what gets displayed in the Microsoft .NET Framework 2.0 Configuration tool.
Name	Name of the code group. You will use this to dynamically delete the code group.
RemoveChild()	Method to remove a child code group from the current code group.

Mostly I just use Description and Name like this:

```
codeGroup->Description = "C:\\ ReadOnly permissions in for Application URL";
codeGroup->Name = "ReadOnly Secure Group";
```

But if I am building a code group hierarchy dynamically, then I would also use the child-related property and methods. You will also see the child-related members in use in a later example that shows how to remove a code group from a policy.

Okay, you now have all the parts needed to programmatically update your system's security policy. Let's take a look at the complete example (see Listing 19-3) and fill in the couple of holes.

Listing 19-3. *Adding Your Own ReadOnly Code Group*

```cpp
using namespace System;
using namespace System::Security;
using namespace System::Security::Permissions;
using namespace System::Security::Policy;

void main()
{
    // Create a new permission set
    PermissionSet^ permSet = gcnew PermissionSet(PermissionState::None);

    // Add permissions to the permission set.
    permSet->AddPermission(
        gcnew SecurityPermission(PermissionState::Unrestricted));
    permSet->AddPermission(gcnew UIPermission(PermissionState::Unrestricted));
    permSet->AddPermission(gcnew FileIOPermission(FileIOPermissionAccess::Read,
                                    "C:\\"));

    // Create Policy Statement
    PolicyStatement^ policy = gcnew PolicyStatement(permSet);

    // Create Membership condition
    IMembershipCondition^ membership =
        gcnew UrlMembershipCondition("http://192.168.1.102/Chapter19/*");

    // Create Code group
    CodeGroup^ codeGroup = gcnew UnionCodeGroup(membership, policy);
    codeGroup->Description = "C:\\ ReadOnly permission for Application URL";
    codeGroup->Name = "ReadOnly Secure Group";

    // Find the machine policy level
    System::Collections::IEnumerator^ ph = SecurityManager::PolicyHierarchy();

    while( ph->MoveNext() )
    {
        PolicyLevel^ pl = (PolicyLevel^)ph->Current;
        if( pl->Label == "Machine" )
        {
            // Add code group to Machine policy
            pl->RootCodeGroup->AddChild(codeGroup);
            break;
        }
    }
}
```

```
    // Save changes
    SecurityManager::SavePolicy();

    Console::WriteLine("Added C:\\ ReadOnly Secure Group");
}
```

You've seen most of the code in Listing 19-3 before. What you haven't seen is how to add the newly created code group as a child to the code group hierarchy. In the listing, I added it to the Machine policy code group. There is nothing really tricky about it. All you do is iterate through the enumeration of all policy levels looking for the Machine policy level and then simply add the new code group as a child of the Machine code group hierarchy.

Finding the enumerator for the Policy hierarchy is less obvious. As you can see, see, I found the SecurityManager class's static method PolicyHierarchy().

Oh... and you have to save your work with the SecurityManager class's static method SavePolicy.

Note I use my IP address 192.168.1.102 as the membership condition. This probably will not be the same as yours. Replace the above code with your IP. You can get it by running IPConfig.exe from the command line.

The results of the above example can be seen using the Microsoft .NET Framework 2.0 Configuration application (see Figure 19-7), which you access from your Administration tools.

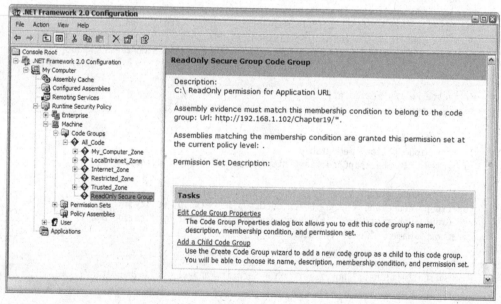

Figure 19-7. *Results shown in the Microsoft .NET Framework 2.0 Configuration application*

Just to complete the circle, I might as well show you how to remove the code group you just added. Listing 19-4 shows how you might do it.

Listing 19-4. *Removing Your Own ReadOnly Code Group*

```
using namespace System;
using namespace System::Security;
using namespace System::Security::Permissions;
using namespace System::Security::Policy;

void main()
{
    CodeGroup^ machine;

    // Iterate through policy hierarchy to get Machine Code group
    System::Collections::IEnumerator^ ph = SecurityManager::PolicyHierarchy();
    while( ph->MoveNext() )
    {
        PolicyLevel^ machinePolicyLevel = (PolicyLevel^)ph->Current;
        if (machinePolicyLevel->Label == "Machine")
        {
            machine = machinePolicyLevel->RootCodeGroup;
            break;
        }
    }

    // Iterate backwards removing all instances of "ReadOnly Secure Group"
    for (int i = machine->Children->Count - 1; i >= 0; i--)
    {
        if(((CodeGroup^)machine->Children[i])->Name == "ReadOnly Secure Group")
        {
            machine->RemoveChild(((CodeGroup^)machine->Children[i]));
        }
    }

    // Save changes
    SecurityManager::SavePolicy();

    Console::WriteLine("Removed C:\\ File ReadOnly Secure Group");
}
```

I think the comments in Listing 19-4 pretty well explain what is happening. First you iterate through the Policy hierarchy until you come to the Machine policy. At this point, grab the Machine policy's code group hierarchy.

The only unusual part is that you next have to iterate backward through the children of Machine's code group during the child removal process. You need to do it backward because as you remove children the machine->Children->Count gets reduced by one as well. Because of this, you will miss one iteration through the hierarchy. This is not an issue in this example since there is only one "ReadOnly Secure Group." However, if you happen to be removing multiple code groups that, for instance, start with "ReadOnly Secure Group," then if the last code group is one you are supposed to delete, it will be missed.

Once you find the code group you want to remove (using the name you so conveniently added during the add process), you call the RemoveChild() method. Incidentally, this will also prune off any grandchildren.

Evidence

Now that you have all the code groups set up, code access security uses an evidence-based method of ultimately determining if a section of code executes.

Evidence is accumulated at the assembly level; therefore, for an assembly to be a part of a code group it must have evidence to support that it adheres to the code group's common membership characteristic or condition. Or in other words, does the assembly originate from a specific site, URL, or zone? Does it have a matching strong name, hash, or publisher? Does it reside in the GAC or Application directory?

The confusing part is that it is still possible for an assembly to run even if it doesn't have the evidence to support that it belongs to a required code group. The catch is that it only runs the code within the assembly that it has the permissions to run. In other words, your assembly may be able to display a UI but the functionality behind the buttons of the interface may require special permissions to run.

Listings 19-5 and 19-6 show this in action. We've shown a simple Windows application that has two buttons: one to read a file and one to write a file.

Listing 19-5. *CAS Example .cpp File*

```
#include "Form1.h"

using namespace CASSecurity;

[STAThreadAttribute]
int main(array<System::String ^> ^args)
{
    // Enabling Windows XP visual effects before any controls are created
    Application::EnableVisualStyles();
    // Create the main window and run it
    Application::Run(gcnew Form1());
    return 0;
}
```

Listing 19-6. *CAS Example .h File*

```
namespace CASSecurity
{
    using namespace System;
    using namespace System::ComponentModel;
    using namespace System::Collections;
    using namespace System::IO;
    using namespace System::Windows::Forms;
    using namespace System::Data;
    using namespace System::Drawing;

    public ref class Form1 : public System::Windows::Forms::Form
    {
    public:
        Form1(void)
        {
            InitializeComponent();
        }
```

```cpp
    protected:
        ~Form1()
        {
            if (components)
            {
                delete components;
            }
        }
    private:
        System::Windows::Forms::Label^  lbOutput;
        System::Windows::Forms::Button^  bnWriteFile;
        System::Windows::Forms::Button^  bnReadFile;
        System::ComponentModel::Container ^components;

#pragma region Windows Form Designer generated code

        void InitializeComponent(void)
        {
            this->lbOutput = (gcnew System::Windows::Forms::Label());
            this->bnWriteFile = (gcnew System::Windows::Forms::Button());
            this->bnReadFile = (gcnew System::Windows::Forms::Button());
            this->SuspendLayout();
            //
            // lbOutput
            //
            this->lbOutput->AutoSize = true;
            this->lbOutput->Location = System::Drawing::Point(68, 71);
            this->lbOutput->Name = L"lbOutput";
            this->lbOutput->Size = System::Drawing::Size(0, 13);
            this->lbOutput->TabIndex = 5;
            //
            // bnWriteFile
            //
            this->bnWriteFile->Location = System::Drawing::Point(170, 30);
            this->bnWriteFile->Name = L"bnWriteFile";
            this->bnWriteFile->Size = System::Drawing::Size(75, 23);
            this->bnWriteFile->TabIndex = 4;
            this->bnWriteFile->Text = L"Write File";
            this->bnWriteFile->UseVisualStyleBackColor = true;
            this->bnWriteFile->Click +=
                gcnew System::EventHandler(this, &Form1::bnWriteFile_Click);
            //
            // bnReadFile
            //
            this->bnReadFile->Location = System::Drawing::Point(48, 30);
            this->bnReadFile->Name = L"bnReadFile";
            this->bnReadFile->Size = System::Drawing::Size(75, 23);
            this->bnReadFile->TabIndex = 3;
            this->bnReadFile->Text = L"Read File";
            this->bnReadFile->UseVisualStyleBackColor = true;
            this->bnReadFile->Click +=
                gcnew System::EventHandler(this, &Form1::bnReadFile_Click);
            //
            // Form1
```

```
                //
                this->AutoScaleDimensions = System::Drawing::SizeF(6, 13);
                this->AutoScaleMode = System::Windows::Forms::AutoScaleMode::Font;
                this->ClientSize = System::Drawing::Size(292, 110);
                this->Controls->Add(this->lbOutput);
                this->Controls->Add(this->bnWriteFile);
                this->Controls->Add(this->bnReadFile);
                this->Name = L"Form1";
                this->Text = L"CAS Security Test";
                this->ResumeLayout(false);
                this->PerformLayout();

            }
#pragma endregion

    private:
        System::Void bnReadFile_Click(System::Object^ sender,
                                      System::EventArgs^ e)
        {
            StreamReader ^sr = File::OpenText("C:\\TestFile.txt");
            String ^s = sr->ReadLine();
            sr->Close();
            lbOutput->Text = s;
        }

    private:
        System::Void bnWriteFile_Click(System::Object^ sender,
                                       System::EventArgs^ e)
        {
            StreamWriter ^sw = File::CreateText("C:\\TestFile.txt");
            sw->WriteLine("This is a test. This is only a test.");
            sw->Close();
            lbOutput->Text = "Wrote text to file.";
        }
    };
}
```

If you have read Chapters 9 and 10, then there should be nothing new here. Just make sure you compile using /clr:safe as it is the only way that you can get code access security to work.

When you run this application from your local machine, it works without any problems. Figure 19-8 shows the normal expected results.

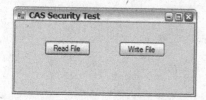

Figure 19-8. *CASSecurity run from the local machine*

On the other hand, if you run it as mobile code via Internet Explorer it loads the interface but the buttons when clicked throw permission exceptions.

Caution Make sure you delete the code group generated with SetSecurity.exe (Listing 19-3) using RemoveSecurity.exe (Listing 19-4) before starting this section, or your results will not be the same.

Running this example from Internet Explorer requires a bit of prep work:

1. In Windows Explorer, right-click the directory that contains the CASSecurity.exe file and select Properties.

2. In the Properties dialog box, select the Web Sharing tab, as shown in Figure 19-9.

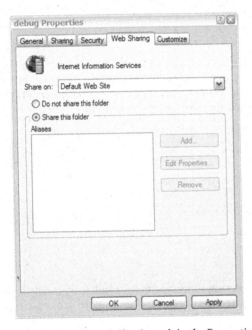

Figure 19-9. *The Web Sharing tab in the Properties dialog box*

3. Select the Share this folder radio button to bring up the Edit Alias dialog box, as shown in Figure 19-10.

4. Type **Chapter19** in the Alias text box.

5. Select the Directory browsing check box (optional).

6. Click OK twice.

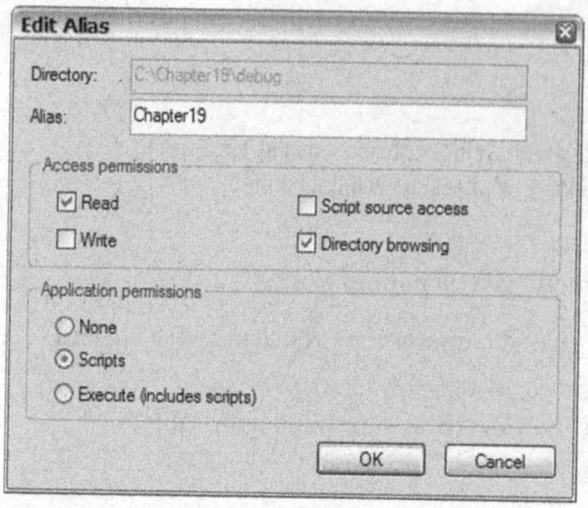

Edit Alias

Directory: C:\Chapter19\debug

Alias: Chapter19

Access permissions

☑ Read   ☐ Script source access
☐ Write   ☑ Directory browsing

Application permissions

○ None
⦿ Scripts
○ Execute (includes scripts)

[OK]   [Cancel]

Figure 19-10. *The Edit Alias dialog box*

Now you can run the application from Internet Explorer. To do this, just type in IE's address line http://192.168.1.102/Chapter19/CASSecurity.exe, substituting my IP address for your own. If you completed step 5 you can simply type in the address line http://192.168.1.102/Chapter19 and click the link to CASSecurity.exe. When you do, you'll see the message in Figure 19-11.

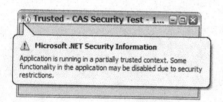

Trusted - CAS Security Test - 1...

⚠ **Microsoft .NET Security Information**

Application is running in a partially trusted context. Some functionality in the application may be disabled due to security restrictions.

Figure 19-11. *Permission warning*

If you ignore the warning and continue, clicking either button will result in a permission exception, as shown in Figure 19-12. Hmmm, not quite what you're expecting, right?

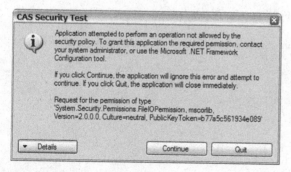

CAS Security Test

ⓘ   Application attempted to perform an operation not allowed by the security policy. To grant this application the required permission, contact your system administrator, or use the Microsoft .NET Framework Configuration tool.

If you click Continue, the application will ignore this error and attempt to continue. If you click Quit, the application will close immediately.

Request for the permission of type 'System.Security.Permissions.FileIOPermission, mscorlib, Version=2.0.0.0, Culture=neutral, PublicKeyToken=b77a5c561934e089'

[▼ Details]   [Continue]   [Quit]

Figure 19-12. *Permission exception*

All is not lost, thanks to all the work you have already done in creating a code group with a URL membership condition of your IP and permissions to allow reading of files off C:\.

Run SetSecurity.exe to add the code group you created earlier. Now when you run CASSecurity.exe from Internet Explorer, the Read File button works but the Write File button still throws an exception. Why is that?

First, the assembly CASSecurity.exe provided evidence that it originates at the URL 192.168.1.102. This satisfies the code group I wrote and the CLR allows the assembly to become a member. Now that it is a member, it has the security permissions of the code group—in this case the right to execute, show a UI, and read files from C:\. Since the code group does not have the permissions to write to C:\, the CLR stops the assembly up short when it tries to do this and throws the permissions exception.

Cool, no?

Securing Your Code Using CAS

One nice thing about the .NET Framework is that it is already configured to work with code access security. Thus, once you have set up your code groups and permission sets, you are basically done, unless you want to secure the resources and functionalities you have written yourself with code access security.

Integrating code access security within your code is done in the same way as with role-based security: using declarative- and imperative-style security. The only real difference between CAS and role-based security is that you use a declarative attribute or imperative class related to the resource or functionality you want to access instead of one related to principal permissions. For example, to declaratively secure the Registry you would use something like this:

```
[RegistryPermissionAttribute(SecurityAction.Demand, Unrestricted=true)]
public class NeedsUnrestrictedRegistrtAccessClass
{
};
```

and to imperatively secure the Registry you would use

```
(gcnew RegistryPermission(PermissionState.Unrestricted))->Demand();
```

The main difference between these two styles is that declarative is evaluated during JIT compiling while imperative is evaluated at runtime.

So far you have only been implementing permission demands, but the demand is only one of the nine actions that can be taken with permissions. Here are all nine:

- Demand
- LinkDemand
- InheritanceDemand
- RequestMinumum
- RequestOptional
- RequestRefuse
- Assert
- Deny
- PermitOnly

Let's take a look at each.

Note Code access security works in conjunction with Windows user account security. Therefore, when your application has permission according to CAS to access a protected resource, if your Windows user account does not have the privilege then the application will throw a permission exception.

Demands

The most common security request type is the Demand type. They also, I think, make the most sense when implementing. Basically, the code protected by the declarative or imperative statement is demanding that the accessing code group have the permissions specified. When the code group has the permissions, the program continues to execute; if not, the CLR throws an exception.

There are three types of demands; each addresses a different process for determining whether or not the demand is successful.

Demand

You have already seen this type in action. You might not know that this form of demand ensures not only that the current code group has the demanded permission but also that all code groups down that call stack also have the required permission.

This means that all assemblies in the call stack below the current call must also have the permissions demanded, not just the one currently executing.

Be aware that the demand occurs every time the protected area is accessed because the stack might contain a different call stack. Therefore, if you call a declaratively protected method repeatedly or execute the imperative Demand method, a security check occurs each time.

One unique implementation of imperative Demand syntax is to enable and disable controls in the UI so that a user does not have the ability to click on a control that he has no privileges for. You need to add the following to the CASSecurity.exe example to implement this:

```
try
{
    (gcnew FileIOPermission(FileIOPermissionAccess::Read, "C:\\"))->Demand();
}
catch(Exception^)
{
    bnReadFile->Enabled = false;
}

try
{
    (gcnew FileIOPermission(FileIOPermissionAccess::Write, "C:\\"))->Demand();
}
catch(Exception^)
{
    bnWriteFile->Enabled = false;
}
```

I placed these lines in the Form1 constructor, but you can place them anywhere as long as they are executed before the controls are displayed. The results are shown in Figure 19-13.

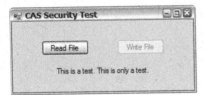

Figure 19-13. *Disabling controls due to lack of permissions*

LinkDemand

The LinkDemand does not have the overhead that the Demand has. It only checks the immediate call to the permission secured area; once the check passes, no subsequent checks are made. In other words, no stack walk occurs and the check is done only once no matter how many times the call is made.

The code to implement LinkDemand is virtually the same as Demand:

```
[ReflectionPermissionAttribute(SecurityAction::LinkDemand, Unrestricted=true)]
void LinkDemandReflectionOperation()
{
}
```

You need to be careful when using LinkDemand, because even though the call is faster, any code that passes the test and thus can reference your code can potentially break security by allowing malicious code to call using the authorized code.

I don't feel the speed gain is worth this possible security problem, so I always use Demand. On the other hand, if you have complete control of the call stack then LinkDemand might work well for you.

Note LinkDemand can only be applied to a method declaratively.

InheritanceDemand

There are two forms of InheritanceDemand. The first is as a class attribute. When used in this form, all classes that inherit from this declaratively secured class must also have the specified permissions.

```
[ZoneIdentityPermissionAttribute(SecurityAction::InheritanceDemand,
                            Zone=SecurityZone::Internet)]
public ref class InheritanceDemandZoneIdentityClass
{
}
```

The second form is an attribute on the virtual method. In this scenario, a class must have the specified permissions of the virtual method to be able to override the virtual method.

```
public ref class InheritanceDemandClass
{
    public:
    [ZoneIdentityPermissionAttribute(SecurityAction::InheritanceDemand,
                            Zone=SecurityZone::Internet)]
    virtual void InheritanceDemandZoneIdentityMethod()
    {
    }
}
```

> **Note** InheritanceDemand can only be applied declaratively.

Requests

Requesting permissions is a different approach to handling permission in code access security. Instead of letting the code run up to the point where the permission is demanded, request permissions don't even let the assembly load into memory.

You apply requests using declarative syntax on the assembly. That way, the CLR can check at the time when the assembly is loading to see if the appropriate permissions are satisfied. If the permissions requested are not satisfied by the evidence, then the assembly itself does not load.

RequestMinimum

The RequestMinimum is an all-or-nothing proposition for an assembly. It is the permission that the code must have to run. The failure to have the permissions causes the CLR to not load the assembly.

```
using namespace System;
using namespace System::IO;
using namespace System::Security;
using namespace System::Security::Permissions;

[assembly:FileIOPermission(SecurityAction::RequestMinimum, Write="C:\\")];

namespace MustWriteTOCRoot
{
}
```

RequestOptional

The RequestOptional allows you to request a set of permissions while refusing all other permissions the CLR might otherwise have given. The RequestOptional does not indicate that all the permissions specified are needed. Instead, it says these are the permissions it is going to let your code have when this assembly runs.

Note that if your code tries to implement a permission not granted by RequestOptional then a SecurityException will be thrown. You might also note that if your code tries to use a permission granted by RequestOptional but not granted to the executing assembly, then the CLR is going to throw an exception just like it would have if you hadn't used any RequestOptional permissions.

To get CASSecurity.exe to run with RequestOptional permissions, you need the following four lines because all of these permissions are required for the application to run successfully:

```
[assembly:FileIOPermission(SecurityAction::RequestOptional, Read="C:\\")];
[assembly:FileIOPermission(SecurityAction::RequestOptional, Write="C:\\")];
[assembly:UIPermission(SecurityAction::RequestOptional,Unrestricted=true)];
[assembly:SecurityPermission(SecurityAction::RequestOptional,
                             Unrestricted=true)];
```

RequestRefuse

RequestRefuse is basically the opposite of RequestOptional. With RequestRefuse you specify which permissions the assembly will refuse. Any other permission that you don't list is allowed.

I normally use RequestOptional instead of RequestRefuse as I feel it provides a more secure environment—you know exactly which permissions you are allowing. The only time I would use RequestRefuse is when I want a very specific set of permissions to be refused. If I were to use RequestRefuse instead of RequestOptional in the CASSecurity.exe example, I would have to include refusals for all the permissions available in .NET except the four lines listed earlier.

The following line shows what you would need to code to refuse an assembly any access to the Registry:

```
[assembly:RegistryPermission(SecurityAction::RequestRefuse,Unrestricted=true)];
```

Overrides

There will come a time where you will find that your application has FullTrust and yet your assembly still throws permission errors. This can't happen, so you must have coded something incorrectly, right? Well, actually you may have coded everything correctly. What most likely happened is one of the assemblies down the stack walk did not have FullTrust or a permission was overridden.

It is with these last three actions on permissions that we override the standard stack walk.

Assert/RevertAssert

The Assert override is probably one of the most dangerous features of code access security and must be used carefully. The reason is that with Assert you can accidentally add permissions that the stack walk would normally have denied. This is because the Assert stops the stack walk at the stack frame where the Assert is made. For those of you more visually inclined, Figure 19-14 might help.

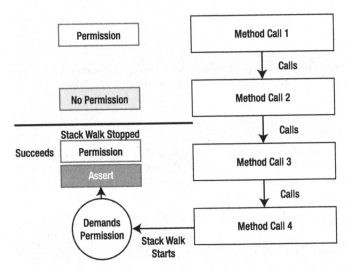

Figure 19-14. *Possible Assert problem*

Caution Microsoft warns that "because calling Assert removes the requirement that all code in the call chain must be granted permission to access the specified resource, it can open up security vulnerabilities if used incorrectly or inappropriately. Therefore, it should be used with great caution."

Personally, I only use Assert when I have complete control of the call stack that is being walked.

Keep in mind that Assert does not grant permission to a demand. The demand works as it normally would for that stack frame, so if that frame would normally have denied the permission the Assert point would also be denied permission.

The actual code involved in an Assert is fairly simple:

```
CodeAccessPermission ^permission =
    gcnew FileIOPermission(FileIOPermissionAccess::Read, "C:\\");

permission->Assert();
// Do stuff
permission->RevertAssert();
```

Since only one Assert is allowed to be in effect at a time for a frame, you should make sure that you call the RevertAssert() method when you are done with your Assert. This basically turns off your Assert.

Deny/RevertDeny

As I'm sure you suspect, this form of override causes the current stack frame to be denied for the resource type specified. Using this override enables you to disable permissions for accessing resources even though the application is running under a code group that has a permission set with the appropriate permissions.

```
CodeAccessPermission ^permissionRead =
    gcnew FileIOPermission(FileIOPermissionAccess::Read, "C:\\");

permissionRead->Deny();
// Do stuff
permissionRead->RevertDeny();
```

The RevertDeny is used to restore the previous permissions to the specified resource. Note that if the resource was denied permissions before the Deny was called, then the resource continues to not have permission.

PermitOnly/RevertPermitOnly

If you want to be specific with which resources are available on a stack walk, then the PermitOnly may be what you want. This override identifies the only resources that will have permissions on the call stack from the time the PermitOnly is specified to its corresponding RevertPermitOnly.

```
CodeAccessPermission ^permissionWrite =
    gcnew FileIOPermission(FileIOPermissionAccess::Write, "C:\\");

permissionWrite->PermitOnly();
// Do Stuff
permissionWrite->RevertPermitOnly();
```

Overrides can be a bit difficult to understand without an example. Listing 19-7 shows how you can use Deny and PermitOnly on the call stack and then have Assert overrule them.

Listing 19-7. *Assert, Deny, and PermitOnly*

```
#include "stdafx.h"

using namespace System;
using namespace System::IO;
using namespace System::Security;
using namespace System::Security::Permissions;

void AssertRead()
{
    CodeAccessPermission ^permission =
        gcnew FileIOPermission(FileIOPermissionAccess::Read, "C:\\");

    permission->Assert();
    StreamReader ^sr = File::OpenText("C:\\TestFile.txt");
    String ^s = sr->ReadLine();
    sr->Close();
    permission->RevertAssert();
    Console::WriteLine("Successful Read");
}

void NoAssertRead()
{
    StreamReader ^sr = File::OpenText("C:\\TestFile.txt");
    String ^s = sr->ReadLine();
    sr->Close();
    Console::WriteLine("Successful Read");
}

void main()
{
    // Deny Reading C:
    CodeAccessPermission ^permissionRead =
        gcnew FileIOPermission(FileIOPermissionAccess::Read, "C:\\");

    permissionRead->Deny();
    try
    {
        AssertRead();
        NoAssertRead();
    }
    catch(SecurityException^)
    {
        Console::WriteLine("Failed To Read");
    }
    permissionRead->RevertDeny();

    // Only allow Writing to C:
    CodeAccessPermission ^permissionWrite =
        gcnew FileIOPermission(FileIOPermissionAccess::Write, "C:\\");
```

```
    permissionWrite->PermitOnly();
    try
    {
        AssertRead();
        NoAssertRead();
    }
    catch(SecurityException^)
    {
        Console::WriteLine("Failed To Read");
    }
    permissionWrite->RevertPermitOnly();
}
```

When you run this example, you do it from the console and thus it has all the rights of the Windows account running it—in my case administrative rights.. Notice that even though I have administrative rights I lose permissions with the Deny and PermitOnly. I only get them back with the Assert.

Figure 19-15 shows AssertDenyPermit.exe in action.

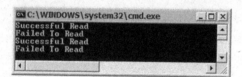

Figure 19-15. *Results of AssertDenyPermit.exe*

Summary

In this chapter you covered .NET security with a specific focus on how to implement it using C++/CLI. You started off with the easier of the two major types of security provided by .NET, role-based security, in particular the identity, principal, and permissions. Next you looked at code access security. You examined permissions, permission sets, policies, code groups, and evidence. Finally, with the basics of CAS covered, you learned how to secure your own code using demands, requests, and overrides.

Now that you have examined safe and managed code, in the next chapter you'll change gears and look at coding with unsafe and unmanaged code.

■■■

PART 3

■■■

Unsafe/Unmanaged C++/CLI

CHAPTER 20

■■■

Unsafe C++ .NET Programming

Well, I think that's enough about safe/managed code. Let's take a look at another major area of C++/CLI: the ability to create unsafe/unmanaged code. Sounds kind of scary, doesn't it?

I'm not sure I understand why C++ .NET books spend so much time on this area of C++ programming as it is (usually) rather simple. It's what C++ programmers have been doing for years, and there are literally hundreds of books on the topic. The only real differences to a C++/CLI code developer are a few extra classes and attributes.

If there really is any complexity, it is on the side of the unsafe/unmanaged code and not the safe/managed code that it interfaces with. Most of this complexity revolves around forcing safe/managed code to be executed within a block of unsafe/unmanaged code, which is really the opposite of what you should normally be doing. Safe/managed code should be the new code being developed, and it should be referencing only when really necessary the old unsafe/unmanaged code.

One nice simplifying feature and a big time saver is that Visual Studio 2005 even auto-generates a lot of the interfacing code for you—most notably in the area of COM development, but I'll get to that in the next chapter.

In this chapter, I will look at some of the more basic areas of unsafe/unmanaged C++/CLI programming. One thing about these more basic areas is that, when used, they are the most common reason you end up not being able to compile your code with the /clr:safe option. Once you finish this chapter, you should be able to figure out what needs to be changed in your code to make it safe/managed.

After we have the basics down in this chapter, I'll then take a look at some of the more advanced topics like interfacing save/managed code with unsafe/unmanaged DLLs and COM objects in the next chapter.

If you are new to unmanaged C++, you might want to consult *Beginning ANSI C++: The Complete Language, Third Edition* by Ivor Horton (Apress, 2004).

Note Basically, unmanaged C++ syntax == ANSI C++ syntax.

What Is Unsafe Code?

I've kind of glossed over it in all the proceeding chapters of the book, but the ability to create safe code is probably the biggest enhancement made to C++/CLI over Managed Extensions for C++. Before C++/CLI, you could only create unsafe C++ code. Yes, Managed Extensions for C++ code enabled memory to be maintained by the CLR, but there was no such thing as safe C++ .NET code, at least not in the sense that it could be verified by the CLR. Of course, you could code C++ in a safe manner, but the user who executed your code was given no guarantee that it was actually safe.

That has all changed in .NET version 2.0 and the C++/CLI compiler, as the `/clr:safe` switch generates verifiable code that the CLR can provide trust levels to, just like it can with C# or Visual Basic .NET.

Note You may have noticed in the examples I provided for download that I almost always use the `/clr:safe` option. Personally, I think it should be the default, as I like the idea of the code being safe. I usually only resort to using the `/clr` option when I'm forced to work with unsafe/unmanaged code.

Unsafe, unmanaged, and native code are all terms that many writers seem to throw around as if they were interchangeable. But actually they are all different things.

When you speak of *unsafe code*, you are talking about the compiler's inability to create verifiable code, which is thus unsafe in regards to security. Unsafe code, when allowed to run by the CLR, has as much control of the computer as you do. If you are, like me (and probably most other developers), an administrator, then the unsafe code has complete control of your computer. Now that is a scary thought.

Unmanaged code is unsafe by its very nature. This type of code has the ability to access and create instances of objects outside of the CLR sandbox. In most cases when you use pointers in your code, you are dealing with unmanaged code. You will see that this is not always true, as C++/CLI provides something called the *interior pointer* that, if handled correctly, can be verified and thus be compiled as safe.

Native code is code that is compiled outside of the C++/CLI world and cannot be verified in any way. Native code is usually in the form of machine language, but again, in theory, it need not be. Native code is usually found in DLLs and COM objects. Native code is generated using a non-.NET compiler or without any type of `/clr` switch if generated with a .NET compiler.

To confuse or simplify things (depending on how you look at it), Microsoft added the ability to place native code within your safe/managed code using the `#pragma unmanaged` directive. Personally, I think it should be called the native directive, because it would reflect more accurately what it is doing and because unmanaged code does not need to be native code.

What does this all mean? Unsafe code is code that contains embedded unmanaged code. Notice I added the word "embedded." The reason for this is it is still possible to have safe code that accesses or runs unmanaged code, so long as the correct interfaces are implemented. What these interfaces do is allow the CLR to know when unsafe code is about to be used and then to use code access security (which I covered in the previous chapter) to determine whether the unsafe code can be executed.

Why Do We Still Need Unsafe Code?

The funny thing is one of the major reasons why unsafe code will continue to exist is due to unsafe code's ability to do things that safe code can't do simply because of its unsafe nature. One of the more obvious of these unsafe features is pointer arithmetic, or the ability to access memory frequently outside of the CLR sandbox and then manipulate the addresses of this memory directly.

Another reason, more obviously, is because there are millions of lines of unsafe code out there already (much of it C++), and it will take an awfully long time to convert to safe code. And, in most cases, there is really no need to do the conversion in the first place, as the code works just fine as it is.

You might think that most of the unsafe code in the case of C++ could simply be recompiled with the `/clr:safe` option and be made safe, but unfortunately in most cases it is not that simple, as pointers and pointer arithmetic are the main means of handling memory in C++ prior to C++/CLI, and as I noted previously, pointers are are in nearly all cases not verifiable, and pointer arithmetic is never verifiable.

Unsafe code is usually needed for interfacing with computer hardware. Most hardware drivers are written in C++, C, or some form of assembly. In most cases, the code relies heavily on pointers to access the hardware, and these pointers point outside of the CLR sandbox.

Another issue about unsafe code is not all of it is in computer languages that can readily be converted to a safe version, as no mainstream .NET compiler is available. (With the growing number of .NET languages, this argument is losing its weight.) Interestingly, the resulting libraries generated by these languages are frequently wrapped by C++, if the function provided by this nonstandard coding language needs to be accessed by third parties. Unfortunately, in most cases the wrapper methods themselves rely heavily on pointers, which even make the interfacing wrapper method unsafe. Now, if you want to generate verifiable code for the main application calling this code, you have the requirement of building a safe wrapper around the unsafe wrapper. Can you say yuck?

Creating Unsafe Code

As I noted earlier, unsafe code is normally created by adding native code to your managed code. It is also possible to create unsafe code with only MSIL code by using unsafe operations or objects.

There are several ways of coding C++/CLI so that it is unsafe. The following are four of the more common ways of making your assembly unsafe. There are others, but these are the methods I've frequently come across in my travels.

- Managed and unmanaged #pragma directives
- Unmanaged arrays
- Unmanaged classes/structs
- Pointers and pointer arithmetic

The Managed and Unmanaged #pragma Directives

The most basic way of creating unsafe code is by mixing managed and unmanaged code together with the directives #pragma managed and #pragma unmanaged. When encountered by the compiler, these directives tell the compiler to generate MSIL (managed) code or native (unmanaged) code. The compiler continues to generate the specified type of code until it encounters a directive to switch the type of code generated.

Listing 20-1 shows a very simple example of using the #pragma managed and #pragma unmanaged directives.

Listing 20-1. *The Managed and Unmanaged #pragma Directives*

```
using namespace System;

#pragma unmanaged

int UMadd(int a, int b)
{
    return a + b;
}

#pragma managed
```

```
int Madd(int a, int b)
{
    return a + b;
}

void main()
{
    Console::WriteLine("Unmanaged Add 2 + 2: {0}", UMadd(2, 2));
    Console::WriteLine("Managed   Add 3 + 3: {0}",  Madd(3, 3));
}
```

By looking at the UMadd() and Madd() methods' code, you will not see much difference. Both are simply standard C++/CLI code. Notice you even call the methods the same way, as long as they are being called within a managed code block.

If you try to call managed code within a native code block, you get the compile time error C3821 'function': managed type or function cannot be used in an unmanaged function. This makes sense as native code does not use the CLR to run, while managed code does, so there is no way for the managed code to be executed within the native code.

Another thing you need to be careful about with these directives is that they are only allowed at the global scope, as shown in Listing 20-1, or at the namespace scope. This means you can't change a method or class partway through. In other words, the whole function or class can be managed or native, but not a combination.

Caution The following code is invalid due to invalid placement of the #pragma directives:

```
int ErrorFunction(int a, int b)
{
#pragma unmanaged
    // Some unmanaged code
#pragma managed
    // Some managed code
}
```

Unsafe Code Since the #pragma unmanaged directive causes unsafe code to be generated, you need to compile it with the /clr option. If you try to compile it with the /clr:safe option, you will get a whole bunch of errors.

So what is the difference between Madd() and UMadd()? To see this, you need to use the ildasm tool, which disassembles an assembly. Figure 20-1 shows Madd() (what little you see of it) and Figure 20-2 shows UMadd().

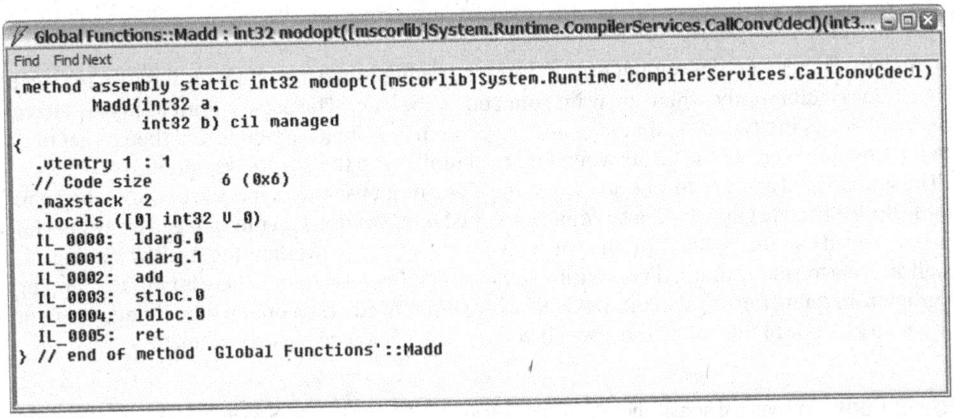

Figure 20-1. *The disassembled Madd()*

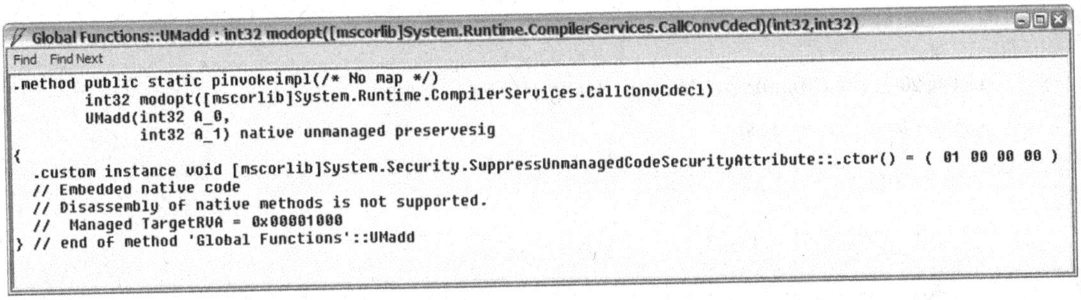

Figure 20-2. *The disassembled UMadd()*

The disassembled version of the Madd() function shows all the MSIL required to execute the function, while the UMadd() function only shows the function declaration and the attribute SuppressUnmanagedCodeSecurityAttribute. What you don't see is the native code that will be invoked when this function is called (if the CLR allows unmanaged code or in this case native code to be run). In a nutshell, behind the scenes the compiler generates MSIL for Madd() and native code for UMadd().

You might be thinking, as I did originally, why is this code unsafe? The CLR has the attributes needed to find out what is unsafe and can allow code access security to do its thing. But, if you think about it, it does sort of make sense. Since the whole assembly is loaded into memory, it might still be possible for someone to access the parts of the assembly that are unsafe. (Don't ask me how, but I'm sure some hacker out there has it figured out.) Therefore, to safeguard against this possibility, the current version of the .NET runtime defines unsafe code at an assembly level, so having any unsafe code in an assembly makes the entire assembly unsafe.

Unmanaged Arrays

One of the first things a C++ developer learns is arrays. Having coded them so long, it is easy to forget that .NET does it differently, when you want your code to be safe. (The usual culprit as to why I have unmanaged arrays in my code is that I cut and paste them in from legacy code and then forget to convert them, until I get all the errors when I try to compile with the /clr:safe option.)

The unmanaged arrays compile and work fine if you don't use the /clr:safe option. When you examine the MSIL code generated, everything looks just fine. So why is an unmanaged array unsafe? If you have coded C++ for a while, I'm sure you know. It is very easy to overflow the stack by looping through an array too many times. (I've done it so many times, I've lost count.) There is nothing stopping a program from doing this with an unmanaged array. A managed array, on the other hand, does not allow you to go beyond the end of the array. If you try, you get a nice big exception.

Unsafe Code Unmanaged arrays, though a legal construct in C++/CLI (so long as they contain fundamental and unmanaged data types) are unsafe. If you want both arrays and safe code, you need to use managed arrays.

Listing 20-2 shows the use of unmanaged arrays within managed code.

Listing 20-2. *The Unmanaged Array in Managed Code*

```
using namespace System;

void main()
{
    int UMarray[5] = {2, 3, 5, 7, 11};

    for (int i = 0; i < 5; i++)
    {
        Console::Write("{0} ", UMarray[i]);
    }
    Console::WriteLine(" -- End of array");
}
```

There is nothing terribly special about the preceding code. But there are specific criteria about what can be contained within an unmanaged array. Personally, I think it's easier to remember what can't be put into them—basically managed data or anything that requires the gcnew command when creating an instance.

One thing of note, as shown in Figure 20-3, is that the code generated by the compiler is MSIL and not native code. Thus, showing unsafe code does not always mean that the code contains native code. (Though you might argue this, as a whole bunch of native code is added to the assembly when /clr or /clr:pure options are used.)

```
[X] Global Functions::main : int32()                                    [_][□][X]
Find  Find Next
.method assembly static int32  main() cil managed
{
  // Code size       79 (0x4f)
  .maxstack  4
  .locals ([0] int32 i,
           [1] valuetype '<CppImplementationDetails>'.$ArrayType$$$BY04H UMarray)
  IL_0000:  ldloca.s    UMarray
  IL_0002:  ldc.i4.2
  IL_0003:  stind.i4
  IL_0004:  ldloca.s    UMarray
  IL_0006:  ldc.i4.4
  IL_0007:  add
  IL_0008:  ldc.i4.3
  IL_0009:  stind.i4
  IL_000a:  ldloca.s    UMarray
  IL_000c:  ldc.i4.8
  IL_000d:  add
  IL_000e:  ldc.i4.5
  IL_000f:  stind.i4
  IL_0010:  ldloca.s    UMarray
  IL_0012:  ldc.i4.s    12
  IL_0014:  add
  IL_0015:  ldc.i4.7
  IL_0016:  stind.i4
  IL_0017:  ldloca.s    UMarray
  IL_0019:  ldc.i4.s    16
  IL_001b:  add
  IL_001c:  ldc.i4.s    11
  IL_001e:  stind.i4
  IL_001f:  ldc.i4.0
  IL_0020:  stloc.0
  IL_0021:  br.s        IL_0027
  IL_0023:  ldloc.0
  IL_0024:  ldc.i4.1
  IL_0025:  add
  IL_0026:  stloc.0
  IL_0027:  ldloc.0
  IL_0028:  ldc.i4.5
  IL_0029:  bge.s       IL_0043
  IL_002b:  ldstr       "{0} "
  IL_0030:  ldloca.s    UMarray
  IL_0032:  ldloc.0
  IL_0033:  ldc.i4.4
  IL_0034:  mul
  IL_0035:  add
  IL_0036:  ldind.i4
  IL_0037:  box         [mscorlib]System.Int32
  IL_003c:  call        void [mscorlib]System.Console::Write(string,
                                                             object)
  IL_0041:  br.s        IL_0023
  IL_0043:  ldstr       " -- End of array"
  IL_0048:  call        void [mscorlib]System.Console::WriteLine(string)
  IL_004d:  ldc.i4.0
  IL_004e:  ret
} // end of method 'Global Functions'::main
```

Figure 20-3. *MSIL generated by UMArray.exe*

Unmanaged Classes/Structs

The next major constructs that a C++ developer learns after the array are the class and the struct. Though similar in many ways to C++/CLI's ref class (which I covered way back in Chapter 3), unmanaged classes have a few major differences that cause them to be unsafe. The most obvious difference, since they are unmanaged, is that they are placed in the CRT heap and not the Managed heap when instantiated. Thus, their memory is not maintained by the .NET garbage collector.

The actual coding of an unmanaged class/struct exactly matches the coding of the traditional (pre-.NET) C++ class/struct, due to the reason that unmanaged C++ code and traditional C++ code are one and the same. So, if you know how to code a C++ class or struct in a non-.NET environment, then you know how to code an unmanaged class or struct.

With .NET version 1.1 and Managed Extensions for C++, the class and struct were given the ability to be managed. With .NET version 2.0 and C++/CLI, the class has been augmented again this time with the ability to be safe as well. The funny thing (at least to me, but I do have a weird sense of humor, just ask my wife) is unmanaged classes and structs remain the default. You have to do specific things to create managed classes, but we covered all that stuff way back in Chapter 3, so let's move on.

Prior to C++/CLI, Managed Extensions for C++ used the exact same syntax for managed and unmanaged classes and structs, except for prefixing managed classes and structs with __gc. From there on, syntax for the two were virtually the same. I know I got confused a few times (but that might be just me) and thus tried to always only use managed classes (and data types, as you may have noted if you have the previous version of this book), as it simplified my life immensely.

C++/CLI has vastly improved the readability of the code over Managed Extensions for C++. Yes, the declaration of managed and unmanaged classes and structs is still very similar (Table 20-1 shows some of the major differences), but the syntax of creating managed classes now is considerably different because of the use of handles [^] and the gcnew command for managed classes instead of pointers [*] and the new command for unmanaged classes. Though this change was primarily to make managed coding easier, it also made life easier when coding unmanaged classes, as now there is no confusing the two.

Table 20-1. *Unmanaged vs. Managed Classes*

Unmanaged class/struct	Managed class/struct
No prefix	ref
Accessed via pointer or reference on the CRT heap or directly within a value type variable	Accessed via handle on the Managed heap or directly within a value type variable
When no explicit base class specified, then class is an independent root	When no explicit base class specified, then class inherits from System::Object
Supports multiple inheritance	Does not support multiple inheritance
Supports friends	Does not support friends
Can only inherit from unmanaged types	Can only inherit from managed types
Can contain data members of type pointer to unmanaged classes but cannot contain a handle to managed classes	Can contain data members of type pointer to unmanaged classes and a handle to managed classes

So what does the comparison of unmanaged and managed classes add up to? I created the nonsense program shown in Listing 20-3, which tries to show the information in Table 20-1 in a different way. I threw in the value class to round out the example, as the value class is sort of an unmanaged managed class. I also did not include friends in the example, as only unmanaged classes support them.

Listing 20-3. *Mixing Managed and Unmanaged Classes*

```cpp
using namespace System;

class       ClassMember  {};
ref class   RefClassMember {};
value class ValueClassMember {};

class Class
{
public:
//  RefClassMember    rc;      // Can't embed instance ref class
//  RefClassMember    ^hrc;    // Can't embed handle to ref class
    ValueClassMember  vc;
//  ValueClassMember  ^hvc;    // Can't embed managed value class
    ValueClassMember  *pvc;
    ClassMember       c;
    ClassMember       *pc;

    int x;
    void write() { Console::WriteLine("Class x: {0}", x); }
};

ref class RefClass
{
public:
    RefClassMember    rc;
    RefClassMember    ^hrc;
    ValueClassMember  vc;
    ValueClassMember  ^hvc;
    ValueClassMember  *pvc;
//  ClassMember       c;       // Can't embed instance of class
    ClassMember       *pc;

    int x;
    void write() { Console::WriteLine("RefClass x: {0}", x); }
};

value class ValueClass
{
public:
//  RefClassMember    rc;      // Can't embed instance ref class
    RefClassMember    ^hrc;
    ValueClassMember  vc;
    ValueClassMember  ^hvc;
    ValueClassMember  *pvc;
//  ClassMember       c;       // Can't embed instance of class
    ClassMember       *pc;

    int x;
    void write() { Console::WriteLine("ValueClass x: {0}", x); }
};
```

```
class ClassChildClassParent : public Class {};                      // OK
//class ClassChildRefClassParent : public RefClass {};              // Error
//class ClassChildValueClassParent : public ValueClass {};          // Error

//ref class RefClassChildClassParent : public Class {};             // Error
ref class RefClassChildRefClassParent : public RefClass {};         // OK
//ref class RefClassChildValueClassParent : public ValueClass {};   // Error

//value class ValueClassChildClassParent : public Class {};         // Error
//value class ValueClassChildRefClassParent : public RefClass {};   // Error
//value class ValueClassChildValueClassParent : public ValueClass {}; // Error

void main()
{
    // Stack
    Class      _class;
    RefClass   refclass;                                // Not really on the stack
    ValueClass valueclass;

    // Handle
//  Class      ^hclass       = gcnew Class();           // Not allowed
    RefClass   ^hrefclass    = gcnew RefClass();
    ValueClass ^hvalueclass  = gcnew ValueClass();

    // Pointer
    Class      *pclass       = new Class();
//  RefClass   *prefclass    = new RefClass();          // Not allowed
    ValueClass *pvalueclass  = & valueclass;

    // Reference
    Class      &rfclass      = *new Class();
//  RefClass   &rfrefclass   = *gcnew RefClass();       // Not allowed
    ValueClass &rfvalueclass = valueclass;

    _class.x      = 1;
    refclass.x    = 2;
    valueclass.x  = 3;
    hrefclass->x  = 4;
    hvalueclass->x = 5;
    pclass->x     = 6;
    pvalueclass->x = 7;
    rfclass.x     = 8;
    rfvalueclass.x = 9;

    _class.write();          // prints 1
    refclass.write();        // prints 2
    valueclass.write();      // prints 9
    hrefclass->write();      // prints 4
    hvalueclass->write();    // prints 5
    pclass->write();         // prints 6
    pvalueclass->write();    // prints 9
    rfclass.write();         // prints 8
    rfvalueclass.write();    // prints 9
}
```

Pointers

If you have spent any time writing C++ code in the past, I'm sure you have come to realize that pointers are essential to C++ development, but also a necessary evil. Basically, it's a "you can't live with them, can't live without them" relationship. Some of the greatest code has been developed using pointers, but also some of the nastiest bugs.

Unmanaged C++ data types can be placed in one of two places, the stack or the heap. When you are dealing with pointers, you are generally dealing with heap data. But pointers can point to almost anything (if the program has the rights), so a pointer can also point to an element of the runtime stack or possibly locations directly within the Windows O/S, though usually that is not allowed. Pointers can be created in a number of ways:

- Placing the address directly into the pointer
- Arithmetically calculated from another pointer
- Copied from an existing object
- Using the new command

Just looking at the preceding list should make it obvious why pointers are not safe. In fact, the first two methods of creating pointers should make you cringe. Think what a field day hackers could have with these methods and thus why they are not supported by handles.

Unsafe Code Pointer arithmetic is probably one of the most powerful and at the same time unsafe operations available to a C++ programmer.

Copying a pointer from an existing object seems harmless enough. But even this has a problem if the object is derived from a managed type. The location of the object pointed to in the managed heap memory can move during the garbage collection process, because not only does the garbage collector delete unused objects in managed heap memory, it also compacts it. Thus, it is possible that a pointer may point to the wrong location after the compacting process. Fortunately, C++/CLI provides two ways of solving pointer movement: the interior pointer and the pinned pointer. I'll cover both in more detail later in the chapter.

Not even using the new command is safe, as the memory allocated is on the CRT heap and is not maintained by the CLR. Using the new command requires you to maintain the allocated memory yourself and when done call the delete command. I know this sounds okay, but I'm afraid very few of us are perfect when it comes to writing code, and I'm pretty sure one day you will forget to deallocate memory, deallocate it too soon, overwrite it, or do any of the other nasty mistakes revolving around pointers.

Interior Pointer

As I harped previously, pointers are extremely powerful, and it would be a great loss to the C++ to lose this aspect of the language. C++/CLI realizes this and has added what it calls *interior pointers*. Interior pointers are fundamentally pointers to managed objects.

I hope your alarms went off with the last sentence. Remember, managed objects can move. So let's be a little more accurate. An interior pointer is a superset of the native pointer and can do anything that can be done by the native pointer. But not only does it point to a managed object, when the garbage collector moves the object, the interior pointer changes its address to continue to point to it.

By the way, interior pointers are safe! Well, I better qualify that. You can use the pointers as you see fit, and they are safe. Just don't change the value of the pointers or manipulate them using pointer arithmetic. Listing 20-4 is a somewhat complicated example showing a safe program using interior pointers.

Listing 20-4. *Safe Interior Pointers*

```
using namespace System;

ref class Point
{
public:
    int X;
};

void main()
{
    Point ^p = gcnew Point();

    interior_ptr<Point^> ip1 = &p;    // Interior pointer to Point

    (*ip1)->X = 1;                    // Assign 1 to the member variable X

    Console::WriteLine("(&ip1)={0:X}\tp->X={1}\t(*ip1)->X={2}",
        (int)&ip1, p->X, (*ip1)->X);

    interior_ptr<int> ip2 = &p->X;    // Pointer to Member variable X

    *ip2 += (*ip1)->X;                // Add X to an interior pointer of itself

    Console::WriteLine("(&ip2)={0:X}\t*ip2={1}", (int)&ip2, *ip2);
}
```

Notice I can assign numbers to the value of the interior pointer. I just can't change the address that the pointer is pointing to. Well, actually, I can, but then the code is no longer safe.

Figure 20-4 shows the results of this little program.

Figure 20-4. *Results of IntPtr.exe*

I've been writing about pointer arithmetic long enough. Let's look at Listing 20-5 and see an example. This example adds the first eight prime numbers together. It does this by adding the value of the same pointer eight times, but each time the value is added the address of the pointer has advanced the size of an int. This example really doesn't need an interior pointer and can be written many other (safe) ways.

Listing 20-5. *Interior Pointer and Pointer Arithmetic and Comparision*

```
using namespace System;

void main()
{
    array<int>^ primes = gcnew array<int> {1,2,3,5,7,11,13,17};

    interior_ptr<int> ip = &primes[0];        // Create the interior pointer

    int total = 0;
    while(ip != &primes[0] + primes->Length)  // Comparing pointers
    {
        total += *ip;
        ip++;                                  // Add size of int to ip not 1
    }

    Console::WriteLine("Sum of the first 8 prime numbers is {0}", total);
}
```

Figure 20-5 shows the results of this little program.

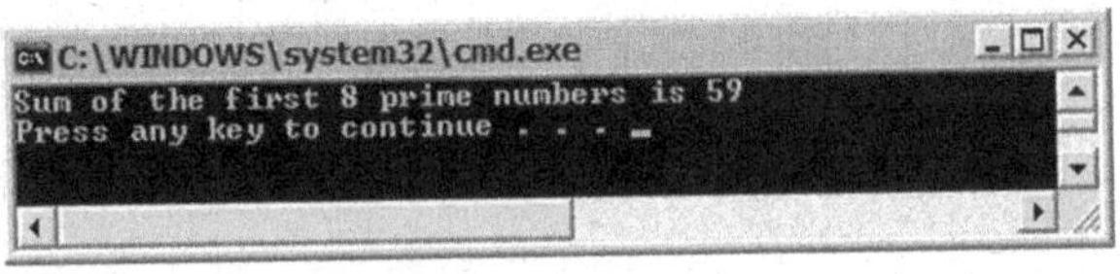

Figure 20-5. *Results of IntPtrArth.exe*

Pinning Pointers

If you are a seasoned traditional C++ programmer, you probably saw immediately a problem with the handle's ability to change addresses. There is no fixed pointer address to access the object in memory. In prior versions of C++/CLI (Managed Extensions for C++), the same syntax was used for addressing managed and unmanaged data. Not only did this lead to confusion, but it also did not make it apparent that the pointer was managed and thus could change. With the new handle syntax, it is far less confusing and readily apparent that the object is managed.

Unfortunately, the volatility of the handle address also leads to the problem that passing a handle to a managed object, as a parameter to an unmanaged function call, will fail. To solve this problem, C++/CLI has added the pin_ptr<> keyword, which stops the CLR from changing its location during the compacting phase of garbage collection. The pointer remains pinned so long as the pinned pointer stays in scope or until the pointer is assigned the value of nullptr.

Unsafe Code The pin_ptr<>, since it deals with providing specific address locations into memory, is an unsafe operation.

The pin_ptr<> uses template syntax where you place the type of object you want to pin within the angle [<>] brackets. For example:

```
pin_ptr<int>
```

I covered templates in Chapter 4.

A pinned pointer can point to a reference handle, a value type, and an element of a managed array. It cannot pin a reference type, but it can pin the members of a reference type. A pinned pointer has all the abilities of a native pointer, the most notable being pointer comparison and arithmetic. Listing 20-6 shows the pin_ptr<> keyword in action.

Listing 20-6. *pin_ptr in Action*

```
#include <stdio.h>

using namespace System;

ref class RTest
{
public:
    int i;
    RTest()
    {
        i = 0;
    }
};

value class VTest
{
public:
    int i;
};

#pragma unmanaged

void incr (int *i)
{
    (*i) += 10;
}

#pragma managed

void incr (VTest *t)
{
    t->i += 20;
}

void main ()
{
    RTest ^rtest = gcnew RTest();   // rtest is a reference type

    pin_ptr<int> i = &(rtest->i);   // i is a pinned int pointer

    incr( i );                      // Pointer to managed data passed as
                                    // parameter of unmanaged function call
```

```
Console::WriteLine ( rtest->i );


VTest ^vtest = gcnew VTest;      // vtest is a boxed value type
vtest->i = 0;

pin_ptr<VTest> ptest = &*vtest; // ptest is a pinned value type.
                                // The &* says give the address of the
                                // indirection of vtest

incr( ptest );                   // Pointer to value type passed as
                                 // parameter of unmanaged function call


Console::WriteLine ( vtest->i );


array<Byte>^ arr = gcnew array<Byte> {'M', 'C', '+', '+'};

pin_ptr<Byte> p = &arr[1];  // ENTIRE array is pinned
unsigned char *cp = p;
printf("%s\n", --cp);           // cp bytes will not move during call
                                // notice the negative pointer arithmetic
                                // into the array.
}
```

Figure 20-6 shows the results of this little program.

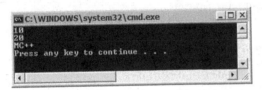

Figure 20-6. *Results of Pinned.exe*

One thing that you might want to be aware of is that, as you can see in the preceding code example, there is no problem including standard include files like stdio.h, but if you do you are going to need to use the /clr switch, as these headers usually cause unmanaged code to be generated.

Pinning Interior Pointers

A major difference between pinned pointers and interior pointers is that pinned pointers cast to native pointers, while interior pointers cannot, due to their ability to change as memory is compacted. Because of this, even though the interior pointer has all the functionality of a native pointer, it still cannot be passed to an unmanaged/native function that is expecting a native pointer.

Fortunately, there is nothing stopping you from pinning an interior pointer as you can see in Listing 20-7.

Listing 20-7. *Pinning an Interior Pointer*

```
using namespace System;

value class Test
{
public:
    int i;
};

#pragma unmanaged

void incr (int *i)
{
    (*i) += 10;
}

#pragma managed

void main ()
{
    Test ^test = gcnew Test();
    interior_ptr<int> ip = &test->i;
    (*ip) = 5;

//  incr( ip );            // Invalid

    pin_ptr<int> i = ip;   // i is a pinned interior pointer

    incr( i );             // Pinned pointer to interior pointer passed to a
                           // native function call expecting a native pointer

    Console::WriteLine ( test->i );
}
```

Including the vcclr.h File

Okay, now that we have all the pieces, let's look at one last thing before we move on to the advanced features in the next chapter.

You have seen that there is no problem placing unmanaged class pointers within a managed class, but you are not able to do the opposite (place an managed class handle into an unmanaged class) due to the garbage collector's inability to maintain member handles in unmanaged classes. (Actually, unmanaged classes don't even understand the handle syntax in the first place, so the garbage collector's inabilities are sort of a mute point.)

```
class      ClassMember  {};
ref class  RefClassMember {};

class Class
{
public:
    RefClassMember  ^hrc;   // Big fat ERROR
};
```

```
ref class RefClass
{
public:
    ClassMember     *pc;      // No problemo
};
```

Well, let's not give up prematurely here... it is not entirely accurate that you can't place a managed class in an unmanaged class. What you can't do is place a handle to a managed class into the unmanaged class. What you use instead of the handle are interior pointers and on occasion pinned pointers. Oh, and you also need to use the .NET Framework class
System::Runtime::InteropServices::GCHandle or the much easier template gcroot<T>. I use gcroot<T>, but feel free to explore GCHandle (if you are a glutton for punishment).

You can find the gcroot<T> template in gcroot.h, but the preferred method of accessing it is via the vcclr.h, as this header file will contain an assortment of utilities. (It only currently contains one utility, but it is still a good practice to follow what Microsoft suggests.)

Essentially, gcroot<T> provides you with the ability to place an interior pointer into your managed class instead of a handle. Listing 20-8 shows a simple example of using gcroot<T>.

Listing 20-8. *Pinning an Interior Pointer*

```
#include "stdio.h"
#include "vcclr.h"

using namespace System;

ref class MClass
{
public:
    int x;
    ~MClass() { Console::WriteLine("MClass disposed"); }
protected:
    !MClass() { Console::WriteLine("MClass finalized"); }
};

#pragma unmanaged   // Works with or without this line

class UMClass
{
public:
    gcroot<MClass^> mclass;

    ~UMClass() { printf("UMClass deleted\n"); }
};

#pragma managed

void main()
{
    UMClass *umc = new UMClass();
    umc->mclass = gcnew MClass();
```

```
    umc->mclass->x = 4;
    Console::WriteLine("Managed Print {0}", umc->mclass->x);
    printf("Unmanaged Print %d\n", umc->mclass->x);

    delete umc;
}
```

Figure 20-7 shows the results of this little program.

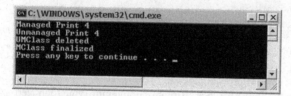

Figure 20-7. *Results of VcclrEx.exe*

I added to the managed class its two destructors (dispose and finalize) to make sure that finalize is being called. This means the garbage collector is doing its job. And, as you can see from Figure 20-7, all is as it should be.

I hinted earlier that vcclr.h also contains one utility function called `PtrToStringChars()`. This utility function converts a managed string into a const interior pointer of type wchar_t. This handy little utility allows you to be more efficient and use the internally stored Char data directly instead of copying it to an unmanaged wchar_t array.

There is one minor catch. Remember, unmanaged functions that are expecting native pointers cannot use interior pointers. Thus, functions like wprintf() will require you to pin the pointer first before you use it.

Listing 20-9 is another "Hello World!" program, this time mixing managed and unmanaged code as well as using the `PtrToStringChars()` function.

Listing 20-9. *Hello World PtrToStringChars() Function Style*

```
#include "stdio.h"
#include "vcclr.h"

using namespace System;

void main()
{
    String ^hstr = "Hello World!";

    pin_ptr<const wchar_t> pstr = PtrToStringChars(hstr);

    wprintf(pstr);
}
```

Summary

This chapter explored the basics of unsafe, unmanaged, and native code. You started off by examining what unsafe code is and how it differs from unmanaged and native code. You then discovered some of the major reasons why you might want to include unsafe code in your applications. Next, you examined some of the ways to make your code unsafe by mixing managed code and unmanaged/native code, unmanaged arrays, unmanaged classes, and pointers. Finally, you took a look at gcroot<T> and the PtrToStringChars() function, which simplify managed code within unmanaged code.

Now with the basics down, I'm going to move on to the final chapter of the book and examine the more advanced mixing of safe/managed code with unmanaged/native DLLs and COM objects.

CHAPTER 21

Advanced Unsafe or Unmanaged C++ .NET Programming

In the previous chapter, you dealt for the most part with the mixing of unsafe (or unmanaged) code directly into your safe (or managed) code. This approach only works if you have access to all the source code. Unfortunately, that is not a luxury that we developers always have. This chapter will address this issue by covering how C++/CLI interfaces with code that

- You don't have access to.

- Accesses objects outside of .NET sandbox and can't be accessed with a .NET language.

- Is written in a language not supported by .NET.

- Has a perfectly acceptable non-.NET implementation; rewriting would be a waste of time, money and/or resources.

There will be other situations where your code interfaces with some external non-.NET code that will not be implemented in .NET.

Basically, this chapter is about interfacing .NET applications with third-party DLLs or COM components. While each requires a different method to perform this interface, neither method is that difficult.

I think it funny (read: waste of time) how some books allocate a large portion of their text covering these interfaces explaining in great detail the internal flow of data and numerous other aspects. Personally, I don't see the point. Just tell me how to do it. That's my approach to this chapter. If you want all the other stuff, there are literally hundreds of Web sites that provide this information.

This chapter will start by examining how to interface with standard unmanaged DLLs using simple data types, and then show how to interface with more complex data types using data marshaling. Finally, I'll move on to interfacing your .NET code with COM components.

P/Invoke

Making calls out of the .NET managed environment to unmanaged DLLs is handled by a mechanism in .NET called P/Invoke (short for Platform Invoke). The basic idea behind P/Invoke is that it finds the DLL and loads it into memory, marshals its arguments (converts from managed format to native format) so that the DLL can understand the call, makes the call to the DLL's function, and then marshals the return value (converts from native format to managed format) so that the managed code understands the results.

Marshaling is a topic all to its own so I cover it a little later. But if you are dealing with primitive types (char, wchar_t, short, int, float, double, etc.), you don't need to do anything special in the way of marshaling anyway.

Calling DLLs without P/Invoke

But before I cover P/Invoke, you should know that you don't need P/Invoke if you are willing to sacrifice safe code, nonprimitive data types, and any language but C or C++. All you have to do is develop the .NET application as you did before .NET existed. If you don't have pre-.NET experience, here is what I mean.

One of the powerful features of C++/CLI is that you can mix and match managed and unmanaged C++ code, in most cases, almost effortlessly. Listing 21-1 shows an example of a .NET console application that uses a third-party DLL (written by me) and a call to the User32.dll's MessageBox.

Listing 21-1. *Mixing Managed and Unmanaged Code Without P/Invoke*

```
#include "stdafx.h"
#include "windows.h"

extern "C" __declspec(dllimport) long square(long value);

using namespace System;

int main(array<System::String ^> ^args)
{
    long Squareof4 = square(4);

    Console::WriteLine(L"The square of 4 is {0}", Squareof4);

    MessageBox(0, L"Hello World!", L"A Message Box", 0);

    return 0;
}
```

As you can see, this code is just some unmanaged and managed C++ code mixed together willy-nilly. If not for the array<> or Console::WriteLine statements, you probably wouldn't even have known that this is a .NET application.

If you have worked with C++ before .NET, you should have no problem with this code. To get access to the MessageBox function, you need to include windows.h, just as you would in any other Windows application without .NET. To access the square function, which resides in a DLL, a dllimport function prototype is needed.

I created the square function within a DLL so that you can see that nothing special is being done behind the scenes with MessageBox. Be careful, though, when you create NativeCode.dll (shown in Listing 21-2). Do not select any of the CLR type projects. Instead, make sure you select the Win32 Project and select DLL in the application settings. Or, if you are compiling the example from the command line, then use the /LD option like this:

```
cl /LD NativeCode.cpp
```

Listing 21-2. *A Very Simple Native Code DLL*

```
#include "stdafx.h"
#include "string.h"

extern "C" __declspec(dllexport) long square(long value)
{
    return value * value;
}
```

To get Listing 21-1 to compile, you need to change the program's properties so that the Linker knows where the User32.lib and NativeCode.lib files are located. To do this, you just replace $(NoInherit) with the path to NativeCode.lib, as seen in Figure 21-1. This kills two birds with one stone. Removing $(NoInherit) causes User32.lib to be added to the link, while replacing it with the path to NativeCode.lib does the same for NativeCode.lib. These .lib files in turn provide information to the compiler on how to interface with their corresponding .dll files.

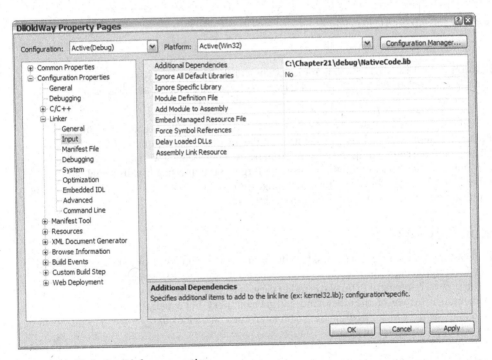

Figure 21-1. *Updating Linker properties*

Once you successfully compile the console application and the DLL, you can now execute the example. You should get something similar to Figure 21-2.

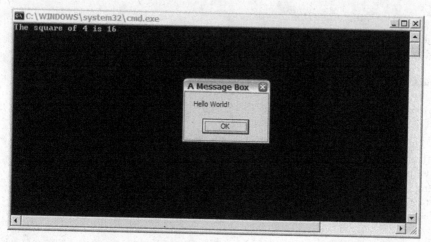

Figure 21-2. *DllOldWay.exe in action*

Caution If when executing DllOldWay.exe you get the error saying "can't find NativeCode.dll", then move NativeCode.dll someplace that the CLR can find it. I moved it to the same directory as DllOldway.exe.

So if you don't need P/Invoke, why I am I even covering it? Whoa there! Remember those restrictions I mentioned earlier? You cannot compile the previous example using /clr:safe, so you can't generate safe code. Things become far from trivial when dealing with factors like ref classes or String objects. And you can probably completely forget about interfacing with Visual Basic, Pascal, or other languages since they do things like change the order in which tasks are done when calling a function and use a different format of the basic data types.

Using P/Invoke

What if you are not willing to sacrifice safe code, nonprimitive data types, or multilanguage development when interfacing with your DLLs? Well, then you need to use P/Invoke.

The code to implement P/Invoke is rather easy. Selecting the correct arguments to use when implementing P/Invoke, on the other hand, can get a bit tricky, but usually the complication revolves around marshaling, which I'm discussing a bit later. Let's take a look at the P/Invoke equivalent to Listing 21-1, shown in Listing 21-3.

Listing 21-3. *A Simple P/Invoke Console Application*

```
#include "stdafx.h"

using namespace System;
using namespace System::Runtime::InteropServices;

[DllImportAttribute("..\\Debug\\NativeCode.dll",
                    CallingConvention=CallingConvention::StdCall)]
extern "C" long square(long value);
```

```
[DllImport("User32.dll", CharSet=CharSet::Auto,
            CallingConvention=CallingConvention::StdCall)]
extern "C" int MessageBox(int hWnd, String^ text, String^ caption,
                          unsigned int type);

int main(array<System::String ^> ^args)
{
    long Squareof4 = square(4);

    Console::WriteLine(L"The square of 4 is {0}", Squareof4);

    MessageBox(0, L"Hello World!", L"A Message Box", 0);

    return 0;
}
```

One nice thing about P/Invoke is that you don't have to go into the project's properties and change settings. Instead, all the information needed to compile and link is included in the source code. Therefore, you can simply compile the previous code and when you execute it you get the same result as shown in Figure 21-3.

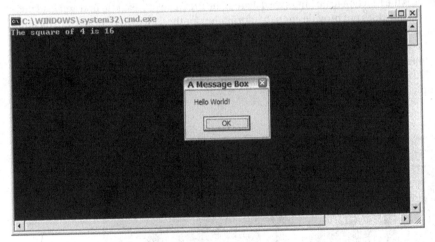

Figure 21-3. *SimplePInvoke.exe in action*

It looks the same as Figure 21-2, doesn't it?

Okay, let's look at the code. Since the code within the main() function is identical to that of Listing 21-1, let's skip that for now (but I will come back to it a little later).

The first thing of interest is the use of the System::Runtime::InteropServices namespace. This namespace contains numerous classes, interfaces, structures, and enumerations used to support platform invoke services and COM Interop (which I'll cover later in the chapter). Though many of these members have been made obsolete for one reason or another, still well over 100 exist—way too many to cover in this chapter. Fortunately (for me anyway), nearly all of these members are for special situations and thus out of the scope of this chapter.

In the previous example, I only need to use three of the namespace members: the DllImportAttribute class, and the CharSet and CallingConvention enumerations. For many of your P/Invoked functions, these will be all you need. In fact, normally you don't have to include CallingConvention enumeration as StdCall is the default. If you are not using String objects, you don't need to use CharSet enumeration, either. So what this boils down to is that you frequently will only use DllImportAttribute.

Note If you feel like saving your fingertips, you can use DllImport instead of DllImportAttribute as they are the same. By the way, you can do this for all attribute classes.

DllImportAttribute

The idea behind P/Invoke is that you create a prototype of the DLL's unmanaged function that you want to call using the DllImportAttribute class. You can declare these prototypes in one of two ways: as global functions or as static methods within a class. You implement these global functions and/or static methods just as you would any other function or method. Of course, you have to use the syntax defined by your prototype.

As the class name suggests, DllImportAttribute is an attribute and is implemented with the special square bracket syntax that is covered in Chapter 18. The DllImportAttribute when compiled generates metadata but no code. This metadata helps the CLR's P/Invoke process figure out where the DLL is and the calling convention to interface with this DLL.

The first and only mandatory positional parameter passed to DllImportAttribute is the name of the DLL that houses the function to be prototyped. Part of the P/Invoke process is to find and load this DLL. If the name alone does not provide enough information for the CLR to find the current location of the DLL, you will get a runtime error stating that the DLL cannot be found (see Figure 21-4). If this occurs, you need to do one of two things. Move the DLL to someplace that the CLR can find it (I usually put it in the same directory as the .exe file or the System32 directory) or, instead of passing just the name of the DLL, provide a full or relative path to the DLL. I show the relative path technique in the previous example.

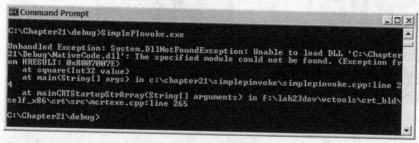

Figure 21-4. *Cannot find DLL error*

Caution Using a full path in the position parameter of the DllImportAttribute can be dangerous as not everyone has their directory structure set up the same as you do. Using a relative path is a little safer as long as the relative path is controlled by your installation process.

Following the DLL's name are six optional named parameters, which further help the CLR P/Invoke process access the DLL and implement the unmanaged function. The named parameters are as follows.

CallingConvention

CallingConvention is an enumeration that defines the calling convention used when passing arguments to the unmanaged function.

The default is StdCall, where the callee cleans the stack.

Other valid values are

- Cdecl, where the caller cleans the stack
- ThisCall, where the first parameter is the this pointer and is stored in the register ECX and other parameters are pushed on the stack
- winapi, where the default platform calling convention is used
- FastCall, which is not currently supported

CharSet

CharSet is an enumeration that defines how strings and characters are marshaled (handled).

The default is Ansi. Other values are Unicode and Auto, which use the format appropriate for the platform. Normally, you should use Auto.

Another feature of CharSet is it can be used to modify the name of the unmanaged function before it is looked up in the export list of the DLL.

A number of Windows methods add an "A" for ANSI version and "W" for Unicode version to the end of the function name; for example, MessageBoxA and MessageBoxW. When you add the CharSet named parameter to the DllImportAttribute, the CLR's P/Invoke process appends the appropriate value for you. You saw this in action in Listing 21-3 and it explains why you used MessageBox and not MessageBoxA or MessageBoxW.

EntryPoint

The EntryPoint string value allows you to specify the name or ordinal number of the function within the DLL for which you create the prototype. When you don't specify an EntryPoint, then the CLR's P/Invoke process will use the name specified in the unmanaged function prototype.

When you specify an EntryPoint value that differs from the unmanaged function prototype name, the EntryPoint takes precedence as the entry point into the DLL. This gives you the ability to rename the unmanaged function. For example, if you wanted the NativeCode.dll's square method to be renamed as Sqr then you would code like this:

```
[DllImportAttribute("NativeCode.dll", EntryPoint="square")]
extern "C" long Sqr(long value);
```

ExactSpelling

I told you earlier that the CharSet enumeration can modify the name of the unmanaged function. I said *can* because this functionality only occurs when ExactSpelling is set to false. The value false happens to be the default value of ExactSpelling, so you don't have to add the ExactSpelling named parameter when you want this functionality to occur. On the other hand, if you only want, let's say, the Unicode version of the unmanaged function to be used, then you would need to set ExactSpelling to true and then specify an EntryPoint or prototype name with the "W" suffix, something like this:

```
[DllImport("user32", CharSet=CharSet::Unicode, ExactSpelling=true)]
extern "C" int MessageBoxW(int hWnd, String^ text, String^ caption,
                           unsigned int type);
```

PreserveSig

The purpose of PreserveSig is to override the default behavior of the unmanaged function's return value. When PreserveSig is set to true (which is the default), the return value works just as you would expect.

On the other hand, if PreserveSig is false the return value takes on a whole different process. The first thing you need to be aware of is that the unmanaged function needs to return a HRESULT and have a parameter of type [out, retval]. With this combination the PreserveSig when set to false causes the [out, retval] parameter to be the actual value returned if the HRESULT is equal to S_OK. But if the HRESULT is something else, then an exception is thrown and the [out, retval] parameter is discarded.

You usually don't have to include the PreserveSig named parameter with a P/Invoked unmanaged function, as it is designed more for COM objects, but this doesn't mean you can't still use it if you are accessing a standard DDL function that uses the HRESULT as a return type and has a [out, retval] parameter.

SetLastError

When SetLastError is set to true, this indicates that the unmanaged function will call SetLastError and the CLR P/Invoke process will call GetLastError to save the error value, preventing any other API function from overwriting this error value as the API stack is walked. You can then get the error using the Marshal::GetLastWinError() within your program. The default value of SetLastError is false.

Static Method in a Class

In the first example, you saw the more common usage of P/Invoke: as a global function. It is also possible to declare a P/Invoke unmanaged function as a static method in a class. There really isn't anything special about it—just a minor syntax change in the prototype declaration, plus you need to call the method just like any other static member method.

Listing 21-4 shows an example of P/Invoke as a static method of the class SimpleClass. The result is identical to the other two previous programs in this chapter, so I won't waste space showing the same figure a third time.

Listing 21-4. *A Simple P/Invoke as a Static Method*

```
#include "stdafx.h"

using namespace System;
using namespace System::Runtime::InteropServices;

ref class SimpleClass
{
public:
    [DllImport("NativeCode")]
    static long square(long value);

    [DllImport("User32", CharSet=CharSet::Auto)]
    static int MessageBox(int hWnd, String^ text, String^ caption,
                          unsigned int type);
};
```

```
int main(array<System::String ^> ^args)
{
    long Squareof4 = SimpleClass::square(4);

    Console::WriteLine(L"The square of 4 is {0}", Squareof4);

    SimpleClass::MessageBox(0, L"Hello World!", L"A Message Box", 0);

    return 0;
}
```

Notice the only change to the code is that the two methods are called within a ref class and you replace extern "C" with static. Oh, and you have to call the static methods prefixed with the class name.

Data Marshaling

Okay, let's take a closer look at the main method of the previous example with and without P/Invoke:

```
int main(array<System::String ^> ^args)
{
    long Squareof4 = square(4);

    Console::WriteLine(L"The square of 4 is {0}", Squareof4);

    MessageBox(0, L"Hello World!", L"A Message Box", 0);

    return 0;
}
```

The code for calling the square method was fairly safe because it only deals with the primitive data type long. On the other hand, I had to be careful when it came to coding the call to the MessageBox() function especially for the non-P/Invoke example because the second and third parameters are pointers to null-terminated wchar_t arrays, which an L "string" happens to be.

If you use the more common System::String type in the non-P/Invoked version, you get an ugly compile time error due to data type incompatibility. To get it to work, you have to pin the string's handle first before calling the function. Here are a couple of ways of doing that:

```
String^ s = L"Hello World";
String^ t = L"A Message Box";

pin_ptr<const wchar_t>ss = &(s->ToCharArray()[0]);
pin_ptr<const wchar_t>tt = PtrToStringChars(t);    // requires vcclr.h
MessageBox(0, ss, tt, 0);
```

In a nutshell, you have to do your own data marshaling.

MarshalAsAttribute

Typically when using P/Invoke with C++/CLI you don't have to worry about marshaling since in most cases the managed and unmanaged formats of the data types are the same. There are exceptions to this; the most common are the String type and classes. Consequently, in most situations there is no need to do anything special when passing and returning simple data types to and from unmanaged DLLs.

That being said, there is nothing stopping you from explicitly defining how parameters are to be marshaled. To do this, you use the attribute System::Runtime::InteropServices::MarshalAsAttribute. The MarshalAsAttribute is a rather easy attribute to work with; it takes one positional enumeration parameter of type System::Runtime::InteropServices::UnmanagedType and is coded like this:

```
[DllImportAttribute("NativeCode.dll")]
extern "C" long square([MarshalAs(UnmanagedType::I4)] long value);
```

The CLR in this example really doesn't need the MarshalAs attribute to help it marshal the value parameter during the P/Invoke process because long and UnmanagedType::I4 are binary equivalent. Some of the more common enumeration values available are shown in Table 21-1.

Table 21-1. *Some Common UnmanagedType Values*

Enumeration	C++/CLI Equivalent	Description
AnsiBStr	String	Length-prefixed ANSI character string
Bool	bool	Win32 BOOL type
BStr	String	Length-prefixed Unicode character string
Currency	Decimal	Decimal is .NET only so marshal as Currency
FunctionPtr	Delegate	C-style function pointer
I1	char	1-byte signed integer
I2	short	2-byte signed integer
I4	int or long	4-byte signed integer
I8	__int64	8-byte signed integer
LPStr	String or StringBuilder	Null-terminated ANSI character string
LPTStr	String or StringBuilder	Null-terminated platform-dependent character string
LPWStr	String or StringBuilder	Null-terminated Unicode character string
R4	float	4-byte floating-point number
R8	double	8-byte floating-point number
TBStr	String	Length-prefixed platform-dependent character string
U1	unsigned char	1-byte unsigned integer
U2	unsigned short	2-byte unsigned integer
U4	unsigned int or unsigned long	4-byte unsigned integer
U8	unsigned __int64	8-byte unsigned integer

Marshaling Strings

Marshaling Strings with P/Invoke as you saw with the MessageBox function earlier is fairly straight-forward. In most cases, as long as you specify the CharSet you don't have to do anything special in the prototype. Personally, I like to add the MarshalAs attribute when passing String parameters, but doing so is up to you.

There is a gotcha, though, due to the fact that .NET Strings are immutable and thus are passed by value. This is normally not an issue, but what happens if you are using the parameter as an in/out value like in the case of the strcpy() function? This function takes one of its string parameters and returns a new string from it. If you use a String type as the in/out parameter, the resulting value returned in the parameter does not get changed. To solve this problem, you use a System::Text::StringBuilder instead of a String, as shown in Listing 21-5.

Listing 21-5. *Marshaling With an In/Out String*

```
using namespace System;
using namespace System::Text;
using namespace System::Runtime::InteropServices;

[DllImport("msvcr70", CharSet=CharSet::Ansi)]
extern "C" int strcpy([MarshalAs(UnmanagedType::LPStr)] StringBuilder^ dest,
                      [MarshalAs(UnmanagedType::LPStr)] String^ source);

void main()
{
    StringBuilder^ dest = gcnew StringBuilder();
    String^ source = "Hello";

    strcpy(dest, source);
    Console::WriteLine(dest);
}
```

Marshaling Ref and Value Classes

One really cool feature of the built-in marshaling functionality of .NET is its ability to marshal between ref (or value) classes and unmanaged classes (or structs) with very little additional code on your part. This might not sound like much, but you have to remember that in .NET memory can move around quite a bit and there is no guarantee that data, though coded to look like it falls sequentially in memory, actually is stored sequentially.

As Listing 21-6 (a snippet of code that I added to NativeCode.cpp) shows, it is possible to pass a class or struct parameter either by pointer or by value in an unmanaged DLL.

Listing 21-6. *Native Passing Parameters by Reference and Value*

```
extern "C"
{
    struct Rec
    {
        int width;
        int height;
    };
```

```
    // By reference
    __declspec(dllexport) bool rIsSquare(Rec *rec)
    {
        return rec->width == rec->height;
    }

    // By value
    __declspec(dllexport) bool vIsSquare(Rec rec)
    {
        return rec.width == rec.height;
    }
}
```

When you are dealing with passing structs or classes as parameters by value, you need to use a value class. When dealing with passing pointers to structs or classes as parameters, you use a ref class.

One problem is that you can't simply use a standard ref or value class as a parameter in the prototype as there is no guarantee that the class's data members will be sequential in memory. In fact, there isn't any guarantee that the order of the members in physical memory will even match since .NET has free reign on how it lays out memory. Instead, you need to add a StructLayoutAttribute of type LayoutKind::Sequential to the class like this:

```
[StructLayout(LayoutKind::Sequential)]
value class vRec
{
};
```

or

```
[StructLayout(LayoutKind::Sequential)]
ref class rRec
{
};
```

Both of these ensure that the class is laid out sequentially, in the order in which the data members appear when exported to unmanaged memory.

One interesting feature of ref or value classes when passing them as a parameter to a P/Invoked function is that you can add member methods to them without impacting anything. Because only the data members are passed, you can safely add constructors, destructors, and any other member methods.

Listing 21-7 shows how to implement passing a ref class and a value class as parameters to a P/Invoked function.

Listing 21-7. *Ref and Value Classes As P/Invoked Parameters*

```
using namespace System;
using namespace System::Runtime::InteropServices;

[StructLayout(LayoutKind::Sequential)]
value class vRec
{
public:
    int width;
    int height;
```

```
    vRec(int iwidth, int iheight)
    {
        width = iwidth;
        height = iheight;
    }
};

[StructLayout(LayoutKind::Sequential)]
ref class rRec
{
public:
    int width;
    int height;

    rRec(int iwidth, int iheight)
    {
        width = iwidth;
        height = iheight;
    }
};

// By value
[DllImportAttribute("NativeCode.dll")]
extern "C" bool vIsSquare(vRec rec);

// by reference
[DllImportAttribute("NativeCode.dll")]
extern "C" bool rIsSquare(rRec^ rec);

void main()
{
    // By Value
    vRec vrec(2,3);
    Console::WriteLine("value rec a square? {0}", vIsSquare(vrec));

    // By Reference
    rRec ^rrec = gcnew rRec(2,3);
    Console::WriteLine("ref rec a square? {0}", rIsSquare(rrec));
}
```

Accessing COM Components from .NET

As a programmer I like the idea of chucking old code and rewriting it. Call me funny, but I think coding is fun and enjoy improving old code. Unfortunately, I don't have all the time or resources in the world, and there comes a time when I have to reuse some old code simply because it just makes more sense to do so. COM and all its derivatives usually fall into this category.

I know I'm going to get some angry letters regarding this statement, but I think COM is a somewhat dated and in most cases obsolete technology. Unfortunately, there is a heck of a lot of it out there and it works just fine, and therefore rewriting it would be a big waste of time. Microsoft saw this and made sure that the .NET/COM interface, better known as COM Interop, was nearly seamless. In fact, in most cases you don't have to write any of the COM Interop code yourself, since Visual Studio 2005 will generate the code for you. For those of you without Visual Studio 2005, you can also manually generate the COM Interop code from the command line. There is no big difference between using Visual Studio 2005 or the command line when it comes to creating the COM Interop code—the results are virtually the same.

Note This chapter assumes that you know how to code, register, etc., your own COM objects and will not cover those topics.

I am including (just for completeness) Listing 21-8, the COM component that I use for all of the examples to follow. As you can see, it is simply a COM-ification of NativeCode.dll from Listing 21-2.

Listing 21-8. *The Chapter's Test COM Component TestCOM*

```cpp
// Compile from command line using
// cl /LD TestCOM.cpp
// regsvr32 TestCOM.dll

#define _ATL_ATTRIBUTES
#include <atlbase.h>
#include <atlcom.h>

[module(name="TestCOM",type="dll")];

// ITestCOM interface with Square method
[dual]
__interface ITestCOM : IDispatch
{
    [id(0x01)] HRESULT Square([in]LONG Value, [out,retval]LONG* Result);
};

// coclass CTestCOM implements the ITestCOM interface
[coclass, threading="both"]
class CTestCOM : public ITestCOM
{
    HRESULT Square(LONG Value, LONG* Result)
    {
        if (Value > 0x0ffff)
        {
            *Result = -1;
            return E_INVALIDARG;
        }
        else
        {
            *Result = Value * Value;
            return S_OK;
        }
    }
};
```

Interop Assembly

To put it bluntly, COM objects and .NET objects are quite different and I'm impressed by the magic invoked by Microsoft to get these square pegs into round holes. This magic is the Interop Assembly. Best of all, you don't have to write a single line of code to create an Interop Assembly!

An Interop Assembly is usually known as a runtime callable wrapper (RCW) because of the functionality it provides. As this name suggests, a RCW is a managed wrapper assembly that enables .NET to understand a COM object at runtime. In other words, not only does it provide marshaling code for parameters and return values, it also does all the prep work required to get the COM object up and running, manages the lifetime of the COM object (I know I don't miss trying to keep the AddRef() and Release() method calls in sync!), identifies and provides interfaces to the members of the COM object, and allows .NET to access these COM object members via dynamic references instead of raw fixed pointers.

Caution With an RCW, you do not have control of when its COM object is garbage collected. On the other hand, you may have heard of the static method System::Runtime::InteropServices::Marshal:: ReleaseComObject(), which you can use to immediately release your RCW. It is true that this method exists, but you must use it with extreme caution (and I mean extreme) as you are removing yourself from the safety net that .NET provides. The ReleaseComObject() method is a very complex topic and I will not cover it further, but if you insist on using the method, make sure you understand completely how it works (there are many Web pages about it) and then test thoroughly.

Creating the Interop Assembly

Since there are two methods of creating the Interop Assembly, let's look at both of them; that way you can make your own decision on which you want to use. (If you don't have Visual Studio 2005, then the choice has already been made for you.)

Type Library Importer

Because not everyone who develops with .NET uses Visual Studio 2005, the .NET Framework provides the developer with a command-line tool called the Type Library Importer (tlbimp) to convert a COM type library into an Interop Assembly. In other words, this command line converts your .tlb file into an RCW.

The default command to run is quite simple:

```
tlbimp.exe <type_library_name>.tlb
```

An example would be the conversion of the .tlb file created from compiling the COM type library TestCOM shown earlier in Listing 21-8:

```
Tlbimp.exe _TestCom.tlb
```

When you use the default command line you get an assembly called TestCom.dll, which contains all the wrapper classes for the COM type library.

Tip When you compile a COM object using only the /LD option, your .tlb file is named vc80.tlb. Before I run tlbimp on this file, I rename and move it to its own directory so I don't accidentally overwrite the actual COM type library DLL file—the default result of running tlbimp is a DLL file with the same name and extension as the originating COM type library.

If you need more specific information generated within the assembly, tlbimp provides a number of optional parameters. Some of the more commonly used parameters are shown in Table 21-2.

Table 21-2. *Common tlbimp Options*

Option	Description
/asmversion:number	Allows you to specify your own version number for the assembly being generated.
/help	Displays help information in the command window.
/keyfile:filename	The filename of the strong name key file that you want to sign the assembly with. You use this parameter along with the /asmversion option to make the generated assembly into a shared assembly that you can place in the GAC. You can create the file using the tool sn.exe covered in Chapter 18.
/namespace:name	Allows you to overrule the default namespace (the name of the type library) with a value of your own choice.
/out:filename	Allows you to specify the output filename. The default value generated is the name of the type library with the extension .dll.
/primary	Creates a primary Interop Assembly containing information about the publisher of the type library. The assembly must be signed with a strong name and have a version number.
/reference:filename	Specifies the name of a file that contains a reference to types defined outside the current type library.
/sysarray	Specifies that COM SafeArrays should be mapped to .NET's System::array.
/unsafe	Creates an interface without .NET security checks. I personally don't recommend you use this since it introduces security risks, but it is available if you absolutely need it.

Now that you have an Interop Assembly, all that is required for a .NET application to reference its members is to add the following to the top of the code:

```
#using <TestCom.dll>
```

And just like you would with any other .NET DLL, make sure that the CLR can reference it by placing it either in the path of the application or in the GAC.

Visual Studio 2005 Generated COM Interop Assembly

If you have Visual Studio 2005, you can let it do all the work. The process is nearly the same as adding a .NET reference to a project, except instead of selecting from the .NET tab you select from the COM tab. Here are the relevant steps:

1. Right-click on the project in the Solution Explorer.

2. Select the Properties menu item.

3. Select Common Properties and then References from the properties navigation tree.

4. Click the Add New Reference button.

5. Select the COM tab in the Add References dialog box.

6. Navigate to and select the COM component you want to add to your project, as shown in Figure 21-5.

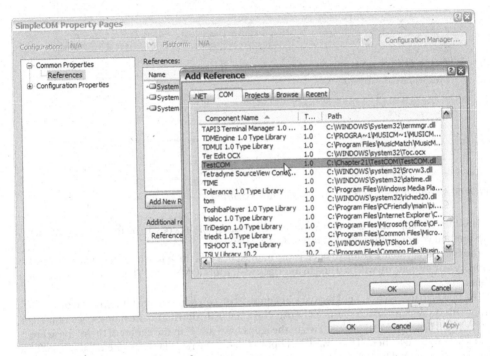

Figure 21-5. *Adding a COM object reference*

7. Click OK twice.

Once you complete these steps, Visual Studio 2005 adds an Interop Assembly called Interop.TestCOM.1.0 to your project.

Invoking the Interop Assembly

If you look at the resulting DLL, created via `tlbimp` on the command line or Visual Studio 2005 using isdasm.exe (see Figure 21-6), you will see that they are nearly identical.

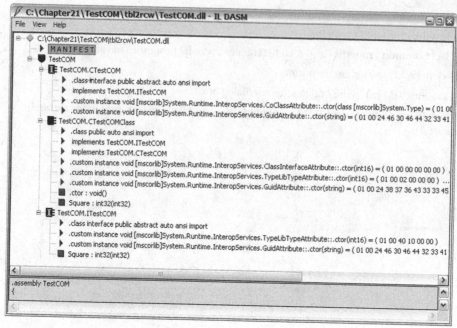

Figure 21-6. *An ildasm view of the TestCOM Interop Assembly*

This makes things easy as it allows the implementation of the code to be the same no matter which method you used to create the Interop Assembly.

The first thing you are going to need is the namespace and the name of the class within the Interop Assembly that you will be using to interface with your COM object. There are three easy ways to obtain this.

The first is to use ildasm. Looking back at Figure 21-6, you'll notice the blue shield icon with a red top. This is the namespace you need to use. Next, navigate down into the namespace branch of the tree. You'll find three class icons. Two of the icons have an "I" in the center of them; these are interfaces. You can use them if you want, but I prefer to use the real class: the one without the "I." This is the RCW created by either tlbimp or VS .NET.

The second method is to use the Object Browser in Visual Studio 2005. The first step is to add a reference to the COM object as I described earlier. This will make the Interop Assembly available to the Object Browser. Next, open the Object Browser by choosing View ➤ Object Browser. This will open a docked window, as shown in Figure 21-7.

Select the COM Object Interop Assembly that you referenced. The namespace you will need to use will be the one next to the curly brackets icon. Expand this icon and you will see three more icons: two interfaces and a class. Again I use the class, but you can use the interface if you prefer.

The third method is a last resort and requires that you know the COM coclass. The namespace will be the name of the Interop Assembly minus any suffixes or prefixes, and the RCW class will be the coclass with a "C" in front and "Class" on the end.

Here is the result of all three methods for the TestCOM assembly:

- Namespace of TestCOM
- RCW of CTestCOMClass

Now all you need to do to use the COM object in your code is to create an instance of the RCW and then call the methods you want, as shown in Listing 21-9.

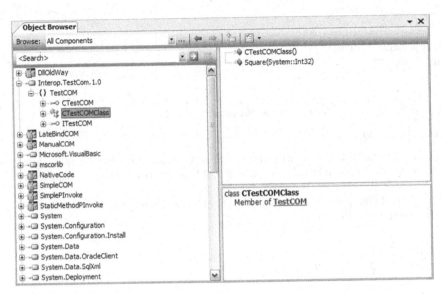

Figure 21-7. *Object Browser*

Listing 21-9. *Invoking the COM Component TestCOM*

```
// #using <TestCom.dll>  // Add if you are not referencing using VS .NET

using namespace System;
using namespace TestCOM;

int main(array<System::String ^> ^args)
{
    CTestCOMClass^ test = gcnew CTestCOMClass();

    long ret = test->Square(4);

    Console::WriteLine("The Square of 4 is {0}", ret);
    return 0;
}
```

As you can see, there is no difference between using an RCW and a standard .NET class. Even IntelliSense works. Like I said, Microsoft performed some major league magic.

Handling COM Object Errors

How return values and errors are handled is hidden in the auto-generated RCW code. All COM methods return a 32-bit HRESULT value and not the nicely marshaled values that .NET presents to the developer. Here is the snippet of the TestCOM code that shows the Square method call:

```
HRESULT Square(LONG Value, LONG* Result)
{
    if (Value > 0x0ffff)
    {
        *Result = -1;
        return E_INVALIDARG;
    }
```

```
        else
        {
            *Result = Value * Value;
            return S_OK;
        }
}
```

And here is the call you make in your .NET application:

```
long ret = test->Square(4);
```

They don't match! What is happening is that the PreserveSig is being set to false, which causes the method to return the [out, retval] parameter if the HRESULT is not an error; otherwise, an exception is thrown.

So, to handle a COM object method error just add a try block around the method call and a catch block to handle the error like this:

```
try
{
    long ret = test->Square(0x10000);
}
catch (Exception^ ex)
{
    Console::WriteLine("Oops an exception occurred: {0}", ex->Message);
}
```

Clean and simple, don't you think?

Late Binding a COM Object

When implementing a COM object with an Interop Assembly, you are performing early binding. In other words, the COM object is connected to the calling application at compile time. In the absence of an Interop Assembly, it is still possible to connect to a COM object as long as the COM object implements IDispatch. This form of connection, which is done at runtime, is called late binding.

To perform late binding on a COM object, you have to know the COM progID, the Registry entry associated with the COM object. Then with the COM progID, you use reflection (see Chapter 18 for a refresher on reflection) to invoke the COM object's methods.

Implementing late binding using reflection for COM objects is very similar to using reflection with assemblies. The big difference is that you use the static method Type::GetTypeFromProgID() to get the Type object (which represents the coclass) instead of the Type::GetType() method.

To help you understand how to code late binding of a COM object, let's look at the full example first and then walk through it step by step. Listing 21-10 provides the same functionality as the early binding example.

Listing 21-10. *Invoking the COM Using Late Binding*

```
using namespace System;
using namespace System::Reflection;

int main(array<System::String ^> ^args)
{
    Type ^typeTestCom = Type::GetTypeFromProgID(L"CTestCOM.CTestCOM");
```

```
if (typeTestCom == nullptr)
{
    Console::WriteLine("Getting CTestCOM.CTestCOM failed");
    return -1;
}

try
{
    Object ^TestComLBnd = Activator::CreateInstance(typeTestCom);

    array<Object^>^ param = gcnew array<Object^> { 4 };

    Object ^ret = typeTestCom->InvokeMember(
            L"Square",
            Reflection::BindingFlags::InvokeMethod,
            nullptr,
            TestComLBnd,
            param);

    Console::WriteLine("Square of 4 is {0}", ret);
}
catch (Exception ^ex)
{
    Console::WriteLine("Error when invoking Square method: {0}",
                        ex->Message);
}
return 0;
}
```

First you get a reference to the Type for which you will invoke members. To do this, you pass the progID to the GetTypeFromProgID() method, which returns a Type object that represents the coclass of the COM object. If the progID cannot be found in the Registry or some other error occurs, the GetTypeFromProgID() method returns a nullptr. Therefore, after I try to get the coclass Type object, I check to see if the value is nullptr and if it is, I quit.

Now that I have the coclass Type, I need to create an instance of it with the static method Activator::CreateInstance(). The CreateInstance() method returns a number of exceptions so I enclose it in a try/catch block, but under normal operations these exceptions should not occur since I have already retrieved a valid coclass Type using the method GetTypeFromProgID().

All that is left is to invoke the member using the aptly named Type member method InvokeMember(). This method takes five parameters:

- The name of the method to invoke.

- The type of operation to perform as a BindingFlag enumeration. In this case, it will normally be InvokeMethod.

- A reference to a binder object (which you can safely ignore so just pass nullptr).

- The reference to an instance of the coclass Type that the operation will be invoked on.

- An array of Objects that you want to pass as arguments.

Just before you call the InvokeMember() method, you need to create the array of Objects you want to pass to the invoked COM object method. If the method doesn't have any parameters, then pass nullptr.

Finally, the InvokeMember() method returns an Object type, so you need to typecast it to the type you want. In the example, WriteLine() handles the typecast for me.

Caution Late binding is less efficient than early binding.

Summary

In this chapter you looked at interfacing with unmanaged DLLs and COM objects. You started off looking at P/Invoke using simple data types. You then moved on to data marshaling with more complex data types. Finally, you looked at interfacing with COM objects using Interop Assemblies using either early binding with RCW or late binding directly with the COM object itself.

Because there is no next chapter to describe, I would like to instead thank you for reading my book. I hope you got as much enjoyment out of reading it as I did writing it.

Index

forums.apress.com

FOR PROFESSIONALS BY PROFESSIONALS™

JOIN THE APRESS FORUMS AND BE PART OF OUR COMMUNITY. You'll find discussions that cover topics of interest to IT professionals, programmers, and enthusiasts just like you. If you post a query to one of our forums, you can expect that some of the best minds in the business—especially Apress authors, who all write with *The Expert's Voice*™—will chime in to help you. Why not aim to become one of our most valuable participants (MVPs) and win cool stuff? Here's a sampling of what you'll find:

DATABASES

Data drives everything.

Share information, exchange ideas, and discuss any database programming or administration issues.

INTERNET TECHNOLOGIES AND NETWORKING

Try living without plumbing (and eventually IPv6).

Talk about networking topics including protocols, design, administration, wireless, wired, storage, backup, certifications, trends, and new technologies.

JAVA

We've come a long way from the old Oak tree.

Hang out and discuss Java in whatever flavor you choose: J2SE, J2EE, J2ME, Jakarta, and so on.

MAC OS X

All about the Zen of OS X.

OS X is both the present and the future for Mac apps. Make suggestions, offer up ideas, or boast about your new hardware.

OPEN SOURCE

Source code is good; understanding (open) source is better.

Discuss open source technologies and related topics such as PHP, MySQL, Linux, Perl, Apache, Python, and more.

PROGRAMMING/BUSINESS

Unfortunately, it is.

Talk about the Apress line of books that cover software methodology, best practices, and how programmers interact with the "suits."

WEB DEVELOPMENT/DESIGN

Ugly doesn't cut it anymore, and CGI is absurd.

Help is in sight for your site. Find design solutions for your projects and get ideas for building an interactive Web site.

SECURITY

Lots of bad guys out there—the good guys need help.

Discuss computer and network security issues here. Just don't let anyone else know the answers!

TECHNOLOGY IN ACTION

Cool things. Fun things.

It's after hours. It's time to play. Whether you're into LEGO® MINDSTORMS™ or turning an old PC into a DVR, this is where technology turns into fun.

WINDOWS

No defenestration here.

Ask questions about all aspects of Windows programming, get help on Microsoft technologies covered in Apress books, or provide feedback on any Apress Windows book.

HOW TO PARTICIPATE:

Go to the Apress Forums site at **http://forums.apress.com/**.
Click the New User link.

Printed in the United States
By Bookmasters